W9-CCT-146

Problems and Materials on the Sale and Lease of Goods

EDITORIAL ADVISORS

Vicki Been
Elihu Root Professor of Law
New York University School of Law

Erwin Chemerinsky
Dean and Distinguished Professor of Law
University of California, Irvine, School of Law

Richard A. Epstein
Laurence A. Tisch Professor of Law
New York University School of Law
Peter and Kirsten Bedford Senior Fellow
The Hoover Institution
Senior Lecturer in Law
The University of Chicago

Ronald J. Gilson
Charles J. Meyers Professor of Law and Business
Stanford University
Marc and Eva Stern Professor of Law and Business
Columbia Law School

James E. Krier
Earl Warren DeLano Professor of Law
The University of Michigan Law School

Richard K. Neumann, Jr.
Professor of Law
Hofstra University School of Law

Robert H. Sitkoff
John L. Gray Professor of Law
Harvard Law School

David Alan Sklansky
Yosef Osheawich Professor of Law
University of California at Berkeley School of Law

Kent D. Syverud
Dean and Ethan A. H. Shepley University Professor
Washington University School of Law

Elizabeth Warren
Leo Gottlieb Professor of Law
Harvard Law School

ASPEN CASEBOOK SERIES

PROBLEMS AND MATERIALS ON THE SALE AND LEASE OF GOODS

SIXTH EDITION

DOUGLAS J. WHALEY
PROFESSOR EMERITUS
MORITZ COLLEGE OF LAW
THE OHIO STATE UNIVERSITY

STEPHEN M. MCJOHN
PROFESSOR OF LAW
SUFFOLK UNIVERSITY LAW SCHOOL

Wolters Kluwer
Law & Business

Copyright © 2012 Douglas J. Whaley and Stephen M. McJohn.

Published by Wolters Kluwer Law & Business in New York.

Wolters Kluwer Law & Business serves customers worldwide with CCH, Aspen Publishers, and Kluwer Law International products. (www.wolterskluwerlb.com)

No part of this publication may be reproduced or transmitted in any form or by any means, electronic or mechanical, including photocopy, recording, or utilized by any information storage or retrieval system, without written permission from the publisher. For information about permissions or to request permissions online, visit us at www.wolterskluwerlb.com, or a written request may be faxed to our permissions department at 212-771-0803.

To contact Customer Service, e-mail customer.service@wolterskluwer.com, call 1-800-234-1660, fax 1-800-901-9075, or mail correspondence to:

> Wolters Kluwer Law & Business
> Attn: Order Department
> PO Box 990
> Frederick, MD 21705

Printed in the United States of America.

1 2 3 4 5 6 7 8 9 0

ISBN 978-1-4548-0723-0

Library of Congress Cataloging-in-Publication Data

Whaley, Douglas J.
  Problems and materials on the sale and lease of goods / Douglas J. Whaley., Stephen M. McJohn. — 6th ed.
      p. cm. — (Aspen casebook series)
  Includes index.
  ISBN 978-1-4548-0723-0
1. Sales — United States. 2. Leases — United States. I. McJohn, Stephen M., 1959- II. Title.
  KF915.W445 2012
  346.7307'2 — dc2

                                                                2012018041

SUSTAINABLE FORESTRY INITIATIVE

Certified Sourcing
www.sfiprogram.org
SFI-01234

SFI label applies to the text stock

About Wolters Kluwer Law & Business

Wolters Kluwer Law & Business is a leading global provider of intelligent information and digital solutions for legal and business professionals in key specialty areas, and respected educational resources for professors and law students. Wolters Kluwer Law & Business connects legal and business professionals as well as those in the education market with timely, specialized authoritative content and information-enabled solutions to support success through productivity, accuracy and mobility.

Serving customers worldwide, Wolters Kluwer Law & Business products include those under the Aspen Publishers, CCH, Kluwer Law International, Loislaw, Best Case, ftwilliam.com and MediRegs family of products.

CCH products have been a trusted resource since 1913, and are highly regarded resources for legal, securities, antitrust and trade regulation, government contracting, banking, pension, payroll, employment and labor, and healthcare reimbursement and compliance professionals.

Aspen Publishers products provide essential information to attorneys, business professionals and law students. Written by preeminent authorities, the product line offers analytical and practical information in a range of specialty practice areas from securities law and intellectual property to mergers and acquisitions and pension/benefits. Aspen's trusted legal education resources provide professors and students with high-quality, up-to-date and effective resources for successful instruction and study in all areas of the law.

Kluwer Law International products provide the global business community with reliable international legal information in English. Legal practitioners, corporate counsel and business executives around the world rely on Kluwer Law journals, looseleafs, books, and electronic products for comprehensive information in many areas of international legal practice.

Loislaw is a comprehensive online legal research product providing legal content to law firm practitioners of various specializations. Loislaw provides attorneys with the ability to quickly and efficiently find the necessary legal information they need, when and where they need it, by facilitating access to primary law as well as state-specific law, records, forms and treatises.

Best Case Solutions is the leading bankruptcy software product to the bankruptcy industry. It provides software and workflow tools to flawlessly streamline petition preparation and the electronic filing process, while timely incorporating ever-changing court requirements.

ftwilliam.com offers employee benefits professionals the highest quality plan documents (retirement, welfare and non-qualified) and government forms (5500/PBGC, 1099 and IRS) software at highly competitive prices.

MediRegs products provide integrated health care compliance content and software solutions for professionals in healthcare, higher education and life sciences, including professionals in accounting, law and consulting.

Wolters Kluwer Law & Business, a division of Wolters Kluwer, is headquartered in New York. Wolters Kluwer is a market-leading global information services company focused on professionals.

For Mary Bush, Tim Ihle, and Pamela Maggied

DJW

To Lorie and Ian

SMM

SUMMARY OF CONTENTS

TABLE OF CONTENTS

This book explores the law of the sale and lease of goods and licenses primarily by focusing on a series of Problems designed to encourage the student to concentrate on the exact statutory language of the Uniform Commercial Code and related statutes. Representative cases and textual notes are also included.

Unfortunately, students reared on the case method sometimes have trouble concentrating on Problem after Problem. Such an attitude here can be academically fatal. As a guide to the degree of concentration required, we have used a hierarchy of signals. When the Problem states "Read §2-302," we mean "Put down this book, pick up the Uniform Commercial Code, and study §2-302 carefully." When the instruction is "See §2-302," the reader need look at the cited section only if unsure of the answer. "Cf. §2-302" or simply "§2-302" are lesser references, included as a guide for the curious.

We have edited many of the footnotes out of the cases; the ones that remain have been stripped of their original numbering and have been consecutively numbered with the other textual footnotes. Unless clearly indicated otherwise, all footnotes in the cases are the court's own.

Finally, we would like to thank all the good people at Aspen Publishers for the assistance they have given us through the years in the production of this and other books. It is a pleasure to work with true professionals. We would also like to express gratitude to our students who have always taught us as much about commercial law as we have taught them.

Douglas J. Whaley
Stephen M. McJohn

June 2012

PROBLEMS AND MATERIALS ON THE SALE AND LEASE OF GOODS

CHAPTER 1
BASIC CONCEPTS

I. INTRODUCTION

Our course primarily concerns the Uniform Commercial Code, a state statute regulating commercial matters that has been enacted, with some variations, in all jurisdictions in the United States. It is divided into different parts called "Articles." The primary focus of this book is Article 2 (Sales), but we will also cover relevant parts of several other Articles, especially Article 2A (Leases), Article 5 (Letters of Credit), and Article 7 (Documents of Title). The Code was written in the middle of the last century, and has been much amended, Article by Article, through the years. Changes to the Code are promulgated by two organizations—the American Law Institute (ALI) and the National Conference of Commissioners on Uniform State Laws (NCCUSL)—and then sent out to the states for adoption. Most states make changes to the various Articles when enacting them, and some of these variations are startlingly different from the official version. In your actual practice of law, make sure you carefully examine the wording of the relevant state statutes to see what changes, if any, were made from the original text, and consider how that will affect the legal advice you give.

A.   The Basics of Article 1

Article 1 of the Uniform Commercial Code is a general Article whose rules are applicable to all the Articles that follow (unless those Articles specifically state otherwise). It contains basic principles such as a section explaining how the Code is to be construed (§1-103), a section preserving the common law unless obviously changed by the Code (§1-103(b)), a command that *good faith* be imposed in all UCC transactions (§1-304), and, most importantly, a huge definition section (§1-201) explaining the meaning of terms used throughout the rest of the statute.

Article 1 itself was rewritten in 2001, and that version was sent out to the states for adoption. Most states have now enacted it, and it is the one you should use in connection with this book.

B.   The Official Comments

The Official Comments to the various sections of the Uniform Commercial Code were not enacted into law, but were written by the drafters of the UCC, and appended thereto. Because they explain what those drafters intended the sections to mean, they are very persuasive in convincing the courts to follow them when litigation arises. On the other hand, if you, future attorney, have a case in which a Comment *hurts* your argument, you might point out that in many jurisdictions the Official Comments were not available to the legislature at the time it adopted the Article concerned (so they are often not even part of the legislative history), and many of these Comments have the look of "Oops, we meant to say . . ." or "We knew we could never get this through the legislature, so we are trying to change the law by Official Comment," and thus can be safely ignored. In any event, the Official Comments are a tool that will be useful to you in your exploration of the Uniform Commercial Code, and you should not hesitate to consult them to help puzzle out the meaning of the various sections.

II.   SCOPE OF ARTICLE 2

A.   "Transactions in Goods"

Article 2 of the Uniform Commercial Code applies to *transactions in goods*. Read §2-102. The word *transactions* is not defined in the Code. Look at §2-106(1); does that help? Much is encompassed within these parameters.

Both the delivery of a multibillion dollar space shuttle to the U.S. Government and the purchase of a package of chewing gum at a local store trigger the application of Article 2 of the Code. *Goods* is defined in §2-105. Read it, and work through the following materials.

PROBLEM 1

Whether Article 2 applies may determine the outcome of a case. If Article 2 applies, its rules may favor one party (such as the implied warranty of merchantability that automatically is given to many buyers). Does Article 2 of the Code apply to the following matters?

(a) The sale of an insurance policy? See Call v. Czaplicki, 72 U.C.C. Rep. Serv. 2d 912 (D.N.J. 2010).

(b) The sale of real property? What about the sale of a house apart from the realty? See §2-107.

(c) The sale of building materials as part of a construction project? See the case following this Problem.

(d) The sale of standing timber? Crops? See §2-107.

(e) A defective spinal plate given a patient in a hospital operating room? See Brandt v. Boston Scientific Corp., 204 Ill. 2d 640, 792 N.E.2d 296, 50 U.C.C. Rep. Serv. 2d 701 (2003). The preparation of false teeth by a dentist? See Carroll v. Grabavoy, 77 Ill. App. 3d 895, 396 N.E.2d 836, 27 U.C.C. Rep. Serv. 940 (1977). The injection of a drug (for which the patient was separately billed) into a patient's eye as part of an operation? See Providence Hospital v. Truly, 611 S.W.2d 127, 30 U.C.C. Rep. Serv. 785 (Tex. Civ. App. 1980).

(f) The sale of membership in a health spa?

(g) The sale of electricity? See GFI Wisconsin, Inc. v. Reedsbury Utility Commn., 440 B.R. 791 (W.D. Wis. 2010).

(h) Devices signed a distribution agreement giving Detail Retail the exclusive right to sell Gooseberry phones in the Midwest. Same result if Detail Retail also agreed to buy 1 million Gooseberry phones directly from Devices? See MidAmerican Distribution, Inc. v. Clarification Technology, Inc., 75 U.C.C. Rep. Serv. 2d 420 (E.D. Ky. 2011); Franklin Publications, Inc. v. General Nutrition Corp., 63 U.C.C. Rep. Serv. 2d 662 (S.D. Ohio 2007).

Milau Associates, Inc. v. North Avenue Development Corp.

Court of Appeals of New York, 1977
42 N.Y.2d 482, 368 N.E.2d 1247, 398 N.Y.S.2d 882, 22 U.C.C. Rep. Serv. 56

WACHTLER, J.

A massive burst in an underground section of pipe, connecting a sprinkler system to the city water line, caused substantial water damage to bolts of textiles stored in a warehouse. The plaintiffs who were commercial tenants of the building sought recovery against both Milau Associates, the general contractor which built the warehouse, and Higgins Fire Protection Inc., the subcontractor that designed and installed the sprinkler system. The suit was brought on the alternative theories of negligence and breach of implied warranty of fitness for a particular purpose.

Evidence adduced at the trial indicated that the break followed the occurrence of a phenomenon known as a "water hammer" — a sudden and unpredictable interruption in the flow from the city water main, followed by a back-surge and build-up of extreme internal pressure when the flow was again released. According to the plaintiffs' experts, this "hoop tension" caused a crack to develop at the root of a V-shaped notch discovered toward the end of the conduit; the fracture traveled along the length of the vulnerable section of pipe with a tearing action and the torrential result.

The "stress-raising" notch was alleged to have been produced by a dull tooth on the hydraulic squeeze cutter used by Higgins to cut sections of the commercially marketed pipe furnished by the subcontractor as specified in the work contract with Milau. Although the 400-foot-long connection had been carefully tested and had functioned properly in conjunction with the remainder of the system inside the building, only a few months in operation had caused enough rusting at the base of the notch, plaintiffs contended, to affect the integrity of the entire system. The defendants produced offsetting expert opinion that the pipe itself was neither defective as manufactured nor improperly installed.

The trial judge, having denied plaintiffs' request to charge that the contractors had impliedly warranted the fractured pipe to be fit for its intended purpose, submitted the case to the jury on the sole question of negligent installation. The jury returned a verdict in favor of the defendants, finding neither want of due care by Higgins nor negligent supervision by Milau.

The textile companies contest the trial court's restrictive rulings on the law of warranty. They assert that the V-shaped notch found in the ruptured section of pipe is adequate proof that this crucial component of the sprinkler system supplied by Higgins was defective. It is their contention that the jury would have been justified in finding a defect in the "goods" furnished under the hybrid sales-services contract without necessarily finding negligence on the part of either defendant. The plaintiffs argue that this defect made the pipe unfit for its intended purpose and that they were entitled to have the jury decide whether there was a breach of an implied warranty under §2-315 of the Uniform Commercial Code or by application of common law warranty principles.

The majority at the Appellate Division found the record to be "devoid of any evidence that the pipe installed by Higgins was unfit for its intended purpose" (56 A.D.2d 587, 588), and concluded that neither the Code nor the case law could be invoked to grant the extension of warranty protection sought by the plaintiffs. While we agree with this result, we have some difficulty with that court's caveat that, "in a proper case, the implied warranty provisions of the Uniform Commercial Code might apply to the 'sale of goods' aspect of a hybrid sales-services contract (see Schenectady Steel Co. v. Trimpoli Gen. Constr. Co., 43 A.D.2d 234 [concurring opn. by Greenblott, J.], *aff'd*, 34 N.Y.2d 939)." (56 A.D.2d, p. 588.)

The sales-services dichotomy has been recognized and developed from the days of the law merchant.[1] In a more contemporary formulation, this court in Perlmutter v. Beth David Hospital (308 N.Y. 100, 104) held that, "when service predominates, and the transfer of personal property is but an incidental feature of the transaction," the exacting warranty standards for imposing liability without proof of fault will not be imported from the law of sales to cast purveyors of medical services in damages. In that case we held that this prohibition could not be circumvented by conceptually severing the sale of goods aspects of the transaction from the overriding service component so that a hospital's act of supplying and even separately charging for impure blood plasma could not in logic or common sense be separated from a physician's contribution in administering the plasma during the course of treatment. Viewed in its entirety, we held in *Perlmutter* that the transaction could not be characterized in part or in its underlying nature as one for the sale of goods, for Mrs. Perlmutter had checked into the hospital to restore her health, not to purchase blood.

The fact that in *Perlmutter* our "service predominates" analysis led to a conclusion of law which was also supported by policy considerations peculiar to the impure blood cases does not strip its analytic approach of vitality. The court made no attempt to mask the fact that reallocating the risk of loss by imposing warranty liability on no greater proof than the adverse result itself would place untoward economic and health-care burdens on hospitals and patients alike. However, the court's sensitivity to these policy considerations, rather than restrict the scope of its holding, should suggest the need to assess all hybrid transactions along the sales-services continuum both legally and pragmatically.

As suggested in *Perlmutter*, those who hire experts for the predominant purpose of rendering services, relying on their special skills, cannot expect infallibility. Reasonable expectations, not perfect results in the face of any

---

1. From its inception, the "English rule" served as a basis for applying the commercial law of sales whenever a transaction resulted in a transfer of chattels. Applying this formulation in Lee v. Griffin (112 Eng. Rep. 716 [K.B. 1861]), Justice Blackburn held that a contract to manufacture and fit a set of false teeth was subject to sales remedies. Courts in this country, however, generally followed the "labor rule," under which the law of sales would not be applied if the contract required a workman "to put materials together and construct an article for the employer" (Mixer v. Howarth, 21 Mass. [4 Pick.] 205, 207 [1838]).

and all contingencies, will be ensured under a traditional negligence standard of conduct. In other words, unless the parties have contractually bound themselves to a higher standard of performance, reasonable care and competence owed generally by practitioners in the particular trade or profession defines the limits of an injured party's justifiable demands (e.g., Aegis Productions, Inc. v. Arriflex Corp., 25 A.D.2d 639 [recognizing that in cases where "the service is performed negligently, the cause of action accruing is for the negligence," and "if it constitutes a breach of contract, the action is for that breach"]).

The parties to the contract underlying this action were perfectly free at the outset, although not after the fact, to adopt a higher standard of care to govern the contractors' performance. Indeed, under a subcontract in which Higgins undertook to design and put together a sprinkler system tailored to the needs of the commercial tenants, the subcontractor was obligated to "furnish and install a wet pipe sprinkler system all in accordance with the requirements of the New York Fire Insurance Rating Organization, including . . . one 84 City water connection from pit at property line to inside of factory building. . . ." Additionally, by affixing its corporate signature to the standard form construction subcontract, the fire protection specialist "expressly warranted" that "all materials and equipment [which it] furnished and incorporated would be new" and that "all *work* under this subcontract shall be of good quality, free from faults and defects and in conformance with the contract documents. All work not conforming to these standards may be considered defective" (emphasis added).

Section 2-313 of the Uniform Commercial Code requires that a "seller's" affirmation of fact to a "buyer" be made as part of the basis of the bargain, that is, the contract for the sale of goods. The express warranty section would therefore be no more applicable to a service contract than the Code's implied warranty provisions. Of course, where the party rendering services can be shown to have expressly bound itself to the accomplishment of a particular result, the courts will enforce that promise (e.g., Robbins v. Finestone, 308 N.Y. 543; Frankel v. Wolper, 181 App. Div. 485, *aff'd*, 223 N.Y. 582).

Here the textile company plaintiffs had the opportunity to plead and test the construction of the written warranty provided in the work subcontract at the trial level. They opted instead to prove fault, and if that failed, to seek enforcement of a warranty imposed by law for the sale of goods unfit for their intended purpose. They were unable to convince a jury that Higgins had performed negligently. And they failed as well to demonstrate that the work subcontract was anything other than precisely what the parties had understood it to be; an agreement outlining the materials to be employed and the performance obligations to be assumed by a construction specialist hired to install a sprinkler system. Both the subcontract and the agreement between Milau and the owner were on their face and at heart no more than a series of performance undertakings, plans, schedules and specifications for the incorporation of the specialized system during the erection of a building — a predominantly labor-intensive endeavor. In the final analysis, the parties contemplated the workmanlike performance of a construction service. The fact that something went wrong less than six months after that service was performed does not change the underlying nature of the agreement governing its performance.

Given the predominantly service-oriented character of the transaction, neither the Code nor the common law of this State can be read to imply an undertaking to guard against economic loss stemming from the non-negligent performance by a construction firm which has not contractually bound itself to provide perfect results (see Schenectady Steel Co. v. Trimpoli Gen. Constr. Co., 43 A.D.2d 234, 238-239; id. pp. 239-240 [Cooke, J., concurring in part]; Ben Constr. Corp. v. Ventre, 23 A.D.2d 44; see also North American Leisure Corp. v. A&B Distributors, Ltd., 468 F.2d 695; 1 Anderson, Uniform Commercial Code [2d ed.] §§2-102:5, 2-105:10; 1955 Report of the N.Y. Law Rev. Commn., p. 361). In fact, where courts in other jurisdictions have purported to apply an implied warranty of fitness to transactions which in essence contemplated the rendition of services, what was actually imposed was no more than a "warranty that the performer would not act negligently" (e.g., Bloomsburg Mills, Inc. v. Sordoni Constr. Co., 401 Pa. 358), or a "warranty of workmanlike performance" imposing only the degree of care and skill that a reasonably prudent, skilled and qualified person would have exercised under the circumstances (e.g., Union Marine & Gen. Ins. Co. v. American Export Lines, Inc., 274 F. Supp. 123; Pepsi Cola Bottling Co. v. Superior Burner Serv. Co., 427 P.2d 833), or an "implied warranty of competence and ability ordinarily possessed by those in the profession" (Wolfe v. Virusky, 306 F. Supp. 519). (See generally Greenfield, Consumer Protection in Service Transactions Implied Warranties and Strict Liability in Tort, 1974 Utah L. Rev. 661, 668-673.) The performance of Higgins and Milau was tested under precisely this standard and found free from any actionable departure.

To be sure, particularly in cases involving personal injury, the absence of an enforceable contractual relationship for the technical sale of goods will not necessarily result in the foreclosure of all remedies, at least where the policies favoring the imposition of strict tort liability for the marketing of defective products are present (see, e.g., Victorson v. Boch Laundry, 37 N.Y.2d 394; Velez v. Craine & Clark Lumber Corp., 33 N.Y.2d 117) or where manufacturing misjudgments create an unreasonably dangerous condition (see Micallef v. Miehle, Co., 39 N.Y.2d 276). However, in the products liability cases, "[r]ather than arising out of the 'will or intention of the parties,' the liability imposed on the manufacturer . . . is predicated largely on considerations of sound social policy" (*Victorson v. Boch Laundry*, supra, p. 401, quoting Codling v. Paglia, 32 N.Y.2d 330, 340-341), including consumer reliance, marketing responsibility and the reasonableness of imposing loss redistribution. Yet the language and policies of the tort-based cases "should not be understood as in any way referring to the liability of a manufacturer [or tradesman] under familiar but different doctrines of the law of contracts for injuries sustained by a customer or other person with whom or for whose benefit the manufacturer previously has made a warranty or other agreement, express or implied" (*Victorson v. Boch Laundry*, supra, p. 400).

The appellants here, however, had at no time in the course of litigation sought to invoke these doctrines to redress their no less real but somehow less impelling economic loss. Additionally, to a much greater extent than professionals and tradesmen in the services arena where standards are usually set contractually, sellers of goods typically encourage mass public reliance on their products' fitness and safety through advertising, packaging and other promotional devices. This phenomenon is reflected in the fact that the Code's warranties attaching to sales of goods are underpinned by an assumption of some form of reasonable reliance by the unleveraged buyer.

No such situation presents itself here and we can find no reasonable basis in policy or in law for reading what would amount to a warranty of perfect results into the contractual relationships defined by the parties to this action.

Accordingly, the order of the Appellate Division should be affirmed.

———————————

The hot issue currently vexing the courts is whether Article 2 applies to transactions involving the sale of software. It is a shame that we don't have more statutory guidance on this and other vital issues affecting electronic commerce, since this form of buying and selling is hugely important. In 2011, online consumer sales constituted an estimated $200 billion in transactions, and business-to-business sales (B2B) were over $1 trillion. This is increasing dramatically each year as people and business eschew the world of paper and telephone and enthusiastically embrace cyberspace. There have been two notable, if unsuccessful, attempts to promulgate uniform laws to address issues of electronic commerce. In 2003, the ALI and NCCUSL promulgated a new version of Article 2, which addressed electronic transactions and sales of software. But, because of prolonged negotiations in its drafting, it was something of an ugly duckling, loved by no one and opposed by many. No states adopted it, and it was withdrawn in 2011. The Uniform Computer Information Transactions Act (UCITA) is a controversial statute proposed by the NCCUSL (but rejected by the ALI), which deals with the sale or licensing of software. There was so much opposition to the statute, which is considered anticonsumer, that it has been enacted (with some changes) only in Maryland and Virginia, and is not likely to be adopted anywhere else. Indeed four states have enacted so-called "bombshelter" statutes, forbidding the application of UCITA to their contracts, even if the parties were to choose UCITA as the relevant law; see Iowa Code §554D.104, N.C. Gen. Stat. §66-329, W. Va. Code §55-8-15, and 9 Vt. Stat. Ann. §2463(a).

In the meantime the courts have taken all sorts of stands on the issue of the applicability of the older version of Article 2 to the sale of software. Some courts say that this is not primarily a transaction in goods, and therefore use the common law instead of the Code; see Honeywell, Inc. v. Minolta Camera Co., Ltd., 41 U.C.C. Rep. Serv. 2d 403 (D.N.J. 1991). Others hold that the sale of software in a package is the sale of goods, but the development of software from scratch is the rendition of services; Pearl Investments, LLC v. Standard I/O, Inc., 257 F. Supp. 2d 326, 50 U.C.C. Rep. Serv. 2d 377 (D. Me. 2003); Olcott Intl. & Co., Inc. v. Micro Data Base Systems, Inc., 793 N.E.2d 1063, 51 U.C.C. Rep. Serv. 2d 352 (Ind. App. 2003). Others use Article 2 either by analogy, see I. Lan Systems, Inc. v. Netscout Service Level Corp., 183 F. Supp. 2d 328, 46 U.C.C. Rep. Serv. 2d 287 (D. Mass. 2002), or because the parties themselves seemed to have assumed that Article 2 governed the transaction. However, the vast majority of courts have routinely applied Article 2, finding that the sale of software is the sale of goods. The leading case is Advent System Ltd. v. Unisys Corp., 925 F.2d 670, 13 U.C.C. Rep. Serv. 2d 669 (3d Cir. 1991); see also Dahlmann v. Sulcus Hospitality Technologies Corp., 63 F. Supp. 2d 772, 39 U.C.C. Rep. Serv. 2d 299 (E.D. Mich. 1999); Softman Products Co., LLC v. Adobe Systems, Inc., 171 F. Supp. 2d 1075, 45 U.C.C. Rep. Serv. 2d 945 (C.D. Cal. 2001).

Analysts Intl. Corp. v. Recycled Paper Products, Inc.

United States District Court, Northern District of Illinois, 1987
1987 WL 12917, 45 U.C.C. Rep. Serv. 746

GRADY, Chief Judge.

This diversity case is before us on the motions of plaintiff/counter-defendant Analysts International Corporation ("AIC") to dismiss the counterclaim of defendant/counterplaintiff Recycled Paper Products, Inc. ("RPP") pursuant to Federal Rule of Civil Procedure 12(b)(6) and for partial summary judgment under Federal Rule of Civil Procedure 56. For the reasons below, we deny the motion for summary judgment and grant the motion to dismiss in part.

FACTS

The facts of this case, although many, are not complex. RPP is an Illinois corporation which publishes and supplies greeting cards and other gift products to retail stores nationwide. RPP's Statement of Facts at 1 ("RPP Facts"). AIC is a Minnesota corporation, with an office in suburban Chicago, which develops, designs, markets, and implements computer software systems. AIC's Statement of Facts at 2 ("AIC Facts"). RPP sought to computerize its system of reordering merchandise; it conceived of a computer-assisted merchandising program ("CAMP") which would automatically process computer-scannable order tickets sent to RPP by its customers. RPP Facts at 2. From the ticket, CAMP would identify the customer, store location and desired product; the computer would analyze the customer's credit, and the product's sales and inventory history, and determine whether to ship the desired product, substitute a different product, or reject the order altogether. Id. at 3. CAMP would also send out invoices and credit the sales force with their commissions. Id.

In late January 1983, RPP drafted the CAMP proposal, which was later refined in August 1983. AIC Facts at 3. RPP decided to hire an outside computer programming firm to develop and implement CAMP. RPP Facts at 3. In the fall of 1983, RPP solicited bids from several software houses, including AIC. AIC supplied RPP with promotional literature. Id. at 4-5. RPP contracted with AIC to send a consultant to conduct a "feasibility study." Id. at 6. After three months of studying RPP's business operations, AIC concluded that it could design, develop and implement the CAMP system. Id. at 7. RPP paid AIC $16,000, calculated at an hourly rate, for the study. Id.

AIC and RPP then entered into a contract. The parties dispute almost every material term of the contract, which was partly in writing and partly oral. On January 17, 1984, AIC sent RPP a letter stating the project would take 36 weeks and would be completed in October 1984, at a price of $278,000. RPP Facts at 8. AIC contends that the price was only a rough estimate and that RPP had agreed to pay AIC on an hourly basis. AIC Facts at 5. RPP claims AIC gave it constant assurances that the price was fixed and that the project would not run past October 1984. RPP Facts at 8-9. The contract was later mutually modified to expand the capacities of CAMP—at an additional cost of $124,210, but the October completion date remained. RPP Counterclaim at ¶24 ("CC"). AIC began to work on the project and submitted biweekly invoices which indicated they were computed on an hourly rate basis; RPP approved and paid the invoices. AIC Facts at 5.

In October 1984, AIC announced the work would not be completed on time; the CAMP system was implemented during the latter part of December 1984. RPP Facts at 13. The system was not tested and personnel were not trained on the system before implementation. Id. RPP states that AIC knew of problems in CAMP all along and did not tell RPP. Id. at 10-12. The program did not perform any of its intended functions. Id. at 13. Between January and June 1985, RPP suffered severe business disruptions.

Id. Among other problems, the system would credit customers with undeserved discounts, orders were erroneously filled, and sales commissions were not properly credited. Id. at 14-17. Throughout this period, AIC tried to fix the program. RPP continued to pay AIC's invoices, totaling $928,689. AIC Facts at 6. RPP hired outside auditors to assess the state of CAMP in May 1985. RPP Facts at 18. The auditors concluded that the system would have to be redone in its entirety. Id. AIC claims that its system was substantially fixed by May 1985. AIC Facts at 6. Nonetheless, AIC worked on CAMP until October 1985, when it left RPP's premises because of RPP's refusal to pay an outstanding bill of $330,386. Id. AIC instituted this lawsuit to recover the unpaid account balance under breach of contract and fraud theories. RPP countersued in a nine-count complaint also alleging breach of contract and warranty, and fraud, among other things. AIC has moved for summary judgment on RPP's breach of contract and warranty counts. It also has moved to dismiss RPP's counts charging common law and statutory fraud, negligent misrepresentation, malpractice, and RICO. We begin with the motion for summary judgment.

MOTION FOR SUMMARY JUDGMENT

AIC moves for summary judgment on RPP's counterclaim for breach of contract and for breach of an express warranty, implied warranty of merchantability and warranty of fitness for a particular purpose. (Counts I-IV respectively.) We begin with Counts III and IV for breach of the implied warranties found in Sections 2-314 and 2-315 of the Uniform Commercial Code, Ill. Rev. Stat. ch. 26, ¶¶2-314, 2-315 (1985) ("UCC"). AIC argues that its agreement with RPP was to provide services, not goods, and that the implied warranties of merchantibility and fitness for a particular purpose apply only to sales of goods. AIC Memorandum in Support of Summary Judgment at 13 ("AIC S/J Mem."). RPP argues that software transactions are governed by the UCC and in any event, the nature of the contract is a disputed question of material fact for the jury. RPP Memorandum in Opposition to Summary Judgment at 13 ("RPP S/J Mem.").

On a motion for summary judgment, the moving party has the burden of establishing that there is no genuine issue of material fact and that it is entitled to judgment as a matter of law. Chrysler v. Gallagher, No. 85C 5930, Memorandum Op. at 6 (N.D. Ill. Jan. 29, 1987) (Grady, J.), citing Cedillo v. International Ass'n of Bridge and Structural Iron Workers, 603 F.2d 7 (7th Cir. 1979). AIC has provided uncontroverted evidence that it did not sell computer hardware, or any "off the shelf" software to RPP. AIC S/J Reply at 2. In further support of its motion, AIC proffers RPP's concession that their agreement entailed substantial design and programming services to be rendered by AIC. AIC S/J Reply at 2; RPP S/J Mem. at 14. This evidence, however, does not establish that AIC is entitled to judgment as a matter of law. The legal issue presented is whether the UCC applies to the purchase of CAMP — a computerized automatic merchandise reordering system. This, in turn, depends on whether the agreement involved is one for a "transaction in goods." 111. Rev. Stat. ch. 26, ¶2-102. AIC argues that agreements to write custom developed computer programs are not transactions in goods. AIC S/J Mem. at 14-15. As support, AIC cites cases holding that the subject of computer program contracts is the skill of the programmers, and not the tangible discs and tapes on which the programs would be stored, so that the transactions were not within Article 2 of the UCC. Data Processing Services, Inc. v. L.H. Smith Oil Corp., 492 N.E.2d 314 (Ind. Ct. App. 1986); Liberty Financial Management Corp. v. Beneficial Data Processing Corp., 670 S.W.2d 40 (Mo. Ct. App. 1984). We are not persuaded by the reasoning found in these cases. Data Processing, for example, found the transaction to be "clear cut" because no "hardware" was sold. 492 N.E.2d at 314. The plaintiff instead retained the computer programmers to develop an "electronic data processing system" to meet its needs. Id. And although the end result would be stored on discs and tapes, it was the programmers' "knowledge, skill, and ability" which was the subject of the contract. Id. at 319. The court mentioned a few paragraphs earlier that plaintiffs contracted for a data processing system. The court's analysis of such a system in terms of discs, on the one hand, and skill on the other, obscures the synthetic nature of software. Software has both tangible and intangible elements. Note, Software and the UCC, 65 Boston U. L. Rev. 129, 131 (1985). Focusing on one aspect of software to the exclusion of the other loses sight of the whole of the contract, which was for a computer system. Obviously the knowledge of the programmer is important, but only insofar as it enables him to produce the software according to the contract. See RRX Industries, Inc. v. LabCon Inc., 772 F.2d 543, 546 (9th Cir. 1985) (programmers' services incidental to contract for software); Triangle Underwriters, Inc. v. Honeywell, Inc., 604 F.2d 737, 742-743 (2d Cir. 1979) (notwithstanding extensive designing services, transaction for computer software was a sale of goods).

AIC next argues that where a transaction primarily involves creative efforts resulting in a unique work product, the contract is one for services. AIC S/J Mem. at 14. AIC cites two Illinois authorities, neither of which we find persuasive. See Nitrin, Inc. v. Bethlehem Steel Corp., 35 Ill. App. 3d 377, 342 N.E.2d 65 (1st Dist. 1976); Boddie v. Litton Unit Handling Systems, 118 Ill. App. 3d 520, 455 N.E.2d 142 (2d Dist. 1983). In *Nitrin*, plaintiffs sued a general contractor for damages sustained when a specially manufactured piece of equipment broke down. The court noted that the 41-page contract between plaintiff and general contractor, drafted by the plaintiff, clearly indicated that the general contractor was responsible only for design and engineering work. Id. at 77. The court held that because the contract did not concern the sale of goods it was not within the purview of the UCC. Id. The situation before us contrasts markedly with *Nitrin*, for the contract between the parties here is hardly explicit; the only written embodiment of their agreement is a letter, drafted by AIC, which refers not to AIC's responsibility for services but for "system delivery" at the end of October. RPP S/J Mem. at Exhibit 8 (Letter of January 19, 1984).

In *Boddie*, plaintiff was a postal worker who was injured by machinery specifically manufactured for the Postal Service. The *Boddie* court explicitly held that the UCC governed the contract under which the machine was sold to the Postal Service's general contractor. 455 N.E.2d at 150, 151. The plaintiff, however, was not in the class of protected people who could seek recovery under the UCC. We do not see how this case supports AIC's position. Furthermore, we can find no Illinois support for AIC's position that specially commissioned goods involving creative efforts are outside of the UCC.

Where an agreement involves both goods and services, Illinois uses the "dominant purpose" test to determine whether an agreement is one for goods rather than for services and is therefore governed by Article 2 of the UCC. Snellman v. A.B. Dick, No. 81 C 3048, Memorandum Op. at 20 (N.D. Ill. Mar. 20, 1987) (Grady, J.). The court must inquire whether the "essence or dominant factor" in the formation of the contract was the provision of goods. *Snellman* at 21 (citing Sally Beauty Co. v. Nexxus Products Co., Inc., 801 F.2d 1001, 1007 (7th Cir. 1986)). RPP has provided much evidence by way of deposition to support its position that the essence of the contract was for a computer program and that the service aspect, though substantial, was an incident to the product. RPP S/J Mem. at Freidmann Dep. 51-52, 81, 109-10, 121-122; Keiser Dep. at 53, 72-73, 105, 171, 182-186, 220-221, 268; Lohmeyer Dep. at 643, 644. AIC has produced no contrary evidence.

We conclude that except for the provision of a good — a computerized reordering system — the agreement in this case would have no purpose. Had RPP gone to a computer store and bought this software off the shelf, there would be no doubt that the software was a good. Because no "off the shelf" software was adequate, AIC was expected to do a great deal of work, to be sure, but that work was to result in the production of a computer program. To call that work "service," implying that it was service rendered to RPP, is to beg the question. Any supplier of a specially designed item must necessarily perform whatever work is required to create or produce the item. But this does not make the undertaking a "service" to the purchaser of the item. AIC itself has admitted that "the end product of [our] services has almost always been an operating computer program or software system designed to conform to the requirements of each specific client." RPP S/J Mem. at Exhibit 18.

We therefore hold that RPP's agreement with AIC was a transaction in goods and was within the purview of the UCC. RPP is entitled to put on proof at trial of breaches of the implied warranties of merchantability and of fitness for a particular purpose. AIC's motion for summary judgment on Counts III and IV is denied. . . .

───────────────

Analysts International held that the contract to "design, develop, and implement" software was a contract for the sale of goods. The opposite result was reached on similar facts in Conwell v. Gray Loon Outdoor Marketing Group, Inc., 906 N.E.2d 805, 812, 69 U.C.C. Rep. Serv. 2d 71 (Ind. 2009):

> A website created under arrangements calling for the designer to fashion, program, and host its operation on the designer's server is neither tangible nor moveable in the conventional sense. To be sure, one can copy a website using tangible, movable objects such as hard drives, cables, and disks. These objects are in themselves just as certainly goods, but it does not necessarily follow that the information they contain classifies as goods as well. The arrangement between POA and Gray Loon contemplated a custom design for a single customer and an ongoing hosting relationship. As such, conventional "predominant thrust" doctrine suggests that the U.C.C. did not apply.

Anthony Pools v. Sheehan

Maryland Court of Appeals, 1983
295 Md. 285, 455 A.2d 434, 35 U.C.C. Rep. Serv. 408

RODOWSKY, J.

This products liability case presents questions of implied warranty and of defense to strict liability in tort involving an in-ground, gunite swimming pool and its diving board. Analysis of whether there is any implied warranty and, if so, whether it can be excluded takes us into the problem of hybrid transactions and into Md. Code (1975), §2-316.1(1) and (2) of the Commercial Law Article (C.L.).[2]

───────────────

2. C.L. §2-316.1 in relevant part provides:

"(1) The provisions of §2-316 do not apply to sales of consumer goods, as defined by §9-109, services, or both.

"(2) Any oral or written language used by a seller of consumer goods and services, which attempts to exclude or modify any implied warranties of merchantability and fitness for a particular purpose or to exclude or modify the consumer's remedies for breach of those warranties, is unenforceable. However, the seller may recover from the manufacturer any damages resulting from breach of the implied warranty of merchantability or fitness for a particular purpose." [This is a non-uniform addition to the UCC, and is not the law in most other states. — EDS.]

Plaintiffs, John B. Sheehan (Sheehan) and his wife, Pilar E. Sheehan, of Potomac Woods, Maryland, sued Anthony Pools, a division of Anthony Industries, Inc. (Anthony) in the Circuit Court for Montgomery County. Sheehan sustained bodily injuries when he fell from the side of the diving board of the plaintiffs' new, backyard swimming pool. The swimming pool had been designed and built by Anthony. Anthony also designed and manufactured the diving board which it installed as part of the swimming pool transaction.

The swimming pool is 16 feet by 40 feet, with a depth from 3 feet to 8 feet. Its style is "Grecian," which means that there is a curved alcove in the center of each of the 16 foot sides. The 6-foot-long diving board in question was installed over an imaginary centerline bisecting the alcove at the deep end of the pool. Anthony had completed its work by mid-June of 1976. On August 21, 1976 the plaintiffs entertained at a pool party. Sheehan testified that he had not previously used the diving board. He said that on that evening he emerged from swimming in the pool, stepped up onto the diving board, and, while walking toward the pool end of the diving board, slipped and fell from the right side of the diving board and struck the coping of the pool.

Plaintiffs advanced two theories of liability. First, skid resistant material built into the surface of the top of the diving board did not extend to the very edge of the board on each side. It stopped approximately one inch short of each edge. This condition, it was claimed, breached an implied warranty of merchantability. Plaintiffs also presented testimony directed toward proving that use of the "defective" diving board, particularly as positioned in the alcove, was unreasonably dangerous.

At the end of the plaintiffs' case, the trial court directed a verdict for Anthony as to liability founded on warranty, because the written contract between the parties conspicuously provided that the express warranties which it contained were in lieu of any other warranties, express or implied. The case went to the jury on a strict liability in tort theory. Verdict was in favor of the defendant, and judgment was so entered.

Plaintiffs appealed to the Court of Special Appeals which reversed and remanded for a new trial. That court said that "the swimming pool package purchased by the Sheehans constitute[d] 'consumer goods'" so that C.L. §2-316.1 rendered ineffective Anthony's attempt to limit the implied warranty of merchantability. Sheehan v. Anthony Pools, 50 Md. App. 614, 619, 440 A.2d 1085, 1088 (1982). The granting of the directed verdict based on the contractual limitation was held to be error. Judgment based on the jury verdict was reversed because of error in the instructions. As to that issue, Judge Moore, writing for the court, concluded:

In the instant case, it is our view that while the trial court was eminently correct in rejecting the defendant's request for a contributory negligence instruction, the matter should not have ended there. On the basis of the facts involved and of the Sheehans' specific request, an instruction should have been granted that Mr. Sheehan's inadvertent or careless use of the diving board and the pool would not bar his recovery. On the other hand, giving such an instruction would also have required an appropriate instruction on assumption of risk, i.e., that the defendant was entitled to prevail if Mr. Sheehan had discovered the defect, was aware of the danger, and then proceeded unreasonably to use the diving board and pool. [Id. at 625-626, 440 A.2d at 1092.]

We granted Anthony's petition for certiorari which raised three questions. In essence, the petition asks us to review (1) the implied warranty issue; (2) the inadvertent use instruction issue; and (3) whether the Court of Special Appeals erred "in holding, as dictum that contributory negligence is not a defense in a strict liability case."

1

The warranty issue, as presented here, involves only the implied warranty of merchantability under C.L. §2-314. Plaintiffs do not argue that their warranty claim is based upon any express warranty or that the diving board was to be used for other than its ordinary purpose. Anthony contends that the Sheehans' swimming pool is not "goods," that exclusion of implied warranties is allowed, and that a directed verdict on the plaintiffs' warranty count was proper. We agree with the Court of Special Appeals that the directed verdict was improper in this case, but we reach that conclusion by a somewhat different route.

Title 2 of the Commercial Law Article is the Maryland Uniform Commercial Code Sales. C.L. §2-101. Unless the context otherwise requires, that title "applies to transactions in goods. . . ." C.L. §2-102. For purposes of title 2, and with certain exclusions not here relevant, "goods" means "all things (including specially manufactured goods) which are movable at the time of identification to the contract for sale. . . ." C.L. §2-105(1). C.L. §2-314(1) in part provides that "[u]nless excluded or modified (§2-316), a warranty that the goods shall be merchantable is implied in a contract for their sale if the seller is a merchant with respect to goods of that kind." C.L. §2-316(2) permits the exclusion or modification of the implied warranty of merchantability by language which mentions merchantability and which, in the case of a writing, is conspicuous. The Maryland UCC, in §2-316.1, then states that the "provisions of §2-316 do not apply to sales of consumer goods, as defined by §9-109, services, or both," and that any "language used by a seller of consumer goods and services, which attempts to exclude or modify any implied warranties . . . is unenforceable." C.L. §9-109(1) provides that goods are "'[c]onsumer goods' if they are used or bought for use primarily for personal, family or household purposes."

The May 25, 1976 contract between Anthony and the plaintiffs is a printed form designed for use in Anthony's Washington, D.C. region. It is a single sheet of paper, approximately 15" by 20", with printing on both sides. The face of the document is three columns wide. The lefthand column on the face is headed "Retail Installment Contract." Under that column are set forth Anthony's contractor license numbers in Virginia, Maryland and the District of Columbia, a statement of the buyer's right to cancel a home solicitation contract, federal truth-in-lending disclosures and a detachable notice of cancellation. The next two columns on the face are entitled "Swimming Pool Construction Agreement." Anthony "agrees to construct for and sell to" the plaintiffs, called "'Buyer,'" the "swimming pool and related equipment described below (herein collectively called the 'work') to be installed at" the plaintiffs' home for a fixed cash price. Below this covenant, under the heading "Plans and Specifications," are two columns listing 47 items, some of which are automatically included and some of which are optional. These items appear under the headings, "General Construction Specifications," "Hydraulic and Filtering Specifications," "Color-Coordinated Exclusive Deck Equip.," "Automatic Pool Equipment" and "Other Anthony Features." In the subject contract Anthony's obligations included pool layout, structural engineering, obtaining construction permits, excavation, use of engineered steel reinforcing throughout the pool structure, guniting the pool structure, finishing the pool interior with hand troweled, waterproof plaster, installation both of a six-inch band of water-line tile and of coping and installation of a filter, a pump, a skimmer and a specified model of six foot diving board. The reverse side of the contract contains two columns of terms and conditions, including the implied warranty exclusion. The subject contract presents a mixed or hybrid transaction. It is in part a contract for the rendering of services and in part a contract for the sale of goods.

Burton v. Artery Company, 279 Md. 94, 367 A.2d 935 (1977) addressed the applicability vel non of the Maryland UCC Sales to hybrid contracts. The issue presented was whether the four-year statute of limitations under §2-725(1), or the general three-year statute, applied to a contract to landscape around a construction project of 13 buildings. The contract called for the furnishing and planting of hundreds of trees, of hundreds of shrubs, and of sod. We there adopted the test enunciated in Bonebrake v. Cox, 499 F.2d 951 (8th Cir. 1974), a case holding that the sale and installation of bowling lanes, with associated equipment, is a contract of sale and not of services. That test is whether "the predominant factor . . . , the thrust, the purpose, reasonably stated, is a transaction of sale with labor incidentally involved," or vice versa. 279 Md. at 114-115, 367 A.2d at 946. Applying that test, the court held the contract in *Burton* to be predominantly a transaction in goods. See also Snyder v. Herbert Greenbaum & Associates, 38 Md. App. 144, 380 A.2d 618 (1977) (contract to furnish and install over 17,000 yards of carpet in 228 apartments was predominantly a sale of goods).

G. Wallach, The Law of Sales Under the Uniform Commercial Code (1981), §11.05[3] at 11-28 describes the current state of the law concerning implied warranties in hybrid transactions to be as follows:

> The general pre-Code approach to this issue was to examine the transaction to see whether the goods aspect or the service aspect of the transaction predominated. If the service aspect predominated, no warranties of quality were imposed in the transaction, not even if the defect or complaint related to the goods that were involved rather than to the services. This mechanical approach remains the most popular method of resolving the issue.[3]

The few reported holdings concerning whether Article 2 of the UCC applies to swimming pool installations have involved a variety of types of pools and are not uniform. A Connecticut trial court decision dealt with the alleged breach of the implied warranty of merchantability in the installation of an aboveground swimming pool. Its sides were plywood panels, braced by a 29"×4" support. A vinyl liner was laid within the sides. That court applied the predominant purpose test. It held that the owners did not offer any adequate evidence on the apportionment between labor and material and equipment, and so they failed to meet the burden of establishing the existence of a warranty under the UCC. Gulash v. Stylarama, Inc., 33 Conn. Supp. 108, 364 A.2d 1221 (1975). A vinyl liner pool was also involved in Riffe v. Black, 548 S.W.2d 175 (Ky. App. 1977). The walls of that pool consisted of prefabricated steel which was set into an excavated site. Sand was troweled for the bottom of the pool. Leaking had resulted from the contractor's failure both to reseal the liner after a wrinkle had developed during installation and to repair the hole which developed later. The Kentucky court applied a predominant purpose test and necessarily classified the contract as one for the sale of goods. It was held that the warranty provisions of that state's UCC "apply to services when the sale is primarily one of goods and the services are necessary to insure that those goods are merchantable and fit for the ordinary purpose." Id. at 177. Judgment for the pool owners was affirmed. Ben Construction Corp. v. Ventre, 23 A.D.2d 44, 257 N.Y.S.2d 988 (1965), is not a UCC case, but it is analogous. It

---

3. Among recent decisions applying the predominant purpose test are: White v. Peabody Construction Co., Inc., 386 Mass. 121, 434 N.E.2d 1015 (1982) (contract for the construction of a housing project was one for services so that there was no warranty implied under the UCC on the windows or frames, which leaked); Milau Associates v. North Avenue Development Corp., 42 N.Y.2d 482, 368 N.E.2d 1247, 398 N.Y.S.2d 882 (1977) (there is no warranty of merchantability on a section of pipe which ruptured and which had been installed as part of a sprinkler system in the course of construction of a new building); Northwestern Equipment, Inc. v. Cudmore, 312 N.W.2d 347 (N.D. 1981) (contract for the repair of the transmission in a used bulldozer is a contract for services and carries no implied warranty of fitness for a particular purpose, even though the charges for parts exceeded the charges for labor).

presented the claim of the pool owners for return of moneys paid, based on a section of the New York Personal Property Law. The pool is described in the opinion only as "installed." Judgment for the defendant contractor was affirmed, 3-2. In the majority's view, the contract was for work, labor and services and was not a sale, while the dissent viewed the transaction as primarily a sale of a swimming pool with an incidental agreement to install.

The Court of Special Appeals has recently held that C.L. §2-601's "perfect tender" provisions do not apply to a contract for the installation of an inground, concrete swimming pool. There was no transaction in goods because the pool was not movable. Chlan v. KDI Sylvan Pools, Inc., 53 Md. App. 123, 452 A.2d 1279 (1982) [No. 192, September Term, 1982, decided December 7, 1982].

Here, Anthony undertook the construction of an inground, steel reinforced, gunite swimming pool with hand finished plaster surfacing, tile trim, and coping. The Sheehans were not buying steel rods, or gunite, or plaster or tiles. The predominant factor, the thrust, the purpose of the contract was the furnishing of labor and service by Anthony, while the sale of the diving board was incidental to the construction of the pool itself. The question thus resolves itself into whether the predominant purpose test, which we applied in *Burton* for the purpose of determining whether the UCC statute of limitations governed that transaction, should be applied to determine whether the sale of the diving board, included in the Anthony-Sheehans transaction, carries an implied warranty of merchantability under §2-314.

Were the predominant purpose test mechanically to be applied to the facts of this case, there would be no quality warranty implied as to the diving board. But here the contract expressly states that Anthony agrees not only to construct the swimming pool, but also to sell the related equipment selected by the Sheehans. The Sheehans are described as "'Buyer.'" The diving board itself is not structurally integrated into the swimming pool. Anthony offered the board as an optional accessory, just as Anthony offered the options of purchasing a pool ladder or a sliding board. When identified to the contract, the diving board was movable. See C.L. §2-105. The board itself remains detachable from its support, as reflected by a photograph in evidence. The diving board, considered alone, is goods. Had it been purchased by the Sheehans in a transaction distinct from the pool construction agreement with Anthony, there would have been an implied warranty of merchantability.

A number of commentators have advocated a more policy-oriented approach to determining whether warranties of quality and fitness are implied with respect to goods sold as part of a hybrid transaction in which service predominates. See Farnsworth, Implied Warranties of Quality in Non-Sales Cases, 57 Colum. L. Rev. 653 (1957); Comment, Sale of Goods in Service-Predominated Transactions, 37 Fordham L. Rev. 115 (1968); Note, Products and the Professional: Strict Liability in the Sale-Service Hybrid Transaction, 24 Hastings L.J. 111 (1972); Note, Contracts for Goods and

Services and Article 2 of the Uniform Commercial Code, 9 Rut.-Cam. L.J. 303 (1978); Comment, Sales-Service Hybrid Transactions: A Policy Approach, 28 Sw. L.J. 575 (1974). To support their position, these commentators in general emphasize loss shifting, risk distribution, consumer reliance and difficulties in the proof of negligence. These concepts underlie strict liability in tort. See Phipps v. General Motors Corp., 278 Md. 337, 363 A.2d 955 (1976).

A leading case applying a policy approach in this problem area is Newmark v. Gimbel's Incorporated, 54 N.J. 585, 258 A.2d 697 (1969). There the patron of a beauty parlor sued for injury to her hair and scalp allegedly resulting from a lotion used in giving her a permanent wave. Because the transaction was viewed as the rendering of a service, the trial court had ruled that there could be no warranty liability. The intermediate appellate court's reversal was affirmed by the Supreme Court of New Jersey which reasoned in part as follows (id., at 593, 258 A.2d at 701):

> The transaction, in our judgment, is a hybrid partaking of incidents of a sale and a service. It is really partly the rendering of service, and partly the supplying of goods for a consideration. Accordingly, we agree with the Appellate Division that an implied warranty of fitness of the products used in giving the permanent wave exists with no less force than it would have in the case of a simple sale. Obviously in permanent wave operations the product is taken into consideration in fixing the price of the service. The no-separate-charge argument puts excessive emphasis on form and downgrades the overall substance of the transaction. If the beauty parlor operator bought and applied the permanent wave solution to her own hair and suffered injury thereby, her action in warranty or strict liability in tort against the manufacturer-seller of the product clearly would be maintainable because the basic transaction would have arisen from a conventional type of sale. It does not accord with logic to deny a similar right to a patron against the beauty parlor operator or the manufacturer when the purchase and sale were made in anticipation of and for the purpose of use of the product on the patron who would be charged for its use. Common sense demands that such patron be deemed a customer as to both manufacturer and beauty parlor operator. [Citations omitted.]

The court was careful to limit its holding to commercial transactions, as opposed to those predominantly involving professional services. Id. at 596-597, 258 A.2d at 702-703.

1 R. Anderson, Uniform Commercial Code (1970), §2-102:5 at 209 refers to *Newmark* as illustrative of a possible trend in the law and states:

> It is probable that a goods-services transaction will come to be subjected to Article 2 of the Code insofar as the contractor's obligations with respect to the goods themselves are involved, at least where the goods involved could have been purchased in the general market and used by the plaintiff-customer.

A warranty of fitness for particular purpose under §2-315 of the UCC was implied in Worrell v. Barnes, 87 Nev. 204, 484 P.2d 573 (1971). In that case a contractor was engaged to do some carpentry work and to connect various appliances in the plaintiff's home to an existing liquified petroleum gas system. The appliances were not supplied by the contractor. Suit was for damage to the plaintiff's home resulting from a fire. The plaintiff produced evidence that the fire was caused by a defective fitting installed by the contractor which had allowed propane to escape. Dismissal of the plaintiff's claims, based on the Nevada version of strict liability in tort and based on implied warranty, was reversed. The court reasoned that, because it had held that the contractor had sold a product so as to bring into operation the doctrine of strict liability, "so also must we deem this case to involve 'goods' within the purview of the Uniform Commercial Code." Id. at 208, 484 P.2d at 576.

1 W. Hawkland, Uniform Commercial Code Series (1982), §2-102:04, at Art. 2, p. 12 has suggested what might be called a "gravamen" test in light of the decision in *Worrell.* He writes:

> Unless uniformity would be impaired thereby, it might be more sensible and facilitate administration, at least in this grey area, to abandon the "predominant factor" test and focus instead on whether the gravamen of the action involves goods or services. For example, in *Worrell v. Barnes*, if the gas escaped because of a defective fitting or connector, the case might be characterized as one involving the sale of goods. On the other hand, if the gas escaped because of poor work by Barnes the case might be characterized as one involving services, outside the scope of the UCC.

In this state, the provisions of C.L. §2-316.1(1) and (2) reflect an implicit policy judgment by the General Assembly which prevents the mechanical application of the predominant purpose test to cases like the one under consideration. Subsection (1) states that §2-316, dealing in part with the manner in which an implied warranty of merchantability may be excluded or modified, does not apply to "consumer goods . . . services, or both." Under subsection (2) language "used by a seller of consumer goods and services" to exclude or modify implied warranties is unenforceable. The hybrid transaction is covered by, or at least embraced within, those terms.

Under the predominant purpose test, as applied by a majority of the courts, a hybrid transaction must first be classified as a sale of goods in order for there to be UCC-based, implied warranties on the goods included in the transaction. If goods predominate and they are consumer goods, §2-316.1 would render contractual disclaimers of implied warranties ineffective because that section applies to a seller of consumer goods. In such cases the result of applying the predominant purpose test is consistent with §2-316.1. If, however, the predominant purpose test results in classifying the transaction as a contract for services there would, under the majority approach, be no UCC-based, implied warranties on goods included in the transaction. But, §2-316.1 declares that a seller of consumer services may not contractually disclaim implied warranties. In the hybrid transaction, at least one effect of §2-316.1 is to render ineffective contractual disclaimers of implied warranties on consumer goods included in a consumer service transaction. Section 2-316.1 is at least partially predicated on a legislative understanding that warranties under the UCC are implied as to the goods included in such transactions. An all or nothing classification of the instant transaction under the predominant purpose test would mean there could be no UCC-based, implied warranties on the diving board and would be contrary to the legislative policy implicit in §2-316.1. Consequently, we cannot use that test in order to determine whether UCC-based warranties are implied as to consumer goods in a transaction that is predominantly for the rendering of consumer services.

The gravamen test of Dean Hawkland suggests the vehicle for satisfying the legislative policy. Accordingly, we hold that where, as part of a commercial transaction, consumer goods are sold which retain their character as consumer goods after completion of the performance promised to the consumer, and where monetary loss or personal injury is claimed to have resulted from a defect in the consumer goods, the provisions of the Maryland UCC dealing with implied warranties apply to the consumer goods, even if the transaction is predominantly one for the rendering of consumer services. The facts of the instant case, however, make it unnecessary for us presently to decide whether §2-316.1 would require that UCC-based, implied warranties also extend to consumer goods which are used up in the course of rendering the consumer service to the consumer.

Thus the diving board which Anthony sold to the Sheehans as part of the swimming pool construction contract carried an implied warranty of merchantability under C.L. §2-314. Anthony's contractual disclaimer of that warranty was ineffective under C.L. §2-316.1. As a result, the trial court erred in relying on the disclaimer as a basis for directing a verdict in favor of Anthony on the warranty count. . . .

Judgment of the court of special appeals affirmed. Costs to be paid by Anthony Industries, Inc.

B. Merchants

PROBLEM 2

Portia Moot, a third-year law student, sold her car to a fellow student. Does Article 2 of the UCC apply to this transaction? Would §2-314 apply to the sale?

Siemen v. Alden

Illinois Appellate Court, 1975

34 Ill. App. 3d 961, 341 N.E.2d 713, 18 U.C.C. Rep. Serv. 884

MORAN, J.

Plaintiff sued defendants to recover for injuries he sustained while operating an automated multi-rip saw. The three-count complaint sought recovery on theories of strict tort liability for sale of a defective product, breach of warranties, and negligence. Plaintiff proceeds on this appeal against defendant Korleski only. He appeals the order of the trial court granting defendant's motion for summary judgment on count one, alleging strict tort liability, and count two, alleging breach of warranties.

Plaintiff had owned and operated a sawmill since 1961. In 1968, he decided to purchase a multi-rip saw to increase his production of decking pallets. Upon the suggestion of a customer, plaintiff contacted Lloyd G. Alden, manufacturer of the saw in question. Alden informed plaintiff that a new saw could not be delivered in less than six months and suggested that plaintiff contact defendant Korleski who owned two of the Alden saws. Plaintiff contacted defendant who advised him that he indeed had two saws: the one he was currently using, and an older one purchased in 1962 which had not been used since 1965. Thereafter the parties met on two occasions at defendant's sawmill to discuss plaintiff's possible purchase of the older saw. At the first meeting, defendant demonstrated the newer saw which operated in the same manner as the one plaintiff was considering purchasing. Plaintiff's son accompanied him to the second meeting at which time plaintiff was first shown the saw in question. It was sitting, partially dismantled, in a corner and was covered with boards and sawdust. Defendant informed plaintiff that it was [not] in operating condition and that plaintiff would have to supply and install saw blades, motor, shiv, belts, pulleys, and a sawdust removal apparatus in order to use it. Thereafter, the parties agreed on a purchase price of $2900.

Plaintiff's injury, which precipitated the instant suit, occurred in 1970 when a cant of wood exploded while being fed through the saw in question.

On appeal, plaintiff contends that summary judgment in favor of defendant should be reversed because (1) defendant had a sufficient relationship to the saw which injured plaintiff to subject him to strict liability for sale of the defective product, and (2) under the Uniform Commercial Code, ch. 26, §2-314 and §2-315 (Ill. Rev. Stat. 1971, ch. 26, §§2-314, 2-315), the defendant is liable for implied warranties.

In Suvada v. White Motor Co., 32 Ill. 2d 612 [2 U.C.C. Rep. Serv. 762] (1965), the Illinois Supreme Court adopted the provisions of Section 402A of the Restatement of the Law of Torts, 2d (1965), which states:

Special Liability of Seller of Product for Physical Harm to User or Consumer

(1) One who sells any product in a defective condition unreasonably dangerous to the user or consumer or to his property is subject to liability for

physical harm thereby caused to the ultimate user or consumer, or to his property, if

    (a) the seller is engaged in the business of selling such a product, and

    (b) it is expected to and does reach the user or consumer without substantial change in the condition in which it is sold.

  (2) The rule stated in Subsection (1) applies although

    (a) the seller has exercised all possible care in the preparation and sale of his product, and

    (b) the user or consumer has not bought the product from or entered into any contractual relation with the seller. [Restatement of the Law of Torts, Second, ch. 14, §402A.]

The plain language of the rule limits the application to a seller engaged in the business of selling the product which proved defective. This limitation is buttressed by the comment accompanying the rule in that the occasional seller is explicitly excluded. (Restatement of Torts, 2d, Comment, page 350. See 55 I.B.J. 906 (1967).) Plaintiff contends that because the sale of the saw occurred within the scope and conduct of defendant's business, and because defendant modified the machine to suit his own purposes thereby creating the condition which led to plaintiff's injury, defendant had a relationship to the saw sufficient to subject him to strict liability. Plaintiff's argument fails to overcome the clear requirement of the rule that the seller be engaged in the business of selling the particular product. In the instant case, defendant asserted and plaintiff has not denied that defendant's only sale of a saw or sawmill equipment was to plaintiff. It is therefore apparent that the sale is an isolated transaction and does not come within the provisions of 402A. Balido v. Improved Machinery Inc., 105 Cal. Rptr. 890, 895 (1973).

Plaintiff claims that under §§2-314 and 2-315 of the Uniform Commercial Code (Ill. Rev. Stat. 1971, ch. 26, §§2-314, 2-315) a genuine issue of material fact exists as to defendant's liability arising from his saw-related knowledge and skill, and plaintiff's ultimate reliance upon this knowledge in purchasing the saw. Section 2-314 states in pertinent part:

Unless excluded or modified . . . a warranty that the goods shall be merchantable is implied in a contract for their sale if the seller is a merchant with respect to goods of that kind. . . .

Section 2-104(1) of the Uniform Commercial Code (Ill. Rev. Stat. 1971, ch. 26, §2-104(1)) defines a merchant as:

[A] person who deals in goods of the kind or otherwise by his occupation holds himself out as having knowledge or skill peculiar to the practices or goods involved in the transaction or to whom such knowledge or skill may be attributed by his employment of an agent or broker or other intermediary who by his occupation holds himself out as having such knowledge or skill.

Defendant [*sic*—Plaintiff?] argues in his reply brief that plaintiff [*sic*—defendant?] falls within the terms of §2-104(1) and is therefore a merchant for purposes of §2-314 by virtue of his "holding himself out as having knowledge or skill." This test, however, is not the standard for determining who is a merchant within the meaning of §2-314. The Committee Notes to §2-104 (S.H.A. 1971, ch. 26, §2-104, Committee Notes ¶2, page 97) and to §2-314 (S.H.A. 1971, ch. 26, §2-314, Committee Comments, ¶3, page 232) make it clear that the definition of merchant within §2-314 is a narrow one and that the warranty of merchantability is applicable only to a person who, in a professional status, sells the particular kind of goods giving rise to the warranty.

> A person making an isolated sale of goods is not a "merchant" within the meaning of the scope of this section [2-314] and, thus, no warranty of merchantability would apply. [S.H.A. 1971, ch. 26, §2-314, Committee Comments, ¶3, page 232.]

The record is clear that defendant is engaged in the sawmill business. The sale in the instant case was an isolated transaction and therefore did not come within the terms of §2-314. *Balido v. Improved Machinery*, supra.

Plaintiff also claims that §2-315 of the Uniform Commercial Code (Ill. Rev. Stat. 1971, ch. 26, §2-315) is applicable to the transaction in the instant case. The provision reads:

> Where the seller at the time of contracting has reason to know any particular purpose for which the goods are required and that the buyer is relying on the seller's skill or judgment to select or furnish suitable goods, there is unless excluded or modified under the next section an implied warranty that the goods shall be fit for such purpose.

This section imposes two requirements: first, that the seller know of the particular purpose for which the goods are required, and second, that the buyer rely on seller's skill or judgment in selecting the product. Here, the first requirement is met in that it is undisputed that defendant knew plaintiff's purpose for buying the saw: the making of pallets. As to the second requirement, plaintiff asserts that the following facts create a genuine issue of material fact as to plaintiff's reliance on seller's expertise: plaintiff neither owned nor had experience with a multi-rip saw whereas defendant had been operating one for about six years; Alden referred other customers to defendant for demonstrations of the saw; and defendant explained safety requirements for operating the saw and made recommendations on operating procedures. Impliedly, according to plaintiff, defendant had expertise due to his experience with the saw, and Alden considered defendant to have that expertise by its referral of other customers to defendant for demonstrations.

Defendant, on the other hand, asserts that there was no genuine issue of material fact indicating that plaintiff relied on defendant's skill or judgment in purchasing the saw, and supports this assertion with the following facts: plaintiff made his original inquiry to purchase an Alden-brand saw upon the advice and suggestion of a customer; after learning of the six-month delivery delay, plaintiff contacted defendant regarding the used Alden saw rather than investigating the purchase of a different brand; plaintiff's statement in his deposition, "in my search for a gang-rip saw I was directed to Ed Korleski," indicates that he had decided to purchase such a saw prior to any contact with defendant; and plaintiff brought his son to view the saw to see "whether he thought [the saw] was what [they] needed," suggesting that plaintiff relied on his son's judgment, not the defendant's.

It is not the facts that are in dispute, but the conclusion or inference to be drawn from them, i.e., do plaintiff's facts raise a question of his reliance on defendant's judgment in selecting the saw sufficient to submit the issue to the jury for determination. We find plaintiff's facts insufficient to raise a question of material fact as to his reliance upon defendant's skill and knowledge; no facts indicated that plaintiff relied on defendant's expertise in making his decision to purchase the saw. Rather, the uncontroverted facts establish that plaintiff had decided to purchase an Alden saw prior to his initial contact with defendant. We hold therefore that the trial court properly granted defendant's motion for summary judgment.

Judgment affirmed.

Notice that the definition of *merchant* in §2-104(1) refers not only to those who deal in the goods involved, but also those merchants who deal in the *practices* of the kind involved in the transaction. Official Comment 2 explains:

> The special provisions as to merchants appear only in this Article and they are of three kinds. Sections 2-201(2), 2-205, 2-207 and 2-209 dealing with the statute of frauds, firm offers, confirmatory memoranda and modification rest on normal business practices which are or ought to be typical of and familiar to any person in business. For purposes of these sections almost every person in business would, therefore, be deemed to be a "merchant" under the language "who . . . by his occupation holds himself out as having knowledge or skill peculiar to the practices . . . involved in the transaction . . ." since the practices involved in the transaction are non-specialized business practices

such as answering mail. In this type of provision, banks or even universities, for example, well may be "merchants." But even these sections only apply to a merchant in his mercantile capacity; a lawyer or bank president buying fishing tackle for his own use is not a merchant.

On the other hand, in Section 2-314 on the warranty of merchantability, such warranty is implied only "if the seller is a merchant with respect to goods of that kind." Obviously this qualification restricts the implied warranty to a much smaller group than everyone who is engaged in business and requires a professional status as to particular kinds of goods. The exception in Section 2-402(2) for retention of possession by a merchant-seller falls in the same class; as does Section 2-403(2) on entrusting of possession to a merchant "who deals in goods of that kind."

A third group of sections includes 2-103(1)(b), which provides that in the case of a merchant "good faith" includes observance of reasonable commercial standards of fair dealing in trade; 2-327(1)(c), 2-603, and 2-605 dealing with responsibilities of merchant buyers to follow seller's instructions, etc.; 2-509 on risk of loss; and 2-609 on adequate assurance of performance. This group of sections applies to persons who are merchants under either the "practices" or the "goods" aspect of the definition of merchant.

PROBLEM 3

Are the following persons merchants?

(a) Amanda, who quit her teaching job on Friday and on Monday opened a hat store?

(b) Tom Tiller, a farmer selling his produce to a wholesaler? Compare Loeb & Co. v. Schreiner, 294 Ala. 722, 321 So. 2d 199, 17 U.C.C. Rep. Serv. 897 (1975) ("Although a farmer might sell his cotton every year, we do not think that this should take him out of the category of a 'casual seller' and place him in the category with 'professionals.'") with Continental Grain Co. v. Brown, 19 U.C.C. Rep. Serv. 52 (W.D. Wis. 1976) ("A sale of 75,000 bushels of corn for a total price in excess of $212,000 is not a 'casual' sale."). See also Vince v. Broome, 443 So. 2d 23, 37 U.C.C. Rep. Serv. 1498 (Miss. 1983) ("Some farming operations are worth millions of dollars. . . . It would stretch the imagination to conclude that all these operations were exempt from coverage under the Commercial Code."); Ohio Grain Co. v. Swisshelm, 40 Ohio App. 2d 203, 318 N.E.2d 428, 15 U.C.C. Rep. Serv. 897 (1973) (the modern farmer is more than "a simple tiller of the soil, unaccustomed to the affairs of business and the marketplace. . . . Only an agribusinessman may hope to survive."); Harvest States Cooperatives v. Anderson, 217 Wis. 2d 154, 577 N.W.2d 381, 36 U.C.C. Rep. Serv. 2d 662 (1998) (man who had some cows and made occasional sales of corn not a merchant).

III.   SCOPE OF ARTICLE 2A

In recent years equipment leasing has become big business. It now accounts for well over $500 billion in outstanding contracts worldwide. Leasing goods (as opposed to purchasing them) has certain advantages. It may be desirable for accounting reasons because the lease obligation is not reflected as an asset/liability, thus improving the balance sheet ratios. At various times there have been tax advantages to leasing goods, though the tax laws have fluctuated on this through the years.[4]

A major problem with all this is that the law of personal property leasing has not been clearly defined. It originally developed from the law of bailments and, by analogy, from the law governing the lease of real property, though it fit comfortably into neither. Where the law was unfavorable or nonexistent, model equipment leases were promulgated by various bodies. See, e.g., Antin, An Equipment Lease Form, 8 A.L.I.-A.B.A. Course Materials J. 117 (1983). Since the adoption of the Uniform Commercial Code, many courts have applied Article 2 to leases, either stating that this was the intention of the drafters — see §2-102, stating that Article 2 applies to "transactions" in goods — or using Article 2 by analogy. Since many of Article 2's sections apply only if a "sale" occurs — defined in §2-106(1) to require the passing of title from the seller to the buyer — the Code's rules have to be stretched a great deal to encompass a true lease of goods.

Added to this difficulty was the fact that many so-called "leases" were not true leases at all, but instead were sales of the goods involved disguised as leases. This was done for various reasons: the bookkeeping and tax considerations mentioned above, plus the desire to escape from the necessity of complying with either Article 2 or the secured transactions rules of Article 9. The original wording of §1-201(37) (defining "security interest") contained a skeletal test for telling a true lease from a disguised sale: if the lessee had the option to become the owner of the leased goods at the end of the lease period for nominal or no consideration, a sale was effected. To this, courts deciding cases under both Article 2 and Article 9 added elaborate tests for telling a true lease from a disguised sale.

In 1987 the last of the various bodies involved approved for adoption a new version of the Uniform Commercial Code containing Article 2A,

---

4. It has always been malpractice for the authors to say the word *tax* out loud, and this book therefore expresses no opinion on the current position of the Internal Revenue Code on this or any other subject.

entitled "Leases." It is modeled in large part (some say too much)[5] on Article 2. Throughout the rest of this book, reference will be made to sections of Article 2A, particularly where those sections deviate from the similar rules in Article 2.[6]

First, however, it is important to appreciate the kind of leases to which Article 2A applies. If a so-called "lease" does not pass the tests described therein, Article 2A is not triggered. Instead, the "lease" will be governed by Articles 2 and 9 because the lease will typically then be a disguised sale on credit, with the "lessor's" interest in reality being nothing more than the reservation of a security interest.[7]

Read the very complicated definition of "security interest" in §1-203, concentrating on the major part of it that attempts to distinguish between a true lease and a security interest (that is, a sale on credit disguised as a lease). What are we to make of this definition? The happiest thing about it (despite its formidable size) is that it does draw some bright lines to help attorneys tell leases from secured transactions:

(1) As under the original definition, if at the end of the lease period the lessee becomes the owner of the property for little or no consideration, a secured transaction and not a lease has been created.

(2) If the contract contains a clause that permits the lessee to terminate the lease at any time and return the leased goods (the so-called "walk away" test), a true lease has resulted. Such a right of termination is not an attribute of a sale of goods.

(3) If the lease is for the entire economic life of the leased goods, with or without renewal, a disguised sale has occurred.

Other than that, each lease must be evaluated on its own. It does not necessarily answer the central question if the lessee pays consideration equal to or even greater than the fair market value of the leased goods as

5. "The Article 2A draftsmen's desire to follow the Article 2 model on occasion resulted in virtual unintelligibility to all but the most experienced and knowledgeable." Report of the Uniform Commercial Code Committee of the Business Law Section of the State Bar of California on Proposed California Commercial Code Division 10 (Article 2A) (1987), reprinted in 39 Ala. L. Rev. at 979, 984 (1988). California has adopted Article 2A with major overhauls to some of its sections. See also Kripke, Some Dissonant Notes About Article 2A, 39 Ala. L. Rev. 791 (1988).

6. The original version of Article 2A contained so many flaws that it was redrafted in 1990. The 1990 version is the one referred to in this book.

7. Professors James White and Robert Summers deal with Article 2A in their splendid treatise on the Uniform Commercial Code: see Chapters 13 to 15 in Volume 2 (5th ed. Practitioner Treatise Series). This work is published in two editions: a multivolume work for practitioners and a one-volume student edition. All further citations, unless noted, are to the student edition: J. White & R. Summers, Uniform Commercial Code (6th ed. 2010) [hereinafter White & Summers].

long as the lease does not cover the total economic life of the goods. Nor does the lessee's assumption of major duties (taxes, risk of loss, etc.) necessarily indicate a lease or a sale of goods.

Use the definition and the above tests to answer the following Problem.

PROBLEM 4

BIG Machines, Inc., leased a computer to Helen's Flower Shoppe for a five-year period. The machine was new and had cost BIG Machines $10,000. Helen's Flower Shoppe promised to pay $225 a month as rent. Is this a lease or a disguised sale? Is your answer affected by the following considerations?

(a) The lease provided that the lessee could terminate the lease at any time and return the computer to the lessor.

(b) Assume there was no such option as described in (a), but the goods had no value at the end of the five-year period.

(c) Assume instead that the rental amount is only $150 a month and the computer will be worth $3,500 at the end of the five-year period. The lease has a clause giving Helen's Flower Shoppe the option to purchase the computer for that amount at that time. Is this a true lease? What if the lease requires the lessee to renew this lease at the end of the five-year period for another five years?

IV. INTERNATIONAL SALES

Effective January 1, 1988, the United States became bound by a treaty: the United Nations Convention on Contracts for the International Sale of Goods [hereinafter CISG]. The Convention covers only issues of contract formation and the rights and duties of the parties thereto. It excludes coverage of products liability issues; it does not address matters touching on contract validity, such as fraud, illegality, etc. As of this writing, 77 countries, including most of the important trading states, are parties.[8] The leading text on the CISG to date is J. Honnold, Uniform Law for International Sales Under the 1980 United Nations Convention (4th ed. 2009).

---

8. As of 2012, the largest trading states not parties to the CISG were Brazil, Hong Kong, India, South Africa, Taiwan, and the United Kingdom. See http://www.uncitral.org/uncitral/en/uncitral_texts/sale_goods/1980CISG_status.html.

PROBLEM 5

Hegemony Enterprises, headquartered in New York, is about to sign a contract for the sale of men's clothing to Cosas Americana, a retailer in Mexico City. You are the lawyer for Hegemony Enterprises, and a company official calls you with the following questions:

(a) Will the CISG apply to this transaction? See CISG Articles 1 and 2.

(b) If Hegemony Enterprises wants the law of New York to apply, can the parties so stipulate in the contract and avoid the CISG? See Article 6.

(c) If Hegemony Enterprises were selling toys to Cosas Americana, would the CISG apply? See Article 2(a).

CHAPTER 2

CONTRACT
FORMATION

The basics of contract formation should be reassuringly familiar to you from Contracts class. Perhaps the UCC approach to the Statute of Frauds, the parol evidence rule, and offer and acceptance were covered there. If not, as you learn these rules rather than review them, contrast the UCC approach with the common law result.

I. THE STATUTE OF FRAUDS

Read §2-201, which is quite a change from the common law Statute of Frauds. At common law, when a contract fell within the Statute, *all* its terms and conditions had to be in writing or the contract was not enforceable. Under §2-201, a contract can be enforced even if a main term is omitted or misstated. The only term necessary for a sufficient memorandum under §2-201(1) is *quantity*.[1] Not only are the standards lessened by the Code, but

---

1. White and Summers note that one could (contrary to the weight of authority) interpret §2-201(1) *not* to require a quantity, but rather to say only that *if* a quantity is specified, that the agreement cannot be enforced beyond that quantity. White & Summers, §3-4, at 97 n.12.

also four exceptions are provided: merchant confirmation letters, special manufacture, part performance, and admission in legal proceedings.

PROBLEM 6

On December 10, James Ross, president of Ross Ice Cream Shoppes, Inc., phoned Robert Scott, president of Amundsen Ice Company, and negotiated the purchase of two tons of ice from Amundsen at $256/ton. As they talked on the phone, Scott picked up a memo pad inscribed "Amundsen Ice Company From the Desk of the President," wrote on it "2 tons Ross Co.," and then scribbled his initials on it. When the parties hung up the phones, Scott placed the memo on a spindle marked "Orders." Ross wrote Scott a letter beginning "Dear Bob: This is to confirm our ice purchase deal . . . ," which described their transaction completely. Scott received the letter on December 14. On January 17, Scott phoned Ross and denied the existence of the contract detailed in the Ross letter. Answer these questions:

(a) Does the memo pad note satisfy §2-201(1)? See §1-201(37) and Official Comment 37.

(b) What legal effect did the December 14 letter have? Same result if Ross's letter failed to mention the quantity? Even if the letter satisfies the Statute of Frauds, is it conclusive as to the existence and terms of the contract? See Hinson-Barr, Inc. v. Pinckard, 292 S.C. 267, 356 S.E.2d 115, 4 U.C.C. Rep. Serv. 2d 36 (1987).

(c) Did Scott's denial of the terms contained in Ross's letter avoid the operation of §2-201(2)? Suppose Scott had immediately written Ross a letter stating, "You haven't stated the terms correctly. We only agreed to sell you 1 ton." Would that letter be a sufficient notice of objection? See Simmons Oil Corp. v. Bulk Sales Corp., 498 F. Supp. 457, 31 U.C.C. Rep. Serv. 1236 (D.N.J. 1980); Annot., 82 A.L.R.4th 709.

St. Ansgar Mills, Inc. v. Streit

Supreme Court of Iowa, 2000
613 N.W.2d 289, 42 U.C.C. Rep. Serv. 2d 58

CADY, Justice.

A grain dealer appeals from an order by the district court granting summary judgment in an action to enforce an oral contract for the sale of corn based on a written confirmation. The district court held the oral contract was unenforceable because the written confirmation was not delivered within a reasonable time after the oral contract as a matter of law. We reverse the decision of the district court and remand for further proceedings.

I. BACKGROUND FACTS AND PROCEEDINGS

St. Ansgar Mills, Inc. is a family-owned agricultural business located in Mitchell County. As a part of its business, St. Ansgar Mills buys corn from local grain farmers and sells corn to livestock farmers for feed. The price of the corn sold to farmers is established by trades made on the Chicago Board of Trade for delivery with reference to five contract months. The sale of corn for future delivery is hedged by St. Ansgar Mills through an off-setting futures position on the Chicago Board of Trade.

A sale is typically made when a farmer calls St. Ansgar Mills and requests a quote for a cash price of grain for future delivery based on the Chicago Board of Trade price for the delivery. The farmer then accepts or rejects the price. If the price is accepted, St. Ansgar Mills protects the price through a licensed brokerage house by acquiring a hedge position on the Chicago Board of Trade. This hedge position, however, obligates St. Ansgar Mills to purchase the corn at the stated price at the time of delivery. Thus, St. Ansgar Mills relies on the farmer who purchased the grain to accept delivery at the agreed price.

Duane Streit formerly resided in Mitchell County and currently practices veterinarian medicine in Carroll County. He also raises hogs. He owns a large hog farrowing operation in Carroll County and a hog finishing operation in Mitchell County near Osage. Streit purchased the Osage farm from his father in 1993. Duane's father, John Streit, resides in Mitchell County and helps Duane operate the Osage finishing facility.

Duane and his father have been long-time customers of St. Ansgar Mills. Since 1989, Duane entered into numerous contracts with St. Ansgar Mills for the purchase of large quantities of corn and other grain products. Duane would generally initiate the purchase agreement by calling St. Ansgar Mills on the telephone to obtain a price quote. If an oral contract was made, an employee of St. Ansgar Mills would prepare a written confirmation of the sale and either mail it to Duane to sign and return, or wait for Duane or John to sign the confirmation when they would stop in to the business.

John would regularly stop by St. Ansgar Mills sometime during the first ten days of each month and pay the amount of the open account Duane maintained at St. Ansgar Mills for the purchase of supplies and other materials. On those occasions when St. Ansgar Mills sent the written confirmation to Duane, it was not unusual for Duane to fail to sign the confirmation for a long period of time. He also failed to return contracts sent to him. Nevertheless, Duane had never refused delivery of grain he purchased by telephone prior to the incident which gave rise to this case.

On July 1, 1996, John telephoned St. Ansgar Mills to place two orders for the purchase of 60,000 bushels of corn for delivery in December 1996 and May 1997. This order followed an earlier conversation between Duane and St. Ansgar Mills. After the order was placed, St. Ansgar Mills completed the written confirmation but set it aside for John to sign when he was expected to stop by the business to pay the open account. The agreed price of the December corn was $3.53 per bushel. The price of the May corn was $3.73 per bushel.

John failed to follow his monthly routine of stopping by the business during the month of July. St. Ansgar Mills then asked a local banker who was expected to see John to have John stop in to the business.

John did not stop by St. Ansgar Mills until August 10, 1996. On that date, St. Ansgar Mills delivered the written confirmation to him.

Duane later refused delivery of the corn orally purchased on July 1, 1996. The price of corn had started to decline shortly after July 1, and eventually plummeted well below the quoted price on July 1. After Duane refused delivery of the corn, he purchased corn for his hog operations on the open market at prices well below the contract prices of July 1. St. Ansgar Mills later told Duane it should have followed up earlier with the written confirmation and had no excuse for not doing so.

St. Ansgar Mills then brought this action for breach of contract. It sought damages of $152,100, which was the difference between the contract price of the corn and the market price at the time Duane refused delivery.

Duane filed a motion for summary judgment. He claimed the oral contract alleged by St. Ansgar Mills was governed by the provisions of the Uniform Commercial Code, and was unenforceable as a matter of law under the statute of frauds. He claimed the written confirmation delivered to John on August 10, 1996 did not satisfy the statute of frauds for two reasons. First, he was not a merchant. Second, the confirmation was not received within a reasonable time after the alleged oral agreement.

The district court determined a jury question was presented on whether Duane was a merchant under the Uniform Commercial Code. However, the district court found the written confirmation did not satisfy the writing requirements of the statute of frauds because the delivery of the confirmation to John, as Duane's agent, did not occur within a reasonable time after the oral contract as a matter of law. The district court found the size of the order, the volatility of the grain market, and the lack of an explanation by St. Ansgar Mills for failing to send the confirmation to Duane after John failed to stop by the business as expected made the delay between July 1 and August 10 unreasonable as a matter of law.

St. Ansgar Mills appeals. It claims a jury question was presented on the issue of whether a written confirmation was received within a reasonable time. . . .

III. STATUTE OF FRAUDS

The statute of frauds is one of the most well-known and venerable rules applicable to contract law. Generally, it establishes an exception to the proposition that oral contracts are enforceable in a lawsuit if sufficiently proven by requiring certain types of contracts to be in writing and signed by the party against whom enforcement is sought. See Iowa Code §554.2201(1).

The statute of frauds originated in 17th century England to combat the use of fraud and perjury by litigants in court proceedings to establish oral contracts. See 2 E. Allan Farnsworth, Contracts §6.1, at 82-83 (2d ed. 1990). At the time, court rules prohibited parties to a lawsuit from testifying as witnesses in their case, and, consequently, an oral contract could only be established with testimony of third parties. See Azevedo v. Minister, 86 Nev. 576, 471 P.2d 661, 663 (1970). This prohibition allowed witnesses to be persuaded to give false testimony on behalf of a party in an effort to establish an oral contract, leaving the other party at a distinct disadvantage. See James J. O'Connell, Jr., Boats Against a Current: The Courts and the Statute of Frauds, 47 Emory L.J. 253, 257 (1998) [hereinafter O'Connell].

In 1677, in response to this unsavory practice of using perjury to establish oral contracts, Parliament enacted the statute of frauds to require certain contracts to be supported by written evidence to be enforceable. 29 Car. 2, ch. 3 (1677) (Eng.); see Hugh E. Willis, Statute of Frauds—A Legal Anachronism, 3 Ind. L.J. 427, 427 (1928). The statute included contracts which were not only particularly susceptible to fraud, but those which posed serious consequences of fraud, including contracts for the sale of goods or property. See O'Connell, 47 Emory L.J. at 258.

Despite a difference in the court rules which gave rise to this statute of frauds, our American legal culture quickly adopted the principle. James J. White & Robert S. Summers, Uniform Commercial Code §2-1, at 50 (2d ed. 1980) [hereinafter White & Summers]. Iowa adopted the statute of frauds in 1851. See Iowa Code §§2409-2410 (1851). The statute of frauds also became a part of the Uniform Sales Act in 1906, which Iowa subsequently adopted in 1924. See 1919 Iowa Acts ch. 396 (initially codified at Iowa Code §§9930-10007 (1924)). This statute required all contracts for the sale of goods to be in writing. Over time, the Uniform Sales Act was replaced by the Uniform Commercial Code.[2] The Uniform Commercial Code contin-

---

2. After six years of deliberating, the National Conference of Commissioners on Uniform State Laws produced the 1952 Official Text of the Uniform Commercial Code. See William A. Schnader, A Short History of the Preparation and Enactment of the Uniform Commercial Code, 22 U. Miami L. Rev. 1, 1-2 (1967). In 1954, Pennsylvania was the first state to formally adopt the text. See 13 Pa. Const. Stat. §§1101 to 9507 (1953). By 1968, the Uniform Commercial Code was effective in 49 states, the District of Columbia, and the Virgin Islands. See Uniform Commercial Code Table, 1 U.L.A. 1-2 (Master ed. 1989). There have been three official revisions, the 1972, the 1978, and the 1987 Official Texts, offered by the Permanent Editorial Board, a board established in 1961 to keep the Code up to

ued to adhere to the statute of frauds, but was limited in its provisions to the sale of goods in excess of $500. Iowa enacted its version of the Uniform Commercial Code in 1966 including the statute of frauds. See 1965 Iowa Acts ch. 413. Iowa's statute of frauds for the sale of goods now provides:

> Except as otherwise provided in this section, a contract for the sale of goods for the price of $500 or more is not enforced by way of action or defense unless there is some writing sufficient to indicate that a contract for sale has been made between the parties and signed by the party against whom enforcement is sought or by that party's authorized agent or broker.

Iowa Code §554.2201(1) (1995).

Although the statute of frauds has been deeply engrained into our law, many of the forces which originally gave rise to the rule are no longer prevalent. White & Summers §2-1, at 51. This, in turn, has caused some of the rigid requirements of the rule to be modified.

One statutory exception or modification to the statute of frauds which has surfaced applies to merchants. Id. §554.2201(2). Under section 554.2201(2), the writing requirements of section 554.2201(1) are considered to be satisfied if, within a reasonable time, a writing in confirmation of the contract which is sufficient against the sender is received and the merchant receiving it has reason to know of its contents, unless written notice of objection of its contents is given within ten days after receipt. Id. Thus, a writing is still required, but it does not need to be signed by the party against whom the contract is sought to be enforced. The purpose of this exception was to put professional buyers and sellers on equal footing by changing the former law under which a party who received a written confirmation of an oral agreement of sale, but who had not signed anything, could hold the other party to a contract without being bound. See White & Summers §2-3, at 55; Kimball County Grain Coop. v. Yung, 200 Neb. 233, 263 N.W.2d 818, 820 (1978). It also encourages the common, prudent business practice of sending memoranda to confirm oral agreements. White & Summers §2-3, at 55.

While the written confirmation exception imposes a specific ten-day requirement for a merchant to object to a written confirmation, it employs a flexible standard of reasonableness to establish the time in which the confirmation must be received. Iowa Code §554.2201(2). The Uniform Commercial Code specifically defines a reasonable time for taking action in relationship to "the nature, purpose and circumstances" of the action. Id. §554.1204(2) [UCC §1-204[3]]. Additionally, the declared purpose of the

---

date. See William A. Schnader, The Permanent Editorial Board for the Uniform Commercial Code: Can it Accomplish its Object?, 3 Am. Bus. L.J. 137, 138 (1965).

3. Now §1-302(b) — EDS.

Uniform Commercial Code is to permit the expansion of commercial practices through the custom and practice of the parties. See Iowa Code Ann. §554.1102 cmt. 2 (course of dealings, usage of trade or course of performance are material in determining a reasonable time). Furthermore, the Uniform Commercial Code relies upon course of dealings between the parties to help interpret their conduct. Iowa Code §554.1205(1). Thus, all relevant circumstances, including custom and practice of the parties, must be considered in determining what constitutes a reasonable time under section 554.2201(2).

Generally, the determination of the reasonableness of particular conduct is a jury question. See Pirelli-Armstrong Tire Co. v. Reynolds, 562 N.W.2d 433, 436 (Iowa 1997); see also Harvey v. Great Atl. & Pac. Tea Co., 388 F.2d 123, 125 (5th Cir. 1968) (passing judgment on the reasonableness of conduct of the parties must be accomplished in light of all the circumstances of the case and should rarely be disposed of by summary judgment). Thus, the reasonableness of time between an oral contract and a subsequent written confirmation is ordinarily a question of fact for the jury. MortgageAmerica Corp. v. American Nat'l Bank, 651 S.W.2d 851, 856 (Tex. Ct. App. 1983); Schiavi Mobile Homes, Inc. v. Gagne, 510 A.2d 236, 238 (Me. 1986) (reasonableness of parties' time for action is a question of fact). It is only in rare cases that a determination of the reasonableness of conduct should be decided by summary adjudication. *Harvey*, 388 F.2d at 125. Summary judgment is appropriate only when the evidence is so one-sided that a party must prevail at trial as a matter of law. Ridgeway v. Union County Comm'rs, 775 F. Supp. 1105, 1109 (S.D. Ohio 1991).

There are a host of cases from other jurisdictions which have considered the question of what constitutes a reasonable time under the written confirmation exception of the Uniform Commercial Code. See Gestetner Corp. v. Case Equip. Co., 815 F.2d 806, 810 (1st Cir. 1987) (roughly five-month delay reasonable in light of merchants "relationship and parties" immediate action under contract following oral agreement); Serna, Inc. v. Harman, 742 F.2d 186, 189 (5th Cir. 1984) (three and one-half month delay reasonable in light of the parties' interaction in the interim, and non-fluctuating prices, thus no prejudice); Cargill, Inc. v. Stafford, 553 F.2d 1222, 1224 (10th Cir. 1977) (less than one-month delay unreasonable despite misdirection of confirmation due to mistaken addressing); Starry Constr. Co. v. Murphy Oil USA, Inc., 785 F. Supp. 1356, 1362-63 (D. Minn. 1992) (six-month delay for confirmation of modification order for additional oil unreasonable as a matter of law in light of Persian Gulf War, thus increased prices and demand); Rockland Indus., Inc. v. Frank Kasmir Assoc., 470 F. Supp. 1176, 1179 (N.D. Tex. 1979) (letter sent eight months after alleged oral agreement for two-year continuity agreement unreasonable in light of lack of evidence supporting reasonableness of delay); *Yung*, 263 N.W.2d at 820 (six-month delay in confirming oral agreement delivered one day prior to last possible day of delivery unreasonable); *Azevedo*, 471 P.2d at 666 (ten-week delay reasonable in light of immediate performance by both parties following oral agreement); Lish v. Compton, 547 P.2d 223, 226-27 (Utah 1976) (twelve-day delay "outside the ambit which fair-minded persons could conclude to be reasonable" in light of volatile price market and lack of excuse for delay other than casual delay). Most of these cases, however, were decided after a trial on the merits and cannot be used to establish a standard or time period as a matter of law. Only a few courts have decided the question as a matter of law under the facts of the case. Compare *Starry*, 785 F. Supp. at 1362-63 (granting summary judgment), and *Lish*, 547 P.2d at 226-27 (removing claim from jury's consideration), with Barron v. Edwards, 45 Mich. App. 210, 206 N.W.2d 508, 511 (1973) (remanding for further development of facts, summary judgment improper). However, these cases do not establish a strict principle to apply in this case. The resolution of each case depends upon the particular facts and circumstances.

In this case, the district court relied upon the large amount of the sale, volatile market conditions, and lack of an explanation by St. Ansgar Mills for failing to send the written confirmation to Duane in determining St. Ansgar Mills acted unreasonably as a matter of law in delaying delivery of the written confirmation until August 10, 1996. Volatile market conditions, combined with a large sale price, would normally narrow the window of reasonable time under section 554.2201(2). However, they are not the only factors to consider. Other relevant factors which must also be considered in this case reveal the parties had developed a custom or practice to delay delivery of the confirmation. The parties also maintained a long-time amicable business relationship and had engaged in many other similar business transactions without incident. There is also evidence to infer St. Ansgar Mills did not suspect John's failure to follow his customary practice in July of stopping by the business was a concern at the time. These factors reveal a genuine dispute over the reasonableness of the delay in delivering the written confirmation, and make the resolution of the issue appropriate for the jury. Moreover, conduct is not rendered unreasonable solely because the acting party had no particular explanation for not pursuing different conduct, or regretted not pursuing different conduct in retrospect. The reasonableness of conduct is determined by the facts and circumstances existing at the time.

Considering our principles governing summary adjudication and the need to resolve the legal issue by considering the particular facts and circumstances of each case, we conclude the trial court erred by granting summary judgment. We reverse and remand the case for further proceedings.

Article 2A has a Statute of Frauds similar to §2-201, though the amount of the lease must be at least $1,000 before a writing is required, and the writing must describe the leased goods and the lease term in order to satisfy the Statute. See §2A-201. There is no "merchant's confirmation" subsection in this section because (according to the Official Comment) that situation does not often arise in lease transactions.

There is no Statute of Frauds for international sales under the CISG unless the country adopting the Convention stipulates that its own Statute of Frauds will apply. See Articles 11 and 96.

PROBLEM 7

The city manager of Thebes, Utah, which is world-famous for its beautiful desert golf course, orally ordered a huge water tank to be made in the shape of a golf ball on a tee from Tanks of America, Inc. The price was agreed to be $30,000, and the city sent Tanks a down payment check for $3,000, signed by the city comptroller and marked "Tank" on the memo line. Tanks of America built the tank and was in the process of painting "City of Thebes" on the side when a representative of a newly elected city administration called and said that the new administration considered the contract unenforceable. Answer these questions:

(a) Does the check satisfy §2-201(1)? Where is the *quantity*? See Beautiful Jewellers Private, Ltd. v. Tiffany & Co., 2007 WL 867202 (S.D.N.Y. 2007).

(b) What legal argument can Tanks of America make based on §§2-201(3)(a) and 2-201(3)(c)? See Harvest States Cooperatives v. Anderson, 217 Wis. 2d 154, 577 N.W.2d 381, 36 U.C.C. Rep. Serv. 2d 662 (1998) (good discussion of specially manufactured goods exception). Does the City of Thebes have a good response to the §2-201(3)(c) argument? See W.I. Snyder Corp. v. Caracciolo, 373 Pa. Super. 486, 541 A.2d 775, 7 U.C.C. Rep. Serv. 2d 993 (1988).

(c) If the city had promised to sign a written contract but had never gotten around to doing so, can promissory estoppel or equitable estoppel be used to circumvent §2-201? Reread §1-103(b), and see Allen M. Campbell Co. v. Virginia Metal Indus., Inc., 708 F.2d 930, 36 U.C.C. Rep. Serv. 384 (4th Cir. 1983); Amber Chemical, Inc. v. Reilly Industries, Inc., 2007 WL 512410 (E.D. Cal. 2007).

PROBLEM 8

Tomorrow, Inc. (a computer software company) and Systems Unlimited (a company specializing in advising other companies how to maximize their computer operations) entered into a written joint venture contract by which Tomorrow, Inc. promised to design and sell to Systems Unlimited software that would enable the latter's customers to receive engineering drawings by phone. The parties agreed that their arrangement was "non-exclusive" (meaning either was allowed to deal with other buyers and sellers of the same product). The contract described the obligations of the parties in some detail and stated that the contract would terminate after two years unless renewed. In fact, after working with Tomorrow, Inc., for only six months, Systems Unlimited decided it could develop its own software more cheaply than buying it from Tomorrow, Inc., so it faxed a letter to the latter stating that their contract was at an end. Systems Unlimited declined to purchase any further software. Tomorrow, Inc., which had incurred substantial startup costs in developing the software for this contract, was astounded and promptly filed suit. Systems Unlimited sought refuge in the Statute of Frauds, arguing that the contract signed by the parties stated no quantity. Does §2-201(1) always require a specific quantity? Look at the statutory language very carefully. Compare §2-306. See also Advent Sys. Ltd. v. Unisys Corp., 925 F.2d 670, 13 U.C.C. Rep. Serv. 2d 669 (3d Cir. 1991); White & Summers, §3-4, at 97 n.12.

PROBLEM 9

Sued by a trusting seller after refusing delivery, Renege Retail's president calmly testifies that he had agreed to buy the goods, but the parties never put anything in writing. Without a signed contract, memorandum, confirmation, or any other writing, is Renege Retail off the hook? See §2-201(3)(b).

At both the federal and state level statutes have been enacted to facilitate electronic commerce as civilization moves from the world of paper into cyberspace. The states acted first, with many of them adopting the Uniform Electronic Transactions Act (UETA), and the federal government followed with the similar Electronic Signatures in Global and National Commerce Act, 15 U.S.C. §7001, commonly known as "E-Sign." The latter statute applies only in jurisdictions not adopting UETA. As of 2012, Illinois, New York, and Washington were the only states not to have enacted UETA. Both statutes should be in your statute book. White and Summers have a clear discussion of the statutes. See White & Summers, §§1-3, 3-9.

The basic thrust of these statutes is to allow electronic records in most commercial transactions even if other statutes, such as the Statute of Frauds, require a writing or a written signature. With certain exceptions (utility cutoff notices, notices of default, repossession, foreclosure and eviction, insurance cancellations, etc.), almost all legal communications by the parties to a transaction can now be accomplished electronically. The statutes provide only that electronic communications may meet the requirements for a writing or signature. They do not provide substantive rules, such as how contracts are formed or what terms will be included in the contract. See Alliance Laundry Systems, LLC v. ThyssenKrupp Materials, NA, 570 F. Supp. 2d 1061, 66 U.C.C. Rep. Serv. 2d 427 (E.D. Wis. 2008).

There are a number of unsettled issues. Both of the statutes mentioned above require that where a consumer is involved, he or she must have *agreed* to electronic disclosures, but it is unclear exactly what this means. The federal statute is broader, requiring that there be *electronic agreement or confirmation of agreement*, and this agreement must be "affirmative"; 15 U.S.C. §7001(c)(1)(C)(ii). This means that the consumer must have agreed electronically to receive electronic records or have confirmed this consent electronically. UETA is less clear about this, though the Comment 4 to §5 indicates that the consumer's agreement to receive electronic communications must be actual and not imposed unconscionably as part of the fine print in a written contract.

There is also no consensus on what electronic communication means. Is it sufficient for the required information to be posted on a website (the so-called "Come and Get It" notice) that the consumer must periodically access (which, of course, most won't do) to keep informed? In the 1990s, AOL posted rate changes only on its website, making customers agree that this was sufficient notice of any hike in the rate, only to back down when 19 Attorneys General objected that the practice was unfair and deceptive. What about e-mail notification? Must it be highlighted in such a way that the consumer will recognize its importance and not delete it as "spam"? If the consumer has switched e-mail addresses, then what? Must the sender do something with bounced-back messages? These matters and others will have to await judicial determination. For a summary of the consumer issues and suggested resolutions, see Jean Braucher, Rent-Seeking and Risk-Fixing in the New Statutory Law of Electronic Commerce: Difficulties in Moving Consumer Protection Online, 2001 Wis. L. Rev. 527.

II.   THE PAROL EVIDENCE RULE

Read §2-202 and its Official Comment.

PROBLEM 10

Lawyers for Swinging Singles Magazine negotiated for an entire year with Space Age Aircraft Co. to obtain a contract for the construction of a special Swinging Singles airplane. (The plane was to be black and silver, with the Swinging Singles emblem painted on the tail; it was to contain a living room, a bed chamber, a swimming pool and hot tubs, and a dance floor.) The resulting 30-page contract also contained a *merger* clause, stating that all prior negotiations were merged into the written contract that contained all the terms of the agreement. The contract was signed by both parties. Does §2-202 bar the introduction of evidence of the following?

(a) An alleged precontract agreement that Space Age would provide free flying lessons to Hi Handsome, president of Swinging Singles, Inc.? The contract says nothing about this. See the test found in Official Comment 3 to §2-202.

(b) An alleged precontract agreement that Swinging Singles could use the plane for two months, and if they did not like it, they could return it for a full refund?

To aid in the construction of agreements, the Code looks to the customs within the industry (called *usage of trade*), the parties' past contacts with one another (called *course of dealing*), and the parties' behavior during the existence of the contract in question (called *course of performance*) and presumes that these matters are relevant in fleshing out the express terms of the contract. See Nanakuli Paving & Rock Co. v. Shell Oil Co., 664 F.2d 772, 32 U.C.C. Rep. Serv. 1025 (9th Cir. 1981) (good discussion of these terms). Read §1-303 carefully. Their relationship to §2-202 is explored in the case below.

Columbia Nitrogen Corp. v. Royster Co.

United States Court of Appeals, Fourth Circuit, 1971
451 F.2d 3, 9 U.C.C. Rep. Serv. 977

BUTZNER, J. . . .

I

Royster manufactures and markets mixed fertilizers, the principal components of which are nitrogen, phosphate and potash. Columbia is primarily a producer of nitrogen, although it manufactures some mixed fertilizer. For several years Royster had been a major purchaser of Columbia's products, but Columbia had never been a significant customer of Royster. In the fall of 1966, Royster constructed a facility which enabled it to produce more phosphate than it needed in its own operations. After extensive negotiations, the companies executed a contract for Royster's sale of a minimum of 31,000 tons of phosphate each year for three years to Columbia, with an option to extend the term. The contract stated the price per ton, subject to an escalation clause dependent on production costs.

Phosphate prices soon plunged precipitously. Unable to resell the phosphate at a competitive price, Columbia ordered only part of the scheduled tonnage. At Columbia's request, Royster lowered its price for diammonium phosphate on shipments for three months in 1967, but specified that subsequent shipments would be at the original contract price. Even with this concession, Royster's price was still substantially above the market. As a result, Columbia ordered less than a tenth of the phosphate Royster was to ship in the first contract year. When pressed by Royster, Columbia offered to take the phosphate at the current market price and resell it without brokerage fee. Royster, however, insisted on the contract price. When Columbia refused delivery, Royster sold the unaccepted phosphate for Columbia's account at a price substantially below the contract price.

II

Columbia assigns error to the pretrial ruling of the district court excluding all evidence on usage of the trade and course of dealing between the parties. It offered the testimony of witnesses with long experience in the trade that because of uncertain crop and weather conditions, farming practices, and government agricultural programs, express price and quantity terms in contracts for materials in the mixed fertilizer industry are mere projections to be adjusted according to market forces.[4]

4. Typical of the proffered testimony are the following excerpts: "The contracts generally entered into between buyer and seller of materials has always been, in my opinion, construed to be the buyer's best estimate of his anticipated requirements for a given period of time. It is well known in our industry that weather conditions, farming practices, government farm control programs, change requirements from time to time. And therefore allowances were always made to meet these circumstances as they arose." "Tonnage requirements fluctuate greatly, and that is one reason that the contracts are not considered as binding as most contracts are, because the buyer normally would buy on historical basis, but his normal average use would be per annum of any given material. Now that can be affected very decidedly by adverse weather conditions such as a drought, or a flood, or maybe governmental programs which we have been faced with for many, many years, seed grain programs. They pay the farmer not to plant. If he doesn't plant, he doesn't use the fertilizer. When the contracts are made, we do not know of all these contingencies and what they are going to be. So the contract is made for what is considered a fair estimate of his requirements. And, the contract is considered binding to the extent, on him morally, that if he uses the tonnage that he will execute the contract in good faith as the buyer. . . ." "I have never heard of a contract of this type being enforced legally . . . ." Well, it undoubtedly sounds ridiculous to people from other industries, but there is a very definite, several very definite reasons why the fertilizer business is always operated under what we call gentlemen's agreements. . . . "The custom in the fertilizer industry is that the seller either meets the competitive situation or releases the buyer from it upon proof that he can buy it at that price. . . . [T]hey will either have the option of meeting it or releasing him from taking additional tonnage or holding him to that price. . . ." And this custom exists "regardless of the contractual provisions." "[T]he custom was that [these contracts] were not worth the cost of the paper they were printed on."

Columbia also offered proof of its business dealings with Royster over the six-year period preceding the phosphate contract. Since Columbia had not been a significant purchaser of Royster's products, these dealings were almost exclusively nitrogen sales to Royster or exchanges of stock carried in inventory. The pattern which emerges, Columbia claimed, is one of repeated and substantial deviation from the stated amount or price, including four instances where Royster took none of the goods for which it had contracted. Columbia offered proof that the total variance amounted to more than $500,000 in reduced sales. This experience, a Columbia officer offered to testify, formed the basis of an understanding on which he depended in conducting negotiations with Royster.

The district court held that the evidence should be excluded. It ruled that "custom and usage or course of dealing are not admissible to contradict the express, plain, unambiguous language of a valid written contract, which by virtue of its detail negates the proposition that the contract is open to variances in its terms. . . ."

A number of Virginia cases have held that extrinsic evidence may not be received to explain or supplement a written contract unless the court finds the writing is ambiguous. E.g., Mathieson Alkali Works v. Virginia Banner Coal Corp., 147 Va. 125, 136 S.E. 673 (1927). This rule, however, has been changed by the Uniform Commercial Code which Virginia has adopted. The Code expressly states that it "shall be liberally construed and applied to promote its underlying purposes and policies," which include "the expansion of commercial practices through custom, usage and agreement of the parties. . . ." §1-102.[5] The importance of usage of trade and course of dealing between the parties is shown by §2-202, which authorizes their use to explain or supplement a contract. The official comment states this section rejects the old rule that evidence of course of dealing or usage of trade can be introduced only when the contract is ambiguous. And the Virginia commentators, noting that "[t]his section reflects a more liberal approach to the introduction of parol evidence . . . than has been followed in Virginia," express the opinion that *Mathieson*, supra, and similar Virginia cases no longer should be followed. §2-202, Va. Comment. See also Portsmouth Gas Co. v. Shebar, 209 Va. 250, 253 n.1, 163 S.E.2d 205, 208 n.1 (1968) (dictum). We hold, therefore, that a finding of ambiguity is not necessary for the admission of extrinsic evidence about the usage of the trade and the parties' course of dealing.

We turn next to Royster's claim that Columbia's evidence was properly excluded because it was inconsistent with the express terms of their agreement. There can be no doubt that the Uniform Commercial Code restates the well established rule that evidence of usage of trade and course of dealing should be excluded whenever it cannot be reasonably construed

---

5. Now §1-103(a)(2) — Eds.

as consistent with the terms of the contract. Division of Triple T Service, Inc. v. Mobil Oil Corp., 60 Misc. 2d 720, 304 N.Y.S.2d 191, 203 (1969), *aff'd mem.*, 311 N.Y.S.2d 961 (1970). Royster argues that the evidence should be excluded as inconsistent because the contract contains detailed provisions regarding the base price, escalation, minimum tonnage, and delivery schedules. The argument is based on the premise that because a contract appears on its face to be complete, evidence of course of dealing and usage of trade should be excluded. We believe, however, that neither the language nor the policy of the Code supports such a broad exclusionary rule. Section 2-202 expressly allows evidence of course of dealing or usage of trade to explain or supplement terms intended by the parties as a final expression of their agreement. When this section is read in light of §1-205(4),[6] it is clear that the test of admissibility is not whether the contract appears on its face to be complete in every detail, but whether the proffered evidence of course of dealing and trade usage reasonably can be construed as consistent with the express terms of the agreement.

The proffered testimony sought to establish that because of changing weather conditions, farming practices, and government agricultural programs, dealers adjusted prices, quantities, and delivery schedules to reflect declining market conditions. For the following reasons it is reasonable to construe this evidence as consistent with the express terms of the contract:

The contract does not expressly state that course of dealing and usage of trade cannot be used to explain or supplement the written contract.

The contract is silent about adjusting prices and quantities to reflect a declining market. It neither permits nor prohibits adjustment, and this neutrality provides a fitting occasion for recourse to usage of trade and prior dealing to supplement the contract and explain its terms.

Minimum tonnages and additional quantities are expressed in terms of "Products Supplied Under Contract." Significantly, they are not expressed as just "Products" or as "Products Purchased Under Contract." The description used by the parties is consistent with the proffered testimony.

Finally, the default clause of the contract refers only to the failure of the buyer to pay for delivered phosphate. During the contract negotiations, Columbia rejected a Royster proposal for liquidated damages of $10 for each ton Columbia declined to accept. On the other hand, Royster rejected a Columbia proposal for a clause that tied the price to the market by obligating Royster to conform its price to offers Columbia received from other phosphate producers. The parties, having rejected both proposals, failed to state any consequences of Columbia's refusal to take delivery — the kind of default Royster alleges in this case. Royster insists that we span this hiatus by applying the general law of contracts permitting recovery of damages upon the buyer's refusal to take delivery according to the written

6. Now §1-303(e) — EDS.

provisions of the contract. This solution is not what the Uniform Commercial Code prescribes. Before allowing damages, a court must first determine whether the buyer has in fact defaulted. It must do this by supplementing and explaining the agreement with evidence of trade usage and course of dealing that is consistent with the contract's express terms; §§1-205(4),[7] 2-202. Faithful adherence to this mandate reflects the reality of the marketplace and avoids the overly legalistic interpretations which the Code seeks to abolish.

Royster also contends that Columbia's proffered testimony was properly rejected because it dealt with mutual willingness of buyer and seller to adjust contract terms to the market. Columbia, Royster protests, seeks unilateral adjustment. This argument misses the point. What Columbia seeks to show is a practice of mutual adjustments so prevalent in the industry and in prior dealings between the parties that it formed a part of the agreement governing this transaction. It is not insisting on a unilateral right to modify the contract.

Nor can we accept Royster's contention that the testimony should be excluded under the contract clause:

> No verbal understanding will be recognized by either party hereto; this contract expresses all the terms and conditions of the agreement, shall be signed in duplicate, and shall not become operative until approved in writing by the Seller.

Course of dealing and trade usage are not synonymous with verbal understandings, terms and conditions. Section 2-202 draws a distinction between supplementing a written contract by consistent additional terms and supplementing it by course of dealing or usage of trade. Evidence of additional terms must be excluded when "the court finds the writing to have been intended also as a complete and exclusive statement of the terms of the agreement." Significantly, no similar limitation is placed on the introduction of evidence of course of dealing or usage of trade. Indeed the official comment notes that course of dealing and usage of trade, unless carefully negated, are admissible to supplement the terms of any writing, and that contracts are to be read on the assumption that these elements were taken for granted when the document was phrased. Since the Code assigns course of dealing and trade usage unique and important roles, they should not be conclusively rejected by reading them into stereotyped language that makes no specific reference to them. Cf. Provident Tradesmen's Bank & Trust Co. v. Pemberton, 196 Pa. Super. 180, 173 A.2d 780 (1961).

---

7. Now §1-303(e) — EDS.

Indeed, the Code's official commentators urge that overly simplistic and overly legalistic interpretation of a contract should be shunned.[8]

We conclude therefore that Columbia's evidence about course of dealing and usage of trade should have been admitted. Its exclusion requires that the judgment against Columbia must be set aside and the case retried. . . .

QUESTION

If the merger clause in the contract between Columbia and Royster had stated that it barred all evidence of usage of trade and course of dealing, would the decision have been different? See Southern Concrete Servs., Inc. v. Mableton Contractors, Inc., 407 F. Supp. 581, 19 U.C.C. Rep. Serv. 79 (N.D. Ga. 1975).

III. OFFER AND ACCEPTANCE

A. General Rules

Common law rules of contract formation had too many technicalities and formalities to suit the drafters of the UCC. If, as often happens, people in business create contracts on a very informal basis, the Code does all it can to give legal meaning to the resulting deal.[9] Read §§2-204, 2-205, and 2-206 before doing the next Problems.

---

8. Referring to the general provisions about course of dealing and trade usage, §1-205, Comment 1 states:

> This Act rejects both the "lay dictionary" and the "conveyancer's" reading of a commercial agreement. Instead the meaning of the agreement of the parties is to be determined by the language used by them and by their action, read and interpreted in the light of commercial practices and other surrounding circumstances. The measure and background for interpretation are set by the commercial context, which may explain and supplement even the language of a formal or final writing.

9. Article 2 specifically addresses the issue of when a binding contract to sell is formed at an *auction*. See §2-328; Gregory Callimanopulos v. Christie's Inc., 621 F. Supp. 2d 127, 69 U.C.C. Rep. Serv. 2d 351 (S.D.N.Y. 2009) (holding that §2-328 authorized auctioneer to reopen bidding, after gavel had fallen on $3 million bid for painting, because auctioneer had not seen another bidder raise her paddle).

PROBLEM 11

Mastervoice TV ordered 20,000 fuses from the Generous Electric Company, the order stating "Reply by return mail." Instead of a formal reply, Generous immediately shipped the fuses. When the fuses arrived, they were found to be defective. Mastervoice, which had to procure substitute goods elsewhere to meet its production schedule, sued Generous Electric for breach of warranty. Answer these questions:

(a) At what moment was the contract formed?

(b) Can Generous make this defense: "There was never any contract since our alleged act of acceptance (the shipment of *defective* goods) did not comply with requirements of Mastervoice's offer (which contemplated only shipment of *good* fuses)"?

(c) Instead of the above, assume that when Generous received the order it discovered that it no longer manufactured the type of fuses Mastervoice wanted, but that it did carry a very similar type of fuse that it believed would suit Mastervoice's needs. The shipping manager for Generous was unable to get through to the relevant people at Mastervoice, so in the end Generous shipped the slightly different fuses along with a cover note saying, "These are similar to the fuses you ordered, but may not be right for you. If they are not suitable, we will gladly take them back without charge." Is Generous now in breach because it shipped nonconforming goods? See §2-206(1)(b).

PROBLEM 12

For years P. Dreamer had wanted a Rolls Royce Silver Shadow with burgundy-colored trim (he had seen one in an ad and salivated). He saw one on the lot of Posh Motors. After Dreamer had dickered loud and long over the terms with Paula Posh, president of Posh Motors, they finally agreed on a price. Dreamer said he wanted to clear the deal with his wife before signing anything, so Posh promised she would hold the car for the Dreamers until the next day at noon. When Mr. and Mrs. Dreamer arrived at the dealership the next morning, the car was gone. Posh had made a better deal with another buyer. Do the Dreamers have a good cause of action? See §2-205. Does §1-103(b) help?

B.   *The Battle of the Forms*

As long as there are merchant buyers and sellers of goods, there will be forms with self-serving boilerplate. And as long as the transactions proceed without incident — which may be after a long while and many sales — their forms will pass like ships on a foggy sea. But when at last one of their transactions sinks, each retreats to the shelter of its favorable terms to claim victory.

Dependable Component Supply, Inc. v. Pace Electronics Inc., 772 So. 2d 582, 43 U.C.C. Rep. Serv. 2d 521 (Fla. App. 2000).

The "battle of the forms" is a much litigated problem that arises from two sources: (1) the business practices of either negotiating deals orally and then exchanging printed forms that no one reads until a dispute arises, or dealing at arm's length with non-matching purchase orders and acknowledgments, and (2) the complexities of §2-207 and its Official Comment.

Subsection (1) to §2-207 is meant to reverse the common law rule that an *acceptance* that was not the *mirror image* of the offer was (impliedly) both a rejection and a counteroffer. Under §2-207(1), an acceptance adding new terms creates a contract based on the original offer, unless the *acceptance* very clearly states otherwise. As to what happens to the additional terms, see §2-207(2).

If, in spite of all logic and business judgment, the parties exchange documents that cannot be reconciled so as to produce a contract, no contract results, and either party may, on discovering this mishap, back out of the deal *if* that party acts prior to the beginning of performance. If performance has begun (with the parties wrongly believing a contract exists), subsection (3) of §2-207 regulates the ensuing mess.

Judges recognize that §2-207 is not a model of clarity: "Referred to as 'a murky bit of prose,' and 'like the amphibious tank that was originally designed to fight in the swamps, but was ultimately sent to fight in the desert,' §2-207 is a defiant, lurking demon patiently waiting to condemn its interpreters to the depths of despair. Nevertheless, §2-207 must and can be conquered." Reaction Molding Technologies, Inc. v. General Electric Co., 585 F. Supp. 1097, 1104, 38 U.C.C. Rep. Serv. 1518 (E.D. Pa. 1984).

PROBLEM 13

The Magic Carpet Co. had a long and profitable business relationship with Alibaba Carpet Manufacturers of Bagdad, Illinois. Fifty-five times Alibaba had sold carpets to Magic Carpet. Each sale was carried out in the following manner. A partner of Magic Carpet telephoned Alibaba's order department and ordered a certain quantity of carpet at the price listed in Alibaba's catalog. After each oral order was placed, the credit department was consulted to determine if Magic Carpet was paid up. Then, if the credit was okay, the order department of Alibaba typed the information from the order on one of its printed acknowledgment forms, each of which had the following paragraph printed conspicuously on its face:

> The acceptance of your order is subject to all of the terms and conditions on the face and reverse side hereof, all of which are accepted by buyer; it supersedes buyer's order form, if any. It shall become a contract either (a) when signed and

delivered by buyer to seller and accepted in writing by seller, or (b) at seller's option, when buyer shall have given to seller specification of assortments, delivery dates, shipping instructions, or instructions to bill and hold as to all or any part of the merchandise herein described, or when buyer has received delivery of the whole or any part thereof, or when buyer has otherwise assented to the terms and conditions hereof.

The provisions on the reverse side of the form provided, among other things, that the seller disclaimed all warranties, express or implied. Each acknowledgment form was signed by an employee in Alibaba's order department and mailed to the Magic Carpet Co. Shortly thereafter, the carpet was shipped. Magic Carpet always received the acknowledgment form before the carpet. They placed each form in a file, accepted delivery of the carpet, and paid for it promptly. On the 56th sale, the accepted and paid-for carpet proved to be nonconforming. Magic Carpet sued Alibaba for breach of warranty. Alibaba replied that its form disclaimed all warranties.

Answer these questions:

(a) Was a contract formed between Magic Carpet and Alibaba? See §2-207(1).

(b) Was the disclaimer of warranties part of that contract? See §2-207(2).

———————————

Problem 13 is based on Dorton v. Collins & Aikman Corp., 453 F.2d 1161, 10 U.C.C. Rep. Serv. 585 (6th Cir. 1972), where the court clearly and competently sorted through the complexities of §2-207. White and Summers discuss §2-207 exhaustively. See White & Summers §2-3.

Diamond Fruit Growers, Inc. v. Krack Corp.

United States Court of Appeals, Ninth Circuit, 1986
794 F.2d 1440, 1 U.C.C. Rep. Serv. 2d 1073

WIGGINS, J.

Metal-Matic, Inc. (Metal-Matic) appeals from judgment entered after a jury verdict in favor of Krack Corporation (Krack) on Krack's third-party complaint against Metal-Matic. Metal-Matic also appeals from the district court's denial of its motion for judgment n.o.v. We have jurisdiction under 28 U.S.C. §1291 (1982) and affirm.

FACTS AND PROCEEDINGS BELOW

Krack is a manufacturer of cooling units that contain steel tubing it purchases from outside suppliers. Metal-Matic is one of Krack's tubing suppliers. At the time this dispute arose, Metal-Matic had been supplying tubing to Krack for about ten years. The parties followed the same course of dealing during the entire ten years. At the beginning of each year, Krack sent a blanket purchase order to Metal-Matic stating how much tubing Krack would need for the year. Then, throughout the year as Krack needed tubing, it sent release purchase orders to Metal-Matic requesting that tubing be shipped. Metal-Matic responded to Krack's release purchase orders by sending Krack an acknowledgment form and then shipping the tubing.

Metal-Matic's acknowledgment form disclaimed all liability for consequential damages and limited Metal-Matic's liability for defects in the tubing to refund of the purchase price or replacement or repair of the tubing. As one would expect, these terms were not contained in Krack's purchase order. The following statement was printed on Metal-Matic's form: "Metal-Matic, Inc.'s acceptance of purchaser's offer or its offer to purchaser is hereby expressly made conditional to purchaser's acceptance of the terms and provisions of the acknowledgment form." This statement and the disclaimer of liability were on the back of the acknowledgment form. However, printed at the bottom of the front of the form in boldface capitals was the following statement: "SEE REVERSE SIDE FOR TERMS AND CONDITIONS OF SALE."

On at least one occasion during the ten-year relationship between Metal-Matic and Krack, Allen Zver, Krack's purchasing manager, discussed the limitations of warranty and disclaimer of liability terms contained in Metal-Matic's acknowledgment form with Robert Van Krevelen, Executive Vice President of Metal-Matic. Zver told Van Krevelen that Krack objected to the terms and tried to convince him to change them, but Van Krevelen refused to do so. After the discussions, Krack continued to accept and pay for tubing from Metal-Matic.

In February 1981, Krack sold one of its cooling units to Diamond Fruit Growers, Inc. (Diamond) in Oregon, and in September 1981, Diamond installed the unit in a controlled-atmosphere warehouse. In January 1982, the unit began leaking ammonia from a cooling coil made of steel tubing.

After Diamond discovered that ammonia was leaking into the warehouse, Joseph Smith, the engineer who had been responsible for building Diamond's controlled-atmosphere warehouses, was called in to find the source of the leak. Smith testified that he found a pinhole leak in the cooling coil of the Krack cooling unit. Smith inspected the coil while it was still inside the unit. He last inspected the coil on April 23, 1982. The coil then sat in a hall at Diamond's warehouse until May 1984, when John Myers inspected the coil for Metal-Matic.

Myers cut the defective tubing out of the unit and took it to his office. At his office, he did more cutting on the tubing. After Myers inspected the tubing, it was also inspected by Bruce Wong for Diamond and Paul Irish for Krack.

Diamond sued Krack to recover the loss in value of fruit that it was forced to remove from the storage room as a result of the leak. Krack in turn brought a third-party complaint against Metal-Matic and Van Huffel Tube Corporation (Van Huffel), another of its tubing suppliers, seeking contribution or indemnity in the event it was held liable to Diamond. At the close of the evidence, both Metal-Matic and Van Huffel moved for a directed verdict on the third-party complaint. The court granted Van Huffel's motion based on evidence that the failed tubing was not manufactured by Van Huffel. The court denied Metal-Matic's motion.

The jury returned a verdict in favor of Diamond against Krack. It then found that Krack was entitled to contribution from Metal-Matic for thirty percent of Diamond's damages. Metal-Matic moved for judgment n.o.v. The court denied that motion and entered judgment on the jury verdict.

Metal-Matic raises two grounds for reversal. First, Metal-Matic contends that as part of its contract with Krack, it disclaimed all liability for consequential damages and specifically limited its liability for defects in the tubing to refund of the purchase price or replacement or repair of the tubing. Second, Metal-Matic asserts that the evidence does not support a finding that it manufactured the tubing in which the leak developed or that it caused the leak. We address each of these contentions in turn. . . .

Discussion

A. Metal-Matic's Disclaimer of Liability for Consequential Damages

If the contract between Metal-Matic and Krack contains Metal-Matic's disclaimer of liability, Metal-Matic is not liable to indemnify Krack for part of Diamond's damages. Therefore, the principal issue before us on this appeal is whether Metal-Matic's disclaimer of liability became part of the contract between these parties.

Relying on Uniform Commercial Code (U.C.C.) §2-207, Or. Rev. Stat. §72.2070 (1985), Krack argues that Metal-Matic's disclaimer did not become part of the contract. Metal-Matic, on the other hand, argues that §2-207 is inapplicable to this case because the parties discussed the disclaimer, and Krack assented to it.

Krack is correct in its assertion that §2-207 applies to this case. One intended application of §2-207 is to commercial transactions in which the parties exchange printed purchase order and acknowledgment forms. See U.C.C. §2-207 comment 1. The drafters of the UCC recognized that "[b]ecause the [purchase order and acknowledgment] forms are oriented to the thinking of the respective drafting parties, the terms contained in them often do not correspond." Id. Section 2-207 is an attempt to provide rules of contract formation in such cases. In this case, Krack and Metal-Matic exchanged purchase order and acknowledgment forms that contained different or additional terms. This, then, is a typical §2-207 situation. The fact that the parties discussed the terms of their contract after they exchanged their forms does not put this case outside §2-207. See 3 R.

Duesenburg & L. King, Sales and Bulk Transfers under the Uniform Commercial Code (Bender's U.C.C. Service) §3.05[2] (1986). Section 2-207 provides rules of contract formation in cases such as this one in which the parties exchange forms but do not agree on all the terms of their contract.

A brief summary of §2-207 is necessary to an understanding of its application to this case. Section 2-207 changes the common law's mirror-image rule for transactions that fall within article 2 of the U.C.C. At common law, an acceptance that varies the terms of the offer is a counteroffer and operates as a rejection of the original offer. See Idaho Power Co. v. Westinghouse Electric Corp., 596 F.2d 924, 926 (9th Cir. 1979). If the offeror goes ahead with the contract after receiving the counteroffer, his performance is an acceptance of the terms of the counteroffer. See C. Itoh & Co. v. Jordan International Co., 552 F.2d 1228, 1236 (7th Cir. 1977); J. White & R. Summers, Handbook of the Law Under the Uniform Commercial Code §1-2 at 34 (2d ed. 1980).

Generally §2-207(1) "converts a common law counteroffer into an acceptance even though it states additional or different terms." Idaho Power, 596 F.2d at 926; see U.C.C. §2-207(1). The only requirement under §2-207(1) is that the responding form contain a definite and seasonable expression of acceptance. The terms of the responding form that correspond to the offer constitute the contract. Under §2-207(2), the additional terms of the responding form become proposals for additions to the contract. Between merchants the additional terms become part of the contract unless the offer is specifically limited to its terms, the offeror objects to the additional terms, or the additional terms materially alter the terms of the offer. U.C.C. §2-207(2); see J. White & R. Summers, §1-2 at 32.

However, §2-207(1) is subject to a proviso. If a definite and seasonable expression of acceptance expressly conditions acceptance on the offeror's assent to additional or different terms contained therein, the parties' differing forms do not result in a contract unless the offeror assents to the additional terms. See J. White & R. Summers, §1-2 at 32-33. If the offeror assents, the parties have a contract and the additional terms are a part of that contract. If, however, the offeror does not assent, but the parties proceed with the transaction as if they have a contract, their performance results in formation of a contract. UCC §2-207(3). In that case, the terms of the contract are those on which the parties' forms agree plus any terms supplied by the UCC. Id.; see Boise Cascade Corp. v. Etsco, Ltd., 39 U.C.C. Rep. Serv. (Callaghan) 410, 414 (D. Or. 1984); J. White & R. Summers, §1-2 at 34.

In this case, Metal-Matic expressly conditioned its acceptance on Krack's assent to the additional terms contained in Metal-Matic's acknowledgment form. That form tracks the language of the §2-207(1) proviso, stating that "Metal-Matic, Inc.'s acceptance . . . is hereby *expressly made conditional* to purchaser's acceptance of the terms and provisions of the acknowledgment form" (emphasis added). See *C. Itoh & Co.*, 552 F.2d at 1235. Therefore, we must determine whether Krack assented to Metal-Matic's limitation of liability term.

Metal-Matic argues that Krack did assent to the limitation of liability term. This argument is based on the discussions between Zver for Krack and Van Krevelen for Metal-Matic. Some time during the ten-year relationship between the companies, these two men discussed Krack's objections to the warranty and liability limitation terms in Metal-Matic's acknowledgment form. Krack attempted to persuade Metal-Matic to change its forms, but Metal-Matic refused to do so. After the discussions, the companies continued to do business as in the past. Metal-Matic contends that Krack assented to the limitation of liability term when it continued to accept and pay for tubing after Metal-Matic insisted that the contract contain its terms.

To address Metal-Matic's argument, we must determine what constitutes assent to additional or different terms for purposes of §2-207(1). The parties have not directed us to any cases that analyze this question and our research has revealed none. We therefore look to the language and structure of §2-207 and to the purposes behind that section to determine the correct standard.

One of the principles underlying §2-207 is neutrality. If possible, the section should be interpreted so as to give neither party to a contract an advantage simply because it happened to send the first or in some cases the last form. See J. White & R. Summers, §1-2 at 26-27. Section 2-207 accomplishes this result in part by doing away with the common law's "last shot" rule. See 3 R. Duesenberg & L. King, §3.05[1][a][iii] at 3-73. At common law, the offeree/counterofferor gets all of its terms simply because it fired the last shot in the exchange of forms. Section 2-207(3) does away with this result by giving neither party the terms it attempted to impose unilaterally on the other. See id. at 3-71. Instead, all of the terms on which the parties' forms do not agree drop out, and the UCC supplies the missing terms.

Generally, this result is fair because both parties are responsible for the ambiguity in their contract. The parties could have negotiated a contract and agreed on its terms, but for whatever reason failed to do so. Therefore, neither party should get its terms. See 3 R. Duesenberg & L. King §3.05 [2] at 3-88. However, as White and Summers point out, resort to §2-207(3) will often work to the disadvantage of the seller because he will "wish to undertake less responsibility for the quality of his goods than the Code imposes or else wish to limit his damages liability more narrowly than would the Code." J. White & R. Summers §1-2 at 34. Nevertheless, White and Summers recommend that §2-207(3) be applied in such cases. Id. We agree. Application of §2-207(3) is more equitable than giving one party its terms simply because it sent the last form. Further, the terms imposed by the code are presumably equitable and consistent with public policy because they are statutorily imposed. See 3 R. Duesenberg & L. King, §3.05 [2] at 3-88.

With these principles in mind, we turn now to Metal-Matic's argument that Krack assented to the disclaimer when it continued to accept and pay for tubing once Metal-Matic indicated that it was willing to sell tubing only if its warranty and liability terms were part of the contract. Metal-Matic's argument is appealing. Sound policy supports permitting a seller to control the terms on which it will sell its products, especially in a case in which the seller has indicated both in writing and orally that those terms are the only terms on which it is willing to sell the product. Nevertheless, we reject Metal-Matic's argument because we find that these considerations are outweighed by the public policy reflected by Oregon's enactment of the UCC.

If we were to accept Metal-Matic's argument, we would reinstate to some extent the common law's last shot rule. To illustrate, assume that the parties in this case had sent the same forms but in the reverse order and that Krack's form contained terms stating that Metal-Matic is liable for all consequential damages and conditioning acceptance on Metal-Matic's assent to Krack's terms. Assume also that Metal-Matic objected to Krack's terms but Krack refused to change them and that the parties continued with their transaction anyway. If we applied Metal-Matic's argument in that case, we would find that Krack's term was part of the contract because Metal-Matic continued to ship tubing to Krack after Krack reaffirmed that it would purchase tubing only if Metal-Matic were liable for consequential damages. Thus, the result would turn on which party sent the last form, and would therefore be inconsistent with §2-207's purpose of doing away with the last shot rule.

That result is avoided by requiring a specific and unequivocal expression of assent on the part of the offeror when the offeree conditions its acceptance on assent to additional or different terms. If the offeror does not give specific and unequivocal assent but the parties act as if they have a contract, the provisions of §2-207(3) apply to fill in the terms of the contract. Application of §2-207(3) is appropriate in that situation because by going ahead with the transaction without resolving their dispute, both parties are responsible for introducing ambiguity into the contract. Further, in a case such as this one, requiring the seller to assume more liability than it intends is not altogether inappropriate. The seller is most responsible for the ambiguity because it inserts a term in its form that requires assent to additional terms and then does not enforce that requirement. If the seller truly does not want to be bound unless the buyer assents to its terms, it can protect itself by not shipping until it obtains that assent. See *C. Itoh & Co.*, 552 F.2d at 1238.

We hold that because Krack's conduct did not indicate unequivocally that Krack intended to assent to Metal-Matic's terms, that conduct did not amount to the assent contemplated by §2-207(1). See 3 R. Duesenberg & L. King, §3.05[1][a][iii] at 3-74....

The jury verdict is supported by the evidence and consistent with the UCC. Therefore, the district court did not err in denying Metal-Matic's motion for a judgment n.o.v.

PROBLEM 14

Would the following clause in the seller's acknowledgment to the buyer's order form be a material alteration under §2-207(2)(b): "Any disputes concerning this contract shall be subject to binding arbitration"? See ICC Chemical Corp. v. Vitol, Inc., 425 Fed. Appx. 57, 74 U.C.C. Rep. Serv. 2d 781 (2d Cir. 2011) (arbitration clause not a material alteration where sometimes used in chemical industry sales); In re Cotton Yarn Antitrust Litigation, 505 F.3d 274 (4th Cir. 2007) (not a material alteration where arbitration was the usage of trade in the textile industry). If this clause were in an acknowledgment of an international sale of goods to which CISG applies, would it be valid? See Article 19; Filanto, S.p.A. v. Chilewich Intl. Corp., 789 F. Supp. 1229 (S.D.N.Y. 1992), *appeal dismissed*, 984 F.2d 58 (2d Cir. 1993); Comment, The U.N. Convention on the International Sale of Goods and the "Battle of the Forms," 13 Fordham Intl. L.J. 649 (1990).

Bayway Refining Co. v. Oxygenated Marketing and Trading A.G.

United States Court of Appeals, Second Circuit, 2000
215 F.3d 219, 41 U.C.C. Rep. Serv. 2d 713

JACOBS, Circuit Judge.

Plaintiff-appellee Bayway Refining Company ("Bayway") paid federal excise tax on a petroleum transaction, as the Internal Revenue Code requires a petroleum dealer to do in a sale to a buyer who has not procured an exemption under the applicable tax provision. In this diversity suit against the buyer, Oxygenated Marketing and Trading A.G. ("OMT"), Bayway seeks to recover the amount of the tax it paid. One question in this "battle of the forms" contract case is whether, under N.Y. U.C.C. §2-207(2)(b) (McKinney 1993), a contract term allocating liability to the buyer for an excise tax is an additional term presumed to have been accepted (as the seller contends) or (as the buyer contends) a material alteration presumed to have been rejected. The United States District Court for the Southern District of New York (McKenna, J.) granted summary judgment in favor of the seller, Bayway.

We conclude that, in the circumstances presented: (i) the party opposing the inclusion of an additional term under §2-207(2)(b) bears the burden of proving that the term amounts to a material alteration; (ii) the district court properly granted summary judgment in favor of the seller, because the additional term here did not materially alter the contract; and (iii) the district court properly admitted evidence of custom and practice in the industry despite the fact that it was first proffered in the moving party's reply papers. Accordingly, we affirm.

BACKGROUND

Bayway and OMT are in the business of buying and selling petroleum products. Bayway contracted to sell to OMT 60,000 barrels of a gasoline blendstock called Methyl Tertiary Butyl Ether ("MTBE"). On February 12, 1998, OMT faxed Bayway a confirmation letter, which operated as the offer, and which stated in pertinent part:

> We are pleased to confirm the details of our purchase from you of MTBE as agreed between Mr. Ben Basil and Roger Ertle on [February 12, 1998]. . . .
> This confirmation constitutes the entire contract and represents our understanding of the terms and conditions of our agreement. . . . Any apparent discrepancies or omissions should be brought to our notice within the next two working days.

Bayway faxed its confirmation to OMT the next day. That document, which operated as the acceptance, stated in pertinent part: "We are pleased to confirm the following verbal agreement concluded on February 12, 1998 with your company. This document cancels and supersedes any correspondence in relation to this transaction." Bayway's acceptance then set forth the parties, price, amount and delivery terms, and undertook to incorporate the company's standard terms:

> Notwithstanding any other provision of this agreement, where not in conflict with the foregoing, the terms and conditions as set forth in Bayway Refining Company's General Terms and Conditions dated March 01, 1994 along with Bayway's Marine Provisions are hereby incorporated in full by reference in this contract.

The Bayway General Terms and Conditions were not transmitted with Bayway's fax, but Paragraph 10 of its General Terms and Conditions states:

> Buyer shall pay seller the amount of any federal, state and local excise, gross receipts, import, motor fuel, superfund and spill taxes and all other federal, state and local taxes however designated, other than taxes on income, paid or incurred by seller directly or indirectly with respect to the oil or product sold hereunder and/or on the value thereof.

This term is referenced as the "Tax Clause."

OMT did not object to Bayway's acceptance or to the incorporation of its General Terms and Conditions (which included the Tax Clause). OMT accepted delivery of the MTBE barrels on March 22, 1998.

The Internal Revenue Code imposes an excise tax, payable by the seller, on the sale of gasoline blendstocks such as MTBE "to any person who is not registered under [26 U.S.C. §4101]" for a tax exemption. 26 U.S.C.A. §4081(a)(1)(A)(iv) (West Supp. 1999). After delivery, Bayway learned that OMT was not registered with the Internal Revenue Service for the tax exemption. The transaction therefore created a tax liability of $464,035.12, which Bayway paid.

Invoking the Tax Clause, Bayway demanded payment of the $464,035.12 in taxes in addition to the purchase price of the MTBE. OMT denied that it had agreed to assume the tax liability and refused to pay that invoice item. In response, Bayway filed this diversity suit alleging breach of contract by OMT.

Upon Bayway's motion for summary judgment, the district court held that the Tax Clause was properly incorporated into the contract. See Tosco Corp. v. Oxygenated Mktg. & Trading A.G., No. 98 Civ. 4695, 1999 WL 328342, at *3-*6 (S.D.N.Y. May 24, 1999). The fact that Bayway had failed to attach a copy of the General Terms and Conditions was irrelevant because OMT could have obtained a copy if it had asked for one. See id. at *3. The court then analyzed the contract-forming documents, applied the "battle of the forms" framework set forth in N.Y. U.C.C. §2-207(2), and concluded that OMT failed to carry its burden of proving that the Tax Clause materially altered the contract. See id. at *3-*6. The court therefore granted summary judgment in favor of Bayway.

DISCUSSION

On appeal, OMT argues (i) that it succeeded in raising genuine issues of fact as to whether the Tax Clause materially altered the Bayway/OMT contract and (ii) that the evidence of custom and practice in the industry, upon which the grant of summary judgment turns, was improperly admitted. . . .

We affirm for substantially the reasons stated by the district court. We hold — on an issue of first impression in this Court — that in a "battle of the forms" case governed by N.Y. U.C.C. §2-207(2)(b), the party opposing the inclusion of an additional term bears the burden of proving that the term works a material alteration. Viewing the evidence in the light most favorable to OMT, we conclude that OMT failed to shoulder that burden. Finally, we hold that the district court properly admitted the evidence concerning industry custom and practice.

A. BATTLE OF THE FORMS

Bayway argued its motion for summary judgment on the basis of New York law, presumably because one of the additional terms incorporated by its acceptance is a New York choice-of-law provision. OMT has accepted New York law as controlling for purposes of Bayway's summary judgment motion. [The court quoted §2-207(1) and (2).]

It was undisputed in the district court that Bayway's confirmation fax is effective to form a contract as an acceptance — even though it stated or referenced additional terms (including the Tax Clause) — because it was not made expressly conditional on OMT's assent to the additional terms. See id. §2-207(1). Therefore, under §2-207(2), the Tax Clause is a proposal for an addition to the contract. See id. §2-207(2). The parties are both merchants within the meaning of the U.C.C. See id. §2-104(1), (3). The Tax Clause therefore is presumed to become part of the contract unless one of the three enumerated exceptions applies. See id. §2-207(2). In its defense, OMT invokes the "material alteration" exception of §2-207(2)(b).

1. Burden of Proof

The allocation of the burden of proof under this exception to §2-207(2) is a question of New York law, see United States v. McCombs, 30 F.3d 310, 323-24 (2d Cir. 1994) (holding that, under the Erie doctrine, federal courts sitting in diversity apply the forum state's law concerning burdens of proof), and is answered in the text of New York's U.C.C. §2-207(2). Section 2-207(2)(b) is an exception to the general rule of §2-207(2) that additional terms become part of a contract between merchants. That general rule is in the nature of a presumption concerning the intent of the contracting parties. Thus if neither party introduced any evidence, the Tax Clause would, by the plain language of §2-207(2), become part of the contract. To implement that presumption, the burden of proving the materiality of the alteration must fall on the party that opposes inclusion. Accordingly, we hold that under §2-207(2)(b) the party opposing the inclusion of additional terms shoulders the burden of proof. In so doing, we join almost every court to have considered this issue. [Citations omitted.]

2. Materiality and Per Se Materiality

A material alteration is one that would "result in *surprise* or *hardship* if incorporated without express awareness by the other party." N.Y. U.C.C. §2-207 cmt. 4 (emphasis added).

Certain additional terms are deemed material as a matter of law. For example, an arbitration clause is per se a material alteration in New York because New York law requires an express agreement to commit disputes to arbitration. See Marlene Indus. v. Carnac Textiles, Inc., 45 N.Y.2d 327, 408 N.Y.S.2d 410, 413, 380 N.E. 2d 239 (1978); see also N.Y. U.C.C. §2-207 cmt. 4 (listing as examples of per se material alterations, inter alia, waivers of warranties of merchantability or fitness for a particular purpose and clauses granting the seller the power to cancel upon the buyer's failure to meet any invoice). OMT characterizes the Tax Clause as a broad-ranging indemnity clause, and analogizes it to these per se material alterations. We reject the analogy. The Tax Clause allocates responsibility for the tax payable on a specific sale of goods. See Union Carbide Corp. v. Oscar Mayer Foods Corp., 947 F.2d 1333, 1335, 1337 (7th Cir. 1991) (distinguishing between "open-ended" tax liability, which is a material alteration, from "responsibility for taxes shown on an individual invoice," which is not). And unlike an arbitration clause, which waives a range of rights that are solicitously protected, the Tax Clause is limited, discrete and the subject of no special protection. Unable to show that the Tax Clause is a material alteration per se, OMT must prove that in this case the Tax Clause resulted in surprise or hardship.[10]

3. Surprise

Surprise, within the meaning of the material alteration exception of §2-207(2)(b), has both the subjective element of what a party actually knew and the objective element of what a party should have known. See American Ins. Co. v. El Paso Pipe & Supply Co., 978 F.2d 1185, 1191 (10th Cir. 1992); In re Chateaugay, 162 B.R. at 956-57. A profession of surprise and raised eyebrows are not enough: "[C]onclusory statements, conjecture, or speculation by the party resisting the motion will not defeat summary judgment." Kulak v. City of New York, 88 F.3d 63, 71 (2d Cir. 1996). To carry the burden of showing surprise, a party must establish that, under the circumstances, it cannot be presumed that a reasonable merchant would have consented to the additional term. See *Union Carbide*, 947 F.2d at 1336.

OMT has adduced evidence that the Tax Clause came as an amazement to OMT's executives, who described the term's incorporation as "contract by ambush" and a "sl[e]ight-of-hand proposal." Thus OMT has sufficiently exhibited its subjective surprise. As to objective surprise, however, OMT has alleged no facts and introduced no evidence to show that a reasonable petroleum merchant would be surprised by the Tax Clause. See In re Chateaugay, 162 B.R. at 957 (including as types of evidence proving objective surprise "the parties' prior course of dealing and the number of written confirmations that they exchanged, industry custom and the conspicuousness of the term"). OMT had no prior contrary course of dealing with Bayway, and offered nothing concerning trade custom or practice.

---

10. Even if an additional term that places the tax liability on the opposing party was a material alteration per se, New York law allows a party to rebut this conclusion in some limited circumstances with a sufficient showing that the additional term reflects the custom and practice in the particular industry. See *Avedon Eng'g*, 126 F.3d at 1285 & n.15 (discussing New York law); Schubtex, Inc. v. Allen Snyder, Inc., 49 N.Y.2d 1, 424 N.Y.S.2d 133, 135, 399 N.E.2d 1154 (1979). As discussed below, Bayway's evidence that the Tax Clause reflects the custom and practice in the petroleum industry is compelling and unrebutted.

Ordinarily, our inquiry into surprise would end here. However, in response to OMT's claim of surprise, Bayway introduced evidence that the Tax Clause reflects custom and practice in the petroleum industry, and on appeal OMT argues that Bayway's own evidence raises a genuine issue of material fact as to whether such a trade practice exists. Although the evidence was introduced by Bayway, we are "obligated to search the record and independently determine whether or not a genuine issue of fact exists." Jiminez v. Dreis & Krump Mfg. Co., 736 F.2d 51, 53 (2d Cir. 1984) (quoting Higgins v. Baker, 309 F. Supp. 635, 639 (S.D.N.Y. 1970)) (internal quotation marks omitted).

Upon our review of the evidence, we conclude that Bayway has adduced compelling proof that shifting tax liability to a buyer is the custom and practice in the petroleum industry. Two industry experts offered unchallenged testimony that it is customary for the buyer to pay all the taxes resulting from a petroleum transaction. One expert stated that "[t]his practice is so universally understood among traders in the industry, that I cannot recall an instance, in all my years of trading and overseeing trades, when the buyer refused to pay the seller for excise or sales taxes."

OMT cites the standard contracts of five major petroleum companies that Bayway introduced to illustrate contract terms similar to the Tax Clause. OMT argues that only three of the five place the tax liability on the buyer, and that there is therefore an issue of fact as to whether the Tax Clause would objectively surprise a merchant in this industry.

OMT misconstrues the evidence. Three of the contracts—those of CITGO Petroleum, Conoco, and Enron—mirror the Tax Clause. A fourth, Chevron's, differs from the others only in that the cost of the taxes is added into the contract price rather than separately itemized. Thus Chevron's standard contract affords OMT no support.

The fifth example, the Texaco contract, is silent as to the tax allocation issue in this case. But on this unrebutted record of universal trade custom and practice, silence supports no contrary inference.

Moreover, common sense supports Bayway's evidence of custom and practice. The federal excise tax is imposed when taxable fuels are sold "to any person who is not registered under [26 U.S.C. §4101]." 26 U.S.C. §4081(a)(1)(A)(iv). The buyer thereby controls whether any tax liability is incurred in a transaction. A trade practice that reflects a rational allocation of incentives (as trade practices usually do) would place the burden of the tax on the party that is in the position to obviate it—here, on OMT as the buyer.

Viewing Bayway's evidence in the light most favorable to OMT, we conclude that allocating the tax liability to the buyer is the custom and practice in the petroleum industry. OMT could not be objectively surprised by the incorporation of an additional term in the contract that reflects such a practice.

4. Hardship

To recapitulate: A material alteration is one that would "result in surprise *or* hardship if incorporated without express awareness by the other party." N.Y. U.C.C. §2-207 cmt. 4 (emphasis added). Although this Official Comment to the U.C.C. seemingly treats hardship as an independent ground for finding that an alteration is material, courts have expressed doubt: "You cannot walk away from a contract that you can fairly be deemed to have agreed to, merely because performance turns out to be a hardship for you, unless you can squeeze yourself into the impossibility defense or some related doctrine of excuse." Union Carbide, 947 F.2d at 1336 ("Hardship is a consequence [of material alteration], not a criterion. (Surprise can be either.)"); see also, e.g., Suzy Phillips Originals, Inc. v. Coville, Inc., 939 F. Supp. 1012, 1017-18 (E.D.N.Y. 1996) (citing *Union Carbide* with approval and limiting the test for material alteration to surprise); In re Chateaugay, 162 B.R. at 957 (same).

We need not decide whether hardship is an independent ground of material alteration, because even if it were, OMT failed to raise a genuine issue of material fact as to hardship. OMT's only evidence of hardship is (generally) that it is a small business dependent on precarious profit margins, and it would suffer a loss it cannot afford. That does not amount to hardship in the present circumstances.

Typically, courts that have relied on hardship to find that an additional term materially alters a contract have done so when the term is one that creates or allocates an open-ended and prolonged liability. See, e.g., St. Charles Cable TV, Inc. v. Eagle Comtronics, Inc., 687 F. Supp. 820, 827 (S.D.N.Y. 1988) (finding a hardship in "shift[ing] all risks for any dispute to the buyers"), *aff'd*, 895 F.2d 1410 (2d Cir. 1989) (unpublished table disposition); Charles J. King, Inc. v. Barge LM-10, 518 F. Supp. 1117, 1120 (S.D.N.Y. 1981).

The Tax Clause places on a buyer a contractual responsibility that bears on a specific sale of goods, that is (at least) not uncommon in the industry, and that the buyer could avoid by registration. The cry of hardship rings hollow, because any loss that the Tax Clause imposed on OMT is limited, routine and self-inflicted.

OMT failed to raise a factual issue as to hardship or surprise. Summary judgment was therefore appropriately granted in favor of Bayway. . . .

For the foregoing reasons, we affirm the judgment of the district court.

PROBLEM 15

The purchase order of the buyer ordered a tugboat, and the fine print demanded that the tugboat be warranted for a two-year period. The tugboat seller's acknowledgment form contained a statement that disclaimed all warranties. Neither party read the other's form, so the tugboat was shipped, accepted, and then had major problems remaining afloat. You are the attorney for the buyer. Advise your client whether the contract includes a warranty.

The last Problem raised the issue of how §2-207 resolves an exchange of forms containing *different* terms. While subsection (1) of the statute talks about both "additional" and "different" terms, subsection (2) mentions only "additional" ones. Official Comment 6 (reprinted below), at first glance, appears to resolve the matter, but a careful reading of it shows that it is addressed only to written confirmations of an oral contract containing different terms, which the Official Comment says cancel each other out. The courts facing the different terms scenario of Problem 15 have divided into two major camps, as discussed in the following case.

Northrop Corporation v. Litronic Industries

United States Court of Appeals, Seventh Circuit, 1994
29 F.3d 1173; 24 U.C.C. Rep. Serv. 2d 407

POSNER, Chief Judge.

"Battle of the forms" refers to the not uncommon situation in which one business firm makes an offer in the form of a preprinted form contract and the offeree responds with its own form contract. At common law, any discrepancy between the forms would prevent the offeree's response from operating as an acceptance. See Poel v. Brunswick-Balke-Collender Co., 216 N.Y. 310, 110 N.E. 619, 621-22 (N.Y. 1915). So there would be no contract in such a case. This was the "mirror image" rule, which Article 2 of the Uniform Commercial Code jettisoned by providing that "a definite and seasonable expression of acceptance or a written confirmation which is sent within a reasonable time operates as an acceptance even though it states terms additional to or different from those offered or agreed upon, unless acceptance is made conditional on assent to the additional or different terms." UCC §2-207(1). See Union Carbide Corp. v. Oscar Mayer Foods Corp., 947 F.2d 1333, 1335-36 (7th Cir. 1991). Mischief lurks in the words "additional to or different from." The next subsection of 2-207 provides that if additional terms in the acceptance are not materially different from those in the offer, then, subject to certain other qualifications (*id.* at 1335-37), they become part of the contract, §2-207(2), while if the additional terms are materially different they operate as proposals and so have no effect unless the offeror agrees to them, UCC §2-207, comment 3; if the offeror does not agree to them, therefore, the terms of the contract are those in the offer. A clause providing for interest at normal rates on overdue invoices, or limiting the right to reject goods because of defects falling within customary trade tolerances for acceptance with adjustment, would be the sort of additional term that is not deemed material, and hence it would become a part of the contract even if the offeror never signified acceptance of it. *Id.*, comment 5.

The Code does not explain, however, what happens if the offeree's response contains *different* terms (rather than additional ones) within the meaning of section 2-207(1). There is no consensus on that question. See James J. White & Robert S. Summers, *Uniform Commercial Code* 33-36 (3d ed. 1988); John E. Murray, Jr., "The Chaos of the 'Battle of the Forms': Solutions," 39 Vand. L. Rev. 1307, 1354-65 (1986). We know there is a contract because an acceptance is effective even though it contains different terms; but what are the terms of the contract that is brought into being by the offer and acceptance? One view is that the discrepant terms in both the nonidentical offer and the acceptance drop out, and default terms found elsewhere in the Code fill the resulting gap. Another view is that the offeree's discrepant terms drop out and the offeror's become part of the contract. A third view, possibly the most sensible, equates "different" with "additional" and makes the outcome turn on whether the new terms in the acceptance are materially different from the terms in the offer — in which event they operate as proposals, so that the offeror's terms prevail unless he agrees to the variant terms in the acceptance — or not materially different from the terms in the offer, in which event they become part of the contract. John L. Utz, "More on the Battle of the Forms: The Treatment of 'Different' Terms Under the Uniform Commerical Code," 16 U.C.C. L.J. 103 (1983). This interpretation equating "different" to "additional," bolstered by drafting history which shows that the omission of "or different" from section 2-207(2) was a drafting error, Utz, *supra*, 16 U.C.C. L.J. at 110-12; Murray, *supra*, 39 Vand. L. Rev. at 1355, substitutes a manageable inquiry into materiality, Union Carbide Corp. v. Oscar Mayer Foods Corp., *supra*, 947 F.2d at 1336-37; Schulze & Burch Biscuit Co. v. Tree Top, Inc., 831 F.2d 709, 715 (7th Cir. 1987); Douglas G. Baird & Robert Weisberg, "Rules, Standards, and the Battle of the Forms: A Reassessment of Section 2-207," 68 Va. L. Rev. 1217, 1246 (1982), for a hair-splitting inquiry into the difference between "different" and "additional." It is hair-splitting ("metaphysical," "casuistic," "semantic," in the pejorative senses of these words) because all different terms are additional and all additional terms are different.

Unfortunately, the Illinois courts — whose understanding of Article 2 of the UCC is binding on us because this is a diversity suit governed, all agree, by Illinois law — have had no occasion to choose among the different positions on the consequences of an acceptance that contains "different" terms from the offer. We shall have to choose.

   The battle of the forms in this case takes the form of something very like a badminton game, but we can simplify it a bit without distorting the issues. The players are Northrop, the giant defense firm, and Litronic, which manufactures electronic components, including "printed wire boards" that are incorporated into defense weapon systems. In 1987 Northrop sent several manufacturers, including Litronic, a request to submit offers to sell Northrop a customized printed wire board designated by Northrop as a "1714 Board." The request stated that any purchase would be made by means of a purchase order that would set forth terms and conditions that would override any inconsistent terms in the offer. In response, Litronic mailed an offer to sell Northrop four boards for $ 19,000 apiece, to be delivered within six weeks. The offer contained a 90-day warranty stated to be in lieu of any other warranties, and provided that the terms of the offer would take precedence over any terms proposed by the buyer. Lynch, a purchasing officer of Northrop, responded to the offer in a phone conversation in which he told Litronic's man, Lair, that he was accepting the offer up to the limit of his authority, which was $24,999, and that a formal purchase order for all four boards would follow. Litronic was familiar with Northrop's purchase order form, having previously done business with Northrop, which had been using the same form for some time. Had Lair referred to any of the previous orders, he would have discovered that Northrop's order form provided for a warranty that contained no time limit.

   Lynch followed up the phone conversation a month later with a "turn on" letter, authorizing Litronic to begin production of all four boards (it had done so already) and repeating that a purchase order would follow. The record is unclear when the actual purchase order was mailed; it may have been as much as four months after the phone conversation and three months after the turn-on letter. The purchase order required the seller to send a written acknowledgment to Northrop. Litronic never did so, however, and Northrop did not complain; it does not bother to follow up on its requirement of a signed acknowledgment.

   Although Litronic had begun manufacturing the boards immediately after the telephone call from Lynch, for reasons that are unknown but that Northrop does not contend are culpable Litronic did not deliver the first three boards until more than a year later, in July of 1988. Northrop tested the boards for conformity to its specifications. The testing was protracted, either because the boards were highly complex or because Northrop's inspectors were busy, or perhaps for both reasons. At all events it was not until December and January, five or six months after delivery, that Northrop returned the three boards (the fourth had not been delivered), claiming that they were defective. Litronic refused to accept the return of the boards, on the ground that its 90-day warranty had lapsed. Northrop's position of course is that it had an unlimited warranty, as stated in the purchase order.

As an original matter one might suppose that this dispute is not over the terms of the warranty but over whether Northrop waited more than the "reasonable time" that the Uniform Commercial Code allows the buyer of nonconforming goods to reject them. UCC §2-602(1). That in fact is how the magistrate judge framed the issue, as we shall see. But the parties continue to treat it as a "warranty" case. Their implicit view is that Litronic's 90-day warranty, if a term of the contract, not only barred Northrop from complaining about defects that showed up more than 90 days after the delivery of the boards but also limited to 90 days the time within which Northrop was permitted to reject the boards because of defects that rendered them nonconforming. We accept this view for purposes of deciding these appeals.

Litronic's appeal concerns the breach of its warranty on the No. 1714 boards. It wins if the warranty really did expire after only 90 days. The parties agree that Litronic's offer to sell the No. 1714 boards to Northrop, the offer made in response to Northrop's request for bids, was — the offer. So far, so good. If Northrop's Mr. Lynch accepted the offer over the phone, the parties had a contract then and there, but the question would still be on what terms. Regarding the first question, whether there was a contract, we may assume to begin with that the acceptance was sufficiently "definite" to satisfy the requirement of definiteness in section 2-207(1); after all, it impelled Litronic to begin production immediately, and there is no suggestion that it acted precipitately in doing so. We do not know whether Lynch in his conversation with Lair made acceptance of the complete contract expressly conditional on approval by Lynch's superiors at Northrop. We know that he had authority to contract only up to $24,999, but we do not know whether he told Lair what the exact limitation on his authority was or whether Litronic knew it without being told. It does not matter. The condition, if it was a condition, was satisfied and so drops out.

We do not think that Northrop's acceptance, via Lynch, of Litronic's offer could be thought conditional on Litronic's yielding to Northrop's demand for an open-ended warranty. For while Lynch's reference to the purchase order might have alerted Litronic to Northrop's desire for a warranty not limited to 90 days, Lynch did not purport to make the more extensive warranty a condition of acceptance. So the condition, if there was one, was not an express condition, as the cases insist it be. See, e.g., McCarty v. Verson Allsteel Press Co., 89 Ill. App. 3d 498, 411 N.E.2d 936, 945, 44 Ill. Dec. 570 (Ill. App. 1980); Clifford-Jacobs Forging Co. v. Capital Engineering & Mfg. Co., 107 Ill. App. 3d 29, 437 N.E.2d 22, 24, 62 Ill. Dec. 785 (Ill. App. 1982); Dorton v. Collins & Aikman Corp., 453 F.2d 1161, 1168 (6th Cir. 1972); White & Summers, *supra*, at 39.

There was a contract, therefore; further, and, as we shall note, decisive, evidence being that the parties acted as if they had a contract — the boards were shipped and paid for. The question is then what the terms of the warranty in the contract were. Lynch's reference in the phone conversation to the forthcoming purchase order shows that Northrop's acceptance contained different terms from the offer, namely the discrepant terms in the purchase order, in particular the warranty—for it is plain that the Northrop warranty was intended to be indefinite in length, so that, at least in the absence of some industry custom setting a limit on warranties that do not specify a duration (cf. UCC §2-207, comments 4 and 5), a point not raised, any limitation on the length of the warranty in the offer would be a materially different term. Daitom, Inc. v. Pennwalt Corp., 741 F.2d 1569, 1577 (10th Cir. 1984); cf. Owens-Corning Fiberglas Corp. v. Sonic Development Corp., 546 F. Supp. 533, 538 (D. Kan. 1982). Of course the fact that Northrop preferred a longer warranty than Litronic was offering does not by itself establish that Northrop's acceptance contained different terms. But Lynch did not accept Litronic's offer and leave it at that. He said that he would issue a Northrop purchase order, and both he and Lair knew (or at least should have known) that the Northrop purchase order form contained a different warranty from Litronic's sale order form. And we have already said that Lynch did not, by his oral reference to the purchase order, condition Northrop's purchase on Litronic's agreeing to comply with all the terms in the purchase order form, given the courts' insistence that any such condition be explicit. (Judges are skeptical that even businesspeople read boilerplate, so they are reluctant, rightly or wrongly, to make a contract fail on the basis of a printed condition in a form contract.) But Lynch said enough to make clear to Lair that the acceptance contained different terms from the offer.

The Uniform Commercial Code, as we have said, does not say what the terms of the contract are if the offer and acceptance contain different terms, as distinct from cases in which the acceptance merely contains additional terms to those in the offer. The majority view is that the discrepant terms fall out and are replaced by a suitable UCC gap-filler. E.g., Daitom, Inc. v. Pennwalt Corp., *supra*, 741 F.2d at 1578-80; St. Paul Structural Steel Co. v. ABI Contracting, Inc., 364 N.W.2d 83 (N.D. 1985); Challenge Machinery Co. v. Mattison Machine Works, 138 Mich. App. 15, 359 N.W.2d 232, 236-38 (Mich. App. 1984) (per curiam). The magistrate judge followed this approach and proceeded to section 2-309, which provides that nonconforming goods may be rejected within a "reasonable" time (see also §2-601(1)), and she held that the six months that Northrop took to reject Litronic's boards was a reasonable time because of the complexity of the required testing. The leading minority view is that the discrepant terms *in the acceptance* are to be ignored, Valtrol, Inc. v. General Connectors Corp., 884 F.2d 149, 155 (4th Cir. 1989); Reaction Molding Technologies, Inc. v. General Electric Co., 588 F. Supp. 1280, 1289 (E.D. Pa. 1984), and that would give the palm to Litronic. Our own preferred view—the view that assimilates "different" to "additional," so that the terms in the offer prevail over the different terms in the acceptance only if the latter are not materially different, has as yet been adopted by only one state, California. Steiner v. Mobil Oil Corp., 20 Cal. 3d 90, 569 P.2d 751, 759 n.5, 141 Cal. Rptr. 157 (Cal. 1977). Under that view, as under what we are calling the "leading" minority view, the warranty in Litronic's offer, the 90-day warranty, was the contractual warranty, because the unlimited warranty contained in Northrop's acceptance was materially different.

Because Illinois in other UCC cases has tended to adopt majority rules, e.g., Rebaque v. Forsythe Racing, Inc., 134 Ill. App. 3d 778, 480 N.E.2d 1338, 1341, 89 Ill. Dec. 595 (Ill. App. 1985), and because the interest in the uniform nationwide application of the Code — an interest asserted in the Code itself (see §1-102) — argues for nudging majority views, even if imperfect (but not downright bad), toward unanimity, we start with a presumption that Illinois, whose position we are trying to predict, would adopt the majority view. We do not find the presumption rebutted. The idea behind the majority view is that the presence of different terms in the acceptance suggests that the offeree didn't *really* accede to the offeror's terms, yet both parties wanted to contract, so why not find a neutral term to govern the dispute that has arisen between them? Of course the offeree may not have had any serious objection to the terms *in the offer* at the time of contracting; he may have mailed a boilerplated form without giving any thought to its contents or to its suitability for the particular contract in question. But it is just as likely that the discrepant terms in the offer itself were the product of a thoughtless use of a boilerplate form rather than a considered condition of contracting. And if the offeror doesn't want to do business other than on the terms in the offer, he can protect himself by specifying that the offeree must accept all those terms for the parties to have a contract. UCC §2-207(2)(a); Tecumseh International Corp. v. City of Springfield, 70 Ill. App. 3d 101, 388 N.E.2d 460, 463, 26 Ill. Dec. 745 (Ill. App. 1979). Now as it happens Litronic did state in its offer that the terms in the offer "take precedence over terms and conditions of the buyer, unless specifically negotiated otherwise." But, for reasons that we do not and need not fathom, Litronic does not argue that this language conditioned the existence of the contract on Northrop's acceding to the 90-day warranty in the offer; any such argument is therefore waived.

It is true that the offeree likewise can protect himself by making his acceptance of the offer conditional on the offeror's acceding to any different terms in the acceptance. But so many acceptances are made over the phone by relatively junior employees, as in this case, that it may be unrealistic to expect offerees to protect themselves in this way. The offeror goes first and therefore has a little more time for careful specification of the terms on which he is willing to make a contract. What we are calling the leading minority view may tempt the offeror to spring a surprise on the offeree, hoping the latter won't read the fine print. Under the majority view, if the offeree tries to spring a surprise (the offeror can't, since his terms won't prevail if the acceptance contains different terms), the parties move to neutral ground; and the offeror can, we have suggested, more easily protect himself against being surprised than the offeree can protect *himself* against being surprised. The California rule dissolves all these problems, but has too little support to make it a plausible candidate for Illinois, or at least a plausible candidate for our guess as to Illinois's position.

There is a further wrinkle, however. The third subsection of section 2-207 provides that even if no contract is established under either of the first two subsections, it may be established by the "conduct of the parties," and in that event (as subsection (3) expressly provides) the discrepant terms vanish and are replaced by UCC gap fillers. This may seem to make it impossible for the offeror to protect himself from being contractually bound by specifying that the acceptance must mirror his offer. But subsection (3) comes into play only when the parties have by their conduct manifested the existence of a contract, as where the offeror, having specified that the acceptance must mirror the offer yet having received an acceptance that deviates from the offer, nonetheless goes ahead and performs as if there were a contract. That is one way to interpret what happened here but it leads to the same result as applying subsection (2) interpreted as the majority of states do, so we need not consider it separately.

Given the intricacy of the No. 1714 boards, it is unlikely that Northrop would have acceded to a 90-day limitation on its warranty protection. Litronic at argument stressed that it is a much smaller firm, hence presumably unwilling to assume burdensome warranty obligations; but it is a curious suggestion that little fellows are more likely than big ones to get their way in negotiations between firms of disparate size. And Northrop actually got only half its way, though enough for victory here; for by virtue of accepting Litronic's offer without expressly conditioning its acceptance on Litronic's acceding to Northrop's terms, Northrop got not a warranty unlimited in duration, as its purchase order provides, but (pursuant to the majority understanding of UCC §2-207(2)) a warranty of "reasonable" duration, courtesy the court. If special circumstances made a 90-day warranty reasonable, Litronic was free to argue for it in the district court.

On the view we take, the purchase order has no significance beyond showing that Northrop's acceptance contained (albeit by reference) different terms. The fact that Litronic never signed the order, and the fact that Northrop never called this omission to Litronic's attention, also drop out of the case, along with Northrop's argument that to enforce the 90-day limitation in Litronic's warranty would be unconscionable. But for future reference we remind Northrop and companies like it that the defense of unconscionability was not invented to protect multi-billion dollar corporations against mistakes committed by their employees, and indeed has rarely succeeded outside the area of consumer contracts. Original Great

American Chocolate Chip Cookie Co. v. River Valley Cookies, Ltd., 970 F.2d 273, 281 (7th Cir. 1992); Salt River Project Agricultural Improvement & Power District v. Westinghouse Electric Corp., 143 Ariz. 368, 694 P.2d 198, 204 (Ariz. 1984); White & Summers, *supra*, §4-9.

AFFIRMED.

The interpretation of §2-207(2) adopted in *Northrup* is often called the "knockout" rule, on the theory that the respective parties knock out each other's additional or different terms; see discussion in Reilly Foam Corp. v. Rubbermaid Corp, 206 F. Supp. 2d 643 (E.D. Pa. 2002).

Courts call the clause that ends subsection (1) of §2-207 ("unless acceptance is expressly made conditional on assent to the additional or different terms") the *proviso* clause. The proviso clause acts just like a railroad switch. If it is *not* used as part of the accepting form, then the purported acceptance does create a contract, and the parties are directed to subsection (2) to determine its terms. If the proviso is put into the accepting document, the exchange of forms does not create a contract, and the parties are directed to subsection (3) to see what results from their dealings. The point is this: the presence or absence of the proviso shunts the parties into either subsection (2) or subsection (3), *but never both*.

PROBLEM 16

On April 25, Plastic Furniture Mart sent a purchase order for 100 tables to the Ersatz Manufacturing Company. In addition to the usual boilerplate language, the purchase order also stated: "BUYER OBJECTS IN ADVANCE TO ANY TERMS PROPOSED BY SELLER THAT DIFFER IN ANY WAY FROM THE TERMS OF THIS PURCHASE ORDER." Ersatz received the order, and on May 3 it sent back its own acknowledgment form, which disclaimed all warranties and contained this clause: "THIS IS NOT AN ACCEPTANCE UNLESS BUYER ASSENTS TO ALL CHANGES MADE BY THIS ACKNOWLEDGMENT FORM." Neither party read the details of the other's form. On May 6, Ersatz shipped the tables. Is there a contract? See §2-207(3). Did Ersatz make a warranty as to the condition of the tables? See §2-314. On May 3 was there a contract?

QUESTION

Assume that you are an associate at a law firm that represents a seller who frequently receives purchase orders triggering §2-207's rules. Your client wants to disclaim warranties, and the senior partner asks you to come up with a way of doing this. What do you advise?

PROBLEM 17

Through a series of phone calls the parties reached a complete oral agreement on the terms of a sales contract. Seller then sent the buyer an e-mail saying "I'm delighted we've made this deal. The contract is attached." The attachment was seller's usual Acknowledgement Form, and it first disclaimed warranties (which had not been discussed in the oral communications), and then clearly tracked the language of §2-207(1)'s proviso, by stating that this was not an acceptance unless the buyer expressly agreed to the seller's new terms. Buyer responded by sending payment, and the seller promptly shipped the goods. When the goods proved to be unmerchantable, buyer sued, and the seller pointed to the disclaimer of warranties in its Acknowledgement Form. Can the seller use the proviso in this situation? See Air Prods. & Chem., Inc. v. Fairbanks Morse, Inc., 58 Wis. 2d 193, 206 N.W.2d 414, 422-423 (1973).

Klocek v. Gateway, Inc.

United States District Court, Kansas, 2000
104 F. Supp. 2d 1332, 41 U.C.C. Rep. Serv. 2d 1059

VRATIL, District Judge.

William S. Klocek brings suit against Gateway, Inc. and Hewlett-Packard, Inc. on claims arising from purchases of a Gateway computer and a Hewlett-Packard scanner. . . . For reasons stated below, the Court overrules Gateway's motion to dismiss, sustains Hewlett-Packard's motion to dismiss, and overrules the motions filed by plaintiff.

I. GATEWAY'S MOTION TO DISMISS

Plaintiff brings individual and class action claims against Gateway, alleging that it induced him and other consumers to purchase computers and special support packages by making false promises of technical support. *Complaint*, ¶¶3 and 4. Individually, plaintiff also claims breach of contract and breach of warranty, in that Gateway breached certain warranties that its computer would be compatible with standard peripherals and standard internet services. *Complaint*, ¶¶2, 5, and 6.

Gateway asserts that plaintiff must arbitrate his claims under Gateway's Standard Terms and Conditions Agreement ("Standard Terms"). Whenever it sells a computer, Gateway includes a copy of the Standard Terms in the box which contains the computer battery power cables and instruction manuals. At the top of the first page, the Standard Terms include the following notice:

Note to the Customer:

This document contains Gateway 2000's Standard Terms and Conditions. By keeping your Gateway 2000 computer system beyond five (5) days after the date of delivery, you accept these Terms and Conditions.

The notice is in emphasized type and is located inside a printed box which sets it apart from other provisions of the document. The Standard Terms are four pages long and contain 16 numbered paragraphs. Paragraph 10 provides the following arbitration clause:

DISPUTE RESOLUTION. Any dispute or controversy arising out of or relating to this Agreement or its interpretation shall be settled exclusively and finally by arbitration. The arbitration shall be conducted in accordance with the Rules of Conciliation and Arbitration of the International Chamber of Commerce. The arbitration shall be conducted in Chicago, Illinois, U.S.A. before a sole arbitrator. Any award rendered in any such arbitration proceeding shall be final and binding on each of the parties, and judgment may be entered thereon in a court of competent jurisdiction.[11]

Gateway urges the Court to dismiss plaintiff's claims under the Federal Arbitration Act ("FAA"), 9 U.S.C. §1 et seq. The FAA ensures that written arbitration agreements in maritime transactions and transactions involving interstate commerce are "valid, irrevocable, and enforceable." 9 U.S.C. §2. Federal policy favors arbitration agreements and requires that we "rigorously enforce" them. Shearson/American Exp., Inc. v. McMahon, 482 U.S. 220, 226, 107 S. Ct. 2332, 96 L. Ed. 2d 185 (1987) (quoting Dean Witter Reynolds, Inc. v. Byrd, 470 U.S. 213, 105 S. Ct. 1238, 84 L. Ed. 2d 158 (1985)); *Moses,* 460 U.S. at 24, 103 S. Ct. 927. "[A]ny doubts concerning the scope of arbitrable issues should be resolved in favor of arbitration." *Moses,* 460 U.S. at 24-25, 103 S. Ct. 927.

FAA Section 3 states:

If any suit or proceeding be brought in any of the courts of the United States upon any issue referable to arbitration under an agreement in writing for such arbitration, the court in which such suit is pending, upon being satisfied that the issue involved in such suit or proceeding is referable to arbitration

---

11. Gateway states that after it sold plaintiff's computer, it mailed all existing customers in the United States a copy of its quarterly magazine, which contained notice of a change in the arbitration policy set forth in the Standard Terms. The new arbitration policy afforded customers the option of arbitrating before the International Chamber of Commerce ("ICC"), the American Arbitration Association ("AAA"), or the National Arbitration Forum ("NAF") in Chicago, Illinois, or any other location agreed upon by the parties. Plaintiff denies receiving notice of the amended arbitration policy. Neither party explains why—if the arbitration agreement was an enforceable contract—Gateway was entitled to unilaterally amend it by sending a magazine to computer customers.

under such agreement, shall on application of one of the parties stay the trial of the action until such arbitration has been had in accordance with the terms of the agreement, providing the applicant for the stay is not in default in proceeding with such arbitration.

9 U.S.C. §3.... [T]he Court concludes that dismissal is appropriate if plaintiff's claims are arbitrable.

Gateway bears an initial summary-judgment-like burden of establishing that it is entitled to arbitration. [Citations omitted.] Thus, Gateway must present evidence sufficient to demonstrate the existence of an enforceable agreement to arbitrate. See, e.g., Oppenheimer & Co. v. Neidhardt, 56 F.3d 352, 358 (2d Cir. 1995). If Gateway makes such a showing, the burden shifts to plaintiff to submit evidence demonstrating a genuine issue for trial. Id.; see also Naddy v. Piper Jaffray, Inc., 88 Wash. App. 1033, 1997 WL 749261, *2, Case Nos. 15431-9-III, 15681-8-III (Wash. App. Dec. 4, 1997). In this case, Gateway fails to present evidence establishing the most basic facts regarding the transaction. The gaping holes in the evidentiary record preclude the Court from determining what state law controls the formation of the contract in this case and, consequently, prevent the Court from agreeing that Gateway's motion is well taken.

Before granting a stay or dismissing a case pending arbitration, the Court must determine that the parties have a written agreement to arbitrate. *See* 9 U.S.C. §§3 and 4; Avedon Engineering, Inc. v. Seatex, 126 F.3d 1279, 1283 (10th Cir. 1997). When deciding whether the parties have agreed to arbitrate, the Court applies ordinary state law principles that govern the formation of contracts. First Options of Chicago, Inc. v. Kaplan, 514 U.S. 938, 944, 115 S. Ct. 1920, 131 L. Ed. 2d 985 (1995). The existence of an arbitration agreement "is simply a matter of contract between the parties; [arbitration] is a way to resolve those disputes—but only those disputes—that the parties have agreed to submit to arbitration." *Avedon,* 126 F.3d at 1283 (quoting *Kaplan,* 514 U.S. at 943-945, 115 S. Ct. 1920). If the parties dispute making an arbitration agreement, a jury trial on the existence of an agreement is warranted if the record reveals genuine issues of material fact regarding the parties' agreement. See *Avedon,* 126 F.3d at 1283....

The Uniform Commercial Code ("UCC") governs the parties' transaction under both Kansas and Missouri law. See K.S.A. §84-2-102; V.A.M.S. §400.2-102 (UCC applies to "transactions in goods."); Kansas Comment 1 (main thrust of Article 2 is limited to sales); K.S.A. §84-2-105(1) V.A.M.S. §400.2-105(1) ("'Goods' means all things . . . which are movable at the time of identification to the contract for sale. . . ."). Regardless whether plaintiff purchased the computer in person or placed an order and received shipment of the computer, the parties agree that plaintiff paid for and received a computer from Gateway. This conduct clearly demonstrates a contract for the sale of a computer. See, e.g., Step-Saver Data Sys., Inc. v. Wyse Techn., 939 F.2d 91, 98 (3d Cir. 1991). Thus the issue is whether the contract of sale includes the Standard Terms as part of the agreement.

State courts in Kansas and Missouri apparently have not decided whether terms received with a product become part of the parties' agreement. Authority from other courts is split. Compare *Step-Saver*, 939 F.2d 91 (printed terms on computer software package not part of agreement); Arizona Retail Sys., Inc. v. Software Link, Inc., 831 F. Supp. 759 (D. Ariz. 1993) (license agreement shipped with computer software not part of agreement); and U.S. Surgical Corp. v. Orris, Inc., 5 F. Supp. 2d 1201 (D. Kan. 1998) (single use restriction on product package not binding agreement); with Hill v. Gateway 2000, Inc., 105 F.3d 1147 (7th Cir.), *cert. denied*, 522 U.S. 808, 118 S. Ct. 47, 139 L. Ed. 2d 13 (1997) (arbitration provision shipped with computer binding on buyer); ProCD, Inc. v. Zeidenberg, 86 F.3d 1447 (7th Cir.1996) (shrinkwrap license binding on buyer)[12] and M.A. Mortenson Co., Inc. v. Timberline Software Corp., 140 Wash. 2d 568, 998 P.2d 305 (2000) (following *Hill* and *ProCD* on license agreement supplied with software).[13] It appears that at least in part, the cases turn on whether the court finds that the parties formed their contract *before* or *after* the vendor communicated its terms to the purchaser. Compare *Step-Saver*, 939 F.2d at 98 (parties' conduct in shipping, receiving and paying for product demonstrates existence of contract; box top license constitutes proposal for additional terms under §2-207 which requires express agreement by purchaser); *Arizona Retail*, 831 F. Supp. at 765 (vendor entered into contract by agreeing to ship goods, or at latest by shipping goods to buyer; license agreement constitutes proposal to modify agreement under §2-209 which requires express assent by buyer); and *Orris*, 5 F. Supp. 2d at 1206 (sales contract concluded when vendor received consumer orders; single-use language on product's label was proposed modification under §2-209 which requires express assent by purchaser); with *ProCD*, 86 F.3d at 1452 (under §2-204 vendor, as master of offer, may propose limitations on kind

---

12. The term "shrinkwrap license" gets its name from retail software packages that are covered in plastic or cellophane "shrinkwrap" and contain licenses that purport to become effective as soon as the customer tears the wrapping from the package. See *ProCD*, 86 F.3d at 1449.

13. The *Mortenson* court also found support for its holding in the proposed Uniform Computer Information Transactions Act ("UCITA") (formerly known as proposed UCC Article 2B) (text located at *www.law.upenn.edu/library/ulc/ucita/UCITA_99.htm*), which the National Conference of Commissioners on Uniform State Laws approved and recommended for enactment by the states in July 1999. See *Mortenson*, 998 P.2d at 310 n.6, 313 n.10. The proposed UCITA, however, would not apply to the Court's analysis in this case. The UCITA applies to computer information transactions, which are defined as agreements "to create, modify, transfer, or license computer information or informational rights in computer information." UCITA, §§102(11) and 103. In transactions involving the sale of computers, such as our case, the UCITA applies only to the computer programs and copies, not to the sale of the computer itself. See UCITA §103(c)(2).

of conduct that constitutes acceptance; §2-207 does not apply in case with only one form); *Hill*, 105 F.3d at 1148-49 (same); and *Mortenson*, 998 P.2d at 311-314 (where vendor and purchaser utilized license agreement in prior course of dealing, shrinkwrap license agreement constituted issue of contract formation under §2-204, not contract alteration under §2-207).

Gateway urges the Court to follow the Seventh Circuit decision in *Hill*. That case involved the shipment of a Gateway computer with terms similar to the Standard Terms in this case, except that Gateway gave the customer 30 days — instead of 5 days — to return the computer. In enforcing the arbitration clause, the Seventh Circuit relied on its decision in *ProCD*, where it enforced a software license which was contained inside a product box. See *Hill*, 105 F.3d at 1148-50. In *ProCD*, the Seventh Circuit noted that the exchange of money frequently precedes the communication of detailed terms in a commercial transaction. See *ProCD*, 86 F.3d at 1451. Citing UCC §2-204, the court reasoned that by including the license with the software, the vendor proposed a contract that the buyer could accept by using the software after having an opportunity to read the license.[14] *ProCD*, 86 F.3d at 1452. Specifically, the court stated:

> A vendor, as master of the offer, may invite acceptance by conduct, and may propose limitations on the kind of conduct that constitutes acceptance. A buyer may accept by performing the acts the vendor proposes to treat as acceptance.

ProCD, 86 F.3d at 1452. The *Hill* court followed the *ProCD* analysis, noting that "[p]ractical considerations support allowing vendors to enclose the full legal terms with their products." *Hill*, 105 F.3d at 1149.[15]

---

14. Section 2-204 provides: "A contract for sale of goods may be made in any manner sufficient to show agreement, including conduct by both parties which recognizes the existence of such contract." K.S.A. §84-2-204; V.A.M.S. §400.2-204.

15. Legal commentators have criticized the reasoning of the Seventh Circuit in this regard. See, e.g., Jean R. Sternlight, Gateway Widens Doorway to Imposing Unfair Binding Arbitration on Consumers, Fla. Bar J., Nov. 1997, at 8, 10-12 (outcome in Gateway is questionable on federal statutory, common law and constitutional grounds and as a matter of contract law and is unwise as a matter of policy because it unreasonably shifts to consumers search cost of ascertaining existence of arbitration clause and return cost to avoid such clause); Thomas J. McCarthy et al., Survey: Uniform Commercial Code, 53 Bus. Law. 1461, 1465-66 (Seventh Circuit finding that UCC §2-207 did not apply is inconsistent with official comment); Batya Goodman, Honey, I Shrink-Wrapped the Consumer: the Shrinkwrap Agreement as an Adhesion Contract, 21 Cardozo L. Rev. 319, 344-352 (Seventh Circuit failed to consider principles of adhesion contracts); Jeremy Senderowicz, Consumer Arbitration and Freedom of Contract: A Proposal to Facilitate Consumers' Informed Consent to Arbitration Clauses in Form Contracts, 32 Colum. J.L. & Soc. Probs. 275, 296-299 (judiciary (in multiple decisions, including *Hill*) has ignored issue of consumer consent to an arbitration clause). Nonetheless, several courts have followed the Seventh Circuit decisions in *Hill* and *ProCD*. See, e.g., M.A. Mortenson Co., Inc. v. Timberline Software Corp., 140 Wash. 2d 568, 998 P.2d 305 (license agreement supplied with software); Rinaldi v.

The Court is not persuaded that Kansas or Missouri courts would follow the Seventh Circuit reasoning in *Hill* and *ProCD*. In each case the Seventh Circuit concluded without support that UCC §2-207 was irrelevant because the cases involved only one written form. See *ProCD*, 86 F.3d at 1452 (citing no authority); *Hill*, 105 F.3d at 1150 (citing *ProCD*). This conclusion is not supported by the statute or by Kansas or Missouri law. Disputes under §2-207 often arise in the context of a "battle of forms," see, e.g., Diatom, Inc. v. Pennwalt Corp., 741 F.2d 1569, 1574 (10th Cir. 1984), but nothing in its language precludes application in a case which involves only one form. The statute provides:

> Additional terms in acceptance or confirmation.
>
> (1) A definite and seasonable expression of acceptance or a written confirmation which is sent within a reasonable time operates as an acceptance even though it states terms additional to or different from those offered or agreed upon, unless acceptance is expressly made conditional on assent to the additional or different terms.
>
> (2) The additional terms are to be construed as proposals for addition to the contract [if the contract is not between merchants]. . . .

K.S.A. §84-2-207; V.A.M.S. §400.2-207. By its terms, §2-207 applies to an acceptance or written confirmation. It states nothing which requires another form before the provision becomes effective. In fact, the official comment to the section specifically provides that §2-207(1) and (2) apply "where an agreement has been reached orally . . . and is followed by one or both of the parties sending formal memoranda embodying the terms so far agreed and adding terms not discussed." Official Comment 1 of UCC §2-207. Kansas and Missouri courts have followed this analysis. See Southwest Engineering Co. v. Martin Tractor Co., 205 Kan. 684, 695, 473 P.2d 18, 26 (1970) (stating in dicta that §2-207 applies where open offer is accepted by expression of acceptance in writing or where oral agreement is later confirmed in writing); Central Bag Co. v. W. Scott and Co., 647 S.W.2d 828, 830 (Mo. App. 1983) (§2-207(1) and (2) govern cases where one or both parties send written confirmation after oral contract). Thus, the Court concludes that Kansas and Missouri courts would apply §2-207 to the facts in this case. Accord *Avedon*, 126 F.3d at 1283 (parties agree that §2-207 controls whether arbitration clause in sales confirmation is part of contract).

Iomega Corp., 1999 WL 1442014, Case No. 98C-09-064-RRC (Del. Super. Sept. 3, 1999) (warranty disclaimer included inside computer Zip drive packaging); Westendorf v. Gateway 2000, Inc., 2000 WL 307369, Case No. 16913 (Del. Ch. March 16, 2000) (arbitration provision shipped with computer); Brower v. Gateway 2000, Inc., 246 A.D.2d 246, 676 N.Y.S.2d 569 (N.Y. App. Div. 1998) (same); Levy v. Gateway 2000, Inc., 1997 WL 823611, 33 U.C.C. Rep. Serv. 2d 1060 (N.Y. Sup. Oct. 31, 1997) (same).

In addition, the Seventh Circuit provided no explanation for its conclusion that "the vendor is the master of the offer." See *ProCD*, 86 F.3d at 1452 (citing nothing in support of proposition); *Hill*, 105 F.3d at 1149 (citing *ProCD*). In typical consumer transactions, the purchaser is the offeror, and the vendor is the offeree. See Brown Mach., Div. of John Brown, Inc. v. Hercules, Inc., 770 S.W.2d 416, 419 (Mo. App. 1989) (as general rule orders are considered offers to purchase); Rich Prods. Corp. v. Kemutec Inc., 66 F. Supp. 2d 937, 956 (E.D. Wis. 1999) (generally price quotation is invitation to make offer and purchase order is offer). While it is possible for the vendor to be the offeror, see *Brown Machine*, 770 S.W.2d at 419 (price quote can amount to offer if it reasonably appears from quote that assent to quote is all that is needed to ripen offer into contract), Gateway provides no factual evidence which would support such a finding in this case. The Court therefore assumes for purposes of the motion to dismiss that plaintiff offered to purchase the computer (either in person or through catalog order) and that Gateway accepted plaintiff's offer (either by completing the sales transaction in person or by agreeing to ship and/or shipping the computer to plaintiff).[16] Accord *Arizona Retail*, 831 F. Supp. at 765 (vendor entered into contract by agreeing to ship goods, or at latest, by shipping goods).

Under §2-207, the Standard Terms constitute either an expression of acceptance or written confirmation. As an expression of acceptance, the Standard Terms would constitute a counter-offer only if Gateway expressly made its acceptance conditional on plaintiff's assent to the additional or different terms. K.S.A. §84-2-207(1); V.A.M.S. §400.2-207(1). "[T]he conditional nature of the acceptance must be clearly expressed in a manner sufficient to notify the offeror that the offeree is unwilling to proceed with the transaction unless the additional or different terms are included in the contract." *Brown Machine*, 770 S.W.2d at 420. Gateway provides no evidence that at the time of the sales transaction, it informed plaintiff that the transaction was conditioned on plaintiff's acceptance of the Standard Terms. Moreover, the mere fact that Gateway shipped the goods with the terms attached did not communicate to plaintiff any unwillingness to proceed without plaintiff's agreement to the Standard Terms. See, e.g., *Arizona Retail*, 831 F. Supp. at 765 (conditional acceptance analysis rarely appropriate where contract formed by performance but goods arrive with conditions attached); Leighton Indus., Inc. v. Callier Steel Pipe & Tube, Inc., 1991 WL 18413, *6, Case No. 89-C-8235 (N.D. Ill. Feb. 6, 1991) (applying Missouri law) (preprinted forms insufficient to notify offeror of

---

16. UCC §2-206(b) provides that "an order or other offer to buy goods for prompt or current shipment shall be construed as inviting acceptance either by a prompt promise to ship or by the prompt or current shipment. . . ." The official comment states that "[e]ither shipment or a prompt promise to ship is made a proper means of acceptance of an offer looking to current shipment." UCC §2-206, Official Comment 2.

conditional nature of acceptance, particularly where form arrives after delivery of goods).

Because plaintiff is not a merchant, additional or different terms contained in the Standard Terms did not become part of the parties' agreement unless plaintiff expressly agreed to them. See K.S.A. §84-2-207, Kansas Comment 2 (if either party is not a merchant, additional terms are proposals for addition to the contract that do not become part of the contract unless the original offeror expressly agrees). Gateway argues that plaintiff demonstrated acceptance of the arbitration provision by keeping the computer more than five days after the date of delivery. Although the Standard Terms purport to work that result, Gateway has not presented evidence that plaintiff expressly agreed to those Standard Terms. Gateway states only that it enclosed the Standard Terms inside the computer box for plaintiff to read afterwards. It provides no evidence that it informed plaintiff of the five-day review-and-return period as a condition of the sales transaction, or that the parties contemplated additional terms to the agreement.[17] See *Step-Saver*, 939 F.2d at 99 (during negotiations leading to purchase, vendor never mentioned box-top license or obtained buyer's express assent thereto). The Court finds that the act of keeping the computer past five days was not sufficient to demonstrate that plaintiff expressly agreed to the Standard Terms. Accord *Brown Machine*, 770 S.W.2d at 421 (express assent cannot be presumed by silence or mere failure to object). Thus, because Gateway has not provided evidence sufficient to support a finding under Kansas or Missouri law that plaintiff agreed to the arbitration provision contained in Gateway's Standard Terms, the Court overrules Gateway's motion to dismiss. . . .

There are many cases disagreeing with the court's analysis and requiring arbitration or allowing warranty disclaimers in spite of §2-207's provisions. These courts typically find that an "approve or return" clause in the paperwork arriving with the goods prevents formation of the contract until the buyer assents to the new terms (usually by doing nothing more than retaining the goods); see Fiser v. Dell Computer Corp., 142 N.M. 331, 165 P.3d 328 (2007). These decisions are all of a piece with the *ProCD* and *Hill* opinions discussed in the last case, which while ignoring §2-207 as irrelevant, create so-called "rolling" or "layered" contracts through the negotiations plus the shipment with new terms, followed by the buyer's failure to object to the changes first mentioned in documents that come with the shipment.

17. The Court is mindful of the practical considerations which are involved in commercial transactions, but it is not unreasonable for a vendor to clearly communicate to a buyer—at the time of sale—either the complete terms of the sale or the fact that the vendor will propose additional terms as a condition of sale, if that be the case.

CHAPTER 3

WARRANTIES

A warranty is a contractual obligation by the seller to remedy certain possible defects in the goods. It may be useful to think of it as a sort of insurance policy issued by the seller to the buyer at the time of sale. The law of warranty has borrowed its concepts from the legal coffers of tort, contract, and property. The UCC divides warranties into two basic types: warranties of *title* and warranties of *quality*. Read §2-312.

I. *THE WARRANTY OF TITLE*

PROBLEM 18

Fast Eddie stole Mabel Stanley's car from a shopping center in Phoenix. He drove it to Las Vegas, where he sold it for $500 to Sealed Lips Used Cars. This firm somehow obtained a Nevada certificate of title for the car, which showed clean title in Sealed Lips. The car was then sold for $2,000 to a bona fide purchaser, Frederick Duty. Duty drove it for a month until a bad run at the roulette wheel forced him to sell it in order to finance further recreational activity. Another bona fide purchaser, Samuel Pirate, bought the car from

Duty for $1,900. He drove it for only one week before the Nevada State Police impounded it and returned it to Mabel in Phoenix. Pirate sued Duty for breach of the warranty of good title.

(a) Duty argues that he *thought* he had good title, and since he was not negligent or in any way at fault in so believing, the warranty was not breached. Does this defense succeed? See Brokke v. Williams, 766 P.2d 1311, 7 U.C.C. Rep. Serv. 2d 1404 (Mont. 1989).

(b) Duty argues that he *did* have good title, and hence the warranty was not breached. Did he? See §2-403(1); Inmi-Etti v. Aluisi, 63 Md. App. 293, 492 A.2d 917, 40 U.C.C. Rep. Serv. 1612 (1985) (*Nemo dat qui non habet—* "He who hath not cannot give").

(c) Would your answer to (b) change if Fast Eddie had bought the car from Mabel with a bad check? See §2-403; Allan Nott Ents., Inc. v. Nicholas Starr Auto, L.L.C. 110 Ohio St. 3d 112, 851 N.E.2d 479 (2006).

(d) Does the law give any relief to Duty? See §2-607(5)(a) (describing a procedure known as *vouching in*).

PROBLEM 19

Before the Nevada State Police found Mabel's car, discussed in the last Problem, they accidentally impounded a very similar car owned by P.T. Boss. Boss had recently purchased the car from Croupier Motors. In order to convince the police that they had made a mistake and should release the car to him, Boss had to hire an attorney, Arnold Sunglasses. The latter did retrieve the car and then sent Boss a bill for $400. Boss forwarded the bill to Croupier Motors, along with a cover letter to the effect that title problems were the seller's headache per §2-312. Should the car dealership pay Sunglasses's bill? See Official Comment 1 to §2-312; White & Summers §10-15(b) at 501-502; Saber v. Dan Angelone Chevrolet, Inc., 811 A.2d 644, 49 U.C.C. Rep. Serv. 2d 352 (R.I. 2002). See also §2-607(5).

PROBLEM 20

Sellers can sometimes evade or disclaim the warranty of title. Determine if the warranty is present in the following situations:

(a) The sales contract has this clause: "The product is sold 'As Is' and seller makes no warranties, express or implied, as part of this sale." See Official Comment 6 to §2-312.

(b) Repossession Motors sold a car on credit to a customer who returned it after failing to make the first payment. It then conducted an Article 9–type resale. (See §9-610(d).) Does the resale buyer get the benefit of a §2-312 warranty? See Official Comment 5.

(c) Ted Traveler walked into the men's room of the bus depot and, to his surprise, was offered an expensive watch at a bargain rate from a stranger. He bought the watch. Is there a warranty of title in this transaction? See §1-303(c).

Moore v. Pro Team Corvette Sales, Inc.

Court of Appeals of Ohio, 2002
152 Ohio App. 3d 71, 786 N.E.2d 903, 48 U.C.C. Rep. Serv. 2d 528

WALTERS, J.

Plaintiff-Appellant, Bryon Moore, brings this appeal from a Henry County Common Pleas Court decision which dismissed his action against Defendant-Appellee, Pro Team Corvette Sales, Inc., regarding a contract for the sale of a 1974 Chevrolet Corvette, which was subsequently discovered to be stolen. On appeal, Moore argues that terms within the agreement did not effectively disclaim the implied warranty of title under U.C.C. 2-312. Because U.C.C. 2-312 provides for a buyer's basic needs with respect to the type of title he in good faith expects to acquire by his purchase, namely, a good, clean title transferred to him in a rightful manner, we find that the provision lacks sufficient specificity to disclaim the implied warranty of title. Accordingly, we reverse the judgment of the trial court.

Facts and procedural history relevant to issues raised on appeal are as follows: In October 1994, Moore drove from his Grosse Isle, Michigan residence to Pro Team Corvette Sales, Inc. ("Pro Team"), located in Napoleon, Ohio, in order to purchase a Chevrolet Corvette. On October 17, 1994, he signed an agreement to purchase a 1974 Corvette, as well as a separate agreement to trade in his 1975 Corvette. When Moore attempted to register the car with the Michigan Bureau of Motor Vehicles, he learned that the car had been reported stolen in Texas, and therefore could not be registered. The Michigan State Police subsequently confiscated the car and returned it to Texas.

On October 15, 1996, Moore filed suit against Pro Team, arguing that its failure to provide good title to the vehicle was negligent. He also claimed unjust enrichment, breach of statutory warranties, and violations of Ohio's Consumer Sales Practices Act. Pro Team denied all liability, claiming that it had excluded all warranties, including the warranty of title, in the purchase agreement. Pro Team also filed a third-party complaint against the dealership that sold the car to Pro Team, as well as the person who sold the car to that dealer, the Michigan State Police, and the sheriff of San Patricio County, Texas.

In defending the suit, Pro Team relied upon language in its contract indicating that the Corvette was being sold "as is" and that the all warranties, including the warranty of title, were excluded from the agreement. Moore sought summary judgment, arguing that the language contained in the agreement was not sufficient to constitute a valid disclaimer of statutorily implied warranties of title. This motion was denied. Moore subsequently dismissed all counts unrelated to the warranty provisions. In February 2002, the trial court dismissed his remaining claims, concluding that the language contained in the agreement was sufficiently specific to permit exclusion of the warranty of title under U.C.C. 2-312.

Moore appeals the trial court's judgment, presenting the following single assignment of error for our review: "The Trial Court erred when it concluded that the dealer's contract properly excluded the warranty of title."

In Ohio, "a seller warrants that he will convey good title free from any security interest or other lien or encumbrance of which the buyer is without knowledge when the contract is made." This implied warranty of title is codified in U.C.C. 2-312 [which the court then quoted].

Accordingly, "[u]nless excluded or modified, U.C.C. 2-312(1) adds to a sales contract a warranty by the seller that the title conveyed shall be good and its transfer rightful." As provided by U.C.C. 2-312(2), a warranty of title may be excluded or modified by specific language giving the purchaser reasons to know that the vendor is only selling what title he possesses.

> [T]his code section provides for a buyer's basic needs in respect to the type of title he in good faith expects to acquire by his purchase, namely, a good, clean title transferred to him in a rightful manner so that he will not be exposed to a lawsuit in order to protect it. . . . In the usual case, the buyer expects to get a good title, and regards disclaimers as affecting only risks with regard to quality.[1]

The Michigan Court of Appeals, in *Jones v. Linebaugh,* held that "very precise and unambiguous language must be used to exclude a warranty so basic to the sale of goods as is title." Specific language is necessary to relieve the buyer of the idea that any disclaimer of warranty relates only to quality.[2] In *Sunseri v. RKO-Stanley Warner Theaters, Inc.,*[3] the court found language stating that the seller "shall in nowise be . . . liable . . . upon or under guaranties [*sic*] or warranties . . . including, but not limited to, the implied warrant[y] of title" lacked sufficient specificity to disclaim the warranty of title. The court reasoned that the language used was ineffective because it was "couched in negative terminology," expressing what the seller will not be liable for rather than what the buyer is or is not receiving. The

1. 1 Hawkland UCC Series (2001) §2-312:5, Disclaimer of Warranty of Title-Contractual Terms.

2. 1 Hawkland UCC Series (2001) §2-312:5, Disclaimer of Warranty of Title-Contractual Terms.

3. Sunseri v. RKO-Stanley Warner Theaters, Inc. (1977), 248 Pa. Super. 111, 374 A.2d 1342, 1344.

inadequacy of such a caveat is best illustrated by juxtaposing it with title disclaimer provisions suggested by authorities in the subject area. For example, 18 Am. Jur. Legal Forms 2d §253:825 (1974), provides:

> Seller makes no warranty as to the title to the goods, and buyer assumes all risks of nonownership of the goods by seller. . . . [W]here the language in a purported disclaimer expresses how the seller's liability will be limited rather than what title (or lack thereof) the seller purports to transfer, the purported disclaimer is ineffective.[4]

The relevant portion of the sale contract states: "All warranties pursuant to U.C.C.2-312 are hereby excluded from this transaction." In light of the foregoing discussion, we find this language to be akin to that which expresses how the seller's liability will be limited, rather than what title the seller purports to transfer, and conclude that the provision lacks sufficient specificity to disclaim the implied warranty of title. Accordingly, Moore's assignment of error is sustained.

Having found error prejudicial to the appellant herein, in the particulars assigned and argued, the judgment of the trial court is hereby reversed and the matter is remanded for further proceedings in accordance with this opinion.

Judgment reversed and cause remanded.

QUESTION

Why is the court being so picky here? What policy is at work? Could this case have better been decided on the grounds that a disclaimer of "UCC 2-312" is always insufficient because no one will know what that means? If you, future attorney, are going to draft a clause disclaiming liability for breach of the warranty of title, how should it be phrased?

Note that the warranty of title also includes:

(1) a warranty that there are no security interests (or other liens) on the goods other than those of which the buyer knows (§2-312(1)(b)), and

(2) a warranty given by merchant sellers against claims based on patent infringement or the like (§2-312(3)).

See Big Lots Stores, Inc. v. Luv N' Care, 62 U.C.C. Rep. Serv. 2d 522 (S.D. Ohio 2007) (breach of warranty of title to supply inventory bearing infringing

---

4. Kel-Keef, 738 N.E.2d at 536.

trademark); Phoenix Solutions, Inc. v. Sony Electronics, Inc., 637 F. Supp. 2d 683, 69 U.C.C. Rep. Serv. 2d 721 (N.D. Cal. 2009) (breach of warranty of title where buyer subject to patent infringement claim).

If the buyer furnishes specifications to the seller (which happens where the goods are to be specially manufactured to the buyer's order), the *buyer* automatically makes a warranty to the seller that protects the latter from infringement claims. Section 2-312(3). This is the *only* situation under the UCC where the buyer is the warrantor.

Entrustment. Closely related to the warranty of title is the doctrine of entrustment, under which a merchant may give good title to goods someone has entrusted to the merchant, even though the merchant neither owns the goods nor has authority to sell them.

PROBLEM 21

Prost leaves her car with Grand Auto for repairs. Grand Auto restores it to A1 condition, then sells it to Stewart. Can Prost recover the car? §2-403(2) and (3).

Kerstin Lindholm v. Peter M. Brant et al.

Supreme Court of Connecticut, 2007
283 Conn. 65, 925 A.2d 1048, 63 U.C.C. Rep. Serv. 2d 431

SULLIVAN, J.

[Lindholm entrusted her painting, *Red Elvis* by Andy Warhol, to Malmberg, a respected art dealer, who arranged for it to be displayed at several leading museums in the United States and Europe — and then sold it for $2.9 million to Brant. Brant had ordered a lien search and a search of the Art Loss Register, neither of which disclosed any problems with title. Brant's pre-sale efforts to get documents showing that the art dealer indeed owned the painting he was selling were unsuccessful.]

Section 42a-2-403 (2) provides that "[a]ny entrusting of possession of goods to a merchant who deals in goods of that kind gives him power to transfer all rights of the entruster to a buyer in ordinary course of business." "'Entrusting'" is defined as "any delivery and any acquiescence in retention of possession regardless of any condition expressed between the parties to the delivery or acquiescence and regardless of whether the procurement of the entrusting or the possessor's disposition of the goods have been such as to be larcenous under the criminal law." General Statutes §42a-2-403 (3).

There is no dispute in the present case that the plaintiff's March 20, 2000 letter authorizing the Guggenheim to release *Red Elvis* to Malmberg constituted an entrustment under §42a-2-403 (3), or that Malmberg, an art dealer, is a merchant dealing in "goods of that kind"—works of art— under §42a-2-403 (2). Under the plain language of §42a-2-403 (2) and (3), therefore, Malmberg, as a merchant dealing in art entrusted with the painting, had the power to transfer all the rights of the entruster to a buyer in the ordinary course of business.

A "'[b]uyer in [the] ordinary course of business'" is defined as "a person that buys goods in good faith, without knowledge that the sale violates the rights of another person in the goods, and in the ordinary course from a person . . . in the business of selling goods of that kind. A person buys goods in the ordinary course if the sale to the person comports with the usual or customary practices in the kind of business in which the seller is engaged or with the seller's own usual or customary practices. . . ." General Statutes §42a-1-201 (9). A person buys goods in good faith if there is "honesty in fact and the observance of reasonable commercial standards of fair dealing" in the conduct or transaction concerned. General Statutes §42a-1-201 (20).

We are required, therefore, to determine whether the defendant followed the usual or customary practices and observed reasonable commercial standards of fair dealing in the art industry in his dealings with Malmberg. As we have indicated, the defendant presented expert testimony that the vast majority of art transactions, in which the buyer has no reason for concern about the seller's ability to convey good title, are "completed on a handshake and an exchange of an invoice." It is not customary for sophisticated buyers and sellers to obtain a signed invoice from the original seller to the dealer prior to a transaction, nor is it an ordinary or customary practice to request the underlying invoice or corroborating information as to a dealer's authority to convey title. Moreover, it is not customary to approach the owner of an artwork if the owner regularly worked with a particular art dealer because any inquiries about an art transaction customarily are presented to the art dealer rather than directly to the principal. It is customary to rely upon representations made by respected dealers regarding their authority to sell works of art. A dealer customarily is not required to present an invoice establishing when and from whom he bought the artwork or the conditions of the purchase.

We are compelled to conclude, however, that the sale from Malmberg to the defendant was unlike the vast majority of art transactions. The defendant had good reason to be concerned that Lindholm might have claims to the painting. Several courts have held that, under such circumstances, a handshake and an exchange of invoice is not sufficient to confer status as a buyer in the ordinary course. In Porter v. Wertz, 416 N.Y.S.2d 254, 68 A.D.2d 141 (1979), *aff'd*, 53 N.Y.2d 696, 421 N.E.2d 500, 439 N.Y.S.2d 105 (1981), for example, the owner of a painting entrusted it to an individual with whom he previously had conducted art transactions for display in the individual's home. This individual then used the services of a delicatessen employee, posing as an art dealer, to sell the painting to a merchant art buyer. Id., 145-46. In discussing the good faith obligation of a merchant, the court stated that although the definition of good faith "by its terms embraces the reasonable commercial standards of fair dealing in the trade, it should not — and cannot — be interpreted to permit, countenance or condone commercial standards of sharp trade practice or indifference as to the provenance, i.e., history of ownership or the right to possess or sell an object d'art. . . ." (Internal quotation marks omitted.) Id., 146. The buyer made no inquiry as to whether the purported art dealer, who was in fact a delicatessen employee, was the owner of the painting or had been authorized by the owner to sell the painting. Id. Because a simple telephone call would have revealed the fact that the defendant was not an art merchant, thereby leading to doubt that would have required further verification, the court concluded that the buyer could not claim buyer in the ordinary course of business status. Id., 146-47.

In *Howley v. Sotheby's, Inc.*, New York Law Journal, Vol. 195 (February 20, 1986), p. 6, col. 3B, the owner of a painting sought its recovery from the defendant art dealer. The defendant had purchased the painting from the caretaker of the owner's home, who had posed as the owner's nephew, even though the defendant was unsure whether the "owner's nephew" had authority to sell the painting. Id. The court concluded that, because the defendant was a professional art dealer, he should have been "scrupulously concerned with taking proper title in anything he purchases." Id. Because the defendant had not taken any steps to verify title, even after the "owner's nephew" informed him that the sale first needed the owner's approval, the defendant did not fulfill his obligation and was liable for conversion. Id.

In Cantor v. Anderson, 639 F. Supp. 364, 367-68 (S.D.N.Y.), *aff'd,* 833 F.2d 1002 (2d Cir. 1986), the court, citing *Howley,* imposed a duty upon a sophisticated buyer to inquire into a painting's ownership when circumstances dictate. In *Cantor,* the buyer and the seller had engaged in numerous previous art transactions. Id., 366. When the buyer sought the return of several of his artworks that were on consignment with the seller, the seller gave the buyer a painting, to which he claimed ownership, as security for the artworks on consignment. Id., 367. The buyer, who had been aware of the seller's financial difficulties and was familiar with the seller's practice of selling works on consignment, had reason to doubt the seller's ownership of the painting. Id., 368. This doubt led to a duty to obtain some verification that the seller had good title. Because the buyer had made no efforts to verify title to the painting, choosing to rely solely on the seller's assurances, the court concluded that the buyer had not fulfilled his duty and was liable for conversion. Id., 368-69.

Finally, in Morgold, Inc. v. Keeler, 891 F. Supp. 1361, 1369 (N.D. Cal. 1995), the court held that an art dealer buyer had obtained good title to a painting by satisfying "the reasonable commercial standards in the art industry. . . ." In that case, the buyer and the seller had engaged in previous art transactions for several years. Id., 1364. When the buyer purchased the painting from the seller, he was unaware that the seller had only a one-half interest in the painting. Id., 1363-65. The court imposed a duty on "dealers in art [to] take reasonable steps to inquire into the title to a painting, particularly if there are warnings that something is wrong with a transaction." Id., 1368. In *Morgold, Inc.*, the buyer had engaged in previous art transactions with the seller and had contacted an expert on the artist, who gave no indication of problems with the painting's title. Id., 1365. Because there were no other warning signs indicating problems with title, the court concluded that the buyer had fulfilled his duty to make a reasonable inquiry and had acquired good title and a right to possession of the painting. Id., 1369.

We agree with these courts that a merchant buyer has a heightened duty of inquiry when a reasonable merchant would have doubts or questions regarding the seller's authority to sell. We further conclude that the steps that a merchant must take to conform to reasonable commercial standards before consummating a deal depend on all of the facts and circumstances surrounding the sale. In the present case, the defendant had concerns about Malmberg's ability to convey good title to *Red Elvis* because he believed that Lindholm might have had a claim to the painting. The defendant also was concerned that Malmberg had not yet acquired title to the painting or that the transaction might be a "flip."

Because of his concern that Lindholm might make a claim to *Red Elvis*, the defendant took the extraordinary step of hiring counsel to conduct an investigation and to negotiate a formal contract of sale on his behalf. He also insisted on and obtained a formal contract containing representations and warranties that Malmberg had title to the painting. In addition, during the course of the investigation, the defendant's counsel conducted both a lien search and an Art Loss Register search that revealed no competing claims to *Red Elvis*. Although the defendant was cautioned that the searches provided only minimal assurance that Malmberg had good title to the painting, such searches typically are not conducted during the course of a normal art transaction and, therefore, provided the defendant with at least some assurance that Lindholm had no claims to the painting.

Moreover, the evidence was sufficient for the trial court reasonably to conclude that at all times during the transaction, both Malmberg and Holm had reputations as honest, reliable, and trustworthy art dealers. This is not like the situation in *Porter v. Wertz*, supra, 68 A.D.2d 146, in which the court concluded that the buyer was not a buyer in the ordinary course of business because he did not know the dealer or his reputation. The defendant had little reason to doubt Malmberg's claim that he was the owner of *Red Elvis*, and any doubts that he did have reasonably were allayed by relying on Holm's assurances that Malmberg had bought the painting from the plaintiff because she needed money due to her divorce. The defendant established at trial that it is customary to rely on the assurances of respected art dealers when conducting a transaction, and the defendant had no reason to depart from this practice.

The defendant's concerns were further allayed when Malmberg delivered *Red Elvis* to a bonded warehouse in Denmark, the delivery location the parties had agreed to in the contract of sale. At the time of the sale, the painting was on loan to the Guggenheim, whose policy it was to release a painting on loan only to the true owner, or to someone the true owner had authorized to take possession. The defendant was not informed that the plaintiff had authorized release to Malmberg for the sole purpose of lending the painting to a museum in Denmark. Knowing that the Guggenheim would release the painting to an authorized party only, it was reasonable for the defendant to believe that Malmberg was the true owner of the painting. We conclude that these steps were sufficient to conform to reasonable commercial standards for the sale of artwork under the circumstances and, therefore, that the defendant had status as a buyer in the ordinary course of business.

We recognize that the customary practice in the art industry of not requiring a merchant buyer to obtain documentary proof that the seller owns the work of art whenever there are reasonable doubts or questions regarding the seller's authority to sell imposes risks on persons who entrust art to an art dealer. Section 42a-1-201 (9) evinces a legislative desire, however, for courts to respect "the usual or customary practices in the kind of business in which the seller is engaged. . . ." We are not entitled to impose the type of business practices that we would prefer.

Moreover, the evidence presented at trial established that the reason that documentary proof of ownership customarily is not required is to protect the confidentiality of the owner and the buyer. Requiring a merchant buyer to obtain an invoice or other supporting documentation proving the seller's ownership would in every transaction destroy the privacy and confidentiality that buyers and sellers have come to desire and expect. Accordingly, only when circumstances surrounding the sale cast severe doubt on the ownership of the artwork are merchant buyers required to obtain documentary assurance that the seller has good title. In this instance, the Swedish-English letter was produced at Holm's suggestion to give the defendant assurance that the *plaintiff* had good title when she sold the painting to Malmberg. In light of the customary practices in the industry, the defendant reasonably could have concluded that Malmberg was unwilling to produce a signed copy of the letter because of his desire to protect the owner's expectation of confidentiality in their transaction. The purpose of the letter was not to give the defendant assurance that *Malmberg* had good title to the painting, and any concerns about Malmberg's title that could be inferred from the refusal to show the defendant a signed copy of the letter were quickly allayed by Malmberg's subsequent delivery of the painting to Denmark. Accordingly, we conclude, on the basis of all the circumstances surrounding this sale, that the defendant's failure to obtain an invoice from the plaintiff to Malmberg or a signed copy of the Swedish-English letter does not strip him of his status as a buyer in the ordinary course of business. For the same reasons, we conclude that the defendant was not required to contact directly the plaintiff or other parties who might have had knowledge concerning *Red Elvis'* title.

We conclude that the trial court properly determined that the defendant was a buyer in the ordinary course of business and, therefore, took all rights the plaintiff had to the painting pursuant to §42a-2-403 (2).

The judgment is affirmed.

PROBLEM 22

Going on a family vacation, Kahr stowed sterling silver and credit cards in a bag in the attic. Not long after returning, Kahr took several bags of clothing to donate to Goodwill — and unknowingly brought along the bag of valuables. Kahr handed the bags over to Goodwill, and signed a form describing the donation as "used clothing." After sorting through the bags, a Goodwill employee set the credit cards aside, but put the silver out for sale. A bargain hunter soon snapped it up. Can Kahr recover the silver? See §2-403(2) and (3); Kahr v. Markland, 543 N.E. 2d 579 (Ill. App. 1989).

II. WARRANTIES OF QUALITY

A. Express Warranties

An express warranty arises when the seller does something affirmative to create buyer expectations about the characteristics or performance of the goods. Typically this means that the seller will make oral or written representations about the product in advertisements, the verbal sales pitch, or the written contract. These representations must have some substance to them (more than mere "puffing") to rise to the dignity of an express warranty. In the Code's words, they must "relate to the goods" (an obvious requirement) and become part of the *basis of the bargain* (a not-so-obvious or explainable requirement). Under the now-replaced Uniform Sales Act (§12), the buyer had to prove *reliance* on the statement alleged to be an express warranty. Does *basis of bargain* mean this? Read Official Comment 3 to §2-313. Most courts (but not all) have not required a buyer to prove any specific reliance, but instead hold that a statement goes to the basis of the bargain if its natural tendency is to induce the buyer to purchase (even though that is not the sole reason). See In re General Motors Corp. Dex-Cool Products Liability Litigation, 62 U.C.C. Rep. Serv. 2d 115 (S.D. Ill. 2007); White & Summers §10-5. This means that if the statement, however made, has any substance to it so that it *might* have played some part in the buyer's decision to buy, the burden is on the *seller* to prove that the buyer did *not* rely. If the seller cannot meet this burden, the buyer has the benefit of an express warranty. See Official Comment 8 to §2-313.

PROBLEM 23

(a) The salesman at the lot of Smiles Pre-Owned Vehicles told the woman buying the car that it was in "A-1 shape." She bought the car, but it broke down the next day, stranding her in the country. Was this oral statement mere puffing? See Wat Henry Pontiac Co. v. Bradley, 202 Okla. 82, 210 P.2d 348 (1949); White & Summers §10-4. Is it an easier case if the seller tells the buyer that the used car is in "mint condition"? See Taylor v. Alfama, 481 A.2d 1059, 39 U.C.C. Rep. Serv. 1235 (Vt. 1984); Nigro v. Lee, 882 N.Y.S.2d 346 (App. Div. 2009) (no express warranty, where eBay seller described Mercedes-Benz automobile as "gorgeous," with "minor blemishes," but sold "as is").

(b) When the farmer looked over the young chickens he was contemplating purchasing from the poultry company, he complained that they looked pretty scruffy. The salesman explained that that was because they were on half-feed and that when they were placed on full-feed, they would "bloom out, straighten up, and fly right," and they would "do a good job in your chicken house." The farmer purchased the chickens, and two months later they started dying in droves. The farmer sued, claiming breach of an express warranty. Is he right? Is this a question of law or of fact for the jury? See Woodruff v. Clark County Farm Bureau Coop. 153 Ind. App. 31, 286 N.E.2d 188, 11 U.C.C. Rep. Serv. 498 (1972).

(c) Portia Moot, a third-year law student, had taken the course in Sales, so when she went to buy a used car, she listened very carefully to the sales pitch. The smarmy salesman was quite friendly, but he only made two statements about the car she bought: "This is a great car!" and "You're going to love it!" In fact, the car broke down a great deal, and Portia quickly grew to hate it. Does she have a cause of action here?

(d) Assume that the car salesman told Portia that the used car she was contemplating purchasing had been thoroughly inspected by the car dealership's crack repair department and was "mechanically in perfect condition." Is that an express warranty? See Bobholz v. Banaszak, 655 N. W.2d 547, 49 U.C.C. Rep. Serv. 2d 25 (Wis. App. 2002). Portia was suspicious about the reliability of the car and before she bought it, she took it to her own favorite mechanic for an inspection. She didn't buy the car until her mechanic cleared it as fine. When the car broke down a few days later, she decided to bring suit on the express warranty. What defense will the car dealership raise?

In re Toshiba America HD DVD Marketing and Sales Practices Litigation

United States District Court, New Jersey, 2009
69 U.C.C. Rep. Serv. 2d 1085

DEBEVOISE, Senior District Judge.

[Plaintiffs bought an HD DVD Player from Toshiba after the company had decided to discontinue its future production of the product because it had lost the technological battle for its format's supremacy, but while Toshiba was still advertising the player as "For Today, Tomorrow and Beyond." When Plaintiffs discovered this deception, they sued for, among other things, breach of an express warranty.]

High Definition Digital Versatile Disc ("HD DVD") is an optical disc storage format for encoding audio-visual entertainment such as movies, and is available for playback on compatible HD DVD players, including Toshiba's HD DVD Player. ([Consolidated Class Action Complaint ("CCAC")] ¶13.) Toshiba developed the HD DVD format to be a "next generation" format to succeed the standard DVD. (*Id.*) The HD DVD Player allows consumers to view movies in higher definition and fidelity than allowed by previous technologies. (*Id.*)

Toshiba introduced the HD DVD Player for sale to consumers in the United States in April 2006. (*Id.* ¶14.) At that time the list prices ranged from $499 to $799. (*Id.*) Plaintiffs allege that these prices were 200% to 500% of the cost of standard DVD players without high definition capabilities. (*Id.*)

The HD DVD Player faced competition from Blu-ray Disc, an optical disc format largely developed and supported by the Sony Corporation ("Sony"). (*Id.* ¶18.) Blu-ray Disc was also marketed as a "next generation" format for the encoding and playback of audio-visual entertainment. (*Id.*) Several major movie studios, which regularly release movies in the DVD format, chose to release movies in Blu-ray format rather than HD DVD. (*Id.* ¶25.) Disney (including Touchstone and Miramax), Sony Pictures (including MGM/Columbia Tristar) and 20th Century Fox all supported Blu-ray technology rather than HD DVD. (*Id.*) Plaintiffs allege that Toshiba "consistently failed to disclose to its customers" this information regarding the support of certain movie studios for Blu-ray rather than HD DVD technology. (*Id.*) In what the Plaintiffs characterize as "a desperate attempt by Toshiba to increase its market share and garner HD DVD movie studio support," on August 21, 2007, *The New York Times* reported that Paramount and Dream Works Animation would receive approximately $150 million in financial incentives for their commitment to HD DVD. (*Id.*)

The competition between Blu-ray and HD DVD was well reported in the media and was likened to the competition 30 years ago between the VHS and Betamax formats for home video recording. (Certification of David E. Sellinger, February 17, 2009 ("Sellinger Cert.") Ex. C at 2 and Ex. E at 1.) As *Business Week* reported in its December 6, 2007 edition,

> For two years now, rival camps have been battling over which new DVD format will prevail: Blu-ray, which is backed by Sony (SNE) and a consortium of 170 other companies, or HD DVD, which is being championed by Toshiba (TOSBF), Microsoft (MSFT), and others. Both technologies promise crisper video that looks better on the new generation of flat-panel, high definition TVs. And the winner stands to control a lucrative new market worth billions. Each side has been competing to win the backing of the major movie studios. Only Warner Bros. (TWX), which currently uses both formats, is still playing hard to get.

(Sellinger Cert. Ex. D at 1.) That same article reported that there were rumors that "Warner [was] coming aboard [Sony] soon," meaning that Warner Brothers was planning to discontinue production of movies in the HD DVD format and instead use the Blu-ray format. (*Id.*; CCAC ¶35.) *Business Week* also reported that the head of Toshiba's HD DVD business in Japan had made three trips since the summer to meet with Warner Brothers regarding its HD DVD business. (Sellinger Cert. Ex. D at 1; CCAC ¶35.) On December 10, 2007, *The New York Times* reported that Warner Brothers had signaled that it would choose one format-HD DVD or Blu-ray-after the 2007 holiday shopping season and that its choice would be determined by which format sold more DVDs during that season. (CCAC ¶35.)

Toshiba continued to market its HD DVD Players, with the slogan "For Today, Tomorrow and Beyond," throughout the 2007 holiday shopping seasons and thereafter. (*Id.* ¶27.) During that season, Plaintiffs allege that Toshiba lowered prices on its Players in order to induce additional sales. (*Id.*)

On January 4, 2008, Warner Brothers announced that it would no longer release movies in the HD DVD format. (*Id.* ¶26.) This announcement led to "a chain reaction in the industry," which included decisions by Best Buy, Wal-Mart and Circuit City to drop HD DVD from their stores. (*Id.*) Once Warner Brothers decided in favor of Blu-ray, that system's market share increased from 49% to 70%. (*Id.* ¶35.)

Toshiba continued marketing its HD DVD Players in January and the first weeks of February 2008. On January 14, 2008, Toshiba issued a press release stating "that it [was] stepping up its successful marketing campaign for HD DVD as it experienced record-breaking unit sales in the fourth quarter of 2007" (*Id.* ¶28.) That press release also stated that "HD DVD is proven to be the format of choice for consumers" and that Toshiba planned to execute an extended advertising campaign to further enhance consumer awareness of the benefits of HD DVD and drive sales. (*Id.*) On February 3, 2008, Toshiba ran an ad during the Super Bowl, "highlighting its HD-A3, HD-A30 and HD-A35 Players," which the Plaintiffs allege "thereby [characterized] the long-term viability of the Players." (*Id.* ¶29.)

Plaintiffs allege that "[m]arket insiders" predicted that Blu-ray would win the battle with the HD DVD format if for no other reason than the fact that Blu-ray was backed by Disney. (*Id.* ¶35.) Plaintiffs also allege that "Toshiba was aware of market trends and knew, despite its misleading marketing campaign, that it was only a matter of time before the company withdrew from the marketplace abandoning its customer base." (*Id.* ¶35.) Plaintiffs claim that, as a "direct result of Toshiba's abrupt exit from the HD DVD market," their investments in the HD DVD Players "lost significant value." (*Id.* ¶31.) . . .

An express warranty by a seller is created by: "[a]ny affirmation of fact or promise made by the seller to the buyer which relates to the goods and becomes part of the basis of the bargain," or "[a]ny description of the goods which is made part of the basis of the bargain." N.J.S.A. §12A:2-313(1)(a) & (b); Cal. Comm. Code §2313(1)(a) & (b); Fla. Stat. Ann. 672.313(1)(a) & (b); Idaho Code §28-2-313(1)(a) & (b); 810 Ill. Comp. Stat. 5/2-313(1)(a) & (b); Mich. Comp. Laws §440.2313(1)(a) & (b). The use of "formal words of promise or that the seller have a specific intention to warrant the good" is not necessary to create an express warranty. Liberty Lincoln-Mercury, Inc. v. Ford Motor Co., 171 F.3d 818, 824 (3d Cir. 1999) (citing N.J. Stat. Ann. §12A:2-313(2)). But "an affirmation merely of the value of the goods or a statement purporting to be merely the seller's opinion or commendation of the goods does not create a warranty." N.J. Stat. Ann §12A:2-313(2); Cal. Comm. Code §2313(2); Fla. Stat. Ann. 672.313(2); Idaho Code §28-2-313(2); 810 Ill. Comp. Stat. 5/2-313(2); Mich. Comp. Laws §440.2313(2).

Plaintiffs allege that Toshiba's "affirmations of fact and/or promises relating to the [HD DVD] Players created express warranties that Toshiba would continue to support the HD DVD format and continue to manufacture such players." (CCAC ¶117.) They allege that Toshiba breached these warranties when it announced in February 2008 that it would exit the HD DVD market. (*Id.* ¶118.) Specifically, Plaintiffs argue that "Toshiba warranted that its [HD DVD] Players could play HD DVDs 'Today, Tomorrow, and Beyond.'" (Plts.' Opp'n Br. 17.) Yet there is no allegation that the HD DVD Players cannot still play HD DVDs. Rather, the problem is that the availability of new HD DVDs has severely decreased. Plaintiffs further argue that the long-term viability of the HD DVD market "was a large part of the basis of the bargain between Toshiba and the putative Class, because consumers were concerned with choosing a high definition DVD player which would have long term viability." (*Id.* 17 & 18.) Toshiba's exit from the HD DVD market has, according to Plaintiffs, "substantially limited that viability." (*Id.* 18.)

Plaintiffs do not allege that their HD DVD Players no longer can play HD DVDs. Rather, they argue that Toshiba's tag line that its HD DVD Players were for "Today, Tomorrow, and Beyond" created an express warranty that, essentially, Toshiba would remain in the HD DVD market forever. As discussed with respect to the Plaintiffs' consumer fraud claims, the statement that HD DVD Players were for "Today, Tomorrow, and Beyond" is puffery and not specific enough to create an express warranty. Plaintiffs cite to L.S. Heath & Son, Inc. v. AT & T Information Systems, Inc., 9 F.3d 561, 570 (7th Cir. 1993), where the Court of Appeals for the Seventh Circuit, applying New Jersey law, noted that, "A statement can amount to a warranty, even if unintended to be such by the seller, 'if it could fairly be understood . . . to constitute an affirmation or representation that the [product] possesse[s] a certain quality or capacity relating to future performance.'" *Id.* (quoting Gladden v. Cadillac Motor Car Div., Gen. Motors Corp., 83 N.J. 320, 416 A.2d 394, 396 (N.J. 1980)). While it is certainly true that a statement relating to future performance *may* create an express warranty, even if not intended by the seller, Toshiba's statement regarding its HD DVD Players does not rise to that level. In *L.S. Heath & Son*, the court found that AT & T's statement that its "complete intregated [sic] data processing and voice/data communications network [will] satisf[y] all of your aforementioned objectives," may have constituted an express warranty. *Id.* AT & T's statement was far more specific than Toshiba's statement that its HD DVD Players were for "Today, Tomorrow, and Beyond." Additionally, even if Toshiba created an express warranty of future *performance*, there is no allegation that the HD DVD Players do not perform as they are intended—i.e., to play HD DVDs.

The CCAC fails to state a claim for breach of express warranty. Count Five of the CCAC is therefore dismissed.

PROBLEM 24

Upon graduation from law school, Andrew Loner hung out his shingle and waited. Mr. and Mrs. Consumer were his first clients, and they told him the following story. Two weeks earlier they had visited a wallpaper store, Paper & Paste, Inc., and inquired about vinyl wallpaper for their dining room.

The salesman told them that the "finest" wallpaper in the store was Expenso-Paper, a vinyl wallpaper selling at $25 a roll. When he learned that the Consumers had never before put up wallpaper, the salesman assured them that Expenso-Paper "goes up easily, can be put on with any paste, and dries immediately." He said that it "would look wonderful" and, moreover, that Expenso-Paper "was used by Mary Magic," the famous movie star, in her dining room. He showed them a sample book, and they picked out a pattern they liked and ordered ten rolls. When the paper arrived the next week, it proved to be very stiff and hard to work with. It tore easily and refused to stay flat on the wall (it either bubbled or, due to its heavy weight, fell down on drying). In addition, it was dyed a darker color than the version of the pattern in the sample book. The final result was that the Consumers' dining room looked terrible. To top it all off, the Consumers discovered that Mary Magic did not own a home (she lived exclusively in hotels).

Upon complaining to Paper & Paste, the Consumers were told by the manager that Expenso-Paper needs a special brand of paste, to wit, Expenso-Paste. They were also told that Expenso-Paper was an inferior brand and that next time they should buy Super Wall, a better product that the store carried.

The Consumers told Loner that they signed the contract without reading it and that the statement about Mary Magic's dining room was made *after* they signed the agreement. Loner (and you) have to answer these questions:

(a) Which of the salesman's representations amount to express warranties?

    (1) finest?

    (2) goes up easily?

    (3) can be put on with any paste?

    (4) dries immediately?

    (5) would look wonderful?

    (6) was used by Mary Magic?

Do you see any other express warranties?

(b) Is the Mary Magic statement part of the *basis of the bargain,* arising as it did after the contract was signed? See §2-209(1); Official Comment 7 to §2-313.

PROBLEM 25

Balding Paul bought a wig from Hair, Inc. He became annoyed when the wig changed colors slightly from season to season. He did not do anything about it until one day, while thumbing through a newspaper, he noticed an ad for Hair, Inc., that claimed that their wigs did not shrink or change color. On checking back, he discovered that Hair, Inc., had run an identical ad during the week prior to his purchase of the wig. He sues. On the witness stand Paul confesses that he never saw the ad until a year after his purchase of the wig. Is this admission fatal to his recovery on a theory of express warranty? See Winston Indus., Inc. v. Stuyvesant Ins. Co., 55 Ala. App. 525, 317 So. 2d 493, 17 U.C.C. Rep. Serv. 924 (1975) (buyer held protected by manufacturer's warranty on mobile home even though he never received a copy).

B. Implied Warranties

In many ways implied warranties are the legal opposites of express warranties. An express warranty is created only where the seller does something *affirmative* (opens his mouth and says something, takes out a newspaper ad, displays a sample). Implied warranties, on the other hand, are *automatically* part of the contract unless the seller (or the circumstance) does something affirmative to get rid of them. Implied warranties are implied as a matter of law; they are sometimes referred to as "children of the law." Like express warranties, the seller's intention to create any implied warranty is completely irrelevant.

1. Merchantability

The implied warranty of merchantability (which is easier to spell and pronounce if you think of it as two words — *merchant* and *ability* — tacked together) is not given a precise definition in the Code. The basic idea is that the item must be saleable and conform to the normal expectations of the parties. Notice that §2-314(2), which you should now read, sets minimum standards for its meaning. Clever lawyers can make much of the laundry list found in that subsection.

Shaffer v. Victoria Station, Inc.

Washington Supreme Court, 1978
91 Wash. 2d 295, 588 P.2d 233, 25 U.C.C. Rep. Serv. 427

DOLLIVER, J.

On March 26, 1974, plaintiff Shaffer ordered a glass of wine at the Victoria Station, a restaurant operated by defendant. In the course of taking his first or second sip, the wine glass broke in Mr. Shaffer's hand, resulting in alleged permanent injury.

Plaintiff brought this action based upon three theories: negligence, breach of implied warranty under the Uniform Commercial Code, and strict liability under the theory of Restatement (Second) of Torts §402A (1965). The manufacturer of the glass was named as a defendant, but was never served. Prior to trial, as counsel and the trial judge were discussing proposed instructions, plaintiff's attorney indicated that he could not prove negligence, and wished to submit the case to the jury on the grounds of breach of warranty and strict liability. Plaintiff then took a voluntary non-suit on the negligence issue. At the same time, the court ruled the case sounded in negligence alone, and granted the defendant's motion for dismissal. The Court of Appeals affirmed. Shaffer v. Victoria Station, Inc., 18 Wash. App. 816, 572 P.2d 737 (1977). We reverse the Court of Appeals.

I

Defendant argues the Uniform Commercial Code does not apply since the restaurant was not a merchant with respect to wine glasses as defined in §2-104 and, since the glass itself was not sold, there was no passing of title as required under §2-106. Plaintiff, however, points to §2-314 as being decisive. We agree. Section 2-314 reads, inter alia:

> (1) Unless excluded or modified (§2-316), a warranty that the goods shall be merchantable is implied in a contract for their sale if the seller is a merchant with respect to goods of that kind. Under this section the serving for value of food or drink to be consumed either on the premises or elsewhere is a sale.
> (2) Goods to be merchantable must be at least such as . . .
>   (c) are fit for the ordinary purposes for which such goods are used; and . . .
>   (e) are adequately contained, packaged, and labeled as the agreement may require; . . . .

It is our opinion that, when the Uniform Commercial Code states "the serving for value of food or drink to be consumed either on the premises or elsewhere is a sale" and that such food and drink must be "adequately contained, packaged, and labeled as the agreement may require," it covers entirely the situation before us. Plaintiff ordered a drink (a glass of wine) from defendant. Defendant sold and served the glass of wine to plaintiff to be consumed by plaintiff on the premises. The wine could not be served as a drink nor could it be consumed without an adequate container. The drink sold includes the wine and the container both of which must be fit for the ordinary purpose for which used. Plaintiff alleges the drink sold — wine in a glass — was unfit and has, therefore, stated a cause of action.

In addition to the language of §2-314, we believe the language of §1-103 is applicable. It states:

> Unless displaced by the particular provisions of this Title, the principles of law and equity, including the law merchant and the law relative to capacity to contract, principal and agent, estoppel, fraud, misrepresentation, duress, coercion, mistake, bankruptcy, or other validating or invalidating cause shall supplement its provisions.

Plaintiff urges that cases which apply the Uniform Commercial Code where the goods are leased rather than sold (see, e.g., Baker v. Seattle, 79 Wash. 2d 198, 484 P.2d 405 (1971)), or are under a bailment for mutual benefit (see, e.g., Fulbright v. Klamath Gas Co., 271 Ore. 449, 533 P.2d 316 (1975)), be extended to the facts before us. We believe this is unnecessary. A more straightforward and less tortuous approach is that adopted in Hadley v. Hillcrest Dairy, Inc., 341 Mass. 624, 171 N.E.2d 293 (1961). In that case, a bottle of milk delivered to the plaintiff's home shattered and cut the plaintiff's hand. The Massachusetts Supreme Judicial Court, relying on the Massachusetts sales act (which was not, as argued by defendant, significantly different in its applicable part from the Uniform Commercial Code), held at 627, "In our view it is immaterial whether or not the property in the jug passed to the plaintiff." The court goes on to cite Geddling v. Marsh, (1920) 1 K.B. 668. In that case, a retailer received bottled mineral water from the manufacturer and was injured by an exploding bottle. The court found the bottles were not sold to the retailer but held the retailer could recover under a breach of an implied warranty of fitness. The court said at 671-672:

> In this case there was only one contract — namely, a contract between the plaintiff and the defendant that the plaintiff should be supplied with mineral waters. Mineral waters could not be supplied except in bottles, and therefore the plaintiff was asking to be supplied with mineral waters in bottles. That undoubtedly is a contract of sale, and I will assume that in that contract there might be a condition that the bottles should not be bought by the plaintiff but should be hired; but the question the county court judge had to consider was whether the bottles were not "supplied under a contract of sale." This was a contract of sale none the less because there was a special provision with regard to the bottles. The section, in my opinion, extends not only to the goods actually bought under the contract but to goods "supplied under the contract of sale." This particular bottle was thus "supplied under a contract of sale," and it follows that it should be reasonably fit for the purpose for which it was supplied. In fact it was not reasonably fit and in consequence of that unfitness the plaintiff was injured.

See also Sartin v. Blackwell, 200 Miss. 579, 28 So. 2d 222 (1946). Plaintiff has a cause of action both on the face of the statute and under the principles of case law elucidated above.

II

We also hold an action lies under the strict liability theory of Restatement (Second) of Torts §402A (1965). The policy questions of strict liability and their application to retailers have been previously determined. See Seattle-First Natl. Bank v. Tabert, 86 Wash. 2d 145, 542 P.2d 774 (1975);

Ulmer v. Ford Motor Co., 75 Wash. 2d 522, 452 P.2d 729 (1969). The only question remaining is whether §402A applies to the transaction here. In addressing this issue, the Court of Appeals expressed concern over an uncontrollable broadening of the doctrine of strict liability:

> Were the wine glass in question held to be a mere facet of the sale of the "glass of wine" and thus a "product" for the purposes of section 402A, the theory of strict liability would be greatly and unnecessarily expanded. The reasonably clear standard of engagement "in the business of selling . . . a product" would be abandoned in deference to a less predictable question — whether the injury-producing aspect of the sale was necessary to the sale. If a wine glass renders a restaurateur strictly liable because he could not sell wine without it, what of other tablewear, the waiters and the bus boys, the furnishings to effect an attractive atmosphere, or the building housing the establishment? The argument could be made that numerous aspects of a restaurant's operation, or that of any other retailer, are integral to each sale. To ignore the fact that this allegedly defective glass was never sold would create great uncertainty as to the limits of strict liability.

Shaffer, at 820-821.

We do not agree with the gloomy view of the Court of Appeals of the consequences of allowing the plaintiff to proceed with this action. We hold the sale of a glass of wine is subject to the strict liability provisions of §402A. If their predictions as to future lawsuits come to pass, we will deal with the litigation at that time. Confirmation of the applicability of §402A to this case is given in comment h, which says:

> The defective condition may arise not only from harmful ingredients, not characteristic of the product itself either as to presence or quantity, but also from foreign objects contained in the product, from decay or deterioration before sale, or from the way in which the product is prepared or packed. No reason is apparent for distinguishing between the product itself and the container in which it is supplied; and the two are purchased by the user or consumer as an integrated whole. Where the container is itself dangerous, the product is sold in a defective condition. Thus a carbonated beverage in a bottle which is so weak, or cracked, or jagged at the edges, or bottled under such excessive pressure that it may explode or otherwise cause harm to the person who handles it, is in a defective and dangerous condition. The container cannot logically be separated from the contents when the two are sold as a unit, and the liability stated in this Section arises not only when the consumer drinks the beverage and is poisoned by it, but also when he is injured by the bottle while he is handling it preparatory to consumption.

Restatement (Second) of Torts §402A, comment h at 351-352 (1965).

Plaintiff has stated a cause of action under theories of implied warranty of fitness and strict liability. The Court of Appeals is reversed.

QUESTIONS

1. Would it be a defense to the restaurant that it was not negligent in any way in connection with its handling of the wine glass? See Official Comment 13 to §2-314; La Fountain v. Sears, Roebuck & Co., 680 F. Supp. 251, 6 U.C.C. Rep. Serv. 2d 1091 (E.D. Mich. 1988).

2. If a casino serves its patrons free drinks at the gaming tables and one of the drinks proves to contain chips of glass, would the Washington Supreme Court reach the same result it did in the last case? See Levondosky v. Marina Assocs., 731 F. Supp. 1210, 11 U.C.C. Rep. Serv. 2d 487 (D.N.J. 1990).

By far the most important segment of §2-314(2) is found in subsection (2)(c): to be merchantable the goods must be "fit for the ordinary purposes for which such goods are used." (Or, as the South Carolina courts have put it since 1793, "a sound price warrants a sound commodity.") When you think about it, a warranty that the goods are fit for their *ordinary purpose* is a big warranty. It is the warranty that the goods will work, and it is typically the only warranty that the buyer needs. When sellers disclaim the implied warranty of merchantability (and they often do), why do buyers not routinely complain?

PROBLEM 26

Consider the following:

(a) Are cigarettes that cause lung cancer merchantable if used over a period of years? See Haglund v. Philip Morris, Inc., 446 Mass. 741, 847 N.E.2d 315 (2006); Franklin E. Crawford, Fit for Its Ordinary Purpose? Tobacco, Fast Food, and the Implied Warranty of Merchantability, 63 Ohio St. L.J. 1165 (2002); White & Summers §10-12; Annot. 80 A.L.R.2d 681. See also Hoyte v. Yum! Brands, Inc., 62 U.C.C. Rep. Serv. 2d 726 (Cal. Ct. App. 2007) (KFC did not breach implied warranty of merchantability, although its products contained trans fats); Bodie v. Purdue Pharma Co., 489 F. Supp. 2d 24 (D.D.C. 2007) (addictive nature of painkiller Oxycontin did not breach warranty of merchantability). If the seller's advertisements stated that the cigarettes were "mild," would that create an express warranty?

(b) To treat menopausal symptoms, plaintiff took medicines manufactured by the defendant, which combined the drug progestin and estrogen. As a consequence she developed breast cancer. Contending that the warranty of merchantability was breached when the defendant failed to warn her of this possibility, she sued. Does that warranty contain a "failure to warn" component? See Hines v. Wyeth, 2011 WL 1990496 (S.D. W. Va. 2011).

(c) Following a recipe in the Exotic Cookbook, Martha prepares puf-ferfish fillet for Thanksgiving. The book, however, neglects to advise chefs to remove the pufferfish's poisonous organs. After a lengthy recuperation, Martha sues the book store and publisher for breach of the implied warranty of merchantability. What result? See Cardozo v. True, 342 So. 2d 1053, 21 U.C.C. Rep. Serv. 69 (Fla. Dist. Ct. App. 1977). *Cardozo* held "It is unthinkable that standards imposed on the quality of goods sold by a merchant would require that merchant, who is a book seller, to evaluate the thought processes of the many authors and publishers of the hundreds and often thousands of books which the merchant offers for sale. One can readily imagine the extent of potential litigation. Is the newsdealer, or for that matter the neighborhood news carrier, liable if the local paper's recipes call for inedible ingredients? We think not." Do you agree?

(d) Officer Krupke, a New York policeman by profession, sold his family car to his next-door neighbor, Maria, telling her it was a "good car." In fact, it was falling apart and blew up the first time she drove it. Has Krupke brea-ched the implied warranty of merchantability? See §2-104(1); Official Comment 3 to §2-314; §1-304. Should §2-314 be extended so that the warranty is made by all sellers? See Ingrid Hillinger, The Merchant of §2-314: Who Needs Him?, 34 Hastings L.J. 747 (1983).

Webster v. Blue Ship Tea Room, Inc.

Massachusetts Supreme Judicial Court, 1964
347 Mass. 421, 198 N.E.2d 309, 2 U.C.C. Rep. Serv. 161

REARDON, J.

This is a case which by its nature evokes earnest study not only of the law but also of the culinary traditions of the Commonwealth which bear so heavily upon its outcome. It is an action to recover damages for personal injuries sustained by reason of a breach of implied warranty of food served by the defendant in its restaurant. An auditor, whose findings of fact were not to be final, found for the plaintiff. On a retrial in the Superior Court before a judge and jury, in which the plaintiff testified, the jury returned a verdict for her. The defendant is here on exceptions to the refusal of the judge (1) to strike certain portions of the auditor's report, (2) to direct a verdict for the defendant, and (3) to allow the defendant's motion for the entry of a verdict in its favor under leave reserved.

The jury could have found the following facts: On Saturday, April 25, 1959, about 1 P.M., the plaintiff, accompanied by her sister and her aunt, entered the Blue Ship Tea Room operated by the defendant. The group was seated at a table and supplied with menus.

This restaurant, which the plaintiff characterized as "quaint," was lo-cated in Boston "on the third floor of an old building in T Wharf which overlooks the ocean."

The plaintiff, who had been born and brought up in New England (a fact of some consequence), ordered clam chowder and crabmeat salad. Within a few minutes she received tidings to the effect that "there was no more clam chowder," whereupon she ordered a cup of fish chowder. Presently, there was set before her "a small bowl of fish chowder." She had previously enjoyed a breakfast about 9 A.M. which had given her no difficulty. "The fish chowder contained haddock, potatoes, milk, water and seasoning. The chowder was milky in color and not clear. The haddock and potatoes were in chunks" (also a fact of consequence). "She agitated it a little with the spoon and observed that it was a fairly full bowl. . . . It was hot when she got it, but she did not tip it with her spoon because it was hot . . . but stirred it in an up and under motion. She denied that she did this because she was looking for something, but it was rather because she wanted an even distribution of fish and potatoes." "She started to eat it, alternating between the chowder and crackers which were on the table with . . . [some] rolls. She ate about 3 or 4 spoonfuls then stopped. She looked at the spoonfuls as she was eating. She saw equal parts of liquid, potato and fish as she spooned it into her mouth. She did not see anything unusual about it. After 3 or 4 spoonfuls she was aware that something had lodged in her throat because she couldn't swallow and couldn't clear her throat by gulping and she could feel it." This misadventure led to two esophagoscopies at the Massachusetts General Hospital, in the second of which, on April 27, 1959, a fish bone was found and removed. The sequence of events produced injury to the plaintiff which was not insubstantial.

We must decide whether a fish bone lurking in a fish chowder, about the ingredients of which there is no other complaint, constitutes a breach of implied warranty under applicable provisions of the Uniform Commercial Code, the annotations to which are not helpful on this point. As the judge put it in his charge, "Was the fish chowder fit to be eaten and wholesome? . . . [N]obody is claiming that the fish itself wasn't wholesome. . . . But the bone of contention here—I don't mean that for a pun—but was this fish bone a foreign substance that made the fish chowder unwholesome or not fit to be eaten?"

The plaintiff has vigorously reminded us of the high standards imposed by this court where the sale of food is involved (see Flynn v. First Natl. Stores Inc., 296 Mass. 521, 523) and has made reference to cases involving stones in beans (Friend v. Childs Dining Hall Co., 231 Mass. 65), trichinae in pork (Holt v. Mann, 294 Mass. 21, 22), and to certain other cases, here and elsewhere, serving to bolster her contention of breach of warranty.

The defendant asserts that here was a native New Englander eating fish chowder in a "quaint" Boston dining place where she had been before; that "[f]ish chowder, as it is served and enjoyed by New Englanders, is a hearty dish, originally designed to satisfy the appetites of our seamen and fishermen"; that "[t]his court knows well that we are not talking of some insipid broth as is customarily served to convalescents." We are asked to rule in such fashion that no chef is forced "to reduce the pieces of fish in the chowder to minuscule size in an effort to ascertain if they contained any pieces of bone." "In so ruling," we are told (in the defendant's brief), "the court will not only uphold its reputation for legal knowledge and acumen, but will, as loyal sons of Massachusetts, save our world-renowned fish chowder from degenerating into an insipid broth containing the mere essence of its former stature as a culinary masterpiece." Notwithstanding these passionate entreaties we are bound to examine with detachment the nature of fish chowder and what might happen to it under varying interpretations of the Uniform Commercial Code.

Chowder is an ancient dish preexisting even "the appetites of our seamen and fishermen." It was perhaps the common ancestor of the "more refined cream soups, purees, and bisques." Berolzheimer, The American Woman's Cook Book (Publisher's Guild Inc., New York, 1941) p. 176. The word "chowder" comes from the French "chaudiere," meaning a "cauldron" or "pot." "In the fishing villages of Brittany . . . 'faire la chaudiere' means to supply a cauldron in which is cooked a mess of fish and biscuit with some savoury condiments, a hodgepodge contributed by the fishermen themselves, each of whom in return receives his share of the prepared dish. The Breton fishermen probably carried the custom to Newfoundland, long famous for its chowder, whence it has spread to Nova Scotia, New Brunswick, and New England." A New England Dictionary (MacMillan and Co., 1893) p. 386. Our literature over the years abounds in references not only to the delights of chowder but also to its manufacture. A namesake of the plaintiff, Daniel Webster, had a recipe for fish chowder which has survived into a number of modern cookbooks[5] and in which the removal of fish bones is not mentioned at all. One old-time recipe recited in the New English Dictionary study defines chowder as "A dish made of fresh fish (esp. cod) or clams, stewed with slices of pork or bacon, onions, and biscuit. Cider and

---

5. "Take a cod of ten pounds, well cleaned, leaving on the skin. Cut into pieces one and a half pounds thick, preserving the head whole. Take one and a half pounds of clear, fat salt pork, cut in thin slices. Do the same with twelve potatoes. Take the largest pot you have. Try out the pork first, then take out the pieces of pork, leaving in the drippings. Add to that three parts of water, a layer of fish, so as to cover the bottom of the pot; next a layer of potatoes, then two tablespoons of salt, 1 teaspoon of pepper, then the pork, another layer of fish, and the remainder of the potatoes. Fill the pot with water to cover the ingredients. Put over a good fire. Let the chowder boil twenty-five minutes. When this is done have a quart of boiling milk ready, and ten hard crackers split and dipped in cold water. Add milk and crackers. Let the whole boil five minutes. The chowder is then ready to be first-rate if you have followed the directions. An onion may be added if you like the flavor." "This chowder," he adds, "is suitable for a large fishing party." Wolcott, The Yankee Cook Book (Coward-McCann, Inc., New York City, 1939) p. 9.

champagne are sometimes added." Hawthorne, in The House of the Seven Gables (Allyn and Bacon, Boston, 1957) p. 8, speaks of "[a] codfish of sixty pounds, caught in the bay [which] had been dissolved into the rich liquid of a chowder." A chowder variant, cod "Muddle," was made in Plymouth in the 1890s by taking "a three or four pound codfish, head added. Season with salt and pepper and boil in just enough water to keep from burning. When cooked, add milk and a piece of butter." The recitation of these ancient formulae suffices to indicate that in the construction of chowders in these parts in other years, worries about fish bones played no role whatsoever. This broad outlook on chowders has persisted in more modern cookbooks. "The chowder of today is much the same as the old chowder. . . ." The American Women's Cook Book, supra, p. 176. The all embracing Fannie Farmer states in a portion of her recipe, fish chowder is made with a "fish skinned, but head and tail left on. Cut fish in 2-inch pieces and set aside. Put head, tail, and backbone broken in pieces, in stew-pan; add 2 cups cold water and bring slowly to boiling point. . . ." The liquor thus produced from the bones is added to the balance of the chowder. Farmer, The Boston Cooking School Cook Book (Little Brown Co., 1937) p. 166.

Thus, we consider a dish which for many long years, if well made, has been made generally as outlined above. It is not too much to say that a person sitting down in New England to consume a good New England fish chowder embarks on gustatory adventure which may entail the removal of some fish bones from his bowl as he proceeds. We are not inclined to tamper with age old recipes by any amendment reflecting the plaintiff's view of the effect of the Uniform Commercial Code upon them. We are aware of the heavy body of case law involving foreign substances in food, but we sense a strong distinction between them and those relative to unwholesomeness of the food itself, e.g., tainted mackerel (Smith v. Gerrish, 256 Mass. 183), and a fish bone in a fish chowder. Certain Massachusetts cooks might cavil at the ingredients contained in the chowder in this case in that it lacked the heartening lift of salt pork. In any event, we consider that the joys of life in New England include the ready availability of fresh fish chowder. We should be prepared to cope with the hazards of fish bones, the occasional presence of which in chowders is, it seems to us, to be anticipated, and which, in the light of a hallowed tradition, do not impair their fitness or merchantability. While we are buoyed up in this conclusion by Shapiro v. Hotel Statler Corp., 132 F. Supp. 891 (S.D. Cal.), in which the bone which afflicted the plaintiff appeared in "Hot Barquette of Seafood Mornay," we know that the United States District Court of Southern California, situated as are we upon a coast, might be expected to share our views. We are most impressed, however, by Allen v. Grafton, 170 Ohio St. 249, where in Ohio, the Midwest, in a case where the plaintiff was injured by a piece of oyster shell in an order of fried oysters, Mr. Justice Taft (now Chief Justice) in a majority opinion held that "the possible presence of a piece of oyster shell in or attached to an oyster is so well known to anyone who eats oysters that we can say as a matter of law that one who eats oysters can reasonably anticipate and guard against eating such a piece of shell. . . ." (p. 259)

Thus, while we sympathize with the plaintiff who has suffered a peculiarly New England injury, the order must be

Exceptions sustained.

Judgment for the defendant.

QUESTIONS

1. Is the court saying that a natural substance does not breach the warranty or that the plaintiff's reasonable expectation should have included the bone? See Phillips v. Town of West Springfield, 405 Mass. 411, 540 N.E.2d 1331, 9 U.C.C. Rep. Serv. 2d 535 (1989).

2. Would the plaintiff have recovered if she had been born and reared in South Dakota and was on her first visit to New England?

3. Would the result be the same if the plaintiff had purchased a *can* of fish chowder and encountered the bone?

PROBLEM 27

Natty Bumpo was driving through upstate New York when a deer ran in front of his car. He swerved to avoid it and ran into a tree. His major injuries came from his sudden contact with the steering wheel and the inside of the driver's door, where he smashed up against sharp points on the dashboard's GPS system. Natty sued the car manufacturer, the Mohican Motor Company, for breach of the warranty of merchantability. His theory was that the manufacturer should have designed a much safer dashboard. The manufacturer's defense was that the car was fit for its ordinary purpose and that Natty had misused it. How should this come out? See Larsen v. General Motors Corp., 391 F.2d 495 (8th Cir. 1968); Comment, Intended Use and the Unsafe Automobile: Manufacturers' Liability for Negligent Design, 28 Md. L. Rev. 386 (1968); Annot., 76 A.L.R.2d 91.

PROBLEM 28

Carry Nation, on the advice of her beautician, Parker Pillsbury, bought a hair dye named "Intoxicating Fragrance" and proceeded to use it in accordance with the instructions on the package. Unfortunately the product contained alcohol, to which Ms. Nation was allergic, and she suffered considerable burn damage to her scalp and ears. When she sued the manufacturer, Harper's Hair Products, Inc., the basic defense was that only 0.5 percent of the population had this allergic reaction. Is this a good defense? See Jeneric/Pentron, Inc. v. Dillon Co., Inc., Chemichl Inc., Chemichl AG, 171 F. Supp. 2d 49, 45 U.C.C. Rep. Serv. 2d 769 (D. Conn. 2001); M. Dixon & F. Woodside, Drug Product Liability (1988); W. Freedman, Allergy and Products Liability (1965); 5 L. Frumer & M. Friedman, Products Liability §49.02 (2011); Comment, Strict Liability and Allergic Drug Reactions, 47 Miss. L.J. 526 (1976); Annot., 53 A.L.R.3d 298.

2.   Fitness for a Particular Purpose

Where the buyer wants to use the goods for something beyond their *ordinary* purpose, a warranty of merchantability is not enough. But the buyer may be able to sue for breach of the implied warranty of fitness for a particular purpose if the buyer can satisfy all of the elements of §2-315. Read the section and its Official Comment.

PROBLEM 29

When Christopher Wren finished building a recreation room in his basement, he wanted a heater for it. He saw an ad for the A-1 Hotblast Heater, which seemed to be what he needed. A good friend of Wren's named Inigo Jones ran a nearby appliance store. Wren went there and told Jones that he wanted the A-1 Hotblast Heater for the new room. Jones knew the room well; he had helped build it. When the heater arrived, it worked perfectly, but it simply did not have the capacity to heat the room. May Wren sue Jones for breach of either §2-314 or §2-315? See Comment 5 to §2-315. See Englebreacht v. W.D. Brannan & Sons, Inc., 501 S.W.2d 707, 13 U.C.C. Rep. Serv. 1015 (Tex. Civ. App. 1973).

PROBLEM 30

Harold Thumbs went to the Easy Paint Store and bought a can of green paint, which the store mixed on the premises from various pigments. Harold used the paint on his dining room walls, but due to a miscalculation on his part, he ran out when he was half finished. He took the empty paint can back to the store. He told the clerk that he was only half done with the job and needed another can, which the clerk promptly mixed and sold him. Harold finished the painting and then noticed two things: (1) the dried paint gave off an offensive odor, and (2) the paint from the second can did not match the first. What cause(s) of action does he have?

PROBLEM 31

Donald Souse ordered a martini at the Tired Executives Club. When he bit into the olive, he cracked his new $2,000 dentures on a pit. Is there a cause of action under either §2-314 or §2-315? See Hochberg v. O'Donnell's Restaurant, Inc., 272 A.2d 846, 8 U.C.C. Rep. Serv. 674 (D.C. 1971).

———————

Courts faced with this last Problem (harmful substances in food) have split into two camps: those that deny liability if the object is a *natural substance*, as opposed to a *foreign object*, and those that permit recovery even where the consumer is injured by a natural substance as long as the biter's "reasonable expectation" is that it would have been removed. The problem reoccurs in the cases as gourmands encounter stones in cherry pies, pits in olives, or, as in the *Webster* case above, bones in fish. See Annot., 7 A.L.R.2d 1027.

C.   *Warranty Disclaimers and Limitations*

1.   **Disclaiming Express Warranties**

The drafters of the Uniform Commercial Code thought that it was basically unfair for a seller to create an express warranty and then try to disclaim it, so they drafted §2-316(1) in such a way as to make disclaimer of an express warranty virtually impossible. Read it. The proper way to avoid liability for an express warranty is *not to make it in the first place*. Note that express warranties are created by *affirmative* seller conduct. The seller must take out an ad, publish a booklet, say something orally about the product, or point to a sample or model, or the warranty will never arise. Having done one of these things and created buyer expectations that the product will comply with the representations made, the seller must live with the liability assumed. See Official Comment 4 to §2-313; Travis v. Washington Horse Breeders Assn., 111 Wash. 2d 396, 759 P.2d 418, 6 U.C.C. Rep. Serv. 2d 1093 (1988).

Bell Sports, Inc. v. Yarusso

Supreme Court of Delaware, 2000
759 A.2d 582, 42 U.C.C. Rep. Serv. 2d 714

WALSH, Justice:

This is an appeal from a Superior Court denial of judgment as a matter of law, or alternatively, for a new trial following an award of damages in a product liability action. The defendant-appellant claims error on the part of the trial judge in ruling on the qualifications of plaintiff's expert witnesses and in permitting the substance of that testimony to establish a jury question on claims for breach of warranty. The appellant further asserts that the jury verdict was internally inconsistent and that the Superior Court should have declared a mistrial after discharging a juror for cause during trial. Upon careful review of the record, we conclude that the Superior Court did not abuse its discretion in permitting the testimony of plaintiff's experts nor in submitting the issues of breach of warranty to the jury. We further conclude that the jury's verdict did not lack consistency and that the refusal to grant a mistrial was not error.

I

On October 20, 1991, Brian J. Yarusso ("Yarusso"), then 22 years of age, was riding his off-road motorcycle[6] at a dirt motocross track located off Church Road in Newark, Delaware. Yarusso was wearing a full complement of safety equipment in addition to the helmet that is the subject of this dispute. While traveling over a series of dirt moguls, or bumps, Yarusso hit one of the moguls in such a way that he was catapulted over the handlebars of the motorcycle. He landed on his head, flipped over and came to rest face down in the dirt. As a result of his fall, Yarusso sustained a burst fracture of the C5 vertebral body and was rendered a quadriplegic.[7]

Yarusso filed suit in the Superior Court against Bell Sports, Inc. ("Bell"), the manufacturer of the Bell Moto-5 helmet he was wearing at the time of the accident. Yarusso's suit against Bell was predicated on a claim that the enhanced injuries he suffered were the proximate result of a defect in the helmet's design. The Bell Moto-5 is a full-face motocross helmet that was designed for off-road use. It complies with federal Department of Transportation ("DOT") standards and is also certified by the Snell Foundation, a leading worldwide helmet research and testing laboratory. The helmet is constructed of a fiberglass outer shell, an inner crushable liner, and a retention system consisting of a chinstrap and D-ring pull-tab. While all three of these components are designed to interact, the inner

6. "Off-road" motorcycles are equipped with motors, tires, seats and suspension components specifically designed to function effectively under adverse riding conditions typical of motocross tracks, woods and fields. They are generally much lighter in weight than motorcycles designed for street use, have a higher degree of suspension clearance/compliance and are usually not equipped with horns, lights and other features required for legal street operation.

7. Dr. Joseph Cusick, a neurosurgeon, described Yarusso's specific injuries. He testified that Yarusso's C5 vertebral body sustained major damage due to a "severe axiocompression load, usually . . . without much extension or flexion." The magnitude of the load was sufficient to crack the bone, push the spinal disk into the soft bone, and "explode" the disc into the spinal cord and some of the other disks.

liner is considered the most important safety feature of the helmet. The expanded polystyrene material of which this liner is primarily constructed is designed to compress upon contact with a solid object.

Yarusso's complaint contained alternative grounds for recovery. He alleged negligence in the design and construction of the helmet, breach of express warranties and breach of an implied warranty of merchantability. Yarusso's express warranty claim arose from specific textual representations in the helmet's accompanying owner's manual (the "manual"), the relevant portions of which are as follows (emphasis printed in manual also reproduced below):

> Five Year Limited Warranty: Any Bell helmet found by the factory to be defective in materials or workmanship within five years from the date of purchase will be repaired or replaced at the option of the manufacturer, free of charge, when received at the factory, freight pre-paid. . . . This warranty is expressly in lieu of all other warranties, and any implied warranties of merchantability or fitness for a particular purpose created hereby, are limited in duration to the same duration as the express warranty herein. Bell shall not be liable for any incidental or consequential damages. . . .
>
> Introduction: Your new Moto-5 helmet is another in the long line of innovative off-road helmets from Bell. . . . (T)he primary function of a helmet is to reduce the harmful effects of a blow to the head. However, it is important to recognize that the wearing of a helmet is not an assurance of absolute protection. NO HELMET CAN PROTECT THE WEARER AGAINST ALL FORESEEABLE IMPACTS.
>
> Helmet Performance: The Moto-5 is designed to absorb the force of a blow first by spreading it over as wide an area of the outer shell as possible, and second by the crushing of the non-resilient inner liner. Damage to the helmet after an impact is not a sign of any defect in the helmet design or construction. It is exactly what the helmet is designed to do.
>
> NOTICE: No helmet can protect the user from all foreseeable impacts. To obtain the maximum protection offered by any helmet, it must fit firmly on the head and the chinstrap must be securely fastened.

Yarusso testified at trial that he purchased this particular helmet based on the specific assertions, quoted above, that "(t)he primary function of a helmet is to reduce the harmful effects of a blow to the head."

Yarusso's implied warranty of merchantability claim arose out of his contention that the helmet was not merchantable because it was sold as an off-road helmet but was designed to function for "on-road" use. Because the helmet met DOT street helmet standards, Yarusso claimed that it was actually designed with a very stiff liner that would effectively function for on-road use but would not protect a rider against foreseeable off-road falls, where the impact surface could conceivably be softer.

A pivotal factual issue at trial was whether the helmet liner properly crushed, as designed, at the time Yarusso's head impacted the ground after his fall. Yarusso claimed that the injuries to his neck were caused by the stiffness or density of the liner material at the helmet crown. At trial, he offered expert testimony by Maurice Fox ("Fox"), a safety consultant who had been employed by a helmet manufacturer during the 1970s. Fox opined that Yarusso's helmet sustained the majority of the fall's impact at its crown where the liner was too dense to crush sufficiently, thereby transmitting excessive force to Yarusso's neck, resulting in his paralysis. Fox's testimony however, was directed primarily at Yarusso's negligence claim against Bell, which the jury subsequently rejected.

Joseph Cusick, M.D. ("Cusick"), a neurological expert, similarly testified that the neck injuries sustained by Yarusso were consistent with impact at the top, or crown, of the helmet. Cusick further testified that a 20-30% reduction of force to Yarusso's body would have been sufficient to avoid injury because his body would have been able to withstand this lower level of force.

Richard Stalnaker, Ph.D. ("Stalnaker"), a biomechanical engineer, also testified on behalf of Yarusso and largely affirmed Fox's opinion. His testimony was crucial in the jury's determination that Bell had breached express and implied warranties. Stalnaker determined that the force of Yarusso's impact with the ground was equivalent to 60 foot pounds, and that adequate crush of the helmet liner would have reduced it significantly to avert injury. Although Stalnaker modified the analytical process used to reconstruct the accident to coincide with that presented by Bell's expert reconstruction witness at trial, Bell's counsel rejected an opportunity to delay the trial and requested only a mistrial. Because the trial judge determined that the factual foundation for Stalnaker's testimony was unchanged despite his use of an alternative analytical, she denied the motion for mistrial leaving the matter for attack through cross-examination.

Bell offered its own expert testimony at trial disputing the helmet's point of impact from the accident and asserting the inability of any helmet to protect its user from severe neck injuries. The principal designer of the helmet, James Sundahl ("Sundahl"), testified that any helmet must be designed to protect its user from a multitude of accident types. He further opined that in circumstances involving a helmet's impact with a soft surface, the surface itself, rather than the helmet, absorbs a greater portion of the energy. When questioned about the representation in the helmet's manual, Sundahl testified that it was "wrong."

James McElhaney, Ph.D. ("McElhaney"), a professor of biomechanics at Duke University, testified for Bell and disputed Yarusso's contention that the helmet was impacted at its crown. McElhaney testified that the front of Yarusso's helmet liner was crushed in a fashion indicating a substantial blow to that area. Both Sundahl and McElhaney presented evidence of industry-wide research to the effect that no helmet can offer "any significant protection of the neck because the mass of the torso is so much more than the energy levels that a helmet can manage." Bell's experts claimed that this helmet and helmets in general are designed to protect users from head and brain injuries and the helmet in this case did precisely that.

Upon the conclusion of Yarusso's case, he abandoned his failure to warn claim. At the close of all the evidence, Bell moved for judgment as a matter of law as to liability. The trial court granted judgment as a matter of law on Yarusso's breach of implied warranty for a particular purpose claim, but denied Bell's motion on the remaining counts. The jury was then charged on the remaining claims of negligence, breach of implied warranty of merchantability and breach of express warranty.

On the second day of jury deliberations, one juror notified the trial court that he had reviewed outside information regarding motorcycle helmets in connection with securing a motorcycle licensing examiner's certificate. The jury also notified the court that they were deadlocked. The trial judge subsequently interrogated the juror who had disclosed his outside knowledge out of the presence of the remaining jurors. The trial judge determined that while the juror had not yet shared this extraneous information with other jurors, he had violated the direct instruction to decide the case solely from the evidence presented. The trial judge dismissed the juror prompting a motion from Bell for a mistrial, which was denied. Because both parties had agreed at the outset of the trial to accept a jury of eleven members, the remaining jurors were permitted to deliberate.

Through specific answers to interrogatories, the jury ultimately found that Bell was not negligent, but had breached an express or implied warranty, which proximately caused Yarusso's enhanced injury. Yarusso was awarded $1,812,000 in damages. Bell objected that the verdict was inconsistent and renewed its motions for judgment as a matter of law or alternatively for a new trial on liability only, all of which were denied by the Superior Court. This appeal followed. . . .

II

By its verdict, the jury specifically determined that Bell had not negligently designed the Moto-5 helmet but that Bell had breached "an express or implied warranty" when it sold the helmet and that "conduct proximately caused Brian Yarusso to suffer enhanced injuries." Bell argues on appeal that Yarusso failed, as a matter of law, to establish an evidentiary basis for recovery under either express or implied warranty and the trial court should have granted judgment in its favor as to those claims.

Preliminarily, we note that the jury was permitted to find liability under alternative forms of breach of warranty, express or implied, without differentiating between the two. Bell did not object to the warranty claims being submitted in that format and, thus, the verdict may be sustained if there is record and legal support for recovery under either theory.

A.

The statutory basis for a claim for damages based on breach of an express warranty arising out of a sale of goods under Delaware law is found in this State's counterpart of the Uniform Commercial Code. Title 6, section 2-313 [which the court quotes — Eds.].

The official commentary to that section under the U.C.C. indicates that the drafters intended its warranty provisions to be construed and applied liberally in favor of a buyer of goods. See U.C.C. §2-313 cmt. 1 (1977) ("Express warranties rest on 'dickered' aspects of the individual bargain, and go so clearly to the essence of that bargain that words of a disclaimer in a form are repugnant to the basic dickered terms."); U.C.C. §2-313 cmt. 3 ("In actual practice affirmations of fact made by a seller about the goods during a bargain are regarded as part of the description of those goods; hence no particular reliance on such statements need be shown in order to weave them into the fabric of the agreement."); U.C.C. §2-313 cmt. 4 ("[A] contract is normally a contract for a sale of something describable and described. A clause generally disclaiming 'all warranties, express or implied' cannot reduce the seller's obligation with respect to such description. . . ."). The language of the U.C.C.'s official commentary may be applied by analogy to the sale of goods governed by 6 Del. C. §2-313 in the reconciliation of any ensuing express warranty disputes. Thus, Bell's argument in this case that the express warranty terms in the manual are strictly limited to the "Five Year Limited Warranty" section, which also contained a purportedly effective disclaimer of those terms, is unfounded.

Formal wording is not necessary to create a warranty and a seller does not have to express any specific intention to create one. See Pack & Process, Inc. v. Celotex Corp., Del. Super., 503 A.2d 646, 658-59 (1985). Here the additional terms found in the manual's "Introduction" and "Helmet Performance" sections (stating that "the primary function of a helmet is to reduce the harmful effects of a blow to the head . . ." and ". . . the [helmet] is designed to absorb the force of a blow by spreading it over as wide an area of the outer shell as possible . . .") are textual representations constituting affirmations of fact upon which a buyer is entitled to rely. While this Court does not appear to have specifically addressed the issue, other courts have held that express warranties can arise from similar textual representations found in owners' manuals even where not specifically labeled as such. See e.g., Kinlaw v. Long Mfg. N.C., Inc., 298 N.C. 494, 259 S.E.2d 552, 557 (1979); Hawkins Constr. Co. v. Matthews Co., 190 Neb. 546, 209 N.W.2d 643, 654-55 (1973).

The restrictive provision of 6 Del. C. §2-316(1), renders Bell's effort to disclaim any express warranties in the manual's "Five Year Limited Warranty" ineffective as a matter of law. See U.C.C. §2-316(1) cmt. 1 (stating that "this section . . . seeks to protect a buyer from unexpected and unbargained language of disclaimer by denying effect to such language when inconsistent with language of express warranty. . . ."). While the manual contains disclaimers warning potential users that the helmet cannot prevent all injuries, other representations were made to assure a potential buyer that the helmet's liner was designed to reduce the harmful effects of a blow to the head. Those representations constituted essential elements of a valid express warranty that may not be effectively disclaimed as a matter of law. See Jensen v. Seigel Mobile Homes Group, 105 Idaho 189, 668 P.2d 65, 71-72 (1983) (holding that one principle of the law of warranty is to hold a seller responsible for its representations and assuring that a buyer receives that which he bargained for).

Bell argues that even if an express warranty was created and not effectively disclaimed here, the manual's textual representations promise only to prevent injuries to the head, not to a user's neck. Furthermore, Bell argues, the helmet's liner did crush as designed, thereby precluding a finding that the warranty was breached. Yarusso counters this argument by pointing out that injuries to the neck may logically follow a blow to the head, the helmet's liner did not sufficiently crush to prevent his injury and, as a result, he did not get what he bargained for. Upon review of the evidence, much of which was admittedly supplied by testimony of Yarusso's experts, the jury came to a logical conclusion that an express warranty was made in the helmet's manual. Upon consideration of this representation in relation to the specific facts of this case, they also concluded that the warranty was breached. In view of the evidence presented by the experts for both parties on the relationship between the helmet's design and the risk of neck injury, a factual predicate existed for the jury to determine whether there was a basis for recovery under the express warranty claim. The Superior Court did not err in submitting that issue to the jury.

B.

Our holding sustaining the jury's verdict on the claim of breach of express warranty renders an in-depth consideration of Bell's implied warranty arguments unnecessary, since the jury was permitted to find a breach of warranty on alternative grounds. The Superior Court in rejecting Bell's post-trial motions also declined to rule on the merits of Bell's attack on the implied warranty finding in view of the jury's finding of liability on the express warranty claim. We also are not required to address Bell's contention that Yarusso was obligated, as a matter of law, to present evidence of a safer alternative design. See Mazda Motor Corp. v. Lindahl, Del. Supr., 706 A.2d 526, 530 (1998). We note, however, that Yarusso's experts never claimed that a helmet can reduce the probability of a user's neck injury in all circumstances, and they were not required to present evidence that a helmet could be designed to achieve this. Expert evidence was presented, however, that a helmet could be designed with a softer liner that would, in theory, limit the amount of force placed on the user's neck, thereby reducing the probability of partial-load direct downward neck injuries, particularly upon impact with harder surfaces. There was, thus, a sufficient factual predicate for submission of the implied warranty claim to the jury.

III

In a related vein, Bell next argues that the jury's finding for Yarusso on breach of express and implied warranties is inconsistent with its finding that Bell was not negligent. Because the jury found no product defect leading to negligent conduct on Bell's part, it could not have properly found, the argument runs, that a defect existed in the helmet upon which any warranty claims relied. See Ruffin v. Shaw Indus., Inc., 4th Cir., 149 F.3d 294, 301 (1998) (holding that the requirements of both actions are nearly alike and that a finding on one claim often "applies equally" to the other); Prentis v. Yale Mfg. Co., 421 Mich. 670, 365 N.W.2d 176, 186 (1984) (both actions "involve identical evidence and require proof of exactly the same elements"). In essence, Bell contends that because its product was not defective, a verdict in favor of Yarusso on warranty and negligence claims was precluded.

A claim for breach of warranty, express or implied, is conceptually distinct from a negligence claim because the latter focuses on the manufacturer's conduct, whereas a breach of warranty claim evaluates the product itself. See Cline v. Prowler Indus. of Md., Inc., Del. Supr., 418 A.2d 968, 978, n.19 (1980) (the focus of a negligence claim is the manufacturer's conduct and the breach of an accepted standard of conduct); Borel v. Fibreboard Paper Prod. Corp., 5th Cir., 493 F.2d 1076, 1094 (1973) (in a products liability case with inconsistent verdicts, it is within the jury's prerogative so long as evidence supports the finding); Community Television Serv. v. Dresser Indus., Inc., D.S.D., 435 F. Supp. 214, 216 (1977) (jury could find defendant neither negligent nor strictly liable while finding as a matter of law that representations in a brochure created an express warranty that defendant breached). Based on the foregoing authorities, we find no fatal inconsistency between the jury's verdict negating negligence but finding breach of warranty. . . .

The judgment of the Superior Court is AFFIRMED.

PROBLEM 32

When Portia Moot went to buy a new car, she asked the salesman how many miles to the gallon it would get. He replied that it would get "between 30 and 35 MPG in the city and 40 to 45 on the highway." Delighted, she bought the car. The very best the car ever did, even in highway driving, was

27 MPG, and Portia was upset. When she threatened a lawsuit, the dealership pointed out the following three clauses in the contract she had signed that it relied on to avoid liability. This contract said nothing about miles per gallon of gas. In your opinion is there any way around these clauses?

(1) "This is the entire contract, and there are no other matters agreed to by the parties that are not contained herein."

(2) "There are no other express or implied warranties except those contained herein."

(3) "No salesperson has the authority to give express warranties other than those contained herein." (As to this last clause, see White & Summers §13-4, and the brief reference to the matter in Official Comment 2 to §2-316.)

2. Disclaiming Implied Warranties

In contrast to express warranties, implied warranties are much more easily disclaimed. Since they are created by the legislature of the enacting state and not by seller conduct, there is less unfairness in their destruction as long as the seller or the circumstances alert the buyer to the disclaimer. Read §§2-316(2) and 2-316(3) carefully.

Cate v. Dover Corp.

Texas Supreme Court, 1990
790 S.W.2d 559, 12 U.C.C. Rep. Serv. 2d 47

DOGGETT, J.

We consider the enforceability of a disclaimer of implied warranties. The trial court upheld the disclaimer and granted summary judgment in favor of Dover Corporation. The court of appeals affirmed. 776 S.W.2d 680. We reverse the judgment of the court of appeals and remand this cause to the trial court for further proceedings consistent with this opinion.

In September 1984, Edward Cate, doing business as Cate's Transmission Service, purchased from Beech Tire Mart three lifts manufactured and designed by Dover Corporation to elevate vehicles for maintenance. Despite repairs made by Beech and Dover, the lifts never functioned properly. Dover contends that Cate's subsequent claim against it for breach of the implied warranty of merchantability is barred by a disclaimer contained within a written, express warranty.

This warranty is set forth on a separate page headed in blue half inch block print, with the heading: "YOU CAN TAKE ROTARY'S NEW 5-YEAR WARRANTY AND TEAR IT APART." The statement is followed by bold black type stating, "And, when you are through, it'll be just as solid as the

No. 1 lift company in America, Rotary." The text of the warranty itself is in black type, contained within double blue lines, and appears under the blue three-eighths inch block print heading "WARRANTY." The disclaimer of implied warranties, although contained in a separate paragraph within the warranty text, is in the same typeface, size, and color as the remainder of the text.

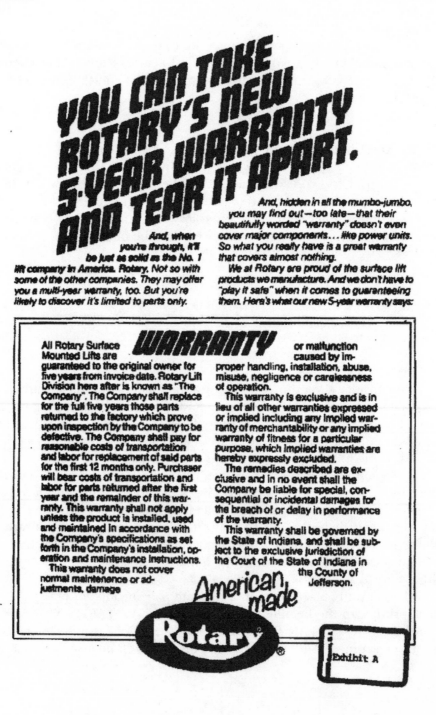

An implied warranty of merchantability arises in a contract for the sale of goods unless expressly excluded or modified by conspicuous language. Tex. Bus. & Com. Code Ann. §§2.314(a), 2.316(b) (Vernon 1968). Whether a particular disclaimer is conspicuous is a question of law to be determined by the following definition:

> A term or clause is conspicuous when it is so written that a reasonable person against whom it is to operate ought to have noticed it. A printed heading in capitals (as: NON-NEGOTIABLE BILL OF LADING) is conspicuous. Language in a body of a form is conspicuous if it is larger or of other contrasting type or color. But in a telegram, any stated term is conspicuous.

Id. §1.201(10). Further explanation is provided by comment 10 thereto:

> This [section] is intended to indicate some of the methods of making a term attention-calling. But the test is whether attention can reasonably be expected to be called to it.

In interpreting this language, Dover argues that a lesser standard of conspicuousness should apply to a disclaimer made to a merchant, such as Cate. Admittedly, an ambiguity is created by the requirement that disclaimer language be conspicuous to "a reasonable person *against whom it is to operate.*" Comment 10, however, clearly contemplated an objective standard, stating the test as "whether attention can reasonably be expected to be called to it."

We then turn to an application of an objective standard of conspicuousness to Dover's warranty. The top forty percent of the written warranty is devoted to extolling its virtues. The warranty itself, contained within double blue lines, is then set out in five paragraphs in normal black type under the heading "WARRANTY." Nothing distinguishes the third paragraph, which contains the exclusionary language. It is printed in the same typeface, size and color as the rest of the warranty text. Although the warranty in its entirety may be considered conspicuous, the disclaimer is hidden among attention-getting language purporting to grant the best warranty available. . . .

Although this is a case of first impression in Texas, the facts here parallel those reviewed in other states. In Massey-Ferguson, Inc. v. Utley, 439 S.W.2d 57, 59 (Ky. Ct. App. 1969), a disclaimer hidden under the heading "WARRANTY and AGREEMENT" was found not to be conspicuous:

> It is true that the *heading was* in large, bold-face type, but there was nothing to suggest that an exclusion was being made; on the contrary, the words of the headings indicated a *making* of warranties rather than a *disclaimer.*

(Emphasis in original.) Similarly, in Hartman v. Jensen's, Inc., 289 S.E.2d 648 (S.C. 1982), the court found that placing a disclaimer under the bold heading "Terms of Warranty" failed to alert the consumer to the fact that an exclusion was intended. Dover's disclaimer similarly fails to attract the attention of a reasonable person and is not conspicuous. . . .

Dover argues that even an inconspicuous disclaimer should be given effect because Cate had actual knowledge of it at the time of the purchase. Because the object of the conspicuousness requirement is to protect the buyer from surprise and an unknowing waiver of his or her rights, inconspicuous language is immaterial when the buyer has actual knowledge of the disclaimer. This knowledge can result from the buyer's prior dealings with the seller, or by the seller specifically bringing the inconspicuous waiver to the buyer's attention. The Code appears to recognize that actual knowledge of the disclaimer overrides the question of conspicuousness. For example, §2.316(b) does not mandate a written disclaimer of the implied warranty of merchantability but clearly provides that an oral disclaimer may be effective.[8] Similarly, §2.316(c)(3) allows an implied warranty to be excluded or modified by methods other than a conspicuous writing: course of dealing, course of performance, or usage of trade. When the buyer is not surprised by the disclaimer, insisting on compliance with the conspicuousness requirement serves no purpose. See R. Anderson, Uniform Commercial Code §2-316:49-50 (1983). The extent of a buyer's knowledge of a disclaimer of the implied warranty of merchantability is thus clearly relevant to a determination of its enforceability. See Singleton v. LaCoure, 712 S.W.2d 757, 759 (Tex. App. Houston [14th Dist.] 1986, *writ ref'd n.r.e.*) (relying in part on buyer's acknowledgement to enforce disclaimer). The seller has the burden of proving the buyer's actual knowledge of the disclaimer.

As this is a summary judgment case, the issue on appeal is whether Dover met its burden by establishing that there exists no genuine issue of material fact thereby entitling it to judgment as a matter of law. City of Houston v. Clear Creek Basin Authority, 589 S.W.2d 671, 678 (Tex. 1979). All doubts as to the existence of a genuine issue of material fact are resolved against the movant, and we must view the evidence in the light most favorable to the Petitioner. Great American Reserve Ins. Co. v. San Antonio Plumbing Supply Co., 391 S.W.2d 41, 47 (Tex. 1965). In support of its claim

---

8. Tex. Bus. & Com. Code §2.136, comment 1 (section seeks to protect buyer from unexpected and unbargained language of disclaimer by permitting exclusion of implied warranties only by conspicuous language or other circumstances which protect buyer from surprise); see also Weintraub, Disclaimer of Warranties and Limitation of Damages for Breach of Warranty Under the UCC, 53 Tex. L. Rev. 60, 66 (1974); J. White & R. Summers, Uniform Commercial Code §12-5, n.76 (2d ed. 1980) (seller may effectively disclaim by orally explaining inconspicuous written disclaimer, provided word "merchantability" used).

that Cate had actual knowledge of the disclaimer, Dover relies on Cate's deposition testimony, as follows:

> *Q:* you know, or do you remember what kinds of warranties you received when you bought the lifts?
> *A:* I may be wrong, but I think it was a five year warranty.
> *Q:* What was your understanding of that warranty?
> *A:* Any problems would be taken care of within the five year period.
> *Q:* Do you know if that warranty was from Beech Equipment, or from Dover?
> *A:* I believe it was from Dover.
> *Q:* Did you receive any written documentation in regard to that warranty?
> *A:* Yes, ma'am.

Although it is clear that Cate understood the warranty to extend for only five years, it is not clear that he understood any other limitations or exclusions. Merely providing a buyer a copy of documents containing an inconspicuous disclaimer does not establish actual knowledge. Dover has failed to establish that as a matter of law Cate had actual knowledge of the disclaimer.

We hold that, to be enforceable, a written disclaimer of the implied warranty of merchantability made in connection with a sale of goods must be conspicuous to a reasonable person. We further hold that such a disclaimer contained in text undistinguished in typeface, size or color within a form purporting to grant a warranty is not conspicuous, and is unenforceable unless the buyer has actual knowledge of the disclaimer. For the reasons stated herein, we reverse the judgment of the court of appeals and remand to the trial court for further proceedings consistent with this opinion.

SPEARS, J. concurs and files a separate opinion (in which MAUZY, J. joins).

RAY, J. files a concurring and dissenting opinion.

SPEARS, J. Although I concur in the court's opinion, I write separately to declare that the time has come for the legislature to consider the realities of the marketplace and prohibit all disclaimers of the implied warranties of merchantability and fitness.

These implied warranties, created by common-law courts long before the adoption of the UCC, developed to protect purchasers from losses suffered because of "the frustration of their expectations about the worth, efficacy, or desirability" of a product. W. Keeton, Prosser and Keeton on the Law of Torts §95A (5th ed. 1984). Implication of these warranties into every goods contract, without regard to the parties' actual assent to their terms, served "to police, to prevent, and to remedy" unfair consumer transactions. Llewellyn, On Warranty of Quality, and Society, 39 Colum. L. Rev. 699, 699 (1936); Humber v. Morton, 426 S.W.2d 554, 557-558 (Tex. 1968). These implied warranties also serve other important purposes: they create incentives to produce and market higher quality products; they discourage shoddy workmanship and unethical trade practices; and they place responsibility on those who profit from the sale of goods, have the greatest control over the products, and are better able to bear the risk of loss. See *Humber*, 426 S.W.2d at 562; Decker & Sons v. Capp, 139 Tex. 609, 610, 164 S.W.2d 828, 829 (1942). Section 2-316 of the U.C.C., however, subverts all of these purposes by giving sellers almost unlimited license to disclaim implied warranties.

We live in an age when sellers of goods "saturate the marketplace and all of our senses" with the most extraordinary claims about the worth of their products. Anderson, The Supreme Court of Texas and the Duty to Read the Contracts You Sign, 15 Tex. Tech L. Rev. 517, 544 (1984); Henningsen v. BloomField Motors, Inc., 161 A.2d 69, 84 (N.J. 1960). Yet, the same sellers under the carte blanche granted them by §2-316 of the U.C.C. refuse to guarantee and indeed expressly disclaim that their products are merchantable or even fit for their intended purposes. Under §2-316, not much is actually required for an effective disclaimer. To disclaim the implied warranty of merchantability the seller need only include the word "merchantability" in a conspicuous fashion. Tex. Bus. & Com. Code Ann. §2-316(b) (Vernon 1968). To disclaim the implied warranty of fitness the seller must use a writing and must make the disclaimer conspicuous. Id. at §2-316(2). No particular form of words is needed to disclaim an implied warranty of fitness, nor does §2-316 require the buyer to be actually aware of the disclaimer before it will be enforced. All implied warranties can be disclaimed by the mere inclusion of expressions like "as is" or "with all faults." Id. at §2-316, comment 1. Finally, as today's majority makes clear, §2-316 does not even require the disclaimer to be conspicuous if the buyer's actual knowledge of the disclaimer can be shown.

By establishing specific "requirements" for disclaimers §2-316 ostensibly "seeks to protect a buyer from unexpected and unbargained-for language of disclaimer." Tex. Bus. & Com. Code §2-316, comment 1 (Vernon 1968). In reality, however, §2-316 completely undermines implied warranties. Implicitly, §2-316 adopts the position that disclaimers should be enforced because society benefits when parties to a contract are allowed to set *all* the terms of their agreement. The problem with this position, and with §2-316 generally, is two-fold: it ignores the fact that governmental implication of protective terms into private contracts is commonplace (e.g., the *implied* warranties of merchantability and fitness); and, more importantly, it rests on the faulty premise that contractual disclaimers are generally freely bargained for elements of a contract.

Freedom of contract arguments generally, and §2-316 specifically, presuppose and are based on "the image of individuals meeting in the marketplace" on equal ground to negotiate the terms of a contract. Rakoff, Contracts of Adhesion: An Essay in Reconstruction, 96 Harv. L. Rev. 1174, 1216 (1983). At one time, this image may have accurately reflected marketplace realities. However, the last half of the twentieth century has witnessed "the rise of the corporation" and, increasingly, the displacement of physical persons as sellers in consumer and commercial contracts. Phillips, Unconscionability and Article 2 Implied Warranty Disclaimers, 62 Chi.-Kent L. Rev. 199, 239 (1985). This development has led to innumerable situations in which consumers deal from an unequal bargaining position, the most prominent example being the ubiquitous standard form contract which is now used by most sellers of goods and which invariably contains an implied warranty disclaimer. See Melody Home Mfg. Co. v. Barnes, 741 S.W.2d 349, 355 (Tex. 1987); *Henningsen*, 161 A.2d at 86-89; Slawson, Standard Form Contracts and Democratic Control of Lawmaking Power, 84 Harv. L. Rev. 529, 529 (1971) ("standard form contracts probably account for more than ninety-nine percent of all the contracts now made"); L. Vold, Handbook of the Law of Sales 447 (2d ed. 1959) (dramatic rise in corporate power has yielded the standard form contract whose terms are drafted by the seller and usually contain implied warranty disclaimers).

The great majority of buyers never read an implied warranty disclaimer found in a standard form contract.[9] Even when implied warranty disclaimers are read, their legal significance is not generally understood. Such disclaimers include unfamiliar terminology (e.g., "implied warranty of merchantability"), and comprehending their legal effect requires one not only to understand what substantive rights are involved, but also to grasp that these rights have been lost via the disclaimer. Phillips, Unconscionability and Article 2 Implied Warranty Disclaimers, 62 Chi.-Kent L. Rev. 199, 243 (1985); see also Federal Trade Commission, Facts for Consumers (Mar. 23, 1979) (more than 35% of those surveyed mistakenly believed that an

---

9. See Restatement (Second) of Contracts §211, Comment b (1981):

> A party who makes regular use of a standardized form of agreement does not ordinarily expect his customers to understand or even to read the standard terms. One purpose of standardization is to eliminate bargaining over details of individual transactions, and that purpose would not be served if a substantial number of customers retained counsel and reviewed the standard terms. . . . Customers do not in fact ordinarily understand or even read the standard terms.

Id.; see also Rakoff, Contracts of Adhesion: An Essay in Reconstruction, 96 Harv. L. Rev. 1174, 1179 n.21 (1983) (citing numerous commentators who declare that standard terms not read or understood, and some empirical studies asserting same proposition); Phillips, Unconscionability and Article 2 Implied Warranty Disclaimers, 62 Chi.-Kent L. Rev. 199, 243 (1985) (many sales do not involve a written sales contract that is presented before the goods change hands; usually, the disclaimer is inside the package and is not seen until after the sale is completed).

"as is" disclaimer meant the dealer would have to pay some, if not all, costs if a car broke down within 25 days of a sale). Finally, even if a buyer reads and understands an implied warranty disclaimer, chances are he will be without power to either strike these terms or "shop around" for better ones. If the buyer attempts the former, he will likely run into an employee who is unauthorized to alter the form contract; if he attempts the latter, he will likely confront a competitor who offers substantially the same form terms. *Henningsen*, 161 A.2d at 87. In short, the "marketplace reality" suggests that freedom of contract in the sale of goods is actually nonexistent; a buyer today can either take the contract with the disclaimer attached or leave it and go without the good. . . .

The realities of the modern marketplace demand that the legislature prohibit implied warranty disclaimers by repealing §2-316 of the U.C.C. Without such action, Texas courts will be forced to rely on "covert tools," such as the unconscionability provision in §2-302 or the "conspicuous" requirement in §2-316, to reach a just and fair result in disclaimer suits. When these tools are used, guidance, predictability and consistency in the law is sacrificed, while limited judicial resources are spent policing unjust bargains that could have been avoided. Were it up to the judicial branch, the courts could declare such disclaimers void as against public policy. If the legislature has the interests of Texas citizens at heart, it will repeal §2-316 because, no matter how conspicuous, such disclaimers are abusive of consumers.

MAUZY, J. joins in this concurring opinion.

RAY, J. I concur in that portion of the court's opinion requiring that a written disclaimer of the implied warranty of merchantability must be conspicuous to a reasonable person. I write separately, however, to take issue with the court's immediate erosion of that standard by permitting a showing of actual knowledge of the disclaimer to override a lack of conspicuousness.

The statute, on its face, provides for no actual knowledge exception. There is no room for judicial crafting of those omitted by the legislature. I would hold that the extent of a buyer's knowledge of a disclaimer is irrelevant to a determination of its enforceability under §2-316(b) of the U.C.C.

The effect of actual knowledge is subject to debate among leading commentators on commercial law. The purpose of the objective standard of conspicuousness adopted by the court today reflects the view that "the drafters intended a rigid adherence to the conspicuousness requirement in order to avoid arguments concerning what the parties said about the warranties at the time of the sale." J. White and R. Summers, Uniform Commercial Code §12-5 (2d ed. 1980). An absolute rule that an inconspicuous disclaimer is invalid, despite the buyer's actual knowledge, encourages sellers to make their disclaimers conspicuous, thereby reducing the need for courts to evaluate swearing matches as to actual awareness in particular cases. See W. Powers, Texas Products Liability Law §2.0723 (1989). Today's decision condemns our court to a parade of such cases.

PROBLEM 33

(a) A statement buried in the fine print of a used car purchase agreement states that "There are no express or implied warranties that are part of this sale." See §§2-316(2), 1-201(10).

(1) Are the implied warranties effectively disclaimed?

(2) If the car dealership asks you to redraft this clause so as to comply with the Code, what changes would you make in the language? See the extended discussion, particularly in the dissent, in Hicks v. Superior Court, 8 Cal. Rptr. 3d 703, 52 U.C.C. Rep. Serv. 2d 576 (Cal. App. 2004).

(3) What changes would you make in the physical appearance of the clause in the contract? Is it all right to put the disclaimer in a clause labeled *WARRANTY?* See Hartman v. Jensen's, Inc., 289 S.E.2d 648, 33 U.C.C. Rep. Serv. 889 (S.C. 1982).

(4) Can the car dealer win the legal dispute by arguing that usage of trade (§1-303(c)) permits the burial of warranty disclaimers in the fine print? (For an annotation collecting the automobile warranty disclaimer cases, see Annot., 54 A.L.R.3d 1217.)

(b) The words *AS IS* are written with soap in large letters across the front windshield of the used car. See §2-316(3)(a). Is this effective to disclaim implied warranties? Express warranties? Annot., 24 A.L.R.3d 465. Must the "as is" language be conspicuous? See §2-316(3)(a); Lumber Mut. Ins. Co. v. Clarklift of Detroit, Inc., 224 Mich. App. 737, 569 N.W.2d 681, 33 U.C.C. Rep. Serv. 2d 1105(1997); R. J. Robertson, Jr., A Modest Proposal Regarding the Enforceability of "As Is" Disclaimers of Implied Warranties: What the Buyer Doesn't Know Shouldn't Hurt Him, 99 Com. L.J. 1 (1994).

(c) The car salesman asks the buyer, "Would you like to examine the car?" and the buyer, who is in a hurry, says, "No." Effective disclaimer? See §2-316(3)(b); see also Official Comment 8.

(d) Remember Ted Traveler (Problem 20), who walked into the men's room of the bus depot and bought an expensive watch? We decided there was no warranty of title in that transaction. However, a warranty of quality is a separate question. Are there implied warranties in this sale? See §2-316(3)(c).

PROBLEM 34

Joe College bought a new car from Flash Motors, relying on the seller's extravagant claims about the car's superior qualities. He signed a purchase order on August 1, and the car was delivered two weeks later. In the glove compartment he found the warranty booklet and on reading it was dismayed to learn that the actual written warranty was very limited in coverage. Is he bound by the written warranty's terms? What argument can he make? See Comment 7 to §2-313; §2-209; White & Summers §13-5 at 582-583.

Bowdoin v. Showell Growers, Inc.

United States Court of Appeals, Eleventh Circuit, 1987
817 F.2d 1543, 3 U.C.C. Rep. Serv. 2d 1366

WISDOM, J.

This appeal raises a single question: whether the defendants effectively disclaimed the implied warranties of fitness and merchantability with respect to a high pressure spray rig that caused injuries to the plaintiffs. The district court concluded that a disclaimer found in the instruction manual that accompanied the spray rig when it was delivered to the purchaser was conspicuous and therefore effective. We disagree. Even assuming that the disclaimer was otherwise conspicuous, it was delivered to the purchaser *after* the sale. Such a post-sale disclaimer is not effective because it did not form a part of the basis of the bargain between the parties to the sale. The decision of the district court is therefore reversed.

FACTS

At the time this controversy arose, the plaintiffs in this action, Rachel and Billy Bowdoin, raised chickens in Sampson, Alabama, for Showell Growers, Inc., a Maryland corporation. Under their contract with Showell Growers, the Bowdoins were required once a year to give a thorough cleaning to their chicken house and the chicken coop pallets. To aid them in this annual task, Showell Growers lent the Bowdoins a high pressure spray rig. In December 1980, Mrs. Bowdoin was using the spray rig to clean the pallets when an article of her clothing caught in the safety shield covering the spray rig's power take-off shaft. Mrs. Bowdoin was pulled into the shaft and suffered severe injuries.

The spray rig in question was manufactured by FMC Corporation, an Illinois corporation. The safety shield and drive shaft component was manufactured for FMC by NEAPCO, Inc., a Pennsylvania corporation. Showell purchased the spray rig from FMC through an FMC dealer, Brushy Mountain Co-op of Moravian Falls, North Carolina. Two weeks after the sale, the spray rig was shipped to Brushy Mountain and then delivered to Showell Growers. An instruction manual was included with the spray rig when it was delivered to Showell Growers. The last page of the instruction manual included a purported warranty disclaimer, which stated: "*The foregoing warranty is expressly in lieu of any and all other warranties, express, implied, statutory or otherwise (including, but without limitation, the implied warranties of merchantability and fitness for a particular purpose). . . ."*

Usually, FMC required its dealer and the purchaser to complete an "agriculture delivery report" before a sale. The report contains a disclaimer of the implied warranties of fitness and merchantability. The purchaser is required to read the report and sign it acknowledging that he has read the warranty information. The report is then returned to FMC. The record shows that no agriculture delivery report was completed in connection with the purchase by Showell Growers.

In 1982, the Bowdoins filed a diversity action against Showell Growers and FMC in the United States District Court for the Northern District of Florida. The Bowdoins later added NEAPCO as a defendant. The Bowdoins sought to recover on a number of counts including one count alleging breach by FMC and NEAPCO of the implied warranties of fitness and merchantability. FMC and NEAPCO moved for summary judgment on this count. The district court concluded that the law of Alabama applied to the warranty claims and that under Alabama law, FMC and NEAPCO had effectively disclaimed the implied warranties with the disclaimer in the instruction manual. The district court therefore granted summary judgment in favor of FMC and NEAPCO, and dismissed with prejudice the Bowdoins' implied warranties claims.

The Bowdoins now appeal that ruling. The sole issue on appeal is whether the district court correctly determined that FMC and NEAPCO had effectively disclaimed the implied warranties. The Bowdoins contend that the district court's ruling in favor of FMC and NEAPCO is erroneous for several reasons: the disclaimer was not part of the bargain and is therefore ineffective; the disclaimer is not conspicuous as required under Alabama law; the spray rig comes within the classification of "consumer goods" and therefore a manufacturer cannot disclaim implied warranties; the disclaimer is unconscionable; and finally, even if the disclaimer is effective as to FMC, it is ineffective as to NEAPCO, which manufactured the drive shaft and safety shield component. We conclude that the disclaimer is ineffective as to both FMC and NEAPCO because it did not form a part of the basis of the bargain. We therefore do not reach the Bowdoins' other arguments.

DISCUSSION

Under the Uniform Commercial Code as adopted by Alabama and virtually every other state, a manufacturer may disclaim the implied warranties of merchantability and fitness provided that the disclaimer is in writing and conspicuous, and provided that the disclaimer is part of the parties' bargain. If a disclaimer was conspicuous to the purchaser *before the sale,* a court will generally hold the disclaimer effective based on the assumption that the disclaimer formed a part of the basis of the bargain. If, however, the disclaimer was not presented to the purchaser before the sale, the court will hold such a disclaimer ineffective because it did not form a part of the basis of the bargain. This "basis of the bargain" rule protects purchasers from unexpected and coercive disclaimers.

We turn now to determine whether the FMC disclaimer was a part of the basis of the bargain. The parties agree that for purposes of this analysis, the Bowdoins stand in the shoes of Showell Growers. The question therefore is whether the disclaimer is effective as to Showell Growers. We conclude that it is not.

Showell Growers purchased the spray rig at least two weeks before it was delivered. When the rig was delivered, an instruction manual was enclosed, and in that instruction manual is the disclaimer upon which FMC and NEAPCO rely. The disclaimer was never brought to Showell's attention.

Such a post-sale disclaimer is ineffective. "By definition, a disclaimer that appears for the first time after the sale in something supplied by the seller is not a part of the basis of the bargain and therefore is not binding on the buyer. Thus, the buyer is not bound by the disclaimer to which he had never agreed at the time of the sale and which first appears in the manufacturer's manual delivered to the buyer with the goods [or] the manufacturer's printed material brochure, or warranty booklet that accompanies the goods. . . ."[10]

The leading Alabama decision on disclaimers of implied warranties is in harmony with this position. In *Tiger Motor Co. v. McMurtry*, the Alabama Supreme Court addressed the validity of a disclaimer of implied warranties with respect to an automobile. The evidence showed that the day after the sale took place, the automobile was delivered to the purchaser along with the disclaimer. The evidence also showed that the disclaimer was never called to the purchaser's attention before the sale. The court concluded that the disclaimer was ineffective. Decisions of other courts construing the same provisions of the Uniform Commercial Code have also concluded that a post-sale disclaimer is not effective. [Citations omitted.]

FMC attempts to distinguish these cases on three grounds. First, FMC argues that unlike the purchasers involved in most of the cases, who were, for the most part, individual consumers, Showell Growers is a sophisticated commercial enterprise. But FMC has not offered and we have not found a post-sale disclaimer case in which such a distinction was material. Indeed, several of the cases in other states did involve commercial transactions between sophisticated commercial enterprises or businessmen, and the results reached were not affected: Courts consistently held that post-sale disclaimers were ineffective.

10. R. Anderson, 3 Uniform Commercial Code §2-316:32, p.345 (footnotes omitted).

FMC next argues that here the post-sale disclaimer was effective because it was conspicuous. Specifically, FMC asserts that the cases which have held post-sale disclaimers ineffective involved "egregious facts involving the combination of the failure of a disclaimer to be conspicuous and its appearance subsequent to the parties' transaction."

FMC's argument is, however, wrong on both the facts and the law. Several of the cases holding post-sale disclaimers ineffective did not even mention whether the disclaimer was otherwise conspicuous. And the cases to which FMC is apparently referring typically involved not one disclaimer but two: one in the sales contract and the other in a document delivered after the sale, such as an instruction manual or a warranty. In those cases, the courts held both disclaimers ineffective: the disclaimer in the sales contract because it was in small print and therefore not conspicuous, and the post-sale disclaimer because it was not a part of the basis of the bargain. In these cases, as in the cases involving only a post-sale disclaimer, the courts generally did not discuss whether the disclaimer was otherwise conspicuous. The absence of such a discussion is not surprising, because as a general rule the conspicuousness of a post-sale disclaimer is immaterial. By definition, a post-sale disclaimer is not conspicuous in the full sense of that term because the reasonable person against whom it is intended to operate could not have noticed it before the consummation of the transaction. A post-sale disclaimer is therefore not effective merely because it was otherwise conspicuous.

Finally, FMC argues that its post-sale disclaimer is effective because of prior dealings with Showell Growers that put Showell on notice that FMC's practice was to disclaim implied warranties with respect to high pressure spray rigs. Showell Growers had previously purchased an FMC spray rig similar to the one that caused Mrs. Bowdoin's injuries. The instruction manual accompanying the first spray rig contained a disclaimer of implied warranties, and according to one Showell employee, that instruction manual appeared to be identical to the one accompanying the spray rig in question. From this, FMC argues that Showell was on notice that FMC was disclaiming the implied warranties with respect to the second spray rig.

This argument misses the point. Even assuming that the mere similar appearance of two instruction manuals could put a purchaser on notice that a disclaimer in the first would also be found in the second, FMC's argument fails for the same reason its argument that a post-sale disclaimer can be effective if it was otherwise conspicuous failed. A disclaimer must be conspicuous before the sale, for only then will the law presume that the disclaimer was part of the bargain. In this case, Showell Growers did not receive the second instruction manual until after the second sale was consummated. The disclaimer in that instruction manual was therefore without significance. This is not less true merely because earlier Showell had received a similar instruction manual. Until it received the second instruction manual, it could not know what it would look like or what it would contain.

CONCLUSION

We conclude that the post-sale disclaimer of implied warranties found in the instruction manual that accompanied the FMC spray rig is ineffective because it did not form a part of the basis of the bargain. The decision of the district court is therefore reversed, and the district court is instructed to reinstate the Bowdoins' breach of implied warranties of fitness and merchantability claims against FMC and NEAPCO.

Rinaldi v. Iomega Corp.

Delaware Superior Court, 1999
41 U.C.C. Rep. Serv. 2d 1143

COOCH, J.

I.   INTRODUCTION: FACTUAL AND PROCEDURAL HISTORY

This proposed class action was commenced in September 1998 on behalf of all persons who have purchased purportedly defective "Zip drives" from January 1, 1995 to the present. The Zip drives are manufactured by defendant Iomega Corporation, a computer storage device maker incorporated in Delaware and based in Utah. A Zip drive is a large capacity personal computer data storage drive. The complaint alleges inter alia that the alleged defect, said by Plaintiffs to be commonly known as the "Click of Death," causes irreparable damage to the removable magnetic media storage disks on which the drives store data. Plaintiffs also allege that the defect renders the data on the disks unreadable and that when another drive attempts to read the data from a disk that has been infected, the defect transfers to the second drive, causing further damage.

Plaintiffs' complaint has four counts. Count I alleges that Defendant breached the implied warranty of merchantability by manufacturing a product that was not fit for the ordinary purpose for which such products are used and that Defendant's disclaimer of the implied warranty of merchantability contained in the packaging of the product was ineffective because it was not sufficiently "conspicuous" as required by 6 Del. C. §2-316(2). Count II alleges that Defendant was negligent in manufacturing and designing the Zip drive without using the reasonable care, skill, and diligence required when placing such a product into the stream of commerce. Count III alleges that Defendant committed consumer fraud in violation of the Delaware Consumer Fraud Act by falsely misrepresenting through advertising to the consuming public that the Zip drives were suitable for their intended purpose. Count IV alleges that Defendant was negligent in failing to warn the consuming public about the risks of its product when it knew or should have known that the product could cause damage when used for its intended purpose. . . .

Defendant's Motion to Dismiss Count I on the grounds that Plaintiffs have failed to state a claim for breach of the implied warranty of merchantability is GRANTED since the Court finds that the disclaimer is "conspicuous." . . .

Defendant contends that Plaintiffs' claim for breach of the implied warranty of merchantability has failed to state a claim because Defendant's disclaimer of the implied warranty of merchantability, contained within the packaging of the Zip drive, effectively disclaimed all liability. The sole issue to be resolved here is whether Count I of the complaint should be dismissed because Defendant's disclaimer of the implied warranty of merchantability was not "conspicuous," as required by 6 Del. C. §2-316, because the disclaimer was contained within the packaging of the Zip drive product itself and therefore not "discovered" by the purchaser prior to the purchaser's purchase of the product.

Defendant's disclaimer inside the Zip drive package provides:

EXCEPT AS STATED ABOVE IN THIS PARAGRAPH, THE FOREGOING WARRANTIES ARE IN LIEU OF ALL OTHER CONDITIONS OR WARRANTIES, EXPRESS, IMPLIED, OR STATUTORY, INCLUDING, WITHOUT LIMITATION, ANY IMPLIED CONDITION OR WARRANTY OF MERCHANTABILITY OR FITNESS FOR A PARTICULAR PURPOSE AND OF ANY OTHER WARRANTY OBLIGATION ON THE PART OF IOMEGA (capitals in original).

The above disclaimer appears near the bottom of a document labeled "IOMEGA LIMITED WARRANTY" located inside the packaging.

6 Del. C. §2-316(2) provides, in pertinent part, ". . . to exclude or modify the implied warranty of merchantability or any part of it the language must mention merchantability and in the case of a writing must be conspicuous. . . ." 6 Del. C. §2-316(2) is identical to §2-316(2) of the Uniform Commercial Code.

The usual arguments concerning the conspicuousness requirement of U.C.C. §2-316(2) have been based on issues such as the size of the type set and the location of the disclaimer in the warranty itself. Defendant contends that the conspicuousness requirement has been met regardless of the location of the disclaimer inside the Zip drive package so long as the disclaimer is "noticeable and easily readable." Defendant asserts that "modern commercial realities of how contracts are formed with consumers of prepackaged products necessitates that the terms of [its] warranty disclaimer be given effect."

Plaintiffs do not claim that the disclaimer was improperly worded, that the text of the disclaimer was improperly placed in the rest of the warranty or that the typeface of the disclaimer was too small, but instead argue that the disclaimer, located in the packaging of the product, could not realistically be called to the attention of the consumer until after the sale had been consummated, thus rendering the disclaimer not "conspicuous" as a matter or law and therefore ineffective. Although similar issues of additional terms to a contract such as a shrinkwrap license,[11] an arbitration clause[12] and a license agreement,[13] each physically located within the packaging of the product, has been litigated in other jurisdictions, the parties have cited no case directly addressing the effectiveness, under U.C.C. §2-316(2), of a disclaimer of the implied warranty of merchantability by virtue of its location within the packaging of a product itself, nor has the Court found any such case.

The issue of conspicuousness, generally, under §2-316 has been the topic of various law review articles, periodicals and texts,[14] and has been the subject of much litigation. As stated, however, no authorities have been located that squarely addressed the issue in this case. The traditional focus has been on the "mention"[15] of merchantability and the visible characteristics of the disclaimer, such as type set and location within the warranty document itself. In determining if a disclaimer of the implied warranty of merchantability is effective as being "conspicuous," the secondary authorities and courts have often looked to the purpose of §2-316.[16] The purpose of that section is to "protect a buyer from unexpected and unbargained for language of disclaimer."[17] That purpose is the real backbone in determining if a disclaimer is conspicuous when looking at factors beyond the mentioning of merchantability and type set.

---

11. ProCD, Inc. v. Zeidenberg, 7th Cir., 86 F.3d 1447 (1996).

12. Hill v. Gateway 2000, Inc., 7th Cir., 105 F.3d 1147 (1997), *cert. denied*, 118 S. Ct. 47 (1997).

13. M.A. Mortenson Co. v. Timberline Software Corp., Wash. App., 970 P.2d 803 (1999).

14. See, e.g., Bernard F. Kistler, Jr., U.C.C. Article Two Warranty Disclaimers and the "Conspicuousness" Requirement of Section 2-316, 43 Mercer L. Rev. 943, 945-953 (1992); Jeffrey C. Selman and Christopher S. Chen, Steering the Titanic Clear of the Iceberg: Saving the Sale of Software From the Perils of Warranties, 31 U.S.F. L. Rev. 531, 533-536 (1997); William H. Danne, Jr., Construction and Effect of UCC §2-316(2) Providing That Implied Warranty Disclaimer Must Be "Conspicuous," 73 A.L.R.3d 248, Vol. 73 (1976).

15. 6 Del. C. §2-316(2).

16. Ronald A. Anderson, Anderson on the Uniform Commercial Code, §2-316:144-153 (3d ed. 1983); Debra L. Goetz, Special Project: Article Two Warranties in Commercial Transactions, An Update, 72 Cornell L. Rev. 1159, 1264-1275 (1978).

17. U.C.C. §2-316 cmt. 1 (1962).

Analogous support for this Court's conclusion that the physical location of the disclaimer of the implied warranty of merchantability inside the Zip drive packaging does not make the disclaimer inconspicuous can be found in some cases from other jurisdictions. In *ProCD, Inc. v. Zeidenberg*,[18] the Seventh Circuit held that a shrinkwrap license located inside the packaging of the computer program was enforceable as an additional term of the contract, and stated that the commercial practicalities of modern retail purchasing dictate where terms such as a shrinkwrap license should be located. The *ProCD* court held that it would be otherwise impractical for these additional terms to be located on the outside of the box in "microscopic" type. The *ProCD* court stated, "[t]ransactions in which the exchange of money precedes the communication of detailed terms are common." The *ProCD* court then looked to other sections of the U.C.C. that dealt with the issue in terms of acceptance and rejection of goods: "A buyer accepts goods under §2-606(1)(b) when, after an opportunity to inspect, [the buyer] fails to make an effective rejection under §2-602(1). [The seller] extended an opportunity to reject if a buyer should find the license unsatisfactory." The *ProCD* court continued its analysis and observed that

> [c]onsumer goods work the same way. Someone who wants to buy a radio set visits a store, pays and walks out with a box. Inside the box is a leaflet containing some terms, the most important of which usually is the warranty, read for the first time in the comfort of home. By [the buyer's] lights, the warranty in the box is irrelevant; every consumer gets the standard warranty implied by the UCC in the event the contract is silent; yet so far as we are aware no state disregards warranties furnished with consumer products.[19]

Plaintiffs argue that *ProCD* is inapposite because it specifically concerned the validity of a shrinkwrap license which is not governed by U.C.C. §2-316(2). Although that is correct, *ProCD* stressed that "the U.C.C. . . . permits parties to structure their relations so that the buyer has a chance to make a final decision after a detailed review" of the contract terms.[20] All of the additional terms, which included the shrinkwrap license, became part of the contract in *ProCD*.

In *Hill v. Gateway 2000, Inc.*,[21] the Seventh Circuit relied on *ProCD* in holding that an arbitration clause located inside the packaging of a computer was enforceable as an additional term to the contract, and stated, "[p]ractical considerations support allowing vendors to enclose the full legal terms with their products. . . . [C]ustomers as a group are better off when vendors skip costly and ineffectual steps such as telephonic recitation,

18. 7th Cir., 86 F.3d at 1447.
19. Id. at 152.
20. Id. at 1453.
21. 7th Cir., 105 F.3d at 1147.

and use instead a simple approve-or-return device."[22] In holding that the arbitration clause was effective, the Hill court concluded that an additional term physically located outside of the contract was nevertheless an enforceable term of the contract.

In *M.A. Mortenson Co. v. Timberline Software Corp.*,[23] the Washington Court of Appeals relied on *ProCD* and *Hill* and held that a licensing agreement located inside the packaging of a software program was enforceable as an additional term to the contract. In *Mortenson* the court stated, ". . . the terms of the present license agreement are part of the contract as formed between parties. We find that [the purchaser's] installation and use of the software manifested its assent to the terms of the license. . . ."[24] As in *ProCD* and *Hill,* the *Mortenson* court held that a licensing agreement located within the packaging of the product, not in the contract itself, was an enforceable additional term of the contract.

Other courts have also addressed the issue of the physical location of the disclaimer of the implied warranty of merchantability from different perspectives. Thus in *Step-Saver Data Systems, Inc. v. Wyse Technology*,[25] the United States District Court for the Eastern District of Pennsylvania discussed the location of a disclaimer of the implied warranty of merchantability inside computer software packaging and held the location of an additional term (in *Step-Saver*, a disclaimer) is to be considered independently of conspicuousness. The *Step-Saver* court held that "[t]here is no question that pursuant to the U.C.C., limitation of warranty and remedies are valid when packaged with the product so long as the limitation is clear, conspicuous and one that a reasonable person would have noticed and understood."[26] The holding in *Step-Saver* that conspicuousness and location are to be considered independently is not directly on point with the issue at bar. However, the *Step-Saver* court relied on the purpose behind §2-316 in finding that so long as a disclaimer of the implied warranty of merchantability is one that could be noticed and understood, the disclaimer is conspicuous.

This Court has addressed the issue of conspicuousness under §2-316(2) in *Lecates v. Hertrick Pontiac Buick Co.*[27] In *Lecates*, a case on which Plaintiffs rely, the issue was whether the implied warranties were effectively disclaimed by an automobile dealer when the car that was sold malfunctioned, causing physical injuries. The court held that the seller's disclaimer of the implied warranty of merchantability located in a sales invoice satisfied the conspicuous requirement of §2-316(2). In *Lecates*, the specific question was whether

---

22. Id. at 1149.
23. 970 P.2d at 803.
24. Id. at 831.
25. E.D. Pa., C.A. No. 89-7203, 1990 WL 87334, Broderick, J. (June 21, 1990).
26. Id. at *7.
27. Del. Super., 515 A.2d 163 (1986).

or not the disclaimer had been delivered by the seller to the buyer only after the sale had already been consummated. The *Lecates* court addressed this narrow issue in light of the specific facts in that case and observed that disclaimer clauses have been held ineffective "if it appeared that the documents in which such clauses appeared were given to the buyer after the sale had been consummated."[28]*Lecates* addressed the issue of what terms and conditions were a part of the contract at the point of contract consummation, but here, Defendant's disclaimer of the implied warranty of merchantability was an additional term of each contract between each plaintiff and Defendant to purchase the Zip drives. Defendant's sales of the Zip drives to the six plaintiffs were each not "consummated" until after each plaintiff had had an opportunity to inspect and then to reject or to accept the product with the additional terms that were enclosed within the packaging of the Zip drive.

The commercial practicalities of modern retail purchasing make it eminently reasonable for a seller of a product such as a Zip drive to place a disclaimer of the implied warranty of merchantability within the plastic packaging. The buyer can read the disclaimer after payment for the Zip drive and then later have the opportunity to reject the contract terms (i.e., the disclaimer) if the buyer so chooses. This Court concludes that Defendant's disclaimer of the implied warranty of merchantability was effective despite its physical placement inside the packaging of the Zip drive and has satisfied the conspicuousness requirement of 6 Del. C. §2-316(2).

Defendant's Motion to Dismiss Count I on the grounds that Plaintiffs have failed to state a claim for breach of the implied warranty of merchantability is granted. . . .

QUESTION

Do these last two cases conflict? If so, which is right and which wrong? The second case, of course, is part of the "rolling contracts" theory of offer and acceptance advanced in cases such as the Seventh Circuit's famous *ProCD* opinion, discussed earlier in this book at pages 73-80.

We will return to the issue of whether the buyer can return a defective item directly to the manufacturer in Problem 64 later in the book. Note that even if a seller disclaimed all express and implied warranties, there could still be liability for breach of the obligation of good faith, such as where the goods sold were virtually unusable. See Accessdata Corporation, v. Alste Technologies GmbH, 2009 WL 2338172 (D. Utah 2009).

---

28. Id. at 170.

3. Limitations on the Warranty

Sometimes a seller is willing to give a warranty to the buyer, but wants in some way to limit the scope of the liability that a breach creates. The Code permits such a limitation, but puts various restrictions on its use. Read §§2-316(4) and 2-719.

Wilson Trading Corp. v. David Ferguson, Ltd.

Court of Appeals of New York, 1968
23 N.Y.2d 398, 244 N.E.2d 685, 297 N.Y.S.2d 108, 5 U.C.C. Rep. Serv. 1213

JASEN, J.

The plaintiff, the Wilson Trading Corporation, entered into a contract of sale with the defendant, David Ferguson, Ltd., for the sale of a specified quantity of yarn. After the yarn was delivered, cut and knitted into sweaters, the finished product was washed. It was during this washing that it was discovered that the color of the yarn had "shaded"—that is, "there was a variation of color from piece to piece and within the pieces." This defect, the defendant claims, rendered the sweaters "unmarketable."

This action for the contract price of the yarn was commenced after the defendant refused payment. As a defense to the action and as a counter-claim for damages, the defendant alleges that "[p]laintiff has failed to perform all of the conditions of the contract on its part required to be performed, and has delivered . . . defective and unworkmanlike goods."

The sales contract provides in pertinent part:

> 2. No claims relating to excessive moisture content, short weight, count variations, twist, quality or shade shall be allowed *if made after weaving, knitting, or processing*, or more than 10 days after receipt of shipment. . . . The buyer shall within 10 days of the receipt of the merchandise by himself or agent examine the merchandise for any and all defects. [Emphasis supplied.]
>
> 4. This instrument constitutes the entire agreement between the parties, superseding all previous communications, oral or written, and no changes, amendments or additions hereto will be recognized unless in writing signed by both seller and buyer or buyer's agent. It is expressly agreed that no representations or warranties, express or implied, have been or are made by the seller except as stated herein, and the seller makes no warranty, express or implied, as to the fitness for buyer's purposes of yarn purchased hereunder, seller's obligations, except as expressly stated herein, being limited to the *delivery of good merchantable yarn of the description stated herein*. [Emphasis supplied.]

Special Term granted plaintiff summary judgment for the contract price of the yarn sold on the ground that "notice of the alleged breach of warranty for defect in shading was not given within the time expressly limited and is not now available by way of defense or counterclaim." The Appellate Division affirmed, without opinion.

The defendant on this appeal urges that the time limitation provision on claims in the contract was unreasonable since the defect in the color of the yarn was latent and could not be discovered until after the yarn was processed and the finished product washed.

Defendant's affidavits allege that its sweaters were rendered unsaleable because of latent defects in the yarn which caused "variation in color from piece to piece and within the pieces." This allegation is sufficient to create a question of fact concerning the merchantability of the yarn (Uniform Commercial Code, §2-314, subd. [2]). Indeed, the plaintiff does not seriously dispute the fact that its yarn was unmerchantable, but instead, like Special Term, relies upon the failure of defendant to give notice of the breach of warranty within the time limits prescribed by paragraph two of the contract.

Subdivision (3) (par. [a]) of section 2-607 of the Uniform Commercial Code expressly provides that a buyer who accepts goods has a reasonable time after he discovers or should have discovered a breach to notify the seller of such breach. (Cf. 5 Williston, Contracts [3d ed.] §173.) Defendant's affidavits allege that a claim was made immediately upon discovery of the breach of warranty after the yarn was knitted and washed, and that this was the earliest possible moment that the defects could reasonably be discovered in the normal manufacturing process. Defendant's affidavits are, therefore, sufficient to create a question of fact concerning whether notice of the latent defects alleged was given within a reasonable time. (Cf. Ann., 17 A.L.R.3d 1010, 1112-1115 [1968]).

However, the Uniform Commercial Code allows the parties, within limits established by the code, to modify or exclude warranties and to limit remedies for breach of warranty. The courts below have found that the sales contract bars all claims not made before knitting and processing. Concededly, defendant discovered and gave notice of the alleged breach of warranty after knitting and washing.

We are, therefore, confronted with the effect to be given the time limitation provision in paragraph two of the contract. Analytically, paragraph two presents separate and distinct issues concerning its effect as a valid limitation on remedies for breach of warranty (Uniform Commercial Code, §§2-316, subd. [4]; 2-719) and its effect as a modification of the express warranty of merchantability (Uniform Commercial Code, §2-316, subd. [1]) established by paragraph four of the contract.

Parties to a contract are given broad latitude within which to fashion their own remedies for breach of contract (Uniform Commercial Code, §2-316, subd. [4]; §§2-718; 2-719). Nevertheless, it is clear from the official section 2-719 of the Uniform Commercial Code that it is the very essence of a sale contract that at least minimum adequate remedies be available for its breach. "If the parties intend to conclude a contract for sale within this Article they must accept the legal consequence that there be at least a fair quantum of remedy for breach of the obligations or duties outlined in the contract. Thus any clause purporting to modify or limit the remedial provisions of this Article in an *unconscionable manner* is subject to deletion and in that event the remedies made available by this Article are applicable as if the striken clause had never existed." (Uniform Commercial Code, §2-719, official comment 1; emphasis supplied.)

It follows that contractual limitations upon remedies are generally to be enforced unless unconscionable. This analysis is buttressed by the fact that the official comments to section 2-302 of the Uniform Commercial Code, the code provision pertaining to unconscionable contracts or clauses, cites Kansas City Wholesale Grocery Co. v. Weber Packing Corp. (93 Utah 414 [1937]), a case invalidating a time limitation provision as applied to latent defects, as illustrating the underlying basis for section 2-302. . . .

However, it is unnecessary to decide the issue of whether the time limitation is unconscionable on this appeal for section 2-719, subd. (2) of the Uniform Commercial Code provides that the general remedy provisions of the code apply when "circumstances cause an exclusive or limited remedy to fail of its essential purpose." As explained by the official comments to this section: "where an apparently fair and reasonable clause because of circumstances fails in its purpose or operates to deprive either party of the substantial value of the bargain, it must give way to the general remedy provisions of this Article." (Uniform Commercial Code, §2-719, official comment 1.) Here, paragraph 2 of the contract bars all claims for shade and other specified defects made after knitting and processing. Its effect is to eliminate any remedy for shade defects not reasonably discoverable within the time limitation period. It is true that parties may set by agreement any time not manifestly unreasonable whenever the code "requires any action to be taken within a reasonable time" (Uniform Commercial Code, §1-204, subd. [1][29]), but here the time provision eliminates all remedy for defects not discoverable before knitting and processing and section 2-719, subd. (2) of the Uniform Commercial Code therefore applies.

Defendant's affidavits allege that sweaters manufactured from the yarn were rendered unmarketable because of latent shading defects not reasonably discoverable before knitting and processing of the yarn into sweaters. If these factual allegations are established at trial, the limited remedy established by paragraph two has failed its "essential purpose" and the buyer is, in effect, without remedy. The time limitation clause of the contract must give way to the general code rule that a buyer has a

---

29. Now §1-302(b) —Eds.

reasonable time to notify the seller of breach of contract after he discovers or should have discovered the defect. (Uniform Commercial Code, §2-207, subd. [3], par. [a].) As indicated above, defendant's affidavits are sufficient to create a question of fact concerning whether notice was given within a reasonable time after the shading defect should have been discovered.

It can be argued that paragraph two of the contract, insofar as it bars all claims for enumerated defects not reasonably discoverable within the time period established, purports to exclude these defects from the coverage of the express warranty of merchantability. By this analysis, the contract not only limits its remedies for its breach, but also purports to modify the warranty of merchantability. An attempt to both warrant and refuse to warrant goods creates an ambiguity which can only be resolved by making one term yield to the other (cf. Hawkland, Limitation of Warranty under the Uniform Commercial Code, 11 How. L.J. 28 [1965]). Section 2-316 (subd. [1]) of the Uniform Commercial Code provides that warranty language prevails over the disclaimer if the two cannot be reasonably reconciled.

Here, the contract expressly creates an unlimited express warranty of merchantability while in a separate clause purports to indirectly modify the warranty without expressly mentioning the word merchantability. Under these circumstances, the language creating the unlimited express warranty must prevail over the time limitation insofar as the latter modifies the warranty. It follows that the express warranty of merchantability includes latent shading defects and defendant may claim for such defects not reasonably discoverable within the time limits established by the contract if plaintiff was notified of these defects within a reasonable time after they should have been discovered. . . .

In sum, there are factual issues for trial concerning whether the shading defects alleged were discoverable before knitting and processing, and if not, whether notice of the defects was given within a reasonable time after the defects were or should have been discovered. If the shading defects were not reasonably discoverable before knitting and processing and notice was given within a reasonable time after the defects were or should have been discovered, a further factual issue of whether the sweaters were rendered unsaleable because of the defect is presented for trial.

The order of the Appellate Division should be reversed, with costs, and plaintiff's motion for summary judgment should be denied.

Chief Judge FULD (concurring). I agree that there should be a reversal but on the sole ground that a substantial question of fact has been raised as to whether the clause limiting the time in which to make a claim is "manifestly unreasonable" (Uniform Commercial Code, §1-204[30]) as

---

30. Now §1-302(b) — EDS.

applied to the type of defect here complained of. In this view, it is not necessary to consider the relevancy, if any, of other provisions of the Uniform Commercial Code (e.g., §§2-302, 2-316, 2-719), dealing with "unconscionable" contracts or clauses, exclusion of implied warranties or limitations on damages.

PROBLEM 35

On November 1, Jack Frost of Portland, Maine, bought a snowmobile from King Cold Recreationland. Jack used the snowmobile to get to work during the week in the winter and for fun on the weekends. The contract that he signed stated that the seller warranted that the vehicle was merchantable, but that, in the event of breach, "the buyer's remedy was limited solely to repair or replacement of defective parts." Moreover, the contract conspicuously stated that the seller was not responsible for "any consequential damages."

One week after he received the snowmobile, Jack noticed a strange rumble in the engine. He took the machine back to the King Cold service department. The machine was returned to him in three days allegedly repaired. These events repeated themselves three times over the next three weeks. Four weeks after he bought the snowmobile, Frost was seriously injured when it blew up while he was riding it. The machine, which cost $1,200, was destroyed. Frost temporarily lost the use of his left arm, incurred hospital expenses of $2,500, and lost pay of $1,600. Moreover, when he did return to work, he had to rent a snowmobile for $40 a week until spring (16 weeks — spring is very late in Maine). In addition, a $350 camera he was carrying was also destroyed. Frost brought suit against King Cold. King Cold defended on the ground that its liability was limited to the cost of repair or replacement. Frost argued that the remedy limitation was "unconscionable" and failed of its "essential purpose." All the parties pointed to §§2-316(4), 2-302, 2-719, and 2-715. How should this suit come out? See Beal v. General Motors Corp., 354 F. Supp. 423 (D. Del. 1973); Earl M. Jorgensen Co. v. Mark Constr., Inc., 56 Haw. 466, 540 P.2d 978, 17 U.C.C. Rep. Serv. 1126 (1975).

———————————

The New Jersey Supreme Court has produced two leading opinions on the validity of a disclaimer of liability for consequential damages in automobile tire blowout cases. In Collins v. Uniroyal, Inc., 64 N.J. 260, 315 A.2d 16, 14 U.C.C. Rep. Serv. 294 (1974), a consumer was killed in an automobile accident when his right rear tire failed. The tire manufacturer tried to avoid §2-719(3) by saying that its disclaimer of liability for personal injury damages overcame the prima facie presumption of unconscionability because its warranty made a conspicuous statement limiting the remedy for blowout to repair or replacement. The court held that this argument was not "consonant with the commercial and human realities," and added:

> A tire manufacturer warrants against blowouts in order to increase tire sales. Public advertising by defendant relative to these tires stated: "If it only saves your life once, it's a bargain." The seller should be held to realize that the purchaser of a tire buying it because so warranted is far more likely to have made the purchase decision in order to protect himself and the passengers in his car from death or personal injury in a blowout accident than to assure himself of a refund of the price of the tire in such an event. That being the natural reliance and the reasonable expectation of the purchaser flowing from the warranty, it appears to us patently unconscionable for the manufacturer to be permitted to limit his damages for a breach of warranty proximately resulting in the purchaser's death to a price refund or replacement of the tire.

In a later case, no personal injury occurred, but the car was destroyed when the tire blew. The tire manufacturer argued that since §2-719(3)'s "prima facie unconscionable" language applies only to "injury to the person," the consumer was limited in her recovery to a replacement of the defective tire. The New Jersey Supreme Court, however, still applied §2-719(3) because it found the warranty limitation to be "seriously lacking in clarity." The court stated:

> [T]he booklet presents the owner with a linguistic maze. Throughout the document there is an admixture of terms relating to quality, capacity, and performance, together with disclaimers and exclusions of coverage, as well as limitations and restrictions upon liability and remedies. There are fulsome and repeated references to the term "guarantee," seemingly relating to quality and performance followed by the rather sudden, isolated use of the term "promise," purportedly limiting the entire contractual undertaking to tire replacement. What is thus given to a purchaser is not a simple and straight-forward document defining on the one hand that which constitutes an affirmation of quality or performance and, on the other, the liability which flows from a breach thereof. Rather what is presented is a melange of overlapping, variant, misleading, and contradictory provisions.

Gladden v. Cadillac Motor Car Div., 83 N.J. 320, 333, 416 A.2d 394, 401, 29 U.C.C. Rep. Serv. 369, 380-381 (1980). For a similar result in a commercial setting, see Andover Air Ltd. Partnership v. Piper Aircraft Corp., 7 U.C.C. Rep. Serv. 2d 1494 (D. Mass. 1989) (remedy limitation to repair or replacement held unconscionable where defective and inexpensive bracket caused $100,000 in damages in an airplane crash). Not all courts are this sympathetic to buyers. In NEC Technologies, Inc. v. Nelson, 267 Ga. 390, 478 S.E.2d 769, 31 U.C.C. Rep. Serv. 2d 992 (1996), the Georgia Supreme Court held that a disclaimer of liability for consequential damages was not unconscionable where a TV malfunctioned, burning down the consumer's home but causing no personal injury.

One other point: although §2-719 does not say so, most courts have required that any remedy limitation be *conspicuous* in order to be effective. See, e.g., Stauffer Chem. Co. v. Curry, 778 P.2d 1083, 10 U.C.C. Rep. Serv. 2d 342 (Wyo. 1989) (any other result "absurd"); but see Apex Supply Co. v. Benbow Indus., 189 Ga. App. 598, 376 S.E.2d 694, 9 U.C.C. Rep. Serv. 2d 547 (1988) (conspicuousness not required because a limitation of remedy is not as serious a matter as a disclaimer of warranty).

Pierce v. Catalina Yachts, Inc.

Supreme Court of Alaska, 1999
2 P.3d 618, 41 U.C.C. Rep. Serv. 2d 737

BRYNER, Justice.

I. INTRODUCTION

After finding that Catalina Yachts, a sailboat manufacturer, breached its limited warranty to repair a defect in a boat that it sold to Jim and Karen Pierce, a jury awarded the Pierces monetary damages for the reasonable cost of repair. Before submitting the case to the jury, the trial court dismissed the Pierces' claim for consequential damages, finding it barred by an express provision in the warranty. On appeal, the Pierces contend that they were entitled to consequential damages despite this provision. We agree, holding that because Catalina acted in bad faith when it breached the warranty, the company cannot conscionably enforce the warranty's provision barring consequential damages. Accordingly, we remand for a trial to determine consequential damages.

II. FACTS AND PROCEEDINGS

In June 1992 Jim and Karen Pierce purchased a forty-two-foot sailboat newly built by Catalina Yachts. Catalina gave the Pierces a limited warranty, promising to repair or pay for repair of any below-waterline blisters that might appear in the gel coat—a smooth outer layer of resin on the boat's hull.[31] The warranty expressly disclaimed Catalina's responsibility for consequential damages.

---

31. This limited warranty provided, in relevant part: "Catalina will repair or, at its option, pay for 100% of the labor and material costs necessary to repair any below-the-waterline gel coat blisters that occur within the first year after the boat is placed in the water."

In June 1994 the Pierces hauled the boat out of the water to perform maintenance and discovered gel-coat blisters on its hull and rudder. They promptly notified Catalina of the problem and submitted a repair estimate of $10,645, which included the cost of removing and replacing the gel coat below the waterline. Catalina refused to accept this estimate, insisting that the hull only needed minor patching. Six months later, after their repeated efforts failed to convince Catalina that the gel coat needed to be replaced, the Pierces sued the company, claiming tort and contract damages. They later amended their complaint to allege a separate claim for unfair trade practices. Before trial, the superior court ruled that the limited warranty's provision barring consequential damages was not unconscionable. Based on this ruling, the court later precluded the Pierces from submitting their consequential damages claim to the jury, restricting the Pierces' recovery on their claim of breach of contract to their cost of repair, as specified in the limited warranty. The jury awarded the Pierces $12,445 as the reasonable cost of repair, specifically finding that the Pierces had given Catalina timely notice of the blister problem, that Catalina breached its gel-coat warranty, that it acted in bad faith in failing to honor its warranty obligations, and that the Pierces could not have avoided any of their losses.

The Pierces appeal, contending that the trial court erred in striking their claim for consequential damages, in excluding evidence supporting their unfair trade practices claim, and in calculating the attorney's fee award. Catalina cross-appeals, also contesting the attorney's fee order.

III.   DISCUSSION

A.   THE PIERCES ARE ENTITLED TO CONSEQUENTIAL DAMAGES.

The Pierces' consequential damages argument requires us to consider a question of first impression concerning how a warranty provision that creates a limited remedy interacts with another provision that excludes consequential damages: if the limited remedy fails, should the exclusion of consequential damages survive?

Alaska's commercial code addresses these issues in AS 45.02.719. The first paragraph of this provision, subsection .719(a), authorizes limited warranties, allowing parties entering into commercial transactions to "limit or alter the measure of damages recoverable under [chapter 7 of the U.C.C.], as by limiting the buyer's remedies to . . . repair and replacement of non-conforming goods or parts" and to agree that the limited remedy is "exclusive, in which case it is the sole remedy." But when a limited remedy fails, the second paragraph of AS 45.02.719, subsection .719(b), nullifies the warranty's limitation, restoring the buyer's right to rely on any authorized remedy: "If circumstances cause an exclusive or limited remedy to fail of its essential purpose, remedy may be had as provided in the code."

Courts construing U.C.C. subsection 719(b) agree that a limited warranty to repair "fails of its essential purpose," "when the seller is either unwilling or unable to conform the goods to the contract."[32]

The policy behind the failure of essential purpose rule is to insure that the buyer has "at least minimum adequate remedies." Typically, a limited repair/replacement remedy fails of its essential purpose where (1) the "[s]eller is unsuccessful in repairing or replacing the defective part, regardless of good or bad faith; or (2) [t]here is unreasonable delay in repairing or replacing defective components.[33]

Here, by specifically finding that the Pierces' boat experienced gel-coat blisters, that the Pierces gave Catalina timely notice of the problem, that Catalina thereafter breached its obligations under the limited gel-coat warranty, and that the Pierces could not have avoided their damages, the jury effectively determined that the gel-coat warranty had failed of its essential purpose. Under subsection .719(b), then, the Pierces seemingly can pursue any remedy available under the commercial code, including consequential damages.

But the Pierces' right to consequential damages under subsection .719(b) is not as certain as it seems. The last paragraph of AS 45.02.719, subsection .719(c), separately provides that consequential damages may be limited or excluded "unless the limitation or exclusion is unconscionable." By validating consequential damages exclusions subject only to unconscionability, subsection .719(c) casts doubt upon subsection .719(b)'s implied promise that, when a limited remedy fails, the buyer may claim consequential damages because they are a "remedy . . . provided in the code."

The commercial code does not directly resolve this tension between subsections .719(b) and .719(c).[34] When, as here, a limited repair remedy fails, and a separate provision of the warranty bars consequential damages, the code fails to say whether a court should apply subsection .719(b) by restoring the buyer's right to seek consequential damages, or whether it

---

32. Chatlos Sys., Inc. v. National Cash Register Corp., 635 F.2d 1081, 1085 (3d Cir. 1980).

33. McDermott, Inc. v. Clyde Iron, 979 F.2d 1068, 1073 (5th Cir. 1993) (internal citations omitted), *rev'd on other grounds,* McDermott, Inc. v. AmClyde, 511 U.S. 202, 114 S. Ct. 1461, 128 L. Ed. 2d 148 (1994). See also S.M. Wilson & Co. v. Smith Int'l, Inc., 587 F.2d 1363, 1375 (9th Cir. 1978); Liberty Truck Sales, Inc. v. Kimbrel, 548 So. 2d 1379, 1384 (Ala. 1989). See generally Daniel C. Hagen, Sections 2-719(2) & 2-719(3) of the Uniform Commercial Code: The Limited Warranty Package & Consequential Damages, 31 Val. U. L. Rev. 111, 115 (1996).

34. See S.M. Wilson & Co., 587 F.2d at 1375 ("The failure of the limited repair warranty to achieve its essential purpose makes available . . . the remedies 'as may be had as provided in this code.' This does not mean, however, that the bar to recovery of consequential damages should be eliminated.").

should instead apply subsection .719(c) by enforcing the bar against consequential damages "unless . . . unconscionable."

Courts addressing this dilemma in other jurisdictions have come to differing conclusions. Some have found the two subsections to be dependent, ruling that when a warranty fails, subsection .719(b)'s command to restore all available remedies trumps subsection .719(c)'s approval of a specific clause that bars consequential damages, regardless of whether that clause might itself be unconscionable. [Citations omitted.] Other courts have applied a case-by-case analysis. [Citations omitted.] But the majority of jurisdictions view [*sic*] these subsections to be independent, ruling that when a warranty fails, a separate provision barring consequential damages will survive under subsection .719(c) as long as the bar itself is not unconscionable. [Citations omitted.]

We believe that the majority approach best serves the Uniform Commercial Code's underlying purposes "to simplify, clarify and modernize the law governing commercial transactions; to permit the continued expansion of commercial practices through custom, usage and agreement of the parties; [and] to make uniform the law among the various jurisdictions."[35] Moreover, this approach balances the purposes of subsections .719(b) and (c) by allowing parties latitude to contract around consequential damages, while protecting buyers from unconscionable results.[36] We therefore adopt the independent approach as the most sensible rule in light of precedent, reason, and policy.

Courts applying this approach recognize that contractual provisions limiting remedies and excluding consequential damages shift the risk of a limited remedy's failure from the seller to the buyer; they examine the totality of the circumstances at issue — including those surrounding the limited remedy's failure — to determine whether there is anything "in the formation of the contract or the circumstances resulting in failure of performance that makes it unconscionable to enforce the parties' allocation of risk."[37]

In determining whether an exclusion is unconscionable, courts examine the circumstances existing when the contract was signed, asking whether "there was . . . reason to conclude that the parties could not competently agree upon the allocation of risk."[38] Courts are more likely to

---

35. U.C.C. §1-102(2) (1996).

36. See McKernan v. United Tech. Corp., 717 F. Supp. 60, 71 (D. Conn. 1989). The comments to U.C.C. §2-719 provide that, while "minimum adequate remedies must be available" to the buyer when a contract fails, "parties are left free to shape their remedies to their particular requirements and reasonable agreements limiting or modifying remedies are to be given effect." U.C.C. §2-719 cmt. 1. In discussing subsection 2-719(3), the U.C.C. comments also recognize that clauses limiting consequential damages are "merely an allocation of unknown or undeterminable risks." U.C.C. §2-719 cmt. 3.

37. *Chatlos*, 635 F.2d at 1087.

38. Id. at 1087.

find unconscionability when a consumer is involved, when there is a dis-
parity in bargaining power, and when the consequential damages clause is
on a pre-printed form; conversely, they are unlikely to find unconscionability when "such a limitation is freely negotiated between sophisticated
parties, which will most likely occur in a commercial setting. . . ."[39]

In addition to inquiring into the circumstances at the time of the sale,
courts examine the case "[f]rom the perspective of later events," inquiring
whether "it appears that the type of damage claimed . . . came within the
realm of expectable losses."[40] The reason for the limited warranty's failure
affects this analysis:

> Whether the preclusion of consequential damages should be effective in this
> case depends upon the circumstances involved. The repair remedy's failure
> of essential purpose, while a discrete question, is not completely irrelevant to
> the issue of the conscionability of enforcing the consequential damages ex-
> clusion. The latter term is "merely an allocation of unknown or undeter-
> minable risks." Recognizing this, *the question . . . narrows to the unconscionability*
> *of the buyer retaining the risk of consequential damages upon the failure of the essential*
> *purpose of the exclusive repair remedy.*[41]

And in examining why a limited remedy failed of its essential purpose,
courts consider it significant if the seller acted unreasonably or in bad faith.

In the present case, the nature of the Pierces' warranty and the circumstances surrounding Catalina's breach weigh heavily against enforcing
the consequential damages bar. The contract at issue was a consumer sale,
not a commercial transaction between sophisticated businesses with
equivalent bargaining power. Catalina unilaterally drafted the damages bar
and evidently included it in a preprinted standard limited warranty.
Moreover, the jury's sizable award for the reasonable cost of repairing the
boat's gel coat establishes that Catalina's breach deprived the Pierces of a
substantial benefit of their bargain. Though some gel-coat blistering might
have been foreseeable, a defect of this magnitude does not fit neatly
"within the realm of expectable losses."

But the decisive factor in this case is the nature of Catalina's breach,
which caused the limited remedy to fail of its essential purpose. The jury
specifically found that Catalina acted in bad faith in failing to honor its
warranty. This finding virtually establishes a "circumstance[ ] resulting in
failure of performance that makes it unconscionable to enforce the parties'
allocation of risk." Because the jury found that Catalina consciously

---

39. *Schurtz*, 814 P.2d at 1114; see also Associated Press v. Southern Ark. Radio Co., 34
Ark. App. 211, 809 S.W.2d 695, 697 (1991); Construction Assocs. v. Fargo Water Equip. Co.,
446 N.W.2d 237, 242 (N.D. 1989).
   40. *Chatlos*, 635 F.2d at 1087.
   41. Id. at 1086-87 (internal citation omitted; emphasis added).

deprived the Pierces of their rights under the warranty, the company cannot conscionably demand to enforce its own warranty rights against the Pierces:

> This Court would be in an untenable position if it allowed the defendant to shelter itself behind one segment of the warranty when it has allegedly repudiated and ignored its very limited obligations under another segment of the same warranty, which alleged repudiation has caused the very need for relief which the defendant is attempting to avoid.[42]

Moreover, in light of Catalina's bad faith, allowing the company to enforce the consequential damages bar would conflict with the commercial code's imperative that "[e]very contract or duty in the code imposes an obligation of good faith in its performance or enforcement."[43] Finally, because it is self-evident that the Pierces did not bargain to assume the risk of a bad faith breach by Catalina, enforcing the bar against consequential damages would thwart AS 45.02.719's basic goal of implementing the parties' agreement.

For these reasons, we hold the superior court erred in ruling that it would be conscionable to enforce the warranty's bar against consequential damages and in declining to allow the Pierces to present their consequential damages claim to the jury. We further hold that this error requires us to remand the case for a trial to determine the extent of these damages. . . .

IV. CONCLUSION

For these reasons, we VACATE the judgment and REMAND for a trial to determine the amount of the Pierces' consequential damages.

NOTE

As this decision notes, there was once sharp judicial disagreement on the issue presented in this last case, but the trend in recent years is to read §2-719(2) and (3) as *independent* of one another, so that an essential failure of the remedy limitation's purpose does not automatically create a claim for disclaimed consequential damages; see Razor v. Hyundai Motor America, 222 Ill. 2d 75, 854 N.E.2d 607 (2006). Predictably, consumers have had an easier time recovering disclaimed consequential damages than have commercial buyers.

---

42. Jones and McKnight Corp. v. Birdsboro Corp., 320 F. Supp. 39, 43-44 (N.D. Ill. 1970).

43. See AS 47.01.203; U.C.C. §1-304.

D. *Defenses in Warranty Actions*

1. Notice

In all warranty actions a buyer loses all UCC rights if there is a failure to give the seller *notice* of the breach within a reasonable period of time after the breach should have been discovered. Read §2-607(3)(a) and Official Comment 4 to that section. The reason for this technical requirement is to preserve for the seller the right to inspect the goods (§2-515) and the right to *cure* (§2-508) and, of course, to facilitate an early settlement of the dispute.

PROBLEM 36

Pearl, a farmer, exhibited to Dave samples of her apples, but said that the bulk of the apples had less color and were one fifth smaller in size than the samples. Dave said, "Bring your apples to my warehouse; such size apples are worth $3 a bushel, and I will pay you that for them." Pearl agreed to do so.

The next day Pearl delivered 150 bushels of apples to Dave's warehouse. These apples were not as good, on an average, as the samples and were one third smaller in size than the samples were. Dave, without inspecting the apples, delivered them ten days later to his commission merchant, who the same day sold them on the market, bringing only $1.50 per bushel.

The commission merchant, immediately upon making the sale, called Dave and informed him of the price brought by the apples. Dave was disgusted and decided to wait until Pearl billed him for the apples, at which time he would give her a piece of his mind. Sixty days later Pearl billed Dave in the amount of $450 for the 150 bushels of apples. Dave refused to pay, telling Pearl that the apples had not measured up to the contract. Pearl sues Dave. Dave contends that Pearl breached an express warranty under the Uniform Commercial Code since a contract of sale by sample was involved. What result? Review §2-313.

Fitl v. Strek

Supreme Court of Nebraska, 2005
269 Neb. 51, 690 N.W.2d 605

WRIGHT, J.

NATURE OF CASE

James G. Fitl purchased a baseball card from Mark Strek, doing business as Star Cards of San Francisco. When Fitl discovered that the baseball card had been altered and was of no value, he sued Strek for what he argued was the current fair market value of an unaltered version of the same card. Following a bench trial, judgment was entered against Strek in the amount of $17,750 plus costs. Strek appeals. . . .

FACTS

In September 1995, Fitl attended a sports card show in San Francisco, California, where Strek was an exhibitor. Fitl subsequently purchased from Strek a 1952 Mickey Mantle Topps baseball card for $17,750. According to Fitl, Strek represented that the card was in near mint condition. After Strek delivered the card to Fitl in Omaha, Nebraska, Fitl placed it in a safe-deposit box.

In May 1997, Fitl sent the baseball card to Professional Sports Authenticators (PSA), a grading service for sports cards that is located in Newport Beach, California. PSA reported to Fitl that the baseball card was ungradable because it had been discolored and doctored.

On May 29, 1997, Fitl wrote to Strek and indicated that he planned to pursue "legal methods" to resolve the matter. Strek replied that Fitl should have initiated a return of the baseball card in a timely fashion so that Strek could have confronted his source and remedied the situation. Strek asserted that a typical grace period for the unconditional return of a card was from 7 days to 1 month.

In August 1997, Fitl sent the baseball card to ASA Accugrade, Inc. (ASA), in Longwood, Florida, for a second opinion. ASA also concluded that the baseball card had been refinished and trimmed.

On September 8, 1997, Fitl sued Strek, alleging that Strek knew the baseball card had been recolored or otherwise altered and had concealed this fact from him. Fitl claimed he had reasonably relied upon Strek's status as a reputable sports card dealer. Strek's answer generally denied Fitl's allegations.

In a trial to the court, Fitl appeared with counsel and offered evidence. Strek was represented by counsel but did not appear or offer any evidence. Fitl testified that he was in San Francisco over the Labor Day weekend of 1995, where he met Strek at a sports card show. Fitl subsequently purchased from Strek a 1952 Mickey Mantle Topps baseball card and placed it in a safe-deposit box. In 1997, Fitl retrieved the baseball card and sent it to PSA, a sports card grading service.

Steve Orand testified that he had been a sports card collector for 27 years and that he bought, sold, and traded cards. He testified that PSA originated in 1996 or 1997 and was a leader in the sports card grading industry. He stated that PSA would not grade an altered card because alteration would totally devalue the card. He opined that any touchup or trimming of a card would render the card valueless and that an altered card is worth no more than the paper on which it is printed.

Orand examined the baseball card in question the week before trial and said that the edges of the card had been trimmed and reglued. One spot on the front of the baseball card and a larger spot on the back had been repainted, which left the card with no value. He testified that the standard for sports memorabilia was a lifetime guarantee and that a reputable collector would stand behind what he sold and refund the money if an item were fake or had been altered.

The district court entered judgment for Fitl in the amount of $17,750 and costs. The court found that Fitl had notified Strek as soon as he realized the baseball card was altered and worthless and that Fitl had notified Strek of the defect within a reasonable time after its discovery. The court rejected Strek's theory that Fitl should have determined the authenticity of the baseball card immediately after it had been purchased.

ASSIGNMENT OF ERROR

Strek claims that the district court erred in determining that notification of the defective condition of the baseball card 2 years after the date of purchase was timely pursuant to Neb. U.C.C. §2-607(3)(a) (Reissue 2001).

ANALYSIS

In a bench trial of a law action, a trial court's factual findings have the effect of a jury verdict and will not be set aside on appeal unless clearly erroneous. Webb v. American Employers Group, 268 Neb. 473, 684 N.W.2d 33 (2004). The district court found that Fitl had notified Strek within a reasonable time after discovery of the breach. Therefore, our review is whether the district court's finding as to the reasonableness of the notice was clearly erroneous.

Section 2-607(3)(a) states: "Where a tender has been accepted . . . the buyer must within a reasonable time after he discovers or should have discovered any breach notify the seller of breach or be barred from any remedy[.]" "What is a reasonable time for taking any action depends on the nature, purpose and circumstances of such action." Neb. U.C.C. §1-204(2) (Reissue 2001).

The notice requirement set forth in §2-607(3)(a) serves three purposes. It provides the seller with an opportunity to correct any defect, to prepare for negotiation and litigation, and to protect itself against stale claims asserted after it is too late for the seller to investigate them. See Cheyenne Mountain Bank v. Whetstone Corp., 787 P.2d 210 (Colo. App. 1990). "Whether the notice given is satisfactory and whether it is given within a reasonable time are generally questions of fact to be measured by all the circumstances of the case." Id. at 213.

In Maybank v. Kresge Co., 302 N.C. 129, 273 S.E.2d 681 (1981), the court reviewed the policies behind the notice requirement. The most important one is to enable the seller "to make efforts to cure the breach by making adjustments or replacements in order to minimize the buyer's damages and the seller's liability." Id. at 134, 273 S.E.2d at 684. A second policy is to provide the seller "a reasonable opportunity to learn the facts so that he may adequately prepare for negotiation and defend himself in a suit." Id. A third policy, designated the "least compelling" by the court, is the same as the policy behind statutes of limitation: "to provide a seller with a terminal point in time for liability." Id. at 135, 273 S.E.2d at 684.

Fitl purchased the baseball card in 1995 and immediately placed it in a safe-deposit box. Two years later, he retrieved the baseball card, had it appraised, and learned that it was of no value. Fitl testified that he had relied on Strek's position as a dealer of sports cards and on his representations that the baseball card was authentic. In Cao v. Nguyen, 258 Neb. 1027, 607 N.W.2d 528 (2000), we stated that a party is justified in relying upon a representation made to the party as a positive statement of fact when an investigation would be required to ascertain its falsity. In order for Fitl to have determined that the baseball card had been altered, he would have been required to conduct an investigation. We find that he was not required to do so. Once Fitl learned that the baseball card had been altered, he gave notice to Strek.

As the court noted in *Maybank v. Kresge Co.*, supra, one of the most important policies behind the notice requirement of North Carolina's equivalent to §2-607(3)(a) is to allow the seller to cure the breach by making adjustments or replacements to minimize the buyer's damages and the seller's liability. However, even if Fitl had learned immediately upon taking possession of the baseball card that it was not authentic and had notified Strek at that time, there is no evidence that Strek could have made any adjustment or taken any action that would have minimized his liability. In its altered condition, the baseball card was worthless.

Strek claimed via his correspondence to Fitl that if Strek had received notice earlier, he could have contacted the person who sold him the baseball card to determine the source of the alteration, but there is no evidence to support this allegation. In fact, Strek offered no evidence at trial. His letter is merely an assertion that is unsupported. Earlier notification would not have helped Strek prepare for negotiation or defend himself in a suit because the damage to Fitl could not be repaired. Thus, the policies behind the notice requirement, to allow the seller to correct a defect, to prepare for negotiation and litigation, and to protect against stale claims at a time beyond which an investigation can be completed, were not unfairly prejudiced by the lack of an earlier notice to Strek. Any problem

Strek may have had with the party from whom he obtained the baseball card was a separate matter from his transaction with Fitl, and an investigation into the source of the altered card would not have minimized Fitl's damages.

Strek represented himself as a sports card dealer at a card show in San Francisco. After Fitl expressed interest in a specific baseball card, Strek contacted Fitl to sell him just such a card. Orand stated that a reputable dealer will stand behind what he sells and refund the money if an item is fake or has been altered. In the context of whether a rejection of goods was made in a reasonable amount of time, we have stated that "when there is no precise rule of law which governs, the question of what, under the circumstances of a particular case, is a reasonable amount of time is usually a question for the jury." See Smith v. Paoli Popcorn Co., 255 Neb. 910, 917, 587 N.W.2d 660, 664 (1999).

The district court found that it was reasonable to give Strek notice of a defect 2 years after the purchase. This finding was not clearly erroneous. Pursuant to §2-607(4), the burden is on the buyer to show a breach with respect to the goods accepted. Fitl presented evidence that the baseball card was not authentic, as he had been led to believe by Strek's representations. Strek did not refute Fitl's evidence.

CONCLUSION

The judgment of the district court is affirmed.

PROBLEM 37

Icarus Airlines ordered 40 new airplanes from the Daedalus Aircraft Company. Twenty were to be delivered on May 8 and the rest on November 10. The first shipment actually came on September 11, but Icarus did not complain. The second came on January 12 of the next year. On January 30, the president of Icarus wrote Daedalus that "We are very disappointed by your late shipment, which has caused us much expense and inconvenience." Three months later Icarus sued, claiming some $24 million in damages caused by the delayed deliveries. In its answer Daedalus responded by stating that it had received no notice of the breach as to the first shipment and that the notice concerning the second shipment was defective because it did not announce Icarus's intention to claim a breach as a result of the late delivery. At trial, Icarus countered by stating that no notice is required where, as here, the breach is obvious to the seller. As to the lack of formal notice of breach in the January letter, Icarus pointed to Official Comment 4 to §2-607.

As the trial court judge, how would you rule on the notice issues? See Aqualon Co. v. MAC Equipment, Inc., 149 F.3d 262, 36 U.C.C. Rep. Serv. 2d

99 (4th Cir. 1998); Peavey Electronics Corp. v. Baan U.S.A., Inc., 10 So. 3d 945 (Miss. Ct. App. 2009) (noting split among courts and holding that merchant did not give notice by merely giving notice of problems, because notice requirement "exists to prevent commercial bad faith, promote mitigation and cure, enable the seller to collect evidence while still fresh, and promote settlement").What if on January 30 Icarus had filed suit against Daedalus rather than waiting three months? Would the notice requirement have been satisfied? See Armco Steel Co. v. Isaacson Structure Steel Co., 611 P.2d 507, 28 U.C.C. Rep. Serv. 1249 (Alaska 1980). In *Armco*, the court held that filing suit was not sufficient notice. However, the dissenting judge said: "[F]iling suit without prior notice may be impolite but it is not deceptive or dishonest and it certainly is no hindrance to 'normal settlement through negotiation.' Often, in fact, serious settlement negotiations do not take place until a lawsuit is filed." See also In re Bridgestone/Firestone, Inc. Tires Products Liability Litigation, 155 F. Supp. 2d 1069, 45 U.C.C. Rep. Serv. 2d 516 (S.D. Ind. 2001).

PROBLEM 38

Alonso Quijano invited his good friend Sancho to dinner and served him a pheasant for the meal. The wine specially uncorked for the meal had been bottled by La Mancha Vineyards. It proved to be laced with a poisonous chemical, but only Sancho drank enough to have a serious reaction: it put him in the hospital for eight months. When he was discharged, he hired an attorney and filed suit against La Mancha Vineyards, which defended on the lack of notice required by §2-607(3)(a). How should this come out? Read §2-318 and Official Comment 5 to §2-607. If the person who had been injured had been Alonso Quijano and if he had given notice of breach to the retail seller, Carrasco Liquors, would that preserve his rights against the manufacturer, La Mancha Vineyards? See ACE American Ins. Co. v. Fountain Powerboats, Inc., 2007 WL 2438338 (D.N.H. 2007).

2. Burden of Proof

In a warranty suit the plaintiff has the burden of proving (1) the creation of the warranty, (2) its breach, (3) its causal connection to the plaintiff's injury ("proximate cause," your old friend from the Torts course, being the usual measure), and (4) the fact and the extent of the injury. See Martineau v. Walker, 542 P.2d 1165 (Idaho 1975). Proof can be an overwhelming obstacle in many situations.

PROBLEM 39

Richard Sharpe's new car spun off the road and hit a tree immediately after a loud clanking noise was heard from under the vehicle as he was driving it along the highway. The steering column had been ripped open. Does this necessarily violate the manufacturer's warranty that the automobile would be "defect free"?

Flippo v. Mode O'Day Frock Shops of Hollywood

Arkansas Supreme Court, 1970
248 Ark. 1, 449 S.W.2d 692

HARRIS, Chief Justice.

This litigation in occasioned by a spider bite. Gladys Flippo, appellant herein, went into a ladies clothing store in Batesville, operated by Rosie Goforth, and known as Mode O'Day Frock Shops of Hollywood. Mrs. Flippo tried on two pairs of pants, of slacks, which were shown to her by Mrs. Goforth. The first pair proved to be too small, and according to appellant's evidence. when Mrs. Flippo put on the second pair, she suddenly felt a burning sensation on her thigh; she immediately removed the pants, shook them, and a spider fell to the floor which was then stepped upon. An examination of her thigh revealed a reddened area, which progressively grew worse. Mrs. Flippo was subsequently hospitalized for approximately 30 days. According to her physician, the injury was caused by the bite of a brown recluse spider.[44] Suit for damages was instituted against Mode O'Day Frock Shops and Rosie Goforth, the complaint asserting three grounds for recovery, first that a pair of slacks in a defective condition (by reason of the presence of a poisonous spider), and unreasonably dangerous was sold to appellant; second, that both appellees were guilty of several acts of negligence, and third, that there was an implied warranty that the slacks were fit for the purpose for which they were purchased, though actually not fit, because of the poisonous spider concealed therein. On trial, the court refused requested instructions offered by appellant on theories of implied warranty, and strict tort liability, and instructed the jury only on the issue of appellees' alleged negligence as the proximate cause of the injury. The jury returned a verdict for both appellees, and judgment was entered accordingly. From the judgment so entered, appellant brings this appeal, not however, appellant from the finding of no negligence; instead, the appeal

---

44. In "Changing Times, the Kiplinger Magazine," issue of April, 1969, Page 45, there is an interesting article with reference to this spider, entitled "Beware the Brown Recluse." The views of several Arkansas physicians are set out, this state being one with a large infestation of this particular species of spider.

is based entirely upon the court's refusal to submit the case upon implied warranty and strict tort liability theories. Accordingly, for reversal, it is first urged that "there was sufficient evidence to justify a finding that Mrs. Flippo was injured by goods unfit for their intended use, supplied by a merchant with respect to goods of that kind, and therefore the trial court erred in refusing to instruct upon the law of implied warranty of merchantability."

It might be said at the outset that appellant has filed a very thorough and comprehensive brief in support of the positions taken; however, we are unable to agree with the views presented under the circumstances of this case. As pointed out by appellant, there was ample evidence to support a finding that Mrs. Flippo suffered a bite by a brown recluse spider concealed on the slacks furnished her by Mrs. Goforth (it is not conceded by appellees that the bite occurred in this manner). Appellant says:

> ". . . If that be true, then appellant submits that such an article of clothing is not reasonably fit for use as an article of clothing and is thus not merchantable."

It is contended that appellees were bound by the implied warranty of merchantability imposed by Ark. Stat. Ann. §85-2-314 (Add. 1961), this statute providing that, in order to be merchantable, the goods must, inter alia, be fit for the ordinary purposes for which such goods are used. Appellant argues that an article of clothing which conceals a venomous creature is certainly unfit for use, and therefore at the time the slacks were handed to Mrs. Flippo, the garment was unfit for the use for which it was intended, and there was accordingly a breach of the implied warranty of merchantability under either the statute or common law.

We cannot agree that the law of implied warranty of merchantability is applicable to a case of this nature. The pair of pants itself was fit for the ordinary purposes for which stretch pants are used; there was nothing wrong from a manufacturing standpoint. In fact, the evidence reflects that Mrs. Flippo bought this particular pair after being bitten, and she has worn and laundered them since the accident. There is absolutely no evidence that the goods were defective in any manner. It is, of course, readily apparent that the spider was not a part of the product, and there is no evidence that either the manufacturer or retailer had any control of the spider, or caused it to be in the pants. Mrs. Goforth said she receives the shipments once a week in pasteboard cartons sealed with tape, and that upon receiving the cartons, she immediately opens them, places the garments on plastic hangers, and hangs them out. The cartons are delivered by truck line, and the witness stated that the slacks in question had been in the store for some time in excess of 20 days.

Irrespective of whether the spider attached itself to the garment in Kansas City, or in Batesville,[45] it was not a part of the garment. The three cases cited by appellant as authority for the common law implied warranty of merchantability, all deal with a defective product, which is not the situation in the present litigation. Perhaps our position can best be made clear by simply stating that the spider was not a part of the manufactured article, and the injury to Mrs. Flippo was caused by the spider — and not the product. We find no cause of action under either the statute or the common law.

Nor can we agree that the trial court erred in refusing to instruct the jury upon the principles of strick tort liability. In Restatement (Second), Torts §402A, which deals with products that are defective, and thus made unreasonably dangerous to the user or consumer, we find:

> "(1) One who sells any product in a defective condition unreasonably dangerous to the user or consumer or to his property is subject to liability for physical harm thereby caused to the ultimate user or consumer, or to his property, if
>   (a) the seller is engaged in the business of selling such a product, and
>   (b) it is expected to and does reach the user or consumer without substantial change in the condition in which it is sold. . . ."

It is at once obvious that the product sold in the instant case was a pair of slacks, and the slacks were not in a defective condition; nor were they unreasonably dangerous; in fact, they were not dangerous at all; still further, the slacks did not cause any physical harm to Mrs. Flippo. Without elaboration, it is at once apparent that subheadings (a) and (b) are not applicable to this litigation, for no one can really contend that the spider was a part of the product, nor can anyone do more than guess at when the spider attached itself to the slacks. . . .

Affirmed.

3. Privity

Because suits on warranties are contract actions, the buyer must establish that there was in fact and in law a contract between the two parties. This "legal connection" is called *privity*. Where a buyer has purchased the goods directly from the retailer who gave the warranty, there is obviously privity between the two parties. Suppose, however, the warranty was made by the manufacturer, who sold to a wholesaler, who sold to a retailer, who

---

45. The evidence reflected that Mrs. Flippo had, at some previous time, been in the business of raising chickens, and owned a chicken house. She said that she had seen spiders in this chicken house, though not at the time chickens were being raised. It is suggested by appellees that she could have brought the spider into the store with her.

sold to the buyer. If the buyer wishes to sue the manufacturer, the issue of lack of privity arises. At common law the manufacturer could successfully maintain a defense based on lack of privity, because the manufacturer did not deal directly with the buyer. The problem of how far back up the distribution chain the buyer can go is said to be an issue of *vertical privity*. To complicate matters, there is a second type of privity called *horizontal privity*. Horizontal privity deals with identifying to whom the retail seller is liable other than the immediate purchaser. The next Problem illustrates the difference.

PROBLEM 40

The Girard Instruments Corporation manufactured a pocket calculator called the Descartes 1000. It bought the paint used on the machine from the Hamilton Paint Company. Girard sold the calculators to the retailer, Leibnitz Department Store, which sold a calculator to Sylvester Cayley. He in turn gave it to his wife as a birthday gift. The Descartes 1000 was a popular gift. Joan Cayley used it all the time, as did the Cayley children (for homework) and even Mr. Gauss, the mailman, who borrowed it one day to compute the distance he walked on his route. After this last use, Mr. Gauss went home, where his dog, Diophantus, eagerly licked his hand and promptly dropped dead of lead poisoning. It turned out that the paint used on the Descartes 1000 had an extraordinarily high lead content. All the Cayleys and Mr. Gauss became very ill and, on recovery, brought suit for their pain and suffering, lost wages, medical expenses, and, in Mr. Gauss's case, the value of his dog. Whom should they sue?

The privity problem looks like the following diagram.

Hamilton Paint Co.

↕

Girard Inst. Corp.

↕

Leibnitz Dept. Store

↕

Sylvester Cayley ⟷ **Joan Cayley** ⟷ **Children** ⟷ **Mr. Gauss**

The question "Can Mr. Gauss sue the Leibnitz Department Store?" is a question of horizontal privity. The question "Can Mr. Cayley sue the Hamilton Paint Company?" is a question of vertical privity. The question "Can Mr. Gauss sue the Hamilton Paint Company?" is a question involving both horizontal and vertical privity.

If the Hamilton Paint Company had made express warranties (either in ads or in writings contained in the calculator box), most courts would have had no problem finding a cause of action in contract on the warranty in favor of anyone relying thereon. And if negligence could be proved (the doctrine of res ipsa loquitur helps here), a tort action was possible. Another theory Mr. Cayley (the retail buyer) could have tried, where no express warranty was involved, was that he was a third-party beneficiary of the implied warranties made in the sales between Hamilton and Girard and between Girard and Leibnitz. The other potential plaintiffs might also try the third-party beneficiary argument.

However, all these theories have technical, practical, or historical problems. Even with the doctrine of res ipsa loquitur, negligence can be hard to prove. Contract/warranty actions are bound by centuries of "no privity — no lawsuit" decisions. And, as we have seen, warranty suits have upheld requirements like that in §2-607(3)(a) — *notice* within a reasonable amount of time (a requirement the mailman is not likely to meet even if his attorney remembers it).

The original 1962 version of the UCC had §2-318, which spoke in a limited fashion to the question of how much horizontal privity was excused under the Code. That version (now called Alternative A) protected the retail buyer's family and house guests from personal injury. Official Comment 3 to §2-318 invited the courts to extend warranty protection. But this version did not help the buyer's employees or casual bystanders, nor did it protect property losses (for example, the loss of the dog by Mr. Gauss). In 1966, the UCC's Permanent Editorial Board proposed two more versions of §2-318: Alternative B, which spoke to privity in terms of a foreseeable personal injury test, and Alternative C, which protected even property damage and nonnatural persons (for example, corporations). Read these versions and the Official Comments (especially Official Comment 3).

Does §2-318 restrict the limits of *vertical* privity so as to answer the question "Can Sylvester Cayley sue the Hamilton Paint Company?" See Official Comment 3 to §2-318, second sentence; Hyundai Motor America, Inc. v. Goodin, 822 N.E.2d 947 (Ind. 2005) (no privity required for manufacturer's breach of an implied warranty); but see Gill v. Blue Bird Body Co., 147 Fed. Appx. 807, 2005 WL 1413293 (11th Cir. 2005) (applying Georgia law, implied warranty claim not allowed against manufacturer where no privity with ultimate buyer).

Reed v. City of Chicago

United States District Court, Northern District of Illinois, 2003 263 F. Supp. 2d 1123, 50 U.C.C. Rep. Serv. 2d 146

MORAN, Senior District Judge.

Plaintiff Ruby Reed brought this action against defendants City of Chicago (City), police officers Timothy Gould, Bruce Young, Brian Pemberton, and Susan Madison (officers), and Edwards Medical Supply, Inc. (Edwards), Cypress Medical Products, Ltd. and Cypress Medical Products, Inc. (together, Cypress), and Medline Industries (Medline) arising from her son's death in a Chicago jail cell. Defendant Cypress filed a motion to dismiss count VI of the complaint—breach of warranty—pursuant to Federal Rule of Civil Procedure 12 (b)(6). For the following reasons, Cypress' motion is denied.

BACKGROUND

Plaintiff Ruby Reed filed this suit as the special administrator of her son J.C. Reed's estate. On November 12, 2000, J.C. Reed (Reed) was allegedly arrested and brought to the City's Fifth District Police Station, where he was placed in a detention cell controlled and managed by the officers. The officers allegedly knew that Reed was mentally unstable, had witnessed him attempting suicide by slitting his wrists, and failed to adequately monitor the cell. The officers removed his clothing and provided him with a paper isolation gown. Plaintiff claims that Reed used this gown to hang himself, and that officers found him in the cell and failed to give him proper medical care, resulting in his death.

Plaintiff further alleges that the gown was manufactured and designed by defendants Edwards, Cypress and Medline, and that these defendants breached implied and express warranties when the gown failed to tear away when used by Reed in an attempt to hang himself.

DISCUSSION

The single issue we must decide is whether plaintiff, as a non-purchaser, can recover from the manufacturer and designer of the gown for breach of warranty. Historically, Illinois law has required plaintiffs suing for breach of warranty to establish both horizontal and vertical privity.[46] [The court quotes Alternative A to §2-318, the version adopted in Illinois—EDS.]

---

46. Lack of vertical privity occurs when a consumer seeks to sue a remote manufacturer who was not involved in the sale to the consumer. Lack of horizontal privity occurs when a user of the product, beside the consumer, is injured. See Thomas v. Bombardier-Rotax Motorenfabrik, 869 F. Supp. 551, 557 n.7 (N.D. Ill. 1994).

The Illinois Supreme Court has determined that the privity is no longer an absolute requirement for breach of warranty actions. Berry v. G.D. Searle & Co., 56 Ill. 2d 548, 309 N.E.2d 550 (Ill. 1974) (stating "privity is of no consequence when a buyer who purportedly has sustained personal injuries predicates recovery against a remote manufacturer for breach of an implied warranty under the code"); see also Suvada v. White Motor Co., 32 Ill. 2d 612, 210 N.E.2d 182 (Ill. 1965), *overruled on other grounds* (holding, prior to the enactment of the UCC in Illinois, that the privity requirement should be abolished in food and drug cases). While section 2-318 lists specific exceptions to the privity requirement, Illinois courts have noted that this list is not necessarily exhaustive. See Wheeler v. Sunbelt Tool Co., Inc., 181 Ill. App. 3d 1088, 1099, 537 N.E.2d 1332, 1340, 130 Ill. Dec. 863, 871 (1989); see also UCC §2-318, comment 3 (stating that "the section in this form is neutral and is not intended to enlarge or restrict the developing case law on whether the seller's warranties, given to his buyer who resells, extend to other persons in the distributive chain").

The vast majority of cases examining the limits of section 2-318 in Illinois have dealt with the employment context, expanding the class of potential breach of warranty plaintiffs to employees of the ultimate purchaser. [Citing cases.] In these cases courts have allowed employees to sue for breach of warranty despite a lack of horizontal privity.

In [Whitaker v. Lian Feng Mach. Co., 156 Ill. App. 3d 316, 509 N.E.2d 591 (1987)] plaintiff was injured while using a band-saw that had been purchased by his employer. . . . The court determined that section 2-318 does not state any limitation on the rights of persons to recover for breach of warranty, nor does it differentiate between horizontal and vertical privity (id. at 593-94). It reasoned that the purpose of warranties is to determine what the seller has agreed to sell . . . , quoting UCC §2-313, comment 4. The employee was essentially a third-party beneficiary to the sale in that the employee's safety while using the bandsaw was "either explicitly or implicitly part of the basis of the bargain when the employer purchased the goods" (id. at 595). . . .

While no Illinois courts have expanded the plaintiff class for breach of warranty actions beyond employees, we believe that the law requires us to do so here. The beneficiary of any warranty made by the manufacturer and designer of the gown is necessarily a potentially suicidal detainee like Reed. If protection is not provided to plaintiffs like Reed, any warranty as to the safety of the gown would have little, if any, effect. In designing and manufacturing the gown, defendants contemplated that the users of the gown would be detainees. Moreover, the safety of these detainees was necessarily a part of the bargain, whether explicitly or implicitly, between the seller and buyer. For these reasons, a detainee of the City like Reed must be able to enforce the protections of any warranties made by the manufacturer and designer of the gown.

Conclusion

For the foregoing reasons, defendants' motion to dismiss count VI of the complaint is denied.

4. A Note on Strict Products Liability

About the same time that the UCC drafters were wrestling with §2-318, another legal revolution was occurring: the development of *strict products liability*. See W. Prosser, Torts 692 (5th ed. 1984). This concept has been described by Professor Prosser as "a freak hybrid born of the illicit intercourse of tort and contract." Prosser, The Fall of the Citadel (Strict Liability to the Consumer), 50 Minn. L. Rev. 791, 800 (1966). Basically, strict products liability permits recovery by an injured consumer in a suit against the manufacturer as long as the consumer can prove that the manufacturer distributed into commerce a product that contained a dangerous defect. There is no necessity of proving either negligence or privity.

The primary source of the doctrine is §402A of the Restatement (Second) of Torts:

> §402A. *Special Liability of Seller of Product for Physical Harm to User or Consumer*
>
> (1) One who sells any product in a defective condition unreasonably dangerous to the user or consumer or to his property is subject to liability for physical harm thereby caused to the ultimate user or consumer, or to his property, if
> (a) the seller is engaged in the business of selling such a product, and
> (b) it is expected to and does reach the user or consumer without substantial change in the condition in which it is sold.
>
> (2) The rule stated in Subsection (1) applies although
> (a) the seller has exercised all possible care in the preparation and sale of his product, and
> (b) the user or consumer has not bought the product from or entered into any contractual relation with the seller.[47]

---

47. In 1997, the American Law Institute published a new Restatement Third, Torts, Products Liability, designed to update the law in this field. The new promulgation answers a host of questions that had been raised under old Restatement §402A, and is a lot more complicated than its predecessor. The primary change made by Restatement Third is that while it retains strict liability for manufacturing defects, it shifts to a negligence standard for design defects and injuries caused by failure to give a proper warning. See Restatement (Third) Torts, Products Liability §2. For a summary of the new Restatement, see David G. Owen, M. Stuart Madden, and Mary J. Davis, 1 Madden & Owen on Products Liability §§5.10-5.12 (2000).

Strict products liability as a separate cause of action has been adopted by most (but not all) courts. Starting with Henningsen v. Bloomfield Motors, Inc., 32 N.J. 358, 161 A.2d 69 (1960), and proceeding through landmark opinions such as Greenman v. Yuba Power Prods., Inc., 59 Cal. 2d 57, 377 P.2d 897, 27 Cal. Rptr. 697 (1962); Seely v. White Motor Co., 63 Cal. 2d 9, 403 P.2d 145, 45 Cal. Rptr. 17, 2 U.C.C. Rep. Serv. 915 (1965); State ex rel. Western Seed Prod. Corp. v. Campbell, 250 Or. 262, 442 P.2d 215 (1968); and Kassab v. Central Soya, 432 Pa. 217, 246 A.2d 848, 5 U.C.C. Rep. Serv. 925 (1968), the courts have worked one by one what Prosser has called "the most rapid and altogether spectacular overturn of an established rule in the entire history of the law of torts." W. Prosser, Torts 690 (5th ed. 1984). A cause of action based on strict products liability is very similar to the UCC implied warranty of merchantability ("fitness for ordinary purpose" is only slight degrees away from freedom from "unreasonably dangerous" defects, the §402A test), and some courts have held the two doctrines are to be measured by the same rules as to privity and defenses. See, e.g., Gregory v. White Truck & Equip. Co., 163 Ind. App. 240, 323 N.E.2d 280, 16 U.C.C. Rep. Serv. 644 (1975) (held contributory negligence is not a defense in a §2-315 suit nor in a §402A suit unless it amounts to an assumption of the risk so that plaintiff proceeded to encounter a known danger); see also Annot., 4 A.L.R.3d 501, and Annot., 46 A.L.R.3d 240, on the defense of contributory negligence in warranty/products liability suits.

Lincoln General Insurance Co. v. Detroit Diesel Corp.

Supreme Court of Tennessee, 2009
293 S.W.3d 487

Janice M. Holder, C.J.

* * *

FACTS AND PROCEDURAL HISTORY

Senators Rental, Inc. ("Senators Rental"), an insured of Lincoln General Insurance Company ("Lincoln General"), purchased a bus manufactured by Prevost Car (US) Inc. ("Prevost"). The engine in the bus was produced by Detroit Diesel Corporation ("Detroit Diesel"). On May 8, 2006, the bus was traveling south on Interstate 65 near Goodlettsville, Tennessee, when it caught fire due to an alleged engine defect. The fire did not cause personal injury or damage to any property other than the bus itself. Lincoln General paid Senators Rental $405,250 for the fire damage pursuant to its insurance policy.

Lincoln General filed a complaint against Prevost and Detroit Diesel. The complaint included counts of breach of express and implied warranties, negligence, and strict products liability. Prevost and Detroit Diesel removed the case to the United States District Court for the Middle District of Tennessee. Prevost filed a motion to dismiss for failure to state a claim pursuant to Federal Rule of Civil Procedure 12(b)(6), arguing that Lincoln General's tort claims are barred by the economic loss doctrine.

On July 1, 2008, the United States District Court certified one question of law to this Court, which we accepted pursuant to Tennessee Supreme Court Rule 23. . . .

ANALYSIS

The United States District Court certified the following question of law: Does Tennessee law recognize an exception to the economic loss doctrine under which recovery in tort is possible for damage to the defective product itself when the defect renders the product unreasonably dangerous and causes the damage by means of a sudden, calamitous event?

This certified question presupposes that Tennessee recognizes the economic loss doctrine, a judicially created principle that reflects an attempt to maintain separation between contract law and tort law by barring recovery in tort for purely economic loss. See generally, Vincent R. Johnson, The Boundary-Line Function of the Economic Loss Rule, 66 Wash. & Lee L. Rev. 523 (2009). Although this Court has never expressly adopted the economic loss doctrine, we expressed agreement with the policies underlying the doctrine in Ritter v. Custom Chemicides, Inc., 912 S.W.2d 128 (Tenn. 1995). In Ritter, this Court stated that "Tennessee has joined those jurisdictions which hold that product liability claims resulting in pure economic loss can be better resolved on theories other than negligence. . . . In Tennessee, the consumer does not have an action in tort for economic damages under strict liability." Id. at 133 (footnote omitted); see also First Nat'l Bank of Louisville v. Brooks Farms, 821 S.W.2d 925, 930-31 (Tenn. 1991) (finding that actions under the Tennessee Products Liability Act are limited to those brought on account of personal injury, death, or property damage and do not include actions brought for pecuniary loss).

The economic loss doctrine is implicated in products liability cases when a defective product damages itself without causing personal injury or damage to other property. In this context, "economic loss" is defined generally as "the diminution in the value of the product because it is inferior in quality and does not work for the general purposes for which it was manufactured and sold." Comment, Manufacturers' Liability to Remote Purchasers for "Economic Loss" Damages — Tort or Contract?, 114 U. Pa. L. Rev. 539, 541 (1966). Two types of economic loss, direct and consequential, occur when a defective product is damaged. See, e.g., Restatement (Third) of Torts: Products Liability §21, cmt. d (1998). Direct economic loss may be measured by the defective product's cost of repair or replacement. Id. Consequential economic losses, such as lost profits, result from the product owner's inability to use the product. Id.

The question certified presents us with our first opportunity to examine the proper application of the economic loss doctrine when only the defective product is damaged. In the seminal case of East River Steamship Corp. v. Transamerica Delaval, Inc., 476 U.S. 858, 868-71, 106 S. Ct. 2295, 90 L. Ed. 2d 865 (1986), the United States Supreme Court examined three approaches to the economic loss doctrine used by various state and federal courts, which it described as the "majority," "minority," and "intermediate" positions, and adopted the majority approach. In *East River*, a shipbuilder contracted with a manufacturer for the production of turbines to propel four oil-transporting super tankers. While at sea, the turbines malfunctioned due to design and manufacturing defects. Only the turbines themselves were damaged. In a unanimous decision, the Supreme Court held that the economic loss doctrine barred the shipbuilder's products liability suit in admiralty against the manufacturer.

In adopting the "majority approach" to the economic loss doctrine, the Supreme Court chose a bright-line rule that precludes recovery in tort when a product damages itself without causing personal injury or damage to other property. In reaching this conclusion, the Supreme Court observed that "[w]hen a product injures only itself the reasons for imposing a tort duty are weak and those for leaving the party to its contractual remedies are strong." Id. at 871, 106 S. Ct. 2295. Specifically, the Supreme Court reasoned that damage to a defective product is merely a failure of the product to meet the purchaser's expectations, a risk that the parties had the opportunity to allocate by negotiating contract terms and acquiring insurance. Id. at 871-72, 106 S. Ct. 2295. In contrast, the "'cost of an injury and the loss of time or health may be an overwhelming misfortune,' and one the person is not prepared to meet." Id. at 871, 106 S. Ct. 2295 (quoting Escola v. Coca Cola Bottling Co., 24 Cal. 2d 453, 150 P.2d 436, 441 (1944)). Finally, the Supreme Court expressed concern that permitting recovery in tort for purely economic loss could subject the manufacturer to an indefinite amount of damages. Id. at 874, 106 S. Ct. 2295. A warranty action, on the other hand, has a "built-in limitation on liability." Id.

In contrast, the "minority approach" to the economic loss doctrine permits tort recovery for purely economic loss. The Supreme Court explained that jurisdictions following the minority approach do not distinguish between economic loss and personal injury or property damage because in either circumstance, the damage was caused by the defendant's conduct. Id. at 869, 106 S. Ct. 2295; see Farm Bureau Ins. Co., 878 S.W.2d at 743. In the minority view, the manufacturer's duty to produce non-defective products and tort law's corresponding concern with safety apply equally when the harm is purely economic. *E. River S.S. Corp.*, 476 U.S. at 868-69, 106 S. Ct. 2295; see *Thompson*, 647 P.2d at 337. Ultimately, the Supreme

Court rejected the minority approach because it "fails to account for the need to keep products liability and contract law in separate spheres and to maintain a realistic limitation on damages." *E. River S.S. Corp.*, 476 U.S. at 870-71, 106 S. Ct. 2295.

Lincoln General urges us to recognize a variation of the third approach to the economic loss doctrine, the "intermediate approach." States that follow the intermediate approach permit tort recovery for damage to the defective product alone under limited exceptions that "turn on the nature of the defect, the type of risk, and the manner in which the injury arose." Id. at 870, 106 S. Ct. 2295. The exception advanced by Lincoln General would permit recovery for unreasonably dangerous products that cause damage to themselves during sudden, calamitous events. This exception would require courts to distinguish between those products that expose a product owner to an unreasonable risk of injury during an abrupt and disastrous occurrence and those products that merely disappoint a product owner's expectations. See id. at 869-70, 106 S. Ct. 2295.

The *East River* Court rejected the dichotomy between disappointed and endangered product owners as "too indeterminate to enable manufacturers easily to structure their business behavior." Id. at 870, 106 S. Ct. 2295. The Court also found unpersuasive an exception that focuses on the manner in which the harm occurred:

> We realize that the damage may be qualitative, occurring through gradual deterioration or internal breakage. Or it may be calamitous. But either way, since by definition no person or other property is damaged, the resulting loss is purely economic. Even when the harm to the product itself occurs through an abrupt, accident — like event, the resulting loss due to repair costs, decreased value, and lost profits is essentially the failure of the purchaser to receive the benefit of its bargain — traditionally the core concern of contract law.

Id. (citations omitted).

We agree with the United States Supreme Court that the owner of a defective product that creates a risk of injury and was damaged during a fire, a crash, or other similar occurrence is in the same position as the owner of a defective product that malfunctions and simply does not work. It follows that the remedies available to these similarly situated product owners should derive from the parties' agreements, not from the law of torts, lest we disrupt the parties' allocation of risk. See Prosser & Keeton on the Law of Torts §101(3), at 709 (5th ed. 1984) ("[R]isk of harm to the product itself due to the condition of the product would seem to be a type of risk that the parties to a purchase and sale contract should be allowed to allocate pursuant to the terms of the contract."). To hold otherwise would make it more difficult for parties to predict the consequences of their business transactions, the cost of which ultimately falls on consumers in the form of increased prices. See *E. River S.S. Corp.*, 476 U.S. at 872, 106 S. Ct. 2295 ("The increased cost to the public that would result from holding a manufacturer liable in tort for injury to the product itself is not justified."); Bocre Leasing Corp. v. Gen. Motors Corp. (Allison Gas Turbine Div.), 84 N.Y.2d 685, 692, 621 N.Y.S.2d 497, 645 N.E.2d 1195 (1995) ("In essence, all consumers would subsidize or 'pay premiums' for purchasers of assertedly 'unduly dangerous' products.").

It is difficult, moreover, for parties and courts to apply a rule that focuses on the degree of risk and the manner in which the product was damaged as opposed to a rule that hinges on harm the plaintiff actually sustains. Lincoln General suggests, nonetheless, that adopting the bright-line rule espoused in *East River* would come at too great a price — the decreased safety of Tennessee citizens. We believe, however, that deterrence is adequately promoted by existing law that permits tort recovery for personal injury and damage to property other than the product itself. As explained by the Illinois Supreme Court, "[b]ecause no manufacturer can predict with any certainty that the damage his unsafe product causes will be confined to the product itself, tort liability will continue to loom as a possibility." Trans States Airlines v. Pratt & Whitney Can., Inc., 177 Ill.2d 21, 224 Ill. Dec. 484, 682 N.E.2d 45, 53 (1997).

Finally, Lincoln General argues that adopting the *East River* approach is inconsistent with the General Assembly's intentions under the Tennessee Products Liability Act of 1978, Tenn. Code Ann. §§29-28-101 to 108 (2000). We disagree. Application of the Tennessee Products Liability Act is limited to "actions brought for or on account of personal injury, death or property damage." Tenn. Code Ann. §29-28-102(6) (emphasis added). We interpret "property damage" to mean damage to property other than the defective product. See Progressive Ins. Co. v. Gen. Motors Corp., 749 N.E.2d 484, 487-89 (Ind. 2001). A product's self-destruction is naturally understood as "economic loss" because it "is indistinguishable in consequence from the product's simple failure to function." Progressive Ins. Co., 749 N.E.2d at 488. This Court previously held in *Ritter* that the Tennessee Products Liability Act does not afford the right to recover purely economic losses. 912 S.W.2d at 132-33; see also *First Nat'l Bank*, 821 S.W.2d at 931 ("[T]he rights and liabilities of parties to actions based on diminished economic expectations can be better adjudicated on other legal theories."); Olin Corp. v. Lambda Elecs., Inc., 39 F. Supp. 2d 912, 914 (E.D. Tenn. 1998). In the almost fourteen years since our decision in *Ritter*, the General Assembly has not amended the Tennessee Products Liability Act to permit claims for purely economic loss.

In our view, the *East River* approach fairly balances the competing policy interests and clearly delineates between the law of contract and the law of tort. We therefore hold that Tennessee law does not recognize an exception to the economic loss doctrine under which recovery in tort is possible for damage to the defective product itself when the defect renders the product unreasonably dangerous and causes damage by means of a sudden, calamitous event.

In so holding, we join the majority of state appellate courts that have considered the adoption of an exception to the economic loss doctrine based on unreasonably dangerous products; sudden, calamitous events; or both. [Citations omitted.]

Finally, our holding is consistent with the Restatement (Third) of Torts: Products Liability (1998). Section 21 specifically excludes harm to "the defective product itself" from the definition of "harm to persons or property" for which economic loss is recoverable. Comment (d) to section 21 further explains:

> A plausible argument can be made that products that are dangerous, rather than merely ineffectual, should be governed by the rules governing products liability law. However, a majority of courts have concluded that the remedies provided under the Uniform Commercial Code — repair and replacement costs and, in appropriate circumstances, consequential economic loss — are sufficient. Thus, the rules of this Restatement do not apply in such situations.

CONCLUSION

In addressing the United States District Court's certified question, we are persuaded that the rationale proffered by the United States Supreme Court in *East River* is sound. We therefore hold that Tennessee does not recognize an exception to the economic loss doctrine under which recovery in tort is possible for damage to the defective product itself when the defect renders the product unreasonably dangerous and causes the damage by means of a sudden, calamitous event. The costs of this appeal are taxed to the respondent, Lincoln General Insurance Company, for which execution may issue if necessary.

———————

Strict products liability suits are largely similar to implied warranty suits, though some courts struggle mightily to draw distinctions between the two causes of action; see Denny v. Ford Motor Co., 87 N.Y.2d 248, 662 N.E.2d 730, 28 U.C.C. Rep. Serv. 2d 15 (N.Y. 1995). Typically, either a suit under §402A or a suit for breach of the implied warranty of merchantability can be a viable legal alternative under the same facts. There are some differences that are immediately visible:

(1) A §402A cause of action does not require notice; a UCC cause of action does. See §2-607(3)(a).

(2) In a §402A cause of action, damages are limited to those for physical injury; the damages in a UCC cause of action are not. See §2-715.

(3) A §402A cause of action has the statute of limitations imposed by state law for tort actions; the UCC action is governed by §2-725. The time periods may differ significantly.

(4) A §402A cause of action is not affected by disclaimers or remedy limitations; a UCC action may be so limited. See §§2-316, 2-719.

(5) Privity is not an issue in §402A suits; privity may be an issue in UCC suits.

(6) Section 402A requires that the product contain a "defect," but a UCC warranty may be breached even if the product is not defective. For example, a perfectly good product may neither fulfill the express warranty nor be fit for the particular purpose for which the buyer needs the goods. See Malawy v. Richards Mfg. Co., 150 Ill. App. 3d 549, 501 N.E.2d 376, 3 U.C.C. Rep. Serv. 2d 511 (1986).

PROBLEM 41

The axle on Monty Python's new car snapped in two while he was driving at a high rate of speed on the interstate. Python's car skidded across the median and ran into a hitchhiker, Thumbs Bystander, killing him instantly. As Bystander's attorney, decide which is the best cause of action: negligence, §402A, or §2-314. Whom should you sue? See Martin v. Ryder Truck Rental, Inc., 353 A.2d 581, 18 U.C.C. Rep. Serv. 870 (Del. 1976).

E. UCC Warranties and the Magnuson-Moss Act

In 1975, Congress passed the Magnuson-Moss Warranty Act,[48] which applies to all consumer products manufactured after July 4, 1975, that are covered by a written warranty. Magnuson-Moss was enacted in response to many years of consumer complaints about warranties — in particular about manufacturers' statements that were labeled warranties, but that upon testing in the courts took away more rights than they gave. The stated purposes of the statute are to improve the adequacy of information available to consumers, to prevent deception, and to improve competition in the marketing of consumer products.[49] For a comprehensive study, see

---

48. The full name of the statute is the Magnuson-Moss Warranty — Federal Trade Commission Improvement Act, 15 U.S.C. §§2301-2312 (1975). Title I deals with consumer product warranties. Title II deals with Federal Trade Commission powers. Only Title I will be discussed in this text.

49. Title I, 15 U.S.C. §2302(a).

C. Reitz, Consumer Protection Under the Magnuson-Moss Warranty Act (1978).

To apply Magnuson-Moss, the warranty given must fall within its scope. Read Mag.-Moss §101,[50] and answer the following Problems.

PROBLEM 42

Attorney Sam Ambulance formed a professional corporation, Ambulance, LPC, under which he practices law. When the corporation buys a company car, is it entitled to the protection of the Magnuson-Moss Warranty Act? See §101(1) and (3).

PROBLEM 43

(a) When Tom Jeffire bought his car from Sharp Sam's Used Car lot, Sam said, "I refuse to warrant my cars in any way." Is there a possible Magnuson-Moss action? See Mag.-Moss §102(b)(2). Is there a UCC warranty?

(b) When Michele Bean bought her car from Sharp Sam, she demanded that he warrant the car. Sam said, "I promise that this car has a sound engine that will last five years." Is there a possible Magnuson-Moss action? See Mag.-Moss §102(a). Is there a UCC warranty?

(c) When Norman Anderson bought his car from Sharp Sam, he demanded that Sam write down his warranty. Sam wrote the following: "I guarantee that the only person to ever own this car was a little old lady who only drove it to church every Sunday." If it turns out that in fact the car was owned by Hotdog Harry, a speedway racer, is there a possible Magnuson-Moss action? See Mag.-Moss §101(6). Is there a UCC warranty? See Skelton v. General Motors Corp., 500 F. Supp. 1181 (N.D. Ill. 1981).

(d) When Ann Leonard bought her car from Sharp Sam, she, too, demanded a written warranty. Before the sale Sam took her into his salesroom and pointed out two loose-leaf binders. Inside one of the binders under the model name of the car that Ann desired, Super Z, there was written the following statement:

The Super Z Has a Full Life-Time Guarantee.

Has Sam subjected himself to Magnuson-Moss? See Mag.-Moss §104. Is there a UCC warranty?

---

50. Citations styled Mag.-Moss § _____ refer to 15 U.S.C. §2301 et seq., Magnuson-Moss Warranty—Federal Trade Commission Improvement Act (1975). Note: section enumeration in textbooks is not always consistent with the enumeration in the U.S.C. In some texts, §2301 of the U.S.C. is labeled as §101, §2302 is labeled as §102, etc.

(e) Mammoth Motors phones you, its corporate counsel, and says that it has heard that two types of written warranties are possible under Magnuson-Moss: a *Full* (statement of duration, e.g., 1 year or 90 days) *Warranty* and a *Limited Warranty*. It is very proud of the performance of its vehicles and is considering giving the full warranty. What differences are there between the two types? See Mag.-Moss §§103, 104, 105, 108. What do you advise?

The most important intersection between the UCC and the Magnuson-Moss Act lies in the area of implied warranties. Read Mag.-Moss §108.

PROBLEM 44

Fenton Hardy bought a new car from Dixon Motors. The car carried a full three-month warranty, which guaranteed all the parts except the tires as defect-free. The warranty conspicuously stated that "this warranty is in lieu of all other warranties, express or implied, particularly the warranty of merchantability." One day after the three-month period expired, every part in the car (except the tires) malfunctioned. Hardy sued in state court using UCC §2-314 as his theory. Was the warranty disclaimer effective? See Mag.-Moss §108. Would it have been effective had Dixon offered only a "limited warranty"? See Mag.-Moss §108 again. In an action based on §2-314, may Hardy recover his attorney fees? See Mag.-Moss §110(d); Champion Ford Sales, Inc. v. Levine, 49 Md. App. 547, 433 A.2d 1218, 33 U.C.C. Rep. Serv. 108 (1981).

Ventura v. Ford Motor Corp.

New Jersey Superior Court, Appellate Division, 1981
180 N.J. Super. 45, 433 A.2d 801, 31 U.C.C. Rep. Serv. 59

BOTTER, J.

Ford Motor Company (Ford) appeals from the final judgment in this action in which plaintiff, the purchaser of a new 1978 Mercury Marquis Brougham, sued Ford's authorized dealer, Marino Auto Sales, Inc. (Marino Auto), and Ford, as manufacturer, for damages due to defects in the vehicle. Marino Auto cross-claimed against Ford for indemnification. The final judgment (a) granted plaintiff rescission of the purchase and damages of $6,745.59 against Marino Auto Sales (representing the purchase price of $7,847.49 less an allowance for plaintiff's use of the car and the sales tax), (b) awarded damages in favor of Marino Auto against Ford on the cross-claim in the sum of $2,910.59 (representing $6,745.59 less the resale value of the car), and (c) awarded counsel fees to plaintiff against Ford in the sum of $5,165. Plaintiff's demands for interest, punitive damages in excess of $2,000,000 and treble damages were denied. The trial court's published opinion was limited to the issue of counsel fees awarded under the Magnuson-Moss Warranty—Federal Trade Commission Improvement Act, 15 U.S.C. §2301 et seq., 173 N.J. Super. 501 (Ch. Div. 1980).

Plaintiff took delivery of the automobile on April 12, 1978. According to the testimony of plaintiff and his wife they experienced engine hesitation and stalling problems early in their use of the car which continued without interruption despite repeated attempts by Marino Auto to cure the problem. Stanley Bednarz, Ford's zone service manager and mechanical specialist who assists dealers in satisfying customers, inspected the vehicle on July 13, 1978 and recommended replacing the exhaust regulator valve. Plaintiff testified that he was told by Bednarz that there was nothing wrong with the car and he would "have to live with this one." Plaintiff also testified that later in July 1978 he returned to Marino Auto intending to ask Mr. Marino to take the car back if it could not be fixed but that he was prevented from doing so and was forcibly removed from the premises. . . .

We reject the contention that, lacking expert proof, plaintiff failed to establish that a defective mechanism for which Ford was responsible caused the engine to hesitate and stall. This conclusion could be reached by inferences from the evidence. [Citations omitted.] The findings that Ford breached its express warranty and that the car was substantially impaired were supported by sufficient credible evidence and must be affirmed on appeal. Rova Farms Resort, Inc. v. Investors Ins. Co. of America, 65 N.J. 474, 483-484 (1974).

At the conclusion of plaintiff's case against Ford the trial judge announced his findings and conclusions that Ford had breached its warranty, that the car was substantially impaired because of persistent and continual stalling and hesitation, but that plaintiff had not proven damages against Ford. He held that the only remedy to which plaintiff was entitled was rescission or revocation of acceptance against Marino Auto, see §2-608; Herbstman v. Eastman Kodak Co., 68 N.J. 1, 9-10 (1975), except that plaintiff would also have a claim for attorney's fees against Ford under the Magnuson-Moss Warranty Act, supra, 15 U.S.C. §2310(d)(2). Various reasons were given for affording plaintiff the right to rescind the purchase and receive a refund of the purchase price from Marino Auto. At one point in his oral decision the trial judge alternatively relied upon the theory of strict liability in tort and breach of an implied warranty of merchantability and fitness. In his written opinion he stated that this result "pierced through the dealership system, granting rescission against the selling dealer Marino, based upon defects in breach of the manufacturer Ford's express warranty." 173 N.J. Super. At 504. He also said: "The only remedy under the Magnuson-Moss Warranty Act for Ford's violation of the act was rescission against the selling dealer Marino"; and he viewed Marino Auto as Ford's "authorized agent to remedy defects. . . ." Id. Punitive damages against Ford were denied because of the absence of "deliberate, willful, malicious fraud or wanton and gross negligence or unconscionable commercial practice. . . ." Thus, the case was continued to permit plaintiff to claim a refund of the purchase price, less an allowance for the use of the car, on a rescission basis against Marino Auto, and to permit Marino Auto to claim indemnification against Ford. Ford was to be afforded the opportunity to defend by establishing Marino Auto's fault in failing properly to repair the auto.

On the next trial date Marino Auto stipulated the sale of the car to plaintiff and seemingly conceded at one point that plaintiff would be entitled to a judgment against Marino Auto based on the finding of Ford's breach of warranty on the proofs offered by plaintiff against Ford. The issues to be tried, then, were declared to be damages on rescission or revocation of acceptance, §2-608, i.e., the purchase price less the value of the car to be returned to the dealer, minus an allowance for the limited use of the car. (There was evidence that plaintiff was financially compelled to continue to use the vehicle in its imperfect state. Upon the seller's breach the buyer has the right to "cover" by acquiring substituted goods but is not barred from any other remedy if he fails to effect "cover." Sections 2-711 and 712. See also §2-711(3) which gives the buyer a security interest in and the right to retain or resell goods after revocation of acceptance.) The case proceeded on the cross-claim although Ford contended that no claim ever could arise until plaintiff recovered a judgment against Marino Auto. On the assumption that proof of Ford's breach of an express warranty established plaintiff's right to recover against Marino Auto, 173 N.J. Super. at 503-504, the trial judge ordered the trial to proceed on Marino Auto's indemnification claim. Proof of plaintiff's damage claim was also anticipated before a final judgment was to be entered on the complaint and cross-claim.

Proofs were presented by Ford to show that the car was not defective and that there could be other causes for engine hesitation or stalling, such as contaminated fuel. Although Ford contends that Marino Auto was negligent in not checking the fuel system, there was no proof that contaminated fuel was the actual cause of the problem. Thus, there was no proof that the defect in the vehicle would have been discovered but for Marino Auto's lack of reasonable care in attempting to repair the car. Marino Auto cannot be denied indemnification because it failed to successfully diagnose the cause of the problem. Ford's expert could find nothing wrong with the car, and, on the facts of this case the trial judge could properly have rejected Ford's contention that Marino Auto was at fault for not correcting it, regardless of where the burden of proving Marino Auto's negligence was placed.

At the conclusion of this testimony Marino Auto contended that there was no proof of any wrongdoing by Marino Auto and no basis for rescission.

However, Marino Auto also claimed indemnification from Ford for any damage award granted to plaintiff against Marino Auto. Ford contended that no judgment should be entered against Marino Auto, that there was no basis for rescission and therefore no need for indemnification. Ford also protested the lack of sufficient notice of plaintiff's complaints about the car's performance.

We have considered the merits of this appeal on the assumption that, although Marino Auto has not appealed the judgment against it, Ford can contend that no judgment should have been entered against Marino Auto. Ford has an interest in the judgment against Marino Auto since it was the basis for Ford's indemnification obligation. In fact, the trial judge did consider Ford's arguments against Marino Auto's liability to plaintiff.

Our reasoning through the body of law applicable to this commonplace contractual skein, which binds consumers, car dealers and manufacturers together, differs from that of the trial judge. But we affirm plaintiff's recovery. We conclude that, despite Marino Auto's attempted disclaimer of all warranties, plaintiff can recover from Marino Auto for the breach of implied warranty of merchantability. We also uphold the award of counsel fees against Ford pursuant to the Magnuson-Moss Warranty Act.

The contract of sale between Marino Auto and plaintiff conspicuously contained the following legend on its face:

> The seller, MARINO AUTO SALES, Inc., hereby expressly disclaims all warranties, either expressed or implied, including any implied warranty of merchantability or fitness for a particular purpose, and MARINO AUTO SALES, Inc., neither assumes nor authorizes another person to assume for it any liability in connection with the sale of the vehicle.

On the back of this sales order-contract were the following terms which were made part of the contract:

> 7. It is expressly agreed that there are no warranties, express or implied, made by either the selling dealer or the manufacturer on the motor vehicle, chassis or parts furnished hereunder except, in the case of a new motor vehicle the warranty expressly given to the purchaser upon the delivery of such motor vehicle or chassis.
>
> The selling dealer also agrees to promptly perform and fulfill all terms and conditions of the owner service policy.

For the purpose of this opinion we will assume that the disclaimer of implied warranties of merchantability and fitness was effective under the Uniform Commercial Code §2-316. Since the dealer passed on to the purchaser a warranty from the manufacturer, we will not consider whether the attempted disclaimer by Marino Auto should be voided as unconscionable and contrary to public policy under §2-302 even though such disclaimer could foreclose rescission or other remedies against the dealer and, without privity between buyer and manufacturer, rescission has been held ordinarily unavailable under the Code against the manufacturer. Edelstein v. Toyota Motors Distributors, 176 N.J. Super. 57, 64 (App. Div. 1980); see Henningsen v. Bloomfield Motors, Inc., 32 N.J. 358, 372-373, 406-408 (1960); Gladden v. Cadillac Motor Car Div., 83 N.J. 320, 330-331 (1980); Herbstman v. Eastman Kodak Co., supra, 68 N.J. at 9-10; cf. Santor v. A. & M. Karagheusian, Inc., 44 N.J. 52 (1965). Section 2-316(1) provides that "words or conduct tending to negate or limit warranty shall be construed wherever reasonable as consistent with each other; but subject to the provisions of this Chapter on parol or extrinsic evidence (§2-202) negation or limitation is inoperative to the extent that such construction is unreasonable." It may be argued that the dealer's conduct in transmitting Ford's warranty to plaintiff, the reference to such warranty in paragraph 7 on the back of the purchase order-contract, and the undertaking "to promptly perform and fulfill all terms and conditions of the owner service policy," are inconsistent with a disclaimer of all warranties and that such a disclaimer is an unreasonable construction. See Gladden v. Cadillac Motor Car Div., supra, 83 N.J. at 330; Henningsen v. Bloomfield Motors, Inc., supra, 32 N.J. at 407-408; cf. Murray v. Holiday Rambler, Inc., 83 Wis. 2d 406, —, 265 N.W.2d 513, 519 (Sup. Ct. 1978). The contract in the *Henningsen* case contained the identical obligation to perform all terms and conditions of the owner service policy. Id. The combination of the dealer's undertaking and the automobile manufacturer's warranty was interpreted in *Henningsen* to rebut the disclaimer of implied warranty of merchantability by the dealer. The court held that the attempt to limit liability to the replacement of defective parts was contrary to public policy and void with respect to a claim for personal injuries resulting from an accident caused by defects in an automobile. However, we need not explore these issues further because the Magnuson-Moss Warranty Act has solved many of the problems posed by the intricacies confronting consumers under the preexisting law of sales.

The Magnuson-Moss Warranty—Federal Trade Commission Improvement Act, supra, was adopted on January 4, 1975, 88 Stat. 2183. Its purpose was to make "warranties on consumer products more readily understandable and enforceable." Note, 7 Rutgers-Camden L.J. 379 (1976). The act enhances the consumer's position by allowing recovery under a warranty without regard to privity of contract between the consumer and warrantor, by prohibiting the disclaimer of implied warranties in a written warranty, and by enlarging the remedies available to a consumer for breach of warranty, including the award of attorneys' fees. Id. The requirement of privity of contract between the consumer and the warrantor has been removed by assuring consumers a remedy against all warrantors of the product.[51] A consumer is defined in 15 U.S.C. §2301(3) as follows:

> (3) The term "consumer" means a buyer (other than for purposes of resale) of any consumer product, any person to whom such product is transferred during the duration of an implied or written warranty (or service contract) applicable to the product, and any other person who is entitled by the terms of such warranty (or service contract) or under applicable State law to enforce against the warrantor (or service contractor) the obligations of the warranty (or service contract).

A "supplier" is defined as any person engaged in the business of making a consumer product directly or indirectly available to consumers, §2301(4), and a "warrantor" includes any supplier or other person who gives or offers to give a written warranty or who is obligated under an implied warranty. §2301(5). The term "written warranty" is defined in §2301(6) to include:

> (A) any written affirmation of fact or written promise made in connection with the sale of a consumer product by a supplier to a buyer which relates to the nature of the material or workmanship and affirms or promises that such material or workmanship is defect free or will meet a specified level of performance over a specified period of time, or
>
> (B) any undertaking in writing in connection with the sale by a supplier of a consumer product to refund, repair, replace or take other remedial action with respect to such product in the event that such product fails to meet the specifications set forth in the undertaking.

The Magnuson-Moss Warranty Act provides for two types of written warranties on consumer products, those described as "full" warranties and those described as "limited" warranties. 15 U.S.C. §2303. The nature of the "full" warranty is prescribed by §2304. It expressly provides in subsection (a)(4) that a consumer must be given the election to receive a refund or replacement without charge of a product or part which is defective or malfunctions after a reasonable number of attempts by the warrantor to correct such condition. For the breach of any warranty, express or implied, or of a service contract (defined in 15 U.S.C. §2301(8)), consumers are given the right to sue for damages and "other legal and equitable relief afforded under state or federal law, 15 U.S.C.A. §2310(d); 15 U.S.C. §2311(b)(1).

Appellant Ford contends that the trial judge improperly invoked section 2304 of the act as a basis for allowing "rescission" in the case since the warranty given by Ford was a limited warranty and not a full warranty. 15

---

51. In Miller and Kanter, "Litigation Under Magnuson-Moss: New Opportunities in Private Actions," 13 U.C.C. L.J. 10, 21-22 (1980), the authors discuss the broad definition of a consumer and state that "an assumption is now created that no privity restriction exists."

U.S.C. §2303(a)(2) provides that all warranties that do not meet federal minimum standards for warranty contained in §2304 shall be conspicuously designated a "limited warranty." "Limited warranties" protect consumers by prohibiting disclaimers of implied warranties, §2308, but are otherwise not described in the act. Note, supra 7, Rutgers-Camden L.J. at 381. Clearly, Ford's warranty, which is quoted later in this opinion, was a limited warranty.

15 U.S.C. §2308 provides as follows:

(a) No supplier may disclaim or modify (except as provided in subsection (b) of this section) any implied warranty to a consumer with respect to such consumer product if (1) such supplier makes any written warranty to the consumer with respect to such consumer product, or (2) at the time of sale, or within 90 days thereafter, such supplier enters into a service contract with the consumer which applies to such consumer product.

(b) For purposes of this chapter (other than section 2304(a)(2) of this title), implied warranties may be limited in duration to the duration of a written warranty of reasonable duration, if such limitation is conscionable and is set forth in clear and unmistakable language and prominently displayed on the face of the warranty.

(c) A disclaimer, modification, or limitation made in violation of this section shall be ineffective for purposes of this chapter and State law.

We will first consider the application of this act to the dealer, Marino Auto. As quoted above, paragraph 7 of the purchase order-contract provides that there are no warranties, express or implied, made by the selling dealer or manufacturer except, in the case of a new motor vehicle, "the warranty expressly given to the purchaser upon delivery of such motor vehicle. . . ." This section also provides: "The selling dealer also agrees to promptly perform and fulfill all terms and conditions of the owner service policy." Ford contended in the trial court that Marino Auto had "a duty" to properly diagnose and make repairs, that such duty was "fixed both by the express warranty . . . which they passed on . . . and by the terms of [paragraph 7 of the contract with plaintiff]" by which Marino Auto expressly undertook "to perform its obligations under the owner service policy." See 15 U.S.C. §2310(f); 16 C.F.R. §700.4 (1980). The provision in paragraph 7 in these circumstances is a "written warranty" within the meaning of §2301(6)(B) since it constitutes an undertaking in connection with the sale to take "remedial action with respect to such product in the event that such product fails to meet the specifications set forth in the undertaking. . . ." In our view the specifications of the undertaking include, at the least, the provisions of the limited warranty furnished by Ford, namely:

LIMITED WARRANTY (12 MONTHS OR 12,000 MILES/19,312 KILO-METRES) 1978 NEW CAR AND LIGHT TRUCK

Ford warrants for its 1978 model cars and light trucks that the Selling Dealer will repair or replace free any parts, except tires, found under normal use in the U.S. or Canada to be defective in factory materials or workmanship within the earlier of 12 months or 12,000 miles/19,312 km from either first use or retail delivery.

All we require is that you properly operate and maintain your vehicle and that you return for warranty service to your Selling Dealer or any Ford or Lincoln-Mercury Dealer if you are traveling, have moved a long distance or need emergency repairs. Warranty repairs will be made with Ford Authorized Service or Remanufactured Parts.

THERE IS NO OTHER EXPRESS WARRANTY ON THIS VEHICLE.[52]

The record does not contain a written description of the "owner service policy" which the dealer agreed to perform. Nevertheless, since Ford is the appellant here, we take its contentions at trial and documents in the record to establish the dealer's obligation to Ford and to plaintiff to make the warranty repairs on behalf of Ford (subject to the right of reimbursement or other terms that may be contained in their agreement). For the purpose of this appeal we are satisfied that the dealer's undertaking in paragraph 7 constitutes a written warranty within the meaning of 15 U.S.C. §2301(6)(B). Accordingly, having furnished a written warranty to the consumer, the dealer as a supplier may not "disclaim or modify [except to limit in duration] any implied warranty to a consumer. . . ." The result of this analysis is to invalidate the attempted disclaimer by the dealer of the implied warranties of merchantability and fitness. Being bound by those implied warranties arising under state law, §§2-314 and 315, Marino Auto was liable to plaintiff for the breach thereof as found by the trial judge, and plaintiff could timely revoke his acceptance of the automobile and claim a refund of his purchase price. Sections 2-608 and 2-711. Zabriskie Chevrolet, Inc. v. Smith, 99 N.J. Super. 441 (L. Div. 1968). In this connection we note that the trial judge found that plaintiff's attempted revocation of acceptance was

---

52. The warranty also provided:

TO THE EXTENT ALLOWED BY LAW:
    1. ANY IMPLIED WARRANTY OF MERCHANTABILITY OR FITNESS IS LIMITED TO THE 12 MONTH OR 12,000-MILE/19,312-KM DURATION OF THIS WRITTEN WARRANTY.
    2. NEITHER FORD NOR THE SELLING DEALER SHALL HAVE ANY RESPONSIBILITY FOR LOSS OF USE OF THE VEHICLE, LOSS OF TIME, INCONVENIENCE, COMMERCIAL LOSS OR CONSEQUENTIAL DAMAGES.

Some states do not allow limitations on how long an implied warranty lasts or the exclusion or limitation of incidental or consequential damages, so the above limitations may not apply to you.
    This warranty gives you specific legal rights, and you also may have other rights which vary from state to state.

made in timely fashion, and that finding has adequate support in the evidence.

As the trial judge noted, 15 U.S.C. §2310(d)(1) provides that a consumer who is damaged by the failure of a warrantor to comply with any obligation under the act, or under a written warranty or implied warranty or service contract, may bring suit "for damages and other legal and equitable relief. . . ." Although the remedy of refund of the purchase price is expressly provided by the Magnuson-Moss Warranty Act for breach of a full warranty, granting this remedy under state law for breach of a limited warranty is not barred by or inconsistent with the act. 15 U.S.C. §2311(b)(1) provides that nothing in the act restricts "any right or remedy of any consumer under State law or other Federal law." See also 15 U.S.C. §2311(c)(2). Thus, for breach of the implied warranty of merchantability, plaintiff was entitled to revoke acceptance against Marino Auto, and a judgment for the purchase price less an allowance for the use of the vehicle was properly entered against Marino Auto. Sections 2-608 and 711. Cf. 15 U.S.C. §2301(12) which defines "refund" as the return of the purchase price "less reasonable depreciation based on actual use where permitted" by regulations.

Plaintiff also could have recovered damages against Ford for Ford's breach of its written limited warranty. Marino Auto was Ford's representative for the purpose of making repairs to plaintiff's vehicle under the warranty. See Henningsen v. Bloomfield Motors, Inc., supra, 32 N.J. at 374; cf. Conte v. Dwan Lincoln-Mercury, Inc., 172 Conn. 112, —, 374 A.2d 144, 149-150 (Sup. Ct. 1976). The limited warranty expressly required the purchaser to return the vehicle "for warranty service" to the dealer or to any Ford or Lincoln-Mercury dealer if the purchaser is traveling or has moved a long distance or needs emergency repairs. Ford contends that it put purchasers on notice that they should advise Ford's district office if they have problems with their cars that a dealer is unable to fix. The record contains a document listing "frequently asked warranty questions" which states:

> The Dealership where you purchased your vehicle has the responsibility for performing warranty repairs; therefore, take your vehicle to that Dealership. . . .
>
> If you encounter a service problem, refer to the service assistance section of your Owner's Guide for suggested action.

We do not read these provisions as requiring notice to Ford as a condition of relief against Ford when Ford's dealer has failed after numerous attempts to correct defects under warranty. . . .

One question posed by this case is whether recovery of the purchase price from the manufacturer was available to plaintiff for breach of the manufacturer's warranty. If the warranty were a full warranty plaintiff would have been entitled to a refund of the purchase price under the Magnuson-Moss Warranty Act. Since Ford's warranty was a limited warranty we must look to state law to determine plaintiff's right to damages or other legal and equitable relief. 15 U.S.C. §2310(d)(1). Once privity is removed as an obstacle to relief we see no reason why a purchaser cannot also elect the equitable remedy of returning the goods to the manufacturer who is a warrantor and claiming a refund of the purchase price less an allowance for use of the product. See Seely v. White Motor Co., 45 Cal. Rptr. 17, —, 403 P.2d 145, 148 (Sup. Ct. 1965); Durfee v. Rod Baxter Imports, Inc., supra, 262 N.W.2d at 357-358, where the Minnesota Supreme Court held as a matter of state law that lack of privity does not bar a purchaser of a foreign car from revoking acceptance and recovering the purchase price from the distributor of such cars as distinguished from the local dealer. The decision was made without regard to the Magnuson-Moss Warranty Act.

We are dealing with the breach of an express contractual obligation. Nothing prevents us from granting an adequate remedy under state law for that breach of contract, including rescission when appropriate. Under state law the right to revoke acceptance for defects substantially impairing the value of the product (§2-608) and to receive a refund of the purchase price (§2-711) are rights available to a buyer against a seller in privity. Where the manufacturer gives a warranty to induce the sale it is consistent to allow the same type of remedy as against that manufacturer. See Durfee v. Rod Baxter Imports, Inc., supra; cf. Seely v. White Motor Co., supra. Only the privity concept, which is frequently viewed as a relic these days, Koperski v. Husker Dodge, Inc., 208 Neb. 29, —, 302 N.W.2d 655, 664 (Sup. Ct. 1981); see Kinlaw v. Long Mfg. N.C., Inc., 298 N.C. 494, 259 S.E.2d 552 (Sup. Ct. 1979), has interfered with a rescission-type remedy against the manufacturer of goods not purchased directly from the manufacturer. If we focus on the fact that the warranty creates a direct contractual obligation to the buyer, the reason for allowing the same remedy that is available against a direct seller becomes clear. Although the manufacturer intended to limit the remedy to the repair and replacement of defective parts, the failure of that remedy, see §2-719(2); Goddard v. General Motors Corp., 60 Ohio St. 2d 41, 396 N.E.2d 761 (Sup. Ct. 1979); Seely v. White Motor Co., supra, and the consequent breach of the implied warranty of merchantability which accompanied the limited warranty by virtue of the Magnuson-Moss Warranty Act, make a rescission-type remedy appropriate when revocation of acceptance is justified. Durfee v. Rod Baxter Imports, Inc., supra, 262 N.W.2d at 357.

Lastly, we consider Ford's contention that a counsel fee was improperly granted to plaintiff since no judgment was entered in favor of plaintiff against Ford and Ford contends it was not given adequate notice of the defects in the car. 15 U.S.C. §2310(d)(2) provides that a consumer who "prevails in any action brought [in any court] under paragraph (1) of this subsection . . . may be allowed by the court to recover as part of the judgment . . . expenses (including attorneys' fees based on the actual time expended). . . ." This section is subject to the provisions contained in §2310(e). Subsection (e) provides that, with certain exceptions, no action based upon breach of a written or implied warranty or service contract may be prosecuted unless a person obligated under the warranty or service contract "is afforded a reasonable opportunity to cure such failure to comply." Here that opportunity was given to Ford's designated representative to whom the purchaser was required to bring the car. A direct employee of Ford, Bednarz, also met with plaintiff or his wife and was made aware of some difficulty with the car. We are not certain of the extent of Ford's knowledge of those difficulties. However, in our view the opportunities given to Marino Auto to repair the vehicle satisfied the requirements of 15 U.S.C. §2310(e) in this case.

As noted, Ford also contends that a counsel fee could not be awarded against Ford because plaintiff did not recover a judgment against Ford. The Magnuson-Moss Warranty Act permits a prevailing consumer to recover attorney's fees "as part of the judgment." The trial judge found that Ford had breached its warranty and that the car's value was substantially impaired. He entered no damage judgment against Ford. However, in the absence of proof of actual damages, plaintiff was entitled to a judgment against Ford for nominal damages. Ruane Dev. Corp. v. Cullere, 134 N.J. Super. 245, 252 (App. Div. 1975); Ench v. Bluestein, 52 N.J. Super. 169, 173-174 (App. Div. 1958); Winkler v. Hartford Accident and Indem. Co., 66 N.J. Super. 22, 29 (App. Div.), *cert. den.*, 34 N.J. 581 (1961); Packard Englewood Motors, Inc. v. Packard Motor Car Co., 215 F.2d 503, 510 (3d Cir. 1954). Ford was not prejudiced by the failure of the trial judge to enter a judgment for nominal damages to which the award of attorney's fees could be attached. See Nobility Homes, Inc. v. Ballentine, 386 So. 2d 727, 730-731 (Sup. Ct. Ala. 1980). The award of counsel fees fulfills the intent of the Magnuson-Moss Warranty Act. Without such an award consumers frequently would be unable to vindicate warranty rights accorded by law.

As to the amount of counsel fees allowed by the trial judge, we find no abuse of discretion. The allowance was for actual time spent at an hourly rate of $75.00. Consideration could properly be given to the fact that plaintiff's attorney undertook this claim on a contingency basis with a relatively small retainer. D.R. 2-106(A)(8). The normal breach of warranty case ought not require four separate appearances before the trial court. To some extent this was not in the control of plaintiff's attorney; and plaintiff might have obtained all the relief required against Ford on the first day of trial. But it did not work out that way. In other cases it may be possible to stipulate damages and simplify the issues, thus limiting the cost of this type of litigation for consumers and suppliers alike. But the issues raised in this case were novel in this state, and no one can be faulted for the difficulty and time consumed in this litigation. . . .

Affirmed.

Pursuant to the Act's command, the Federal Trade Commission has promulgated rules to supplement the statute; see 40 Fed. Reg. 60188 (1975), 16 C.F.R. §§701 et seq. These regulations have delineated the precise information required for the §102 warranties, provided for presale availability of the warranty through signs or warranty binders to be kept at the place of sale, and specified the makeup and procedure to be followed by entities (called *mechanisms*) engaging in §110's informal settlement of disputes.

F. Warranties and Article 2A

The warranty rules for the lease of goods found in Article 2A are, with minor variations, mere carbon copies of the Article 2 rules. There is one major difference, however, which arises in what Article 2A calls a "finance lease."

PROBLEM 45

Chemicals of Tomorrow Corp. decided that the safest way to work with hazardous materials was through the use of an advanced robot. It persuaded Aurora Robotics, Inc., to design a robot that would meet its needs. To finance the purchase of the robot, Chemicals of Tomorrow went to Octopus National Bank, which bought the robot from Aurora Robotics and then leased it to Chemicals of Tomorrow. The robot was subject to both express and implied warranties, which became important when the robot ran amuck in one of Chemicals of Tomorrow's laboratories and caused extensive damage. Answer these questions:

(a) Is this a "finance lease"? What factors do and do not influence this decision? See §2A-103(1)(g) and its Official Comment (g); Information Leasing Corp. v. King, 155 Ohio App. 3d 201, 800 N.E.2d 73, 52 U.C.C. Rep. Serv. 2d 443 (2003). As the leasing officer for the bank, what steps would you have recommended to make sure that a court would hold that this lease so qualified? See De Lage Landen Financial Services, Inc. v. M.B. Management Co., Inc., 888 A.2d 895 (Pa. Super. 2005).

(b) What name does Article 2A give to Aurora Robotics in this situation? See §2A-103(1)(x).

(c) Does Chemicals of Tomorrow have the benefit of whatever warranties Aurora Robotics gave to Octopus National Bank? See §2A-209 and its Official Comment.

(d) Is Octopus National Bank responsible for breach of the implied warranty of merchantability? See §2A-212.

(e) If Octopus National Bank's leasing officer had told Chemicals of Tomorrow's president, "We have investigated this robot, and I guarantee you it will cause you no trouble," must the lessor then respond in a warranty lawsuit to a claim for damages? See §2A-210 and Official Comment (g), third paragraph, to §2A-103.

(f) The lease between Octopus National Bank and Chemicals of Tomorrow contained a clause stating that the lessee had to pay the lessor even if the goods did not work, a "hell or high water" clause, so-called because the lessee binds itself to pay the lessor no matter what happens in connection with the performance of the leased goods. After the robot ruins the laboratory, must Chemicals of Tomorrow nonetheless pay Octopus National Bank? See §2A-407 and its Official Comment. Would we reach the same result if the lessee were a consumer?

Colonial Pacific Leasing Corp. v. McNatt Datronic Rental Corp.

Georgia Supreme Court, 1997
268 Ga. 265, 486 S.E.2d 804, 33 U.C.C. Rep. Serv. 2d 1135

BENHAM, Chief Justice.

We granted a writ of certiorari to the court of appeals to review its decision in McNatt v. Colonial Pacific Leasing Corp., 221 Ga. App. 768 (472 S.E.2d 435) (1996). We expressed particular concern with whether the "hell or high water" clause in the equipment finance leases at issue insulated the assignees of the lessor from the lessee's claim of fraud allegedly perpetrated by agents of the supplier of the equipment. We conclude that a "hell or high water" clause does not insulate a lessor's assignee from a claim of fraud where an agency relationship can be established between the assignee and the perpetrators of the alleged fraud.

In early 1991, Linda and William McNatt, sole shareholders and president and secretary-treasurer, respectively, of Quick-Trip Printers, Inc., entered into negotiations with representatives of Itex Systems Southeast, Inc., for the acquisition of an Itex computer printing system. The McNatts selected the equipment Quick-Trip Printers desired to obtain from Itex and, on June 10, 1991, executed equipment finance leases with Burnham Leasing Company, whereby Burnham agreed to purchase the equipment chosen by Quick-Trip Printers from the supplier with which Quick-Trip had dealt, and to then lease the equipment to Quick-Trip for a monthly rental payment. Burnham Leasing immediately assigned its interest in the leases to appellants Colonial Pacific Leasing Corporation and Datronic Rental Corporation.[53] Though she did not later recall signing it, Linda McNatt's signature appears on an "Acknowledgment and Acceptance of Equipment by Lessee,"[54] dated June 11, 1991. Linda McNatt also purportedly executed a personal guaranty of the lease agreement on June 10, 1991.[55]

Quick-Trip Printers experienced problems with the equipment, and the assignee/lessors delayed payment to Itex. While Itex was ultimately paid for the equipment, Quick-Trip Printers never made a lease payment to the assignee/lessors because the equipment never performed as the Itex agents led the McNatts to believe it would. The lessors repossessed the equipment and, four months after it signed the leasing documents, Quick-Trip Printers filed suit against the equipment supplier, the manufacturer, and the lessors, seeking, among other things, rescission of the leases. In an amended pleading, Quick-Trip Printers sought damages for the assignee/lessors' alleged negligent release of funds to Itex. Colonial Pacific and Datronic each filed a counterclaim seeking payment pursuant to the leases assigned to them. The trial court granted summary judgment in favor of the assignee/lessors on the main claims, relying on Quick-Trip Printers' disclaimer of all warranties concerning the suitability of the equipment,[56] and a finding that lessee Quick-Trip Printers had authorized the release of

53. The leases executed by Quick-Trip Printers and Burnham Leasing authorized Burnham to assign its interest in the lease, and stated that any assignee of Burnham would have all of the rights but none of the obligations of Burnham under the lease. Quick-Trip Printers, as lessee, agreed that it would not assert against the assignee/lessor any defense, counterclaim, or set-off that it might have against Burnham.

54. In that document, Quick-Trip acknowledged that the specified equipment had been received "in good condition and repair, has been properly installed, tested, and inspected, and is operating satisfactorily in all respects for all of Lessee's intended uses and purposes." The document went on to state that "Lessee hereby accepts unconditionally and irrevocably the Equipment" and "specifically authorizes and requests Lessor to make payment to the supplier of the Equipment." Just above the signature line, in upper-case letters, was the lessee's acknowledgment and agreement "THAT LESSEE'S OBLIGATIONS TO LESSOR BECOME ABSOLUTE AND IRREVOCABLE AND LESSEE SHALL BE FOREVER ESTOPPED FROM DENYING THE TRUTHFULNESS OF THE REPRESENTATIONS MADE IN THIS DOCUMENT."

55. While acknowledging that the signature on the personal guaranty looked like her signature, Mrs. McNatt questioned whether she had signed the document, noting that she was not acquainted with the person who purportedly witnessed her signature. The witness, an employee of Burnham Leasing, executed an affidavit in which she stated she had witnessed Mrs. McNatt sign the personal guaranty.

56. Prominently displayed on the front page of both leases signed by Quick-Trip was Burnham Leasing's disclaimer of warranties and claims:

> THERE ARE NO WARRANTIES BY OR ON BEHALF OF LESSOR. Lessee acknowledges and agrees by his signature below as follows: (a) LESSOR MAKES NO WARRANTIES EITHER EXPRESS OR IMPLIED AS TO THE CONDITION OF THE EQUIPMENT, ITS MERCHANTABILITY, ITS FITNESS OR SUITABILITY FOR ANY PARTICULAR PURPOSE, ITS DESIGN, ITS CAPACITY, ITS QUALITY, OR WITH RESPECT TO ANY CHARACTERISTICS OF THE EQUIPMENT; . . . (e) If the Equipment is not properly installed, does not operate as represented or warranted by the supplier or manufacturer, or is unsatisfactory for any reason, re-

the funds. The trial court also granted the assignee/lessors summary judgment on their counterclaims, "pursuant to the terms of their respective equipment leases." [57]

The court of appeals reversed the trial court's judgment on the main claims, finding issues of material fact on Quick-Trip's assertion of failure of consideration and on Quick-Trip's claim that the assignee/lessors negligently released funds to the equipment supplier. The appellate court reversed the grant of summary judgment to the assignee/lessors on their counterclaim for the unpaid rent, holding that the leases' requirement that the rental payments be made even if the equipment were damaged, defective, or unfit could not be enforced when it was alleged that employees of the equipment vendor, Itex, had fraudulently induced Quick-Trip to acquire the equipment. That is to say, the "hell or high water" clauses in the leases requiring payment to the assignee/lessors were of no moment where the lessee alleged the lease was procured by the fraudulent misrepresentations of the vendor's agents.

1. The leases in question are classic examples of "lease financing," described by one commentator as possibly "'the most important single source of funds to support business expenditures for capital equipment.' [Cit.]" Amelia H. Boss, The History of Article 2A: A Lesson for Practitioner and Scholar Alike, 39 Ala. L. Rev. 575, 577 (1988). The tax laws, rulings of the Comptroller of the Currency, as well as amendments to the Bank Holding Company Act and government regulations have fueled the trend toward equipment leasing. Edwin E. Huddleson III, Old Wine in New Bottles: UCC Article 2A — Leases, 39 Ala. L. Rev. 615, 616, n.1 (1988). As of 1992, it was estimated that 30 percent of capital equipment in the United States was acquired through leasing. Robert D. Strauss, Equipment Leases under U.C.C. Article 2A — Analysis and Practice Suggestions, 43 Mercer L. Rev. 853, 854 (1992). Most finance lessors view the "hell or high water" clause at issue in the cases at bar as sacrosanct. Huddleson, supra, 39 Ala. L. Rev. at 666.

---

gardless of cause or consequence, Lessee's only remedy, if any, shall be against the supplier or manufacturer of the Equipment and not against Lessor.

57. In each lease, Quick-Trip Printers "acknowledge[d] and agree[d]" that "NO DEFECT, DAMAGE OR UNFITNESS OF THE EQUIPMENT FOR ANY PURPOSE SHALL RELIEVE LESSEE OF THE OBLIGATION TO PAY RENT OR RELIEVE LESSEE OF ANY OTHER OBLIGATION UNDER THIS LEASE." It further agreed to pay the total rent, that it would not "abate, set off, deduct any amount, or reduce any payment for any reason," that the lease was not cancelable or terminable by Quick-Trip, and that it would not "assert against the [lessor's] assignee any defense, counterclaim, or setoff that [Quick-Trip] may have against [Burnham Leasing]." The requirement that the lessee continue to make payments regardless of the condition of the equipment and that the lessee not assert against the assignee/lessors defenses assertable against the original lessor is commonly referred to as a "hell or high water" clause.

A "finance lease" involves three parties—the lessee/business, the finance lessor, and the equipment supplier. The lessee/business selects the equipment and negotiates particularized modifications with the equipment supplier. Instead of purchasing the equipment from the supplier, the lessee/business has a finance lessor purchase the selected equipment, and then leases the equipment from the finance lessor.

> Traditionally, a finance lessor has been thought of as a passive lessor, whose transactions remain functionally the equivalent of an extension of credit. It is typically the lessee, not the lessor, who selects the goods in a "finance lease." Moreover, a finance lessor often has neither the opportunity nor the expertise to inspect the goods in order to discover defects in them. Given the limited function of the lessor, the lessee relies almost entirely on the supplier for representations, covenants, and warranties.

Huddleson, supra, 39 Ala. L. Rev. at 660.

> In effect, the [lessee/business] is relying upon the [supplier] to provide the promised goods and to stand by its promises and warranties; the [lessee/business] does not look to the [finance lessor] for these. The [finance lessor] is only a finance lessor, and deals largely in paper, rather than goods. In that situation it makes no sense to treat the [finance lessor] as a seller to the [business/lessee] with warranty liability, nor does it make any sense to free the [supplier] from liability for breach of promises and warranties that it would have given in an outright sale to the [business/lessee]. Usually, the [finance lessor] expects to be paid, even though the [equipment] might prove to be defective or totally unsuitable for the [lessee/business's] particular business.

2 J. White & R. Summers, Uniform Commercial Code, §13-3(a) (4th ed. 1995).

2. In Georgia, all lease contracts for "goods," including finance leases, first made or first effective on or after July 1, 1993, are governed by Article 2A of the Uniform Commercial Code. OCGA §11-2A-101 et seq.; Ga. L. 1993, p. 633, §5. Because the leases at issue were executed prior to the effective date of Article 2A, we must look to the Georgia law relating to the lease of personal property that Article 2A supplanted — "a hybrid of the law of bailment, contract, UCC Article 2 (Sales of Goods), UCC Article 9 (Secured Transactions), together with common law principles concerning personal property and real estate leases." Sarah B. King, Commercial Code, Leases: Provide Regulations Relating to Leases of Goods, 10 G.S.U. L. Rev. 34 (1993).

Under pre-Article 2A Georgia law, the conduct of the parties to a lease finance transaction is governed by the terms of the lease. Citicorp Industrial Credit v. Rountree, 185 Ga. App. 417, 420 (364 S.E.2d 65) (1987). Georgia case law generally upholds the bargains struck by parties, as long as the contract is not the product of fraud (OCGA §13-4-60), or is not violative of the public policy of this State. Emory Univ. v. Porubiansky, 248 Ga. 391, 393 (282 S.E.2d 903) (1981). A finance lessor's disclaimer of warranties expressed clearly and unambiguously is not prohibited by law or public policy (Petroziello v. United States Leasing Corp., 176 Ga. App. 858, 860 (338 S.E.2d 63) (1985)), and a finance lease may authorize a lessor to assign its rights in the contract free from claims and defenses which the lessee might have against the original lessor. Short v. General Electric Credit Corp., 113 Ga. App. 476 (148 S.E.2d 450) (1966). A contractual requirement that the lessee make its rental payments is valid in the absence of fraud on the part of or imputed to the finance lessor. Woods v. Advanta Leasing Corp., 201 Ga. App. 844(1) (412 S.E.2d 607) (1991). See Holcomb v. Commercial Credit Svcs. Corp., 180 Ga. App. 451 (349 S.E.2d 523) (1986).

The inclusion of a "hell or high water" clause, however, does not resolve the issue in favor of the assignee/lessors. In Doss v. Epic Healthcare Mgt. Co., 901 S.W.2d 216 (Mo. App. 1995), the Court of Appeals of Missouri held that the clause did not protect an assignee who knew at the time of assignment that the agreement was in default, that the lessee no longer possessed the chattel, and that the agreement had been terminated. In Louisiana, the clause may not be enforced when the lessee withholds payment because the assignee lessor has not provided the lessee with peaceful possession of the equipment for the term of the lease. Angelle v. Energy Builders Co., 496 So. 2d 509 (La. App. 1986). Most recently, the Kansas Court of Appeals concluded that the clause did not preclude a lessee from asserting equitable estoppel. Toshiba MasterLease v. Ottawa Univ., 927 P.2d 967 (Kan. App. 1996).

Each of the leases in the cases at bar clearly exclude warranty and promissory liability of the finance lessor and its assignees to Quick-Trip Printers, each states that Quick-Trip agreed to pay the full amount of the rental agreement to assignee/lessors, regardless of defect, damage, or unfitness of the equipment for any purpose, and each states that the lessee agreed not to assert against the assignee lessors defenses it could assert against the original lessor. Thus, the contract precludes the business lessee from asserting the fraud of or imputable to the original finance lessor as a defense against the assignee lessors' claim for payment.

However, the business lessee in the case at bar did not wait until it was sued by the assignee/lessors to allege fraud. Instead, Quick-Trip Printers took the offensive, filing suit in an effort to enforce its statutory right (OCGA §13-4-60) to rescind its lease contracts with the assignee/lessors on the ground that the equipment supplier's employees fraudulently induced Quick-Trip to enter into the equipment lease contracts with the original finance lessor. In order for the purported fraud of the employees of the equipment supplier to authorize rescission of the finance lease, their actions must somehow be imputed to the assignee lessors through the finance lessor. Although the finance leases clearly stated that Quick-Trip acknowledged that the employees of the equipment supplier were not the agents of the finance lessor, such a contractual statement is "not necessarily conclusive as to the non-existence of such a relationship." Potomac Leasing Co. v. Thrasher, 181 Ga. App. 883(1) (354 S.E.2d 210) (1987). In *Potomac*, evidence that the supplier's employees were trained with regard to completing the finance leasing documents and were authorized by the finance lessor to negotiate a finance lease for the finance lessor was sufficient to defeat the finance lessor's motion for directed verdict. However, the supplier's employee who merely submitted a business/lessee's credit application to the finance lessor for review and decision is not, as a matter of law, an agent of the finance lessor. Gulf Winds v. First Union Bank, 187 Ga. App. 383(1) (370 S.E.2d 508) (1988).

In the cases at bar, appellee William McNatt testified on deposition that the equipment supplier's employees who purportedly made the fraudulent statements to the McNatts wanted the McNatts to sign a lease and told Mr. McNatt the monthly leasing costs. Mr. McNatt provided a financing statement to the supplier's employees as part of the effort to secure a finance lease, and the lease documents were presented to the McNatts by the supplier's employees. Mr. McNatt stated unequivocally on deposition that the equipment supplier's employees never represented themselves as being agents of the finance lessors, and Mrs. McNatt, who was also deposed, stated that the employees of the equipment supplier never discussed being employees of the finance lessors. We conclude from our review of the record that the equipment supplier's employees acted only as a conduit of information between the business lessee and the finance lessor; there is no evidence that the finance lease was negotiated by the supplier's employees pursuant to authorization given them by the finance lessor. In other words, there is no evidence of a relationship pursuant to which the purported fraud of the supplier's employers could be imputed to the finance lessor and vitiate the contracts executed by Quick-Trip with the finance lessor. Woods v. Advanta Leasing Corp., supra, 210 Ga. App. 844; Holcomb v. Commercial Credit Svcs., supra, 180 Ga. App. 451. Contrary to the holding of the Court of Appeals, there is no material issue of fact concerning the imputation of fraud to the assignee/lessors and whether Quick-Trip was entitled to rescission of the assigned leases. As there is no evidence of fraud imputable to the assignee/lessors, the leases are not rescindable under §13-4-60, and the "hell or high water" clauses contained in the lease are viable.

3. Quick-Trip Printers cited failure of consideration as a defense to the assignee/lessors' counterclaims for the unpaid rent. In light of its contractual agreement not to assert against the assignee/lessors any defense it might have against the original lessor, Quick-Trip is estopped to assert

failure of consideration as a defense to the assignee/lessors' counterclaims. Furthermore, in the absence of fraud, a lessee is precluded from asserting the defense of failure of consideration against the assignee/lessors of a contract in which the lessee waived all express and implied warranties. United States Leasing Corp. v. Jones Pharmacy, 144 Ga. App. 26 (240 S.E.2d 300) (1977). As was discussed in Division 2, supra, there is no evidence of fraud imputable to the finance lessors. The court of appeals, citing its decision in Granite Equip. Leasing Corp. v. Folds, 133 Ga. App. 856 (212 S.E.2d 490) (1975), concluded that the contractual waiver of warranty was not effective against Quick-Trip since Quick-Trip asserted that the equipment received was not as orally promised by the supplier's employees (the alleged fraud which permeates these cases), and the serial numbers on the equipment received did not match the serial numbers contained in the leasing contract. In *Granite*, the court of appeals held that the lessee's defense of failure of consideration had not been waived by the disclaimer of warranty because the disclaimer applied to the type of machine for which the contract called, "a 'factory rebuilt' press," and not to that which was actually delivered — "a 'reconditioned' press." (Emphasis supplied.) See also Avery v. Key Capital Corp., 186 Ga. App. 712(1) (368 S. E.2d 364) (1988) (disclaimers in lease applicable to 1984 vehicle described therein, but not to 1983 model delivered). Linda McNatt testified in her deposition that the equipment listed in the lease agreements was delivered to Quick-Trip. Her husband did not dispute that the pieces received were the type of machine for which the contract called. He testified only that he noted discrepancies between the serial numbers listed on the contract for individual pieces, and the serial numbers of the parts actually delivered. There being no discrepancy in the type of equipment contractually promised and that actually delivered, the contractual waiver of warranty was effective and defeated Quick-Trip's defense of failure of consideration.

4. Lastly, we address Quick-Trip's contention that the assignee lessors are liable to Quick-Trip for the negligent release of funds to Itex. Despite having an "Acknowledgement and Acceptance of Equipment by Lessee" which authorized the assignee/lessors to pay the equipment supplier, the assignee/lessors withheld payment from the supplier due to the business lessee's verbal notification, in response to inquiries made by the assignee/lessors, that the equipment was defective. According to the assignee/lessors, the funds were released to the supplier upon notification from the business lessee that the equipment problems had been resolved. The business lessee disputes the assignee/lessors' version of the facts. As there appears to be a genuine issue of material fact concerning the claim that the assignee/lessors negligently released the funds to the equipment supplier, we agree with the Court of Appeals that summary judgment in favor of the assignee/lessors on the business lessee's claim was inappropriate.

Judgment affirmed in part and reversed in part.

G. Warranties in International Sales

The warranty provisions of the CISG for the international sale of goods are very similar to the UCC rules. The major difference is not one of substance, but one of terminology: the treaty drafters, wanting to write on a clean slate, eschewed use of the term "warranty" and all the historical baggage that comes with it. Read Articles 35 to 44 of the Convention, and see whether you can nevertheless find within them counterparts to the following:

(a) a warranty of title;

(b) express warranty liability; and

(c) implied warranties of merchantability and/or fitness for a particular purpose.

How are warranties disclaimed under the treaty? See Articles 6 and 35.

CHAPTER 4

TERMS OF THE CONTRACT

I. *FILLING IN THE GAPS*

In the nineteenth and early twentieth centuries, if the parties left a major term out of the contract, the courts typically found no legally enforceable agreement. Judges declared themselves powerless to "make a contract for the parties." In recent years the courts were more willing to save the contract by implying reasonable terms where possible. The drafters of the Code fueled this practice by giving the courts statutory guidance in their gap-filling role. Glance through §§2-305 to 2-311.

PROBLEM 46

Edwin Drake wrote to the Watsons Flat Motor Oil Company and said that he wanted to buy 100 cases of its motor oil, some cases to be Type A (the expensive oil) and some to be Type B (a cheaper kind). He said he would let the company know later how much he wanted of each type. The company told him that Type B was selling for $30 a case, but that since the price of Type A was fluctuating, the sale price would have to be set by the company at the time of delivery. Drake agreed. The parties signed a written contract for the delivery of 100 cases, types to be specified by Drake one week prior to the delivery date, which was set for April 8. On April 1, the agent of the oil company called Drake to ask how much he would take of each type. Drake said, "April Fool! I'm not taking any," and hung up the phone. The company calls you, its attorney, for advice. In the past dealings that it has had with Drake, he always has ordered 100 cases and has taken 50 to 65 percent in Type A and the rest in Type B. The usual price for Type A has been $50 a case, but due to a Middle East oil situation, the price has now jumped to $125 a case. What should the company do? See §§2-305, 2-311, 1-205. If this were an international sale of goods under the CISG, what result? See Article 65. What if Drake had simply said, "April Fool!" and hung up? Is this a definite repudiation? See §§2-610, 2-611. What action can the oil company take to clear up Drake's ambiguous statement? Read §2-609 and its Official Comment; see Pittsburgh-Des Moines Steel Co. v. Brookhaven Manor Water Co., 532 F.2d 572, 18 U.C.C. Rep. Serv. 931 (7th Cir. 1976).

Section 1-304 provides that every contract or duty within the Uniform Commercial Code "imposes an obligation of good faith in its performance and enforcement." Many of the UCC provisions specifically require good faith. Good faith is defined in §1-201(20) to include a subjective component ("honesty in fact") and an objective component ("observance of reasonable commercial standards of fair dealing"). Courts often struggle to determine whether good faith limits a party's ability to enforce the literal terms of the contract and the relevant provisions of the UCC.

Casserlie v. Shell Oil Co.

Supreme Court of Ohio, 2009
121 Ohio St. 3d 25, 902 N.E.2d 1, 68 U.C.C. Rep. Serv. 2d 310

MOYER, C.J.

I

Appellants' proposition of law proposes that "[t]he definition of Good Faith under the [Uniform Commercial Code] incorporating an 'honesty in fact' component requires a subjective inquiry." We disagree and affirm the judgment of the court of appeals.

II

Appellants, Donald Casserlie and others, are a group of independent Shell lessee-dealers in the greater Cleveland area (collectively, "the dealers"). The appellees in this case are Shell Oil Company, its partners, and its successors (collectively, "Shell"), who at various times between 1995 and the time the complaint was filed sold Shell-branded gasoline to the dealers in the greater Cleveland area. The dealers leased gas stations, including equipment and land, from Shell and operated them as franchisees. The parties' contracts obligated the dealers to buy gasoline only from Shell at a wholesale price set by Shell at the time of delivery. This type of term in a contract is known as an open-price term.

The price paid by the dealers is referred to as the dealer-tank-wagon ("DTW") price because it includes the cost of delivery to the stations. Shell charged the dealers a DTW price that was based on market factors including the prices offered by its major competitor, British Petroleum ("BP"), and the street price within areas of Cleveland. In each area of the city, called a price administration district ("PAD"), Shell charged all dealers the same DTW price.

In 1998, Shell, Texaco, and Saudi Aramco formed Equilon Enterprises L.L.C.; Shell's agreements with service stations in Cleveland were assigned to Equilon. In November 1999, Equilon and appellee Lyden Company entered into a joint venture called True North Energy, L.L.C. True North became the distributor of Shell-branded gasoline in the Cleveland area, including to the stations operated by the dealers. True North set the DTW price as the wholesale price it had paid Equilon for gasoline plus six or seven cents per gallon.

Shell also sold gasoline to "jobbers," which were independent companies operating non-Shell-owned gas stations. Jobbers purchased gasoline directly at the oil company's terminal and paid the "rack" price, which was the cost of purchasing gasoline at the oil company's terminal and thus did not include delivery costs.

In 1999, the dealers filed suit against Shell, alleging, among other claims, that Shell had engaged in bad faith when it set the DTW price. The dealers alleged that the rack price was often substantially lower than the DTW price. This allowed jobbers, including Lyden Company, to offer wholesale DTW prices that were substantially lower than the DTW price charged to the dealers. The dealers contend that this pricing is unreasonable and is part of a marketing plan proposed by Shell that was designed to drive them out of business. The dealers assert that Shell's goal was to eliminate them so that Shell could take over operation of the gas stations, thus profiting from all of the sales, including nonfuel sales, at the stations, and not just from wholesale gasoline sales to and rental income from the dealers.

The parties agreed to bifurcate the proceedings and move forward only on the bad-faith claim. On April 13, 2005, the trial court granted summary judgment for Shell. The court found that Shell did not violate R.C. 1302.18, which codifies Uniform Commercial Code ("UCC") section 2-305 and requires a price to be fixed in good faith, when it set the DTW price and that the dealers had not proven that the price had been set in a commercially unreasonable manner.

The dealers appealed, arguing that bad faith may be shown either by evidence of a party's intent, a subjective standard, or by evidence of its commercial unreasonableness, which is an objective standard. The court of appeals affirmed the trial court's ruling and adopted an objective standard based on Tom-Lin Ents. v. Sunoco, Inc. (R&M) (C.A.6, 2003), 349 F.3d 277. The court determined that the dealers failed to show that Shell's prices were not commercially reasonable. The cause is before this court upon our acceptance of a discretionary appeal.

III

As a preliminary matter, we review de novo the granting of summary judgment. Comer v. Risko, 106 Ohio St. 3d 185, 2005 Ohio 4559, 833 N.E.2d 712, ¶ 8.

The parties agree that Shell has authority pursuant to the dealer agreements to set the price of gasoline at the time of delivery. They agree that the price must be set subject to R.C. 1302.18, which requires the price to be "reasonable." R.C. 1302.18(A). Pursuant to R.C. 1302.18(B) (UCC section 2-305(2)), the price must be set "in good faith." "Good faith" is defined generally as "honesty in fact in the conduct or transaction concerned," R.C. 1301.01(S), but in the case of a merchant, "'good faith'... means honesty in fact and the observance of reasonable commercial standards of fair dealing in the trade." R.C. 1302.01(A)(2). It is undisputed that Shell is a "merchant," as defined in R.C. 1302.01(A)(5).

Shell argues that good faith requires an objective inquiry and is demonstrated when a seller's price is within the range of its competitors and the seller has not discriminated between similarly situated buyers. Shell also contends that "an inquiry into the seller's subjective intent is neither permitted nor required." The dealers argue that good faith requires a subjective inquiry and ask, "[H]ow can an open price, specifically calculated to drive a contractual partner out of business, be a 'good faith' price."

The trial court and court of appeals agreed with Shell, relying on Tom-Lin Enters., 349 F.3d 277. In Tom-Lin, the court confronted an agreement nearly identical to the one between the dealers and Shell and concluded, applying Ohio law, that an inquiry into good faith required "an objective analysis of the merchant-seller's conduct." (Emphasis sic and footnote omitted.) Id. at 281-282. Thus, neither the trial court nor the court of appeals considered whether an examination into "good faith" required a subjective inquiry, and neither court engaged in a subjective inquiry.

It is not disputed that the latter half of the definition of good faith, "the observance of reasonable commercial standards of fair dealing in the trade," requires only an objective analysis. The issue before us is whether there is room for a subjective inquiry within the honesty-in-fact analysis in these circumstances.

The UCC does not define the term "honesty in fact." It should also be noted that "[c]ourts and commentators have recognized that the meaning of 'good faith' is not uniform throughout the [UCC]." Mathis v. Exxon Corp. (C.A.5, 2002), 302 F.3d 448, 456. See also Martin Marietta Corp. v. New Jersey Nat'l Bank (C.A.3, 1979), 612 F.2d 745, 751 (noting that good faith is considered subjective in Article 1 but objective in Article 2). Thus, case law defining good faith in other areas of the UCC, such as the Article 1 covenant of good faith and fair dealing, is of somewhat limited value here. Non-UCC cases defining good faith are of even less relevance.

Official Comment 3 to UCC section 2-305 does provide some guidance. That comment provides, in full:

> "[UCC section 2-305(2)], dealing with the situation where the price is to be fixed by one party rejects the uncommercial idea that an agreement that the seller may fix the price means that he may fix any price he may wish by the express qualification that the price so fixed must be fixed in good faith. Good faith includes observance of reasonable commercial standards of fair dealing in the trade if the party is a merchant. (Section 2-103 [R.C. 1302.01]). But in the normal case a 'posted price' or a future seller's or buyer's 'given price,' 'price in effect,' 'market price,' or the like satisfies the good faith requirement."

Comment 3 explains that the purpose of R.C. 1302.18(B) is to restrict the price a seller or buyer may set when the contract price has been left open, by requiring the price to be fixed in good faith. The second sentence of the comment does not remove honesty in fact from the definition of good faith in this context, because it uses the nonexclusive term "includes." The last sentence, however, is not limited to part of the good-faith definition but rather provides a safe harbor where a "posted price" satisfies good faith in its entirety.

A number of cases from other jurisdictions considering open price terms have relied on the posted-price comment. This court has noted in the past that "it is desirable to conform our interpretations of the Uniform Commercial Code to those of our sister states." Edward A. Kemmler Mem. Found. v. 691/733 E. Dublin-Granville Rd. Co. (1992), 62 Ohio St. 3d 494, 499, 584 N.E.2d 695. Relying on the Official Comments to the UCC helps to achieve this uniformity, as does reviewing case law that has previously interpreted particular provisions.

The Supreme Court of Texas addressed the very issue before us here in an essentially identical fact pattern in Shell Oil Co. v. HRN, Inc. (Tex. 2004), 144 S.W.3d 429. Independent gasoline dealers brought suit against Shell, alleging that the prices were not set in good faith under UCC section

2-305(2) because Shell had set the prices intending to put them out of business. 144 S.W.3d 429, 431-432. The court held that Shell did not violate its duty of good faith, because the posted price was both commercially reasonable and nondiscriminatory. Id. at 435-436. It noted that "'[i]t is abundantly clear . . . that the chief concern of the UCC Drafting Committee in adopting §2-305(2) was to prevent discriminatory pricing.'" Id. at 434, quoting *Wayman*, 923 F. Supp. at 1346-1347. A subjective good-faith inquiry "injects uncertainty into the law of contracts and undermines one of the UCC's primary goals — to 'promot[e] certainty and predictability in commercial transactions.'" Id. at 435, quoting Am. Airlines Emps. Fed. Credit Union v. Martin (Tex. 2000), 29 S.W.3d 86, 92, quoting Putnam Rolling Ladder Co., Inc. v. Mfrs. Hanover Trust Co. (1989), 74 N.Y.2d 340, 349, 547 N.Y.S.2d 611, 546 N.E.2d 904. The drafters of the UCC, therefore, incorporated the posted-price safe harbor to prevent extensive litigation involving any open-price term, "while seeking 'to avoid discriminatory prices.'" Id., quoting Malcolm, The Proposed Commercial Code: A Report on Developments from May 1950 through February 1951 (1951), 6 Bus. Law. 113, 186. The court concluded that subjective intent was not intended to stand alone as a basis for liability: "[A]llegations of dishonesty under this section must also have some basis in objective fact which at a minimum requires some connection to the commercial realities of the case." Id. at 435-436.

A few cases note the posted-price comment but conclude that it does not provide a safe harbor where there is subjective bad faith. See Marcoux v. Shell Oil Prods. Co. L.L.C. (C.A.1, 2008), 524 F.3d 33, 50; *Mathis*, 302 F.3d at 455-456; Bob's Shell, Inc. v. O'Connell Oil Assoc., Inc. (Aug. 31, 2005), D. Mass. No. 03-30169, 2005 U.S. Dist. LEXIS 21318, 2005 WL 2365324; see also Allapattah Servs., Inc. v. Exxon Corp. (S.D. Fla. 1999), 61 F. Supp. 2d 1308, 1322 (finding that when the seller double charged for credit-card processing, the action was not a "normal case," because the dispute was not over the actual price charged but over the manner in which the price was calculated; thus, the safe-harbor provision did not apply). Those cases contend that the comment is limited to the "normal case," which does not include a situation where the seller is purposefully trying to drive the buyer out of business.

This interpretation would eviscerate the safe harbor in any action in which the plaintiff alleges circumstantial evidence of an improper motive, leading to drawn-out litigation "even if the prices ultimately charged were undisputedly within the range of those charged throughout the industry." *HRN*, 144 S.W.3d at 435. See Berry, Byers, & Oates, Open Price Agreements: Good Faith Pricing in the Franchise Relationship (2007), 27 Franchise L.J. 45, 49. If a subjective inquiry could determine bad faith, a seller charging a fair price, even exactly the same price as another, good-faith seller, could be deemed to be acting in bad faith. . . .

All of this is not to say that intent is necessarily irrelevant to an analysis of good faith under UCC section 2-305(2), but only that a subjective inquiry is not permitted when the posted-price safe harbor applies. By its language, the safe harbor does not apply when it is not the "normal case" or when the price setter is not imposing a "posted price," "given price," "price in effect," "market price," or the like. As long as a price is commercially reasonable, it qualifies as the "normal case." The touchstone of prices set through open-price term contracts under UCC section 2-305 is reasonableness. A price that is nondiscriminatory among similarly situated buyers correspondingly qualifies as a "posted price" or the like. A discriminatory price could not be considered a "posted" or "market" price, because, in effect, the seller is not being "honest in fact" about the price that it is charging as a posted price, since it is charging a different price to other buyers.

Therefore, a price that is both commercially reasonable and nondiscriminatory fits within the limits of the safe harbor and complies with the statute's good-faith requirement. Given our conclusion below that the safe harbor applies to the facts of this case, we are not required to precisely define good faith as it is used in section 2-305(2). We offer no opinion, in particular, on the role of subjective intent within the good-faith analysis beyond the safe harbor.

IV

The facts of this case demonstrate that the prices set by Shell were both commercially reasonable and nondiscriminatory. Aside from claiming that Shell's goal in setting prices was to drive the dealers out of business, the only evidence of bad faith was that the prices set were too high for dealers to remain profitable and compete with jobbers in the Cleveland area. However, Shell is not required to sell gasoline at a price that is profitable for buyers. "A good-faith price under section [2-305] is not synonymous with a fair market price or the lowest price available." *HRN*, 144 S.W.3d at 437. As noted by the court of appeals: "The trial court . . . found that Shell submitted expert testimony which established that the DTW prices set by the company were within the range set by its competitors." Casserlie v. Shell Oil Co., 2007 Ohio 2633, at P 31. The dealers failed to rebut this evidence. Id.

The dealers also point out that Shell's prices varied throughout the area because of PAD pricing. But the fact that Shell's DTW prices varied by PADs does not itself demonstrate unreasonable or discriminatory pricing. It is reasonable for Shell to adjust according to competition, and there is no evidence that Shell discriminated among similarly situated buyers, such as dealers within a given PAD or dealers in similar PADs.

Finally, the only other argument of discrimination put forth by the dealers is that jobbers were charged significantly less, specifically, the rack price rather than the DTW price. Jobbers and dealers are not, however, similarly situated buyers. The price difference is partially explained by the fact that the DTW price includes a delivery charge, while the rack price does not. We further find the Sixth Circuit Court of Appeals analysis comparing jobbers and dealers in *Tom-Lin* instructive, just as the lower courts did. See *Tom-Lin Ents.*, 349 F.3d at 285-286. *Tom-Lin* noted that jobbers perform additional functions compared to dealers, such as maintaining the properties they own and bearing the risk of environmental liability. Id. at 285. Because jobbers relieve Shell of these obligations, they are charged a lower price. The dealers have not challenged these differences. The disparate pricing between jobbers and dealers is not evidence of discrimination.

V

When a price that has been left open in a contract is fixed at a price posted by a seller or buyer, and the posted price is both commercially reasonable and nondiscriminatory, the price setter has acted in good faith as required by R.C. 1302.18(B), and a subjective inquiry into the motives of the price setter is not permitted. In this case, the dealers have not provided any evidence that the prices set by Shell were commercially unreasonable or discriminatory. The posted-price safe harbor therefore applies, and we affirm the judgment of the court of appeals.

Judgment affirmed.

[A dissenting judge argued that good faith for open-price terms should, as in other contexts, have both subjective and objective components. The Official Comment, in the dissent's view, should not be given such authority, because it was not enacted as law by the Ohio legislature.]

II. UNCONSCIONABILITY

The opposite of the incomplete contract is the one that contains too much. In the name of *freedom of contract, caveat emptor,* and the *duty to read,* courts have permitted some rapacious merchants to insulate themselves in legally formidable contracts that have bordered on fraud and were filled with "I win — you lose" provisions. Early attacks on these *adhesion contracts* (so called because the lesser party had to adhere to the will of the stronger) were made in well-known articles like Friedrich Kessler's Contracts of

Adhesion — Some Thoughts About Freedom of Contract, 43 Colum. L. Rev. 629 (1943). Later, the chief reporter for the UCC, Karl Llewellyn, proposed this famous "true answer" to the problem:

> The answer, I suggest, is this: Instead of thinking about "assent" to boiler-plate clauses, we can recognize that so far as concerns the specific, there is no assent at all. What has in fact been assented to, specifically, are the few dickered terms, and the broad type of the transaction, and but one thing more. That one thing more is a blanket assent (not a specific assent) to any not unreasonable or indecent terms the seller may have on his form, which do not alter or eviscerate the reasonable meaning of the dickered terms. The fine print which has not been read has no business to cut under the reasonable meaning of those dickered terms which constitute the dominant and only real expression of agreement, but much of it commonly belongs in.

K. Llewellyn, The Common Law Tradition: Deciding Appeals 370 (1960).

The UCC tackled the problem in §2-302. This provision caused whole forests to be stripped to supply the paper for scholarly analysis on a grand scale. The redoubtable Professor Arthur Leff set the tone in a celebrated article attacking §2-302 and its unconscionability principle as "an emotionally satisfying incantation" having "no reality referent"; see Leff, Unconscionability and the Code — The Emperor's New Clause, 115 U. Pa. L. Rev. 485 (1967). Professor Leff's chief contribution to the analysis of §2-302 was his division of "unconscionability" into two types: unfair conduct in the formation of the contract (called *procedural unconscionability*), and unfairness in the terms of the resulting bargain (called *substantive unconscionability*). It was Leff's idea that both are required before a court can make a finding of §2-302 unconscionability.

Read §2-302 and its Official Comment, and then answer the following questions.

QUESTIONS

1. Is *unconscionability* defined in the Code? If asked, how would you define the meaning to a judge?

2. Is the unconscionability issue one for the judge or the jury? What is the policy reason for the Code drafters' decision on this matter?

3. Is the §2-302(2) hearing mandatory as a technical step prior to a finding of unconscionability? See Haugen v. Ford Motor Co., 219 N.W.2d 462, 15 U.C.C. Rep. Serv. 92 (N.D. 1974), holding that the hearing *is* mandatory and that summary judgment is inappropriate without such a hearing.

4. Would the answers to these questions change if this were a lease of goods to a consumer? See §2A-108.

PROBLEM 47

Professor Chalk went into the Swank Boating Company and inquired about the possibility of buying a sailboat. He told the salesman that he knew nothing about sailboats, but had always wanted to get into sailing. The salesman showed him a boat, a handsome catamaran, costing $3,150. Chalk, delighted, signed a contract. On his way home from the store, he passed another boat showplace and saw the same type of sailboat advertised at a price of $1,000. Subsequent investigation proved that the highest price any other store was asking for the boat was $1,200. Chalk, who had done no comparison shopping, had not known this. Does §2-302 permit Chalk to avoid the sale? See Morris v. Capitol Furniture & Appliance Co., 280 A.2d 775 (D.C. 1971); Jones v. Star Credit Corp., 59 Misc. 2d 189, 298 N.Y.S.2d 264 (Sup. Ct. 1969); Annot., 38 A.L.R.4th 25. For a historical viewpoint, see Hamilton, The Ancient Maxim Caveat Emptor, 40 Yale L.J. 1133 (1931). See also Ellinghaus, In Defense of Unconscionability, 78 Yale L.J. 757 (1969).

III. *IDENTIFICATION OF THE GOODS*

The Code's provisions on risk of loss, casualty to goods, damages, and other matters frequently draw distinctions based on whether the goods have been *identified* as the specific goods to which the contract refers. Read §2-501, and note the general policy favoring early identification found in Official Comment 2.

PROBLEM 48

Decide if *identification* per §2-501 has occurred in the following situations.

(a) Seller, a fisherman, contracts to sell his entire catch for the coming season. Does identification occur on the making of the contract, on the catching of the fish, or on their packaging with a label indicating they belong to this particular buyer? See Official Comment 6.

(b) Three Ring Circus contracted to sell the unborn calf of the circus's elephant Nancy as soon as the calf was born; the contract was made when Nancy was two-months pregnant. Does the identification occur on the date of contracting, on the calf's birth, or when the calf is marked for shipment?

(c) Farmer Carl agreed to sell to Breakfast Cereals, Inc., one-half of the grain he had stored in Rural Silo, where Farmer Carl's grain was mixed with that of other farmers. Does identification occur on contracting or on segregation of the grain? Read Official Comment 5. See §§2-105(3), 2-105(4).

(d) Wonder Widgets contracted to sell 5,000 widgets to a buyer. Its warehouse contained 2 million widgets, all alike. Does identification occur on contracting or when the goods are picked out and marked as pertaining to this contract? See §1-201(18).

IV.   RISK OF LOSS: NO BREACH

A.   General Rules

Under the old Uniform Sales Act, risk of loss stayed with the person having technical title to the goods and passed to the buyer only when *title* to the goods switched to the buyer. The UCC expressly states that its rules as to who bears the risk of loss have nothing to do with who has technical title (§2-401(1)). This astounded Samuel Williston, the original drafter of the Uniform Sales Act, who called this abandonment of title the "most iconoclastic" idea in the Code; in a famous and rather sad article, he vainly argued against the adoption of the UCC. See Williston, The Law of Sales in the Proposed Uniform Commercial Code, 63 Harv. L. Rev. 561 (1950). Compare Corbin, The Uniform Commercial Code — Sales; Should It Be Enacted?, 59 Yale L.J. 821 (1950), in which Professor Arthur Corbin announced his enthusiastic endorsement of the Code. The general Code rule on the transfer of the risk of loss is that, absent contrary agreement, (1) where the seller is a *merchant*, the risk of loss passes to the buyer on the buyer's actual *receipt* of the goods; and (2) where the seller is not a merchant, risk of loss passes to the buyer when the seller tenders delivery. See §2-509(3).

PROBLEM 49

William College bought a car from Honest John, the friendly car dealer. He paid the price in full, and Honest John promised delivery on the next Monday. On Monday the car was ready, and Honest John phoned College and said, "Take it away." College said he was busy and that he would pick it up the next day, to which Honest John agreed. That night the car was stolen from the lot due to no fault of Honest John, who had taken reasonable precautions against such a thing. Who had the risk of loss? See §2-509(3) and Official Comment 3. Ramos v. Wheel Sports Center, 96 Misc. 2d 646,

409 N.Y.S.2d 505, 25 U.C.C. Rep. Serv. 156 (Civ. Ct. 1978). Might Honest John claim he was a *bailee* so that §2-509(2) applies? See White & Summers §6-3; Galbraith v. American Motor Home Corp., 14 Wash. App. 754, 545 P.2d 561, 18 U.C.C. Rep. Serv. 914 (1976).

PROBLEM 50

Janice Junk decided to hold a garage sale to clean up her home and get some extra cash. In the course of the sale, which was a huge success, her neighbor, Barbara Bargain, offered Junk $200 for her piano, and the two women shook hands. Junk said to Bargain, "Take it away. It's yours." Bargain replied that she would come to get it the next day with four strong friends and a truck. That night Junk's home burned to the ground, and the piano was destroyed. Did the risk of loss pass from Junk to Bargain? See §2-503. If Bargain never picked up the piano and if it was destroyed in a fire *six months* after the sale, what result? See §2-709(1)(a).

Section 2-509(3) applies only when §2-509(1) or §2-509(2) does not. In many contracts, where the goods are in an independent warehouse, the seller must arrange for the warehouse company (bailee) to change its records to show the buyer as the new owner. Subsection (2) of §2-509 sets out the rules as to when the risk of loss passes to the buyer in such a situation. In essence, the risk of loss rests on whoever has control over the bailee. Read §2-509(2).

Since understanding Subsection (2) of §2-509 depends in large part on understanding the nature of warehouse receipts and delivery orders, both negotiable and nonnegotiable, risk of loss under §2-509(2) will be covered in greater depth later in the book, in the Article 7 chapter.

In some contracts the seller is required to ship the goods by independent carrier to the buyer. Such transportation contracts are governed by §2-509(1). Read that section. Note that in transportation contracts the test as to when the risk passes depends on whether the contract requires the seller to "deliver [the goods] at a particular destination." How do you know whether the contract requires the seller to deliver the goods to the buyer or merely to see that they are delivered to the carrier? The next section deals with that problem.

B. *Delivery Terms*

In sales contracts the parties often agree that the seller need only get the goods to the carrier and then the buyer will take the risk of loss. This type of contract is called a *shipment contract.* On the other hand, the parties may agree that the goods must be delivered by the carrier before the risk passes from seller to buyer. Such a contract is called a *destination contract.* According to Official Comment 5 to §2-503, the presumption made by Article 2 is in favor of a shipment contract. Read that Comment. Where the contract is silent on risk of loss, the courts have enforced this presumption that a shipment contract was intended; Wilson v. Brawn of California, Inc., 132 Cal. App. 4th 549, 33 Cal. Rptr. 3d 769 (2005).

Through the years, merchants have developed a set of *delivery terms* like F.O.B. (free on board), F.A.S. (free along-side), C.I.F. (cost, insurance, freight), C. & F. (cost and freight), and ex-ship (off the ship), which are shorthand methods of stating whether the sale calls for a shipment or a destination contract. These terms (and similar ones) are defined and their legal implications stated clearly in §§2-319 through 2-324. Not only are these terms *delivery* terms, defining the passage of the risk of loss, but also they are *price* terms that inform the buyer that the price quoted includes freight paid to the point indicated. Thus, if the seller is in New York and the buyer is in Chicago, a *$2,000 F.O.B. New York* term means that the risk of loss passes on delivery to the carrier and that the price quoted includes only delivery to the carrier (the buyer must pay the freight charges to get the goods to Chicago). Remember:

(1) C.I.F. and C. & F. always indicate a *shipment* contract. C.I.F. means that the price stated includes the *cost* of the item, the *insurance* premium, and the *freight* charge. The law merchant concluded the C.I.F. was obviously a shipment contract (where the buyer takes the risk of loss during shipment) because the buyer agreed to pay insurance as part of the price. If the buyer did not have the risk of loss, why would insurance be needed? C. & F. is the same as C.I.F. without the buyer's agreeing to pay the insurance. Therefore, one might think that C. & F. should indicate a destination contract. It does not for two reasons. First, the buyer frequently asks for a C. & F. price because a blanket insurance policy already covers goods the buyer owns. Second, the law merchant regarded C. & F. as a shipment term, and businesses have arranged their affairs accordingly ever since. Read §2-320.

(2) F.A.S. and ex-ship are delivery terms used in connection with ships. Read §§2-319(2) and 2-322, and use them in answering Problem 51.

(3) F.O.B. can indicate *either* a shipment or a destination contract. In a contract it is always followed by a named place (like F.O.B. Pittsburgh). The risk of loss passes *at the named place.* Thus, if the named place is the seller's warehouse, the F.O.B. term calls for a shipment contract; if it is the buyer's store, a destination contract results. Read §2-319.

PROBLEM 51

Seller in New York City contracted to sell 80 boxes of clothing to buyer in Savannah, Georgia. The delivery term was "$1,800 F.A.S. S.S. Seaworthy,

N.Y.C." Seller delivered the 80 boxes to the dock alongside the *S.S. Sea-worthy* and received a bill of lading from the ship as a receipt. Before the boxes could be loaded, the dock collapsed, and everything thereon disappeared into the water. Under §2-319(2) must buyer pay the $1,800 anyway? What if the delivery term had been "Ex-ship S.S. Seaworthy, Savannah," and the boxes had been properly unloaded just before the dock collapsed? Would §2-322 make the buyer pay?

PROBLEM 52

Seller in Detroit, Michigan, contracted to sell and ship 50 automobiles to buyer in Birmingham, Alabama. Assume lightning strikes, destroying the vehicles *after* the carrier has received them but before they are loaded on board the railroad car that was to take them to Birmingham. Who had the risk of loss if (a) the contract said, "F.O.B. Detroit" (see §2-319(1)(a)); (b) the contract said, "F.O.B. railroad cars Detroit" (see §2-319(1)(c) and Pagano v. Occidental Chem. Corp., 629 N.E.2d 569 (Ill. App. 1994)); or (c) the contract said, "C.I.F. Birmingham" (see §2-320)?

PROBLEM 53

The dispatcher for Perfect Pineapples, Inc., had just finished loading five boxcars of the company's product on board the cars of an independent railroad carrier when he received a notice from PPI's sales department that the company had agreed to sell one boxcar load to Grocery King Food Stores "F.O.B. seller's processing plant." The dispatcher agreed to divert one of the boxcars to Grocery King, but before he could do so, a hurricane destroyed all five boxcars and their contents. Who bears the risk of loss? See Official Comment 2 to §2-509 and §2-501.

Cook Specialty Co. v. Schrlock

United States District Court, Eastern District of Pennsylvania, 1991
772 F. Supp. 1532, 16 U.C.C. Rep. Serv. 2d 360

WALDMAN, J.

Defendant Machinery Systems, Inc. ("MSI") contracted to sell plaintiff a machine known as a Dries & Krump Hydraulic Press Brake. When the machine was lost in transit, plaintiff sued defendants to recover for the loss. Presently before the court is plaintiff's motion for summary judgment and defendant MSI's cross-motion for summary judgment. . . .

II. FACTS

The pertinent facts are not contested and are as follow.

Plaintiff entered into a sales contract with defendant MSI for the purchase of a Dries & Krump Press Brake in August of 1989 for $28,000. The terms of the contract were F.O.B. MSI's warehouse in Schaumburg, Illinois. Defendant R.T.L., also known as Randy's Truck Lines, ("the carrier") was used to deliver the press brake from the defendant's warehouse to the plaintiff in Pennsylvania. MSI obtained a certificate of insurance from the carrier with a face amount of $100,000 and showing a $2,500 deductible. (See dfdt. ex. D.)

On October 20, 1989, the carrier took possession of the press brake at MSI's warehouse. While still in transit, the press brake fell from the carrier's truck. The carrier was cited by the Illinois State Police for not properly securing the load. Plaintiff has recovered damages of $5,000 from the carrier's insurer, the applicable policy limit for this particular incident. The machine was worth $28,000.[1]

III. DISCUSSION

This dispute is governed by the Uniform Commercial Code ("U.C.C.") provisions regarding risk of loss. The parties agree that there is no meaningful distinction between the pertinent law of Pennsylvania and Illinois, both of which have adopted the UCC.

The term "F.O.B., place of shipment," means that "the seller must at that place ship the goods in the manner provided in this Article (§2-504) and bear the expense and risk of putting them into the possession of the carrier." 13 Pa. C.S.A. §2319. Thus, MSI bore the expense and risk of putting the machine into the carrier's possession for delivery. At the time the carrier takes possession, the risk of loss shifts to the buyer. The UCC provides:

> Where the contract requires or authorizes the seller to ship the goods by carrier
>
>   a) if it does not require him to deliver them at a particular destination, the risk of loss passes to the buyer when the goods are duly delivered to the carrier. . . .

13 Pa. C.S.A. §2509.

Goods are not "duly delivered" under §2-509, however, unless a contract is entered which satisfies the provisions of §2-504. See 13 Pa. C.S.A.

---

1. Plaintiff, who also sued for certain consequential damages, asserts a claim for a total of $81,000.

§2509, Official Comment 2. Section 2-504, entitled "Shipment by Seller" provides that:

> Where the seller is required or authorized to send the goods to the buyer and the contract does not require him to deliver them at a particular destination, then unless otherwise agreed he must a) put the goods in the possession of such a carrier and make such a contract for their transportation *as may be reasonable having regard to the nature of the goods* and other circumstances of the case.

13 Pa. C.S.A. §2504 (emphasis added).

Plaintiff argues that the contract MSI made for the delivery of the press brake was not reasonable because defendant failed to ensure that the carrier had sufficient insurance coverage to compensate plaintiff for a loss in transit. Plaintiff thus argues that the press brake was never duly delivered to a carrier within the meaning of §2-509 and accordingly the risk of loss never passed to plaintiff.

Plaintiff relies on two cases. In the first, La Casse v. Blaustein, 93 Misc. 2d 572, 403 N.Y.S.2d 440 (Civ. Ct. 1978), the defendant seller shipped calculators to the plaintiff buyer, a college student, in two cartons by fourth class mail. The buyer authorized the seller to spend up to $50 for shipping and insurance. The seller spent only $9.98 and insured each carton, valued at $1,663, for $200. The seller wrongly addressed one of the cartons, and inscribed a theft-tempting notation on it. The New York County Civil Court held that the defendant had improperly arranged for transportation of the calculators.

La Casse is the only reported case which suggests that a seller's failure to obtain adequate insurance may breach his duty to make a reasonable contract for shipment under §2-504. The dearth of support for plaintiff's position is instructive. A leading UCC authority has remarked: "Under this subsection [§2-504], what constitutes an 'unreasonable' contract of trans-portation? *Egregious* cases do arise." See J. White and R. Summers, Uniform Commercial Code §5-2 (1988). The only such "egregious case" identified by White and Summers is *La Casse,* where "the package was underinsured, misaddressed, shipped by fourth class mail, and bore a 'theft-tempting' inscription." White and Summers, supra, at §5-2.

The actions taken by the defendant in *La Casse* were utterly reckless. Moreover, unlike the defendant in that case, MSI did not undertake the responsibility to insure the shipment, and did not ship the press brake at a lower cost than the plaintiff expressly authorized it to pay.

Plaintiff also relies on Miller v. Harvey, 221 N.Y. 57, 116 N.E. 781 (1917). This pre-Code case is inapplicable. In *Miller,* by failing to declare the actual value of goods shipped on a form provided for that purpose, the seller effectively contracted away the buyer's rights against the carrier. Official Comment 3 to §2-504 states:

[i]t is an improper contract under paragraph (a) for the seller to agree with the carrier to a limited valuation below the true value and thus cut off the buyer's opportunity to recover from the carrier in the event of loss, when the risk of shipment is placed on the buyer.

Thus, a contract is improper if the seller agrees to an inadequate valuation of the shipment and thereby extinguishes the buyer's opportunity to recover from the carrier. That is quite different from a seller's failure to ensure that a carrier has sufficient insurance to cover a particular potential loss, in which case the carrier is still liable to the buyer.

Plaintiff's focus on a single sentence of Official Comment 3 ignores the explicit language of the statute which defines reasonable in the context of "having regard to the nature of the goods," 3 Pa. C.S.A. §2504, and the portion of the Comment which states:

Whether or not the shipment is at the buyer's expense the seller must see to any arrangements, *reasonable in the circumstances*, such as refrigeration, watering of live stock, protection against cold . . . and the like. . . .

Id., Official Comment 3.

The clear implication is that the reasonableness of a shipper's conduct under §2-504 is determined with regard to the mode of transport selected. It would be unreasonable, for example, to send perishables without refrigeration. See Larsen v. A.C. Carpenter, Inc., 620 F. Supp. 1084, 1119 (E.D.N.Y. 1985). No inference fairly can be drawn from the section that a seller has an obligation to investigate the amount and terms of insurance held by the carrier.

The court finds as a matter of law that MSI's conduct was not unreasonable under §2-504. MSI obtained from the carrier a certificate of insurance and did nothing to impair plaintiff's right to recover for any loss from the carrier.[2] Accidents occur in transit. For this reason, the UCC has specifically established mercantile symbols which delineate the risk of loss in a transaction so that the appropriate party might obtain insurance on the shipment. The contract in this case was "F.O.B." seller's warehouse. Plaintiff clearly bears the risk of loss in transit.

There are no material facts in dispute and MSI is entitled to judgment as a matter of law.

---

2. Plaintiff's argument that because the carrier used an allegedly unprofessional sounding name, Randy's Truck Line, and inelegant stationery, MSI was on notice that the carrier was unreliable is untenable. The Philadelphia telephone directory alone lists dozens of moving companies bearing the name, often just the first name, of an individual. Moreover, plaintiff has made no showing that the carrier, which is a party defendant, does not in fact have the means to satisfy a judgment in the amount sought.

Rheinberg-Kellerei GmbH v. Vineyard Wine Co.

North Carolina Court of Appeals, 1981
53 N.C. App. 560, 281 S.E.2d 425, 32 U.C.C. Rep. Serv. 96

Plaintiff, a West German wine producer and exporter, instituted this action to recover the purchase price of a shipment of wine sold to defendant and lost at sea en route between Germany and the United States. Subsequent to a hearing, the court, sitting without a jury, made the following findings of fact.

Plaintiff is a West German corporation engaged in the business of producing, selling, and exporting wine. Defendant, a North Carolina corporation, is a distributor of wine, buying and selling foreign and domestic wines at wholesale. Frank Sutton, d/b/a Frank Sutton & Company and d/b/a The Empress Importing Company, and other names, of Miami Beach, Florida, is a licensed importer and seller of wines. During 1978-1979 Sutton served as an agent for plaintiff and was authorized to sell and solicit orders for plaintiff's wine in the United States. During 1978 and early 1979, Randall F. Switzer, then of Raleigh, North Carolina, was a broker soliciting orders of wine on behalf of several producers and brokers, including Sutton, on a commission basis.

During the summer of 1978, Switzer, on behalf of Frank Sutton, began to solicit orders from prospective customers in North Carolina for wines produced by plaintiff. He contacted Bennett Distributing Company in Salisbury, North Carolina and the defendant in Charlotte, North Carolina, soliciting orders for sale through Sutton of wine produced by plaintiff to be shipped from West Germany consolidated in one container. Switzer, in late August 1978, called the office of Sutton in Miami Beach, Florida, reporting that he had secured orders from Bennett Distributing Company and defendant for 625 cases and 620 cases, respectively, of plaintiff's wines. Switzer then mailed to Sutton a copy of the proposed orders. Switzer also left a copy of the proposed order by defendant with the defendant's sales manager.

On 25 August 1978, the office of Sutton prepared a written confirmation of the orders and mailed them to defendant. Defendant received the written confirmation of orders, but never gave written notice of objection to the contents thereof to plaintiff or plaintiff's agent, Sutton. Written confirmation of the orders together with "Special Instructions" which reflected the instructions to plaintiff regarding the proposed consolidated shipment, were mailed to the plaintiff in West Germany on or about 25 August 1978.

According to the stated prices for the wine, the purchase price of the 620 cases of wine ordered by the defendant was 15.125,00 German marks. On 15 September 1980, the rate of exchange of German marks to United States dollars was such that one German mark equals $.57. Therefore, the purchase price of the 620 cases of wine, 15.125,00 German marks, equals $8,621.25.

Between August and December 1978, defendant's president, Cremilde D. Blank, and Switzer made telephone inquiries to Sutton concerning the status of the wine orders, but were not furnished any information concerning when and how the wine would be shipped or when and where it would arrive. On or about 8 November 1978, Mrs. Blank telephoned Sutton's office and obtained certain details concerning the consolidated order and then wrote to Bennett Distributing Company. Thereafter, in November 1978, Bennett Distributing Company informed Mrs. Blank that it had cancelled its order with the plaintiff, and Switzer thereafter attempted to resell Bennett's share of the order.

On or about 27 November 1978, plaintiff issued notice to Sutton giving the date of the shipment, port of origin, vessel, estimated date of arrival and port of arrival. Sutton did not give any of such information to defendant or to Switzer and did not notify defendant of anything. There was never any communication of any kind between plaintiff and defendant, and defendant was not aware of the details of the shipment.

Plaintiff delivered the wine ordered by defendant, consolidated in a container with the other wine, to a shipping line on 29 November 1978, for shipment from Rotterdam to Wilmington, North Carolina, on board the M.S. Munchen. Defendant did not request the plaintiff to deliver the wine ordered to any particular destination, and plaintiff and its agent, Sutton, selected the port of Wilmington for the port of entry into the United States. The entire container of wine was consigned by plaintiff to defendant, with freight payable at destination by defendant.

After delivering the wine to the ocean vessel for shipment, plaintiff forwarded the invoice for the entire container, certificate of origin and bill of lading, to its bank in West Germany, which forwarded the documents to Wachovia Bank and Trust Company, N.A., in Charlotte, North Carolina. The documents were received by Wachovia on 27 December 1978. The method of payment for the sale was for plaintiff's bank in West Germany to send the invoice, certificate of origin and bill of lading, to Wachovia whereupon defendant was to pay the purchase price to Wachovia and obtain the shipping documents. Wachovia then would forward payment to plaintiff's bank, and defendant could present the shipping documents to the carrier to obtain possession.

Wachovia mailed to defendant on 29 December 1978, a notice requesting payment for the entire consolidated shipment, by sight draft in exchange for documents. The notice was not returned by the Post Office to the sender.

On or about 24 January 1979, defendant first learned that the container of wine had left Germany in early December 1978 aboard the M.S. Munchen, which was lost in the North Atlantic with all hands and cargo aboard between 12 December and 22 December 1978.

Defendant did not receive any wine from plaintiff and did not pay Wachovia for the lost shipment. Plaintiff released the sight draft documents to Frank Sutton. Defendant was not furnished with any copy of said documents until receiving some in March and April 1979 and the others through discovery after this action was filed.

The order and "Special Instructions," mailed by Sutton to plaintiff, but not to defendant, provided inter alia: (1) "Insurance to be covered by purchaser"; (2) "Send a 'Notice of Arrival' to both the customer and to Frank Sutton & Company"; and (3) "Payment may be deferred until the merchandise has arrived at the port of entry."

Based upon the foregoing findings of fact, the trial court made the following pertinent conclusions of law:

2. The defendant agreed to purchase 620 cases of wine from the plaintiff through its agent or broker, Frank Sutton, in late August 1978.

3. Plaintiff failed to comply with §2-504, which provides:

"Where the seller is required or authorized to send the goods to the buyer and the contract does not require him to deliver them at a particular destination, then unless otherwise agreed he must . . .

"(c) promptly notify the buyer of the shipment."

4. The purpose of such notification requirement is so the buyer (as defendant in this instance would have been) may make necessary arrangements for cargo insurance and otherwise to protect itself against any ensuing loss.

5. The plaintiff failed to deliver any such notice to defendant herein prior to the sailing of the ship and the ensuing loss. While plaintiff gave such notice to its agent, Frank Sutton did not pass such information on to defendant, so defendant was unaware of details vital to securing cargo insurance or otherwise protecting itself against loss in transit. The mailing of documents after shipment to Wachovia Bank & Trust Company, N.A. to collect the invoice amount plus freight and charges from defendant by sight draft, of which defendant was unaware until some weeks after the loss of the ship was not prompt notice to the defendant as required by the above statute.

6. Risk of loss of the wine therefore did not pass from the plaintiff to defendant upon delivery of the container of wine to the carrier, as provided in §2-509(1)(a).

7. Plaintiff is not entitled to recover any amount from the defendant due to such lack of notice.

From judgment in favor of the defendant, dismissing plaintiff's action, both plaintiff and defendant have appealed. . . .

WELLS, J.

The first question presented by plaintiff's appeal is whether the trial court was correct in its conclusion that the risk of loss for the wine never passed from plaintiff to defendant due to the failure of plaintiff to give prompt notice of the shipment to defendant. Plaintiff made no exceptions to the findings of fact contained in the judgment and does not contend that the facts found were unsupported by the evidence. Our review on appeal is limited to a determination of whether the facts found support the court's conclusions and the judgment entered. Rule 10(a), N.C. Rules of Appellate Procedure; Swygert v. Swygert, 46 N.C. App. 173, 180-81, 264 S.E.2d 902, 907 (1980).

All parties agree that the contract in question was a "shipment" contract, i.e., one not requiring delivery of the wine at any particular destination. See J. White & R. Summers, Uniform Commercial Code §5-2, at 140-42 (1972). The Uniform Commercial Code, as adopted in North Carolina, dictates when the transfer of risk of loss occurs in this situation. Section 2-509(1)(a) provides, in pertinent part:

> Risk of loss in the absence of breach. — (1) Where the contract requires or authorizes the seller to ship the goods by carrier (a) if it does not require him to deliver them at a particular destination, the risk of loss passes to the buyer when the goods are duly delivered to the carrier even though the shipment is under reservation (§2-505)....

Before a seller will be deemed to have "duly delivered" the goods to the carrier, however, he must fulfill certain duties owed to the buyer. In the absence of any agreement to the contrary, these responsibilities, set out in §2-504, are as follows: [the court quotes §2-504 — EDS.].

The trial court concluded that the plaintiff's failure to notify the defendant of the shipment until after the sailing of the ship and the ensuing loss, was not "prompt notice" within the meaning of §2-504, and therefore, the risk of loss did not pass to defendant upon the delivery of the wine to the carrier pursuant to the provisions of §2-509(1)(a). We hold that the conclusions of the trial court were correct. The seller is burdened with special responsibilities under a shipment contract because of the nature of the risk of loss being transferred. See W. Hawkland, 1 A Transactional Guide to the UCC §1.2104, at 102-107 (1964). Where the buyer, upon shipment by seller, assumes the perils involved in carriage, he must have a reasonable opportunity to guard against these risks by independent arrangements with the carrier. The requirement of prompt notification by the seller, as used in §2-504(c), must be construed as taking into consideration the need of a buyer to be informed of the shipment in sufficient time for him to take action to protect himself from the risk of damage to or loss of the goods while in transit. But see J. White & R. Summers, Uniform Commercial Code §5-2, fn. 12 (1972). It would not be practical or desirable, however, for the courts to attempt to engraft onto §2-504 of the U.C.C. a rigid definition of prompt notice. Given the myriad factual situations which arise in business dealings, and keeping in mind the commercial realities, whether notification has been "prompt" within the meaning of UCC will have to be determined on a case-by-case basis, under all the circumstances. See W. Hawkland, 1 A Transactional Guide to the U.C.C. §1.2104, at 106 (1964).

In the case at hand, the shipment of wine was lost at sea sometime between 12 December and 22 December 1978. Although plaintiff did notify its agent, Frank Sutton, regarding pertinent details of the shipment on or about 27 November 1978, this information was not passed along to defendant. The shipping documents were not received by defendant's bank for forwarding to defendant until 27 December 1978, days after the loss had already been incurred. Since the defendant was never notified directly or by the forwarding of shipping documents within the time in which its interest could have been protected by insurance or otherwise, defendant was entitled to reject the shipment pursuant to the term of §2-504(c). . . .

In the plaintiff's appeal, the judgment is affirmed.

In the defendant's appeal, the appeal is dismissed.

PROBLEM 54

The University of Beijing in China ordered video equipment to be shipped from Applied Technology, Inc., in San Jose, California. If nothing is said about the subject, as a matter of international law, will this create a shipment or a destination contract? See CISG Articles 67 and 69. If the parties had been negotiating for the purchase of this equipment but had not gotten around to signing the contract until the goods were already on board an airplane crossing the Pacific Ocean, does the buyer have the risk of loss only from the moment of the signing of the contract or from the delivery of the equipment to the air carrier? See Article 68.

PROBLEM 55

Dime-A-Minute Rent-A-Car rented a new sports car to Joseph Armstrong. Due to a snafu at the rental office, Armstrong did not sign a rental agreement. As he was leaving the rental car lot, the car was struck by a city bus due to no fault of Armstrong (who was unhurt). The sports car was totaled. Dime-A-Minute demanded that Armstrong look to his insurance to replace the car. Did he have the risk of loss here? See §2A-219. If he had signed a rental agreement making him responsible for the car, would that agreement be valid? See §§1-302 and 2A-108.

The above discussion of risk of loss, both under the UCC and under the CISG, presupposes that neither of the parties is in breach of their agreement at the moment when the risk would normally pass. If this is not true (for instance, when the seller is in breach because the goods do not conform to the warranties made in the contract), §2-509 does not apply (and neither does Article 67 of the CISG); the relevant risk of loss section is §2-510 (§2A-220 for leases and Articles 66 and 70 in the CISG). Before considering §2-510, we need to explore the UCC's definition of *breach*, and that brings us to the standards of performance set by the Code.

CHAPTER 5

PERFORMANCE OF THE CONTRACT

Section 2-301 states that the seller's basic obligation is "to transfer and deliver" and the buyer's is "to pay in accordance with the contract." Thus, the seller must tender (offer to deliver) conforming goods, and the buyer must pay for them. Read and compare §2-507(1) with §2-511(1). They appear to be conflicting, don't they? The conflict disappears when the sections are considered in light of the technical/procedural snarl that they are designed to unravel. It is this: in any contract action, the plaintiff loses unless it can be shown that the other party is in breach. Where a sale of goods is involved, it is frequently true that the parties contemplated a contemporaneous swap of money for the goods. If at the appointed time neither party shows up, the buyer is not in breach because the seller did not tender, and vice versa. If the parties did not intend a contemporaneous swap, but instead contracted so that one or the other's performance was to come first, then either §2-507(1) or §2-511(1) will not apply, since the parties will have "otherwise agreed." When, for example, the parties agree that buyer is to be given six months after delivery in which to pay, failure of the seller to deliver on time is a breach, and the seller may be sued without the buyer's having to allege a §2-511(1) tender of payment. Knowing that the seller's basic duty is to tender conforming goods, and that the buyer's duty is to pay for them, leaves unanswered a host of legal questions. What does the seller's *tender* entail? (Answer: §§2-503 and 2-504.)

What does *conforming* mean? (Answer: §2-106(2).) What means of payment can the buyer use? (Answer: §§2-511(2) and 2-511(3).) These and other questions are the subject of this portion of the book.

I. INSTALLMENT SALES

At common law, successful plaintiffs in contract actions were generally required to prove *substantial performance* (as opposed to technically perfect performance) of the terms of the contract. From your contracts course you may remember Judge Cardozo's opinion in Jacob & Youngs Inc. v. Kent, 230 N.Y. 239, 129 N.E. 889 (1921), the so-called *Reading Pipe* case. The court held that the construction contract was substantially performed even though the contractor installed a different but similar brand of pipe instead of the Reading brand called for under the explicit terms of the contract.

In installment contracts, defined in §2-612(1), substantial performance is still the law. The seller is entitled to payment even where the tender of the goods fails to conform exactly to the contract as long as it "substantially" conforms. Read §2-612. For a good discussion of this section (and many others), see Ellen A. Peters, Remedies for Breach of Contracts Relating to the Sale of Goods Under the Uniform Commercial Code: A Roadmap for Article Two, 73 Yale L.J. 199, 223-229 (1963).

PROBLEM 56

Travis Galleries developed a market in copies of famous statues. It ordered monthly shipments of the statues from Ersatz Imports, agreeing to take 12 shipments of 20 statues each over the coming year. The first month all of the statues arrived upside down in their cartons. The manager of Travis Galleries was amazed that most had survived the trip in this condition. Only one was broken, and a phone call to Ersatz Imports resulted in a promise to ship a replacement at once. The next month the statues were again packaged upside down, and half of them were broken. Does §2-612 permit rejection for this reason? Assume that Ersatz replaced the broken statues within a week, but that the next month the shipment contained no statues at all. Instead, Ersatz had mistakenly shipped Travis poor copies of 20 French Impressionist paintings. Travis Galleries called you, its attorney. May it reject this shipment? Under what theory? May it now cancel the remainder of the Ersatz contract?

Cherwell-Ralli, Inc. v. Rytman Grain Co.

Connecticut Supreme Court, 1980
433 A.2d 984, 29 U.C.C. Rep. Serv. 513

PETERS, J.

This case involves a dispute about which of the parties to an oral installment contract was the first to be in breach. The plaintiff, Cherwell-Ralli, Inc., sued the defendant, Rytman Grain Co., Inc., for the nonpayment of moneys due and owing for accepted deliveries of products known as Cherco Meal and C-R-T Meal. The defendant, conceding its indebtedness, counterclaimed for damages arising out of the plaintiff's refusal to deliver remaining installments under the contract. The trial court, Bordon, J., trial referee, having found all issues for the plaintiff, rendered judgment accordingly, and the defendant appealed.

The trial court's unchallenged finding of fact establishes the following: The parties, on July 26, 1974, entered into an installment contract for the sale of Cherco Meal and C-R-T Meal on the basis of a memorandum executed by the Getkin Brokerage House. As modified, the contract called for shipments according to weekly instructions from the buyer, with payments to be made within ten days after delivery. Almost immediately the buyer was behind in its payments, and these arrearages were often quite substantial. The seller repeatedly called these arrearages to the buyer's attention but continued to make all shipments as requested by the buyer from July 29, 1974 to April 23, 1975.

By April 15, 1975, the buyer had become concerned that the seller might not complete performance of the contract, because the seller's plant might close and because the market price of the goods had come significantly to exceed the contract price. In a telephonic conversation between the buyer's president and the seller's president on that day, the buyer was assured by the seller that deliveries would continue if the buyer would make the payments for which it was obligated. Thereupon, the buyer sent the seller a check in the amount of $9825.60 to cover shipments through March 31, 1975.

Several days later, on April 23, 1975, the buyer stopped payment on this check because he was told by a truck driver, not employed by the seller, that this shipment would be his last load. The trial court found that this was not a valid reason for stoppage of payment. Upon inquiry by the seller, the buyer restated his earlier concerns about future deliveries. Two letters, both dated April 28, 1975, describe the impasse between the parties: the seller again demanded payment, and the buyer, for the first time in writing, demanded adequate assurance of further deliveries. The buyer's demand for assurance was reiterated in its direct reply to the seller's demand for payment. The buyer, however, made no further payments, either to replace the stopped check or otherwise to pay for the nineteen accepted shipments for which balances were outstanding. The seller made no further deliveries after April 23, 1975, when it heard about the stopped check; the buyer never made specific requests for shipments after that date. Inability to deliver the goods forced the seller to close its plant, on May 2, 1975, because of stockpiling of excess material.

The trial court concluded, on the basis of these facts, that the party in breach was the buyer and not the seller. The court concluded that the seller was entitled to recover the final balance of $21,013.60, which both parties agreed to be due and owing. It concluded that the buyer could not prevail on its counterclaim because it had no reasonable grounds to doubt performance from the seller and had in fact received reasonable assurances. Further, the buyer had presented no reasonably accurate evidence to establish the damages it might have sustained because of the seller's failure to deliver.

The buyer on this appeal challenges first the conclusion that the buyer's failure to pay "substantially impaired the value of the whole contract" so as to constitute "a breach of the whole contract," as is required by the applicable law governing installment contracts. U.C.C. §2-612(3). What constitutes impairment of the value of the whole contract is a question of fact; Graulich Caterer, Inc. v. Holterbosch, Inc., 101 N.J. Super. 61, 75, 243 A.2d 253 (1968); Holiday Mfg. Co. v. B.A.S.F. Systems, Inc., 380 F. Supp. 1096, 1102 (D. Neb. 1974). The record below amply sustains the trial court's conclusion in this regard, particularly in light of the undenied and uncured stoppage of a check given to comply with the buyer's promise to reduce significantly the amount of its outstanding arrearages. See Frigiking, Inc. v. Century Tire & Sales Co., 452 F. Supp. 935, 938 (N.D. Tex. 1978).

The buyer argues that the seller in an installment contract may never terminate a contract, despite repeated default in payment by the buyer, without first invoking the insecurity methodology of §2-609. That is not the law. If there is reasonable doubt about whether the buyer's default is substantial, the seller may be well advised to temporize by suspending further performance until it can ascertain whether the buyer is able to offer adequate assurance of future payments. Kunian v. Development Corporation of America, 165 Conn. 300, 312, 334 A.2d 427 (1973); Dangerfield v. Markel, 252 N.W.2d 184, 192-93 (N.D. 1977). But if the buyer's conduct is sufficiently egregious, such conduct will, in and of itself, constitute substantial impairment of the value of the whole contract and a present breach of the contract as a whole. An aggrieved seller is expressly permitted, by §2-703(f), upon breach of a contract as a whole, to cancel the remainder of the contract "with respect to the whole undelivered balance." See Frigiking, Inc. v. Century Tire & Sales Co., supra. Nor is the seller's remedy to cancel waived, as the buyer argues, by a lawsuit seeking recovery for payments due. While §2-612(3) states that a contract is reinstated if the seller "brings an action with respect *only* to past installments" (emphasis added), it is clear in this case that the seller intended, as the buyer well knew, to bring this contract to an end because of the buyer's breach.

The buyer's attack on the court's conclusions with respect to its counterclaim is equally unavailing. The buyer's principal argument is that the seller was obligated, on pain of default, to provide assurance of its further performance. The right to such assurance is premised on reasonable grounds for insecurity. Whether a buyer has reasonable grounds to be insecure is a question of fact. AMF, Inc. v. McDonald's Corp., 536 F.2d 1167, 1170 (7th Cir. 1976). The trial court concluded that in this case the buyer's insecurity was not reasonable and we agree. A party to a sales contract may not suspend performance of its own for which it has "already received the agreed return." At all times, the buyer had received all the goods which it had ordered. The buyer could not rely on its own nonpayments as a basis for its own insecurity. The presidents of the parties had exchanged adequate verbal assurances only eight days before the buyer itself again delayed its own performance on the basis of information that was facially unreliable. Contrary to the buyer's argument, subsequent events proved the buyer's fears to be incorrect, since the seller's plant closed due to a surplus rather than due to a shortage of materials. Finally, it is fatal to the buyer's appeal that neither its oral argument nor its brief addressed its failure to substantiate, with probative evidence, the damages it alleged to be attributable to the seller's nondeliveries.

There is no error.

In this opinion the other judges concurred.

II.   THE PERFECT TENDER RULE

The substantial performance rule has never (at least in theory) applied to single-delivery contracts between merchants. Learned Hand once stated that "There is no room in commercial contracts for the doctrine of substantial performance." Mitsubishi Goshi Kaisha v. J. Aron & Co., 16 F.2d 185, 186 (2d Cir. 1926). To prevail in a single-delivery sale, the seller must make a *perfect tender*, one that complied with all of the terms of the contract, and then show that the buyer refused to take the goods. The reason for this higher standard in single-delivery sales is that in such cases the buyer does not have the same bargaining position a buyer would have in installment sales (where the seller needs to keep dealing with the buyer on repeated occasions and therefore must, as a business matter, keep the buyer happy).

The Code's perfect tender rule is found in §2-601. Read it. (*Commercial unit* is defined in §2-105(6).)

PROBLEM 57

Stella Speculator, a wealthy investor, signed a contract with Swank Motors to buy five new cars. All five were to be delivered on October 1. When the cars arrived, she test drove each of them and then returned two of them, saying she would keep the other three. She rejected the two cars because the audio system did not work in one of them (she was a great music lover) and the carpeting in the trunk of the other was ripping. Swank Motors offered to repair both defects. When Speculator refused to permit repair, Swank sued. Answer these questions:

(a) Does the common law doctrine *de minimis non curat lex* ("the law does not notice small defects") survive §2-601? If so, in spite of the tiny defects, the cars would be conforming. See Official Comment 2 to §2-106; see also D.P. Technology Corp. v. Sherwood Tool, Inc., 751 F. Supp. 1038, 13 U.C.C. Rep. Serv. 2d 686 (D. Conn. 1990) (where goods specially manufactured, buyer not in good faith in rejecting because of insubstantial delay in delivery).

(b) A seller has a right to *cure* in some circumstances; see §2-508. Is this section of use to Swank Motors? See Wilson v. Scampoli, 228 A.2d 848, 4 U.C.C. Rep. Serv. 178 (D.C. 1967), reprinted below.

(c) Suppose Swank can demonstrate that it is common for car sellers to correct small defects. Will Swank succeed if it argues that such correction is a *usage of trade* (§1-303(c)) and thus either that the goods are *conforming* or that because of this usage of trade, the parties have impliedly agreed that a §2-601 perfect tender is not required? See §§1-302, 1-201(b)(3).

III. CURE

If the seller has not made a *perfect* tender, and as a result the buyer has rejected the goods, the seller has the right in some circumstances to *cure* the defective performance. The key section is §2-508. Read it and its Official Comments. For an annotation on the subject, see Annot., 36 A.L.R.4th 544.

PROBLEM 58

On August 8, Francis and Sophie Ferdinand ordered a new car from Princip Motors for $22,000. The car was scheduled for delivery "no later than September 1" (it had special accessories that had to be installed at the factory). On August 15, Princip Motors told the Ferdinands that the car was ready, so they picked it up. Halfway home (three miles from the car dealer), the engine blew up without warning. The Ferdinands were not hurt, but the engine was destroyed. On being informed that the Ferdinands wanted their money back, Princip made the following responses:

(a) Princip offered to take an engine out of a car of the same model and install it in the original automobile (which was otherwise undamaged).

(b) Princip refused to refund the money; instead, it claimed a right to give the Ferdinands a new car to be delivered fresh from the factory on August 20.

Does §2-508 require the Ferdinands to accept either of these cure offers?

In resolving Problem 58, it may help you to know about the *Shaken Faith Doctrine*, developed in a similar situation by the court in a leading case (worth reading):

> For a majority of people the purchase of a new car is a major investment, rationalized by the peace of mind that flows from its dependability and safety. Once their faith is shaken, the vehicle loses not only its real value in their eyes, but becomes an instrument whose integrity is substantially impaired and whose operation is fraught with apprehension. The attempted cure in the present case was ineffective.

Zabriskie Chevrolet, Inc. v. Smith, 99 N.J. Super. 441, 458, 240 A.2d 195, 205, 5 U.C.C. Rep. Serv. 30, 42 (1968).

And, in the words of one pedant, "The court should be willing to take judicial notice of what all modern day consumers 'know': things that do not work well at the start are not likely to work well in the future unless the original defect is minor in nature." Whaley, Tender, Acceptance, Rejection and Revocation — The UCC's "TARR-Baby," 24 Drake L. Rev. 52, 58 (1974).

Wilson v. Scampoli

District of Columbia Court of Appeals, 1967
228 A.2d 848, 4 U.C.C. Rep. Serv. 178

MYERS, J.

This is an appeal from an order of the trial court granting rescission of a sales contract for a color television set and directing the return of the purchase price plus interest and costs.

Appellee purchased the set in question on November 4, 1965, paying the total purchase price in cash. The transaction was evidenced by a sales ticket showing the price paid and guaranteeing ninety days' free service and replacement of any defective tube and parts for a period of one year. Two days after purchase the set was delivered and uncrated, the antennae adjusted and the set plugged into an electrical outlet to "cook out."[1] When the set was turned on, however, it did not function properly, the picture having a reddish tinge. Appellant's delivery man advised the buyer's daughter, Mrs. Kolley, that it was not his duty to tune in or adjust the color but that a service representative would shortly call at her house for that purpose. After the departure of the delivery men, Mrs. Kolley unplugged the set and did not use it.[2]

On November 8, 1965, a service representative arrived, and after spending an hour in an effort to eliminate the red cast from the picture advised Mrs. Kolley that he would have to remove the chassis from the cabinet and take it to the shop as he could not determine the cause of the difficulty from his examination at the house. He also made a written memorandum of his service call, noting that the television "Needs Shop Work (Red Screen)." Mrs. Kolley refused to allow the chassis to be removed, asserting she did not want a "repaired" set but another "brand new" set. Later she demanded the return of the purchase price, although retaining the set. Appellant refused to refund the purchase price, but renewed his offer to adjust, repair, or, if the set could not be made to function properly, to replace it. Ultimately, appellee instituted this suit against appellant seeking a refund of the purchase price. After a trial, the court ruled that "under the facts and circumstances the complaint is justified. Under the equity powers of the court I will order the parties put back in their original status, let the $675 be returned, and the set returned to the defendant."

Appellant does not contest the jurisdiction of the trial court to order rescission in a proper case, but contends the trial judge erred in holding that rescission here was appropriate. He argues that he was always willing to comply with the terms of the sale either by correcting the malfunction by minor repairs or, in the event the set could not be made thereby properly operative, by replacement; that as he was denied the opportunity to try to correct the difficulty, he did not breach the contract of sale or any warranty thereunder, expressed or implied. [The court quotes §2-508—Eds.] A retail dealer would certainly expect and have reasonable grounds to believe that merchandise like color television sets, new and delivered as crated at the factory, would be acceptable as delivered and that, if defective in some way, he would have the right to substitute a conforming tender. The

---

1. Such a "cook out," usually over several days, allows the set to magnetize itself and to heat up the circuit in order to indicate faulty wiring.

2. Appellee, who made his home with Mrs. Kolley, had been hospitalized shortly before delivery of the set. The remaining negotiations were carried on by Mrs. Kolley, acting on behalf of her father.

question then resolves itself to whether the dealer may conform his tender by adjustment or minor repair or whether he must conform by substituting brand new merchandise. The problem seems to be one of first impression in other jurisdictions adopting the Uniform Commercial Code as well as in the District of Columbia.

Although the Official Code Comments do not reach this precise issue, there are cases and comments under other provisions of the Code which indicate that under certain circumstances repairs and adjustments are contemplated as remedies under implied warranties. In L & N Sales Co. v. Little Brown Jug, Inc., 12 Pa. D. & C. 2d 469 (Phila. County Ct. 1957), where the language of a disclaimer was found insufficient to defeat warranties under §§2-314 and 2-315, the court noted that the buyer had notified the seller of defects in the merchandise, and as the seller was unable to remedy them and later refused to accept return of the articles, it was held to be a breach of warranty. In Hall v. Everett Motors, Inc., 340 Mass. 430, 165 N.E.2d 107 (1960), decided shortly before the effective date of the Code in Massachusetts, the court reluctantly found that a disclaimer of warranties was sufficient to insulate the seller. Several references were made in the ruling to the seller's unsuccessful attempts at repairs, the court indicating the result would have been different under the Code.

While these cases provide no mandate to require the buyer to accept patchwork goods or substantially repaired articles in lieu of flawless merchandise, they do indicate that minor repairs or reasonable adjustments are frequently the means by which an imperfect tender may be cured. In discussing the analogous question of defective title, it has been stated that:

> The seller, then, should be able to cure [the defect] under subsection 2-508(2) in those cases in which he can do so without subjecting the buyer to any great inconvenience, risk or loss. [Hawkland, Curing an Improper Tender of Title to Chattels: Past, Present and Commercial Code, 46 Minn. L. Rev. 697, 724 (1962).]

See also Willer & Hart, Forms and Procedures under the U.C.C., §24.07[4]; D.C. Code §28:2-608(1)(a) (Supp. V, 1966).

Removal of a television chassis for a short period of time in order to determine the cause of color malfunction and ascertain the extent of adjustment or correction needed to effect full operational efficiency presents no great inconvenience to the buyer. In the instant case, appellant's expert witness testified that this was not infrequently necessary with new televisions. Should the set be defective in workmanship or parts, the loss would be upon the manufacturer who warranted it free from mechanical defect. Here the adamant refusal of Mrs. Kolley, acting on behalf of appellee, to allow inspection essential to the determination of the cause of the excessive red tinge to the picture defeated any effort by the seller to provide timely repair or even replacement of the set if the difficulty could not be corrected. The cause of the defect might have been minor and easily adjusted or it may have been substantial and required replacement by another new set but the seller was never given an adequate opportunity to make a determination.

We do not hold that appellant has no liability to appellee,[3] but as he was denied access and a reasonable opportunity to repair, appellee has not shown a breach of warranty entitling him either to a brand new set or to rescission. We therefore reverse the judgment of the trial court granting rescission and directing the return of the purchase price of the set.

Reversed.

QUESTIONS

1. Is the court following the perfect tender rule here? See §2-601.
2. What portion of §2-508 is relevant to this case?
3. In this case the buyer rejected the goods but refused to return them to the seller. Is this permissible? See §2-711(3).

IV. REJECTION AND ACCEPTANCE

When the seller makes a tender of the goods, the buyer must choose between two possible legal responses: rejection (§2-602) and acceptance (§§2-606 and 2-607). A buyer cannot do both since rejection and acceptance are mutually exclusive actions. Failure to act results in a technical *acceptance*, since rejection must come within a reasonable period of time after delivery of the goods. Read §2-602. The definition of *acceptance* is found in §2-606, and its legal consequences are spelled out in §2-607. Note two important things about these sections as you read them: (1) a buyer is entitled to a reasonable *trial-use* period to see if the goods conform (this is phrased in the Code as a "reasonable opportunity to inspect"; see §2-513), and (2) on acceptance, the burden of proof as to defects shifts to the buyer (§2-607(4)). Prior to acceptance, the seller must prove that a perfect tender was made under §2-601.

---

3. Appellant on appeal has renewed his willingness to remedy any defect in the tender, and thus there is no problem of expiration of his warranties. He should be afforded the right to inspect and correct any malfunction. If appellee refuses to allow appellant an opportunity to do so, then no cause of action can lie for breach of warranty, express or implied, and the loss must be borne by appellee.

PROBLEM 59

Midwestern Seafoods, headquartered in Iowa, ordered 50 live lobsters from Maine Exports, "F.O.B. Portland." On September 1, Maine Exports loaded the lobsters on board an airplane in Portland, from where they were flown to Boston and then to Des Moines. Maine Exports failed to notify Midwestern Seafoods of the date of the flight until two days later, when Midwestern's purchasing agent called to inquire. He then made a few calls and located the lobsters in Des Moines, where they had been sitting for a day. Midwestern signed a receipt and picked the lobsters up. Twenty of them were clearly dying (15 due to bad handling by Maine Exports before they were handed over to the airline and 5 due to damage in transit); the other 30 were fine. Midwestern decided, for reasons that are unclear, that it wanted none of the lobsters.

(a) Is the seller's failure to notify Midwestern of the shipment a ground for rejection? See §2-504.

(b) May Midwestern reject because of the 20 defective lobsters? See §§2-601, 2-503, 2-509(1), 2-510(1).

(c) How quickly must Midwestern act if it wishes to reject? What technical steps is it required to take? See §§2-602, 1-201(26), 1-204.

(d) Must Midwestern reship the goods to Maine Exports if the latter offers to pay the freight? See §2-602(2) with its Official Comment 2; §§2-603, 2-604.

(e) If Midwestern decides to keep 30 of the lobsters for resale, is this allowed? See §§2-602(2)(a), 2-606; cf. §§2-601, 2-105(6); Annot., 67 A.L.R.3d 363.

(f) If Midwestern rejects the goods, must it give its reasons in the notice of rejection? What penalty is there for not doing so? See §2-605 and its Official Comment 2.

(g) If Midwestern gives a valid notice of rejection within a reasonable period of time after the lobsters are delivered, what should it then do with the lobsters? See §2-602(2).

Ramirez v. Autosport

New Jersey Supreme Court, 1982
88 N.J. 277, 440 A.2d 1345, 33 U.C.C. Rep. Serv. 134

POLLOCK, J.

This case raises several issues under the Uniform Commercial Code ("the Code" and "UCC") concerning whether a buyer may reject a tender of goods with minor defects and whether a seller may cure the defects. We consider also the remedies available to the buyer, including cancellation of the contract. The main issue is whether plaintiffs, Mr. and Mrs. Ramirez, could reject the tender by defendant, Autosport, of a camper van with minor defects and cancel the contract for the purchase of the van.

The trial court ruled that Mr. and Mrs. Ramirez rightfully rejected the van and awarded them the fair market value of their trade-in van. The Appellate Division affirmed in a brief per curiam decision which, like the trial court opinion, was unreported. We affirm the judgment of the Appellate Division.

I

Following a mobile home show at the Meadowlands Sports Complex, Mr. and Mrs. Ramirez visited Autosport's showroom in Somerville. On July 20, 1978, the Ramirezes and Donald Graff, a salesman for Autosport, agreed on the sale of a new camper and the trade-in of the van owned by Mr. and Mrs. Ramirez. Autosport and the Ramirezes signed a simple contract reflecting a $14,100 purchase price for the new van with a $4,700 trade-in allowance for the Ramirez van, which Mr. and Mrs. Ramirez left with Autosport. After further allowance for taxes, title and documentary fees, the net price was $9,902. Because Autosport needed two weeks to prepare the new van, the contract provided for delivery on or about August 3, 1978.

On that date, Mr. and Mrs. Ramirez returned with their checks to Autosport to pick up the new van. Graff was not there so Mr. White, another salesman, met them. Inspection disclosed several defects in the van. The paint was scratched, both the electric and sewer hookups were missing, and the hubcaps were not installed. White advised the Ramirezes not to accept the camper because it was not ready.

Mr. and Mrs. Ramirez wanted the van for a summer vacation and called Graff several times. Each time Graff told them it was not ready for delivery. Finally, Graff called to notify them that the camper was ready. On August 14, Mr. and Mrs. Ramirez went to Autosport to accept delivery, but workers were still touching up the outside paint. Also, the camper windows were open, and the dining area cushions were soaking wet. Mr. and Mrs. Ramirez could not use the camper in that condition, but Mr. Leis, Autosport's manager, suggested that they take the van and that Autosport would replace the cushions later. Mrs. Ramirez counteroffered to accept the van if they could withhold $2,000, but Leis agreed to no more than $250, which she refused. Leis then agreed to replace the cushions and to call them when the van was ready.

On August 15, 1978, Autosport transferred title to the van to Mr. and Mrs. Ramirez, a fact unknown to them until the summer of 1979. Between August 15 and September 1, 1978, Mrs. Ramirez called Graff several times urging him to complete the preparation of the van, but Graff constantly advised her that the van was not ready. He finally informed her that they could pick it up on September 1.

When Mr. and Mrs. Ramirez went to the showroom on September 1, Graff asked them to wait. And wait they did — for one and a half hours. No one from Autosport came forward to talk with them, and the Ramirezes left in disgust.

On October 5, 1978, Mr. and Mrs. Ramirez went to Autosport with an attorney friend. Although the parties disagreed on what occurred, the general topic was whether they should proceed with the deal or Autosport should return to the Ramirezes their trade-in van. Mrs. Ramirez claimed they rejected the new van and requested the return of their trade-in. Mr. Lustig, the owner of Autosport, thought, however, that the deal could be salvaged if the parties could agree on the dollar amount of a credit for the Ramirezes. Mr. and Mrs. Ramirez never took possession of the new van and repeated their request for the return of their trade-in. Later in October, however, Autosport sold the trade-in to an innocent third party for $4,995. Autosport claimed that the Ramirezes' van had a book value of $3,200 and claimed further that it spent $1,159.62 to repair their van. By subtracting the total of those two figures, $4,159.62, from the $4,995.00 sale price, Autosport claimed a $600-700 profit on the sale.

On November 20, 1978, the Ramirezes sued Autosport seeking, among other things, rescission of the contract. Autosport counterclaimed for breach of contract.

II

Our initial inquiry is whether a consumer may reject defective goods that do not conform to the contract of sale. The basic issue is whether under the UCC, adopted in New Jersey as N.J.S.A. 12A:1-101 et seq., a seller has the duty to deliver goods that conform precisely to the contract. We conclude that the seller is under such a duty to make a "perfect tender" and that a buyer has the right to reject goods that do not conform to the contract. That conclusion, however, does not resolve the entire dispute between buyer and seller. A more complete answer requires a brief statement of the history of the mutual obligations of buyers and sellers of commercial goods.

In the nineteenth century, sellers were required to deliver goods that complied exactly with the sales agreement. See Filley v. Polk, 115 U.S. 213, 29 L. Ed. 372, 373 (1885) (buyer not obliged to accept otherwise conforming scrap iron shipped to New Orleans from Leith, rather than Glasgow, Scotland, as required by contract); Columbian Iron Works & Dry-Dock Co. v. Douglas, 84 Md. 44, 34 A. 1118, 1120-1121 (1896) (buyer who agreed to purchase steel scrap from United States cruisers not obliged to take any other kind of scrap). That rule, known as the "perfect tender" rule, remained part of the law of sales well into the twentieth century. By the 1920's the doctrine was so entrenched in the law that Judge Learned Hand declared "[t]here is no room in commercial contracts for the doctrine of substantial performance." Mitsubishi Goshi Kaisha v. J. Aron & Co., Inc., 16 F.2d 185, 186 (2d Cir. 1926).

The harshness of the rule led courts to seek to ameliorate its effect and to bring the law of sales in closer harmony with the law of contracts, which allows rescission only for material breaches. LeRoy Dyal Co. v. Allen, 161 F.2d 152, 155 (4th Cir. 1947). See 5 Corbin, Contracts §1104 at 464 (1951); 12 Williston, Contracts §1455 at 14 (3d ed. 1970). Nevertheless, a variation of the perfect tender rule appeared in the Uniform Sales Act. N.J.S.A. 46:30-75 (purchasers permitted to reject goods or rescind contracts for any breach of warranty); N.J.S.A. 46:30-18 to -21 (warranties extended to include all the seller's obligations to the goods). See Honnold, "Buyer's Right of Rejection, A Study in the Impact of Codification Upon a Commercial Problem," 97 U. Pa. L. Rev. 457, 460 (1949). The chief objection to the continuation of the perfect tender rule was that buyers in a declining market would reject goods for minor nonconformities and force the loss on surprised sellers. See Hawkland, Sales and Bulk Sales Under the Uniform Commercial Code, 120-122 (1958), cited in N.J.S.A. 12A:2-508, New Jersey Study Comment 3.

To the extent that a buyer can reject goods for any nonconformity, the UCC retains the perfect tender rule. Section 2-106 states that goods conform to a contract "when they are in accordance with the obligations under the contract." Section 2-601 authorizes a buyer to reject goods if they "or the tender of delivery fail in any respect to conform to the contract." The Code, however, mitigates the harshness of the perfect tender rule and balances the interests of buyer and seller. See Restatement (Second), Contracts, §241 comment (b) (1981). The Code achieves that result through its provisions for revocation of acceptance and cure. N.J.S.A. 2-608, 2-508.

Initially, the rights of the parties vary depending on whether the rejection occurs before or after acceptance of the goods. Before acceptance, the buyer may reject goods for any nonconformity. N.J.S.A. 2-601. Because of the seller's right to cure, however, the buyer's rejection does not necessarily discharge the contract. N.J.S.A. 2-508. Within the time set for performance in the contract, the seller's right to cure is unconditional. Id., subsec. (1); see id., Official Comment 1. Some authorities recommend granting a breaching party a right to cure in all contracts, not merely those for the sale of goods. Restatement (Second), Contracts, ch. 10, especially §§237 and 241. Underlying the right to cure in both kinds of contracts is the recognition that parties should be encouraged to communicate with each other and to resolve their own problems. Id., Introduction p. 193.

The rights of the parties also vary if rejection occurs after the time set for performance. After expiration of that time, the seller has a further reasonable time to cure if he believed reasonably that the goods would be acceptable with or without a money allowance. N.J.S.A. 2-508(2). The determination of what constitutes a further reasonable time depends on the surrounding circumstances, which include the change of position by and the amount of inconvenience to the buyer. N.J.S.A. 2-508, Official Comment 3. Those circumstances also include the length of time needed by the seller to correct the nonconformity and his ability to salvage the goods by resale to others. See Restatement (Second), Contracts, §241 comment (d). Thus, the Code balances the buyer's right to reject nonconforming goods with a "second chance" for the seller to conform the goods to the contract under certain limited circumstances. N.J.S.A. 2-508, New Jersey Study Comment 1.

After acceptance, the Code strikes a different balance: the buyer may revoke acceptance only if the nonconformity substantially impairs the value of the goods to him. N.J.S.A. 2-608. See Herbstman v. Eastman Kodak Co., 68 N.J. 1, 9 (1975). See generally, Priest, "Breach and Remedy for the Tender of Non-Conforming Goods under the Uniform Commercial Code: An Economic Approach," 92 Harv. L. Rev. 960, 971-973 (1978). This provision protects the seller from revocation for trivial defects. *Herbstman,* supra, 68 N.J. at 9. It also prevents the buyer from taking undue advantage of the seller by allowing goods to depreciate and then returning them because of asserted minor defects. See White & Summers, Uniform Commercial Code, §8-3 at 391 (2d ed. 1980). Because this case involves rejection of goods, we need not decide whether a seller has a right to cure substantial defects that justify revocation of acceptance. See Pavesi v. Ford Motor Co., 155 N.J. Super. 373, 378 (App. Div. 1978) (right to cure after acceptance limited to trivial defects) and White & Summers, supra, §8-4 at 319 n.76 (open question as to the relationship between §§2-608 and 2-508).

Other courts agree that the buyer has a right of rejection for any nonconformity, but that the seller has a countervailing right to cure within a reasonable time. Marine Mart Inc. v. Pearce, 480 S.W.2d 133, 137 (Ark. 1972). See Intermeat, Inc. v. American Poultry, Inc., 575 F.2d 1017, 1024 (2d Cir. 1978); Moulton Cavity & Mold, Inc. v. Lyn-Flex Industries, 396 A.2d 1024, 1027 n.6 (Me. 1979); Uchitel v. F.R. Tripler & Co., 434 N.Y.S.2d 77, 81, 107 Misc. 2d 310 (App. Term 1980); Rutland Music Services, Inc. v. Ford Motor Co., 422 A.2d 248, 249 (Vt. 1980). But see McKenzie v. Alla-Ohio Coals, Inc., 29 U.C.C. Rep. 852, 856-857 (D.D.C. 1979).

One New Jersey case, *Gindy Mfg. Corp. v. Cardinale Trucking Corp.,* suggests that, because some defects can be cured, they do not justify rejection. 111 N.J. Super. 383, 387 n.1 (Law Div. 1970). Accord, Adams v. Tremontin, 42 N.J. Super. 313, 325 (App. Div. 1956) (Uniform Sales Act). But see Sudol v. Rudy Papa Motors, 175 N.J. Super. 238, 240-241 (D. Ct. 1980) (§2-601 contains perfect tender rule). Nonetheless we conclude that the perfect tender rule is preserved to the extent of permitting a buyer to reject goods for any defects. Because of the seller's right to cure, rejection does not terminate the contract. Accordingly, we disapprove the suggestion in *Gindy* that curable defects do not justify rejection.

A further problem, however, is identifying the remedy available to a buyer who rejects goods with insubstantial defects that the seller fails to cure within a reasonable time. The Code provides expressly that when "the buyer rightfully rejects, then with respect to the goods involved, the buyer may cancel." N.J.S.A. 2-711. "Cancellation" occurs when either party puts an end to the contract for breach by the other. N.J.S.A. 2-106(4). Nonetheless, some confusion exists whether the equitable remedy of rescission survives under the Code. Compare Ventura v. Ford Motor Corp., 173 N.J. Super. 501, 503 (Ch. Div. 1980) (rescission under UCC) and Pavesi v. Ford Motor Corp., supra, 155 N.J. Super. at 377 (equitable remedies still available since not specifically superseded, §1-103) with Edelstein v. Toyota Motors Dist., 176 N.J. Super. 57, 63-64 (App. Div. 1980) (under UCC rescission is revocation of acceptance) and Sudol v. Rudy Papa Motors, supra, 175 N.J. Super. at 241-242 (under UCC, rescission no longer exists as such).

The Code eschews the word "rescission" and substitutes the terms "cancellation," "revocation of acceptance," and "rightful rejection." N.J.S.A. 2-106(4); 2-608; and 2-711 & Official Comment 1. Although neither "rejection" nor "revocation of acceptance" is defined in the Code, rejection includes both the buyer's refusal to accept or keep delivered goods and his notification to the seller that he will not keep them. White & Summers, supra, §8-1 at 293. Revocation of acceptance is like rejection, but occurs after the buyer has accepted the goods. Nonetheless, revocation of acceptance is intended to provide the same relief as rescission of a contract of sale of goods. N.J.S.A. 2-608 Official Comment 1; N.J. Study Comment 2. In brief, revocation is tantamount to rescission. See Herbstman v. Eastman Kodak Co., supra, 68 N.J. at 9; accord, Peckham v. Larsen Chevrolet-Buick-Oldsmobile, Inc., 99 Idaho 675, —, 587 P.2d 816, 818 (1978) (rescission and revocation of acceptance amount to the same thing). Similarly, subject to the seller's right to cure, a buyer who rightfully rejects goods, like one who revokes his acceptance, may cancel the contract. N.J.S.A. 2-711 & Official Comment 1. We need not resolve the extent to which rescission for reasons other than rejection or revocation of acceptance, e.g. fraud and mistake, survives as a remedy outside the Code. Compare N.J.S.A. 1-103 and White & Summers, supra, §8-1, p. 295, with N.J.S.A. 2-721. Accordingly, we approve *Edelstein* and *Sudol*, which recognize that explicit Code remedies replace rescission, and disapprove *Ventura* and *Pavesi* to the extent they suggest the UCC expressly recognizes rescission as a remedy.

Although the complaint requested rescission of the contract, plaintiffs actually sought not only the end of their contractual obligations, but also restoration to their pre-contractual position. That request incorporated the equitable doctrine of restitution, the purpose of which is to restore plaintiff to as good a position as he occupied before the contract. Corbin, supra, §1102 at 455. In UCC parlance, plaintiffs' request was for the cancellation of the contract and recovery of the price paid. N.J.S.A. 2-106(4), 2-711.

General contract law permits rescission only for material breaches, and the Code restates "materiality" in terms of "substantial impairment." See Herbstman v. Eastman Kodak Co., supra, 68 N.J. at 9; id. at 15 (Conford, J., concurring). The Code permits a buyer who rightfully rejects goods to cancel a contract of sale. N.J.S.A. 2-711. Because a buyer may reject goods with insubstantial defects, he also may cancel the contract if those defects remain uncured. Otherwise, a seller's failure to cure minor defects would compel a buyer to accept imperfect goods and collect for any loss caused by the nonconformity. N.J.S.A. 2-714.

Although the Code permits cancellation by rejection for minor defects, it permits revocation of acceptance only for substantial impairments. That distinction is consistent with other Code provisions that depend on whether the buyer has accepted the goods. Acceptance creates liability in the buyer for the price, N.J.S.A. 2-709 (1), and precludes rejection. N.J.S.A. 2-607(2); N.J.S.A. 2-606, New Jersey Study Comment 1. Also, once a buyer accepts goods, he has the burden to prove any defect. N.J.S.A. 2-607(4); White & Summers, supra, §8-2 at 297. By contrast, where goods are rejected for not conforming to the contract, the burden is on the seller to prove that the nonconformity was corrected. Miron v. Yonkers Raceway, Inc., 400 F.2d 112, 119 (2d Cir. 1968).

Underlying the Code provisions is the recognition of the revolutionary change in business practices in this century. The purchase of goods is no longer a simple transaction in which a buyer purchases individually-made goods from a seller in a face-to-face transaction. Our economy depends on a complex system for the manufacture, distribution, and sale of goods, a system in which manufacturers and consumers rarely meet. Faceless manufacturers mass-produce goods for unknown consumers who purchase those goods from merchants exercising little or no control over the quality of their production. In an age of assembly lines, we are accustomed to cars with scratches, television sets without knobs and other goods with all kinds of defects. Buyers no longer expect a "perfect tender." If a merchant sells defective goods, the reasonable expectation of the parties is that the buyer will return those goods and that the seller will repair or replace them.

Recognizing this commercial reality, the Code permits a seller to cure imperfect tenders. Should the seller fail to cure the defects, whether substantial or not, the balance shifts again in favor of the buyer, who has the right to cancel or seek damages. N.J.S.A. 2-711. In general, economic considerations would induce sellers to cure minor defects. See generally Priest, supra, 92 Harv. L. Rev. 973-974. Assuming the seller does not cure, however, the buyer should be permitted to exercise his remedies under N.J.S.A. 2-711. The Code remedies for consumers are to be liberally construed, and the buyer should have the option of cancelling if the seller does not provide conforming goods. See N.J.S.A. 1-106.

To summarize, the UCC preserves the perfect tender rule to the extent of permitting a buyer to reject goods for any nonconformity. Nonetheless, that rejection does not automatically terminate the contract. A seller may still effect a cure and preclude unfair rejection and cancellation by the buyer. N.J.S.A. 2-508, Official Comment 2; N.J.S.A. 2-711, Official Comment 1.

III

The trial court found that Mr. and Mrs. Ramirez had rejected the van within a reasonable time under N.J.S.A. 12A:2-602. The court found that on August 3, 1978, Autosport's salesman advised the Ramirezes not to accept the van and that on August 14, they rejected delivery and Autosport agreed to replace the cushions. Those findings are supported by substantial credible evidence, and we sustain them. See Rova Farms Resort v. Investors Ins. Co., 65 N.J. 474, 483-484 (1974). Although the trial court did not find whether Autosport cured the defects within a reasonable time, we find that Autosport did not effect a cure. Clearly the van was not ready for delivery during August, 1978, when Mr. and Mrs. Ramirez rejected it, and Autosport had the burden of proving that it had corrected the defects. Although the Ramirezes gave Autosport ample time to correct the defects, Autosport did not demonstrate that the van conformed to the contract on September 1. In fact, on that date, when Mr. and Mrs. Ramirez returned at Autosport's invitation, all they received was discourtesy.

On the assumption that substantial impairment is necessary only when a purchaser seeks to revoke acceptance under N.J.S.A. 2-608, the trial court correctly refrained from deciding whether the defects substantially impaired the van. The court properly concluded that plaintiffs were entitled to "rescind" — i.e., to "cancel" — the contract.

Because Autosport had sold the trade-in to an innocent third party, the trial court determined that the Ramirezes were entitled not to the return of the trade-in, but to its fair market value, which the court set at the contract price of $4,700. A buyer who rightfully rejects goods and cancels the contract may, among other possible remedies, recover so much of the purchase price as has been paid. N.J.S.A. 2-711. The Code, however, does not define "pay" and does not require payment to be made in cash. . . .

For the preceding reasons, we affirm the judgment of the Appellate Division.

QUESTIONS

1. Did the defendant's grounds for cure fit within §2-508?
2. Is the court creating a right to cure outside of §2-508?

PROBLEM 60

Ulysses Sinon ran a dude ranch in Troy, Colorado. He decided to erect a statue of a giant horse near the entrance to the ranch as a tourist attraction. The horse was specially manufactured by Epeius of Paris and arrived in six boxes to be assembled by Sinon. When the horse was put together, Sinon was displeased with the appearance of the tail. The horse had been designed by Epeius, and the scale model Sinon had seen when he decided to buy the horse had had a different tail. Sinon removed the tail and substituted one of his own design. He returned the original to Epeius along with a letter of rejection. In the meantime, Sinon painted the rest of the horse black (in the delivered state it was white) and used it extensively in advertising for the ranch. The horse failed to attract new business to the ranch. After three months of display, Sinon took it down and shipped it back to Epeius with a letter of rejection that stated that the problem with the tail made the horse unattractive and unusable. Epeius sues. Did Sinon make a rejection or an acceptance? If the tail did not conform to the model, is that a ground for rejection? See §2-601. If Sinon had made a technical acceptance, does that fact preclude a suit for breach of warranty? See §2-607(2). What steps should Sinon take to preserve his legal rights? See §2-607(3)(a). What reasons lie behind the notice requirement? See §§2-508, 2-515.

Plateq Corp. of North Haven v. Machlett Laboratories, Inc.

Connecticut Supreme Court, 1983
189 Conn. 433, 456 A.2d 786, 35 U.C.C. Rep. Serv. 1162

Peters, J.

In this action by a seller of specially manufactured goods to recover their purchase price from a commercial buyer, the principal issue is whether the buyer accepted the goods before it attempted to cancel the contract of sale. The plaintiff, Plateq Corporation of North Haven, sued the defendant, The Machlett Laboratories, Inc., to recover damages, measured by the contract price and incidental damages, arising out of the defendant's allegedly wrongful cancellation of a written contract for the manufacture and sale of two lead-covered steel tanks and appurtenant stands. The defendant denied liability and counterclaimed for damages. After a full hearing, the trial court found for the plaintiff both on its complaint and on the defendant's counterclaim. The defendant has appealed.

The trial court, in its memorandum of decision, found the following facts. On July 9, 1976, the defendant ordered from the plaintiff two lead-covered steel tanks to be constructed by the plaintiff according to specifications supplied by the defendant. The parties understood that the tanks were designed for the special purpose of testing x-ray tubes and were required to be radiation-proof within certain federal standards. Accordingly, the contract provided that the tanks would be tested for radiation leaks after their installation on the defendant's premises. The plaintiff undertook to correct, at its own cost, any deficiencies that this post-installation test might uncover. The plaintiff had not previously constructed such tanks, nor had the defendant previously designed tanks for this purpose. The contract was amended on August 9, 1976, to add construction of two metal stands to hold the tanks. All the goods were to be delivered to the defendant at the plaintiff's place of business.

Although the plaintiff encountered difficulties both in performing according to the contract specifications and in completing performance within the time required, the defendant did no more than call these deficiencies to the plaintiff's attention during various inspections in September and early October, 1976. By October 11, 1976, performance was belatedly but substantially completed. On that date, Albert Yannello, the defendant's engineer, noted some remaining deficiencies which the plaintiff promised to remedy by the next day, so that the goods would then be ready for delivery. Yannello gave no indication to the plaintiff that this arrangement was in any way unsatisfactory to the defendant. Not only did Yannello communicate general acquiescence in the plaintiff's proposed tender but he specifically led the plaintiff to believe that the defendant's truck would pick up the tanks and the stands within a day or two. Instead of sending its truck, the defendant sent a notice of total cancellation which the plaintiff received on October 14, 1976. That notice failed to particularize the grounds upon which cancellation was based.

On this factual basis, the trial court, having concluded that the transaction was a contract for the sale of goods falling within the Uniform Commercial Code, General Statutes §§2-101 et seq., considered whether the defendant had accepted the goods. The court determined that the defendant had accepted the tanks, primarily by signifying its willingness to take them despite their nonconformities, in accordance with General Statutes §2-606(1)(a), and secondarily by failing to make an effective rejection, in accordance with General Statutes §2-606(1)(b). Once the tanks had been accepted, the defendant could rightfully revoke its acceptance under General Statutes §2-608 only by showing substantial impairment of their value to the defendant. In part because the defendant's conduct had foreclosed any post-installation inspection, the court concluded that such impairment had not been proved. Since the tanks were not readily resalable on the open market, the plaintiff was entitled, upon the defendant's wrongful revocation of acceptance, to recover their contract price, minus salvage value, plus interest. General Statutes §§2-703; 2-709(1)(b). Accordingly, the trial court awarded the plaintiff damages in the amount of $14,837.92.

In its appeal, the defendant raises four principal claims of error. It maintains that the trial court erred: (1) in invoking the "cure" section, General Statutes §2-508, when there had been no tender by the plaintiff seller; (2) in concluding, in accordance with the acceptance section, General Statutes §2-606(1), that the defendant had "signified" to the plaintiff its willingness to take the contract goods; (3) in misconstruing the defendant's statutory and contractual rights of inspection; and (4) in refusing to find that the defendant's letter of cancellation was occasioned by the plaintiff's breach. We find no error.

Upon analysis, all of the defendant's claims of error are variations upon one central theme. The defendant claims that on October 11, when its engineer Yannello conducted the last examination on the plaintiff's premises, the tanks were so incomplete and unsatisfactory that the defendant was rightfully entitled to conclude that the plaintiff would never make a conforming tender. From this scenario, the defendant argues that it was justified in cancelling the contract of sale. It denies that the seller's conduct was sufficient to warrant a finding of tender, or its own conduct sufficient to warrant a finding of acceptance. The difficulty with this argument is that it is inconsistent with the underlying facts found by the trial court. Although the testimony was in dispute, there was evidence of record to support the trial court's findings to the contrary. The defendant cannot sustain its burden of establishing that a trial court's findings of fact are clearly erroneous; Practice Book §3060D; Pandolphe's Auto Parts, Inc. v. Manchester, 181 Conn. 217, 221-22, 435 A.2d 24 (1980); by the mere recitation in its brief of conflicting testimony entirely unsupported by reference to pages of the transcript. Practice Book §3060F(b). There is simply no fit between the defendant's claims and the trial court's finding that, by October 11, 1976, performance was in substantial compliance with the terms of the contract. The trial court further found that on that day the defendant was notified that the goods would be ready for tender the following day and that the defendant responded to this notification by promising to send its truck to pick up the tanks in accordance with the contract.

On the trial court's finding of facts, it was warranted in concluding, on two independent grounds, that the defendant had accepted the goods it had ordered from the plaintiff. Under the provisions of the Uniform Commercial Code, General Statutes §32a-2-606(1) "[a]cceptance of goods occurs when the buyer (a) after a reasonable opportunity to inspect the goods signifies to the seller . . . that he will take . . . them in spite of their nonconformity; or (b) fails to make an effective rejection."

In concluding that the defendant had "signified" to the plaintiff its willingness to "take" the tanks despite possible remaining minor defects, the trial court necessarily found that the defendant had had a reasonable opportunity to inspect the goods. The defendant does not maintain that its engineer, or the other inspectors on previous visits, had inadequate access to the tanks, or inadequate experience to conduct a reasonable examination. It recognizes that inspection of goods when the buyer undertakes to pick up the goods is ordinarily at the seller's place of tender. See General Statutes §§42a-2-503, 42a-2-507, 42a-2-513; see also White & Summers, Uniform Commercial Code §3-5 (2d ed. 1980). The defendant argues, however, that its contract, in providing for inspection for radiation leaks after installation of the tanks at its premises, necessarily postponed its inspection rights to that time. The trial court considered this argument and rejected it, and so do we. It was reasonable, in the context of this contract for the special manufacture of goods with which neither party had had prior experience, to limit this clause to adjustments to take place after tender and acceptance. After acceptance, a buyer may still, in appropriate cases, revoke its acceptance, General Statutes §42a-2-608, or recover damages for breach of warranty, General Statutes §42a-2-714. The trial court reasonably concluded that a post-installation test was intended to safeguard these rights of the defendant as well as to afford the plaintiff a final opportunity to make needed adjustments. The court was therefore justified in concluding that there had been an acceptance within §42a-2-606(1)(a). A buyer may be found to have accepted goods despite their known nonconformity; [citations omitted].

The trial court's alternate ground for concluding that the tanks had been accepted was the defendant's failure to make an effective rejection. Pursuant to General Statutes §42a-2-606(1)(b), an acceptance occurs when, after a reasonable opportunity to inspect, a buyer has failed to make "an effective rejection as provided by subsection (1) of section 42a-2-602." The latter subsection, in turn, makes a rejection "ineffective unless the buyer reasonably notifies the seller." General Statutes §42a-2-605(1)(a) goes on to provide that a buyer is precluded from relying, as a basis for rejection, upon unparticularized defects in his notice of rejection, if the defects were such that, with reasonable notice, the seller could have cured by making a substituted, conforming tender. The defendant does not question the trial court's determination that its telegram of cancellation failed to comply with the requirement of particularization contained in §2-605(1). Instead, the defendant argues that the plaintiff was not entitled to an opportunity to cure, under General Statutes §2-508, because the plaintiff had never made a tender of the tanks. That argument founders, however, on the trial court's finding that the seller was ready to make a tender on the day following the last inspection by the defendant's engineer and would have done so but for its receipt of the defendant's telegram of cancellation. The trial court furthermore found that the defendant's unparticularized telegram of cancellation wrongfully interfered with the plaintiff's contractual right to cure any remaining post-installation defects. In these circumstances, the telegram of cancellation constituted both a wrongful and an ineffective rejection on the part of the defendant. See Uchitel v. F.R.

Tripler & Co., 107 Misc. 2d 310, 434 N.Y.S. 2d 77, 81-82 (Supreme Court 1980); White & Summers, supra, §8-3, p. 315.

Once the conclusion is reached that the defendant accepted the tanks, its further rights of cancellation under the contract are limited by the governing provisions of the Uniform Commercial Code. "The buyer's acceptance of goods, despite their alleged non-conformity, is a watershed. After acceptance, the buyer must pay for the goods at the contract rate; General Statutes §2-607(1); and bears the burden of establishing their nonconformity. General Statutes §2-607(4)." Stelco Industries, Inc. v. Cohen, 182 Conn. 561, 563-64, 438 A.2d 759 (1980). After acceptance, the buyer may only avoid liability for the contract price by invoking the provision which permits revocation of acceptance. That provision, General Statutes §2-608(1), requires proof that the "nonconformity [of the goods] substantially impairs [their] value to him." See Superior Wire & Paper Products, Ltd. v. Talcott Tool & Machine, Inc., 184 Conn. 10 (42 C.L.J. 44, pp. 4, 6), 441 A.2d 43 (1981); Conte v. Dwan Lincoln-Mercury, Inc., 172 Conn. 112, 120-21, 374 A.2d 144 (1976). On this question, which is an issue of fact; *Superior Wire & Paper Products, Ltd. v. Talcott Tool & Machine, Inc.*, supra, 6-7; *Conte v. Dwan Lincoln-Mercury, Inc.*, supra, 121; the trial court again found against the defendant. Since the defendant has provided no basis for any argument that the trial court was clearly erroneous in finding that the defendant had not met its burden of proof to show that the goods were substantially nonconforming, we can find no error in the conclusion that the defendant's cancellation constituted an unauthorized and hence wrongful revocation of acceptance.

Finally, the defendant in its brief, although not in its statement of the issues presented, challenges the trial court's conclusion about the remedial consequences of its earlier determinations. Although the trial court might have found the plaintiff entitled to recover the contract price because of the defendant's acceptance of the goods; General Statutes §§2-703(e) and 2-709(1)(a); the court chose instead to rely on General Statutes §2-709(1)(b), which permits a price action for contract goods that cannot, after reasonable effort, be resold at a reasonable price. Since the contract goods in this case were concededly specially manufactured for the defendant, the defendant cannot and does not contest the trial court's finding that any effort to resell them on the open market would have been unavailing. In the light of this finding, the defendant can only reiterate its argument, which we have already rejected, that the primary default was that of the plaintiff rather than that of the defendant. The trial court's conclusion to the contrary supports both its award to the plaintiff and its denial of the defendant's counterclaim.

There is no error.

V. REVOCATION OF ACCEPTANCE

Having made a technical acceptance, a buyer may still bring a breach of warranty action provided that a proper §2-607(3)(a) notice has been given. If the buyer wins, damages based on §§2-714 and 2-715 will be awarded, and the buyer will still have the goods. If the buyer does not want the goods, but wants the return of the price, the proper UCC method is called *revocation of acceptance*. Read §2-608. At common law this action was called *rescission*. However, revocation of acceptance differs from common law rescission because the buyer not only recovers the price, but may recover consequential damages as well. See Official Comment 1 to §2-608; cf. §§2-711(1), 2-715 (also note Official Comment 1 to §2-715).

In both rejection and revocation of acceptance, the buyer in essence disclaims the goods. The standards under which a buyer can revoke acceptance are more difficult to meet than are the standards for rejection. In rejection, a buyer can in theory reject if the goods "fail in any respect"; however, to revoke an acceptance, the buyer must show that the defect "substantially impairs the value" of the goods. See Annot., 98 A.L.R.3d 1183.

Waddell v. L.V.R.V. Inc.

Supreme Court of Nevada, 2006
122 Nev. 15, 125 P.3d 1160, 58 U.C.C. Rep. Serv. 2d 655

Gibbons, J.

**1 This is an appeal and cross-appeal from a district court judgment allowing revocation of acceptance of a contract and an order awarding attorney fees and costs.

Respondent/cross-appellant L.V.R.V. Inc., D/B/A Wheeler's Las Vegas RV (Wheeler's) sold a 1996 Coachmen Santara motor home (the RV) to appellants/cross-respondents Arthur R. Waddell and Roswitha M. Waddell (the Waddells). The Waddells noticed numerous problems with the RV and "continually" had to return it to Wheeler's service department for repairs. Eventually, the Waddells stopped attempting to have Wheeler's make repairs and filed a complaint seeking to revoke their acceptance of the RV or, in the alternative, money damages. Wheeler's answered the complaint and filed a third-party complaint seeking indemnification from respondent Coachmen Recreational Vehicle Company, Inc. (Coachmen). After a bench trial, the district court granted judgment in favor of the Waddells and Coachmen.

On appeal, Wheeler's argues that (1) the district court erred in allowing the Waddells to revoke their acceptance, (2) the district court abused its discretion by admitting two documents into evidence, (3) the district court erred in denying Wheeler's motion for attorney fees, and (4) the district court erred in denying indemnification from Coachmen. The Waddells argue on cross-appeal that the district court erred in denying them (1) computerized research costs and (2) post-judgment interest on their attorney fees award.

FACTS

In 1996, the Waddells served jointly as president of the Las Vegas area Coachmen Association Camping Club. During the course of that group's meetings, the Waddells spoke with Tom Pender, Wheeler's sales manager, about upgrading from the motor home they then owned to a "diesel pusher" motor coach. As a result of that conversation, Pender took the Waddells to the Wheeler's lot and showed them a 1996 Coachmen Santara model diesel pusher coach.

The Waddells test-drove and eventually agreed to purchase the RV and an extended warranty. Before they took possession of the RV, the Waddells requested that Wheeler's perform various repairs. The Waddells' request included a service on the RV's engine cooling system, new batteries, and alignment of the door frames. Wheeler's told Arthur Waddell that the repairs had been performed as requested. The Waddells took delivery of the RV on September 1, 1997.

The Waddells first noticed a problem with the RV's engine shortly after they took possession of it. They drove the RV from Las Vegas to Hemet, California. On the return trip, the entry door popped open and the RV's engine overheated while ascending a moderate grade to such a degree that Mr. Waddell had to pull over to the side of the road and wait for the engine to cool down.

When the Waddells returned from California, they took the RV back to Wheeler's for repairs. Despite Wheeler's attempts to repair the RV, the Waddells continually experienced more problems with the RV, including further episodes of engine overheating. Between September 1997 and March 1999, Wheeler's service department spent a total of seven months during different periods of time attempting to repair the RV.

**2 On June 9, 2000, the Waddells filed a complaint in district court seeking both equitable relief and money damages. Wheeler's answered the complaint and ultimately filed a third-party complaint against Coachmen seeking equitable indemnification and contribution.

Following a three-day bench trial, the district court issued its findings of fact, conclusions of law, and judgment. The district court concluded that the RV's nonconformities substantially impaired its value to the Waddells. The district court allowed the Waddells to revoke their acceptance of the RV and ordered Wheeler's to return all of the Waddell's out-of-pocket expenses, but further concluded that Wheeler's was not entitled to indemnification from Coachmen. Following entry of judgment, the district court awarded the Waddells $15,000 in attorney fees, entered supplemental findings of fact and conclusions of law, issued an amended judgment, entered a separate order denying post-judgment interest on the attorney fee award, and denied the Waddells' motion to retax their costs to include computerized research fees. This timely appeal and cross-appeal followed.

Discussion

Wheeler's argues that the district court erred in allowing the Waddells to revoke their acceptance of the RV because the Waddells failed to prove that the RV suffered nonconformities that substantially impaired its value. We disagree.

The district court found that despite Wheeler's good-faith attempts to repair the RV, the nonconformities persisted and rendered the RV unfit for its intended use. Some of those nonconformities identified by the district court included: the bedroom air conditioning does not cool, the front air conditioning does not cool, the dash heater does not blow hot air, RV batteries do not stay charged, and chronic engine overheating. The district court concluded that these nonconformities and others substantially impaired the RV's value to the Waddells and that the Waddells had revoked their acceptance of the RV within a reasonable time.

Substantial Impairment

NRS 104.2608(1) provides that a buyer may revoke his acceptance if the item suffers from a "nonconformity [that] substantially impairs its value *to him*" and (a) the buyer accepted the goods on the understanding that the seller would cure the nonconformity or (b) the buyer was unaware of the nonconformity and the nonconformity was concealed by the difficulty of discovery or by the seller's assurances that the good was conforming. (Emphasis added.)

We have never before determined when a nonconformity substantially impairs the value of a good to the buyer. Other jurisdictions treat this determination as an issue of fact,[4] which "is made in light of the 'totality of the circumstances' of each particular case, including the number of deficiencies and type of nonconformity and the time and inconvenience spent in downtime and attempts at repair."[5]

---

4. See, e.g., Frontier Mobile Home Sales, Inc. v. Trigleth, 256 Ark. 101, 505 S.W.2d 516, 517 (1974); Rester v. Morrow, 491 So. 2d 204, 209 (Miss. 1986); McCullough v. Bill Swad Chrysler-Plymouth, 5 Ohio St. 3d 181, 449 N.E.2d 1289, 1294 (1983).

5. Fortin v. Ox-Bow Marina, Inc., 408 Mass. 310, 557 N.E.2d 1157, 1162 (1990) (quoting *Rester*, 491 So. 2d at 210).

The Supreme Court of Oregon has established a two-part test to determine whether a nonconformity, under the totality of the circumstances, substantially impairs the value of the goods to the buyer. The test has both an objective and a subjective prong:

> **3 Since [the statute] provides that the buyer may revoke acceptance of goods "whose nonconformity substantially impairs its value to him," the value of conforming goods to the plaintiff must first be determined. This is a subjective question in the sense that it calls for a consideration of the needs and circumstances of the plaintiff who seeks to revoke; not the needs and circumstances of an average buyer. The second inquiry is whether the nonconformity in fact substantially impairs the value of the goods to the buyer, having in mind his particular needs. This is an objective question in the sense that it calls for evidence of something more than plaintiff's assertion that the nonconformity impaired the value to him; it requires evidence from which it can be inferred that plaintiff's needs were not met because of the nonconformity.[6]

Since Nevada, like Oregon, adopted Uniform Commercial Code §2-608 verbatim, we conclude that this test applies to NRS 104.2608. Accordingly, we adopt the Supreme Court of Oregon's two-part test for determining whether a nonconformity substantially affects the good's value to the buyer under NRS 104.2608(1).

SUBJECTIVE VALUE TO THE WADDELLS

Arthur Waddell testified that he purchased the RV to enjoy the RV lifestyle. Before purchasing the RV, the Waddells owned similar vehicles that they used both as a residence and for camping trips. In fact, Mr. Waddell testified that he and his wife intended to sell their house and spend two to three years traveling around the country.

Mr. Waddell further testified that he shopped at Wheeler's based on Wheeler's advertisements. Marlene Wheeler, president and chief operating officer, testified that Wheeler's advertising encouraged the purchase of an RV to find unlimited freedom. When Mr. Waddell spoke with Tom Pender, sales manager at Wheeler's, about upgrading to an RV for those purposes, Pender told him that he had an RV on the lot that would meet his needs.

Mr. Waddell's testimony demonstrates that the RV's subjective value to the Waddells was based on their ability to spend two or three years driving

---

6. Jorgensen v. Pressnall, 274 Or. 285, 545 P.2d 1382, 1384-85 (1976) (footnote omitted), quoted with approval in McGilbray v. Scholfield Winnebago, Inc., 221 Kan. 605, 561 P.2d 832, 836 (1977); see also Milicevic v. Mercedes-Benz USA, LLC, 256 F. Supp. 2d 1168, 1176 (D. Nev. 2003) (applying a two-part test that addressed both objective and subjective considerations); Haight v. Dales Used Cars, Inc., 139 Idaho 853, 87 P.3d 962, 966 (App. 2003) (applying a similar two-part test).

the RV around the country. Thus, we must consider whether the RV's nonconformities substantially impaired the value of the RV based on the Waddells' particular needs.

OBJECTIVE IMPAIRMENT

Mr. Waddell testified that as a result of the RV's defects, he and his wife were unable to enjoy the RV as they had intended. Mr. Waddell further testified that the RV's engine would overheat within ten miles of embarking if the travel included any climbing. As a result of the overheating, the Waddells were forced to park on the side of the road and wait for the engine to cool down before continuing. Consequently, the RV spent a total of 213 days, or seven months and one day, at Wheeler's service department during the eighteen months immediately following the purchase. This testimony is sufficient to demonstrate an objective, substantial impairment of value.

**4 The Supreme Court of Ohio has stated that a nonconformity effects a substantial impairment of value if it "shakes the buyer's faith or undermines his confidence in the reliability and integrity of the purchased item."[7] The Supreme Judicial Court of Massachusetts has recognized that "even cosmetic or minor defects that go unrepaired . . . or defects which do not totally prevent the buyer from using the goods, but circumscribe that use . . . can substantially impair the goods' value to the buyer."[8] The United States District Court for the District of Nevada recently reiterated that "'the [seller's] inability to correct defects in [motor] vehicles creates a major hardship and an unacceptable economic burden on the consumer.'"[9]

In this case, the chronic engine overheating shook the Waddells' faith in the RV and undermined their confidence in the RV's reliability and integrity. Not only did this problem make travel in the RV unreliable and stressful to the Waddells, the overheating made travel in the vehicle objectively unsafe.

Accordingly, we conclude that substantial evidence exists to support revocation of acceptance under NRS 104.2608(1).

REASONABLE TIME FOR REVOKING ACCEPTANCE

Wheeler's argues that the Waddells should not have been allowed to revoke their acceptance because they did not attempt to revoke within a reasonable time after purchasing the RV. We disagree.

---

7. *McCullough*, 449 N.E.2d at 1294; see also *Rester*, 491 So. 2d at 210-11.
8. *Fortin*, 557 N.E.2d at 1162.
9. *Milicevic*, 256 F. Supp. 2d at 1176 (quoting Berrie v. Toyota Motor Sales, USA, Inc., 267 N.J. Super. 152, 630 A.2d 1180, 1181 (1993)).

Under NRS 104.2608(2), "[r]evocation of acceptance must occur within a reasonable time after the buyer discovers or should have discovered the ground for it and before any substantial change in condition of the goods which is not caused by their own defects." The statute further provides that revocation "is not effective until the buyer notifies the seller of it." We have never before determined a reasonable timeline for revocation of acceptance. However, other jurisdictions have held that the reasonable time determination "depends upon the nature, purpose and circumstances of the transaction."[10] The reasonable time determination is generally considered to be an issue of fact for the trial court.

Here, the district court found that the Waddells were entitled to revoke their acceptance since they notified Wheeler's of their intent to revoke within a reasonable time. Mr. Waddell testified that he first noticed the RV's defects immediately after his purchase. Mr. Waddell took the RV to Wheeler's service department whenever he noticed a defect and Wheeler's always attempted, often unsuccessfully, to repair the RV. In September 1998, Mr. Waddell took the RV to Wheeler's after continued engine overheating. As a result of these defects, Wheeler's service department kept the RV for approximately seven months of the eighteen months that the Waddells owned the RV. Roger Beauchemin, a former employee of Wheeler's service department, testified that Wheeler's was unable to repair some of the defects, including the engine's chronic overheating problems. In January 1999, the Waddells again brought the RV to Wheeler's complaining of persistent engine overheating. The Waddells demanded a full refund of the purchase price in March 1999 and sought legal counsel. Through counsel, the Waddells wrote to Wheeler's during the summer of 1999 to resolve the matter. Wheeler's did not respond to these inquiries until early 2000. Unable to resolve the dispute with Wheeler's, the Waddells revoked their acceptance of the RV in June 2000.

**5 The seller of nonconforming goods must generally receive an opportunity to cure the nonconformity before the buyer may revoke his acceptance. However, as the Supreme Court of Mississippi has recognized, the seller may not "postpone revocation in perpetuity by fixing everything that goes wrong."[11] Rather, "[t]here comes a time when . . . [the buyer] is entitled to say, 'That's all,' and revoke, notwithstanding the seller's repeated good faith efforts to [cure]."

Furthermore, the seller's attempts to cure do not count against the buyer regarding timely revocation. The United States District Court for the

---

10. DeVoe Chevrolet-Cadillac v. Cartwright, 526 N.E.2d 1237, 1240 (Ind. Ct. App. 1988); see also Golembieski v. O'Rielly R.V. Center, Inc., 147 Ariz. 134, 708 P.2d 1325, 1328 (Ariz. Ct. App. 1985) (noting that "[r]easonableness of the time for revocation is a question of fact unique to the circumstances of each case").

11. See *Rester*, 491 So. 2d at 210.

District of Nevada has held that the "time for revocation of acceptance will be tolled while the seller attempts repairs."[12] Tolling the reasonable time for revocation of acceptance is appropriate given "the buyer's obligation to act in good faith, and to afford the seller a reasonable opportunity to cure any defect in the goods."

The Waddells gave Wheeler's several opportunities to repair the defects before revoking their acceptance. Because Wheeler's was unable to repair the defects after a total of seven months, the Waddells were entitled to say "that's all" and revoke their acceptance, notwithstanding Wheeler's good-faith attempts to repair the RV. Also, the reasonable time for revocation was tolled during the seven months that Wheeler's kept the RV and attempted to repair the defects. Accordingly, the district court's determination is supported by substantial evidence and is not clearly erroneous. . . .

CONCLUSION

**7 The district court did not err in allowing the Waddells to revoke their acceptance of the RV within a reasonable time because chronic engine overheating problems substantially impaired the RV's value to the Waddells. . . .

QUESTIONS

1. Sometimes the buyer will return the car to the seller when giving a notice of revocation. Need the buyer do this? Read carefully §§2-711(3) and 1-201(37); cf. §2-706. See Mobile Home Sales Management, Inc. v. Brown, 562 P.2d 1378, 21 U.C.C. Rep. Serv. 1040 (Ariz. App. 1977) ("when the buyer has a security interest in the goods and the seller makes no request for their return, the buyer should not be penalized by making tender back a prerequisite to revocaton of acceptance"). See also Deaton, Inc. v. Aeroglide Corp., 99 N.M. 253, 657 P.2d 109, 35 U.C.C. Rep. Serv. 130 (1982). What if the buyer did not have a security interest in the car? See §§2-608(3), 2-602.

2. Should the court when allowing revocation make an allowance for the use the buyer got from the car? Is the seller entitled to a setoff for the amount of benefits the purchaser received? See §1-103; compare Barco Auto Leasing Corp. v. House, 202 Conn. 106, 520 A.2d 162, 3 U.C.C. Rep.

---

12. Sierra Diesel Injection Service v. Burroughs Corp., 651 F. Supp. 1371, 1378 (D. Nev. 1987).

Serv. 2d 122 (1987) with Moore v. Howard Pontiac-American, Inc., 492 S.W.2d 227, 12 U.C.C. Rep. Serv. 676 (Tenn. App. 1973).

3. If the buyer keeps the car after revoking acceptance, may the buyer keep driving it without negating the effectiveness of the revocation of acceptance? See §§2-606(1)(c), 2-602(2)(a)(b). Compare Computerized Radiological Serv. v. Syntex Corp., 786 F.2d 72, 42 U.C.C. Rep. Serv. 1656 (2d Cir. 1986) (use of CAT scanner for 22 months after sending letter of revocation constituted acceptance), Wadsworth Plumbing & Heating Co., Inc. v. Tallycraft Corp., 277 Ore. 433, 560 P.2d 1080, 21 U.C.C. Rep. Serv. 502 (1977) ("such use would appear to be an 'act inconsistent with the seller's ownership'"), and Fecik v. Capindale, 54 Pa. D. & C. 2d 701, 10 U.C.C. Rep. Serv. 1391 (1971) (post-revocation use destroys buyer's §2-608 suit), with Deere & Co. v. Johnson, 271 F.3d 613, 46 U.C.C. Rep. Serv. 2d 433 (5th Cir. 2001) (farmer's continued use of combine excused where replacement cost high); Stroh v. American Recreation & Mobile Home Corp. of Colo., 35 Colo. App. 196, 530 P.2d 989, 16 U.C.C. Rep. Serv. 726 (Colo. App. 1975) (continued use of mobile home after revocation was not acceptance, but seller could recover damages for buyer's post-revocation use), Fargo Mach. & Tool Co. v. Kearney & Trecker Corp., 428 F. Supp. 364 (E.D. Mich. 1977) ("in 'exceptional circumstances' subsequent use is permissible"), and Keller v. Inland Metals All Weather Conditioning, Inc., 76 P.3d 977, 51 U.C.C. Rep. Serv. 2d 303 (Idaho 2003) (use of rejected dehumidifier excused where unavoidable). In a leading case involving vehicles, the Kansas Supreme Court permitted post-revocation use (with a setoff to seller for the benefit buyer received thereby): Johnson v. General Motors Corp., 233 Kan. 1044, 668 P.2d 139, 36 U.C.C. Rep. Serv. 1089 (1983) ("Here buyers were placed in a position where if they stored the truck . . . they would not have had a vehicle for transportation. . . . With little or no low-cost public transportation available to the public, private transportation has changed from a luxury to a necessity."). The Massachusetts Supreme Judicial Court has agreed with this, stating that a jury should be instructed to consider a number of circumstances in deciding the reasonableness of the buyer's actions: the seller's instructions to the buyer after revocation of acceptance; the degree of economic and other hardship that the buyer would suffer if he or she discontinued using the defective goods; the reasonableness of the buyer's use after revocation as a method of mitigating damages; the degree of prejudice to the seller; and whether the seller acted in bad faith; Liarikos v. Mello, 418 Mass. 669, 639 N.E.2d 716, 27 U.C.C. Rep. Serv. 2d 136 (1994).

Given this, if your client tells you, the attorney, that it is necessary to continue to use the goods following rejection/revocation, what do you advise? Cf. §2-714.

4. Is the seller entitled to more than one opportunity to cure? See Car Transportation Brokerage Company, Inc. v. Blue Bird Body, 322 Fed. Appx.

891, 68 U.C.C. Rep. Serv. 2d 777 (11th Cir. 2009) (holding that because the electrical system for a motor coach is a complex piece of equipment, buyer must give seller more than one chance to cure before revoking acceptance).

NOTE: LEMON LAWS

A number of states have enacted so-called *Lemon Laws* that resolve some of the disputes we have been exploring when they arise in connection with a consumer's purchase of an automobile. For example, the issue addressed in Question 2 above is specifically covered by many of these statutes. New York General Business Law §198a says that a refund from the defendant may be reduced by "a reasonable allowance for the consumer's use of the vehicle in excess of the first 12,000 miles of operation and a reasonable allowance for any damage not attributable to normal wear or improvements." For an exploration of what the various states have done, see Annot., 51 A.L.R.4th 872.

PROBLEM 61

The day after Alice Bluegown bought her new car, the right rear fender fell off. May she use §2-608 or must she give the car dealer a right to cure? Pretend she is sitting in your office expecting an immediate answer; glance at §2-608 and decide. The next day she took the car back to have the fender repaired; this made her late for work. The dealer fixed it, and the fender gave her no more trouble. However, the first time it rained all the paint washed off the car. May she revoke now? She took the car back to the dealer when the rain stopped and rode the bus to work (late again). The car dealer did a nice job repainting the car. Two weeks later the engine quit on her when she was in the middle lane of a superhighway at rush hour. The car had to be towed to the car dealer, and Alice missed an important sales meeting. The car dealer fixed the engine. Now Alice is back in your office. The car's trunk will not open. Must she permit them to fix it, or can she revoke? See Foss, The Seller's Right to Cure When the Buyer Revokes Acceptance: Erase the Line in the Sand, 16 S. Ill. U. L.J. 1 (1991). She has missed enough work to worry about hurting her career. She's also concerned that the car is going to keep breaking down right through and past the warranty period. What do you advise? Is §2-609 of use to her? If she decides to revoke acceptance and if the court agrees that this is allowed, would it also permit her to recover for the cost of a rental car used as substitute transportation while she was attempting to purchase a new car? See McGinnis v. Wentworth Chevrolet Co., 295 Ore. 494, 668 P.2d 365, 37 U.C.C. Rep. Serv. 130 (1983). If she goes out and buys a *new* car, can she make the first car dealer pay for it? See §2-712.

PROBLEM 62

Suppose in the last Problem the contract between the dealer and Bluegown explicitly limits the remedy for breach to repair or replacement of defective parts. The dealer argues that all defects have been promptly and successfully repaired and that the remedy of revocation of acceptance is therefore unavailable to Bluegown. See §2-719(2); Durfee v. Rod Baxter Imports, Inc., 262 N.W.2d 349, 22 U.C.C. Rep. Serv. 945 (Minn. 1977); see also Andover Air Ltd. Partnership v. Piper Aircraft Corp., 7 U.C.C. Rep. Serv. 2d 1494 (D. Mass. 1989).

PROBLEM 63

Arthur Author ordered an expensive computer (the ION #740) from ION Business Machines. ION sent him model #745, a newer and better version of the machine he had ordered, at the same price. When he saw the computer, he liked it and wrote them a letter of acceptance, enclosing a check in payment. However, when he began to use it, he was horrified to learn that the computer was turned on by a hidden switch under the front panel. Arthur Author's father had lost a finger when he reached under a machine to activate it. Arthur had witnessed the accident as a child. Arthur sent a notice of revocation of acceptance to ION, stating that the #740 had a visible switch and explaining that the hidden switch on the #745 brought back childhood memories that kept him from wanting the computer. Does §2-608 permit him to revoke for this reason? See Official Comment 2. Is §2-508(2) relevant? How would you advise ION to respond to Arthur Author's letter? See Annot., 98 A.L.R.3d 1183.

PROBLEM 64

After his car had broken down with the same defect six times, Zack Taylor decided to revoke acceptance and return the car to Fillmore Motors, the dealership that had sold him the vehicle but that had been unable to repair it. To Zack's dismay, he discovered that Fillmore Motors had gone bankrupt and was out of business. Zack is now in your office with this issue: may he revoke acceptance against the *manufacturer* of the car (which had covered its product with a limited warranty)? Compare Fode v. Capital RV Center, Inc., 575 N.W.2d 682, 36 U.C.C. Rep. Serv. 2d 696 (N.D. 1998), with Gasque v. Mooers Motor Car Co., Inc., 227 Va. 154, 313 S.E.2d 384 (1984); Gregory J. Krabacher, Revocation of Tripartite Rolling Contracts: Finding a Remedy in the Twenty-First Century Usage of Trade, 66 Ohio St. L.J. 397 (2005). Note that the Magnuson-Moss Warranty Act might help consumers win this battle. Section 110(d) of the Act allows a civil action against the warrantor that includes both legal and *equitable* relief (and, revocation of acceptance, being a form of rescission, qualifies as an equitable remedy). Revocation of acceptance, being a form of rescission, arguably qualifies as an equitable remedy, but the courts have split on whether it can be used in Magnuson-Moss actions against a manufacturer not in privity with the consumer; compare Mydlach v. DaimlerChrysler Corp., 364 Ill. App. 3d 135, 846 N.E.2d 126 (2005), and Shuldman v. DaimlerChrysler Corp., 1 A.D.3d 343, 768 N.Y.S.2d 214 (2003), with Chaurasia v. General Motors Corp., 212 Ariz. 18, 126 P.3d 165 (Ariz. App. 2006).

Just as the United Nations CISG treaty does not use the value-loaded word *warranty*, it substitutes the word *avoidance* for concepts such as rescission, rejection, and revocation of acceptance, while keeping much of the substance. The concept of avoidance under the treaty is the subject of the next Problem.

PROBLEM 65

Jeans of the World, a retail clothing outlet in Helsinki, Finland, ordered 20 boxes of jeans from Grey Goods of Manhattan in New York, to be delivered September 1. Use the CISG to answer these questions:

(a) If the goods arrive on July 20, must Jeans of the World take them? See Article 52(1).

(b) If the goods arrive on the appointed date, but there are only 18 boxes, must Jeans of the World accept them? See Articles 35, 49, 51, and 25. Can the buyer get the other two boxes? See Article 46. If the buyer avoids the contract, can the seller reinstate it by delivering the missing two boxes? See Articles 48 and 49.

(c) If a flood causes water damage to the boxes before Jeans of the World tries to avoid the contract, does this affect its ability to do so? See Article 82.

PROBLEM 66

Ambiance Hotel decided to acquire ten horse-carriages to be specially designed to carry its guests around the tourist areas of the scenic city in which it is located. It had the plans for the carriages transmitted to Buggies, Inc., a carriage manufacturer, which assured Ambiance that there would be no problem with the creation of the carriages. Ambiance financed this transaction by having Octopus National Bank purchase the carriages from Buggies, Inc., and then lease them to ambiance for a ten-year period. Assume that this transaction qualifies as a finance lease; see §2A-103(1)(g).

(a) If the carriages are delivered to the hotel and Ambiance rejects them because they are the wrong color, must Ambiance pay the lease amounts to Octopus National Bank? (You may assume that the finance lease contained a "hell or high water" clause.) See §§2A-407(1), 2A-515.

(b) If the hotel accepts the carriages, but becomes upset when they constantly break down, can it revoke its acceptance and refuse to pay the lessor? See §§2A-407, 2A-516 and its Official Comment, 2A.

VI. RISK OF LOSS: BREACH

The Code's general rules on risk of loss are found in §2-509, but that section applies only where neither party has breached the sales contract. If a breach has occurred, §2-510 is the relevant section. Read it.

Jakowski v. Carole Chevrolet, Inc.

New Jersey Superior Court, 1981
180 N.J. Super. 122, 433 A.2d 841, 31 U.C.C. Rep. Serv. 1615

NEWMAN, J.

Plaintiff seeks summary judgment on Count I alleging breach of a new car sales contract by the defendant, Carole Chevrolet.

The essential facts are not in dispute. On March 8, 1980 plaintiff, Jakowski, (hereinafter referred to as buyer), entered into a contract of sale with defendant, Carole Chevrolet, (hereinafter referred to as seller), calling for the purchase by plaintiff of one brand new 1980 Chevrolet Camaro. The parties also agreed that the car would be both undercoated and that its finish would have a polymer coating. While there is some disagreement as to exactly when the buyer ordered the coatings, it is undisputed that prior to delivery the seller agreed to deliver the car with the coatings applied. Likewise, it is undisputed that the car in question was delivered to the buyer without the required coatings on May 19, 1980.

The next day, May 20, 1980, the seller contacted the buyer and informed him that the car delivered to him lacked the coatings in question and seller instructed buyer to return the car to seller so that the coatings could be applied. On May 22, 1980, the buyer returned the auto to the seller for application of the coatings. Sometime during the evening of the 22nd or the morning of the 23rd the car was stolen from seller's premises and it was never recovered. Seller has refused to either provide a replacement auto to buyer or to refund the purchase price. Buyer remains accountable on the loan, provided through GMAC, for the purchase of the car.

The narrow question thus presented is upon whom, as between buyer and seller, this loss should fall. In UCC terminology, on May 22, 1980, which party bore the risk of the car's loss.

Seller argues that the risk of loss passed to the buyer upon his receipt of the auto. This is consistent with U.C.C. §2-509(3) pursuant to which the risk of loss passes to the buyer upon his receipt of the goods. Section 2-509(4), however, expressly provides that the general rules of §2-509 are subject to the more specific provisions of §2-510 which deals with the effect of breach upon risk of loss.

Buyer relies upon §2-510(1) which provides:

> Where a tender or delivery of goods so fails to conform to the contract as to give a right of rejection the risk of their loss remains on the seller until cure or acceptance.

Application of this section to the instant facts requires that three questions be answered. First, did the car "so fail to conform" as to give this buyer a right to reject it? If so, did the buyer "accept" the car despite the non-conformity? Finally, did the seller cure the defect prior to the theft of the auto?

The first question must be answered in the affirmative. The contract provided that the car would be delivered with undercoating and a polymer finish and it is undisputed that it was delivered without these coatings. The goods were thus clearly non-conforming and despite seller's assertion to the contrary, the degree of their non-conformity is irrelevant in assessing the buyer's concomitant right to reject them. Section 2-106 is clear in its intent to preserve the rule of strict compliance; that is, the "perfect tender" rule:

> Goods . . . are "conforming" or conform to the contract *when they are in accordance with* the obligations under the contract. [Section 2-106(2). (Emphasis supplied.) See also Comment 2 to §2-106.]

The language of §2-510(1), "so fails to conform," is misleading in this respect: no particular quantum of non-conformity is required where a single delivery is contemplated. The allusion is to §2-612 which substitutes a rule of substantial compliance where, *and only where,* an installment deal is contemplated. White & Summers, Uniform Commercial Code (2d ed. 1980), §5.5 at 187-188.

Secondly, did buyer "accept" the auto by taking possession of it? This question was presented in Zabriskie Chevrolet, Inc. v. Smith, 99 N.J. Super. 441 (Law Div. 1968). In *Zabriskie* it was held that the mere taking of possession by the purchaser is not equivalent to acceptance. Before he can be held to have accepted, a buyer must be afforded a "reasonable opportunity to inspect" the goods. *Zabriskie*, supra, at 452-453; §2-606.

Seller's actions in this matter preclude analysis in conventional "acceptance" terms. Buyer had no opportunity, indeed, no reason, to reject given seller's own communication to buyer shortly after delivery, to the effect that the goods did not conform and that the seller was exercising its right to cure said non-conformity. See §2-508 (seller's right to cure). This communication, in effect an acknowledgment of non-conformity, obviated the need for a formal rejection on buyer's part, if, indeed, §2-510(1) imposes such an obligation. Put another way, it precluded the buyer from rejecting the car. Consistent with this analysis, I find as a matter of law that there was no acceptance by buyer of this non-conforming auto.

As to the final question of whether the seller effected a cure, there is no evidence, in fact defendant does not even contend, that cure was ever effected.

Given the undisputed facts the operation of §2-510(1) is inescapable. The goods failed to conform, the buyer never accepted them and the defect was never cured. Accordingly, the risk of loss remained on the seller and judgment is granted for plaintiff.

A further note on the law is in order. It is possible to conjure up a host of hypotheticals leading to seemingly perverse results under §2-510. The section has been the subject of some scholarly criticism. See, e.g., White & Summers, supra, §5.5 at 187. Williston, "The Law of Sales in the Proposed Uniform Commercial Code," 63 Harv. L. Rev. 561, 583 (1950).

The fact is, however, that those courts considering it have had little difficulty in applying it as written. See, e.g., United Airlines, Inc. v. Conductron Corp., 69 Ill. App. 3d 847, 26 Ill. Dec. 344, 387 N.E.2d 1272 (Ill. App. 1979) (Flight trainer destroyed in fire after delivery to buyer); Southland Mobile Home v. Chyrchol, 255 Ark. 366, 500 S.W.2d 778 (Ark. Sup. 1973) (Mobile home destroyed in fire after delivery to buyer); Graybar Elec. Co. v. Shook, 283 N.C. 213, 195 S.E.2d 514 (N.C. Sup. 1973) (Nonconforming cable stolen while in buyer's possession); Wilkie v. Cummins Diesel Eng. Inc., 252 Md. 611, 250 A.2d 886 (Md. Ct. App. 1969) (Engine block frozen while in buyer's possession).

The rule is simple enough: under §2-510(1) where goods fail to conform to the contract of sale, the risk of loss remains on the seller until the buyer accepts the goods or until the seller cures the defect. In the aforecited cases, such was the result even though in all of them the goods were still in the *buyer's* possession at the time of their destruction.

For present purposes it is adequate to hold simply that where a seller obtains possession of the goods in an effort to cure defects in them so as to comply with his end of the bargain, he is under a contractual duty to redeliver them to the buyer. In failing to do so, he has breached the contract.

Pursuant to §2-711 buyer is entitled to a refund of so much of the purchase price as has been paid to seller. Included in the cost of the automobile are the finance charges incurred by the buyer who secured financing from GMAC pursuant to a retail installment sales contract entered into with the seller. There is no dispute about including these charges in the purchase cost and the buyer, as of March 30, 1981, indicated the total amount due on any judgment to be $9,398.75. However, since this case was first heard some additional time has passed and a current pay off figure should be obtained for inclusion in this judgment. Plaintiff is directed to submit an appropriate order.

PROBLEM 67

The Lamia Museum's director, Mandrake Griffin, ordered three new pieces for the museum: an Egyptian sphinx, an Old World gargoyle, and an Etruscan statue of a centaur. These objets d'art were purchased under separate contracts from Empusa Exports of London, England. All were to be shipped "F.A.S. S.S. Titanic" on or about April 9, on their way to the museum, which was located in New Jersey. The parties agreed that New Jersey law would apply. Prior to April 9, Empusa Exports received a call from Griffin cancelling the purchase of the centaur statue. Empusa protested the cancellation, but agreed to ship the other two pieces. Empusa's manager discovered that the sphinx was a phony, but kept her mouth shut and shipped it anyway. She also discovered that the gargoyle's condition was such that it could not survive the exposure to sea air, so she decided to send it by air in spite of the contract's F.A.S. Titanic term. This decision proved wise since the *Titanic* encountered an obstacle on its sea voyage and foundered, taking the sphinx with it. The gargoyle arrived in good condition, and Griffin wrote a letter to Empusa accepting the gargoyle and enclosing the museum's check. A week later Griffin learned that the gargoyle was not from the "Old World," but instead had been cast in Hoboken many years ago, had somehow found its way to Europe, and now was home again. He sent Empusa a letter demanding that the museum's money be returned and stating that he canceled the sale. Before Empusa could respond, two things happened: the museum burned to the ground, and the centaur statue was stolen from Empusa's warehouse (through no fault of Empusa, which was not negligent in guarding it). Both the museum and Empusa were fully insured. Answer these questions:

(a) By shipping the other two objects after the museum refused to take the centaur statue, did Empusa waive its right to sue for the repudiation? See

§§2-209(1), 2-106(3), 2-106(4). Would §1-308 have helped Empusa? What should it have done to use this section?

   (b) Which party took the risk of loss on
      (1) the centaur?
      (2) the sphinx?
      (3) the gargoyle?

   (c) When Empusa shipped the gargoyle by air instead of by sea, could Lamia have treated this as an imperfect tender and rejected the gargoyle for that reason? See §§2-503(1), 2-503(2), 2-504, 2-614.

   (d) The Lamia Museum's insurance policy with the Pegasus Insurance Company contains two clauses relevant to §2-510. One provided that on payment of a claim the insurance company was subrogated to any claim its insured had against any other person. The other stated that the policy should not be deemed to provide protection for any claim where the risk of loss rested with another person. What is the effect of these provisions? See Official Comment 3 to §2-510; White & Summers §§6-7.

VII.   IMPOSSIBILITY OF PERFORMANCE

   The Code has four provisions designed to straighten out the legal tangles created by those unexpected events of life that make the performance of a contract impossible or (the UCC equivalent) *commercially impracticable*. By creating a new standard of commercial impracticability, the Code drafters intended to broaden the common law concept of *impossibility*. Many commentators believe that the courts have essentially ignored the drafters' intentions and treated commercial impracticability as synonymous with common law impossibility. See Annot., 93 A.L.R.3d 584.

   Read §§2-613 to 2-616, and work through the following Problems.

PROBLEM 68

   Virgil Escapement had always wanted a sundial for his garden, and he ordered one for $250 from Horology Timepieces, Inc. The latter had 12 sundials of the type Escapement ordered in its storage room when an earthquake shook the building. All 12 fell over, and all but three were smashed. The remaining three were slightly damaged. Escapement, on being informed of the problem, insisted on the right to look over the three remaining sundials and to select one for his purchase, possibly at a reduced price due to the damage. Horology comes to you. Is §2-613 or §2-615 relevant? Must it let Escapement pick out a sundial, and must it offer to let him purchase at a reduced price, or can it simply cancel without fear of legal liability? For the test for impossibility of performance in international sales, see CISG Article 79; cf. Articles 71 and 72.

If the agreed-upon delivery or payment means become unavailable, §2-614 may require use of a substitute. See Macromex v. Globex International, 69 U.C.C. Rep. Serv. 2d 349 (2009) (under §2-614, Romanian importation ban triggered obligation to change delivery location, where facilities unavailable).

PROBLEM 69

Suppose the following, using the basic facts of the last Problem. When Horology received Virgil's order, one of their salespersons immediately put a red tag on one of the sundials. It said, "Hold for Virgil Escapement." Then the earthquake occurred, and miraculously only Virgil's sundial was destroyed. The other 11 sundials, all exactly like Virgil's, were undamaged. When Virgil demanded his sundial, Horology pleaded §2-613. Will that section excuse them? See Valley Forge Flag Co. v. New York Dowel & Molding Import Co., 90 Misc. 2d 414, 395 N.Y.S. 2d 138, 21 U.C.C. Rep. Serv. 1320 (Civ. Ct. 1977).

Arabian Score v. Lasma Arabian Ltd.

United States Court of Appeals, Eighth Circuit, 1987
814 F.2d 529, 3 U.C.C. Rep. Serv. 2d 590

WOLLMAN, J.

Beating dead horses is the sport of appellate judges, a generally harmless pastime painful only to the readers of appellate opinions. Paying for the promotion of dead horses can be an expensive proposition, however, as the facts of this case make abundantly clear.

Arabian Score (Arabian), a Minnesota limited partnership, appeals from the district court's orders granting summary judgment in favor of Lasma Arabian Ltd. (Limited), a Florida limited partnership, and Lasma Corporation (Lasma), an Arizona corporation. We affirm.

On October 27, 1983, Arabian entered into an agreement to purchase from Limited an Arabian colt named Score. The agreement, which the parties agreed would be governed by and construed in accordance with the laws of Arizona, provided that Arabian would pay Limited $1 million "for the purchase of Score and the performance by Lasma of various services in the promotion of Score." The contract required Lasma to spend $250,000 for the performance of those services which consisted of advertising and promoting Score as a 2 Star Stallion under a license agreement with Lasma Star Stallion, Inc., a separate corporation that is not a party to this lawsuit.

Paragraph 4 of the agreement provided that for a period of five years after the date of his purchase, Score would be a 2 Star Stallion, as defined by the Star Stallion license agreement, with the result that Score's foals would be eligible for nomination to all Lasma-sponsored sales open to the get of Lasma stallions.[13] If Lasma Star Stallion, Inc., in its sole discretion, determined that Score was not eligible to participate in the Star Stallion Program, Lasma would, at Arabian's option, replace Score with an eligible stallion or refund to Arabian the unused portion of the money Lasma would otherwise be required to spend promoting Score pursuant to the terms of the paragraph 5 of the agreement.

Paragraph 5 of the agreement provided that for five consecutive calendar years commencing with 1984, Lasma would implement a complete annual program for the promotion of Score as a 2 Star Stallion. Lasma was to pay $70,000 for the 1984 program and $45,000 for each of the remaining four annual programs. The annual programs were to "include advertising in various trade publications, direct mail programs and the training, boarding, conditioning and showing of SCORE by Lasma."

Pursuant to paragraph 6 of the agreement, Lasma guaranteed that Score was not infertile.

Paragraph 9 of the agreement provided: "Except as provided by paragraphs 4 and 6 above, the Partnership accepts SCORE *AS IS*, all implied warranties being excluded. Risk of loss passes upon closing. All incidental and consequential damages are excluded."

On February 8, 1984, Arabian obtained a mortality insurance policy from Transit Casualty Company insuring Score for his actual cash value. Alas — memento mori — Score went to his reward within the year, dying on September 11, 1984, having sired two foals during his brief life. Misfortune compounding, Transit Casualty Company (its name bespeaks its character?) went broke. Lasma having expended only $52,891.14 for the promotion of Score, Arabian brought suit against Lasma and Limited, seeking recovery of the $197,108.86 not expended from the $250,000 that the purchase agreement allocated for the promotion of Score.

Count I of Arabian's complaint (later dismissed by stipulation) alleged that Lasma and Limited had breached the contract by not promoting Score. Count II sought recovery of the unspent portion of the $250,000 on the ground of impossibility of performance. Count III sought recovery under paragraph 4 of the purchase agreement.

---

13. As near as we can tell from the materials presented to the trial court, the Star Stallion program is to the ranking of Arabian horses what the Mobil Guide is to the ranking of restaurants. This may not be a totally accurate description, but it will do for the purposes of this case.

The district court ruled that because Score's death was a foreseeable risk that was assumed by Arabian by the terms of the purchase agreement, neither the doctrine of impossibility nor of commercial frustration was applicable. Likewise, because the unrebutted evidence established that it is not unusual for Lasma Star Stallions, Inc. and Lasma to promote deceased horses, it was not an arbitrary, capricious, or irrational exercise of discretion by Lasma to determine that Score was still eligible postmortem to participate in the Star Stallion Program.

As provided by the agreement, we look to Arizona law to resolve the issues presented by Arabian's complaint.

In Garner v. Ellingson, 18 Ariz. App. 181, 501 P.2d 22 (1972), the Arizona Court of Appeals defined commercial frustration as circumstances beyond the control of the parties which render performance of the contract impossible and exonerate the party failing to perform. The court did not limit the doctrine to strict impossibility but included impracticability caused by extreme or unreasonable difficulty or expense. Id. at 23. The court did require, however, proof that the supervening frustrating event was not reasonably foreseeable. Id. at 24.

In Mohave County v. Mohave-Kingman Estates, 120 Ariz. 417, 586 P.2d 978, 983 (1978), the Arizona Supreme Court stated that "while Arizona recognizes the doctrine of commercial frustration . . . we do not see fit to interpret it as general absolution whenever performance under the contract becomes difficult or expensive. Proper application of this doctrine requires us to examine whether the allegedly frustrating event was reasonably foreseeable." In that case, the court refused to apply the doctrine where a zoning change had affected the economic feasibility of a contract to buy and develop land. The court reasoned that "the doctrine of commercial frustration does not apply to the instant case because the risk of change in the zoning ordinances was an event properly foreseeable by the defendants, and one which they would have contracted against." Id. at 984.

Arizona rejects the application of the commercial frustration doctrine when a party assumes the risk of the frustrating event. Kintner v. Wolfe, 102 Ariz. 164, 426 P.2d 798 (1967). In *Kintner*, the Arizona Supreme Court rejected a commercial frustration claim by a guarantor who had agreed to remain liable for the rent due on a liquor license lease "without respect to future changes in conditions." A change in law made renting liquor licenses illegal, but the court required the guarantor to pay, stating: "If the parties to a contract have agreed in express or implied terms that the risk of loss shall fall upon one or the other of the parties, full effect is given to such provision." Id. at 803.

We conclude that the trial court was correct in holding that the commercial frustration doctrine is inapplicable in this case, both because Score's death was foreseeable, as evidenced by Arabian's purchase of insurance, and because Arabian assumed the risk that Score might die prematurely. Moreover, the doctrine of impossibility/commercial frustration is not applicable because the party obligated to perform — Lasma — does not contend that it is unable or unwilling to complete its duty to promote Score.

Arabian further contends that by virtue of his death Score is no longer eligible to participate in the Star Stallion Program; consequently, paragraph 4 of the agreement obligates Lasma to return any unspent portion of the funds earmarked for promotional purposes.

As indicated earlier, Lasma Star Stallion, Inc. is not a party to this lawsuit, and there are no findings by the district court that Lasma or Limited controls Lasma Star Stallion, Inc. in the exercise of its discretion. Because Lasma Star Stallion, Inc. has not declared Score to be ineligible for the Star Stallion Program, the condition precedent to Lasma's obligation under paragraph 4 of the agreement has not been satisfied.

Even if it were within Lasma's discretion to declare Score ineligible to participate in the Star Stallion Program, we could not say that the decision that Score is still eligible for the program was an arbitrary or capricious abuse of discretion.

Arabian argues that the decision to promote a dead horse is per se arbitrary.[14] As indicated above, however, Lasma's unrebutted evidence shows that Lasma Star Stallion, Inc. and Lasma regularly promote deceased horses. This is done to enhance the owning entity's reputation and to increase the value of the stallion's progeny. Further, the language of paragraph 4 was not intended to cover the risk of death but of ineligibility for other reasons, such as infertility or substandard offspring.

It is with some reluctance that we affirm the district court's grant of summary judgment. That reluctance stems from the thought that spending $197,108.86 to promote a dead horse borders on the bizarre. The parties to this agreement were sophisticated and, we assume, well-heeled businesspersons, however, and that which we find to be somewhat unusual may be commonplace to those who inhabit the wealthy world of the horsey set.

The judgment dismissing Arabian's complaint is affirmed.

PROBLEM 70

In the mid-1960s, in an effort to boost sales of its nuclear reactors, Westinghouse Corporation agreed to sell 27 utility companies 80 million pounds of uranium over the next 20 years. The average sale price per pound was $10. When Westinghouse made the sale, it actually owned only 15 million pounds of uranium. By the mid-1970s, the price of uranium had risen

---

14. At oral argument, counsel for Arabian asked, rhetorically we assume, "How are you going to show a dead horse?" Considerations of judicial decorum and a due regard for the financial loss suffered by Arabian dissuaded us from suggesting the construction of a mausoleum — an equestrian Lenin's Tomb, if you will.

to $40 a pound. In late 1975, Westinghouse announced that it would not honor its contract. The utilities sued. Westinghouse argued that the best evidence in the late 1960s and early 1970s indicated uranium prices would be stable over the long term. Westinghouse claimed that the price rise was unforeseeable and that the contracts were excused under §2-615 as "commercially impracticable." In particular, Westinghouse blamed the 1973 oil embargo and worldwide price fixing for the "unpredictable" price rises. See Official Comments 4 and 5 to §2-615. How should the dispute be resolved? See Publicker Indus. v. Union Carbide Corp., 17 U.C.C. Rep. Serv. 989 (E.D. Pa. 1975); Ecology Services, Inc. v. Granturk Equipment, Inc., 443 F. Supp. 2d 756 (D. Md. 2006); Eagan, The Westinghouse Uranium Contracts: Commercial Impracticability and Related Matters, 18 Am. Bus. L.J. 281 (1980); Rochester Gas & Electric Corp. v. Delta Star, Inc., 68 U.C.C. Rep. Serv. 2d 130 (W.D.N.Y. 2009) (seller of goods at a fixed price was not relieved of obligation where price of component increased due to Hurricane Katrina). If you could advise Westinghouse on how to avoid this problem in the future, what would you suggest? See §2-305.

Louisiana Power & Light Co. v. Allegheny Ludlum Industries, Inc.

United States District Court, Eastern District of Louisiana, 1981
517 F. Supp. 1319, 32 U.C.C. Rep. Serv. 847

GORDON, J.

This breach of contract case is before the court on plaintiff's motion for summary judgment. The material facts which are not in dispute are as follows:

Plaintiff, Louisiana Power & Light Company (hereinafter referred to as "LP & L"), entered into a contract with defendants, Allegheny Ludlum Industries, Inc. and Allegheny Ludlum Steel Corporation (hereinafter referred to collectively as "Allegheny"), in which Allegheny agreed to supply condenser tubing to LP & L for use at LP & L's Waterford 3 nuclear power plant. The contract was awarded to Allegheny Ludlum Steel Corporation, then a division of Allegheny Ludlum Industries, Inc., after the solicitation of bids by LP & L's agent, Ebasco Services, Incorporated. The contract, dated February 8, 1974, was accepted by Allegheny in mid-March of 1974.

Pursuant to the terms of the contract Allegheny undertook to furnish, fabricate and deliver to LP & L stainless steel condenser tubing in accordance with the specifications of LP & L's agent, Ebasco. Equal shipments of the tubing were to be made on June 1, 1976, June 15, 1976, and July 1, 1976, for a total price of $1,127,387.82. The contract also provided that if LP & L delayed shipment beyond August 31, 1976, but not later than January 31, 1977, the contract price would be increased by three percent (3%). A further adjustment at the rate of ten percent (10%) would take place if LP & L delayed shipment beyond January 31, 1977, but not later than January 31, 1978. No other escalation clauses were included in the contract.

On May 19, 1975, Allegheny sent a letter to LP & L seeking "additional compensation" for performance under the contract. Allegheny informed LP & L that subsequent to the formulation of the contract its "costs [had] risen at such a high rate that escalators built into our contracts have in no way adequately compensated for them. For example, since March of 1974 the price of electrolytic nickel has increased 24%, low carbon ferrochrome 185% and labor 21%." Allegheny sought the opportunity to meet with representatives of LP & L in order to discuss Allegheny's price increases and possible solutions to Allegheny's problem. Allegheny suggested a renegotiation of the contract price, but LP & L chose not to meet with Allegheny to discuss the matter.

In October of 1975, LP & L, through Ebasco, advised Allegheny that it considered Allegheny's price increases to be business risks which must be absorbed by Allegheny. On November 4, 1975, Allegheny informed LP & L, by letter from C. R. Hastings, General Manager of Allegheny's Wallingford Tubular Products Division, that a "[c]urrent review of this matter suggests that Allegheny Ludlum might be well advised not to perform under the contract." On November 19, 1975, Ebasco wrote to Allegheny's Wallingford Tubular Products Division, and demanded written assurances within thirty days, pursuant to §2-609 of the New York Commercial Code,[15] that Allegheny would fully and properly perform under the contract.

As of January 19, 1976, LP & L had not received any such written assurance of performance from Allegheny and on January 30, 1976, LP & L notified Allegheny by letter that it considered the contract repudiated by Allegheny. Thereafter, on February 17, 1976, C. R. Hastings at Allegheny wrote to LP & L informing it that Allegheny was willing to "make delivery under the subject purchase order at $1.80 per lb. . . . [Allegheny's] full cost of producing the material. . . ."

LP & L rejected Allegheny's offer to supply the tubing at Allegheny's cost and through its agent, Ebasco, LP & L solicited bids from other vendors for supply of the requisite condenser tubing. LP & L steadfastly rejected the offer of Allegheny to supply the tubing at Allegheny's cost, a price higher than that specified in the LP & L/Allegheny contract. On June 16, 1976, LP & L, through Ebasco, entered into a contract with Trent Tube Division of Crucible, Inc. for the purchase of condenser tubing at a price of $1,729,278.

---

15. The contract between LP & L and Allegheny stated that the contract was to be governed by the laws of the State of New York, hence the invocation of §2-609 of the New York Commercial Code.

Allegheny intended that the condenser tubing which was the subject of its contract with LP & L would be supplied by its Wallingford Tubular Products Division at Wallingford, Connecticut. C. R. Hastings, General Manager of the Wallingford Tubular Division, stated in his deposition that performance under the terms of the LP & L/Allegheny contract would have caused Allegheny to sustain a projected loss of $428,500 on the contract. Hastings indicated that such a loss would have reduced the planned profit for 1976 at the Wallingford plant from $1,018,000 to $589,500.

Plaintiff seeks by way of its lawsuit to recover from Allegheny the costs of its "cover," the monetary difference between the LP & L/Allegheny contract and the LP & L/Trent Tube contract, plus the expenses which it incurred in the re-solicitation of bids for the tubing. Allegheny has defended this action on four principal bases: commercial impracticability, mutual mistake, unconscionability and alleged bad faith conduct by LP & L. Plaintiff's claim and Allegheny's defenses will be considered in accord with the appropriate standards for summary judgment motions.

LP & L claims that Allegheny breached its contract to supply condenser tubing to LP & L. The first evidence which LP & L received that indicated that Allegheny would not perform under the contract as written was Allegheny's letter of May 19, 1975, to LP & L in which Allegheny sought "additional compensation" for supplying the condenser tubing. In response to that submission, LP & L sent a letter to Allegheny, invoking the provisions of §2-609 of the New York Uniform Commercial Code and requesting assurance from Allegheny that it would perform under the contract.

The pertinent provisions of §2-609 of the UCC, invoked by LP & L, provide:

§2-609. *Right to Adequate Assurance of Performance*

(1) A contract for sale imposes an obligation on each party that the other's expectation of receiving due performance will not be impaired. When reasonable grounds for insecurity arise with respect to the performance of either party the other may in writing demand adequate assurance of due performance. . . .

(4) After receipt of a justified demand failure to provide within a reasonable time not exceeding thirty days such assurance of due performance as is adequate under the circumstances of the particular case is a repudiation of the contract.

The letter which LP & L received from Allegheny requesting "additional compensation" provided LP & L with a reasonable basis for insecurity as to Allegheny's performance under the contract. LP & L's letter of November 19, 1975, to Allegheny constituted an adequate demand on Allegheny for an assurance of performance. When LP & L failed to receive such an assurance by January 19, 1976, it was justified in characterizing the contract as repudiated. LP & L notified Allegheny of that fact on January 30, 1976. Subsequently, Allegheny indicated to plaintiff that it would perform under the contract for added compensation. Such a belated and qualified offer of performance cannot, however, be viewed as an assurance of performance under §2-609 of the U.C.C. Allegheny's failure to supply an assurance of performance within the allotted time period operated as a repudiation of the contract.

The UCC provides that:

> When either party repudiates the contract with respect to a performance not yet due the loss of which will substantially impair the value of the contract to the other, the aggrieved party may . . . (b) resort to any remedy for breach (Section 2-703 or Section 2-711). . . . [Uniform Commercial Code §2-610.]

One available remedy in the event of a breach is for the buyer to obtain a "cover" by purchasing goods in substitution for the goods due from the seller. A buyer and non-breaching party may then seek to recover from the seller and breaching party the price of such substituted goods plus incidental and consequential damages. See U.C.C. §2-711 and §2-712. It is just such a claim that plaintiff is making in the instant case. Based on the undisputed facts in this case, plaintiff is entitled to recover on that claim, unless Allegheny prevails on one of its defenses.

COMMERCIAL IMPRACTICABILITY

The first of Allegheny's defenses to be considered is that of commercial impracticability. The Uniform Commercial Code provides that performance under a contract may be excused if performance under the contract is commercially impracticable. Section 2-615 of the UCC, upon which Allegheny relies in its defense of commercial impracticability, states in pertinent part:

> §2-615. *Excuse by Failure of Presupposed Conditions*
> Except so far as a seller may have assumed a greater obligation and subject to the preceding section on substituted performance:
> (a) Delsy in delivery or non-delivery in whole or in parts by a seller who complies with paragraphs (b) and (c) is not a breach of his duty under a contract for sale if performance as agreed has been made impracticable by the occurrence of a contingency the non-occurrence of which was a basic assumption on which the contract was made. . . .

In reliance upon that rule of law Allegheny argues that its performance under the contract with LP & L was rendered commercially impracticable because of a "severe shortage of critical raw materials and an increase in the cost of labor, an unexpected contingency which caused a dramatic increase in the price of those raw materials and the condenser tubing. The non-occurrence of such was a basic assumption on which the contract was founded and altered the essential nature of performance."

There are three conditions which must be met pursuant to §2-615 before performance under a contract can be excused because of commercial impracticability: "(1) a contingency must occur, (2) performance must thereby be made 'impracticable' and (3) the non-occurrence of the contingency must have been a basic assumption on which the contract was made." Neal-Cooper Grain Co. v. Texas Gulf Sulphur Co., 508 F.2d 283, 293 (7th Cir. 1974).

The rule has also been stated as "excus[ing] delay or nondelivery when the agreed upon performance has been rendered 'commercially impracticable' by an unforeseen supervening event not within the contemplation of the parties at the time the contract was entered into." Eastern Air Lines, Inc. v. McDonnell Douglas Corp., 532 F.2d 957, 988 (5th Cir. 1976). The rationale behind the doctrine of commercial impracticability is that when an event occurs which renders performance so "vitally different" from that which is anticipated, the contract cannot be reasonably considered to govern and performance under that contract is excused. *Eastern Air Lines, Inc.*, supra, at 991.

The burden of proof on a claim of commercial impracticability rests with the party making the claim, in this case the defendants. Allegheny must meet its burden as to each of the requisite three elements in order to be successful in this defense. See Eastern Air Lines, Inc. v. Gulf Oil Corp., 415 F. Supp. 429, 438 (S.D. Fla. 1975), citing Ocean Air Tradeways, Inc. v. Arkay Realty Corp., 480 F.2d 1112, 1117 (9th Cir. 1973).

The undisputed facts in this case show that Allegheny has not and cannot meet its burden of proof as to this defense because it is unable to show that performance under the contract was commercially impracticable. Allegheny contacted LP & L in May of 1975 and informed LP & L that between March of 1974 and May of 1975, its costs for electrolytic nickel had risen by 24%, for low carbon ferrochrome had risen by 185%, and that its labor costs had risen by 21%. C. R. Hastings, General Manager of Allegheny's Wallingford Tubular Division stated in his deposition that had Allegheny performed under the contract as written, it would have sustained a loss of $428,500 on the contract and that the planned profitability of the Wallingford plant would have been reduced to an overall profit of $589,500 for the year of performance.

There are no facts which indicate that Allegheny's costs increased by more than the amount indicated to LP & L in the Allegheny letter of May 19, 1975. Moreover, there are no facts which indicate that Allegheny would have sustained a greater loss than that attested to by C. R. Hastings had it performed under the contract. There are also no facts which indicate that

Allegheny would have been unprofitable during 1976 in either its overall corporate structure or in its Wallingford Tubular Division had it performed under the contract as written. Hastings testified in his deposition that a profit was anticipated for the Wallingford plant even had Allegheny been required to perform under the contract's terms. The material facts in this regard are clear, simple and undisputed. When viewed in the context of a claim of commercial impracticability, as that term has been interpreted in the case law, it must be said that performance under the contract was not commercially impracticable.

The mere fact that performance under the contract would have deprived Allegheny of its anticipated profit and resulted in a loss on the contract is not sufficient to show commercial impracticability. Rather, ". . . [t]he party seeking to excuse his performance must not only show that he can perform only at a loss but also that the loss will be especially severe and unreasonable." Gulf Oil Corp. v. Federal Power Commission, 563 F.2d 588, 600 (3d Cir. 1977), *cert. denied*, 434 U.S. 1062 (1978), *petition for cert. dismissed*, 435 U.S. 911 (1978).

Allegheny's loss by performance would not have been especially severe and unreasonable in this case. On the contrary, by Allegheny's own estimate its costs of performance under the contract increased only 38% over the original contract price of $1,127,387.82. While no seller desires to be called upon to perform under a contract when performance will result in a financial loss, such are the realities of commercial life. Whereas the law quite properly provides relief for situations in which performance can only be had at an excessive and unreasonable cost, see Transatlantic Financing Corp. v. United States, 363 F.2d 312 (D.C. Cir. 1960), Allegheny's cost of performance did not increase to the extent necessary to excuse its performance under the doctrine of commercial impracticability.[16]

Eastern Air Lines, Inc. v. Gulf Oil Corp., 415 F. Supp. 429, 438 (S.D. Fla. 1975) is instructive:

> The modern U.C.C. §2-615 doctrine of commercial impracticability has its roots in the common law doctrine of frustration or impossibility and finds its most recognized illustrations in the so-called "Suez Cases," arising out of the various closings of the Suez Canal and the consequent increases in shipping costs around the Cape of Good Hope. Those cases offered little encouragement to those who would wield the sword of commercial impracticability. As a leading British case arising out of the 1957 Suez closure declared, the unforeseen cost increase that would excuse performance "must be more than merely onerous or expensive. It must be positively unjust to hold the parties bound." Ocean Tramp Tankers v. V/O Sovfracht (The Eugenia), 2 Q.B. 226,

---

16. When consideration is given to Allegheny's anticipated profitability in 1976, it becomes more apparent that this was not a situation wherein performance under the contract would have been especially severe and unreasonable.

239 (1964). To the same effect are Tsakiroglou and Co. Ltd. v. Noblee Thorl G.m.b.H., 2 Q.B. 348, (1960), *aff'd*, A.C. 93 (1962), and Caparanoyoti & Co., Ltd. v. E. T. Green, Ltd., 1 Q.B. 131, 148 (1959). These British precedents were followed by the District of Columbia Circuit, which gave specific consideration to UCC §2-615, Comment 4, in Transatlantic Financing Corp. v. United States, 124 U.S. App. D.C. 183, 363 F.2d 312, 319 (1966).

In *Transatlantic Financing Corp.*, supra, Judge J. Skelly Wright considered a claim of commercial impracticability and impossibility in connection with a suit seeking additional compensation for transport of a cargo of wheat around the Cape of Good Hope. The plaintiff was forced to abandon its customary route through the Suez Canal when Egypt obstructed the canal and closed it to traffic. Plaintiff argued that it was subjected to an additional expense of $43,972.00 above the contract price of $305,842.92 because of the longer journey necessitated by the closing of the canal. The court stated:

> . . . While it may be an overstatement to say that increased cost and difficulty of performance never constitute impracticability, to justify relief there must be more of a variation between expected cost and the cost of performing by an available alternative than is present in this case, where the promisor can legitimately be presumed to have accepted some degree of abnormal risk, and where impracticability is urged on the basis of added expense alone. [363 F.2d at 319.] The court affirmed the dismissal of the plaintiff's action because performance under the contract had not been rendered legally impossible.

In a similar case resulting from the closure of the Suez Canal, it was held that extra expense of 31.6% of the contract price, incurred in bringing the vessel around the Cape of Good Hope, was not sufficient to constitute commercial impracticability. American Trading and Production Corp. v. Shell International Marine, Ltd., 453 F.2d 939 (2d Cir. 1972). In discussing the degree of increase in costs that would constitute impossibility or commercial impracticability, it was stated that:

> Mere increase in cost alone is not a sufficient excuse for non-performance (Restatement of Contracts §467 (1932)). It must be an "extreme and unreasonable" expense (Restatement of Contracts §454 (1932)). While in the *Transatlantic* case supra, the increased cost amounted to an increase of about 14% over the contract price, the court did cite with approval the two leading English cases Ocean Tramp Tankers Corp. v. V/O Sovfracht (The Eugenia), [1964] 2 Q.B. 226, 233 (C.A. 1963) (which expressly overruled Societe Franco Tunisienne D'Armement v. Sidemar S.P.A. (The Messalia), [1961] 2 Q.B. 278 (1960), where the court had found frustration because the Cape route was highly circuitous and involved an increase in cost of approximately 50%), and Tsakiroglou & Co. Ltd. v. Noblee Thorl G.m.b.H., [1960] 2 Q.B. 318, 348, *aff'd*, [1962] A.C., 93 (1961) where the House of

Lords found no frustration though the freight costs were exactly doubled due to the Canal closure. [453 F.2d at 942.]

In Iowa Electric Light and Power Company v. Atlas Corp., 467 F. Supp. 129 (N.D. Iowa 1978), the court held that an increase in seller's costs by 52.2%, resulting in the seller's loss of approximately $2,673,125.00, failed to constitute commercial impracticability thereby precluding judicial adjustment or discharge of the contract for supply of uranium concentrate. In making such a determination, the court noted that cost increases of 50-58 percent had generally not been considered of sufficient magnitude to excuse performance under a contractual agreement.

As the jurisprudence indicates, Allegheny's performance under the contract was not commercially impracticable. Even if Allegheny were to show that its increased costs constituted a contingency, the non-occurrence of which was a basic assumption on which the contract was made, it still could not show that performance had been rendered commercially impracticable as a result. Allegheny bears the burden of proof as to each of the requisite three elements on its claim of commercial impracticability. Being unable to prove all three elements, its defense must fall.

Allegheny has suggested that claims of commercial impracticability are inherently insusceptible of resolution by summary judgment. That position is incorrect. While great care should be exercised in granting summary judgment motions in cases of this sort, the mere invocation of the term "commercial impracticability" is not a talisman behind which a defaulting seller may hide and be guaranteed a trial in the absence of a dispute as to the material facts in the matter. Were that the case, every seller or buyer caught in a burdensome position under a contract would find it hard to resist the natural temptation to compel renegotiation of unprofitable contracts by threatening to invoke a claim of commercial impracticability, knowing that it would be assured of a trial on the merits and knowing that even if it lost at trial, it would be required to do no more than fulfill its obligation under the contract. Such a rule of law would constitute a misuse of the protections afforded by the doctrine of commercial impracticability, particularly in cases of this sort where the facts are clear and undisputed and in which the seller in breach has been unable to cite a case wherein a claim of commercial impracticability has been upheld under similar factual circumstances.[17]

17. In Aluminum Company of America v. Essex Group, Inc., 499 F. Supp. 53 (W.D. Pa. 1980), a claim of commercial impracticability was upheld. The facts surrounding the claim of commercial impracticability in *Alcoa* are, however, distinguishable from those in the instant case. Plaintiff stood to lose $60,000,000.00 in *Alcoa* if its performance under the contract was compelled while the defendant stood to gain a concomitant "windfall profit." There are no comparable facts in the instant case. Allegheny stood to lose $428,500 on a $1,127,387.82 contract. It cannot be said that LP & L would be the beneficiary of a "windfall profit" like that in *Alcoa*.

The clear undisputed facts require resolution of the commercial impracticability defense in plaintiff's favor. Allegheny is unable to meet its burden of proof....

UNCONSCIONABILITY

Section 4 of the Supplementary Terms and Conditions of the LP & L/Allegheny contract provides that:

4. Provision for Cancellation
    At any time after the acceptance of this Order the Purchaser shall have the absolute right to cancel the entire Order upon the payment to the Seller for all disbursements and expenses which the Seller has incurred or become obligated for prior to date of notice of cancellation, less the reasonable resale value of equipment which shall have been obtained or ordered to become an integral part of the Equipment plus a sum as profit bearing the same ratio to the profit that the Seller would have received upon completing the Work as that portion of Work done bears to the entire amount of Work to be done by the Seller under this Order.

Allegheny argues that the aforementioned cancellation provision is unconscionable, that it taints the contract in its entirety and that as a result the contract is unenforceable. Accordingly, Allegheny urges that LP & L be barred from any recovery for damages.

The unconscionability which Allegheny suggests is rooted in the alleged one-sidedness of the provision which provides a right of cancellation to LP & L with no concomitant right given to Allegheny. The defendants submit that until production commenced, LP & L could cancel its order with impunity and would only be required to pay a penalty for cancellation "if Allegheny would be making a profit on the order, which LP & L now knew it would not...."

Section 2-302 of the U.C.C., which is the basis for Allegheny's claim of unconscionability states: [the court quotes §2-302—EDS.].

Comment 1 to U.C.C. §2-302 sets forth the standards to be used in making a determination on an unconscionability claim. "The basic test is whether in the light of the general commercial background and the commercial needs of the particular trade or case, the clauses involved are so one-sided as to be unconscionable under the circumstances existing at the time of the making of the contract.... The principle is one of prevention of oppression and unfair surprise...and not of disturbance of allocation of risks because of superior bargaining power."

Allegheny's allegation of unconscionability presents a question of law to be decided by the court. It is not a jury issue. U.C.C. §2-302. W.L. May Co., Inc. v. Philco-Ford Corp., 543 P.2d 283 (Or. 1975). However, plaintiff's claim that the cancellation clause and the contract were unconscionable entitles the parties to "a reasonable opportunity to present evidence as to . . . commercial setting, purpose and effect to aid the court in making . . . [its] determination." U.C.C. §2-302(2). The unconscionability claim is not susceptible of resolution by summary judgment. The court's determination of the issue cannot be made without a hearing. *Zicari v. Joseph Harris Co.*, 304 N.Y.S.2d 918 (N.Y. 1969). Accordingly, plaintiff's motion for summary judgment must be denied in this regard.

BAD FAITH

Allegheny also asserts that bad faith conduct by LP & L serves as a defense to LP & L's claim for breach of contract. The basis of Allegheny's allegation of bad faith is that LP & L refused to meet with it in a timely fashion to discuss renegotiation of the contract. Allegheny argues that its bad faith allegation must be resolved at trial by the finder of fact.

The Uniform Commercial Code imposes an obligation of good faith on the performance or enforcement of contracts under the Code. U.C.C. §1-203.[18] "Good faith" is defined as "honesty in fact and the observance of reasonable commercial standards of fair dealing in the trade." U.C.C. §2-103(1)(b).

Allegheny's defense of bad faith based on LP & L's failure to engage in timely renegotiation of the contract is without merit. There is no obligation imposed under law which would have required LP & L to engage in renegotiation or even discuss renegotiation of its contract with Allegheny. See *Missouri Public Service Company v. Peabody Coal Co.*, 583 S.W.2d 721, 725 (Mo. App. 1979), *cert. denied*, 444 U.S. 865. Allegheny has not attempted to show any requirement for renegotiation. Allegheny's claim that LP & L was in bad faith for failure to do what it had no obligation to do cannot withstand scrutiny. It cannot survive the test of plaintiff's summary judgment motion.

Insofar, however, as Allegheny makes a claim of bad faith conduct in connection with LP & L's purchase of goods in substitution for those due from Allegheny, the "cover" under U.C.C. §2-712(1), that defense relates to the damages portion of LP & L's lawsuit. The issue awaits resolution with LP & L's claim for damages.

In that regard, this court cannot now say that there are no genuine issues of material fact surrounding LP & L's claim for damages. The facts surrounding the obtaining of a "cover," timeliness, mitigation of damages, good faith and costs cannot be decided at this time. Unlike the liability portion of plaintiff's claim and consideration of certain of Allegheny's defenses, the issue of LP & L's damages awaits resolution at trial.

18. Now §1-304 — EDS.

CONCLUSION

Based on the foregoing authorities and analysis, the court hereby grants the motion of Louisiana Power & Light Co. for summary judgment on the issue of liability and Allegheny's defenses of commercial impracticability, mistakes of fact and bad faith. The motion for summary judgment must be denied insofar as Allegheny's defense of unconscionability and the issue of LP & L's damages are concerned.

CHAPTER 6
REMEDIES

I. SPECIAL REMEDIES

The 2-700s of the UCC are the basic remedy provisions (though some remedies, such as rejection and revocation of acceptance, which we covered earlier, are found in other parts of Article 2). The 2-700s may be further divided into two parts: the seller's remedies when the buyer is in breach (§§2-703 to 2-710) and the buyer's remedies when the seller is in breach (§§2-711 to 2-717). These two areas will be discussed below; but before getting to them, pedagogical tidiness calls for a quick look at some special situations.

A. Remedies on Insolvency

When one contracting party becomes insolvent while in possession of goods that have been identified to the contract, the other may in some circumstances elect to forgo damages and try to get the goods themselves. This action is called *reclamation*. The key Code sections are §§2-502 and 2-702; read them. Both refer to the "insolvency" of the seller as a triggering event, but what does that term mean? In the Bankruptcy Code, it is defined as having more liabilities than assets, a bookkeeping test that is hard to determine without much investigation. The equitable definition of "insolvency," therefore, defined the term as being unable to pay one's debts as they matured, a much easier thing to prove. Which of these does the UCC adopt? See §1-201(b)(23).

PROBLEM 71

Ratchett Tools delivered a truckload of inventory to Madoff Hardware. The next day, Ratchett Tools read that Madoff Hardware had shut its doors, failed to pay its many creditors, and has few assets to go after. Can Ratchett get the inventory back? See §2-702(2). Would it help sellers to include a clause in their sales contract forms making buyers promise they had the wherewithal to pay for goods ordered? See §2-702(2). What if Ratchett had learned of the financial distress before delivery? §2-702(1). What if Madoff Hardware files for bankruptcy? See 11 U.S.C. §546(c), which should be in your statute book as part of the Bankruptcy Code.

———————————

Quite often a battle develops between a party (buyer or seller) seeking to reclaim the goods and either a trustee in bankruptcy or a secured creditor of the party with the goods. If the battle is between the reclaiming seller and the trustee in bankruptcy, a section of the Bankruptcy Reform Act, revised in 2005, protects a seller's reclamation right from the trustee's avoiding powers even more broadly than §2-702; see 11 U.S.C.A. §546(c) (allowing seller to reclaim goods that were delivered to insolvent buyer within 45 days before buyer's bankruptcy). The battle between the secured creditor and the reclaiming party is governed by meshing Article 2 with Article 9, not always an easy task. The leading case is In re Samuels & Co., 510 F.2d 139 (5th Cir. 1975), *rev'd on other grounds*, 526 F.2d 1238 (5th Cir. 1976), *cert. denied*, 429 U.S. 834 (1976), where the secured creditor wins over an unpaid cash seller. See also White & Summers, §24-7 (suggesting that courts are likely to continue to favor secured creditors, under the revised version of Bankruptcy Code §546(c)).

B.   Liquidated Damages

At common law, if the parties put a liquidated damages clause in their contract, it was upheld by the courts only if the parties truly intended the figure named to be compensatory and had made in good faith an attempt to pre-estimate the damages. The courts struck the clause and made the aggrieved party prove actual damages if the courts decided that the parties had intended the liquidated figure to be a penalty amount to be forfeited in the event of breach. See Equitable Lumber Co. v. IPA Land Dev. Corp., 38 N.Y.2d 516, 344 N.E.2d 391, 381 N.Y.S.2d 459, 18 U.C.C. Rep. Serv. 273 (1976); J. Calamari & J. Perillo, Contracts §§14-31, 14-32 (3d ed. 1987).

The Code's liquidated damages provision is §2-718(1). It makes little change from the common law rules except that it provides that the validity of the liquidated damages clause is to be tested, in part, against the *actual* harm caused by the breach (a criterion of no importance at common law). See Note, A New Standard for Liquidated Damage Provisions Under the Uniform Commercial Code?, 38 Ohio St. L.J. 437 (1977); see also Annot., 98 A.L. R.3d 586. Interestingly enough, the liquidated damages provision in Article 2A for the leasing of goods no longer refers to actual damages, specifically allows a *formula* to be used to compute damages, and drops all reference to the effect of an unreasonably large liquidated damages clause. Read §2A-504 and its Official Comment. Would this section permit the parties to contract for an outrageous amount (obviously a penalty) in the event of lessee default? See Benfield, Lessor's Damages Under Article 2A After Default by the Lessee as to Accepted Goods, 39 Ala. L. Rev. 915, 953 (1988).

C. *The Breaching Buyer's Restitution*

PROBLEM 72

The zoo officials for the Minerun (West Virginia) Zoo contracted to buy an elephant from the zoo in White Cliffs, Delaware. The terms of the deal were that the West Virginia zoo would deliver a black bear worth $300 as a down payment and pay $100 a month for 20 months, at the end of which time the Delaware zoo would deliver the elephant. The bear was tendered and accepted. The West Virginia zoo duly made its $100 payments for 15 months before it ran out of money and could pay no more. The West Virginia zoo comes to you. Can it recover the $1,500 it has paid? The bear? Look at §§2-718(2), 2-718(3), and 2-718(4). Assuming the bear was and is still worth $300, calculate the amount that the West Virginia zoo is likely to recover in a restitution action.

II. SELLER'S REMEDIES

The plan of the 2-700s is to describe briefly the seller's remedies in §2-703 and the buyer's in §2-711, and then to flesh out these brief descriptions in the sections immediately following. All of these remedies sections are to be read in light of the Code's guiding remedial principle, §1-305(a):

> The remedies provided by this Act shall be liberally administered to the end that the aggrieved party may be put in as good a position as if the other party had fully performed but neither consequential or special nor penal damages may be had except as specifically provided in this Act or by other rule of law.[1]

Now read §2-703 and its Official Comment.

A.   Accepted Goods

The seller's recovery of damages is measured by §2-709 (Action for the Price) if the buyer has made a technical *acceptance* of the goods or if the goods are destroyed within a commercially reasonable period of time after the risk of loss shifts to the buyer. In effect, §2-709 is the equivalent of a specific performance remedy for the seller. As discussed below, if the seller still has possession of the goods (or had the risk of loss at the time of their destruction), damages are measured by other sections in the 2-700s. For now, read §2-709. This section is annotated in 90 A.L.R.3d 1141.

PROBLEM 73

Backslappers Auto Sales sold a new blue sports car to Dwane Diletante on credit. He accepted the car and drove it for a month. He then sent Backslappers a notice of revocation of acceptance and gave as his reason the recent repainting of his garage in a color that clashed with the blue car. The notice stated that Diletante had parked the car down the block from his home (away from the clashing garage) and that Backslappers should come and get it. Dwane also refused to make any more car payments. Three days after Backslappers received the notice, the car disappeared and has never been found. May the seller recover the price under §2-709? Who had the risk of loss? See §§2-608(1) and (3), 2-606(1), 2-510; note Official Comment 5 to §2-709. There is a good discussion of this problem in White & Summers §8-3. Would it make a difference if Diletante had *rejected* the goods for the same reason?

---

1. The Wyoming Supreme Court has read this section as prohibiting punitive damages awards in suits alleging fraud; Waters v. Trenckmann, 503 P.2d 1187, 11 U.C.C. Rep. Serv. 712 (Wyo. 1972). Other courts have disagreed; see the discussion in Seaton v. Lawson Chevrolet-Mazda, Inc., 821 S.W.2d 137, 16 U.C.C. Rep. Serv. 2d 1070 (Tenn. 1991).

B.   Unaccepted Goods

When the buyer repudiates before delivery or rejects the goods, the relevant Code section is §2-706 if the seller resells the goods to someone else. If no resale occurs, damages are measured under §2-708. Other relevant sections are cited in the following Problems.

PROBLEM 74

Lannie Light was the sole proprietor of Light's Bulbs, a lighting fixtures business in Austin, Texas. She contracted to sell 80 neon light fixtures to Signs, Inc., a firm in San Antonio. The price was $1,500 "F.O.B. Austin," and the shipment date was to be March 15. On March 5, Signs, Inc., phoned Light and told her that the deal was off, but Lannie refused to agree to a cancellation. She went to her warehouse and picked 80 of the fixtures from her large stock. Then she posted a notice on the bulletin board near the cash register in her store, stating that 80 of the fixtures would be sold to the person making the best offer. Carl Customer (who was always buying these types of items) saw the sign and offered Light $1,000 for the fixtures. Light sold Customer the goods and took payment. Now Light comes to you. She tells you that on March 5 the fixtures were selling on the open market at $800 for 80 and that on March 15 the price for 80 such fixtures was $900 in Austin and $800 in San Antonio. Answer these questions:

(a) Does the UCC permit Light to select goods from the warehouse *after* the buyer repudiates? See §2-704.

(b) Was the resale proper? See §2-706 and Official Comment 2.

(c) If Light's damages are measured under §2-708(1), what amount may she collect? What amount under §2-706?

(d) Does Light have the choice between the §2-706 (Resale) computation and the §2-708 (Repudiation) computation? See Official Comment 1 to §2-703; White & Summers §8-7.

PROBLEM 75

Fun in the Sun, Inc., sells swimming pools. Its president comes to your law office with this problem. A customer named Esther Swimmer ordered one of the standard above-ground pools, retailing for $2,000. The pool's components are purchased by Fun in the Sun at a wholesale price of $800 and are assembled into the finished product. The assembly process costs the seller $400. Swimmer has now repudiated the contract, and Fun in the Sun wants to sue. The current market price is $2,000 for such a pool. Fun in the Sun is sure it can find another buyer at that price if it resells the pool. Does it have damages? How are they measured? See §2-708(2), along with Official Comment 2. See also White & Summers §§8-8 to 8-13.

The problem with sellers in Fun in the Sun's position (sellers having an unlimited supply of goods) is that if the law forces them to measure damages under §2-706 or §2-708(1), they lose the profit they would have made from the sale to the second customer. A seller in such a position is called a *lost volume seller*. The drafters meant for §2-708(2) to rescue such a seller from this dilemma, but the actual mechanics of the operation of the section are not clear. The problem arises in part from the undefined phrase "profit (including reasonable overhead)," which contains accounting terms having no fixed legal meaning. For an analysis of their import, see Speidel & Clay, Seller's Recovery of Overhead Under U.C.C. Section 2-708(2): Economic Cost Theory and Contract Remedial Policy, 57 Cornell L. Rev. 681 (1972). See also Scott, The Case for Market Damages: Revisiting the Lost Profits Puzzle, 57 U. Chi. L. Rev. 1155 (1990).

Teradyne, Inc. v. Teledyne Industries, Inc.

United States Court of Appeals, First Circuit, 1982
676 F.2d 865, 33 U.C.C. Rep. Serv. 1669

WYZANSKI, J.

In this diversity action, Teradyne, Inc. sued Teledyne Industries, Inc. and its subsidiary for damages pursuant to §2-708(2) of the U.C.C. Teledyne does not dispute the facts that it is bound as a buyer under a sales contract with Teradyne, that it broke the contract, and that Teradyne's right to damages is governed by §2-708(2). The principal dispute concerns the calculation of damages.

The district court referred the case to a master whose report the district court approved and made the basis of the judgment here on appeal.

The following facts, derived from the master's report, are undisputed.

On July 30, 1976 Teradyne, Inc. ["the seller"], a Massachusetts corporation, entered into a Quantity Purchase Contract ["the contract"] which, though made with a subsidiary, binds Teledyne Industries, Inc., a California corporation ["the buyer"]. That contract governed an earlier contract resulting from the seller's acceptance of the buyer's July 23, 1976 purchase order to buy at the list price of $98,400 (which was also its fair market value) a T-347A transistor test system ["the T-347A"]. One consequence of such governance was that the buyer was entitled to a $984 discount from the $98,400 price.

The buyer canceled its order for the T-347A when it was packed ready for shipment scheduled to occur two days later. The seller refused to accept the cancellation.

The buyer offered to purchase instead of the T-347A a $65,000 Field Effects Transistor System ["the FET"] which would also have been governed by "the contract." The seller refused the offer.

After dismantling, testing, and reassembling at an estimated cost of $614 the T-347A, the seller, pursuant to an order that was on hand prior to the cancellation, sold it for $98,400 to another purchaser [hereafter "resale purchaser"].

Teradyne would have made the sale to the resale purchaser even if Teledyne had not broken its contract. Thus if there had been no breach, Teradyne would have made two sales and earned two profits rather than one.

The seller was a volume seller of the equipment covered by the July 23, 1976 purchase order. The equipment represented standard products of the seller and the seller had the means and capacity to duplicate the equipment for a second sale had the buyer honored its purchase order.

Teradyne being of the view that the measure of damages under §2-708(2) was the contract price less ascertainable costs saved as a result of the breach—see Jericho Sash and Door Company, Inc. v. Building Erectors, Inc., 362 Mass. 871, 872, 286 N.E.2d 343 (1972) [hereafter "*Jericho*"]—offered as evidence of its cost prices its Inventory Standards Catalog ["the Catalog"]—a document which was prepared for tax purposes not claimed to have been illegitimate, but which admittedly disclosed "low inventory valuations." Relying on that Catalog, Teradyne's Controller, McCabe, testified that the *only* costs which the seller saved as a result of the breach were:

direct labor costs associated with production	$3,301
material charges	17,045
sales commission on one T-347A	492
expense	1,800
Total	$22,638

McCabe admitted that he had not included as costs saved the labor costs of employees associated with testing, shipping, installing, servicing, or fulfilling 10-year warranties on the T-347A (although he acknowledged that in forms of accounting for purposes other than damage suits the costs of those employees would not be regarded as "overhead"). His reason was that those costs would not have been affected by the production of one machine more or less. McCabe also admitted that he had not included fringe benefits which amounted to 12% in the case of both included and excluded labor costs.

During McCabe's direct examination, he referred to the 10-K report which Teradyne had filed with the SEC. On cross-examination McCabe admitted that the 10-K form showed that on average the seller's revenues were distributed as follows:

profit	9%
"selling and administrative" expense	26%
interest	1%
"costs of sales and engineering" (including substantial research and development costs incidental to a high technology business)	64%

He also admitted that the average figures applied to the T-347a.

Teledyne contended that the 10-K report was a better index of lost profits than was the Catalog. The master disagreed and concluded that the more appropriate formula for calculating Teradyne's damages under §2-708(2) was the one approved in *Jericho*, supra — "'gross' profit including fixed costs but not costs saved as a result of the breach." He then stated:

> In accordance with the statutory mandate that the remedy "be liberally administered to the end that the aggrieved party may be put in as good a position as if the other party had fully performed," MGL c106 §1-106(1),[2] I find that the Plaintiff has met its burden of proof of damages, and has established the accuracy of its direct costs and the ascertainability of its variable costs with reasonable certainty and "whatever definiteness and accuracy the facts permit." Comment 1 to §1-106(1) of the U.C.C.

In effect, this was a finding that Teradyne had saved only $22,638 as a result of the breach. Subtracting that amount and also the $984 quantity discount from the original contract price of $98,400, the master found that the lost "profit (including reasonable overhead)" was $74,778. To that amount the master added $614 for "incidental damages" which Teradyne incurred in preparing the T-347A for its new customer. Thus he found that Teradyne's total §2-708(2) damages amounted to $75,392.

The master declined to make a deduction from the $75,392 on account of the refusal of the seller to accept the buyer's offer to purchase an FET tester in partial substitution for the repudiated T-347A.

At the time of the reference to the master, the court, without securing the agreement of the parties, had ordered that the master's costs should be paid by them in equal parts.

Teradyne filed a motion praying that the district court (1) should adopt the master's report allowing it to recover $75,392, and (2) should require Teledyne to pay all the master's costs. The district court, without

---

2. Now §1-305(a) — EDS.

opinion, entered a judgment which grants the first prayer and denies the second. Teledyne appealed from the first part of the judgment; Teradyne appealed from the second part.

1. The parties are agreed that §2-708(2) applies to the case at bar. Inasmuch as this conclusion is not plain from the text, we explain the reasons why we concur in that agreement.

Section 2-708(2) applies only if the damages provided by §2-708(1) are inadequate to put the seller in as good a position as performance would have done. Under §2-708(1) the measure of damages is the difference between unpaid contract price and market price. Here the unpaid contract price was $97,416 and the market price was $98,400. Hence no damages would be recoverable under §2-708(1). On the other hand, if the buyer had performed, the seller (1) would have had the proceeds of two contracts, one with the buyer Teledyne and the other with the "resale purchaser" and (2) *it seems* would have had in 1976-7 one more T-347A sale.

A literal reading of the last sentence of §2-708(2) — providing for "due credit for payments or proceeds of resale" — would indicate that Teradyne recovers nothing because the proceeds of the resale exceeded the price set in the Teledyne-Teradyne contract. However, in light of the statutory history of the subsection, it is universally agreed that in a case where after the buyer's default a seller resells the goods, the proceeds of the resale are not to be credited to the buyer if the seller is a lost volume seller[3] — that is, one who had there been no breach by the buyer, could and would have had the benefit of both the original contract and the resale contract.[4]

Thus, despite the resale of the T-347A, Teradyne is entitled to recover from Teledyne what §2-708(2) calls its expected "profit (including reasonable overhead)" on the broken Teledyne contract.[5]

---

3. The term "lost volume seller" was apparently coined by Professor Robert J. Harris in his article A Radical Restatement of the Law of Seller's Damages: Sales Act and Commercial Code Results Compared, 18 Stan. L. Rev. 66 (1965). The terminology has been widely adopted. See Famous Knitwear Corp. v. Drug Fair Inc., 493 F.2d 251, 254 n.5 (4th Cir. 1974); Snyder v. Herbert Greenbaum & Assoc. Inc., 38 Md. App. 144, 157, 380 A.2d 618, 624 (1977); Publicker Industries, Inc. v. Roman Ceramics Corp., 652 F.2d 340, 346 (3d Cir. 1981). See Restatement (Second) Contracts §347 Comment f; J. White and R. Summers, Uniform Commercial Code, 2d ed. (1980) [hereinafter "White and Summers"] §7-9, particularly p. 276 first full paragraph.

4. Famous Knitwear Corp. v. Drug Fair Inc., supra, 493 F.2d 254 n.7; Snyder v. Herbert Greenbaum & Assoc. Inc., supra, 380 A.2d 625-626; Neri v. Retail Marine Corp., 30 N.Y.2d 393, 399, 285 N.E.2d 311, 314 (1972). See White and Summers, §7-13, particularly 284-285.

5. Ibid. White and Summers at pp. 284-285 give the following supposititious case which parallels the instant case. Boeing is able to make and sell in one year 100 airplanes. TWA contracts to buy the third plane off the assembly line, but it breaks the contract and Boeing resells the plane to Pan Am which had already agreed to buy the fourth plane. Because of the breach Boeing sells only 99 aircraft during the year. White and Summers say that the right result, despite the words of §2-708(2), is that Boeing recovers from TWA both the net profit and the overhead components of the TWA contract price, no credit being given for any part of the proceeds Boeing received from its sale to Pan Am.

2. Teledyne not only "does not dispute that damages are to be calculated pursuant to §2-708(2)" but concedes that the formula used in Jericho Sash & Door Co. v. Building Erectors Inc., 362 Mass. 871 (1972), for determining lost profit including overhead—that is, the formula under which direct costs of producing and selling manufactured goods are deducted from the contract price in order to arrive at "profit (including reasonable overhead)" as that term is used in §2-708(2)—"is permissible provided all variable expenses are identified."

What Teledyne contends is that all variable costs were not identified because the cost figures came from a catalog, prepared for tax purposes, which did not fully reflect all direct costs. The master found that the statement of costs based on the catalog was reliable and that Teledyne's method of calculating costs based on the 10-K statements was not more accurate. Those findings are not clearly erroneous and therefore we may not reverse the judgment on the ground that allegedly the items of cost which were deducted are unreliable. Fed. R. Civ. P. 52(a); Merrill Trust Co. v. Bradford, 507 F.2d 467, 468 (1st Cir. 1974); Van Alen v. Dominick & Dominick, Inc., 560 F.2d 547, 551 (2d Cir. 1977).

Teledyne's more significant objection to Teradyne's and the master's application of the Jericho formula in the case at bar is that neither of them made deductions on account of the wages paid to testers, shippers, installers, and other Teradyne employees who directly handled the T-347A, or on account of the fringe benefits amounting in the case of those and other employees to 12 per cent of wages. Teradyne gave as the reason for the omission of the wages of the testers, etc. that those wages would not have been affected if each of the testers, etc. handled one product more or less. However, the work of those employees entered as directly into producing and supplying the T-347A as did the work of a fabricator of a T-347A. Surely no one would regard as "reasonable overhead" within §2-708(2) the wages of a fabricator of a T-347A even if his wages were the same whether he made one product more or less. We conclude that the wages of the testers, etc. likewise are not part of overhead and as a "direct cost" should have been deducted from the contract price. A fortiori fringe benefits amounting to 12 per cent of wages should also have been deducted as direct costs. Taken together we cannot view these omitted items as what Jericho called "relatively insignificant items." We, therefore, must vacate the district court's judgment. In accordance with the procedure followed in Publicker Industries, Inc. v. Roman Ceramics Corp., 603 F.2d 1065, 1072-3 (3d Cir. 1979) and Famous Knitwear Corp. v. Drug Fair, Inc., 493 F.2d 251, 255-256 (4th Cir. 1974), we remand this case so that with respect to the omitted direct labor costs specified above the parties may offer further evidence and the court may make findings "with whatever definiteness and accuracy the facts permit, but no more." Jericho, p. 872.

There are two other matters which may properly be dealt with before the case is remanded to the district court.

3. Teledyne contends that Teradyne was required to mitigate damages by acceptance of Teledyne's offer to purchase instead of the T-347A the FET system.

That point is without merit.

The meaning of Teledyne's offer was that if Teradyne would forego its profit-loss claim arising out of Teledyne's breach of the T-347A contract, Teledyne would purchase another type of machine which it was under no obligation to buy. The seller's failure to accept such an offer does not preclude it from recovering the full damages to which it would otherwise be entitled. As Restatement (Second) Contracts, §350 Comment c indicates, there is no right to so-called mitigation of damages where the offer of a substitute contract "is conditioned on surrender by the injured party of his claim for breach." "One is not required to mitigate his losses by accepting an arrangement with the repudiator if that is made conditional on his surrender of his rights under the repudiated contract." 5 Corbin, Contracts 2d (1964) §1043 at 274. Acc. Campfield v. Sauer, 189 F. 576 (6th Cir. 1911); Stanspec Corp. v. Jelco, Inc., 464 F.2d 1184, 1187 (10th Cir. 1972). Teradyne acted in a commercially reasonable manner in refusing to accept Teledyne's offer. . . .

The district court's judgment is vacated and the case is remanded to the district court to proceed in accordance with this opinion.

QUESTIONS

1. Exactly who qualifies as a "lost volume seller"? If a college student advertises his guitar for sale in the campus newspaper, he contracts to sell it to a caller, the caller then backs out, and the student sells the guitar to someone else, can the student qualify as a lost volume seller?

2. Why does the court draw a distinction between overhead costs and variable expenses (which the court calls "direct costs")? Which was which here?

3. Section 2-708(2) specifically requires a subtraction of the "proceeds of resale." Doesn't this language always defeat the lost volume seller, who will typically have resold the unaccepted goods? See R.E. Davis Chem. Corp. v. Diasonics, Inc., 826 F.2d 678, 4 U.C.C. Rep. Serv. 2d 369 (7th Cir. 1987).

4. For a case requiring the seller to measure damages at no more than the lost profit amount where the market price/contract price differential under §2-708(1) would overcompensate the seller, see Purina Mills, L.L.C. v. Less, 295 F. Supp. 2d 1017, 52 U.C.C. Rep. Serv. 2d 310 (N.D. Iowa 2003).

5. The lost volume concept also applies to lessors of goods. See §2A-529's Official Comment 2 and C.I.C. Corp. v. Ragtime, Inc., 319 N.J. Super. 662, 726 A.2d 316, 38 U.C.C. Rep. Serv. 2d 21 (N.J. App. 1999).

PROBLEM 76

Milo Veep, sales agent for the Complex Computer Corporation (CCC), negotiated a contract whereby his company was to design and manufacture a special computer that would regulate the timing of subway trains for the City of Plantation, Mississippi. The price was $20,000 F.O.B. CCC's plant was in Atlanta, Georgia. When the computer was half completed, the City of Plantation underwent a change of administration, and the new city leaders decided to dump the subway renovations. They phoned CCC and canceled the computer order. Now Veep phones your law office for advice. To help in your decision, Veep states that as scrap, the computer and its components are now worth $5,000. Veep has heard that three other cities have subway systems similar to Plantation's, and if the computer is finished, they might be enticed to buy it at a price between $15,000 and $20,000. On the other hand, it will cost CCC $9,000 to complete the computer.

(a) Should CCC stop the manufacture of the computer and sell it for scrap or complete manufacture and then try to resell it? See §2-704(2) and its Official Comment 2.

(b) If CCC completes manufacture and then, after a good faith effort, is unable to find a new buyer for the computer, can it make Plantation pay for the finished product? See §2-709(1)(b); Official Comment 1 to §2-704.

The remedies provided for the parties in a lease of goods by Article 2A have been slavishly copied from the corresponding provisions in Article 2. For the most part this does no harm, but the Article 2A equivalent to §2-709's "Action for the Price" has generated a lot of discord. Read §2A-529, "Lessor's Action for the Rent."

PROBLEM 77

Lawyer Portia Moot decided to rent a computer from Machines Unlimited and use it in her office. The computer arrived, and Portia found it most satisfactory, but her struggling practice made it difficult for her to make the lease payments on time. After she had missed two payments in a row, Machines Unlimited sent a goon to her office to repossess the computer. Portia was not there at the time, but her loyal administrative assistant protested mightily when the goon grabbed the machine — at one point blocking the door with her body — but she was shoved aside and the computer was taken. The lease still had a year to run, with payments of $100 due each month. Machines Unlimited sued Portia for $1,200.

(a) Was Machines Unlimited's repossession valid? See §2A-525. What remedy does Portia have if it was not?

(b) Assuming there was no problem with the repossession, is the lessor required to try to mitigate damages by re-leasing the machine? See §2A-529 and its Official Comment.

(c) Could the lessor avoid any possible duty to mitigate by so stipulating in the lease agreement? See §§1-302, 2A-503; Homer Kripke, Some Dissonant Notes About Article 2A, 39 Ala. L. Rev. 792, 795-796 (1988).

III. BUYER'S REMEDIES

The general list of the buyer's remedies is found in §2-711. This section also gives the buyer a right to cancel and recover the price if the buyer has already paid. In most circumstances, the buyer has further recoverable damages, as identified in other sections. All the sections are designed to follow §1-305's admonition that the Code's goal is to put the aggrieved party in as good a position as performance would have. As for which sections are appropriate in a given case as far as monetary damages are concerned, the answer depends on whether the buyer has *accepted* the goods or not.

A. Accepted Goods

If a technical §2-606 acceptance of the goods has been made and is not later revoked, the buyer may still sue for breach of warranty (or other breach of contract) if a notice of the defect has been given to the seller within a reasonable time after the defect should have been discovered; §2-607(3)(a). Damages are then measured by §§2-714 and 2-715. Read those sections. See Annot., 96 A.L.R.3d 299.

PROBLEM 78

The world-famous pianist Bart Cristofori made $50,000 a year giving concerts. Recently he decided to experiment with some new sounds. He purchased an electric piano for $3,000 from the Silbermann Electronic Music

Company. The purchase was negotiated orally; there was no written contract. Cristofori practiced day and night to master the new instrument. After three months of arduous practice, he noticed a strange ringing in his ears. Subsequent medical examination revealed that Cristofori was going deaf. The cause was a high-pitched whine (above the level of human perception) emanating from the electric piano. On learning that the piano had done this to him, Cristofori took an axe and chopped the piano into unrecognizable bits. (This action ended his ability to revoke his acceptance; §§2-608(3), 2-602(2)(b).) When he calmed down, he brought suit against the piano company for breach of warranty. His damages were claimed as $1,755,505, based on the following elements: $3,000 was the cost of the piano, $2,000 was doctor's fees, $500 was paid to experts to examine the piano and determine if it was the cause of the ear problem, $750,000 was lost income for the next 15 years, $1,000,000 was the value of Cristofori's hearing, and $5 was for the axe. Silbermann Electronic Music defended by (1) denying that it had warranted the piano in any way and (2) proving that the whine was harmless to everybody in the world except Cristofori. (The company proved that the accident occurred to him only because of the bone structure of his skull coupled with the fact that he had a metal plate installed in his head as a result of an auto accident in his youth.) Answer these questions:

(a) What warranty, if any, did the Silbermann Company breach? Does the company's care in manufacturing the piano or the freakishness of the injury keep the warranty from being breached?

(b) Which, if any, of Cristofori's damages are recoverable under §2-714?

(c) Which, if any, of the items claimed are *incidental damages* under §2-715(1)?

(d) The §2-715(2)(a) test of consequential damages with its "reason to know" language is a restatement of our old friend *Hadley v. Baxendale*. Is it relevant here?

(e) If you were the judge of both the facts and the law, what amount would you award Cristofori, and why?

PROBLEM 79

Sheila Spin made it to the finals of the USA Yo-Yo Championship, where she was widely thought to be a cinch to win the $10,000 first prize. The day of the competition she went into the Smalltime Drug Store owned by her Uncle Mort and told him that she wanted to buy a four-foot nylon yo-yo cord to use in the competition. Mort sold her one for $1.50 (he put it on her bill) and wished her luck. That she did not have. The cord was defective and broke during her first trick, thus eliminating her from the competition. When the bill came from the drug store, Sheila refused to pay it. In fact, she filed suit against Mort, asking for $50,000 consequential damages. Every expert witness who testified stated that Sheila's ability with the yo-yo was the greatest in the world. Mort defended on two grounds: (1) merely knowing about the intended use of the yo-yo in the competition was not enough to impose liability on him unless the parties had agreed to put this risk on him, and (2) her damages were too speculative. Answer these questions:

(a) Does the UCC permit Sheila to refuse to pay the bill? See §2-717. If the buyer feels obligated to pay only part of the bill, what procedure should be followed? See §3-311 (dealing with payment-in-full checks).

(b) Are the consequential damages for which Sheila asked too speculative? See Official Comment 4 to §2-715; White & Summers §11-4. Cf. Wachtel v. National Alfalfa Journal, 190 Iowa 1293, 176 N.W. 801 (1920) (leading contender in canceled contest entitled to value of the chance of winning).

(c) Is knowledge of the possible consequential damages alone sufficient to impose liability on a seller? Or is Mort right in saying that the liability for consequential damages attaches only if the seller has agreed (expressly or impliedly) to assume the risk? See Official Comment 2 to §2-715; White & Summers §11-4; Beal v. General Motors Corp., 354 F. Supp. 423, 12 U.C.C. Rep. Serv. 105 (D. Del. 1973).

(d) May Sheila recover her attorney fees as consequential damages? See Equitable Lumber Corp. v. IPA Land Dev. Corp., 38 N.Y.2d 516, 344 N.E.2d 391, 381 N.Y.S.2d 459, 18 U.C.C. Rep. Serv. 273 (1976) (may be recovered if the contract so provides, but any specified amount must be valid as a liquidated damages provision); Indiana Glass Co. v. Indiana Michigan Power Co., 692 N.E.2d 886, 37 U.C.C. Rep. Serv. 2d 332 (Ind. App. 1998) (not unless another statute so provides); Cady v. Dick Loehr's, Inc., 100 Mich. App. 543, 299 N.W.2d 69 (1980) (trial court has discretion to award attorney fees as consequential damages); Modine Mfg. Co. v. North East Indep. Sch. Dist., 503 S.W.2d 833, 14 U.C.C. Rep. Serv. 317 (Tex. Civ. App. 1974) (no, because such fees are penal in nature and the Code does not authorize punitive damages).

PROBLEM 80

Rambo Trucks, Inc., sold Hercules Moving Company a large moving van. The contract of sale limited the buyer's remedy for breach of warranty to replacement or repair only and clearly disclaimed liability for consequential damages. The first day on the job, the truck proved incapable of climbing even small hills, so Hercules Moving Company revoked its acceptance of the truck. It claimed a security interest in the truck pursuant to §2-711(3) and pending sale, stored it at a truck depot, which charged it $50 a day for storage.

Must Rambo Trucks pay the storage charges, or is the company protected by the disclaimer of consequential damages? See §§2-719(3), 2-715(1); Commonwealth Edison Co. v. Allied Chem. Nuclear Prods., Inc., 684 F. Supp. 1429, 6 U.C.C. Rep. Serv. 2d 380 (N.D. Ill. 1988) (storage charges of $293,000,000!).

B. Unaccepted Goods

Where the seller never delivers the goods or where the buyer rejects or revokes acceptance, §2-711 states that the buyer may recover the price and other damages. These generally include incidental and consequential damages under §2-715. See Official Comment 1 to that section. In addition, the buyer may seek specific performance or replevin under §2-716. Read §2-716 and its Official Comment.

As Comment 1 indicates, the drafters intended to "liberalize" the application of the doctrine of specific performance. Thus, §2-716 provides for the use of specific performance not only when goods are unique, but also "in other proper circumstances." What are "proper circumstances"? See Laclede Gas Co. v. Amoco Oil Co., 522 F.2d 33, 17 U.C.C. Rep. Serv. 447 (8th Cir. 1975), *rev'd on other grounds*, 531 F.2d 942 (8th Cir. 1975) (the court gave the buyer, a distributor of propane gas, a mandatory injunction against the seller, who had promised to supply gas over a long term); Eastern Airlines Inc. v. Gulf Oil Corp., 415 F. Supp. 429, 19 U.C.C. Rep. Serv. 721 (S.D. Fla. 1975) (Gulf Oil was enjoined from breaching its contract with Eastern for jet fuel); Sedmak v. Charlie's Chevrolet, Inc., 622 S.W.2d 694, 31 U.C.C. Rep. Serv. 851 (Mo. Ct. App. 1981) (holding buyers entitled to specific performance of contract to buy one of a limited edition of Corvette automobiles); Annot., 26 A.L.R.4th 294.

An important buyer remedy is found in §2-712, where the buyer is authorized to *cover*—that is, purchase substitute goods. If a buyer covers properly, the damages are measured by a comparison of the original contract price and the cost of the cover. Read §2-712.

PROBLEM 81

Mr. and Mrs. Transient ordered a 2014 Blocklong model mobile home for $8,000 from the Home on Wheels Sales Corporation, delivery to be made on May 20. The Transients planned on spending an additional $500 to build a foundation that the Blocklong trailer had to have for maximum utility. Due to widespread industry strikes, the price of trailers rose dramatically in the early spring, and on May 10, Home on Wheels informed the Transients that the deal was off. The Transients shopped around and on September 25 bought a 2014 Behemoth model mobile home for $15,000 from another dealer. The Behemoth was larger than the Blocklong model (it had a basement and a laundry room), but it did not require a foundation. The Transients then brought suit. Home on Wheels defended by offering to show that (a) the Behemoth was selling for $10,000 up to September 5 when the price rose to $15,000, and (b) the Behemoth always sells for $2,000 more than the Blocklong since the former is a snazzier trailer. What damages can the Transients get under §2-712? See Official Comment 2 of that section; White & Summers §7-3; Annot., 79 A.L.R.4th 844.

Hughes Communications Galaxy, Inc. v. United States

United States Court of Appeals, Federal Circuit, 2001
271 F.3d 1060, 46 U.C.C. Rep. Serv. 2d 453

RADER, Circuit Judge.

Following a trial on damages for breach of contract, the United States Court of Federal Claims awarded Hughes Communications Galaxy, Inc. $102,680,625. Hughes Communications Galaxy, Inc. v. United States, 47 Fed. Cl. 236 (2000) (*Hughes V*). Because the Court of Federal Claims did not abuse its discretion in calculating damages, this court affirms.

I.

This case has received extensive factual analysis in prior opinions. . . . This appeal addresses only the Court of Federal Claims' breach of contract damage determination in *Hughes IV* and *Hughes V*.

In December 1985, NASA and Hughes entered into a Launch Services Agreement (LSA), which required NASA to use its "best efforts" to launch ten of Hughes' HS-393 satellites on space shuttles. The LSA required NASA to continue using its best efforts to launch Hughes' HS-393s until it launched all ten HS-393s or until September 30, 1994, whichever was earlier. NASA compiled "manifests" of all shuttle payloads scheduled for launch on shuttles. NASA reissued these manifests periodically to account for changed circumstances. The manifests listed commercial payloads in order of their planned or firm launch dates and scheduled a shuttle for each launch. After NASA and Hughes entered the LSA, NASA assigned Hughes' satellites specific slots on a manifest.

In January 1986, the space shuttle Challenger exploded. Following the Challenger explosion, NASA suspended operation of the shuttles until September 1988. Further, in August 1986, President Reagan announced that NASA would no longer launch commercial satellites on shuttles. On July 10, 1986, NASA completed the last manifest before President Reagan's announcement. It projected that NASA would launch eight Hughes satellites on shuttles by September 1994. Thereafter, NASA compiled a new manifest that only included "shuttle unique" and "national security and foreign policy" payloads. That manifest did not list any Hughes satellites. Later NASA informed Hughes that it would almost certainly not launch any Hughes satellites on shuttles.

After 1986, Hughes launched three of its HS-393s on expendable launch vehicles (ELVs), one of which was the JCSAT-1. Hughes also launched several similar satellites on ELVs, including six HS-601 satellites. The HS-601s are similar to the HS-393s, except they are more powerful and better suited for ELV launches. While the ELV launches provided an alternative to shuttle launch services under the LSA, Hughes incurred more costs by launching satellites on ELVs rather than on shuttles.

Hughes sued the United States Government for breach of contract and for taking its property without providing just compensation. The Court of Federal Claims granted summary judgment to the Government on both claims based on the sovereign act defense. *Hughes I*, 26 Cl. Ct. at 144-46. This court reversed that summary judgment and remanded. *Hughes II*, 998 F.2d at 959. On remand, the Court of Federal Claims granted summary judgment for Hughes for breach of contract. *Hughes III*, 34 Fed. Cl. at 634. Before holding a trial on damages, the Court of Federal Claims ruled that the Government could not produce evidence to reduce its damages by the amount Hughes had passed on to its customers in increased prices. *Hughes IV*, 38 Fed. Cl. at 582.

At the damages trial, Hughes sought to prove damages by showing its increased costs in launching satellites on ELVs, rather than on shuttles. Hughes presented two main methods for calculating the increased costs. The first method, the Ten HS-393 Satellites Method, compared the costs of launching ten HS-393s on shuttles under the LSA with the costs of launching ten HS-393s on ELVs. Because Hughes had actually launched only three HS-393s on ELVs, the method based the ELV launch costs on the actual costs of launching the three HS-393s. The second method, the Primary Method, compared Hughes' actual costs of launching ten satellites on ELVs with the costs that Hughes would have incurred by launching ten satellites on shuttles under the LSA. The ten satellites included the three HS-393s, the six HS-601s, and one HS-376.

The Court of Federal Claims used the Ten HS-393 Satellites Method to calculate Hughes' increased costs of "cover." *Hughes V*, 47 Fed. Cl. at 244. However, the court modified the method in several important respects. First, the court found that even using its best efforts, NASA would have only launched five HS-393s under the LSA. Accordingly, the court only awarded Hughes increased costs for five satellites, rather than ten. Id. Second, the court averaged the costs of launching on shuttles the three HS-393s that were actually launched on ELVs and used that average for the fourth and fifth satellites, rather than individually calculating the cost of launching each satellite on a shuttle, as Hughes' expert had done. Id. at 244 n.12. Third, in calculating the ELV launch costs for the fourth and fifth satellites, the court escalated the costs using the midpoint between March 1989 and September 1994, rather than the midpoint between March 1989 and December 1995, as Hughes' expert had done. Id. at 244. Fourth, the court refused to award Hughes prejudgment interest on its damages. Id. at 244-45. Fifth, the court refused to award Hughes reflight insurance costs and increased launch insurance costs for the five satellites. Id. at 245-46.

Based on its modified HS-393 method, the court awarded Hughes $102,680,625 in damages for its increased launch costs. Id. at 247. Hughes and the Government both appeal. This court has jurisdiction under 28 U.S.C. §1295(a)(3) (1994).

II. . . .

"The general rule in common law breach of contract cases is to award damages sufficient to place the injured party in as good a position as he or she would have been had the breaching party fully performed." San Carlos Irrigation & Drainage Dist. v. United States, 111 F.3d 1557, 1562-63 (Fed. Cir. 1997). Thus, "[a] plaintiff must show that but for the breach, the damages alleged would not have been suffered." Id. Moreover, the damages must have been foreseeable at the time the parties entered the contract, which requires that they "be the natural and proximate result of the breach." Locke v. United States, 151 Ct. Cl. 262, 283 F.2d 521, 526 (Ct. Cl. 1960). The LSA itself further limits damages to "direct damages only" and excludes consequential damages from any recovery.

The Court of Federal Claims awarded Hughes its increased costs of "cover." If a seller breaches a contract for goods, the buyer may "cover" or, in other words, obtain substitute goods from another seller. U.C.C. §2-712 (1997); E. Allan Farnsworth, Farnsworth on Contracts, §12.11 (2d ed. 1998). Additionally, courts often award an analogous remedy for breach of service contracts such as the LSA. Farnsworth, supra, §12.11. While the cover remedy of the Uniform Commercial Code does not govern this analogous remedy under the LSA, the Uniform Commercial Code provides useful guidance in applying general contract principles. Because both parties and the Court of Federal Claims have referred to this remedy as a "cover" remedy, this court will also use this term to refer to the remedy for Hughes' increased costs of obtaining substitute launch services.

The substitute goods or services involved in cover need not be identical to those involved in the contract, but they must be "commercially usable as reasonable substitutes under the circumstances." U.C.C. §2-712 cmt. 2. Whether cover provides a reasonable substitute under the circumstances is a question of fact. Bigelow-Sanford, Inc. v. Gunny Corp., 649 F.2d

1060, 1065 (5th Cir. 1981) (stating that whether cover is reasonable is a "classic jury issue" (quoting Transammonia Export Corp. v. Conserv, Inc., 554 F.2d 719, 724 (5th Cir. 1977))).

When a buyer of goods covers, the buyer's remedy for the seller's breach as to those goods equals the difference between the cost of the replacement goods and the contract price plus other losses. U.C.C. §2-712; Farnsworth, supra, §12.11. Similarly, if the seller breaches a contract for services, the buyer's remedy for cover equals the difference between the cost of the substitute services and the contract price plus other losses. Farnsworth, supra, §12.11 (where a building contractor breaches a first contract and the owner obtains substitute performance under a second contract, the owner can recover "any additional amount required by the second contract beyond what the owner would have had to pay under the first").

The Government cross appeals, arguing that Hughes should only be able to recover damages for the three HS-393s that it actually launched. While Hughes did not actually launch the fourth and fifth HS-393s that the Court of Federal Claims used to calculate damages, Hughes did incur costs in launching the HS-601s. The Court of Federal Claims found that Hughes developed the HS-601s to replace the HS-393s because the HS-601s were better suited for ELV launches, and that Hughes would have launched ten HS-393s on shuttles, given the opportunity. *Hughes V*, 47 Fed. Cl. at 240-41. The Government disputes these findings, asserting that Hughes developed the HS-601s for independent business reasons, specifically, the more powerful HS-601s were more marketable. On this point, however, the Court of Federal Claims specifically credited testimony of Hughes' witnesses that Hughes would not have developed the HS-601 if the Government had not breached the LSA and that Hughes could have designed the HS-393 to accommodate the additional power of the HS-601. Id. at 240. This testimony directly supports the Court of Federal Claims' finding that "the HS-393 could have been used in place of the HS-601" for HS-601 launches during the contract period. *Hughes V*, 47 Fed. Cl. at 240. Thus, the trial court found that the HS-601 launches were reasonable substitutes under the circumstances of this breach.

Additionally, the Court of Federal Claims specifically found that no credible evidence supported the Government's attack on the HS-601 as a reasonable substitute. Specifically, the Government argues that at the time of contracting, the Government could not have foreseen "the demise of the HS-393" as a result of its breach. However, the Court of Federal Claims' damages method does not compensate Hughes for the "demise of the HS-393." Rather it compensates Hughes for increased launch costs. Had Hughes kept using the HS-393s, it would likely have incurred the same damages that the Court of Federal Claims awarded.

In sum, the Court of Federal Claims hinged its determination of this issue on credibility. Such determinations are virtually never clear error. First Interstate Bank v. United States, 61 F.3d 876, 882 (Fed. Cir. 1995). Furthermore, while the damages calculation might have been easier if Hughes had kept launching HS-393s on ELVs, ease of proof in potential future litigation is not sufficient justification to require Hughes to continue launching satellites that were ill-suited for ELV launches. As the victim of the breach, Hughes was within its rights to obtain commercially reasonable substitute launch services even if the substitute services were not identical to those covered by the LSA. The Court of Federal Claims thus did not clearly err in holding that Hughes successfully covered by launching HS-601s on ELVs. Accordingly, this court rejects the Government's cross appeal.

The Court of Federal Claims' use of increased HS-393 launch costs provided reasonable certainty in calculating damages. The trial court compared the costs of launching HS-393s on ELVs with the costs of launching the same HS-393s on shuttles. That comparison provided a basis for assessing Hughes' increased costs in launching the HS-601s. Under this method, the Court of Federal Claims accounted for any measurable difference in value to Hughes between the HS-393 launches and the HS-601 launches. See Farnsworth, supra, §12.11 ("[A]ny measurable difference in quality [of a substitute] can be compensated for by a money allowance."). Accordingly, the Court of Federal Claims used the increased costs for HS-393s as a reasonable approximation of the increased costs incurred by Hughes in launching the substitute HS-601s. Under this method, the trial court did not abuse its discretion. See S.W. Elecs. & Mfg. Corp. v. United States, 228 Ct. Cl. 333, 655 F.2d 1078, 1088 (Ct. Cl. 1981) (the trial court need only "make a fair and reasonable approximation").

The LSA states that damages "shall be limited to direct damages only and shall not include any loss of revenue, profits or other indirect or consequential damages." As discussed above, the increased costs represent direct damages incurred by Hughes in obtaining substitute launch services. Additionally, the damages do not include any lost revenues or profits, only increased costs. Finally, the damages are not consequential. The Uniform Commercial Code is instructive on this point. It allows recovery of the difference between the cost of cover and the contract price "together with any incidental and consequential damages," U.C.C. §2-712 (emphasis added), thereby distinguishing between consequential damages and the direct cost of cover. In sum, the Court of Federal Claims did not abuse its discretion by awarding Hughes damages for its increased costs incurred by obtaining substitute launch services for two HS-601s in addition to the three HS-393s.

Hughes decided to launch the JCSAT-1 satellite, a particular HS-393, on an ELV several months before President Reagan's announcement in

1986 that NASA would no longer launch commercial satellites on shuttles. NASA only breached its best efforts obligation after President Reagan's announcement. *Hughes III*, 34 Fed. Cl. at 630-34; *Hughes V*, 47 Fed. Cl. at 243. However, the LSA is not limited to launching particular satellites, such as the JCSAT-1. Rather, the LSA specifies a particular type of satellite (HS-393) in its preamble, and refers to the ten satellites as "HC-9 through HC-18." Thus, Hughes could have substituted another HS-393 for JCSAT-1, and Hughes still would have launched ten HS-393s on shuttles if NASA had provided those services under the LSA. Accordingly, the Court of Federal Claims did not abuse its discretion by awarding Hughes damages for the increased costs of launching the JCSAT-1.

III.

The Court of Federal Claims found that NASA could have launched five HS-393s during the LSA contract period using its best efforts. The Court of Federal Claims based this finding on the July 1986 manifest, but credited a report by Barrington Consulting Group that unexpected delays beyond NASA's control reduced the number of shuttle launches below the projections in the July 1986 manifest. *Hughes V*, 47 Fed. Cl. at 243. Under the priorities in the July 1986 manifest, the Barrington report concluded that NASA would have launched five HS-393 satellites.

If NASA had given commercial satellites priority over NASA satellites, Hughes asserts, NASA would have launched ten HS-393s. However, before President Reagan's statement, NASA did not elevate commercial launches above its other priorities. NASA did not breach its best efforts obligation before President Reagan's statement. The priorities before President Reagan's statement gave approximately equal priority to commercial and NASA payloads. As the Court of Federal Claims correctly reasoned, Hughes could not have reasonably expected NASA priorities to elevate commercial satellites above other goals for the remainder of the contract period.

Similarly, the LSA's best efforts requirement did not obligate NASA to use the 1984 policy announced in a House sub-committee hearing. In the event of shuttle scheduling conflicts, the 1984 policy gave commercial satellites priority over NASA research and development missions. Under this policy, Hughes asserts, NASA would have launched all ten HS-393s. The LSA itself specifically included a 1982 listing of priorities, but said nothing about the 1984 policy. Without the 1984 policy in the contract, the LSA did not incorporate those priorities into NASA's best efforts obligation.

The Court of Federal Claims also correctly found that circumstances prevented NASA from increasing its launch rates to include all ten HS-393s. In testimony to Congress in 1992, NASA asserted its ability to launch more shuttles than its budget allowed. According to Hughes, the Government chose to limit the number of launches by limiting NASA's budget. The record amply supports the trial court's finding that the post-Challenger investigation and technical problems prevented NASA from launching more shuttles. *Hughes V*, 47 Fed. Cl. at 242-43. The record shows that, in all years except 1994, the Government budgeted for more shuttle launches than NASA was able to launch. In 1994, the Government budgeted for eight launches and NASA actually launched eight. Thus, the Court of Federal Claims did not clearly err in finding that technical obstacles, rather than budget choices, prevented NASA from launching more shuttles during the LSA contract period.

Additionally, Mr. Kiraly, the Government's expert, estimated the number of HS-393s that NASA's best efforts could have launched at between one and six. The variance in this estimate does not undercut the Court of Federal Claims' finding. The Court of Federal Claims relied on the Barrington report, which specifically concluded that NASA's best efforts would have launched five HS-393s. Id. at 243. Thus, the Court of Federal Claims did not clearly err in finding that NASA's best efforts would have produced five HS-393 launches.

IV.

Because Hughes actually launched only three HS-393s, the Court of Federal Claims calculated the average costs of launching those three satellites on shuttles. Then, using the report of Hughes' expert, Mr. Hammer, the trial court applied that average to project the shuttle launch costs of the fourth and fifth satellites. Id. at 244. Hughes asserts that the Court of Federal Claims should have used the shuttle launch costs for each individual satellite shown in Mr. Hammer's report. However, the trial court's method is symmetrical with its calculation of the costs of ELV launches. For ELV launch costs, the trial court averaged the actual ELV launch costs for the three HS-393s and applied that average to project the ELV launch costs of the fourth and fifth satellites. Id. at 244. Hughes does not disagree with the method of calculating ELV launch costs; the Court of Federal Claims merely did the same thing with the shuttle launch costs. The trial court reasonably exercised its discretion in using this symmetrical approach in calculating damages. . . .

IX.

The Government sought to reduce Hughes' damages by the amount Hughes recouped by increasing prices to customers, in other words, by the amount Hughes "passed through" to its customers. The Court of Federal Claims did not allow the Government to assert this defense at the damages trial. *Hughes IV*, 38 Fed. Cl. at 582. According to the Court of Federal Claims, this type of mitigation is too remote to consider. Id.

Although not in the breach of contract context, the Supreme Court has addressed this issue. In Southern Pacific Co. v. Darnell-Taenzer Lumber Co., 245 U.S. 531, 38 S. Ct. 186, 62 L. Ed. 451 (1918), a railroad overcharge case, the Court addressed the reduction of damages because the damaged party allegedly passed the unreasonable charge on to its customers. The Court stated: "The answer is not difficult. The general tendency of the law, in regard to damages at least, is not to go beyond the first step. As it does not attribute remote consequences to a defendant so it holds him liable if proximately the plaintiff has suffered a loss." Id. at 533-34, 38 S. Ct. 186. In an antitrust case, the Court noted that calculating pass-through damages reductions would present "the nearly insuperable difficulty of demonstrating that the particular plaintiff could not or would not have raised his prices absent the overcharge or maintained the higher price had the overcharge been discontinued." Hanover Shoe, Inc. v. United Shoe Mach. Corp., 392 U.S. 481, 493, 88 S. Ct. 2224, 20 L. Ed. 2d 1231 (1968). Similarly, allowing a pass-through damages reduction in a breach of contract action would destroy symmetry between reduction and escalation of damages. Moreover a standard for pass-through reductions would entail extremely difficult burdens for the trial court. Thus, the Supreme Court's reasoning also applies to this breach of contract action. The Court of Federal Claims did not abuse its discretion by disallowing pass-through damages reductions.

CONCLUSION

Because the Court of Federal Claims did not abuse its discretion in determining Hughes' damages for the Government's breach of the LSA, this court affirms.

————————

Technically, a buyer does not have to cover. If a buyer fails to cover in an appropriate situation, however, consequential damages that could have been avoided are denied. See §2-715(2)(a). If a buyer decides to cover, the legal effect of the steps taken, as well as when cover should be effectuated, is measured against a standard of reasonableness in the given factual situation. Financial inability is an excuse for non-cover. See REB, Inc. v. Ralston Purina Co., 525 F.2d 749, 18 U.C.C. Rep. Serv. 122 (10th Cir. 1975). One practical test by which to gauge the reasonableness of the buyer's covering actions is to ask if the buyer would have made the same arrangements if there was no prospect of a successful suit against the breaching seller. See White & Summers §7-3, at 287-288.

If the buyer does not cover, damages may be measured under the next section, §2-713, a much criticized provision. See Childres, Buyer's

Remedies: The Danger of Section 2-713, 72 Nw. U. L. Rev. 837 (1978). Read §2-713.

PROBLEM 82

The Student Bar Association (SBA) of the Gilberts Law School decided to hold a mammoth wine- and cheese-tasting party for the students, faculty, staff, and alumni. The SBA ordered the wine from Classy Caterers. They agreed to pay $1,000 for it, the wine to be delivered on March 30, the day of the party. Classy Caterers ordered the wine from Grapes Vineyards in California, "F.O.B. San Francisco" for $750, but Grapes Vineyards went bankrupt on March 25. Classy Caterers was able to find identical wine in its own city for $750, and it bought the wine on March 25 for that amount. On March 25, the price of similar wine in San Francisco was $900. The cost of transporting the wine from San Francisco to the site of the party would have been $100. The SBA paid Classy Caterers $1,000 for the wine. Classy Caterers filed claims for damages in the bankruptcy proceeding of its defaulting supplier.

(a) Compute the damages due Classy for the failure to deliver the wine under §2-712. Now do it under §2-713. See Official Comment 5 to §2-713; White & Summers §7-4.

(b) What role does the $100 transportation cost play in computing damages? Note the definition of "market place" in §2-723.

Tongish v. Thomas

Kansas Court of Appeals, 1992
16 Kan. App. 2d 809, 829 P.2d 916, 18 U.C.C. Rep. Serv. 2d 161,
aff'd on opinion below, 251 Kan. 728, 840 P.2d 471,
20 U.C.C. Rep. Serv. 2d 936

WALTON, J., assigned.

The Decatur Coop Association (Coop) (third-party intervenor/appellant) appeals a breach of contract damages award it received from Denis Tongish (plaintiff/appellee), alleging damages should have been the difference between the market price of sunflower seeds and the contract price under K.S.A. 84-2-713. We agree that the trial court applied the wrong measure of damages. We reverse the damages award and remand with directions that the trial court determine the damages under K.S.A. 84-2-713.

On April 28, 1988, Coop contracted with Denis Tongish to purchase all the sunflower seeds grown by him. The contract required Tongish to plant 160 acres of sunflower seeds but was later reduced to 116.8 acres. The seeds were to be delivered one-third by December 31, 1988, one-third by March

31, 1989, and one-third by May 31, 1989. The price for the seeds was $13 per hundred pounds for large seeds and $8 per hundred pounds for small seeds.

Coop also contracted with Bambino Bean & Seed, Inc., to sell it all the sunflower seeds Coop purchased from the farmers. Bambino paid Coop the same price Coop paid the farmers.

Coop retained a $.55 per hundred pounds handling charge for the seeds it received from the farmers and then delivered the seeds to Bambino. Therefore, Coop had no risk on fluctuating market prices in its contract with Tongish. The only profit anticipated by Coop was the handling fees for the seeds.

In October and November, Tongish delivered sunflower seeds to Coop as the contract required. In January, a disagreement occurred between Tongish and Coop over the amount of dockage[6] found in the seeds Tongish delivered. Coop readjusted the amount and paid Tongish an extra $222.33.

By January the market price of sunflower seeds had doubled from the Tongish-Coop contract price. On or about January 13, 1989, Tongish informed Coop that he was not going to honor the contract.

In May 1989, Tongish delivered 82,820 pounds of sunflower seeds to Danny Thomas for a price of $14,714.89. After dockage, the price was about $20 per hundred pounds. Tongish testified that if he sold all of these seeds to Coop under the contract price for large seeds, he would receive about $9,561.76. Therefore, Tongish would receive $5,153.13 more from Danny Thomas than he would by performing under the contract with Coop.

Tongish filed a petition against Danny Thomas to collect the balance due from their sunflower seed sale. Thomas paid $7,359.61 into the court and was later dismissed as a party. Coop intervened as a third-party defendant. Coop alleged that Tongish breached their contract and it was entitled to damages.

A trial was held on May 14, 1991. The trial court found that Tongish had breached the contract and there was no basis for that breach. The court also determined that Coop was entitled to damages in the amount of $455.51, the expected profit for handling charges in the transaction. Coop timely appealed.

The trial court decided the damages to Coop should be the loss of expected profits. Coop argues that K.S.A. 84-2-713 entitles it to collect as damages the difference between the market price and the contract price. Tongish argues that the trial court was correct and cites K.S.A. 84-1-106 as support for the contention that a party should be placed in as good a position as it would be in had the other party performed. Therefore, the only disagreement is how the damages should be calculated.

---

6. *Dockage* means the removable waste material in grains. — EDS.

The measure of damages in this action involves two sections of the Uniform Commercial Code: K.S.A. 84-1-106 and K.S.A. 84-2-713. The issue to be determined is which statute governs the measure of damages. Stated in another way, if the statutes are in conflict, which statute should prevail? The answer involves an ongoing academic discussion of two contending positions. The issues in this case disclose the problem.

If Tongish had not breached the contract, he may have received under the contract terms with Coop about $5,153.13 less than he received from Danny Thomas. Coop in turn had an oral contract with Bambino to sell whatever seeds it received from Tongish to Bambino for the same price Coop paid for them. Therefore, if the contract had been performed, Coop would not have actually received the extra $5,153.13.

We first turn our attention to the conflicting statutes and the applicable rules of statutory construction. K.S.A. 84-1-106(1)[7] states:

> The remedies provided by this act shall be liberally administered to the end that the aggrieved party may be put in as good a position as if the other party had fully performed but neither consequential or special nor penal damages may be had except as specifically provided in this act or by other rule of law.

If a seller breaches a contract and the buyer does not "cover," the buyer is free to pursue other available remedies. K.S.A. 84-2-711 and 84-2-712. One remedy, which is a complete alternative to "cover" (K.S.A. 84-2-713, Official comment, ¶5), is K.S.A. 84-2-713(1), which provides:

> Subject to the provisions of this article with respect to proof of market price (section 84-2-723), the measure of damages for nondelivery or repudiation by the seller is the difference between the market price at the time when the buyer learned of the breach and the contract price together with any incidental and consequential damages provided in this article (section 84-2-715), but less expenses saved in consequence of the seller's breach. . . .

The statutes do contain conflicting provisions. On the one hand, K.S.A. 84-1-106 offers a general guide of how remedies of the UCC should be applied, whereas K.S.A. 84-2-713 specifically describes a damage remedy that gives the buyer certain damages when the seller breaches a contract for the sale of goods.

The cardinal rule of statutory construction, to which all others are subordinate, is that the purpose and intent of the legislature governs. [Citations omitted.] When there is a conflict between a statute dealing generally with a subject and another statute dealing specifically with a certain phase of it, the specific statute controls unless it appears that the

---

7. Now §1-305 — EDS.

legislature intended to make the general act controlling. State v. Wilcox, 245 Kan. 76, Syl. ¶1, 775 P.2d 177 (1989). The Kansas Supreme Court stated in Kansas Racing Management, Inc. v. Kansas Racing Commn., 244 Kan. 343, 353, 770 P.2d 423 (1989): "General and special statutes should be read together and harmonized whenever possible, but to the extent a conflict between them exists, the special statute will prevail unless it appears the legislature intended to make the general statute controlling."

K.S.A. 84-2-713 allows the buyer to collect the difference in market price and contract price for damages in a breached contract. For that reason, it seems impossible to reconcile the decision of the district court that limits damages to lost profits with this statute.

Therefore, because it appears impractical to make K.S.A. 84-1-106 and K.S.A. 84-2-713 harmonize in this factual situation, K.S.A. 84-2-713 should prevail as the more specific statute according to statutory rules of construction.

As stated, however, Coop protected itself against market price fluctuations through its contract with Bambino. Other than the minimal handling charge, Coop suffered no lost profits from the breach. Should the protection require an exception to the general rule under K.S.A. 84-2-713? . . .

There is authority for appellee's position that K.S.A. 84-2-713 should not be applied in certain circumstances. In Allied Canners & Packers, Inc. v. Victor Packing Co., 162 Cal. App. 3d 905, 209 Cal. Rptr. 60, 61 (1984), Allied contracted to purchase 375,000 pounds of raisins from Victor for 29.75 cents per pound with a 4% discount. Allied then contracted to sell the raisins for 29.75 cents per pound expecting a profit of $4,462.50 from the 4% discount it received from Victor. 162 Cal. App. 3d at 907-908, 209 Cal. Rptr. 60.

Heavy rains damaged the raisin crop and Victor breached its contract, being unable to fulfill the requirement. The market price of raisins had risen to about 80 cents per pound. Allied's buyers agreed to rescind their contracts so Allied was not bound to supply them with raisins at a severe loss. Therefore, the actual loss to Allied was the $4,462.50 profit it expected, while the difference between the market price and the contract price was about $150,000. 162 Cal. App. 3d at 908-909, 209 Cal. Rptr. 60.

The California appellate court, in writing an exception, stated: "It has been recognized that the use of the market-price contract-price formula under §2-713 does not, absent pure accident, result in a damage award reflecting the buyer's actual loss. [Citations omitted.]" 162 Cal. App. 3d at 912, 209 Cal. Rptr. 60. The court indicated that §2-713 may be more of a statutory liquidated damages clause and, therefore, conflicts with the goal of §1-106. The court discussed that in situations where the buyer has made a resale contract for the goods, which the seller knows about, it may be appropriate to limit §2-713 damages to actual loss. However, the court cited a concern that a seller not be rewarded for a bad faith breach of contract. 162 Cal. App. 3d at 912-914, 209 Cal. Rptr. 60.

In *Allied*, the court determined that if the seller knew the buyer had a resale contract for the goods, and the seller did not breach the contract in bad faith, the buyer was limited to actual loss of damages under §1-106. 162 Cal. App. 3d at 915, 209 Cal. Rptr. 60.

The similarities between the present case and *Allied* are that the buyer made a resale contract which the seller knew about. (Tongish knew the seeds eventually went to Bambino, although he may not have known the details of the deal). However, in examining the breach itself, Victor could not deliver the raisins because its crop had been destroyed. Tongish testified that he breached the contract because he was dissatisfied with dockage tests of Coop and/or Bambino. Victor had no raisins to sell to any buyer, while Tongish took advantage of the doubling price of sunflower seeds and sold to Danny Thomas. Although the trial court had no need to find whether Tongish breached the contract in bad faith, it did find there was no valid reason for the breach. Therefore, the nature of Tongish's breach was much different than Victor's in *Allied*.

Section 2-713 and the theories behind it have a lengthy and somewhat controversial history. In 1963, it was suggested that §2-713 was a statutory liquidated damages clause and not really an effort to try and accurately predict what actual damages would be. Peters, Remedies for Breach of Contracts Relating to the Sale of Goods Under the Uniform Commercial Code: A Roadmap for Article Two, 73 Yale L.J. 199, 259 (1963).

In 1978, Robert Childres called for the repeal of §2-713. Childres, Buyer's Remedies: The Danger of Section 2-713, 72 Nw. U. L. Rev. 837 (1978). Childres reflected that because the market price/contract price remedy "has been the cornerstone of Anglo-American damages" that it has been so hard to see that this remedy "makes no sense whatever when applied to real life situations." 72 Nw. U. L. Rev. at 841-842.

In 1979, David Simon and Gerald A. Novack wrote a fairly objective analysis of the two arguments about §2-713 and stated:

> For over sixty years our courts have divided on the question of which measure of damages is appropriate for the supplier's breach of his delivery obligations. The majority view, reinforced by applicable codes, would award market damages even though in excess of plaintiff's loss. A persistent minority would reduce market damages to the plaintiff's loss, without regard to whether this creates a windfall for the defendant. Strangely enough, each view has generally tended to disregard the arguments, and even the existence, of the opposing view.

Simon and Novack, Limiting the Buyer's Market Damages to Lost Profits: A Challenge to the Enforceability of Market Contracts, 92 Harv. L. Rev. 1395, 1397 (1979).

Although the article discussed both sides of the issue, the authors came down on the side of market price/contract price as the preferred damages theory. The authors admit that market damages fly in the face "of the familiar maxim that the purpose of contract damages is to make the injured party whole, not penalize the breaching party." 92 Harv. L. Rev. at 1437. However, they argue that the market damages rule discourages the breach of contracts and encourages a more efficient market. 92 Harv. L. Rev. at 1437.

The *Allied* decision in 1984, which relied on the articles cited above for its analysis to reject market price/contract price damages, has been sharply criticized. In Schneider, UCC Section 2-713: A Defense of Buyers' Expectancy Damages, 22 Cal. W. L. Rev. 233, 266 (1986), the author stated that Allied "adopted the most restrictive [position] on buyer's damages. This Article is intended to reverse that trend." Schneider argued that by following §1-106, "the court ignored the clear language of §2-713's compensation scheme to award expectation damages in accordance with the parties' price allocation of risk as measured by the difference between contract price and market price on the date set for performance." 22 Cal. W. L. Rev. at 264.

Recently in Scott, The Case for Market Damages: Revisiting the Lost Profits Puzzle, 57 U. Chi. L. Rev. 1155, 1200 (1990), the *Allied* result was called "unfortunate." Scott argues that section 1-106 is "entirely consistent" with the market damages remedy of 2-713. 57 U. Chi. L. Rev. at 1201. According to Scott, it is possible to harmonize sections 1-106 and 2-713. Scott states, "Market damages measure the expectancy ex ante, and thus reflect the value of the option; lost profits, on the other hand, measure losses ex post, and thus only reflect the value of the completed exchange." 57 U. Chi. L. Rev. at 1174. The author argues that if the nonbreaching party has laid off part of the market risk (like Coop did) the lost profits rule creates instability because the other party is now encouraged to breach the contract if the market fluctuates to its advantage. 57 U. Chi. L. Rev. at 1178.

We are not persuaded that the lost profits view under *Allied* should be embraced. It is a minority rule that has received only nominal support. We believe the majority rule or the market damages remedy as contained in K.S.A. 84-2-713 is more reasoned and should be followed as the preferred measure of damages. While application of the rule may not reflect the actual loss to a buyer, it encourages a more efficient market and discourages the breach of contracts.

The majority rule further permits the parties to measure the expectancy of what might happen if the seller does not perform the contract. The buyer has an option at the beginning of the contract to take actions to protect against an uncertain future. The parties both know that the option is an election that can be exercised by the buyer to protect against future losses. This generates stability in the market by discouraging the seller from breaching the contract when the market fluctuates to his advantage. The rule is further in accord with the rule of statutory construction that a specific statute shall prevail over a conflicting general statute dealing with the same subject matter unless the legislature intended to make the general statute control.

For the reasons stated, we hold that the provisions of K.S.A. 84-2-713 provide the proper measure of damages in this case. We reject the holding in *Allied* that the provisions of §2-713 of the Uniform Commercial Code (K.S.A. 84-2-713) are more of a statutory liquidated damages clause that conflicts with the goal of §1-106 of the U.C.C. (K.S.A. 84-1-106) to mandate the creation of an exception when a buyer protects itself from market price fluctuations through a contract with another.

The damage award is reversed and the case is remanded with directions that the trial court determine and award damages pursuant to the provisions of K.S.A. 84-2-713.

In affirming the above opinion, which it adopted, the Kansas Supreme Court added this paragraph:

> At first blush, the result reached herein appears unfair. However, closer scrutiny dissipates this impression. By the terms of the contract Coop was obligated to buy Tongish's large sunflower seeds at $13 per hundredweight whether or not it had a market for them. Had the price of sunflower seeds plummeted by delivery time, Coop's obligation to purchase at the agreed price was fixed. If loss of actual profit pursuant to K.S.A. 84-1-106(1) would be the measure of damages to be applied herein, it would enable Tongish to consider the Coop contract price of $13 per hundredweight plus 55 cents per hundredweight handling fee as the "floor" price for his seeds, take advantage of rapidly escalating prices, ignore his contractual obligation, and profitably sell to the highest bidder. Damages computed under K.S.A. 84-2-713 encourage honoring of contracts and market stability.

Remedies Under the Treaty. The damages provisions in the CISG for the international sale of goods are modeled after the similar provisions of the UCC and should look reassuringly familiar to you. Read Articles 74 to 78. There are some new words that the treaty must teach American ears. One is the concept of "fundamental breach," an idea that comes from the civil law. Read Articles 46(2) and 25. Fundamental breach is roughly equivalent to "material breach" (the opposite of "substantial performance)." The Restatement (Second) of Contracts §241 states:

Section 241. Circumstances Significant in Determining Whether a Failure Is Material
    In determining whether a failure to render or to offer performance is material, the following circumstances are significant:

(a) the extent to which the injured party will be deprived of the benefit which he reasonably expected;

(b) the extent to which the injured party can be adequately compensated for the part of that benefit of which he will be deprived;

(c) the extent to which the party failing to perform or to offer to perform will suffer forfeiture;

(d) the likelihood that the party failing to perform or to offer to perform will cure his failure, taking account of all the circumstances including any reasonable assurances;

(e) the extent to which the behavior of the party failing to perform or to offer to perform comports with standards of good faith and fair dealing.

Another new concept is *Nachfrist* (German for "extension"). It is illustrated in the following Problem.

PROBLEM 83

Experimental Transportation, Inc., of Los Angeles designed an all-terrain vehicle for rugged hill country travel (called the "Clod Jumper") and agreed to sell one for $30,000 to Dingo Ranch of Australia. Neither party was willing to be bound by the laws of the other's country, so they agreed to adopt the law of the CISG. Experimental Transportation was supposed to deliver the Clod Jumper by December 1, but it had problems with Customs and that date came and went with no activity. Dingo Ranch sent a letter to Experimental Transportation proposing that the date of delivery be moved to February 1. Having sent such a letter, is it now bound to wait until that date before suing? See Article 47. Is it bound to wait even if Experimental Transportation's reply is "Go to hell!"? What if instead of the buyer proposing the *Nachfrist*, the seller, Experimental Transportation, is the one to propose a grace period? Can this be done? Compare Articles 48 and 63. If the machine is delivered and then fails to work, can Dingo Ranch force Experimental Transportation to fix it? See Article 46(3). Is this remedy available in American law? See Uniform Commercial Code §2-716.

———————

The treaty has a strong presumption in favor of specific performance. See Articles 46 and 62. However, Article 28 does not require specific performance if the court that would be asked to grant it would not do so if its own law applied. For example, in the United States there are major limits on equitable remedies (there must be no adequate remedy at law—i.e., damages; the court must not become involved in undue supervision of the resulting performance; etc.), and an American court might use these rules to duck an order for specific performance.

IV.   ANTICIPATORY REPUDIATION

Ever since the classic case of Hochster v. De La Tour, 2 El. & Bl. 678, 118 Eng. Rep. 922 (Q.B. 1853), it has been settled that if one party to a contract makes a definite repudiation of the contract before the date set for performance, the other party could treat the repudiation as a breach and sue immediately. But the common law also permitted the innocent party to ignore the repudiation and await the performance date to see if the repudiator would retract the repudiation. As long as the innocent party had not changed position in reliance on the repudiation (say, by covering), the repudiator was free to retract the repudiation, reinstate the contract, and perform as originally agreed.

To what extent has the Code changed these common law rules? Read §§2-610 and 2-611. These sections do not define *repudiation*, which is, of course, their triggering event. A repudiation must be a definite refusal to perform; mere equivocation is not enough. See Official Comment 1 to §2-610; White & Summers §7-2; Copylease Corp. of Am. v. Memorex Corp., 403 F. Supp. 625, 18 U.C.C. Rep. Serv. 317 (S.D.N.Y. 1975). The equivocating party can be forced into performance or repudiation by use of the procedure outlined in §2-609 (Right to Adequate Assurance of Performance).

Unfortunately, in the process of drafting the Code's damages sections, the drafters became careless when dealing with the time for measuring damages in an anticipatory repudiation situation, and the UCC sections simply do not fit together. The following Problem should help you see the difficulty.

PROBLEM 84

The United States Army contracted with the Hawaiian Cattle Company for the purchase of 1,000 pounds of beef. Delivery was set six months later, on October 8, the agreed price to be $5,000. Shortly thereafter, the price of beef rose sharply, and Hawaiian Cattle repudiated the contract on July 10, when the price was $6,000. The Army's procurement officer scrambled around and on July 15 discovered it was possible to cover by buying similar cattle from Texas at a cost of $7,000. Instead, the Army sent Hawaiian Cattle a telegram stating that it did not accept or recognize the repudiation and expected performance on October 8. By October 8 the price had risen to $8,000. The Army decided not to cover at all and instead served the troops beans. As general counsel for the Army, advise the Army of the amount it can recover from Hawaiian Cattle. Read §§2-610, 2-713, and 2-723(1). Does it help reconcile these sections to know that the drafters of §2-713 were thinking of a buyer who learns of the repudiation *after* the date set for the original performance, not (as in this Problem) before the due date?

V. THE STATUTE OF LIMITATIONS

The Code drafters decided that it was important to have a uniform statute of limitations for transactions in goods, and they chose four years "as the most appropriate to modern business practice. This is within the normal commercial record keeping period." Official Comment to §2-725. Read §2-725, and note that the four-year period begins to run at the *accrual* of the cause of action (the moment a suit could be brought). The parties may reduce the period by agreement down to one year, but they may not extend it beyond four. One court has decided that an agreement so reducing the limitation period need not be conspicuous to be enforced. Jandreau v. Sheesley Plumbing & Heating Co., 324 N.W.2d 266, 34 U.C.C. Rep. Serv. 785 (S.D. 1982). In most jurisdictions the statute of limitations is an affirmative defense and is waived if not pleaded and proved. See, e.g., Mysel v. Gross, 70 Cal. App. 3d 10, 138 Cal. Rptr. 873, 21 U.C.C. Rep. Serv. 1338 (1977).

PROBLEM 85

Four years and two days after delivery of his new car, Joe Suburb came out of his house to discover he had a flat tire. He changed it and, for the first time, put on the spare tire. That afternoon as he was driving on the interstate, the tire burst due to a manufacturing flaw. Joe was killed. Has the statute of limitations run under these situations?

(a) The tire warranty read: "These tires are merchantable." If this were a lease of goods, would Article 2A reach a different result? See §2A-506.

(b) The tire warranty read: "These tires have a lifetime guarantee." See Kelleher v. Lumber, 152 N.H. 813, 891 A.2d 477 (2005); Rawls v. Associated Materials, LLC, 2011 WL 3297622 (S.D. W. Va. 2011); Annot., 93 A.L.R.3d 690.

(c) The sales material said with regard to the tires: "Many tires are still on the road after five years." See Jones & Laughlin Steel Corp. v. Johns-Manville Sales Corp. v. Brown & Kerr, Inc., 626 F.2d 280, 29 U.C.C. Rep. Serv. 1184 (3d Cir. 1980) (relying on precedent stating that statement of future performance is "explicit" if it does not arise by implication, but is instead "distinctly stated; plain in language; clear; not ambiguous; express; unequivocal").

(d) The tire warranty read: "These tires are warranted for seven years from date of purchase." If a tire first malfunctioned at the beginning of the third year, when would the statute of limitations expire? See Joswick v. Chesapeake Mobile Homes, Inc., 765 A.2d 90, 43 U.C.C. Rep. Serv. 2d 479 (Md. 2001).

(e) There were no express warranties given with regard to the tires; there were also no warranty disclaimers. See Note, When Does the Statute of Limitations Begin to Run on Breaches of Implied Warranties?, 30 Baylor L. Rev. 386 (1978).

Mydlach v. DaimlerChrysler Corp.

Supreme Court of Illinois, 2007
226 Ill.2d 307, 875 N.E.2d 1047, 314 Ill. Dec. 760, 64 U.C.C. Rep. Serv. 2d 44

Justice FITZGERALD delivered the judgment of the court, with opinion:

BACKGROUND

On June 20, 1998, plaintiff purchased a used 1996 Dodge Neon, manufactured by defendant, from McGrath Buick-Nissan (McGrath) in Elgin, Illinois. The vehicle was originally put into service on June 24, 1996, with a three-year/36,000-mile limited warranty. The warranty provided, in relevant part, as follows:

> "The 'Basic Warranty' begins on your vehicle's Warranty Start Date which is the earlier of (1) the date you take delivery of your new vehicle, OR (2) the date the vehicle was first put into service. . . .
>
> The 'Basic Warranty' covers the cost of all parts and labor needed to repair any item on your vehicle (except as noted below) that's defective in material, workmanship, or factory preparation. You pay nothing for these repairs.
>
> The 'Basic Warranty' covers every Chrysler supplied part of your vehicle, EXCEPT its tires and cellular telephone. . . .
>
> These warranty repairs or adjustments (parts and labor) will be made by your dealer at no charge using new or remanufactured parts.
>
> The 'Basic Warranty' lasts for 36 months from the vehicle's Warranty Start Date OR for 36,000 miles on the odometer, whichever occurs first."
> (Emphasis in original.)

At the time of plaintiff's purchase in 1998, the car's mileage was 26,296. Thus, the warranty had approximately one year or 10,000 miles remaining.

Beginning July 7, 1998, plaintiff brought the car to McGrath and another authorized dealership several times for a variety of problems, including a recurring fluid leak. Plaintiff claimed that the dealerships' repair attempts were unsuccessful and, as a result, she could not use the vehicle as intended. Plaintiff ultimately filed suit against defendant on May 16, 2001, seeking legal and equitable relief, as well as attorney fees and costs, under the Magnuson-Moss Act. . . .

III

Although the Magnuson-Moss Act provides a private right of action for breach of a written warranty, the Act does not contain a limitations provision for such an action. Where a federal statute fails to specify a limitations period for suits under it, "courts apply the most closely analogous statute of limitations under state law." DelCostello v. International Brotherhood of Teamsters, 462 U.S. 151, 158, 103 S. Ct. 2281, 2287, 76 L. Ed. 2d 476, 485 (1983); accord Wilson v. Garcia, 471 U.S. 261, 268, 105 S. Ct. 1938, 1942, 85 L. Ed. 2d 254, 261 (1985); Teamsters & Employers Welfare Trust v. Gorman Brothers Ready Mix, 283 F.3d 877, 880 (7th Cir. 2002). In suits brought under the Magnuson-Moss Act, our appellate court, as well as courts in other jurisdictions, generally consider the UCC to be the most closely analogous statute and have borrowed the limitations provision contained therein. See, e.g., Nowalski, 335 Ill. App. 3d at 628, 269 Ill. Dec. 781, 781 N.E.2d 578 (collecting Illinois cases); Hillery v. Georgie Boy Manufacturing, Inc., 341 F. Supp. 2d 1112, 1114 (D. Ariz. 2004); Poli v. Daimler-Chrysler Corp., 349 N.J. Super. 169, 181, 793 A.2d 104, 111 (2002); Murungi v. Mercedes Benz Credit Corp., 192 F. Supp. 2d 71, 79 (W.D.N.Y. 2001); Keller v. Volkswagen, 1999 PA Super. 153, ¶5, 733 A.2d 642. We agree with the foregoing authorities and will look to the limitations provision contained in the UCC to determine the timeliness of plaintiff's complaint. Specifically, we will look to article 2 of the UCC, which applies to "transactions in goods." 810 ILCS 5/2-102 (West 2006).

Section 2-725 of the UCC, titled "Statute of limitations in contracts for sale," generally provides a four-year limitations period:

"(1) An action for breach of any contract for sale must be commenced within 4 years after the cause of action has accrued. By the original agreement the parties may reduce the period of limitation to not less than one year but may not extend it.

(2) A cause of action accrues when the breach occurs, regardless of the aggrieved party's lack of knowledge of the breach. A breach of warranty occurs when tender of delivery is made, except that where a warranty explicitly extends to future performance of the goods and discovery of the breach must await the time of such performance the cause of action accrues when the breach is or should have been discovered." 810 ILCS 5/2-725 (West 2006).

Preliminarily, we note that the future-performance exception to the four-year limitations period, set forth in subsection (2) above, is not at issue in this case. As will be discussed in greater detail below, a repair or replacement warranty like the one issued by defendant here "has nothing to do with the inherent quality of the goods or their future performance." *Cosman*, 285 Ill. App. 3d at 261, 220 Ill. Dec. 790, 674 N.E.2d 61. See also C. Reitz, Manufacturers' Warranties of Consumer Goods, 75 Wash. U. L.Q. 357, 364 n.24 (1997) ("Promises to repair or replace refer to future performance of sellers, not to future performance of goods"); L. Lawrence, Lawrence's Anderson on the Uniform Commercial Code §2-625:129, at 332 (3d ed. 2001) (discussing difference between a warranty of future performance and a covenant to repair or replace). Accordingly, we turn our attention to the balance of the statute and the parties' arguments relative thereto.

Defendant argues that section 2-725 should be applied as written. Thus, because the statute provides that a "breach of warranty occurs when tender of delivery is made," and tender of delivery of the Dodge Neon was first made in June 1996, plaintiff's suit, filed in May 2001, was untimely. See *Nowalski*, 335 Ill. App. 3d at 632, 269 Ill. Dec. 781, 781 N.E.2d 578 (holding that cause of action for breach of three-year/36,000-mile limited warranty accrued when the vehicle was delivered and not when defendant failed to successfully repair the vehicle). Plaintiff argues that a repair warranty cannot be breached until the manufacturer fails to repair the vehicle after a reasonable opportunity to do so, and that the appellate court did not err in finding her complaint was timely filed. See *Cosman*, 285 Ill. App. 3d at 260, 220 Ill. Dec. 790, 674 N.E.2d 61 (holding that breach of six-year/60,000-mile limited power-train warranty "cannot occur until Ford refuses or fails to repair the powertrain if and when it breaks"); Belfour v. Schaumburg Auto, 306 Ill. App. 3d 234, 241, 239 Ill. Dec. 383, 713 N.E.2d 1233 (1999) (following *Cosman* and holding that breach of three-year/50,000-mile repair warranty "cannot occur until Audi refuses or fails to repair the defect"); *Cogley*, 368 Ill. App. 3d at 96-97, 306 Ill. Dec. 243, 857 N.E.2d 336 (following *Cosman* and holding that suit for breach of three-year/36,000-mile repair warranty filed within four years of repair attempt was timely).[8]

We begin our analysis by turning to the language of article 2 of the UCC. Section 2-725(2) plainly states that "[a] breach of warranty occurs when tender of delivery is made." 810 ILCS 5/2-725(2) (West 2006). The *Nowalski* opinion, on which defendant relies, concluded that once article 2

8. The same divergence of opinion on the limitations issue that is exemplified by *Nowalski* and *Cosman* exists among our sister states. See generally L. Garvin, Uncertainty and Error in the Law of Sales: The Article Two Statute of Limitations, 83 B.U. L. Rev. 345, 377-81 (2003) (discussing the split among state courts in their approach to repair or replacement promises).

of the UCC is chosen as the analogous state statute from which to borrow the statute of limitations, the analysis begins and ends with the "tender of delivery" language quoted above. *Nowalski*, 335 Ill. App. 3d at 632, 269 Ill. Dec. 781, 781 N.E.2d 578. We disagree.

Although courts generally consider article 2 of the UCC to be the statute most closely analogous to the Magnuson-Moss Act, the two enactments are not identical. For example, article 2 addresses warranties that are created by the "seller." See 810 ILCS 5/2-312, 2-313, 2-314, 2-315 (West 2006). The Magnuson-Moss Act, however, addresses warranties from a "supplier" or "warrantor" who may or may not be the immediate seller. See 15 U.S.C. §§2301(4), (5), (6) (1994). In addition, the term "warranty," as used in the two enactments, is not the same. As discussed above, the Act speaks of implied warranties and written warranties, the latter of which may be either full or limited. 15 U.S.C. §§2301(6), (7), 2303 (1994). In contrast, the UCC speaks of express warranties (which may be oral or written), implied warranties, and warranty of title. 810 ILCS 5/2-312, 2-313, 2-314, 2-315 (West 2006).

Although the parties agree that defendant's warranty is a "written warranty" under the Magnuson-Moss Act, they disagree as to whether the warranty is an "express warranty" under the UCC. Defendant argues that the repair warranty qualifies as an express warranty and that plaintiff's claim is therefore governed by the tender-of-delivery rule in section 2-725(2). Plaintiff argues that it does not qualify as an express warranty and that her claim is not subject to the tender-of-delivery rule.

Section 2-313 of the UCC explains how express warranties are created.

> "Express warranties by the seller are created as follows:
>
> (a) Any affirmation of fact or promise made by the seller to the buyer which relates to the goods and becomes part of the basis of the bargain creates an express warranty that the goods shall conform to the affirmation or promise.
>
> (b) Any description of the goods which is made part of the basis of the bargain creates an express warrant
>
> (c) Any sample or model which is made part of the basis of the bargain creates an express warranty that the whole of the goods shall conform to the sample or model." 810 ILCS 5/2-313(1) (West 2006).

The UCC makes plain that an express warranty is related to the quality or description of the goods. See Moorman Manufacturing Co. v. National Tank Co., 91 Ill. 2d 69, 78, 61 Ill. Dec. 746, 435 N.E.2d 443 (1982) (observing that UCC warranty rules "determine the quality of the product the manufacturer promises and thereby determine the quality he must deliver"); Alloway v. General Marine Industries, L.P., 149 N.J. 620, 630, 695 A.2d 264, 269 (1997) (stating that "the U.C.C. provides for express warranties regarding the quality of goods"); Allis-Chalmers Credit Corp. v. Herbolt, 17 Ohio App. 3d 230, 233, 17 OBR 496, 479 N.E.2d 293, 297 (1984) (identifying UCC express warranties as one of the "warranties of quality"); 1 W. Hawkland, Uniform Commercial Code Series §2-313.4, at 546 (2002) ("express warranties relate exclusively to quality, description and title of the goods and have nothing to do with the other terms of the contract").

In other words, an express warranty, for purposes of the UCC, obligates the seller to deliver goods that conform to the affirmation, promise, description, sample or model. If a seller delivers conforming goods, the warranty is satisfied. If the seller delivers nonconforming goods, the warranty is breached at that time. Even if the buyer is unaware that the goods, as delivered, do not conform to the seller's affirmation, promise, description, sample or model, the warranty has been breached. Under this scenario, the statutory pronouncement that "[a] breach of warranty occurs when tender of delivery is made" (810 ILCS 5/2-725(2) (West 2006)) makes perfect sense, and the four-year limitations period commences at that time. See M. Klinger, The Concept of Warranty Duration: A Tangled Web, 89 Dick. L. Rev. 935, 939 (1985) ("Section 2-725(2) presumes that all warranties, expressed or implied, relate only to the condition of the goods at the time of sale" and "[a]s a result, the period of limitations begins to run at that time"); L. Garvin, Uncertainty and Error in the Law of Sales: The Article Two Statute of Limitations, 83 B.U. L. Rev. 345, 379 (2003) ("Article Two defines a range of express and implied warranties" which "[a]ll go to the quality of the goods at tender").

The warranty in the present case, however, is not related to the quality or description of the goods at tender. It does not warrant that the vehicle will conform to some affirmation, promise, description, sample or model. Rather, the warranty promises only that the manufacturer will repair or replace defective parts during the warranty period. As defendant made clear in its brief before this court:

"DaimlerChrysler's limited warranty was not a promise that the vehicle would be defect free and in the event of a breach of warranty, Plaintiff would be limited to repair or replacement of the vehicle. Rather, DaimlerChrysler's limited warranty promised to cover the cost to repair or replace defective parts in the automobile for the time period covering 36 months or 36 thousand miles."

Although defendant's warranty qualifies as a "written warranty" under the Act, it is not an "express warranty" under the UCC, and is thus not the type of warranty that can be breached on "tender of delivery" (810 ILCS 5/2-725(2) (West 2006)). See *Cogley*, 368 Ill. App. 3d at 96, 306 Ill. Dec. 243, 857 N.E.2d 336; *Cosman*, 285 Ill. App. 3d at 258-60, 220 Ill. Dec. 790, 674 N.E.2d 61; C. Dewitt, Note, Action Accrual Date for Written Warranties to

Repair: Date of Delivery or Date of Failure to Repair, 17 U. Mich. J.L. Reform 713, 722 n.35 (1984) (promise to repair "relates not to the goods and their quality, but to the manufacturer and its obligation to the purchaser," and thus "a repair 'warranty' falls beyond the scope of . . . the on-delivery rule"); C. Reitz, Manufacturers' Warranties of Consumer Goods, 75 Wash. U. L.Q. 357, 364 n.24 (1997) (tender-of-delivery date for commencement of four-year UCC limitations provision is "completely inappropriate to promises to repair or replace goods that are later determined to be defective"). Accordingly, we reject defendant's argument that the four-year limitations period for breach of the repair warranty commenced upon delivery of the Dodge Neon in 1996, and we overrule the *Nowalski* opinion on which defendant relies.

Our conclusion that the repair warranty is not a UCC express warranty, and thus not subject to the tender-of-delivery rule set forth in the second sentence of section 2-725(2), does not render section 2-725(2) irrelevant for purposes of determining when the limitations period began on plaintiff's claim under the Magnuson-Moss Act. The first sentence of section 2-725(2) remains applicable. The first sentence states: "[a] cause of action accrues when the breach occurs, regardless of the aggrieved party's lack of knowledge of the breach." (Emphasis added.) 810 ILCS 5/2-725(2) (West 2006). Although the UCC does not expressly state when the breach of a repair promise occurs, we may refer to the law that exists outside of the UCC. See 810 ILCS 5/1-103 (West 2006) ("Unless displaced by the particular provisions of this Act, the principles of law and equity . . . shall supplement its provisions"); L. Lawrence, Lawrence's Anderson on the Uniform Commercial Code §2-725:99, at 301 (3d ed. 2001) (because the UCC provides no assistance as to when a nonwarranty breach of contract "occurs" for purposes of computing the limitations period, "it is necessary to resort to the general non-Code law of contracts," which "has not been displaced by the Code and therefore continues in force").

Generally, "[w]hen performance of a duty under a contract is due any non-performance is a breach." Restatement (Second) of Contracts §235, at 211 (1979). Performance under a vehicle manufacturer's promise to repair or replace defective parts is due not at tender of delivery, but only when, and if, a covered defect arises and repairs are required. In that event, if the promised repairs are refused or unsuccessful, the repair warranty is breached and the cause of action accrues, triggering the four-year limitations period. See *Cosman*, 285 Ill. App. 3d at 260, 220 Ill. Dec. 790, 674 N.E.2d 61 (holding that breach of six-year/60,000-mile limited power-train warranty "cannot occur until Ford refuses or fails to repair the powertrain if and when it breaks"); *Belfour*, 306 Ill. App. 3d at 241, 239 Ill. Dec. 383, 713 N.E.2d 1233 (holding that breach of three-year/50,000-mile repair warranty "cannot occur until Audi refuses or fails to repair the defect"); *Cogley*, 368 Ill. App. 3d at 96-97, 306 Ill. Dec. 243, 857 N.E.2d 336 (holding that suit for breach of three-year/36,000-mile repair warranty filed within four years of repair attempt was timely). See also Monticello v. Winnebago Industries, Inc., 369 F. Supp. 2d 1350, 1356-57 (N.D. Ga. 2005) (under Georgia law, a written warranty that provides for repair or replacement of parts is breached when the purchaser returns the product to the dealer for repair and repair is refused or unsuccessful); *Poli*, 349 N.J. Super. at 180, 793 A.2d at 110-11 (under New Jersey law, cause of action for breach of seven-year/70,000-mile power-train warranty would not have accrued when the car was delivered, but rather when persistent problems appeared or when DaimlerChrysler was unable to repair the defect); Long Island Lighting Co. v. Imo Industries Inc., 6 F.3d 876, 889-90 (2d Cir. 1993) (under New York law, cause of action for breach of a repair promise accrued when the generator malfunctioned and the seller refused to make the necessary repairs).

This is the approach advocated by some commentators. For example, in his discussion of the appropriate treatment of a manufacturer's express warranty to repair or replace defective parts, Professor Lawrence states:

> "The sounder approach is to recognize that the failure to repair or replace is merely a breach of contract and not a breach of warranty, and therefore no cause of action arises until the seller has refused to repair or replace the goods. This is because until the seller has failed or refused to make the repairs or provide a replacement, the buyer, not being entitled to such a remedy, has no right to commence an action for damages. As a result, the action is timely if brought within four years of the seller's failure or refusal."
> L. Lawrence, Lawrence's Anderson on the Uniform Commercial Code §2-725:101, at 303 (3d ed. 2001).

Accord L. Garvin, Uncertainty and Error in the Law of Sales: The Article Two Statute of Limitations, 83 B.U. L. Rev. 345, 381 (2003).

The correctness of this approach is manifest when we consider consumer claims for breach of repair warranties that run for periods longer than the three years/36,000 miles at issue here. For example, consider the case of a consumer who purchases a vehicle carrying a five-year/50,000-mile repair warranty. If the four-year limitations period commences at "tender of delivery," the limitations period for a breach of the repair promise occurring in year five will expire before the breach even occurs, thus rendering the repair warranty unenforceable during its final year. Statutes of limitations, however, are intended "to prevent stale claims, not to preclude claims before they are ripe for adjudication." Guzman v. C.R. Epperson Construction, Inc., 196 Ill. 2d 391, 400, 256 Ill. Dec. 827, 752 N.E.2d 1069 (2001). Even a four-year warranty could be rendered unenforceable if breach of the repair promise occurred near the end of the warranty period. In that case, the buyer would have only the briefest of periods in which to file suit. See *Nationwide Insurance Co.*, 533 Pa. at 434, 625 A.2d at 1178.

Defendant argues that concerns about the enforceability of longer-term repair warranties are inapplicable to the facts of this case and without merit. We disagree. Although the repair warranty at issue here ran for three years, our holding in this case will apply equally to longer-term warranties. Such warranties are common in the automobile industry. Adoption of defendant's position would be an invitation to manufacturers and sellers of automobiles, as well as other goods, to engage in misleading marketing. That is, a manufacturer or seller could use the marketing advantage of a longer repair warranty, yet escape the accompanying obligations of that warranty by pleading the statute of limitations in defense. C. Williams, The Statute of Limitations, Prospective Warranties, and Problems of Interpretation in Article Two of the UCC, 52 Geo. Wash. L. Rev. 67, 105 (1983). Such a result is contrary to the very purpose of the Magnuson-Moss Act: "to improve the adequacy of information available to consumers" and "prevent deception." 15 U.S.C. §2302(a) (1994).

Defendant also argues that unless the tender-of-delivery rule in section 2-725 is given effect, the limitations period for breach of limited warranty actions will be "limitless" and "uncertain." This argument is without merit. Because the promise to repair or replace defective parts is only good during the warranty period, the latest a breach of warranty can occur is at the very end of that period. Accordingly, the statute of limitations will expire, at the latest, four years after the warranty period has run. If breach of a repair warranty occurs earlier in the warranty period, the limitations period for that breach will expire sooner, but in no event will the warrantor's exposure extend beyond the warranty period, plus four years. Thus, contrary to defendant's argument, commencing the four-year limitations period from the date the warrantor fails or refuses to repair the vehicle does not result in a limitless limitations period.

We recognize, of course, that a fact question may arise as to the date on which a repair warranty was breached which, in turn, would create some uncertainty as to when the four-year limitations period should commence. Fact questions of this nature, however, frequently arise in cases where the statute of limitations has been pled in defense. Resolution of this type of uncertainty is a classic function of the trier of fact. See, e.g., County of Du Page v. Graham, Anderson, Probst & White, Inc., 109 Ill. 2d 143, 153-54, 92 Ill. Dec. 833, 485 N.E.2d 1076 (1985) (remanding the matter to the circuit court for a factual determination as to when the statute of limitations began to run against the county on its claims for defective design and construction of the county's administration building); Knox College v. Celotex Corp., 88 Ill. 2d 407, 417, 58 Ill. Dec. 725, 430 N.E.2d 976 (1981) (holding that trier of fact must determine when the plaintiff had sufficient information as to the roof defect to start the running of the limitations period); Witherell v. Weimer, 85 Ill. 2d 146, 156, 52 Ill. Dec. 6, 421 N.E.2d 869 (1981) ("In many, if not most, cases the time at which an injured party knows or reasonably should have known both of his injury and that it was wrongfully caused will be a disputed question to be resolved by the finder of fact"). We therefore reject defendant's argument that commencing the limitations period when the warrantor fails or refuses to repair the defect—rather than at tender of delivery—will create unacceptable uncertainty in the limitations period.

Turning to the facts of this case, the record indicates that plaintiff brought her vehicle to McGrath and another authorized dealer on several occasions beginning in July 1998. At that point, assuming the alleged defects were covered defects, defendant was obligated (through its authorized dealer) to make good on its repair promise. Plaintiff's lawsuit, filed in May 2001, is therefore timely. Accordingly, we affirm that portion of the judgment of the appellate court which reversed the grant of summary judgment in favor of defendant as to count I of the complaint.

Affirmed in part and reversed in part; cause remanded.

PROBLEM 86

If the manufacturer of a vehicle sold it to the dealership, and the dealership then resold the vehicle to a consumer, would the four-year period on the manufacturer's *implied* warranty start running on the date of delivery to the dealership or on the date of the sale to the ultimate consumer? See Wilson v. Class, 605 A.2d 907, 17 U.C.C. Rep. Serv. 2d 1166 (Del. Super. 1992). Would we reach the same result on an *express* warranty given by the manufacturer?

PROBLEM 87

Painter Sally Smock had no luck selling her own works, but made good money by creating phony works supposedly by Salvador Dali, signing Dali's name to them, and selling them to DaDa Gallery. In 2015, DaDa Gallery unwittingly sold two of Smock's forgeries to Mr. and Mrs. America, tourists who paid $150,000. The Americas proudly exhibited the supposed Dalis in their Cincinnati living room, until 2020 when Smock made the national news as she went to jail for art forgery. The Americas then sued DaDa Gallery for breach of express warranty, only to be met with the argument that the statute of limitations under §2-725 had run out. How should this come out? See Balog v. Center Art Gallery, 745 F. Supp. 1556, 12 U.C.C. Rep. Serv. 2d 962 (D. Haw. 1990); Doss, Inc. v. Christie's Inc., 70 U.C.C. Rep. Serv. 2d 884 (S.D.N.Y. 2009) (holding that a cause of action for selling painting, which had been stolen by the Nazis from a Paris art dealer, accrued in 1991 when the painting was sold by Christie's, not in 2006 when there was challenge to buyer's ownership).

PROBLEM 88

In 2015, Notheby's Auction Company sold Max Collector a painting expressly warranted to be by Degas, for $1 million. Experts hired by Notheby's had all agreed it was created by Degas in 1886. In 2032, Max Collector sold the painting to Grandiose Museum for $5 million, making an express warranty that it was by Degas. Two years later, the museum learned conclusively that the painting was in fact a forgery created in 1923. It sued Max Collector for return of the purchase price. Does Max Collector have an indemnification action against Notheby's, or has the statute of limitations expired on that claim? See §2-725 and the following case.[9]

Central Washington Refrigeration, Inc. v. Barbee

Supreme Court of Washington, 1997
133 Wash. 2d 509, 946 P.2d 760

SANDERS, Justice.

We are asked whether a buyer of goods may bring an indemnity action against the seller for liability incurred to a third party for a defect in the goods, and, if so, when the statute of limitations begins to run. We hold a buyer may maintain such indemnity action and that the statute of limitations begins to run when the buyer pays damages to the third party or the third party obtains judgment against the buyer, whichever is first in time.

In 1987 petitioner Central Washington Refrigeration, Inc. (Central) contracted with a Yakima orchard to install a set of cold storage rooms to store apples and other fruit. Central in turn contracted with respondent McCormack Engineering (McCormack) to purchase the refrigeration coils which Central was to install. Pursuant to the sales agreement McCormack specially manufactured the coils according to Central's specifications and timely delivered them in August 1987 at which time Central installed the coils in the cold storage rooms.

From the start, however, the orchard experienced problems with the cold storage rooms. After several repair attempts and an intervening bankruptcy by the orchard, the orchard defaulted on payments for the cold

---

9. Some states regulate art authenticity problems by special statute; see L. Garvin, Uncertainty and Error in the Law of Sales: The Article Two Statute of Limitations, 83 B.U. L. Rev. 345, 371 n.116 (2003), citing Fla. Stat. Ann. §686.504; Mich. Comp. Laws Ann. §442.322; N.Y. Arts & Cult. Aff. Law §13.01; R.I. Gen. Laws §5-62-9(1), cited in Mydlach v. DaimlerChrysler Corp., above.

storage rooms and Central subsequently sued for payment. In March 1989 the orchard counterclaimed for damages asserting Central misdesigned the cold storage system, used poor workmanship in building it, installed improper components, and failed to repair the system.

On May 22, 1992 — over four-and-a-half years after McCormack delivered the coils — Central filed a third-party complaint against McCormack alleging the coils were defective and caused all the problems, seeking contribution and/or indemnity from McCormack for any damages due the orchard from Central. [The court below held that] to the extent Central's claim was either contractual or for indemnity, it was barred by the four-year U.C.C. statute of limitations governing contracts. *Central Washington Refrigeration, Inc. v. Barbee*, 81 Wash. App. 212, 220, 223-24, 913 P.2d 836 (1996). We granted review to determine whether a buyer may maintain an indemnity action against the seller based on breach of warranty, and, if so, when the applicable statute of limitations commences to run. . . .

Indemnity in its most basic sense means reimbursement (Black's Law Dictionary 769 (6th ed. 1990)) and may lie when one party discharges a liability which another should rightfully have assumed. *Stevens v. Security Pac. Mortgage Corp.*, 53 Wash. App. 507, 517, 768 P.2d 1007, review denied, 112 Wash. 2d 1023 (1989) ("Indemnity requires full reimbursement and transfers liability from the one who has been compelled to pay damages to another who should bear the entire loss.").[10]

While indemnity sounds in contract and tort it is a separate equitable cause of action. The variety of indemnity relevant to this case is implied contractual indemnity, also referenced to as "implied in fact" indemnity. Such arises when one party incurs a liability the other party should discharge by virtue of the nature of the relationship between the two parties. . . . The nature of the relationship between the parties gives rise to the right of implied indemnity. . . .[11] The question here is whether the contractual relationship between buyer and seller under the U.C.C. is sufficient to give rise to an implied right of indemnity when a defect in the good

10. See also *McDermott v. City of New York*, 50 N.Y.2d 211, 406 N.E.2d 460, 462, 428 N.Y.S.2d 643 (1980) ("Conceptually, implied indemnification finds its roots in the principles of equity. It is nothing short of simple fairness to recognize that '[a] person who, in whole or in part, has discharged a duty which is owed by him but which as between himself and another should have been discharged by the other, is entitled to indemnity' (Restatement, Restitution, §76). To prevent unjust enrichment, courts have assumed the duty of placing the obligation where in equity it belongs.").

11. See 42 C.J.S. Indemnity §31, at 121 (1991) ("A right to indemnity, while not implied in every contract or contractual relationship, may be claimed on the basis of an implied contract, which can arise either from the conduct of the parties or be implied from the nature of their relationship, whether it be a contractual or other legal relationship, and from given warranties and covenants, or be otherwise implied from unique special factors indicating the parties' intent that the party from whom indemnity is sought should be ultimately liable.") (citations omitted).

causes damage to a third party user and such defect constitutes breach of seller's warranties.

A minority of courts addressing the issue under comparable facts has found the contractual relationship between buyer and seller under the U.C.C. insufficient to give rise to an indemnity action. See, e.g., Perry v. Pioneer Wholesale Supply Co., 681 P.2d 214, 219 (Utah 1984). Jurisdictions following this minority rule are Utah, Idaho, and South Dakota. The minority rule would view Central's claim as nothing more than a claim for damages under a sales contract between merchants for breach of implied warranties resulting in consequential damages owed to a third party.[12] Use of the label "indemnity" would not alter the perception that the action still sounds in contract. The claim would be governed in whole by the U.C.C. Under the U.C.C. actions for breach of contract must be commenced within four years of date of delivery of goods regardless of when the buyer discovers the defect. Because Central failed to bring its claim against McCormack within four years of delivery, its suit would be time-barred under the minority rule. The Court of Appeals chose to follow the minority rule.

Central, however, argues the minority rule errs in failing to recognize an indemnity claim here. We agree. Central points to the majority of courts addressing the issue which have ruled the contractual relationship between buyer and seller under the U.C.C. is a sufficient relationship to give rise to an implied right of indemnity. Jurisdictions following the majority rule include California, Maine, Michigan, Minnesota, Missouri, Nebraska, New Hampshire, New York, North Carolina, Pennsylvania, and Virginia.

A clear statement of the majority rule appears in Bellevue South Assocs. v. HRH Constr. Corp., 78 N.Y.2d 282, 579 N.E.2d 195, 574 N.Y.S.2d 165 (1991). In Bellevue a subcontractor installed defective floor tiles in an apartment complex and was sued by the apartment complex owner. The subcontractor eventually sued the tile manufacturer for indemnity, seeking to shift the entire liability, alleging the manufacturer breached the implied warranties. The manufacturer argued the suit was nothing more than one on the contract and thus the U.C.C. four-year statute of limitations must govern to bar the suit. The New York high court rejected the manufacturer's argument, concluding the contractual relationship and the

---

12. Two legal commentaries argue the minority rule has it right. See Paul J. Wilkinson, An Ind. Run Around the U.C.C.: The Use (or Abuse?) of Indemnity, 20 Pepp. L. Rev. 1407, 1438 (1993) (such "indemnity" actions are nothing more than actions for consequential damages resulting from breach of contract and there is no reason to treat consequential damages paid to a third party any differently from any other damages incurred as a result of a breach of contract); Thomas A. Leggette, When Can an Implied Indemnity Cause of Action be Used to End-Run a Limitations Bar?, 42 Fed'n Ins. & Corp. Couns. Q. 33, 33 (1991) (a party should not be able to end-run the strict four-year U.C.C. statute of limitations period for suing on contracts by simply denominating the action one for "indemnity").

U.C.C.'s implied warranties provided "the requisite basis for an indemnification claim." Id., 574 N.Y.S.2d at 171, 579 N.E.2d at 201.

We adopt the majority rule and hold a contractual relationship under the U.C.C., with its implied warranties, provides sufficient basis for an implied indemnity claim when the buyer incurs liability to a third party as a result of a defect in the goods which would constitute a breach of the seller's implied or express warranties. In so holding we acknowledge "[t]here is a substantial difference between an instance where a product simply fails as opposed to a situation where the product fails and causes damage to a third party." Carrier Corp. v. Detrex Corp., 4 Cal. App. 4th 1522, 6 Cal. Rptr. 2d 565, 569 (1992). We also understand our decision to join the majority camp comports with the equitable principles underlying indemnity.[13]

The remaining question is when the statute of limitations commences to run on the indemnity claim. Indemnity actions are distinct, separate causes of action from the underlying wrong and are governed by separate statutes of limitations. It is settled law that indemnity actions accrue when the party seeking indemnity pays or is legally adjudged obligated to pay damages to a third party. The statute of limitations on the indemnity action therefore begins to run at that point. . . .

Thus, the statute of limitations on Central's alleged indemnity claim began to run when Central paid the orchard to settle the orchard's claims. Because Central brought suit at the same time it settled, we hold its indemnity action is not time barred. Central's indemnification suit must be determined on its merits. The Court of Appeals is reversed, the case is remanded for trial and Central shall recover its costs on appeal.

GUY, Justice (dissenting).

Article 2 of the Uniform Commercial Code (U.C.C.) establishes one general law governing all commercial sales for the purpose of providing predictability and consistency for all commercial sales transactions. In my view the majority opinion is inconsistent with this purpose. By holding contract-based indemnity claims are outside the U.C.C.'s four-year statute

---

13. See, e.g., City of Willmar v. Short-Elliott-Hendrickson, Inc., 512 N.W.2d 872, 874 (1994) (indemnity is an equitable action and "is not based on contract or tort, although either may secondarily be involved, but on one party paying more than its fair share."); City of Clayton v. Grumman Emergency Prods., Inc., 576 F. Supp. 1122, 1127 (E.D. Mo. 1983) ("A party who buys and then resells a product is not in a position to discover the latent defect within the warranty's limitation period because the product is in the hands of the consumer during that time. Only when the consumer sues the retailer does the retailer gain notice of the latent defect."). We note indemnity may not be available when equity does not so require. See Sheehan v. Morris Irr., Inc., 460 N.W.2d 413, 417 (S.D. 1990); Farmers Nat'l Bank v. Wickham Pipeline Constr., 114 Idaho 565, 759 P.2d 71, 75 (1988) (equity does not require an indemnity action to be recognized where parties could have sued at law but slept on their rights). As the parties have not so requested, we refrain from assessing the particular equities in this case.

of repose, RCW 62A.2-725, the majority leaves commercial retailers susceptible to indemnity claims indefinitely.[14] Therefore, I dissent.

The transaction between Central and McCormack was a sale of goods. I would hold that any claim stemming from this commercial sales transaction, including one for indemnity, is governed by article 2 of the U.C.C. and its four-year statute of repose. Further, I would hold that Central's claim for indemnity was time barred since it was raised after the four-year time period had expired.

The majority is compelled by the belief that this court must follow the lead of other jurisdictions and find that when commercial buyers have paid damages to a third party due to defective products purchased from a commercial retailer, the buyer has two avenues for compensation. The jurisdictions on which the majority relies found that such commercial buyers not only have a breach of warranty claim against the commercial retailer under article 2 but also have an implied right of indemnity against the retailer founded in common law and governed by general statutes of limitations. The majority does not thoroughly discuss why this policy decision is correct but instead places great importance on the fact that a "majority" of other jurisdictions follow it. Contrary to the majority's conclusion, there is no majority/minority view on whether indemnity claims are independent of the U.C.C. Rather, there exists a split of authority. Four states, South Dakota, Idaho, Utah and Georgia, find that such claims fall exclusively under the U.C.C. Courts in six states, Minnesota, California, New York, Nebraska, New Hampshire and Maine, hold indemnity claims may be raised independent of the U.C.C. Therefore, there exists authority from other jurisdictions to support both sides of this policy debate as to whether all contract-based claims, including those of indemnity, are bound by the U.C.C. I would hold that a decision finding contract-based indemnity claims are governed by the U.C.C. is correct because it creates a policy consistent with the purpose of the U.C.C. — one of predictability and uniformity.

Although the jurisdictions cited by the majority claim fairness requires that a commercial buyer who pays out-of-pocket damages to a third party has a remedy unrestricted by a statute of repose, I believe at some point the law must recognize commercial practices and concepts, including the concept of bargained-for risk. Commercial buyers do not purchase items with the notion they are receiving an implied lifetime guarantee. They

14. Although a third party's claim against a commercial buyer for breach of warranty continues to be bound by the four-year time period, under the majority opinion there is no predictability as to how long a commercial retailer will be held liable for indemnity. Because accrual of an indemnity claim against a commercial retailer does not occur until a judgment is entered against a commercial buyer or when a commercial buyer pays damages to a third party, a commercial retailer cannot predict on what date an action for indemnity will accrue against it.

know products may not last forever. However, there does exist an implied warrantability that lasts for four years after delivery, in order to create a balance between fairness and bargained-for risk. The U.C.C. has identified this four-year period, commencing at the time of delivery, as a fair period of time for a commercial buyer to expect guaranteed warrantability and a commercial retailer to expect to be held liable.

Section 2-725 was adopted to "[take] sales contracts out of the general laws limiting the time for commencing contractual actions and selects a four year period as the most appropriate to modern business practice. This is within the normal commercial record keeping period." RCWA 62A.2-725 U.C.C. cmt. at 415 (Purposes). Section 2-725 provides "a time when [a merchant] ought to be secure in his reasonable expectation that the slate has been wiped clean of ancient obligations, and he ought not to be called on to resist a claim when 'evidence has been lost, memories have faded, and witnesses have disappeared.'" Paul J. Wilkinson, Comment, An Ind. Run Around the U.C.C.: The Use (or Abuse?) of Indemnity, 20 Pepp. L. Rev. 1407, 1412 (1993) (quoting Developments in the Law, Statutes of Limitations, 63 Harv. L. Rev. 1177, 1185 (1950)). These comments illustrate the U.C.C.'s goal to establish an across-the-board governing law for all commercial sales transactions that adequately addresses fairness and bargained-for risk. By allowing a common law remedy in a commercial sale relationship, the majority contradicts this goal. In order to remain consistent with the purpose of the U.C.C., I would hold that Central's action against McCormack is governed by article 2 and that section 2-725 applies.

I would also hold that Central's action, under article 2, is barred under section 2-725. In my view, section 2-725 is a statute of repose, not a statute of limitation. A statute of limitation bars plaintiffs from bringing an already accrued claim after a specified period of time; a statute of repose terminates a right of action after a specified time, even if the injury has not yet occurred. . . .

The language of U.C.C. §2-725 unambiguously creates a statute of repose. Because it is unambiguous, the meaning of the statute is derived from the words of the statute. State v. McDougal, 120 Wash. 2d 334, 350, 841 P.2d 1232 (1992); State v. Olson, 47 Wash. App. 514, 516, 735 P.2d 1362 (1987). The statute states a claim must be made within "four years after the cause of action has accrued." RCW 62A.2-725(1). According to the statute "[a] cause of action accrues when the breach occurs," and "[a] breach of warranty occurs when tender of delivery is made. . . ." RCW 62A.2-725(2). Therefore, all claims must be made no more than four years after delivery, whether or not the buyer is aware of the product's defect. Based on this clear language, I would hold that Central's contractual indemnity claim, based on the breach of an implied warranty, was barred when the action was filed in May 1992, since the coils were delivered more than four and a half years earlier—in August 1987.

Section 2-725 actually "poses few problems: it simply bars a buyer from bringing an action for breach of warranty more than four years after tender of delivery. This straight-forward rule forces buyers to sue when evidence is most readily available and allows sellers to continue with their businesses without fear of suit after a reasonable definite period." Debra L. Goetz et al., Project, Article Two Warranties in Commercial Transactions: An Update, 72 Cornell L. Rev. 1159, 1324-29 (1987).

I would find that Central's claim is governed by U.C.C. §2-725, a statute of repose, and was properly dismissed by the trial court. I would affirm the decision of the Court of Appeals.

CHAPTER 7
DOCUMENTS OF
TITLE

Article 7 of the Code deals with the legal problems created by *documents of title* (defined in §1-201(16)) — items (whether tangible paper or electronic records) issued for the purpose of actually representing title to goods. The two primary types of documents of title are bills of lading (§1-201(6)) and warehouse receipts (§1-201(42)).[1] Article 7 was revised in 2003,[2] primarily to allow the creation of electronic forms of documents of title, and §§7-106 and 7-105 (in that order) deal with such creatures.[3]

The creation of paper representing the right of ownership of the goods became inevitable as soon as merchants wanted to borrow money and pledge goods that they owned as collateral. If the goods were large enough to store in a warehouse, the money lender was normally unwilling to take physical possession of the goods. The money lender was also normally unwilling to give the borrower possession of the collateral for fear the goods would be sold to someone else or taken by the buyer's other creditors. The solution to the problem was to store the goods with a bailee and have the bailee issue a

---

1. For treatises on point, see W. Towle, Warehousing Law (1988), and R. Henson, Documents of Title Under the Uniform Commercial Code (2d ed. 1990).

2. Citations in this chapter referencing Article 7 refer to the 2003 version, which has been adopted by the vast majority of states.

3. For an article on point, see Susan Beecher, Can the Electronic Bill of Lading Go Paperless?, 40 Int'l Law. 627 (2006).

paper stating that the goods belonged to the owner of the paper. In this fashion, the paper, representing the obligation of the bailee to deliver the goods to the holder, could be freely transferred, discounted, and rediscounted without the necessity of moving the goods into the physical control of each new owner. Any holder of the paper could surrender it and require the bailee (*issuer*) to turn over the goods. Read §7-403 carefully. Note that under subsection (c) the person claiming the goods *must* (except in the §7-503 situation discussed later) surrender the negotiable document of title for cancellation in order to receive the goods. If the document has been lost, the holder can get the goods only by procuring a court order directing the bailee to turn over the goods. Read §7-601. Documents of title are negotiable or nonnegotiable depending on whether they contain order or bearer language (§7-104). Since under §7-403(c) the bailee can demand only the surrender of negotiable paper, only negotiable documents of title truly represent absolute ownership of the goods. Nonnegotiable paper simply evidences the contract between the bailor and the bailee, which is to do whatever the contract says. Nonnegotiable documents normally state exactly to whom the bailee will deliver the goods and under what conditions. Therefore, for reasons of safety, lenders prefer to loan money against negotiable documents. With nonnegotiable documents, lenders run the risk that there has already been a delivery of the goods to someone else.

I. WAREHOUSE RECEIPTS

A. Form

The front of a *negotiable* warehouse receipt states the name of the warehouse that is issuing the receipt and states in large type that:

> This is to certify that we have received in storage for the account of _____ in apparent order, except as noted hereon (contents, condition, and quality being unknown), the following described property, subject to all of the terms and conditions on the front or back of this contract, such property to be delivered to _____ or order, upon payment of all storage, handling and other charges and the surrender of this Warehouse receipt properly endorsed.

Following this statement usually there are the following:

(1) a space for listing the goods stored,
(2) a statement of the warehouse company's intention to claim a lien against the goods until the storage charges are paid,

(3)   a statement as to the amount of the storage charge, and
(4)   the official signature of the warehouse company.

The back of the warehouse receipt contains a space in which the agent of the warehouse can note *partial* deliveries to the holder of the document (later holders can claim only the amount of goods the document shows were not delivered to prior holders). The back also has the *standard contract terms* in small print (these standard terms were adopted by a 1926 conference of experts and approved by the Department of Commerce); the terms cover the fact that the storage is on a month-to-month basis and spell out in detail the warehouse company's position as to insurance, limitation of liability, right to move the goods, etc.

A nonnegotiable warehouse receipt looks substantially the same except:

(1)   It is not made deliverable to anyone. The warehouse engages to deliver the goods as per instructions received from the person storing the goods (the bailor). *Order* language is not used.
(2)   There is no space on the back for notation of partial deliveries. This is because surrender of the document is not required to take out all or part of the goods. Section 7-403(c) applies only to *negotiable* documents.

Negotiable warehouse receipts normally have the word NEGOTIABLE stamped across their face in large letters (and the documents tend to have fancy and ornate borders, designed to make counterfeiting more difficult). Nonnegotiable documents have NONNEGOTIABLE stamped on the front.

Glance through §7-202.

As can be seen from the above, the warehouse receipt plays three roles: it is (1) a *receipt* for the goods, (2) a *contract* for storage, and (3) if negotiable, a *physical embodiment* of the concept of *title* to the goods.

B.   Basic Bailment Law

All document-of-title situations start with the bailment of the goods and the issuance of a receipt by the bailee. Bailment law is relevant to fill in the gaps in Article 7 and the federal statutes. The most important bailment concept needed to supplement the Code is that the bailee is required to make proper delivery of the goods to the bailor when the bailment ends or is to be responsible for nondelivery. Section 7-403(a) gives very few excuses for nondelivery. An *unauthorized* delivery of the goods by a bailee is conversion. Restatement (Second) of Torts §234; cf. §7-601(b). Read §7-404. A "bailee is absolutely liable for misdelivering cargo, unless his mistake as to the person entitled to receive the goods was induced by the bailor." David Crystal, Inc. v. Cunard Steam-Ship Co., Ltd., 339 F.2d 295, 298 (2d Cir. 1964); Met-Al, Inc. v. Hansen Storage Co., 828 F. Supp. 1369, 21 U.C.C. Rep. Serv. 2d 1107 (E.D. Wis. 1993) ("Equitable defenses to allegations of misdelivery are disfavored."); Singer Co. v. Stott & Davis Motor Express, Inc., 79 A.D.2d 227, 463 N.Y.S.2d 508, 31 U.C.C. Rep. Serv. 658 (App. Div. 1981) ("Once a plaintiff establishes delivery of goods and the failure of the bailee to return them on demand, a prima facie case of negligence is made and the burden of coming forward with evidence tending to show due cause shifts to the bailee. . . ."); People v. Wallace, 2011 WL 1662860 (N.Y. App. Div. 2011) ("A person need not knowingly or intentionally act wrongfully for a conversion to occur"). These principles are best illustrated by one of the cases rising out of the famous Salad Oil scandal.

Procter & Gamble Distributing Co. v. Lawrence American Field Warehouse Corp.

New York Court of Appeals, 1965
16 N.Y.2d 344, 213 N.E.2d 897, 266 N.Y.S.2d 765,
3 U.C.C. Rep. Serv. 157, 21 A.L.R.3d 1320

VAN VOORHIS, J.

This is an action against a warehouse corporation based upon the nondelivery of the merchandise for which it issued its warehouse receipts. The theory of action is conversion. Plaintiff (hereafter called P & G) asserts that in the absence of any explanation of the disappearance of these goods, the defendant (hereafter called Field) is liable for the market value of this merchandise at the times when it was delivered to the warehouse. Plaintiff is correct in these contentions, we have concluded, and is entitled to summary judgment in this amount. We agree with the Appellate Division that no triable issue is presented concerning the liability of defendant, but consider that the Appellate Division erred in directing an assessment of damages and in not awarding to plaintiff the undisputed market value of the merchandise delivered to defendant at the time of its delivery, which was as high as at any subsequent time or times prior to notification to plaintiff of its disappearance. The basic issue is simple, but it has been encrusted with a complex of fact and legal argument which makes it necessary to discuss the case in more detail.

Allied Crude Vegetable Oil Refining Corp. (hereinafter called Allied) is not a party to this action, but this cause of action against defendant arose through a course of dealings between plaintiff and Allied, which traded in vegetable oils manufactured by various producers including plaintiff. Originally plaintiff sold such merchandise outright on sight draft with bill of lading attached. In the early Fall of 1962, however, in order more fully to utilize its working capital, Allied persuaded plaintiff to engage in a practice known as field warehousing. Allied had leased oil storage tanks at Bayonne, New Jersey, formerly owned by the Tidewater Associated Oil Company. These were sublet to Field, a wholly owned subsidiary of American Express Company (hereafter called Amexco), which thereupon operated as an independent warehouse company. When Allied purchased vegetable oils from plaintiff, and other producers, as it did f.o.b. seller's plant or warehouse, Bayonne, New Jersey, the oil would be shipped to Bayonne to the seller's order, and stored for the seller's account in Field's warehouses. Down payments were made, described in the contract as "Margin Requirements on Consigned Shipments," amounting to about 20% of the purchase price, at the time of receipt of the oil at Field's warehouse, and the balance by sight draft with bill of lading attached, or cash in advance of shipment to buyer, as Allied disposed of the oil.

In accordance with this procedure, plaintiff shipped 9,206,740 pounds of fully refined soybean oil under bills of lading to plaintiff itself as consignee at Bayonne, New Jersey, which was delivered for storage and safe keeping to Field at said warehouse for plaintiff's account. Field, the defendant, issued five warehouse receipts for this oil dated March 22, April 1 and April 9, 1963. Each warehouse receipt recited the number of the bill of lading for the tank car in which it had been contained, amounting in total to 151 tank carloads. Not only was the presence of this oil in defendant's tanks attested by these nonnegotiable receipts issued in plaintiff's name, but also by a series of month-end statements, issued by defendant indicating that the oil was in the warehouse. Both the warehouse receipts and these month-end statements, based on defendant's books, are evidence that the oil was received by defendant at its tank warehouse in Bayonne, New Jersey. In the absence of any evidentiary facts showing that defendant did not receive the oil in the suit, its warehouse receipts, month-end statements and books of account are conclusive against defendant on this point. Mere suspicion that the oil was stolen before reaching defendant's tanks is not sufficient to overcome this documentary evidence. . . . The usual measure of damage, in event of non-delivery of goods by a bailee, is the market value on the date of the conversion . . . not the date when the bailor learns of the loss or presents his warehouse receipt and demands his merchandise. Where, as here, the date of the conversion has not been identified, the Appellate Division has held that the value should be fixed as of the date when the bailor received notice of the loss. This, we think, was error. The circumstances regarding the loss of bailed property are more likely to be known by the bailee than by the bailor, and, where the time and manner of the loss is unknown, it ought not lie in the power of the bailee to choose the date for determining market value by electing when to notify the bailor that the goods have disappeared and cannot be accounted for. The rule that the loss is to be measured as of the time of the conversion, when the conversion date is known, should not be reshaped to designate the date when the bailor is notified of the conversion if the conversion date is unknown. That would place the bailee in a better legal position by pleading ignorance of the circumstances of the loss than if he knew or revealed the circumstances. . . .

[I]t follows that the bailor should be awarded damages measured by the highest value of the property between the date when the bailment commenced and the date when the bailor has received notice that the property has been lost. . . .

On its appeal defendant (Field) contends that there is a triable issue respecting whether it exercised reasonable care as bailee of this oil. Defendant points to section 7-204 of the Uniform Commercial Code, in effect in New Jersey at the time, providing that a warehouseman is liable for damages for loss or injury to the goods "caused by his failure to exercise such care in regard to them as a reasonably careful man would exercise under like circumstances but unless otherwise agreed he is not liable for damages which could not have been avoided by the exercise of such care." Section 7-403 of the same statute provides that the bailee must deliver the goods to a person under the document unless and to the extent that the bailee established "damage to or delay, loss or destruction of the goods for which the bailee is not liable."

These sections of the Uniform Commercial Code appear not to have altered for present purposes the prior law . . . that a warehouseman shall not be liable for loss or injury to the goods which could not have been avoided by the exercise of reasonable care, and section 8 (General Business Law, former §95), like section 7-403 of the Uniform Commercial Code, stated that a warehouseman is liable for nondelivery of bailed goods "in the absence of some lawful excuse provided by this article." Citing these sections, the Appellate Division correctly stated . . . that a warehouseman "has the burden of explanation for any loss or disappearance of the property bailed. . . . It is not enough to assert that care was taken, describing the practices used, when the disappearance of the oil remains wholly unexplained." . . . In the opinion by the present Chief Judge the rule applicable here was stated in the form of a quotation from Claflin v. Meyer (75 N.Y. 260, 264):

> If he [the bailor] proves the demand upon the warehouseman and his refusal to deliver, these facts unexplained are treated by the courts as prima facie evidence of negligence; but if, either in the course of his proof or that of the defendant, it appears that the goods have been lost by theft, the evidence must show that the loss arose from the negligence of the warehouseman. . . .

The Appellate Division well said that it is self-contradictory for a warehouseman simultaneously to assert due care and total lack of knowledge of what happened, and that it would establish an unwise rule to place a bailee in better position to be excused if he knew less about the disappearance of the goods than if he knew more. That is the underlying reason for the time-honored law of New York and New Jersey requiring a warehouseman to make an explanation of injury or loss in the case of bailed merchandise, which has been continued and not abolished by the Uniform Commercial Code.

The other points raised on the appeal by defendant Field merit but passing mention. One is that plaintiff should be obliged to accept a proportionate share of the conglomerate found on hand in the tanks of these subsidiaries of Amexco. This consisted mostly of acid soap stock, fish oil and water. These mixed fluids were not the edible fully refined vegetable oil delivered to Field by plaintiff. An argument is made that the warehouse receipts showed plaintiff's refined vegetable oil to be fungible, and granted permission to mix it with similar oil owned by other depositors. From that it is said that a warehouseman need do no more than take the word of other customers concerning the nature of the fluids which are being placed in the tanks of the warehouseman, and that if it be soap acid or fish oil then that is plaintiff's misfortune. It is a sufficient answer to that contention that plaintiff is not required to acquit the warehouse in whole or in part by taking in return a commodity or blend of commodities of a different nature from that which was deposited. . . .

No one has ever discovered exactly what happened to the missing salad oil (which was the collateral for millions of dollars worth of loans). N. Miller, The Great Salad Oil Swindle (1965).

As this case indicates, a warehouse company that issues a warehouse receipt is liable to good faith holders even if the warehouse never received the goods. Read §7-203. It is also liable if the goods are incorrectly described. A warehouse is required to keep goods separate unless they are fungible. See §7-207. If the goods are fungible, a "buyer in the ordinary course of business" can purchase the goods and get good title even though there is an outstanding negotiable warehouse receipt (§7-205).

A bailee's duty of care is that which "a reasonably careful man would exercise under the circumstances." Read §7-204 and the following case.

Admiralty Island Fisheries, Inc. v. Millard Refrigerated Services, Inc.

United States District Court, Nebraska, 2007
2007 WL 4051649

LAURIE SMITH CAMP, District Judge.

This matter is before the Court on cross-motions for partial summary judgment. The Plaintiff National Fire Insurance of Hartford as subrogee of

Suram Trading Corporation filed a motion for partial summary judgment (Filing No. 67 reviving Filing No. 35), in which Admiralty Island Fisheries has joined. (Filing No. 68). The Defendant, Millard Refrigerated Services, Inc. ("Millard") has filed a motion for partial summary judgment against those Plaintiffs (Filing Nos. 70 and 72), and Plaintiffs Certain Underwriters at Lloyd's of London as subrogee of Icicle Seafoods, Inc., and Hartford Casualty Insurance Company, as subrogee of Global Fishing, Inc. (Filing Nos. 69 and 71) (hereafter the subrogees and subrogors will be referred to collectively as the "Plaintffs"). The cross-motions ask the Court to determine the legal effect of relevant limitation of liability clauses.

FACTUAL BACKGROUND

Millard operates cold storage warehouses throughout the country. Suram, Icicle, Global, and Admiralty have all stored seafood products in a Millard warehouse. It is undisputed that, as each truckload of seafood was delivered by the Plaintiffs to Millard warehouse, Millard issued a warehouse receipt. The warehouse receipts contain the parties' agreement regarding the storage of the seafood product.

Sometime in March 2006, Millard discovered that several pounds of seafood that were owned by the various Plaintiffs were missing. Millard conducted an internal investigation into the loss and determined that at least some of the seafood had been stolen by some of its employees. Millard ultimately terminated five of its employees for theft of seafood that was supposed be stored in the warehouse. The five employees admitted to stealing only small quantities of the seafood, which was a sufficient basis for terminating their employment. National Fire contends that Millard's former employees stole more than 94,000 pounds of seafood with a fair market value of $455,000. Millard contends that its liability for the loss is limited to 50 cents per pound, or $47,000. The issue presented on these cross-motions for partial summary judgment is whether the limitation of liability clause is enforceable, assuming that the former employees were responsible for the theft.

ANALYSIS

Consistent with the UCC, warehouse receipts may contain a limitation of liability provision that limits the warehouse operator's liability for the stored products in the case of loss or damage. Millard's warehouse receipts include a limitation of liability clause. The Plaintiffs seek a declaration from the Court that the limitation of liability clause contained on the back of the warehouse receipt is of no effect if the Plaintiffs succeed in demonstrating that Millard employees stole the seafood. The Defendant, on the other hand, asks the Court to conclude as a matter of law that the parties' contract permits Millard to limit its liability for the loss of the seafood to 50 cents per pound, regardless of whether the disappearance of the seafood is attributable to theft by the Millard employees.

THE WAREHOUSE RECEIPT

The front of the warehouse receipts in question contain the following provision, in all capital lettering:

Limitation of liablity: Unless the depositor declares a valuation higher than $.50 per pound or $12.00 per cubic foot for stored goods and such declared higher value is agreed to in writing by the warehouseman, the warehouse-man's liability for loss or damage thereto shall be expressly limited as specifically set forth in Section 10(e) of the standard contract terms on the reverse side hereof.

The front of the warehouse receipt also provides:

The goods listed hereon in apparent good order [sic], except as noted hereon (contents, condition and quality unknown) subject to all terms and conditions herein and on the reverse hereof. Such property to be delivered to the Depositor upon the payment of all storage, handling and other charges.

On the back of the receipt is Section 10(e), copied below in the same manner that it appears in the receipt, states:

IN THE EVENT OF LOSS, DAMAGE OR DESTRUCTION TO STORED GOODS FOR WHICH COMPANY IS LEGALLY LIABLE, STORER DECLARES THAT COMPANY'S LIABILITY FOR DAMAGES SHALL BE LIMITED TO THE LESSER OF THE FOLLOWING AMOUNTS: (1) THE ACTUAL COST TO DEPOSITOR OF REPLACING OR REPRODUCING THE DAMAGED GOOD TOGETHER WITH TRANSPORTATION COSTS TO THE WAREHOUSE, (2) THE FAIR MARKET VALUE OF THE GOODS ON THE DATE DEPOSITOR IS NOTIFIED OF LOSS, DAMAGE OR DESTRUCTION, (3) 50 TIMES THE MONTHLY STORAGE CHARGE APPLICABLE TO SUCH LOST, DAMAGED, OR DESTROYED GOODS OR (4) THE GREATER OF (I) $.50 PER POUND NET WEIGHT OF THE GOODS, EXCLUSIVE OF TARE, OR (II) $12.00 PER CUBIC FOOT, PROVIDED, HOWEVER, THAT WITHIN A REASONABLE TIME AFTER RECEIPT OF THIS WAREHOUSE RECEIPT, DEPOSITOR MAY, UPON WRITTEN REQUEST, INCREASE WAREHOUSEMAN'S LIABILITY ON PART OR ALL OF THE GOODS STORED UNDER THE WAREHOUSE RECEIPT, IN WHICH CASE AN INCREASED CHARGE WILL BE MADE BASED UPON SUCH INCREASED VALUATION; FURTHER PROVIDED THAT NO SUCH REQUEST SHALL BE VALID UNLESS MADE BEFORE

LOSS, DAMAGE OR DESTRUCTION TO ANY PORTION OF THE GOODS
STORED UNDER THIS WAREHOUSE RECEIPT HAS OCCURRED.

Section 10(f) states:

The limitation of liability referred to in paragraph (e) above shall be
Depositor's exclusive remedy against Warehouseman for any claim or cause
of action whatsoever relating to loss, damage and/or destruction of the
stored goods and shall apply to all claims including inventory shortage and
mysterious disappearance claims unless Depositor proves by affirmative evidence that Warehouseman converted the good to its own use. Depositor
waives any right to rely upon any presumption of conversion imposed by law.
In no event shall Depositor be entitled to incidental, special, punitive or
consequential damages.

(*See e.g.*, Filing No. 69, Ex. 5).

APPLICABLE PROVISIONS OF THE UNIFORM COMMERCIAL CODE

The Court finds that Uniform Commercial Code §7-204 applies to the
facts presented. Section 7-204, captioned *Duty of Care; Contractual Limitation
of Warehouse's Liability*, states:

(a) A warehouse is liable for damages for loss of or injury to the goods
caused by its failure to exercise care with regard to the goods that a reasonably careful person would exercise under similar circumstances. Unless otherwise agreed, the warehouse is not liable for damages that could not have
been avoided by the exercise of that care.

(b) Damages may be limited by a term in the warehouse receipt or
storage agreement limiting the amount of liability in case of loss or damage
beyond which the warehouse is not liable. *Such a limitation is not effective with
respect to the warehouse's liability for conversion to its own use.* On request of the
bailor in a record at the time of signing the storage agreement or within a
reasonable time after receipt of the warehouse receipt, the warehouse's liability may be increased on part or all of the goods covered by the storage
agreement or the warehouse receipt. In this event, increased rates may be
charged based on an increased valuation of the goods.

PLAINTIFFS' MOTION FOR PARTIAL SUMMARY JUDGMENT

Because a warehouse operator would not be liable at all absent a
failure of due care, a failure of due care by Millard must be established
before the enforcement of the limitation of liability clause even becomes an
issue. The Plaintiffs ask the Court to assume that they can prove their
seafood disappeared due to employee theft. The Court might assume, for
purposes of this motion, that Millard was negligent in hiring the former

employees without checking their backgrounds for criminal history or in failing to maintain security over the seafood after it was deposited at the warehouse. These assumptions relate to the threshold issue of Millard's lack of due care. For purposes of this motion only, the Court will assume that Millard was negligent in failing to prevent the former employees' theft of the Plaintiffs' property.

Under Nebraska law, conversion is "any unauthorized or wrongful act of dominion exerted over another's personal property which deprives the owner of his property permanently or for an indefinite period of time." Roth v. Farmers Mutual Insurance Company of Nebraska, 371 N.W.2d 289, 291 (Neb. 1985). Under this definition, there is no dispute that the former Millard employees committed an intentional conversion of the Plaintiffs' property. Assuming Millard's liability arising out ordinary negligence under Section 7-204(a), the limitation of liability provision applies according to Section 7-204(b), unless the warehouse operator's liability arises out of a conversion "for its own use." The Court agrees with the observation of the commentators that "conversion for it [sic] own use" as used in Section 7-204(a) must mean something more and different than simple conversion. See Comment Note No. 4, UCC §7-204 (2005) (explaining that "[c]onversion to its own use" is narrower than the idea of conversion generally" and disapproving "[c]ases such as Lipman v. Peterson, 575 P.2d 19 (Kan. 1978) holding to the contrary. . . .")

The limitation of liability provision applies in the presence of ordinary negligence unless there is proof that the former employees' theft, the conversion, was for the purpose of advancing Millard's interests. Enforcement of a limitation of liability clause is not a complete defense to liability, but it must be raised as would an affirmative defense because it benefits the defendant. For that reason, the Court concludes that the burden of proof should be on the warehouse operator to demonstrate that the conversion of the bailor's property was not for its own use. In reaching this legal conclusion, the Court acknowledges its rejection of Millard's attempt to place the burden on the Plaintiffs as stated in the warehouse receipts' paragraph 10(f). To place the burden of proof on the Plaintiffs, as bailors, would ignore the policy arguments that support the enforcement of limitation of liability provisions in commercial contracts.[4]

---

4. According to at least one commentator, there are good reasons to place the burden of proof on the warehouse operator. First, the warehouse operator is in the best position to explain the loss because the operator has taken control of the goods and has determined the manner in which they are stored. Second, placing the burden on the warehouse operator to show that it acted with due care will encourage warehouse operators to act with care and caution in the handling and storage of bailed goods and to maintain adequate tracking systems that will withstand judicial scrutiny. Third, placing the burden on operators will also have a beneficial effect on the industry because those warehouses that are unable to establish that their storage practices are reasonable will incur increased operating costs, eventually forcing poorly-run facilities out of business. Last, placing the burden on the

Millard has come forward with evidence that the conversion was not for its own use. Millard's general manager, Michael McTier, conducted an investigation into the Plaintiffs' losses. As a result of the investigation, five employees were fired for theft. McTier believes, based on the investigation, that all losses were caused by the former employees' theft. (Filing No. 79, McTier Dep. 159). At least one of the former employees has stated that the seafood was sold to a third-party. McTier has testified that Millard did not benefit in any way from the theft.

The Plaintiffs have not come forward with any evidence to create a genuine issue of material fact regarding whether the conversion — the theft — was for Millard's own use. Plaintiffs argue that the conversion was for Millard's own purposes because it 1) was committed within the authorized space and time of the employees' employment, 2) was committed while they were performing duties for which they were hired, and 3) "was actuated, at least in part, by a purpose to serve the master [Millard]." (Filing No. 82, p. 12). The crux of Plaintiffs' argument is that Millard's interests were furthered by the conversion because Millard was paying the former employees to work while they were also stealing; the former employees used Millard's equipment, including pallets, forklifts, and trucks, to accomplish the theft; and the former employees conducted the theft during hours when they were "also" working. I do not agree that these facts are evidence that the conversion was to Millard's own use. The former employees' abuse of their employment position does not automatically transform their conversion to a conversion for Millard's own use. Absent undisputed facts that the conversion was for Millard's own use, the Court concludes that the Plaintiff's motion for partial summary judgment is denied.

MILLARD'S MOTION FOR PARTIAL SUMMARY JUDGMENT

Millard also moves for partial summary judgment asking the Court to confirm the enforceability of the limitation of liability clauses in its warehouse receipts. Because there are genuine issues related to the degree of Millard's negligence, Millard's motion will be denied. The Court, assuming ordinary negligence on the part of Millard, has found that the Plaintiffs have failed to come forward with evidence to create a genuine issue regarding whether the former employees stole the seafood to further Millard's own interests. There is no evidence that the conversion was to Millard's own use. It would seem to follow that the limitation of liability

---

warehouses will give the operators incentive to procure insurance on all bailed goods entrusted to them which the operators can procure, presumably at a lower cost than would be incurred if each bailor had to procure its own insurance. "A Warehouse's Burden of Proof," Ralph Anzivino, *UCC Law Journal* (Spring 2004).

clause is enforceable to limit the damages that Millard may owe to the Plaintiffs.

This case does not present a relationship involving a monopoly or parties of unequal bargaining power that might make the contract unenforceable. Where ordinary commercial relationships exist, the Eighth Circuit Court has upheld "the strong public policies of recognizing parties' liberty to contract and enforcing contracts as written." Sander v. Alexander Richardson Investments, 334 F.3d 712, 719 (8th Cir. 2003). The Plaintiffs had an opportunity to negotiate for a higher price per pound to be paid under the limitation of liability clause in the event of loss, but Plaintiffs did not. As a result, they were not obligated to pay the higher storage costs that likely would have come with a limitation of liability clause that was more advantageous to them. Rather, the parties agreed that the risk of loss greater than 50 cents per pound would be borne by the Plaintiffs.

However, in opposition to Millard's motion, the Plaintiffs argue that the limitation of liability clause should not be enforced as against public policy. The Plaintiffs contend that it will show at trial that Millard acted with gross negligence in failing to prevent the theft. If the Plaintiffs are able to demonstrate at trial that the failure of due care on the part of Millard constitutes gross negligence, not just ordinary negligence, then enforcement of the limitation of liability clause may be contrary to public policy. *See* New Light Company, Inc. v. Wells Fargo Alarm Services, 525 N.W.2d 25, (Neb. 1994) (holding that exculpatory clause in parties' agreement was void as against public policy to the extent that it purported to relieve fire alarm company from liability for its own gross negligence or willful and wanton misconduct). "Whether a particular exculpatory clause in a contractual agreement violates public policy depends upon the facts and circumstances of the agreement and the parties involved." *Id.* (noting that the greater the risk to human life and property, the stronger the argument in favor of voiding attempts by a party to insulate itself from damages caused by that party's gross negligence or willful and wanton misconduct.) "Gross negligence" has been defined as:

> [G]reat and excessive negligence; that is, negligence in a very high degree. It indicates the absence of slight care in the performance of a duty. . . . Willful and wanton misconduct exists where a defendant had actual knowledge that because of its actions, a danger existed to the plaintiff and the defendant intentionally failed to act to prevent a harm that was reasonably likely to result.

Id. at 30. Both the Plaintiffs and Millard have offered evidence relative to the degree of care exercised by Millard in connection with the seafood. There is some evidence that Millard knew of the thefts or should have known of them several months before Millard did anything about it.

Because there are genuine issues of fact regarding the reasonableness of the security steps Millard took and did not take, whether Millard's conduct rises to the level of gross negligence is an issue for the jury. Accordingly, Millard's motion for partial summary judgment will also be denied.

IT IS ORDERED:

1. The Plaintiffs' Motions for Partial Summary Judgment . . . are denied; and

2. The Defendant's Motions for Partial Summary Judgment as to the Plaintiffs . . . are denied.

QUESTIONS

1. Would the court have reached the same result if the limitation was buried in the fine print on the receipt? See Keefe v. Bekins Van & Storage Co., 540 P.2d 1132, 17 U.C.C. Rep. Serv. 1286 (Colo. App. 1975) (limitation effective even though not called to customer's attention); Sanfisket Inc. v. Atlantic Cold Storage Corp., 347 So. 2d 647, 21 U.C.C. Rep. Serv. 1155 (Fla. Dist. App. 1977) (inconspicuous limitation held effective); Jasphy v. Osinsky, 834 A.2d 426, 51 U.C.C. Rep. Serv. 2d 1215 (N.J. Super. 2003) (limitation of liability to $1 held unconscionable).

2. Could the bailee depend on a clause in the receipt that completely disclaimed liability for its own negligence? See §1-302; Blue Valley Co-op. v. National Farmers Organization, 600 N.W.2d 786, 39 U.C.C. Rep. Serv. 2d 633 (Neb. 1999) (disclaimer in crop storage); Gonzalez v. A-1 Self Storage, Inc., 795 A.2d 885, 411 U.C.C. Rep. Serv. 2d 1119 (N.J. Super. 2000) (disclaimer in consumer goods storage).

C. Bailee's Lien

All bailees (including warehousemen and carriers) are given a statutory lien in the bailed goods to the extent of the charges for storage and expenses incident to the bailment contract (expenses necessary to preserve the goods, for instance). For warehouses, this lien is described in §§7-209 and 7-210; for carriers, §§7-307 and 7-308. These bailee's liens are possessory liens only; the bailee loses its lien if it voluntarily surrenders the goods (or wrongfully refuses to surrender them). See Darby v. Baltimore & Ohio Ry. Co., 259 Md. 493, 270 A.2d 652, 8 U.C.C. Rep. Serv. 375 (1970). If the bailor does not pay the bailee's charges, the latter may foreclose its lien by public or private sale (the rules of which are described in the above-named sections). The Code primarily requires the foreclosure sale to be held in a "commercially reasonable manner." For a case exploring the details of a bailee lien foreclosure on stored household goods, see Bradford v. Muinzer, 498 F. Supp. 1384, 29 U.C.C. Rep. Serv. 1597 (N.D. Ill. 1980).

D. Delivery Orders

You will remember that if the goods are stored under a nonnegotiable warehouse receipt, the bailee can deliver the goods without requiring surrender of the warehouse receipt. Many nonnegotiable warehouse forms state that delivery will be made "on *detached written* authority *without* the return of this receipt." When the owner (bailor) wants the order delivered, the owner simply sends a letter (called a *delivery order*) to the bailee, explaining to whom the goods are to be delivered.

Storing goods in bulk under a nonnegotiable warehouse receipt and then breaking them up into smaller units by separate delivery orders is a convenient way to merchandise commodities. The delivery orders, which need take no particular form, can be negotiable or nonnegotiable. A delivery order is negotiable if it directs the bailee to deliver the goods to someone, "or his order," or "to bearer"; otherwise, it is nonnegotiable. In many ways a delivery order is directly analogous to an Article 3 draft, only it is an order to deliver goods instead of to pay money. Like a draft, it imposes no liability on the bailee until the bailee *accepts* the order (no liability to the holder of the delivery order, that is; the bailee who refuses to accept a delivery order may be in breach of the bailment contract and, if so, is liable to the bailor). See §7-502(a)(4), especially the last sentence.

All of this ties in with how a seller of bailed goods makes *tender* to the buyer under Article 2 of the Code. Read §§2-509(2) and 2-503(4) carefully. Where a *negotiable* document of title is involved, both §§2-509(2) and 2-503(4)(a) make it clear that the risk of loss shifts to the buyer on delivery of the document if the goods conform to the contract (if not, §2-510 applies). However, these sections do *not* apply to negotiable delivery orders, which are lumped in with the rules governing nonnegotiable documents in §§2-509(2)(c) and 2-503(4)(b) ("record directing the bailee to deliver" means a delivery order). Where no documents are involved (say, a pet dog is boarded at a kennel and then sold), §2-509(2)(b) passes the risk of loss to the buyer on the bailee's acknowledgment of the buyer's right to possession. See Whately v. Tetrault, 29 Mass. App. Dec. 112, 5 U.C.C. Rep. Serv. 838 (1964).

PROBLEM 89

Fred Bandanna, a farmer, took two truckloads of his cotton to Rural Warehouse for storage. The first truckload of 80 bales he stored under a negotiable warehouse receipt issued by Rural. For the second truckload of 80 bales, he obtained a nonnegotiable warehouse receipt. Fred took the documents to the offices of Harold Fastbuck, a commodity merchant. Harold bought both the negotiable receipt covering the first truckload and the nonnegotiable receipt covering the second truckload of cotton from Fred. Harold asked, however, that Fred divide the 80 bales represented by the nonnegotiable receipt into two equal lots so that Harold could resell them more easily. Fred sat down and wrote out two delivery orders addressed to Rural, each requiring the warehouse to turn over 40 bales to "Harold Fastbuck or order." As soon as Fred left his office, Harold sold one of the delivery orders to another commodity merchant, Sue Fourthparty. He endorsed on the back of the delivery order "Deliver to Sue Fourthparty or order, (signed) Harold Fastbuck." Sue phoned Rural Warehouse and said that she was the owner of 40 bales of the Fred Bandanna cotton under a delivery order. The warehouse agent agreed that Sue could pick up the bales the next day. That night lightning struck the warehouse, and all the cotton burned. Who took the risk of loss as to each segment of the cotton? See §§2-509(2), 2-503(4)(b), and 7-502(a)(4).

E.   Terminology: The Issuer

Under the Code, the person primarily liable on a document of title is the *issuer* of the document. Since the *bailee* (warehouse or carrier) is almost always the person who *issues* (creates) the document, there is a temptation to think of *issuer* as synonymous with *bailee*. This would be correct except for the fact that the issuer of a delivery order (which *is* a document of title according to §1-201(16)) is the *bailor*. Read §§7-102(a)(5) and 7-102(a)(8). This fact will become important later on when we get to talking about *due negotiation* and the duties of the issuer. Question: who was (were) the issuer(s) in Problem 89?

II.   BILLS OF LADING

Just as warehouses issue negotiable or nonnegotiable receipts for bailed goods, carriers (such as railroads, airlines, ocean liners, and trucking firms) issue similar documents on the receipt of goods for transportation across the country or the world. These documents, called *bills of lading*, may be negotiable or nonnegotiable (depending on whether order or bearer language is used). As with warehouse receipts, the bill of lading is, simultaneously, a receipt for the goods, a contract of transportation, and tangible evidence of ownership of the bailed goods.

A. *Federal Law*

Article 7 of the Code covers only intrastate shipments. If the goods are to cross state lines, the documents issued by the carrier are governed by the Federal Bills of Lading Act (the Pomerene Act of 1916), 49 U.S.C. §81 et seq. If the goods are to cross water, they will be governed by a host of federal statutes including the Shipping Act, 46 U.S.C. §801 et seq.; the Intercoastal Shipping Act, 46 U.S.C. §843 et seq.; and (most important) the Carriage of Goods by Sea Act, 46 U.S.C. §1300 et seq. (For those of you who will have commercial bailees as clients, note at this point that all interstate carriers and warehouses are subject to federal regulation of their trade. The Federal Aviation Administration, for example, formulates rules and regulations for the airlines involved in interstate and foreign air carriage. The Department of Agriculture regulates warehouses storing agricultural products. See the United States Warehouse Act, 7 U.S.C. §241 et seq. There will also be special state statutes and regulations that deal with warehouses and carriers.)

Fortunately, the basic law set out in the Federal Bills of Lading Act is more or less the same as that in Article 7, and unless the wording is particularly crucial, language of the federal act will not be mentioned. What is important is that you remember that Article 7 does *not* apply (except by analogy) to any bill of lading issued for goods that are to leave the state. For such a bill you need to refer to the exact language of the relevant federal statutes.

B. *The Basic Idea*

Do not confuse *shipper* with *carrier* or *issuer*. The *shipper* is the original owner (bailor) of the goods who turns them over to the carrier for transportation. The *carrier* then issues a bill of lading (thus becoming an *issuer*) to the shipper. If the bill is negotiable, the carrier (issuer) will not turn over the goods at the destination until the negotiable bill of lading is surrendered (§7-403(c) applies to carriers as well as warehouses). This means that the shipper must send the bill of lading to the person who is to receive the goods (normally the buyer) before the latter can get possession of the goods. Often the shipper will not surrender the bill of lading to the buyer until the latter has paid for the goods (or has *accepted* a draft drawn on it; see the discussion below); this is called requiring *payment against documents*. As soon as the buyer pays the seller (or seller's agent), the buyer gets possession of the negotiable bill of lading and can claim the goods from the carrier. A carrier that delivers the goods to the buyer without demanding surrender of an outstanding negotiable bill of lading has converted the goods and is liable to the holder of the negotiable bill. See BII Finance Co.

v. U-States Forwarding Serv. Corp., 115 Cal. Rptr. 2d 312, 46 U.C.C. Rep. Serv. 2d 827 (Cal. App. 2002). Review §7-403(3), and read §§7-404 and 7-601(2).

C.   Form

1.   Negotiable

The word *consign* means to send or hand over goods to another. A negotiable bill of lading is called an order bill of lading because the goods are consigned to the "order of _____."

In bill of lading terminology, the goods are entrusted to the carrier by the *consignor* (the shipper) for delivery to the *consignee* (the person to whom the goods will belong at the end of their journey, normally the buyer). The consignee is *not* the carrier-bailee. If Sam Seller in Toledo sells goods to Betty Buyer in Atlanta via the Monopoly Railroad, using a negotiable bill of lading issued by the railroad, then Sam is the consignor, Betty is the consignee, and the Monopoly Railroad is the carrier-issuer (the agent of the consignor who carries out the consignment contract). Order (negotiable) bills of lading are yellow in color, as required by Interstate Commerce Commission (ICC) regulations.

An order bill states that the goods have been received in apparent good order, except as otherwise indicated, and states the contract of transportation (including rates), incorporating all the fine print on the back of the contract. On the front is space for describing the goods covered by the document and blanks to be filled in showing, among other things,

(1) shipper's (consignor's) name and address,
(2) to whose order the goods are consigned,
(3) the destination of the goods, and
(4) whom the carrier is to notify when the goods arrive (normally the buyer).

A negotiable bill also contains sentences like this one in large print on the front: "Surrender of this original order bill of lading properly indorsed is required prior to the delivery of the property. Inspection of such property will not be permitted by anyone prior to delivery unless permission is indorsed hereon or given in writing by the consignor." (As to inspection rights, see note §2-513(3), which agrees with this language.)

2. Nonnegotiable

A nonnegotiable bill of lading is called a *straight* bill of lading because the goods are delivered straight to the consignee whether or not the nonnegotiable bill is surrendered. Straight bills are to be printed on white paper by ICC regulation. The carrier will take the goods to their destination, notify the consignee of their arrival, and await instructions as to whom the goods are to be delivered.

Frequently the consignor consigns the goods to *itself*, thereby making the consignor and the consignee the same entity. This happens on negotiable as well as nonnegotiable bills. The reason that this is often done is to make it clear that the consignor is at all times the owner of the goods, and for that reason it is called a "shipment under reservation" (meaning a reservation of *title*). When the buyer pays for them, the seller will indorse a negotiable bill over to the buyer or, if a nonnegotiable bill is used, will issue a *delivery order* (the same as with warehouse receipts) to the carrier telling it to deliver the goods to the buyer. In effect, consigning the goods to itself gives the seller a security interest in the goods until the purchase price is paid. The Code recognizes that the *equitable* interest is in the buyer even though the legal title is in the seller. Read §2-505 carefully.

PROBLEM 90

Homer Widget, of South Bend, Indiana, the inventor of the three-dimensional widget, contracted to sell 5,000 widgets to Ned's Novelty Store in Evansville, Indiana. Homer delivered the goods to the Overnight Trucking Company, consigning the goods to himself but writing "Notify Ned's Novelty Store on arrival" on the straight bill of lading. (The carrier keeps a duplicate copy of the bill of lading with the goods; the original is, of course, turned over to the consignor.) Homer mailed the original bill to his cousin Wilbur Widget, who lived in Evansville. Along with the bill he sent a delivery order signed by himself and addressed to the trucking company telling the company to deliver the goods to Ned's Novelty Store. Homer's cover letter to his cousin stated that Wilbur should take the delivery order down to Ned at the store and turn it over to Ned only if Ned paid Wilbur cash for the goods. Wilbur did present the delivery order as Homer directed, but Ned was short on funds and could not pay. Wilbur, confused, mailed all the documents back to Homer with a letter saying Ned would not pay. Meanwhile, the goods arrived at Evansville, and John ("Slow") Burly, the company's truck driver, had to decide what to do with the widgets. Reading the bill of lading, he discovered that the consignee lived in South Bend. By checking the phone book, he learned that Homer Widget had no address in Evansville. Then the truck driver noticed that he was to notify Ned's Novelty Store, which did have an Evansville address, so he delivered the widgets to Ned.

(a) Was the carrier's delivery to Ned improper? Read §7-303 carefully; see Mistletoe Express Serv. v. Sanchez, 721 S.W.2d 418, 2 U.C.C. Rep. Serv. 2d 1648 (Tex. App. 1986).

(b) If the widgets were destroyed in an auto accident prior to Ned's refusal to pay, who would have had the risk of loss if the contract was "F.O.B. truck South Bend"? See §2-509(1). See also Sternheim v. Silver Bell of Roslyn, Inc., 66 Misc. 726, 321 N.Y.S.2d 965, 9 U.C.C. Rep. Serv. 465 (Cty. Ct. 1971). As to the carrier's duty of care, read §7-309(1).

(c) Would the result with regard to the risk of loss or proper delivery change if the bill of lading had been an order bill? See §§7-403(c), 2-509.

PROBLEM 91

Blue Skies Air Lines was about to deliver a shipment of frozen fish to the buyer to whom it was consigned under a straight bill issued by the airline when the phone rang. The seller-consignor was on the phone, and she forbade the delivery, telling Blue Skies to return the fish to her, since she had learned that the "buyer is a bum." If Blue Skies returns the goods to the seller, is it risking liability to the buyer? See §§7-303, 2-505, 2-705 (plus Official Comment 1 to §2-705); Clock v. Missouri-Texas R.R., 407 F. Supp. 448, 19 U.C.C. Rep. Serv. 224 (E.D. Mo. 1976).

PROBLEM 92

Jane Pitchfork, a southern Iowa farmer, had an excellent pumpkin crop (1,700 pumpkins) this year. She stored 1,000 pumpkins with the Pumpkin Warehouse, Inc., located in Des Moines, taking a negotiable warehouse receipt for 500 and a nonnegotiable receipt for the other 500. She also contracted to sell 700 other pumpkins to Peter P. Pumpkineater, who lived in Sioux City, Iowa. The terms of the contract required her to ship Pumpkineater 700 stemless pumpkins "F.O.B. railroad car Fort Madison, Iowa." Jane was too lazy to cut off the stems, but she thought Pumpkineater really would not care, so she loaded 700 pumpkins on board an Iowa Pacific Railroad car at Fort Madison, Iowa. She received a negotiable bill of lading consigned to her own order and made a proper contract for carriage of the pumpkins to Sioux City. She sold the 1,000 warehouse pumpkins to Mom's Pies, Inc., of Cedar Rapids. She indorsed the negotiable warehouse receipt over to Mom's Pies for the first 500 stored pumpkins and gave them a nonnegotiable delivery order for the other 500 stored pumpkins. Before Mom's Pies could contact the warehouse, the Iowa Pacific Railroad train carrying the pumpkins passed through Des Moines and derailed (due to the negligence of the train's engineer). The train ran off the track and went through the center of the Pumpkin Warehouse, destroying all 1,700 pumpkins. Jane Pitchfork, a dejected woman, comes to you. The railroad is, of course, going to be liable to whoever took the risk of loss as to the pumpkins. Advise Jane as to where the risk of loss is placed for each of the pumpkin transactions. See §§2-503, 2-509, 2-510, 2-601, 2-319.

D.   Misdescription

Consider this problem. The bill of lading states that the boxcar contains 42 cartons of widgets. When the goods are delivered to buyer, there are only 32 cartons, or the cartons contain peanuts, or the boxcar (which was loaded and sealed by the shipper) is empty. Is the carrier liable for wrong information (misdescription) on the bill of lading if the shipper furnished the carrier with the information? The problem frequently comes up because carriers (particularly railroads) often permit the shipper to load the goods itself and then to fill out the descriptive section of the bill of lading, which the carrier then signs. Carriers defend this practice by saying that as a practical matter it is impossible for the carrier's agents to police the shipper's loading or to inventory the goods loaded. To guard against possible liability for resulting misdescription, the carrier normally states SHIPPER'S WEIGHT, LOAD, AND COUNT on the bill of lading in order to indicate that the carrier makes no warranties as to these matters. Is this language effective to eliminate the carrier's liability for misdescription? Study §7-301.

The corresponding federal law is the Federal Bills of Lading Act §22, which follows. This section has been much litigated:

> If a bill of lading has been issued by a carrier or on his behalf by an agent or employee the scope of whose actual or apparent authority includes the receiving of goods and issuing bills of lading therefor for transportation in commerce among several States and with foreign nations, the carrier shall be liable to (a) the owner of goods covered by a straight bill subject to existing right of stoppage in transit or (b) the holder of an order bill, who has given value in good faith relying upon the description therein of the goods, or upon the shipment being made upon the date therein shown, for damages caused by the nonreceipt by the carrier of all or part of the goods upon or prior to the date therein shown, or their failure to correspond with the description thereof in the bill at the time of its issue.

GAC Commercial Corp. v. Wilson

United States District Court, Southern District of New York, 1967
271 F. Supp. 242, 4 U.C.C. Rep. Serv. 772

BRYAN, J.

[The St. Lawrence Pulp & Paper Corp. borrowed money from plaintiff G.A.C., which took as collateral straight bills of lading, both interstate and intrastate, issued by defendant Norwood & St. Law. Railroad. The bills of lading indicated that St. Lawrence, as consignor, had shipped various amounts of paper products to different consignees and the plaintiff took the bills with the understanding that the goods had not yet been delivered. Plaintiff loaned St. Lawrence $254,173.42 against the bills of lading, but St. Lawrence went bankrupt anyway. To the great surprise of everyone but some of St. Lawrence's employees, the railroad cars proved to be empty. Plaintiff brought this action against St. Lawrence's officers and the Norwood Railroad.]

The method by which the alleged fraudulent scheme was carried out appears for purposes of this motion to be as follows: the bankrupt St. Lawrence, as part of its facilities in Norfolk, New York, maintained a railroad siding connected with the lines of defendant carrier which had a freight office approximately 1/8th of a mile from the siding. St. Lawrence was permitted to load freight at its spur track in preparation for shipments on defendant's line. The railroad cars were sealed by St. Lawrence with seals provided by the railroad. St. Lawrence also prepared the bills of lading on blanks furnished in quadruplicate by defendant Norwood. The bills thus prepared were then presented to Norwood's agent who signed the original and one copy without inspecting the contents of the cars. No notation such as "contents of packages unknown" or "shipper's weight, load and count" was written on the bills. The signed copies were returned to St. Lawrence and forwarded with the invoices to G.A.C. which made advances on the goods described, which, as it turned out, had not been shipped.

Since sixty of the bills of lading were issued by a common carrier for the transportation of goods in interstate commerce, the issues as to these bills are controlled by the provisions of the Federal Bills of Lading Act, 49 U.S.C. §81. This statute stands as "a clear expression of the determination of Congress to take the whole subject matter of such bills of lading within its control." . . .

Prior to the passage of the Federal Bills of Lading Act "the United States courts held that a carrier was not liable for the act of its agent in issuing a bill of lading for goods where no goods had in fact been received." Josephy v. Panhandle & S.F. Ry., 235 N.Y. 306, 310, 139 N.E. 277, 278 (1923); see, e.g., Clark v. Clyde S.S. Co., 148 F. 243 (S.D.N.Y. 1906). The liability of carriers for acts of their agents was expanded, but not drastically, by the passage of the federal legislation which draws a sharp distinction between order bills of lading and straight bills where in fact the goods are never received for shipment by the carrier. Under §22 of the Act, 49 U.S.C. §102, "[i]f a bill of lading has been issued by a carrier or on his behalf by an agent or employee . . . , the carrier shall be liable to . . . the holder of an order bill, who has given value in good faith, relying upon the description therein of the goods, . . . for damages caused by the nonreceipt by the carrier of all or part of the goods upon or prior to the date therein shown." However, the liability of the carrier for nonreceipt extends only to "the owner of goods covered by a straight bill," provided, of course, he also gives value in good faith in reliance upon the description of goods contained in the bill. See Strohmeyer & Arpe Co. v. American Line S.S. Corp., 97 F.2d 360, 362 (2d Cir. 1938).

It is clear that a party in the position of Norwood is not included within the narrow category of those liable on a straight bill under the federal legislation. In the first place there is no question that the straight bills of lading here involved are non-negotiable. [Citations omitted.] As a consequence plaintiff G.A.C., as apparent transferee of bills and invoices representing accounts receivable under the agreement with St. Lawrence, upon notification to the carrier of the transfer, could only "become the direct obligee of whatever obligations the carrier owed to the transferor of the bill immediately before the notification." 49 U.S.C. §112; see id. §109. Norwood obviously owed St. Lawrence nothing because no goods in fact were received. There was therefore no outstanding obligation to G.A.C. . . .

By no stretch of the imagination does G.A.C. qualify as an "owner of goods covered by a straight bill" who can sue the carrier under §22 of the Federal Bills of Lading Act, 39 U.S.C. §102, for representing that goods in fact had been received. The reason for this is that it is completely illusory to attempt to assign an "owner" to non-existent goods. R. Braucher, Documents of Title 23 (1958); 2 S. Williston, Sales §419a, at 576-77 (rev. ed. 1948). While the consignee is generally deemed to have title to goods shipped under a straight bill of lading, see George F. Hinrichs, Inc. v. Standard Trust & Sav. Bank, 279 F. 382, 386 (2d Cir. 1922), even he cannot sue the carrier for representing in a straight bill that non-existent goods had in fact been received. Martin Jessee Motors v. Reading Co., 87 F. Supp. 318 (E.D. Pa.), *aff'd*, 181 F.2d 766 (3d Cir. 1950). The rationale applied in *Martin Jessee Motors*—that the consignee can prevail against the carrier "only by proving its title to specific property," 181 F.2d at 767—applies a fortiori to bar the claim of G.A.C. Plaintiff's interest in the "aggregate face value of the accounts receivable pledged as security" under no conceivable reading of the statute can be deemed an "[ownership] of goods covered by a straight bill." G.A.C. is not one of the favored few who can recover under the Federal Bills of Lading Act. . . .

Plaintiff G.A.C. fares no better with respect to the two bills of lading representing intrastate shipments in New York. . . . Although the awkward term "owner" in 49 U.S.C. §102 has been replaced by the word "consignee" in the Uniform Commercial Code §7-301 . . . the change is immaterial for purposes of this case. Plaintiff, perhaps an assignee, transferee or pledgee of the non-negotiable bills, though it claims not to be, is certainly not a "consignee," which is the only party protected. 2 Anderson, Uniform Commercial Code 261 n.9 (1961); see R. Braucher, Documents of Title 23-24 (1958). Contrast U.C.C. §7-203. Thus, as with the sixty interstate bills, G.A.C. cannot successfully sue on the two intrastate bills. . . .

It is true that the result dictated by the federal legislation may lead to some inequities. A straight bill under the Federal Bills of Lading Act is obviously not a good security risk. Casenote, 63 Harv. L. Rev. 1439, 1440 (1950). The fraud of the shipper by failing to deliver goods to the carrier can result, as it did here, in misleading statements on the bills of lading, which operate to the detriment of banks and other commercial financers making advances on the basis of the bills. See Oliver Straw Goods Corp. v. Osaka Shosen Kaisha, 27 F.2d 129, 134 (2d Cir. 1928) (A. Hand, J.). Moreover, the carrier can readily prevent such a situation from arising by inserting "in the bill of lading the words, 'Shipper's weight, load, and count,' or other words of like purport" to "indicate that the goods were loaded by the shipper and the description of them made by him." 49 U.S.C. §101.

But the overriding policy considerations in the Act look the other way on the issue of liability. First, "[t]here is nothing in the statute to indicate that the mere omission of the words 'Shipper's weight, load, and count' in and of itself makes the carrier liable for damages to goods improperly loaded. The omission of the statutory words merely serves to shift upon the carrier the burden of proving that the goods were improperly loaded by the shipper, and that the damage ensued from that cause." (D.N.J. 1951); see UCC §7-301(4).[5] According to the allegations the true culprits in this case were the shipper and its agents; there is no reason to saddle defendant Norwood with liability simply because it did not insert the "Shipper's weight, load, and count" language in the bills. In addition, practicality demands loading arrangements such as those here, where the shipper places his goods aboard and seals the railroad car which the carrier has provided. Section 21 of the Act, 4 U.S.C. §101, anticipates that shippers are expected to do much of the counting and loading on their own sidings or spur tracks. The rapid flow of commerce might well be hindered if the carrier in every instance were charged with ascertaining whether in fact there were goods behind every one of its straight bills.

Moreover, denying security value to a straight bill of lading does not work a hardship upon banks and other commercial institutions. G.A.C., as a knowledgeable lender, is fully aware of the risks inherent in straight bills,

5. Now §7-301(d) — EDS.

and could well have required order bills to protect itself. See Chicago & Northwestern Ry. v. Stevens Natl. Bank, 75 F.2d 398 (8th Cir. 1935). It nevertheless chose to rely upon straight bills to lend money to the now bankrupt St. Lawrence at a profitable rate of interest. Wiser now, G.A.C. seeks to shift its loss to Norwood, an undoubtedly solvent defendant. The Federal Bills of Lading Act protects against this type of hindsight by requiring the lender to accept this kind of security subject to the defenses between the carrier and the shipper.

The motion of defendant Norwood for Judgment on the pleadings treated as a motion for summary judgment is granted.

It is so ordered.

Read §7-301.

In the *GAC* case, which involves a straight bill of lading, §22 of the Federal Bills of Lading Act (FBLA) does not protect GAC because there are no goods, and hence there can be no owner. Professor Robert Riegert argues that the protection given owners of straight bills by the FBLA is thus illusory and that Congress did not intend the *GAC* result. See Riegert, Rights of a Transferee of Document of Title Who Is Not Holder by Due Negotiation, 9 Cumb. L. Rev. 27 (1978). The UCC in §7-301 gives protection on a straight bill to the consignee. Is the GAC court right in saying that plaintiff is not protected by §7-301? See §7-102(a)(3).

Both the FBLA and §7-301 protect holders by due negotiation of order bills. Both acts also allow the carrier to disclaim liability under certain circumstances. For a case involving an order bill where the disclaimer did not work, see Chicago & Nw. Ry. Co. v. Stephens Natl. Bank of Fremont, 75 F.2d 398 (8th Cir. 1935). Liability for nonreceipt or misdescription under bills of lading, either negotiable or nonnegotiable, is a tricky subject. See R. Riegert & R. Braucher, Documents of Title 33-41 (3d ed. 1978).

PROBLEM 93

Harry Thief went to the offices of Monopoly Railroad to see his old prison cellmate, Phillip ("Forger") Copy. Copy, under an assumed name, was currently employed by Monopoly as chief shipping clerk. Harry asked Phillip to make out some phony negotiable bills of lading representing nonexistent shipments by Harry to a buyer in California. Harry wanted to sell the bills to a bank and split the money with Phillip. Phillip made out the bills, which Harry discounted at the Octopus National Bank, and the two of them left town. When the bank sued the railroad, the latter defended on the grounds that the phony bills contain the words "Shipper's weight, load, and count." Is this defense good? See §7-301 and its Official Comment 3; Gleason v.

Seaboard Air Line Ry. Co., 278 U.S. 349 (1929); cf. Societe Generale v. Federal Ins. Co., 856 F.2d 461, 6 U.C.C. Rep. Serv. 2d 1236 (2d Cir. 1988).

III. DUE NEGOTIATION

A. The Basic Concept

The word *negotiable* in our law always means that if a piece of paper is in the proper form (a typical requirement is that it be made out either to *bearer* or to the *order* of a named individual), is transferred in the proper manner, and reaches the hands of a bona fide purchaser (BFP) who has no knowledge of problems with the paper, then the BFP may enforce the paper as written and does not take subject to the usual claims or defenses. In Article 3 of the Uniform Commercial Code, the BFP who gets these extraordinary rights is called a *holder in due course*. In Article 7, the BFP is given the jaw-breaking designation of a "holder to whom a negotiable document of title has been duly negotiated" (§7-502). Note well that the whole concept only applies to *negotiable* documents and hence excludes nonnegotiable warehouse receipts and straight bills of lading. Holders of such documents get no special rights (§7-504).

Negotiation of a negotiable document of title (whether warehouse receipt, bill of lading, or delivery order) is accomplished by indorsement and delivery under rules that are virtually interchangeable with the rules for the negotiation of Article 3 drafts and notes: §§7-501(a), 7-501(b) (providing for negotiation of electronic documents of title), 7-501(c) ("Indorsement of a nonnegotiable document of title neither makes it negotiable nor adds to the transferee's rights" (emphasis added)), §7-501(d).

A person cannot become a §7-502 holder until the document has been *duly negotiated*. Due negotiation is a term of art. It is defined in §7-501(a)(5) and (b)(3), which should be read carefully at this point.

Cleveland v. McNabb

United States District Court, Western District of Tennessee, 1970
312 F. Supp. 155, 7 U.C.C. Rep. Serv. 1226

BROWN, C.J.
The plaintiffs here, Dr. W.B. Cleveland and his wife, Katherine Cleveland, are owners of lands situated in Fayette County, Tennessee. On January 17, 1967, these plaintiffs entered into a written lease with the

defendant Jack McNabb which lease provided that, for a period of five years, the tenant McNabb would pay the landlord an annual rental amounting to fifty dollars per acre for all acreage allotted to cotton by the government and ten dollars per acre for all acreage actually planted in soybeans. (This lease is attached to the Amended and Supplemental Complaint as Exhibit A). In this action the plaintiffs sue the defendant McNabb for rent allegedly due and owing from the 1968 crop year. Further, the plaintiffs sue the defendants TFC Marketing Service, Inc., John S. Wilder and W.W. Wilder, individually and as partners doing business as Longtown Supply Company, the Commodity Credit Corporation and the United States of America to enforce landlord's liens for the value of purchased crops to the extent that such liens are necessary to satisfy any unpaid rent. It is undisputed that each of this group of defendants received crops raised by the defendant McNabb on the plaintiffs' lands. (The United States is named as a defendant because the Commodity Credit Corporation is a branch of the United States Department of Agriculture. The named defendant Ralston Purina Company has by consent been dismissed). . . .

As stated previously, the plaintiffs also seek in this action to enforce landlord's liens for the value of crops raised on their lands in 1968 to the extent that such liens are necessary to satisfy any unpaid rent. In this connection it is stipulated that the defendant Commodity Credit Corporation made a loan on and later acquired ownership of cotton grown on the plaintiffs' lands in 1968 and that this cotton had a value of $27,155.40. . . .

To support their contention that they are entitled to liens on all crops grown on their lands in 1968, the plaintiffs rely on the Tennessee Crop Liens Statute, T.C.A. §§64-1201 to 64-1214. In particular the plaintiffs rely on the following sections: [The court quotes the statute, which gives landlords a lien on all crops grown on their land to the amount of rent due, and further provides that the landlord can enforce this lien against a purchaser of the crop "with or without notice" — Eds.].

It is next contended by the defendant United States that the plaintiffs are not entitled to a lien upon crops purchased by the Commodity Credit Corporation because the Commodity Credit Corporation was a good faith purchaser for value of negotiable warehouse receipts. As a result of such negotiation, the United States contends, the Commodity Credit Corporation acquired title to the crops in question free of the plaintiffs' crop lien.

Article Seven of the Uniform Commercial Code, as adopted in Tennessee, provides that, with limited exceptions, a holder to whom a negotiable document of title has been "duly negotiated" thereby acquires title to the goods described in such documents. §7-502. The term "duly negotiated" is defined in the preceding section, §7-501, as follows: [the court quoted the version of §7-501 in effect at the time].

In addition, §1-201[6] provides in part:

(25) A person has "notice" of a fact when ... (c) from all the facts and circumstances known to him at the time in question he has reason to know that it exists.

The United States contends that the Commodity Credit Corporation received the warehouse receipts in question "duly negotiated." The plaintiffs, on the other hand, contend that the negotiation in question was not in the regular course of business and that the Commodity Credit Corporation, from all the facts and circumstances known to it, had reason to know of the plaintiffs' lien. Consequently it is the plaintiffs' position that the Commodity Credit Corporation did not acquire title, through due negotiation, to the crops it purchased.

The proof shows that the defendant McNabb delivered the cotton he had raised on the plaintiffs' lands and later sold to Commodity Credit Corporation to a cotton gin. After the cotton was ginned it was taken directly to a warehouse which issued a negotiable warehouse receipt for each bale of cotton it held. McNabb later received these receipts which were issued in his name as producer at the cotton gin and took them to the Agricultural Stabilization and Conservation Service office, which is the government office administrator of the cotton loan program in Somerville, Tennessee. McNabb left the warehouse receipts at this office and in return ultimately received a "loan." [Under the system, if the loan is not paid, the cotton becomes the property of the government—Eds.]

A clerk from the ASCS office, Mrs. Sally Pat McNeil, testified that she had made no inquiry as to where the defendant McNabb had grown his cotton. The loan papers executed by this clerk show in the space designated for information concerning liens that there was no lien on the cotton grown by McNabb. Mrs. McNeil testified that she obtained this information from McNabb himself. McNabb testified that a copy of his lease with the plaintiffs was on file in the ASCS office. Further, the proof shows that the warehouse receipts referred to cotton gin tickets which in turn indicate that the cotton delivered by McNabb was grown on the plaintiffs' lands.

On this record we find that the warehouse receipts were not "duly negotiated" to the Commodity Credit Corporation so as to cut off the plaintiffs' lien. First, as the plaintiffs point out, the Department of Agriculture's own regulations, specifically 7 C.F.R. 1427.1364, require that cotton going into the loan program be lien-free. This regulation, we think, indicates that some inquiry is to be made by the local ASCS office to determine if there is a lien on cotton which is to be put into the government loan program. McNabb, as a tenant farmer (albeit a large one) could not

6. Now §1-202—Eds.

reasonably be expected to be fully familiar with the Tennessee Lien statutes and therefore limited inquiry from him alone, even if it might reasonably be assumed that he would give an honest answer, was not sufficient, especially since Mrs. McNeil only asked McNabb whether there was a lien on the cotton he had grown, and not whether his farm land was leased. Also, as indicated, the information that McNabb was a tenant farmer was readily available to the ASCS office. Either the government office disregarded the Tennessee Lien statute or was unfamiliar with it. At any rate, we think from all the facts and circumstances known to it, the Commodity Credit Corporation had reason to know of the plaintiffs' lien. Further, we do not believe that the existence of the above-mentioned custom and usage should lead us to the conclusion that the government through its representatives had no reason to know that the lien existed.

In *McNabb*, Commodity Credit Corp. was denied §7-502 holder status because it "had reason to know." Not all courts agree on the amount of knowledge of a claim or defense that is sufficient to deprive one of the §7-502 status. Compare R.E. Huntly Cotton Co. v. Fields, 551 S.W.2d 472, 21 U.C.C. Rep. Serv. 1157 (Tex. Civ. App. 1977) ("access to information sufficient to put [transferees] on notice of claims . . . is immaterial unless defendants had actual knowledge of facts and circumstances that would amount to bad faith").

Under §7-501, the negotiation must also be in the regular course of business or financing to be a due negotiation. Official Comment 1 to §7-501 provides in part:

> There are two aspects to the usual and normal course of mercantile dealings, namely, the person making the transfer and the nature of the transaction itself. The first question which arises is: Is the transferor a person with whom it is reasonable to deal as having full powers? In regard to documents of title the only holder whose possession appears, commercially, to be in order is almost invariably a person in the trade. No commercial purpose is served by allowing a tramp or a professor to "duly negotiate" an order bill of lading for hides or cotton not his own, and since such a transfer is obviously not in the regular course of business, it is excluded from the scope of the protection of subsection (a)(5) or (b)(3).
>
> The second question posed by the "regular course" qualification is: Is the transaction one which is normally proper to pass full rights without inquiry, even though the transferor itself may not have such rights to pass, and even though the transferor may be acting in breach of duty? In raising this question the "regular course" criterion has the further advantage of limiting the effective wrongful disposition to transactions whose protection will really further trade. Obviously, the snapping up of goods for quick resale at a price

suspiciously below the market deserves no protection as a matter of policy: it is also clearly outside the range of regular course.

Any notice on the document sufficient to put a merchant on inquiry as to the "regular course" quality of the transaction will frustrate a "due negotiation". Thus irregularity of the document or unexplained staleness of a bill of lading may appropriately be recognized as negating a negotiation in "regular" course.

A §7-502 holder gets the rights listed in that section. The FBLA is similar. Read §7-502 carefully and do the next Problem.

PROBLEM 94

Wonder Warehouse issued a negotiable warehouse receipt to "bearer" which covered 40 drums of oil. The bailor was Bonanza Petroleum Company. The receipt was pledged by Bonanza to the Octopus National Bank as collateral for a $5,000 loan. While in the bank's possession, the receipt was stolen by the bank's credit manager, Claude McStuffy, who gave it to his cousin Al McStuffy, a disreputable oil products salesman. Al presented the receipt at the warehouse, and the new agent on duty delivered the drums to him. The agent, however, also stupidly returned the receipt to Al. Al sold the drums through his business. He then took the old warehouse receipt to the Antitrust National Bank, where he pledged it as collateral for a $5,000 loan. Al and Claude then skipped town. When both banks make demand on the warehouse for the goods, does the warehouse have any defenses? Remember §7-403? Consider it; then read §7-404.

B. The §7-503(1) Owner

Go back to Article 2 (Sales), and read the *entrusting rule* found in §§2-403(2) and 2-403(3), which we considered when we talked about the warranty of title; see Simson v. Moon, 137 Ga. App. 82, 222 S.E.2d 873, 18 U.C.C. Rep. Serv. 1191 (1975); Annot., 59 A.L.R.4th 567. An understanding of what constitutes an entrusting is essential to understand the Problem and discussion that follow.

PROBLEM 95

Albert Collector took his favorite antique grandfather clock down to the Antique Clock Store to be cleaned. The proprietor assured him it would be ready on Friday. On Thursday, Betty Shopper wandered into the store, saw the clock, and became entranced by it. She made the proprietor an offer he couldn't refuse, so he sold her the clock and she took it home. Albert Collector was furious. He consults you. Can he replevy the clock from Betty? See Lindholm v. Brant, 283 Conn. 65, 925 A.2d 1048 (2007) (reprinted in Chapter 3). Can he sue the proprietor? Using what theory (or theories)? If the proprietor had stored the clock in a warehouse, received a negotiable warehouse receipt therefor, and pledged the receipt to Last National Bank in return for a loan, could Albert Collector retrieve the clock from the warehouse? Compare §§7-403, 7-502, and 7-503.

What *real* defenses are available against a §7-502 holder? The only ones that the Code sets out are listed in §7-403(a): proper delivery to a superior claimant, nonnegligent destruction of the goods, sale to enforce bailee's lien, and "any other lawful excuse" (not further defined in the Code). Who is the *superior claimant* that §7-403(a) permits to get the goods from the bailee even though there is an outstanding negotiable document of title? The answer: a §7-503(a) owner.

A §7-503(a) owner is a person who had a legal interest or perfected security interest in the goods *prior to* the bailee's issuance of a document of title and who was in no way responsible for the creation of a situation permitting a negotiable document of title to come into existence. Read §7-503(a) carefully along with Official Comment 1. Essentially, §7-503(a) means that if the owner of goods *entrusts* them (or documents covering them) or delivers them to anyone so that that person has the *apparent* authority to deal with the goods, the owner is estopped to assert ownership against a subsequent §7-502 holder. See In re Jamestown Farmers Elevator, Inc., 49 Bankr. 661, 41 U.C.C. Rep. Serv. 578 (Bankr. D.N.D. 1985).

Where the owner has entrusted and is thus estopped, *ownership* becomes a *personal* defense and unassertable against a §7-502 holder. *But* when the owner of goods has had them, in effect, stolen by someone other than the owner's agent, then the owner is the very person §7-503(a) was meant to protect. A §7-503(a) owner has a superior right to the goods even against a §7-502 holder. In this case, ownership is a *real* defense, and the true owner can force the bailee to turn over the goods to the §7-503(a) owner without surrendering the negotiable document (though, as a practical matter, the owner will probably either have to get a court order or sign an indemnity agreement with the bailee before the latter will turn over the goods).

The policy here is that — since one of two innocent parties must bear a loss — if the owner has been even slightly at fault by permitting someone else to have the goods (and therefore apparent authority to ship or store them) or the documents, the owner should bear the loss. The owner must learn not to be so trusting in the future — or to insure against employee defalcation. But if the owner has had the goods stolen by someone not permitted to hold onto the goods, then the owner should be able to trace the goods and recover them even if they are found in the possession of a bailee.

Agricredit Acceptance, LLC v. Hendrix

United States District Court, Southern District of Georgia, 2000
82 F. Supp. 2d 1379, 41 U.C.C. Rep. Serv. 2d 242

NANGLE, District Judge.

Before the Court is defendant Hohenberg Bros. Co., Loeb & Company, Inc., Weil Brothers-Cotton, Inc., and the Montgomery Company, Inc.'s (the merchants') motion for summary judgment (Doc. 80). For the reasons that follow, defendants' motion is denied.

I. BACKGROUND . . .

The defendant merchants buy cotton stored in warehouses and resell it to textile mills. Br. Supp. Defs.' Consolidated Mot. Summ. J. at 1 (Doc. 81). These transactions are generally electronic in nature, involving electronic warehouse receipts (EWRs) maintained in the central operating systems of various EWR providers. Id. at 1-2. The sale typically begins with the merchants' receipt of a recap sheet from a prospective seller, which describes a number of bales being offered for sale by grade, quantity and warehouse in which the bales are stored. Id. at 2. The merchant then telephones the seller and submits an offer involving either a fixed price or an "on call" price which is based on the price of cotton futures on the New York market. Id. Once an agreement is reached between the merchant and the seller, the seller transfers the EWRs for the bales sold into the name of the merchant, and the merchant receives a confirmation of this transaction from the EWR provider. Id. When the EWRs are in the name of the merchant, the merchant is able to obtain a list of the bales by receipt number from the central filing system by downloading the list into the merchant's computers. Id. The sale is completed when the merchant pays the seller for the cotton represented by the EWRs. Id.

These sales can also be accomplished via contract for future delivery. Id. at 5. These contracts involve the seller promising to provide some specific number of bales in the future at a provisional price. After the seller acquires the bales, it transfers the EWRs for the bales into the name of the merchant and the process proceeds as above. Id.

Thomas Hendrix's 1997 cotton crop was financed by a loan from plaintiff Agricredit Acceptance Corporation (AAC). Order dated Dec. 21, 1998, at 2. The loan was secured by the cotton crop. Id. AAC's security interest was properly perfected by filing the Security Agreement in the real estate records of the counties wherein the cotton was grown and with the

County clerks' offices. Id. at 3. Sea Island Cotton Trading was designated as a selling agent through which Hendrix would sell the cotton crop, and AAC notified Sea Island of its security interest in accordance with the provisions of the Food Security Act (FSA), 7 U.S.C. §1631. Id. Hendrix's cotton crop was ginned, baled, and stored in various warehouses, including Collins Gin & Warehouse, Candler Gin & Warehouse, Goldkist, Inc., Growers Gin & Warehouse, Inc., and Bulloch Gin. Id.; Br. Supp. Defs.' Mot. Summ. J. at 3. The warehouses issued EWRs for the cotton in the central filing system of the EWR provider to which they were subscribed. Br. Supp. Defs.' Mot. Summ. J. at 3. These receipts were eventually placed in the name of Sea Island. Id. at 4; Order dated Dec. 21, 1998, at 3.

All of the defendant merchants purchased large quantities of cotton from Sea Island in 1997 and 1998, including many bales from Hendrix's 1997 crop. The merchants paid Sea Island for these bales, and the EWRs representing the bales were transferred by Sea Island into the names of the purchasing merchants. Br. Supp. Defs.' Mot. Summ. J. at 4-15. Sea Island never paid AAC or Hendrix for the cotton in violation of its obligations under the FSA notice. Order dated Dec. 21, 1998, at 4. Consequently, plaintiff AAC filed suit against the defendant merchants and others seeking foreclosure of its security interest in the Hendrix cotton, a writ of possession against anyone in possession of the cotton, and a finding of conversion and an award of damages against the cotton merchants, among other things. Id.

The defendant merchants assert that because the EWRs representing the Hendrix cotton were duly negotiated to them by Sea Island and because AAC entrusted the cotton to Hendrix with apparent authority to sell it, the cotton is no longer subject to AAC's security interest. That is, the merchants assert that duly negotiated EWRs have priority over a prior perfected security interest, especially when the secured party entrusts the collateral to the borrower. As this Court found in its Order dated December 21, 1998, the resolution of these issues depends on this Court's interpretation of the Georgia Uniform Commercial Code and its application to the facts of this case. Id. at 13-14.

II. ANALYSIS . . .

In Georgia, a security interest in crops can only be perfected by the filing of a financing statement. O.C.G.A. §11-9-302(1)(h).[7] Generally, a perfected security interest takes priority over other liens, claims or rights to property and to security interests perfected at a later date. O.C.G.A. §§11-9-310 and -312.[8] This general rule is of course subject to exception.

---

7. Section 9-310(a) in the 1999 revision of Article 9 — EDS.
8. Section 9-334 in the 1999 revision of Article 9 — EDS.

For example, a buyer in the ordinary course of business takes free of a security interest created by his seller, O.C.G.A. §11-9-307(1). Furthermore, nothing in Article 9 of the UCC limits the rights of "a holder to whom a negotiable document of title has been duly negotiated . . . and such holders . . . take priority over an earlier security interest even though perfected," O.C.G.A. §11-9-309.[9]

A warehouse receipt is a negotiable document of title if it provides by its terms that the goods are to be delivered to bearer or to the order of a named person. O.C.G.A. §11-7-104(1)(a).[10] These receipts may be in an electronic format. O.C.G.A. §10-4-19(e). A negotiable document running to order is negotiated by indorsement and delivery. O.C.G.A. §§11-7-501(1).[11] A negotiable document running to bearer is negotiated by delivery alone. O.C.G.A. §11-7-501(2).[12]

To be duly negotiated, a document of title must be negotiated "to a holder who purchases it in good faith without any notice of any defense against it or claim to it on the part of any person and for value, unless it is established that the negotiation is not in the regular course of business." O.C.G.A. §11-7-501(4).[13] Good faith is defined by reference to O.C.G.A. §11-1-201(19) as "honesty in fact in the conduct or transaction concerned." "A person has 'notice' of a fact when: (a) He has actual knowledge of it; or (b) He has received a notice or notification of it; or (c) From all the facts and circumstances known to him at the time in question he has reason to know that it exists." O.C.G.A. §11-1-201(25). Finally, in general, a person gives value for rights if he acquires them "in return for any consideration sufficient to support a simple contract." O.C.G.A. §11-1-201(44). Section 11-7-502 provides that a holder to whom a negotiable warehouse receipt has been duly negotiated acquires title to the document, title to the goods, and the direct obligation of the warehouse to deliver the goods, except as provided in O.C.G.A. §11-7-503.

Section 11-7-503[14] provides that:

> (1) A document of title confers no right in goods against a person who before issuance of the document had a legal interest or a perfected security interest in [the goods] and who neither:
>
> (a) Delivered or entrusted [the goods] . . . to the bailor or his nominee with actual or apparent authority to ship, store, or sell . . . ; nor
>
> (b) Acquiesced in the procurement by the bailor or his nominee of any document of title.

---

9. Section 9-331 in the 1999 revision of Article 9 — EDS.
10. Now §7-104(a) — EDS.
11. Now §7-501(a)(1) — EDS.
12. Now §7-501(a)(2) — EDS.
13. Now §7-501(b)(3) — EDS.
14. The same rule is continued with slight wording changes in §7-503 — EDS.

Neither Article 1 nor Article 7 defines the term "entrusted." This term is used elsewhere in the UCC, however. Section 11-2-403(3) defines it as "any delivery and any acquiescence in retention of possession regardless of any condition expressed between the parties." However, Georgia courts have found that this provision only applies to owners of goods, because one cannot entrust goods one does not own. Sunnyland Employees' Fed. Credit Union v. Fort Wayne Mortgage Co., 182 Ga. App. 5, 354 S.E.2d 645, 647 (1987) (holding that party with security interest in mobile home could not be the entruster of it because party was not the owner of the home); United Carolina Bank v. Sistrunk, 158 Ga. App. 107, 279 S.E.2d 272, 274 (1981) (holding party with security interest in car could not be the entruster of it because party was not the owner of the car); McConnell v. Barrett, 154 Ga. App. 767, 270 S.E.2d 13, 15-16 (1980) (holding that non-owners cannot be entrusters and citing Adams v. City Nat'l Bank & Trust Co., 565 P.2d 26, 29 (Okla. 1977)). Acquiescence is not defined anywhere in the UCC.

C. INTERPRETATION AND APPLICATION OF THE UCC.

Defendants' motion for summary judgment is based on two theories: (1) that the EWRs were duly negotiated to the merchants and pursuant to O.C.G.A. §§11-9-309, the merchants' interest in the cotton has priority over AAC's interest, Br. Supp. Defs.' Mot. Summ. J. at 16-19; Defs.' Objections to Dep. Testimony Offered by Pl. at 2-4, 6, 7-8 (Doc. 123); and (2) that AAC waived the priority of its security interest by entrusting the cotton to Hendrix pursuant to O.C.G.A. §§11-7-503, Br. Supp. Defs.' Mot. Summ. J. at 20; Defs.' Objections to Dep. Testimony Offered by Pl. at 7-8; Defs.' Resp. Opp'n AAC's Objection to Affs. at 9-12 (Doc. 120).

1. Due Negotiation and §11-9-309.[15]

For the EWRs to be duly negotiated to the merchants, the merchants must be purchasers in good faith without notice of claims or defenses to the receipts and for value. O.C.G.A. §11-7-501(4).[16] It is undisputed that the merchants purchased the EWRs for value. Consequently, the Court must determine whether the merchants also purchased the EWRs in good faith and without notice.

Good faith as defined in Article 1[17] means "honesty in fact." Plaintiff does not dispute that the merchants acted with honesty in fact in this transaction. Rather, relying on an improper definition of good faith, AAC asserts that good faith requires the merchants to perform a lien check on the cotton before purchase. The Court finds that the "honesty in fact"

---

15. Now §9-331 — Eds.

16. Now §7-501(b)(3) — Eds.

17. In the revised version of Article 1, §1-20(b)(20) defines "good faith" as "honesty in fact and the observance of reasonable commercial standards of fair dealing," thus adding an objective component to the mix — Eds.

definition does not require the merchants to perform a lien check on the cotton prior to purchase. Consequently, the Court holds that the merchants are purchasers in good faith as a matter of law.

However, this finding does not end the inquiry. The merchants must also be purchasers without notice of any defenses or claims to the EWRs. Plaintiff relies on the third prong of Article 1's definition of notice in arguing that the merchants' experience with the cotton industry and its willful ignorance as to the existence of liens on the cotton constitute reason to know that plaintiff's defense to the EWRs existed. Pl's Resp. Opp'n Defs.' Mot. Summ. J. at 22-24 (Doc. 93). While some jurisdictions have required the existence of suspicious circumstances for a finding of "reason to know"; Colin v. Central Penn Nat'l Bank, 404 F. Supp. 638, 640-41 (E.D. Pa. 1975); others hold that willful or deliberate indifference to or ignorance of information is a basis for a finding of "reason to know"; Demoulas v. Demoulas, 428 Mass. 555, 703 N.E.2d 1149, 1167 (1998) ("If a person confronted with a state of facts closes his eyes in order that he may not see that which would be visible and therefore known to him if he looked, he is chargeable with 'knowledge' of what he would have seen had he looked.") (citations omitted); New Bedford Inst. for Savings v. Gildroy, 36 Mass. App. Ct. 647, 634 N. E.2d 920 (1994) ("Further, a holder has no duty to inquire unless 'the circumstances reveal a deliberate desire by the holder to evade knowledge of claims made by the maker.'") (citations omitted).

The Court finds that the evidence in the record indicates that a genuine issue of fact exists concerning the merchants' notice of AAC's claims to the cotton. The merchants testified in deposition that they do not perform lien searches on cotton bought from merchants or gins. Dep. Hohenberg Bros. Co. through John D. Mitchell at 25-27 (Doc. 91); Dep. Weil Brothers-Cotton, Inc. through James A. Wade at 18-19 (Doc. 90); Dep. Loeb & Co., Inc. through James L. Loeb at 24 (Doc. 87); Dep. Montgomery Co. through Jack D. Atkins at 27-28, 42-43 (Doc. 89). However, when buying directly from the producer or when buying in a state with a central lien filing system, most of the merchants do perform lien searches. Dep. Mitchell at 25-26; Dep. Loeb at 24; Dep. Atkins at 28, 42-43. Further, when dealing with sales via contract for future delivery, the merchants include a clause in the contract requiring the seller to warrant that there are no liens on the cotton. Dep. Mitchell at 68-72. These facts imply that the merchants certainly knew of the possibility of the existence of liens. Whether their failure to search for liens amounts to deliberate indifference or ignorance to their existence, however, is less than clear from the facts presently in the record. The Court finds that this issue is one for a jury to decide.

Even if the Court finds that the merchants had no notice of AAC's claims to the cotton, this finding would not automatically provide superiority to the merchants' claims to the cotton. O.C.G.A. §11-9-309[18] provides that

18. Now §9-331 — EDS.

"Nothing in this article limits the rights . . . of a holder to whom a negotiable document of title has been duly negotiated . . . and such holders take priority over an earlier security interest even though perfected." Defendants urge the Court to hold that this Section provides that any duly negotiated EWR automatically trumps a prior perfected security interest in the goods covered by that EWR. Defendants' interpretation of §11-9-309 is in error. Such an interpretation would eviscerate the provisions of O.C.G.A. §11-7-503, which expressly provide that EWRs confer no rights in the goods covered by the EWRs against security interests existing and perfected prior to the issuance of the EWR where there has been no entrustment or acquiescence on the part of the secured party. The proper interpretation of §11-9-309 is that the Section only applies when the negotiable document holder and the secured party are both claiming an interest in the document. Farmers State Bank of Somonauk v. National Bank of Earlville, 230 Ill. App. 3d 881, 172 Ill. Dec. 894, 596 N.E.2d 173, 174-76 (1992). That is, §11-9-309 addresses disputes between competing interests in a negotiable document whereas §11-7-503 covers disputes between competing interests in the underlying goods. Accordingly, even if the EWRs were duly negotiated to the merchants, disposition of the cotton covered by those EWRs depends upon the application of O.C.G.A. §11-7-503.

2. Entrustment

Defendants argue that despite the Georgia courts' interpretation of §11-2-403, this Court is free to find that AAC entrusted the cotton to Hendrix by leaving it in his possession and allowing him to sell it through Sea Island. However, because Article 1 and Article 7 provide no definition for the term "entrusted," this Court must look to the Georgia courts' interpretation of that term as it is used in other sections of the UCC. Banks v. Georgia Power Co., 267 Ga. 602, 481 S.E.2d 200, 202 (1997) (stating that court is required to construe statute with reference to other statutes and decisions of the courts); Poteat v. Butler, 231 Ga. 187, 200 S.E.2d 741, 742 (1973) ("All statutes are presumed to be enacted by the General Assembly with full knowledge of the existing condition of the law . . . and their meaning and effect is to be determined in connection . . . with reference to other statutes and decisions of the courts."). Because the Georgia courts have held in the context of §11-2-403 that a secured party who does not own the goods cannot entrust them; Sunnyland, 354 S.E.2d at 647; United Carolina Bank, 279 S.E.2d at 274; McConnell, 270 S.E.2d at 15-16; this Court must hold similarly in the context of §11-7-503.[19] Consequently, the Court finds that plaintiff did not entrust the cotton to Hendrix as a matter of law.

19. This interpretation does not make the use of the term "entrusted" superfluous in the context of §11-7-503. Rather, that Section also applies to any persons with any legal

Plaintiff may, however, have acquiesced in the procurement of a document of title in the cotton (namely the EWRs) pursuant to §11-7-503(l)(b).[20] When a bank knows that a farmer is attempting to sell his collateral and it acquiesces in his procurement of documents of title to that collateral, the bank has waived its right to assert its security interest in the collateral. Mercantile Bank of Springfield v. Joplin Regional Stockyards, Inc., 870 F. Supp. 278, 283 (W.D. Mo. 1994). The evidence presently before the Court is not sufficient to support a ruling on this issue as a matter of law. Consequently, the question of plaintiff's acquiescence is better left to a jury.

III. CONCLUSION

Because genuine issues of material fact exist,

IT IS HEREBY ORDERED that defendants' motion for summary judgment is denied.

C. *Other Transfers*

Section 7-504, which you should read as soon as you finish this paragraph, sets out the rights acquired by a transferee of a document when there has been no *due negotiation*. Section 7-505 goes on to provide that the indorser of a document of title does not make any *contract* that the bailee will honor the document, but §7-507 (which you should also glance at) provides that any transferor makes the warranties listed there. In addition, since a sale of goods is involved in the transfer of any document of title, a transferor also makes the Article 2 warranties, discussed in the earlier part of this book.

It is a basic rule of all commercial law that a transferee gets whatever legal rights the transferor had. This rule is called the shelter rule because the transferee is said to take shelter in the status of the transferor. In Article 2 (Sale of Goods) the shelter rule is found in §2-403; read it. In Article 3 (Commercial Paper) the rule turns up in §3-203(b), and in Article 8 (Investment Securities) it is reflected in §8-301. For Article 7 the rule is codified in §7-504(a). Read it, and use it to work the following Problem.

PROBLEM 96

The shipping agent for the King Cotton Manufacturing Company wrongfully took for himself 90 bales of cotton that had come under his

---

interest in the goods which was created prior to the issuance of the document of title. When such persons are the owners of the goods, the entrustment provision would apply.

20. Now §7-503(a)(2) — EDS.

control and stored them in the Rural Warehouse, which issued to him a negotiable warehouse receipt. This receipt he took to Octopus National Bank (ONB) and gave as security for a loan. He indorsed the receipt over to ONB. King Cotton discovered the bales were missing and investigated; the shipping agent was arrested. Shortly thereafter, ONB sold the warehouse receipt to Antitrust National Bank (ANB), which bought the document with full knowledge of the above facts. Both ANB and King Cotton made a demand on Rural Warehouse for the cotton. Rural calls you, its attorney, for advice. What do you say? Note §§7-403(c), 7-501 through 7-504, and 7-603.

IV. COLLECTION THROUGH BANKS

A. "Payment Against Documents"

If the seller and buyer deal with each other on a face-to-face basis, delivery of the goods and payment of the price normally occur at the same moment, and neither party need trust the other. Where seller and buyer are separated by great distances, a seller must either trust the buyer to live up to the contract (a sale on *open account* with trust on both sides) or figure out a way to make certain that the buyer cannot get the goods until they are paid for. The easiest way to do this would be to have an agent in the buyer's city who could present the bill of lading covering the goods to the buyer but not turn it over to the buyer until cash was paid for the goods. In effect, this is the solution that sellers have adopted. See §2-503(5)(b). The *agent* that sellers typically use is a bank in the buyer's city. And, instead of a letter of instruction telling the bank-agent what to do, the seller simply draws an Article 3 draft (§3-104(e)) on the buyer (so that the buyer is the drawee) and attaches it to the bill of lading.

A draft is similar to a check; it is an instruction of payment. The seller is the drawer, and the buyer is the drawee. A simple draft will look like this:

```
                                        _____
                                            (Date)

To:  _____      _____
         (Buyer's Name)                   (Amount)
At sight pay to the order of _____
                              (Payee's Name)
_____ dollars and _____ cents.

                                   _____
                                     (Seller's Signature)
```

The payee will be whomever the seller nominates: the seller's bank, one of the seller's creditors, or even the seller itself. The only difference between this draft and your typical check is that the drawee is the buyer and not a bank.

Now that the seller has created the draft, it is combined with other papers for delivery to the buyer. The papers (which will normally include the bill of lading, a sales invoice, and, occasionally, an inspection certificate) along with the seller's draft on buyer are indorsed over to the seller's local bank for collection. Then the normal bank collection machinery in Article 4 is put into motion. Eventually, a bank in buyer's vicinity makes a formal Article 3 *presentment* of the draft (§3-501), and the buyer must either pay or dishonor. In any event, the buyer cannot get the documents (especially the bill of lading) until payment, so the seller is protected from having to trust a buyer in an arm's length transaction. If the buyer dishonors, the seller is notified by the collecting bank. The seller will then give instructions to the bank as to what to do with the goods when they arrive (the bank will be able to claim them from the carrier because it has the bill of lading. Cf. §7-403(c)).

Any draft accompanied by sales documents like those mentioned above is called a *documentary draft*. See §4-104(a)(6). The normal rules for negotiable instruments in Articles 3 and 4 apply to such drafts, but occasionally the sections make special rules for documentary drafts, e.g., §4-202(a)(2) (providing that after dishonor a collecting bank need not return a documentary draft to its transferor).

Sometimes the seller does not demand that the buyer actually pay prior to receiving the documents. Under some contracts, it is enough that buyer *accept* the draft and incur the obligation of an *acceptor* (§3-413), thus becoming primarily liable on the draft (the draft is now commonly called a *trade acceptance*). Typically, these are *time drafts* (as opposed to *sight drafts*, whereby payment is required as soon as buyer sees the draft) because they require payment in 30, 60, or 90 days after "sight" (presentment to buyer). The business reason why this is frequently done is so that buyer can take the goods during the grace period, by manufacturing transform them into other goods, and resell them. In these transactions the seller sends the draft and documents through the banks and asks the collecting bank to call the buyer and make a presentment for acceptance. Read §4-212. The buyer shows up and accepts by writing the buyer's signature on the draft (if the buyer does not show up, the draft is dishonored). After acceptance, the draft is returned to the presenter and may be further negotiated. On acceptance by the buyer, the bank turns over the documents, and in 30, 60, or 90 days (or whatever time period the draft provides) the buyer is required to pay the draft or is in breach of the acceptor's contract. For an article spelling out *payment against documents* in detail, see Farnsworth, Documentary Drafts Under the Uniform Commercial Code, 22 Bus. Law. 479 (1967).

PROBLEM 97

Sam Seller in Dallas signed a sales contract to sell one ton of tennis balls to Beth Buyer in Indianapolis, "FOB truck in Dallas," $800 to be paid by a 60-day time draft on the buyer. Sam boxed the tennis balls and filled out a packaging invoice describing the goods. He drew a draft as follows:

To: Beth Buyer

Sixty days after sight pay to the order of *Sam Seller* $800.
(Signed) *Sam Seller*

He took the tennis balls down to the Texas Trucking Company and asked for a negotiable bill of lading consigned to his own order, with the instructions "notify Beth Buyer on arrival." The trucking company issued the negotiable ("order") bill to Sam.

Sam then took the bill of lading, the invoice describing the goods, and the draft on Buyer down to his local bank, the Lone Star National Bank. He asked Lone Star to collect the draft. On agreeing to the bank's collection charge, Sam indorsed both the draft and the bill of lading over to the bank. Lone Star Bank then forwarded the draft and the documents to the Indianapolis State Hoosier Bank for collection. The Hoosier Bank called Beth Buyer and told her to come by the bank and get the papers. Beth came down that afternoon, wrote her name diagonally on the draft (which the bank dated and kept), and received the other documents. Read §2-514. Two days later the Texas Trucking Company showed up with the goods and promptly notified Buyer of their arrival. Buyer went down to the truck depot and surrendered the bill of lading (as required by §7-403(c)), whereupon she received the tennis balls. Now, to see how Article 2 and Article 7 fit together like one glorious puzzle, answer the following questions:

(a) Can Beth Buyer *inspect* the goods? If so, when? See §2-513.

(b) If the tennis balls are defective (Seller has breached one of his Article 2 warranties), can Buyer reject (§2-602) or revoke her acceptance (§2-608) and refuse to pay?

(c) If the cartons are empty (Sam is a crook), can Buyer sue the Texas Trucking Company, since the bill of lading states that the goods shipped are "ONE TON TENNIS BALLS"?

(d) Can Buyer sue the collecting bank because the documents did not conform to the goods shipped? Read §7-508 to answer this one.

B. Liability of the Collecting Bank

Sometimes a seller in the position of Sam (above) will sell (*discount*) the draft and documents to a local bank. This generally makes no difference in the resulting rights (see, for example, the last sentence of §7-508), but it does give the collecting bank a security interest in the draft and documents (§4-210(a)(3)) and therefore permits it to become a holder in due course (§4-211). Read §2-506.

The last Part of Article 4 contains four sections that deal specifically with the collection of documentary drafts. Read §§4-501 to 4-504 to see how these sections link the sale under Article 2 with the use of Article 7 documents of title.

Rheinberg Kellerei GmbH v. Brooksfield National Bank of Commerce

United States Court of Appeals, Fifth Circuit, 1990
901 F.2d 481, 11 U.C.C. Rep. Serv. 2d 1214

GARZA, J.

American bank did not notify German bank of difficulty in payment on international collection order which came due on arrival of goods in Houston; the collection order was eventually dishonored. The district court held that the American bank did not know, and had no duty to inquire, whether goods had arrived, and entered take nothing judgment. Because we find that the American bank was on notice of the possibility of dishonor and should have told the German bank of the problem in collection, we reverse.

FACTS

In January of 1986, J & J Wine, an American company, ordered a shipment of wine from a German firm, Rheinberg Kellerei GmbH, through an importer, Frank Sutton & Co.[21] Payment was to be made through an international letter of collection handled by Edekabank in Germany and

---

21. The "GmbH" designation means "Gesellschaft mit beschrankter Haftung," or "company with limited liability." GmbH is a common form of corporate organization in Germany and is similar to the "Inc." designation in the American corporate system.

Brooksfield National Bank of Commerce Bank in San Antonio ("NBC Bank").[22] On March 27, NBC Bank received the letter of collection, bill of lading and invoices from Edeka.[23] The letter of collection noted that payment was due "on arrival of goods in Houston harbor," and called for NBC Bank to notify Sutton "in case of any difficulty of lack payment." The invoices noted an estimated time of arrival: April 2, 1986. NBC Bank then presented the documents to J & J Wine on March 27.

There is some dispute as to what, exactly, J & J Wine told NBC Bank about its financial situation at the time, but it is sure that J & J Wine did not pay the amount due, and instead asked NBC Bank to hold the letter for a time while J & J Wine worked to raise the money for payment. NBC Bank did not notify Edeka or Sutton of J & J Wine's failure to pay on presentment. In fact, NBC Bank did nothing further until early May, when Sutton informed them that the wine was still at the Houston port and NBC Bank cabled Edeka for further instructions.

The wine had arrived in Houston on March 31, but NBC Bank did not receive notice of that. Because J & J Wine had not taken delivery of it, the wine sat, exposed, at Houston harbor in metal containers until it had deteriorated completely. U.S. Customs agents eventually sold it at auction. J & J Wine subsequently went out of business, and Rheinberg Kellerei was never paid for the wine.

Rheinberg Kellerei then brought this suit, alleging that NBC Bank had negligently failed to inform it of J & J Wine's failure to pay, and that because of that negligence, the wine had spoiled at Houston harbor. After a bench trial, the district court entered a take-nothing judgment for NBC Bank. The court reasoned that, because payment was not due until the wine's arrival, and NBC Bank had no notice of that arrival and no duty to inquire further, NBC Bank had no knowledge that J & J Wine was in breach of the payment terms. For that reason, the district court held that NBC Bank could not be held liable for failure to inform Edeka of J & J Wine's default.

Complaining that the district court improperly applied the requirements of the International Rules for Collection (the "Rules") and erred in

---

22. In a case like this one, international letters of collection are issued by the seller's bank (Edeka) and sent to the buyer's bank (NBC Bank), which in turn presents the letter and its documents to the buyer. To receive the documents and collect the goods, the buyer pays the amount due to its bank, which then forwards the funds to the seller's bank. Enforcement of these letters is governed by the International Chamber of Commerce's International Rules for Collection.

23. The bill of lading called for notification of Sutton and M.G. Maher & Co., the customs broker, on arrival of the goods in Houston. NBC Bank was not listed on the Bill of Lading or the invoices.

construing the letter of collection itself, Rheinberg Kellerei brought this appeal.

DISCUSSION

I. DUTY TO INFORM

NBC Bank presented the letter of collection and the other documents to J & J Wine for payment on March 27, 1986, before the wine had arrived and before the payment was due. Rheinberg Kellerei argues that, regardless of whether NBC Bank knew when the wine had arrived, once NBC Bank presented the documents, it had a duty to inform Edeka of any problem in collecting J & J Wine's payment. We agree. That duty arises both from the Rules and the collection letter itself.

A. *Letter of Collection*

The letter, which is the primary source of responsibility in this case, instructs NBC Bank to notify Sutton "in case of any difficulty of lack payment."[24] The district court found that section demanded notice only if there were a "lack of payment or failure to pay." Likewise, NBC Bank emphasizes that the trigger for notice is a *lack* of payment. What the court below and NBC Bank ignore is the word "difficulty." The letter did not instruct NBC Bank to notify Sutton only if there were a default, or a failure to pay, or a lack of payment. Rather, NBC Bank was called on to act also if there were any *difficulty* in collecting payment. And the request that NBC Bank hold the letter while J & J Wine sought financing certainly posed a difficulty in collection. Once NBC Bank knew that J & J Wine had asked for time to come up with the money, it should have notified Sutton in accordance with the letter's instructions.

The Rules specify that any special instructions posted on a letter of collection should be "complete and precise." General Provisions, §C. While the instructions given on this letter could have been in clearer language, they are sufficiently precise to make NBC Bank aware of its duty to notify Sutton once difficulty arose in the collection.

B. *International Rules for Collection*

Article 20(iii)(c) of the Rules provides that the "collecting bank [NBC Bank] must send without delay advice on non-payment or advice of non-acceptance to the bank from whom the collecting order was received [Edeka]." The court below and NBC Bank submit that section called on NBC Bank to notify Edeka if J & J Wine had not paid on the letter at the time it came due: on arrival of the goods in Houston harbor. And, they

---

24. Sutton was Rheinberg Kellerei's agent in this sale.

argue, since NBC Bank had no actual notice of the arrival of the goods, it did not breach that duty to notify.

The issue, it seems, is the definition of "non-payment" as it is used in Art. 20(iii)(c). Does it refer to a failure to pay on presentment? Does it require an affirmative statement of intent not to pay? Must the due date have arrived? No court has yet defined the term and its attendant duties, so we must look for guidance elsewhere.

The Rules were adopted to aid in "defining, simplifying and harmonizing the practices and terminology used in international banking." I.C.C. Banking Commission, Statement of Services to Business. They serve, for the international banking community, the same function as the Uniform Commercial Code does for domestic players. There is no reason, then, to ignore the UCC as an advisory source.

Section 4-502 of the UCC governs payment of "on arrival" drafts, such as were presented in our case. Tex. Bus. & Com. Code Ann., §4-502 (Tex. UCC) (Vernon's 1968). Under that section, a bank such as NBC Bank may, but need not, present the documents to the buyer before the goods arrive. But if the buyer does not pay at that time, the bank must notify the seller's bank: "Refusal to pay or accept because the goods have not arrived is not dishonor; *the bank must notify its transferor of such refusal* but need not present the draft again. . . ." UCC §4-502 (emphasis added). The UCC imposes on the presenting bank a duty to notify the seller's bank of any delay or failure to pay on presentment of an "on arrival" draft, *whether or not the draft is yet due.*

If §4-502 were applied to our case, NBC Bank would have a duty to notify Edeka of J & J Wine's failure to pay the letter of collection when it was presented on March 27, even though the goods were not yet in Houston harbor and the payment was not yet due. This is not to say that J & J Wine was in default at that time or had dishonored the letter. Rather, the notice is an act of prudence, an exercise in due care. And, as the aims of the Rules and the UCC are more than consistent, and both demand the exercise of due care, we find that the Rules impose the same duty. NBC Bank should have notified Edeka of J & J Wine's failure to pay at presentment, as that failure constituted a "non-payment" under Art. 20(iii)(c).

NBC Bank and the court below rely heavily on the fact that NBC Bank had no actual knowledge of the wine's arrival in Houston, and had no duty to inquire further. We agree with those premises, but do not feel they affect NBC Bank's duty to notify. That duty arose — under both the Rules and the letter itself — when J & J Wine failed to pay on presentment and asked for time. Arrival of the wine did not trigger it. And NBC Bank cannot avoid liability by hiding from knowledge of arrival and claiming that ignorance as a defense.

II. DAMAGES

State law governs the measure of damages in a case such as this one. Gathercrest, Ltd. v. First American Bank & Trust, 805 F.2d 995, 997 (11th Cir. 1986). Tex. Bus. & Com. Code Ann. §2-709(1) (Tex. UCC) (Vernon's 1968) gives the relevant standard: "the seller may recover, together with any incidental damages under the next section, the price (1) of goods accepted or of conforming goods lost or damaged . . . after risk of their loss has passed to the buyer." Risk of loss had passed to J & J Wine when the goods arrived at Houston harbor and were available for J & J Wine to take delivery. Tex. Bus. & Com. Code Ann., §2-509(1)(b) (Tex. UCC) (Vernon's 1968). The district court found that because the wine was exposed for such a long period in Houston harbor, it was "'over cooked' and had deteriorated, lost its original flavor, freshness, was flat and should not be sold into the market that it was intended." Since the goods were so damaged, Rheinberg Kellerei is entitled to the contract price plus the unpaid freight costs, as provided in UCC [§2-709(1)(a)].

NBC Bank is entitled to a credit for the net proceeds of any resale of the damaged wine. UCC §2-709(2). Customs agents sold the wine at auction, but we have no evidence before us of the price paid or the net amount remaining after customs fees, wharfage, and the costs of the auction were paid. For that reason, we remand this case to the district court for the limited purpose of calculating that net amount. After finding that net amount, the district court should enter judgment for Rheinberg Kellerei for the contract price plus freight charges, less the net proceeds of the customs auction.

CONCLUSION

NBC Bank had a duty to notify Edeka or Sutton, which was triggered when J & J Wine failed to pay the letter of collection on presentment and asked for more time. That duty arose from two sources: the Rules and the letter itself. Though payment was not due until the wine arrived in Houston harbor, that arrival was not a triggering event for the duty to arise, and lack of knowledge of it is no defense. The judgment of the district court is, therefore, reversed, and this cause is remanded for calculation of damages.

It is so ordered.

Up to this point the text has mostly dealt with sales transactions within the United States. To understand sales of goods between sellers and buyers in different countries, Article 5 (Letters of Credit) must now be mastered. In international sales, most sales are carried out through the use of documents of title, with the added complication that letters of credit are also used. International collection of documentary drafts is regulated by Brochure 600 of the International Chamber of Commerce (2007 revision), which the banks regard as "the law." The relevant UCC Articles — 4, 5, and 7 — are similar to its provisions.

CHAPTER 8

LETTERS OF
CREDIT

There are two primary sources for the law relating to letters of credit: Article 5 of the Uniform Commercial Code and the Uniform Customs and Practice for Documentary Credits, 2007 Revision [Brochure 600 of the International Chamber of Commerce, hereinafter the UCP]. Since the two are not significantly different, we shall look primarily to the Code for study purposes. If you should get involved in a letter of credit case, however, remember to study the UCP carefully—it is recognized as a complete statement of prevailing international banking practices in the field; for the relationship of Article 5 to the UCP, see Official Comment 2 to §5-103. The leading treatise on Article 5 is J. Dolan, The Law of Letters of Credit (4th ed. 2007).

I. THE BASIC PROBLEM

Assume you are the proprietor of a business in Detroit, Michigan, that makes and sells men's shirts. One day you get a letter from Germany saying: "I want to buy 50,000 shirts at $7 each United States currency, FOB Frankfurt. (Signed) *Hans Goldschnitt*." Since you have never heard of Hans

Goldschnitt, you are reluctant to ship him 50,000 shirts and risk nonpayment after the shipping costs are incurred. There are no satisfactory credit bureaus similar to Dun and Bradstreet on an international basis. How can you avoid a credit risk? The answer devised by the law merchant is for you to write Herr Goldschnitt and tell him that you will ship the goods only to a *bank* of international repute that is willing to write a letter to you making itself *primarily* and *irrevocably* liable for the payment of the contract price. If Hans Goldschnitt agrees and you agree on the other contract terms, he will go to a major German bank — say, the National Volksbank of Frankfurt (NVF) — and establish credit with the bank. Shortly thereafter you will receive a letter from the bank more or less in the following form:

NATIONAL VOLKSBANK OF FRANKFURT
Credit no. 829-411
November 20, 2015

Dear Detroit Seller:

We hereby establish our **IRREVOCABLE CREDIT** in your favor for the account of Hans Goldschnitt, our customer, up to the aggregate amount of $350,000, U.S. dollars, available by your sight draft on us, to be accompanied by the following documents:

(1) full set of clean bills of lading issued by German Ocean Lines to the order of National Volksbank of Frankfurt, notify Hans Goldschnitt;

(2) signed commercial sales invoices describing the goods;

(3) customs certificates;

(4) packing lists;

(5) inspection certificate by Grey Goods Inspection Service of New York.

Bills of lading must be dated not later than August 1, 2016; drafts must be negotiated within ten days of shipment; all drafts must be marked "Drawn Under Credit No. 829-411." Subject to UCP rules (Brochure 600). This credit will expire on October 1, 2016. We hereby agree with drawers, indorsers, and bona fide holders of drafts drawn under and in compliance with the terms and conditions of this credit to honor the same on due presentation of draft to the drawee.

Yours very truly,

National Volksbank
of Frankfurt

The German bank will probably forward this letter of credit to you through a local Detroit bank (which has translation facilities and better international commercial paper routing procedures than you do). The Detroit bank will give you the letter and tell you that it is willing to transmit the documents and drafts to the German bank at the proper time. In this situation the Detroit bank is called an *adviser*.

On July 6, 2016, per your contract with Hans Goldschnitt, you draw up the packing lists, invoices, and certificates required by the letter of credit and put the goods on board a German Ocean Lines ship. In return you get a *clean* (free of carrier's notation indicating a defect in the goods or packaging) bill of lading to the order of the German bank and draw a draft payable to yourself on the NVF (that is, the German bank will be the drawee). You clip all these documents together and take them down to the Detroit bank, which forwards them to the German bank and makes an Article 3 presentment for you. If the German bank decides that you have complied with the terms of the letter of credit, it will honor the draft (pay it — the money is then remitted to you by the Detroit bank) and receive all the documents. The German bank then calls Hans Goldschnitt and tells him to come pay if he wants the documents he will need to get the goods off the ship. He does so. When the goods arrive, German Ocean Lines notifies Hans pursuant to instructions on their copy of the bill of lading. He presents the bill of lading and receives the goods.

Several variations on the above are possible. If you are unwilling to wait to get your money, you may be able to sell (*discount*) the drafts to the Detroit bank. Or, as part of your initial contract with the buyer, you may have required him to get a *Detroit bank* to issue the letter of credit to you. He can do this as follows: he establishes credit with the NVF; the NVF issues a letter of credit to you through the Detroit bank and asks the Detroit bank to *confirm* it. If the Detroit bank decides to do so (and it will first investigate the credit reputation of the German bank), it will notify you that the NVF has issued a letter of credit to you and that the Detroit bank "hereby confirms it." This makes the Detroit bank a *confirmer* and liable in exactly the same fashion as the issuer. The confirming letter of credit will state that the Detroit bank will honor drafts under the letter of credit if accompanied by the listed documents. The transaction then proceeds as above, except the drafts you draw are drawn on and presented to the Detroit bank for payment. (*Note:* it is possible to draw a *time* draft on the issuing bank whereby it is given 30, 60, or 90 days — as determined by contract — following formal *acceptance* in which to pay. Such a time draft is commonly called a *banker's acceptance*.) The issuing bank may require that the draft be presented for payment not to itself but to another entity with whom it has a contractual arrangement (called a *nominated person* — see §5-102(a)(11), defining the term, and §5-107(b) and its Official Comment 4, explaining the legal status of a nominated person). This is often done, for example, when the issuer does not carry sufficient amounts of the currency called for by the credit or when the issuing bank wants a more experienced institution to examine the documents presented by the beneficiary.

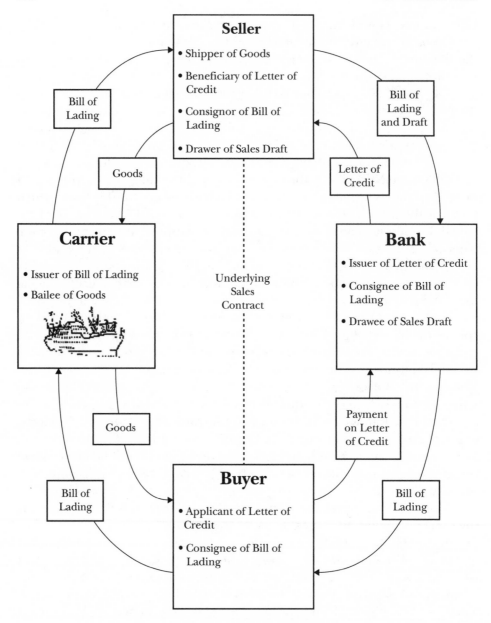

To be distinguished from the above *documentary credit* is the so-called *standby letter of credit*. A standby credit is issued by a bank to be honored only if there is default in an unrelated contract. For example, assume that a contractor agrees to build 50 apartment buildings for the owner of the lots on which the construction will occur. The owner might require the contractor to have its bank issue a standby credit in favor of the owner, to be drawn on only in the event that the contractor does not fulfill its contractual obligation. A standby credit differs from a documentary credit in that the beneficiary of the credit is not required to produce documents along with its draft against the letter of credit; instead, it typically just gives a written notice of breach. Thus, a standby credit is similar to a surety obligation (though not the same).[1] Standby letters of credit are much in use nowadays; in 2011, it was estimated that standby letters of credit in the United States totaled over $600 billion (and double that worldwide).

PROBLEM 98

The U.S. Army wanted to order uniforms for its soldiers from Khaki Clothing, Inc., agreeing to pay a set amount on delivery. The Army, however, had had major problems in past dealings with Khaki, which was always very late at meeting delivery schedules. The purchasing officer for the Army asked the Army's attorney if the contract could contain a penalty clause, imposing a huge penalty on Khaki if it did not deliver the uniforms by the required date. The attorney, mindful of basic contracts law, opined that penalty clauses (even if disguised as liquidated damages clauses) are invalid as a matter of common law, but then he had an idea. He put a clause in the purchasing contract requiring Khaki to get a standby letter of credit in favor of the Army and requiring the issuing bank to pay a huge penalty sum to the Army in the event that Khaki did not deliver the uniforms on time. Octopus National Bank issued such a credit, but when Khaki missed the delivery deadline and the Army tried to collect the penalty specified in the credit, the bank balked and in its defense pointed to the common law rule forbidding penalty clauses in contracts. Will this succeed? See Balboa Ins. Co. v. Coastal Bank, 42 U.C.C. Rep. Serv. 1716 (S.D. Ga. 1986); Telenois, Inc. v. Village of Schaumburg, 628 N.E.2d 581, 23 U.C.C. Rep. Serv. 2d 862 (Ill. App. 1993); McLaughlin, Standby Letters of Credit and Penalty Clauses: An Unexpected Synergy, 43 Ohio St. L.J. 1 (1982).

II. DEFINITIONS AND SCOPE OF ARTICLE 5

Section 5-102(a)(9) addresses itself to the question of who can issue a letter of credit. Section 5-104 describes the formal requirements of such a

---

1. It is *ultra vires* for a bank to act as a surety, so the courts have been careful to draw distinctions between suretyship and the issuance of a standby letter of credit, typically pointing to the fact that a surety is secondarily liable on the contract between the principal and the creditor, but that a bank's liability on a standby letter of credit is an independent obligation. See, e.g., State ex rel. Missouri Highway & Transp. Commn. v. Morganstein, 703 S.W.2d 894, 1 U.C.C. Rep. Serv. 2d 197 (Mo. 1986).

letter (note that electronically generated letters of credit are clearly allowed; see Official Comment 3 to §5-104).

Letters of credit *not* requiring the presentation of documents are called *clean credits* because normally only drafts are tendered. See Housing Sec. Inc. v. Maine Natl. Bank, 391 A.2d 311, 26 U.C.C. Rep. Serv. 750 (Me. 1978). The most startling use of such a letter of credit occurred in 1963, when the Royal Bank of Canada, the Morgan Guaranty Trust Co., and the Bank of America issued letters of credit totaling $106 million as security for the ransom of prisoners from the Cuban Bay of Pigs invasion. See Gerald T. McLaughlin, Remembering the Bay of Pigs: Using Letters of Credit To Facilitate the Resolution of International Disputes, 32 Ga. J. Int'l & Comp. L. 743 (2004).

Now read the definitions in §5-102. In the above hypothetical you were the *beneficiary* of the letter of credit; Hans Goldschnitt was the *applicant* (the former version of Article 5 called Hans the *customer*); the German bank was the *issuer*, and the Detroit bank was the *advisor* or *confirmer*, depending on which part of the hypothetical you are looking at. Read §5-107. Do not get these terms confused.

Now go back and reread §5-102(a)(10), which defines *letter of credit*. Article 7 of the UCP states that an "issuing bank is irrevocably bound to honour as of the time it issues the credit." By contrast, §5-106(a) *presumes* (if not otherwise stated) that a letter of credit is irrevocable. Remember this: *no one wants a revocable letter of credit*. To understand why, see §5-106(b); Official Comment 1 to that section comments that "revocable letters of credit offer unhappy possibilities for misleading the parties who deal with them." See Beathard v. Chicago Football Club, Inc., 419 F. Supp. 1133, 20 U.C.C. Rep. Serv. 164 (N.D. Ill. 1976). Article 2 of the UCC decrees that in sale of goods contracts, a clause requiring a letter of credit means an *irrevocable* letter of credit. Read §2-325. Circle the word *irrevocable* in subsection (3).

III. THE ISSUER — DUTIES AND RIGHTS

When the applicant comes to the issuing bank and asks to establish credit so that the bank will issue a letter of credit to the seller, the bank normally makes the applicant sign an airtight contract absolutely binding the applicant to reimburse the bank *or else*. Cf. §5-108(i)(1). When a bank issues an irrevocable letter of credit, it is under a duty to honor a draft properly drawn there under, §5-108(a), so it wants to protect itself. A bank owes corresponding duties to its applicant. Read §5-108 carefully. It is important to understand that if the issuer honors a draft that it should have dishonored, the issuer may not seek reimbursement from its applicant.[2] See Brenntag Intern. Chemicals, Inc. v. Norddeutsche Landesbank GZ, 70 F. Supp. 2d 399, 42 U.C.C. Rep. Serv. 2d 1107 (S.D.N.Y. 1999). An issuer in this predicament has a potential remedy in the warranty section, §5-110.

The moment of truth for the issuer occurs when the beneficiary presents a draft drawn on the issuer for the amount of the credit, accompanied by all the other items listed in the credit to be presented with the draft. In making the decision whether to pay the credit or to dishonor it (which could lead to a lawsuit alleging wrongful dishonor, with damages measured under §5-111) the issuer is only allowed to consider the documents presented by the beneficiary. What is called the "independence principle" flatly forbids the issuer to bring up matters having to do with the underlying transaction between the beneficiary and the applicant; read §5-103(d).

PROBLEM 99

At the request of its applicant, Greenbaum Construction Company, the Last National Bank issued a letter of credit to Latek Steel Company, obligating itself to pay drafts drawn against it, reflecting steel shipped to Greenbaum Construction under "Invoice #0046." Two weeks after the letter of credit was issued, the buyer and seller changed the shipment dates on the underlying contract and issued a new invoice, this one being "Invoice #0060." Latek Steel Company shipped the steel to Greenbaum Construction Company as agreed and was disturbed to learn that the buyer had filed for bankruptcy two days later. However, it was reassured by the terms of the letter of credit. On Friday, March 27, it submitted a draft to Last National, accompanied by Invoice #0060, and was turned down for payment on April 1. Answer these questions:

(a) Label the parties: who is the *issuer*, the *beneficiary*, the *applicant*?

(b) What is the effect of the bank holding onto the presented draft until April 1? See §5-108(b).

(c) Remembering the doctrine of *de minimis non curat lex* ("the law does not notice small defects"), the attorney for Latek Steel argued that it had substantially complied with the letter of credit, so the bank was guilty of wrongful dishonor and ought to respond in damages under §5-111. Is this right? See Dubose Steel, Inc. v. Branch Banking & Trust Co., 72 N.C. App.

---

2. Failure of the applicant to reimburse the issuer is irrelevant as far as the beneficiary is concerned. In this situation, the beneficiary is not liable to the issuer in quasi-contract under a theory of unjust enrichment. See City Natl. Bank v. Westland Towers Apartments, 152 Mich. App. 136, 2 U.C.C. Rep. Serv. 2d 1623 (1986). The usual explanation is that the beneficiary has not in any way been unjustly enriched; it was paid for goods delivered. Section 5-108(i)(4) clearly bars a restitution action in any situation where the defect was apparent on the face of the documents presented.

598, 324 S.E.2d 859, 41 U.C.C. Rep. Serv. 187 (1985); Dolan, Strict Compliance with Letters of Credit: Striking a Fair Balance, 102 Banking L.J. 18 (1985).

(d) Does the seller have any other remedy? See §2-702; Bankruptcy Code §546(c).

(e) What should Latek Steel have done to avoid all this? See §5-106(b).

Voest-Alpine Trading Co. v. Bank of China

United States District Court, Southern District of Texas, 2000
167 F. Supp. 2d 940, 46 U.C.C. Rep. Serv. 2d 808

GILMORE, District Judge.

On February 16-17 and 21-23, 2000, a bench trial was held in the above-styled case. Having considered the evidence in this case and the applicable law, the Court enters the following findings of fact and conclusions of law.

On June 23, 1995, Plaintiff Voest-Alpine Trading USA Corporation ("Voest-Alpine") entered into a contract with Jiangyin Foreign Trade Corporation ("JFTC") to sell JFTC 1,000 metric tons of styrene monomer at a total price of $1.2 million. To finance the transaction, JFTC applied for a letter of credit through Defendant Bank of China. The letter of credit provided for payment to Voest-Alpine once the goods had been shipped to Zhangjiagang, China and Voest-Alpine had presented the requisite paperwork to the Bank of China as described in the letter of credit. The letter of credit was issued by the Bank of China on July 6, 1995 and assigned the number LC9521033/95. In addition to numerous other typographical errors, Voest-Alpine's name was listed as "Voest-Alpine USA Trading Corp." instead of "Voest-Alpine Trading USA Corp." with the "Trading USA" portion inverted. The destination port was also misspelled in one place as "Zhang-jiagng," missing the third "a." The letter of credit did indicate, however, that the transaction would be subject to the 1993 Uniform Customs and Practice, International Chamber of Commerce Publication Number 500 ("UCP 500").

By the time the product was ready to ship, the market price of styrene monomer had dropped significantly from the original contract price between Voest-Alpine and JFTC. Although JFTC asked for a price concession in light of the decrease in market price, Voest-Alpine declined and, through its agents, shipped the styrene monomer on July 18, 1995. All required inspection and documentation was completed. On August 1, 1995, Voest-Alpine presented the documents specified in the letter of credit to Texas Commerce Bank, the presenting bank. Texas Commerce Bank found discrepancies between the presentation documents and the letter of credit which it related to Voest-Alpine. Because Voest-Alpine did not believe that any of the noted discrepancies would warrant refusal to pay, it instructed Texas Commerce Bank to forward the presentation documents to the Bank of China.

Texas Commerce Bank sent the documents via DHL courier to the Bank of China on August 3, 1995. According to the letter of credit, Voest-Alpine, the beneficiary, was required to present the documents within fifteen days of the shipping date, by August 2, 1995. As the documents were presented on August 1, 1995, they were presented timely under the letter of credit. Bank of China received the documents on August 9, 1995.

On August 11, 1995, the Bank of China sent a telex to Texas Commerce Bank, informing them of seven alleged discrepancies between the letter of credit and the documents Voest-Alpine presented, six of which are the subject of this action. The Bank of China claimed that 1) the beneficiary's name differed from the name listed in the letter of credit, as noted by the presenting bank; 2) Voest-Alpine had submitted bills of lading marked "duplicate" and "triplicate" instead of "original"; 3) the invoice, packing list and the certificate of origin were not marked "original"; 4) the date of the survey report was later than that of the bill of lading; 5) the letter of credit number in the beneficiary's certified copy of the fax was incorrect, as noted by the presenting bank; and 6) the destination was not listed correctly in the certificate of origin and the beneficiary's certificate, as noted by the presenting bank. The telex further stated, "We are contacting the applicant of the relative discrepancy [*sic*]. Holding documents at your risks and disposal."

On August 15, Texas Commerce Bank faxed the Bank of China, stating that the discrepancies were not an adequate basis to refuse to pay the letter of credit and requested that the bank honor the letter of credit and pay Voest-Alpine accordingly. The telex identified Voest-Alpine as the beneficiary in the transaction. Voest-Alpine also contacted JFTC directly in an effort to secure a waiver of the discrepancies but was unsuccessful.

On August 19, 1995, the Bank of China sent another telex to Texas Commerce Bank further explaining what it believed to be discrepancies between the letter of credit and the documentation presented by Voest-Alpine according to the UCP 500. In relevant part, the telex provided: "You cannot say [the discrepancies] are of no consequence. The fact is that our bank must examine all documents stipulated in the credit with reasonable care, to ascertain whether or not they appear, on their face, to be incompliance [*sic*] with the terms and conditions of the credit. According to Article 13 of UCP 500. An irrevocable credit constitutes a definite undertaking of the issuing bank, providing that the stipulated documents are complied with the terms and conditions of the credit according to Article UCP 500. Now the discrepant documents may have us refuse to take up the documents according to article 14(B) of UCP 500."

The Bank of China returned the documents to Voest-Alpine and did not honor the letter of credit.

I.

The commercial letter of credit is a payment device often used in international trade which permits a buyer in a transaction to substitute its financial integrity with that of a stable credit source, usually a bank. *Alaska Textile Co., Inc. v. Chase Manhattan Bank, N.A.*, 982 F.2d 813, 815 (2d Cir. 1992).

"[A letter of credit] transaction usually comprises three separate contracts: '[f]irst, the issuing bank enters into a contract with its customer to issue the letter of credit. Second, there is a contract between the issuing bank and the party receiving the letter of credit. Third, the customer who procured the letter of credit signs a contract with the person receiving it, usually involving the sale of goods or the provision of some service.'" *Resolution Trust Corporation v. Kimball*, 963 F.2d 820, 820 (5th Cir. 1992) (quoting *East Girard Sav. Ass'n v. Citizens National Bank, Etc.*, 593 F.2d 598, 601 (5th Cir. 1979)). The underlying principle of the letter of credit transaction is the independence of the three contracts. *Philadelphia Gear Corp. v. Central Bank*, 717 F.2d 230, 235 (5th Cir. 1983). The issuing bank does not verify that all the terms of the underlying contract have been fulfilled and must pay on a draft properly presented by a beneficiary, without reference to the rights or obligations of the parties to the contract. Tex. Bus. & Comm. Code Ann. §5.108(a), (f)(1) (Vernon's 2000). The issuing bank need only make a facial examination of the presenting documents to determine whether the beneficiary has complied with the terms of the letter of credit, however, the bank bears the risk of any misinterpretation of the beneficiary's demand for payment. Tex. Bus. & Comm. Code Ann. §5.108(i)(4) (Vernon's 2000).

Prior to the amendments to the Texas Business and Commercial Code in 1999, a beneficiary was not required to make its presentation documents strictly comply with the letter of credit, but to present documents that on their face "appear[ed] to comply" with the letter of credit in order to receive payment. Tex. Bus. & Comm. Code Ann. §5.109(b)[3] (Vernon's 1998); see also *Vest v. Pilot Point Nat'l Bank*, 996 S.W.2d 9, 12 (Tex. Civ. App. 1999) (finding that the language in section 5.109 did not mandate strict compliance). The current statutory law requires an issuer to honor a presentation that, as determined by standard practice of financial institutions that regularly issue letters of credit, "appears on its face strictly to comply with the terms and conditions of the letter of credit." Tex. Bus. & Comm. Code Ann. §5.108(a), (e) (Vernon's 2000). Determination of what constitutes standard practice of financial institutions is a "matter of interpretation for the court." Tex. Bus. & Comm. Code Ann. §5.108(e) (Vernon's 2000).

---

3. The prior version of Article 5 — EDS.

The Uniform Customs and Practices for Documentary Credits, first issued in 1930 by the International Chamber of Commerce and revised approximately once every ten years since, is a compilation of internationally accepted commercial practices which may be incorporated into the private law of a contract between parties. Banco General Runinahui, S.A. v. Citibank Int'l, 97 F.3d 480, 482 (11th Cir. 1996) (citing *Alaska Textile*, 982 F.2d at 816). In this case, the parties expressly adopted the UCP 500 as the governing authority in the letter of credit. Where parties explicitly refer to the UCP 500 in their contracts, the UCP has been interpreted to apply to the transaction. *Vest*, 996 S.W.2d at 15. Accordingly, the Court will look to the UCP for guidance in analyzing whether the actions of the Bank of China were in conformity with "standard practice" of financial institutions.

The Bank of China claims that its August 11, 1995 telex to Texas Commerce Bank constituted notice of refusal under the UCP 500 because it contained the required elements listed in Article 14(d). Voest-Alpine argues that the telex did not constitute notice of refusal because there is no clear statement of refusal and because the portion of the telex that indicated that the Bank of China was contacting JFTC to seek a waiver rendered the communication ambiguous.

Article 14(d) of the UCP 500 provides:

> i. If the Issuing Bank . . . decides to refuse the [presentation] documents, it must give notice to that effect by telecommunication or, if that is not possible, by other expeditious means, without delay but no later than the close of the seventh banking day following the day of receipt of the documents. Such notice shall be given to the bank from which it received the documents, or to the Beneficiary, if it received the documents directly from him.
>
> ii. Such notice must state all discrepancies in respect of which the bank refuses the documents and must also state whether it is holding the documents at the disposal of, or is returning them to, the presenter.

International Chamber of Commerce, ICC Uniform Customs and Practice for Documentary Credits, ICC Publication No. 500 20 (1993).

According to Article 14(d), if the issuing bank elects not to honor the presentation documents, it must provide a notice of refusal within seven banking days of receipt of the documents and the notice must contain any and all discrepancies and state the disposition of the rejected documents. The section requires that if a bank wishes to reject a presentation of documents, it "*must give notice to that effect.*" (emphasis supplied)

Here, the Bank of China's notice is deficient because nowhere does it state that it is actually rejecting the documents or refusing to honor the letter of credit or any words to that effect. While it is true that under the UCP 500 the notice must contain a list of discrepancies and the disposition of the documents and the Bank of China's telex of August 11, 1995 does indeed contain these elements, this only addresses the requirements of Article 14(d)(ii). A notice of refusal, by its own terms must actually convey refusal, as specified in Article 14(d)(i). This omission is only compounded by the statement that the Bank of China would contact the applicant to determine if it would waive the discrepancies. As Plaintiff's expert, Professor James Byrne, testified, within the framework of Article 14, this additional piece of information holds open the possibility of acceptance upon waiver of the discrepancies by JFTC and indicates that the Bank of China has not refused the documents.

In the August 19, 1995 telex, the Bank of China stated, "Now the discrepant documents *may have us refuse* to take up the documents according to article 14(B) of UCP 500" (emphasis supplied). This is the bank's first mention of refusal and it is tentative at best. The use of "now" further indicates that the documents were not previously refused in the August 11, 1995 telex. Even if this second telex was sent as a notice of refusal, it came too late. The Court finds that the evidence establishes that the telex was sent on August 19, 1995. Seven banking days, the refusal period allotted by the UCP 500 Article 14(d), would have expired on August 18, 1995. International Chamber of Commerce, ICC Uniform Customs and Practice for Documentary Credits, ICC Publication No. 500 21 (1993). Accordingly, the Court finds that the Bank of China did not provide a notice of refusal within seven banking days of receipt of the presentation documents as required by Article 14(d) of the UCP 500. The Bank of China's failure to formally refuse the documents before the deadline precludes the bank from claiming that the documents are not in compliance with the terms and conditions of the credit, according to Article 14(e) of the UCP 500. Id. Although the Court could properly conclude its analysis here, the Court will analyze the discrepancies listed by the Bank of China in the August 11, 1995 telex.

II.

Voest-Alpine claims that the six remaining discrepancies cited by the Bank of China are mere technicalities and typographical errors that do not warrant the rejection of the documents. Voest-Alpine argues for a "functional standard" of compliance, contending that if the whole of the documents obviously relate to the transaction covered by the credit, the issuing bank must honor the letter of credit. The Bank of China argues that the discrepancies were significant and that if the documents contain discrepancies on their face, it is justified in rejecting them and is not required to look beyond the papers themselves.

Section 13(a) of the UCP 500 provides:

> Banks must examine all documents stipulated in the Credit with reasonable care, to ascertain whether or not they appear, on their face, to be in compliance with the terms and conditions of the Credit. Compliance of the stipulated documents on their face with the terms and conditions of the Credit shall be determined by international standard banking practice as reflected in these Articles. Documents which appear on their face to be inconsistent with one another will be considered as not appearing on their face to be in compliance with the terms and conditions of the Credit.

International Chamber of Commerce, ICC Uniform Customs and Practice for Documentary Credits, ICC Publication No. 500 19 (1993).

The UCP 500 does not provide guidance on what inconsistencies would justify a conclusion on the part of a bank that the documents are not in compliance with the terms and conditions of the letter of credit or what discrepancies are not a reasonable basis for such a conclusion. The UCP 500 does not mandate that the documents be a mirror image of the requirements or use the term "strict compliance."

The Court notes the wide range of interpretations on what standard banks should employ in examining letter of credit document presentations for compliance. Even where courts claim to uphold strict compliance, the standard is hardly uniform. The first and most restrictive approach is to require that the presentation documents be a mirror image of the requirements. See Banco General Runinahui, S.A. v. Citibank Int'l, 97 F.3d 480, 483 (11th Cir. 1996) ("This Court has recognized and applied the 'strict compliance' standard to requests for payment under commercial letters of credit. . . . '[T]he fact that a defect is a mere technicality' does not matter.") (quoting Kerr-McGee Chem. Corp. v. FDIC, 872 F.2d 971, 973 (11th Cir. 1989)); Alaska Textile Co. v. Chase Manhattan Bank, 982 F.2d 813, 816 (2d Cir. 1992) (Noting that documents that are nearly the same as those required by the letter of credit are unacceptable for presentation in a letter of credit transaction).

Second, there are also cases claiming to follow the strict compliance standard but support rejection only where the discrepancies are such that would create risks for the issuer if the bank were to accept the presentation documents. See Flagship Cruises Ltd., v. New England Merchants Nat'l Bank of Boston, 569 F.2d 699, 705 (1st Cir. 1978) ("We do not see these rulings as retreats from rigorous insistence on compliance with letter of credit requirements. They merely recognize that variance between documents specified and documents submitted is not fatal if there is no possibility that the documents could mislead the paying bank to its detriment"); Crist v. J. Henry Schroder Bank & Trust Co., 693 F. Supp. 1429, 1433 (S.D.N.Y. 1988) (where a party who has succeeded by operation of law to the rights of the beneficiary of a letter of credit, refusal was improper, even though the terms of the credit provided for payment only to the beneficiary); Bank of Cochin, Ltd. v. Manufacturers Hanover Trust Co., 612 F. Supp. 1533, 1541 (S.D.N.Y. 1985) (even under the strict compliance standard, a variance is permitted between the documents specified in a letter of credit and the documents presented thereunder where "there is no possibility that the documents could mislead the paying bank to its detriment"); *Vest*, 996 S.W.2d at 14 (noting that strict compliance does not demand "oppressive perfectionism").

A third standard, without much support in case law, is to analyze the documents for risk to the applicant. See Int'l Chamber of Commerce, Comm'n on Banking Technique and Practice, Publication No. 511, UCP 500 & 400 Compared 39 (Charles del Busto ed. 1994) (discussion of a standard that would permit "deviations that do not cause ostensible harm" to the applicant); see also Breathless Assoc. v. First Savings & Loan Assoc., 654 F. Supp. 832, 836 (N.D. Tex. 1986) (noting, under the strict compliance standard, "[a] discrepancy . . . should not warrant dishonor unless it reflects an increased likelihood of defective performance or fraud on the part of the beneficiary").

The mirror image approach is problematic because it absolves the bank reviewing the documents of any responsibility to use common sense to determine if the documents, on their face, are related to the transaction or even to review an entire document in the context of the others presented to the bank. On the other hand, the second and third approaches employ a determination-of-harm standard that is too unwieldy. Such an analysis would improperly require the bank to evaluate risks that it might suffer or that might be suffered by the applicant and could undermine the independence of the three contracts that underlie the letter of credit payment scheme by forcing the bank to look beyond the face of the presentation documents.

The Court finds that a moderate, more appropriate standard lies within the UCP 500 itself and the opinions issued by the International Chamber of Commerce ("ICC") Banking Commission. One of the Banking Commission opinions defined the term "consistency" between the letter of credit and the documents presented to the issuing bank as used in Article 13(a) of the UCP to mean that "the whole of the documents must obviously relate to the same transaction, that is to say, that each should bear a relation (link) with the others on its face. . . ." Int'l Chamber of Commerce, Banking Comm'n, Publication No. 371, Decisions (1975-1979) of the ICC Banking Commission R. 12 (1980). The Banking Commission rejected the notion that "all of the documents should be *exactly* consistent in their wording." Id. (emphasis in original).

A common sense, case-by-case approach would permit minor deviations of a typographical nature because such a letter-for-letter correspondence between the letter of credit and the presentation documents is virtually impossible. See Int'l Chamber of Commerce, Comm'n on Banking Technique and Practice, Publication No. 511, UCP 500 & 400 Compared 39 (Charles del Busto ed. 1994) (noting the difficulty in attaining mirror-image compliance). While the end result of such an analysis may bear a strong resemblance to the relaxed strict compliance standard, the actual calculus used by the issuing bank is not the risk it or the applicant faces but rather, whether the documents bear a rational link to one another. In this way, the issuing bank is required to examine a particular document in light of all documents presented and use common sense but is not required to evaluate risks or go beyond the face of the documents. The Court finds that in this case the Bank of China's listed discrepancies should be analyzed under this standard by determining whether the whole of the documents obviously relate to the transaction on their face.

First, the Bank of China claimed that the beneficiary's name in the presentation documents, Voest-Alpine Trading USA, differed from the letter of credit, which listed the beneficiary as Voest-Alpine USA Trading. While it is true that the letter of credit inverted Voest-Alpine's geographic locator, all the documents Voest-Alpine presented that obviously related to this transaction placed the geographic locator behind "Trading," not in front of it. Furthermore, the addresses corresponded to that listed in the letter of credit and Texas Commerce Bank's cover letter to the Bank of China identified Voest-Alpine Trading USA as the beneficiary in the transaction with JFTC. The letter of credit with the inverted name bore obvious links to the documents presented by Voest-Alpine Trading USA. This is in contrast to a misspelling or outright omission. See Beyene v. Irving Trust Co., 762 F.2d 4 (2d Cir. 1985) (listing beneficiary as "Soran" rather than "Sofan" was sufficient basis for refusal); Bank of Cochin, Ltd. v. Manufacturers Hanover Trust Co., 612 F. Supp. 1533 (S.D.N.Y. 1985) (omitting "Ltd." from corporate name justified rejection). In contrast with these cases, the inversion of the geographic locator here does not signify a different corporate entity. The expert testimony of Professor Byrne supports the finding that this is not a discrepancy that warrants rejection of the presentation documents because the UCP 500 does not impose a standard of exact replication.

Second, the Bank of China pointed out that the set of originals of the bill of lading should have all been stamped "original" rather than "original," "duplicate" and "triplicate." It should be noted that neither the letter of credit nor any provision in the UCP 500 requires such stamping. In fact, the ICC Banking Commission expressly ruled that "duplicate" and "triplicate" bills of lading did not need to be marked "original" and that failure to label them as originals did not justify refusal of the documents. Int'l Chamber of Commerce, Banking Comm'n, Publication No. 565, Opinions of the ICC Banking Comm'n 1995-1996 38 (Gary Collyer ed. 1997). While it is true that this clarification by the ICC came after the transaction at issue in this case, it is clear from the face of the documents that these documents are three originals rather than one original and two copies. The documents have signatures in blue ink [*sic*—that?] vary slightly, bear original stamps oriented differently on each page and clearly state on their face that the preparer made three original bills. Further, one possible definition of duplicate is "[t]o make or execute again" and one definition of triplicate is "[o]ne of a set of three identical things." Webster's II New Riverside University Dictionary 410, 1237 (1994). While the "duplicate" and "triplicate" stamps may have been confusing, stamps do not make obviously original documents into copies.

Third, the Bank of China claimed that the failure to stamp the packing list documents as "original" was a discrepancy. Again, these documents are clearly originals on their face as they have three slightly differing signatures in blue ink. There was no requirement in the letter of credit or the UCP 500 that original documents be marked as such. The ICC's policy statement on the issue provides that, "banks treat as original any document that appears to be hand signed by the issuer of the document." (Int'l Chamber of Commerce, Comm'n on Banking Technique and Practice, The determination of an "Original" document in the context of UCP 500 sub-Article 20(b) July 12, 1999). http://www.iccwbo.org/home/statementsrules/statements/1999/the-determination-of-an-original-document.asp. The failure to mark obvious originals is not a discrepancy.

Fourth, the Bank of China argues that the date of the survey report is after the bill of lading and is therefore discrepant. A careful examination of the survey report reveals that the survey took place "immediately before/after loading" and that the sample of cargo "to be loaded" was taken. The plain language of the report reveals that the report may have been issued after the bill of lading but the survey itself was conducted before the ship departed. The date does not pose a discrepancy.

Fifth, the Bank of China claims that the letter of credit number listed in the beneficiary's certified copy of [*sic*] fax is wrong. The letter of credit number was listed as "LC95231033/95" on the copy of [*sic*] fax instead of "LC9521033/95" as in the letter of credit itself, adding an extra "3" after "LC952." However, adding the letter of credit number to this document was gratuitous and in the numerous other places in the documents that the letter of credit was referenced by number, it was incorrect only in one place. Moreover, the seven other pieces of information contained in the document were correct. The document checker could have easily looked to any other document to verify the letter of credit number, or looked to the balance of the information within the document and found that the document as a whole bears an obvious relationship to the transaction. Madame Gao, the document checker who reviewed Voest-Alpine's presentation documents for the Bank of China, testified that she did not look beyond the face of this particular document in assessing the discrepancy. The cover letter from Texas Commerce Bank, for example, had the correct number.

Finally, the Bank of China claims that the wrong destination is listed in the certificate of origin and the beneficiary's certificate. The certificate of origin spelled Zhangjiagang as "Zhangjiagng" missing an "a" as it is misspelled once in the letter of credit, making it consistent. The beneficiary's certificate, however, spelled it "Zhanjiagng," missing a "g" in addition to the "a," a third spelling that did not appear in the letter of credit. Madame Gao first considered the discrepancy a "misspelling" rather than an indication of the wrong port, according to her notes. There is no port in China called "Zhangjiagng" or "Zhanjiagng." "Gng" is a combination of letters not found in Romanized Chinese, whereas "gang" means "port" in Chinese. The other information contained in the document was correct, such as the letter of credit number and the contract number, and even contained the distinctive phrase "by courie lukdt within 3 days after shipment," presumably meaning by courier within three days after shipment, as in the letter of credit. The document as a whole bears an obvious relationship with the transaction. The misspelling of the destination is not a basis for dishonor of the letter of credit where the rest of the document has demonstrated linkage to the transaction on its face.

Based on the foregoing, the Court finds in favor of the plaintiff, Voest-Alpine.

NOTES

1. This case was decided under the UCP 500, where the so-called *strict compliance* requirement was less markedly pronounced than it currently is in the Uniform Commercial Code. Indeed, in the more recent UCP 600 things get even murkier. Article 14(d) states that "Data in a document, when read in context with the credit, the document itself and international standard banking practice, need not be identical to, but must not conflict with, data in that document, any other stipulated document or the credit." For the tests under the UCC, read §§5-103(d) and 5-108(a) and the following Official Comments: Official Comment 3 to §5-102 and Official Comment 1 to §5-108. Using the tests therein (which have changed since the above case), would the court have reached the same result? In determining whether there is strict compliance with the credit, §5-108(a) refers to "standard practice," as does (e). The International Chamber of Commerce has promulgated a guide as to that called "International Standard Banking Practice for the Examination of Documents under Documentary Credits" (ICC Publication 645).

2. As to the waiver issue in the above case, see §5-108(c).

3. In letter of credit transactions, it should be emphasized that banks issuing the credits do not charge a great deal and therefore should be exposed to a minimum risk. If a bank is going to dishonor the credit, it should make sure that it is playing fair with all the parties involved so that in any ensuing litigation the commercial reasonableness of its actions will attract the sympathy of the court.

PROBLEM 100

Assume in the last Problem that the letter of credit issued by Last National had required that the bill of lading representing the goods be given not to Greenbaum Construction Company, the applicant, but presented to the bank itself. Assume also that Latek Steel has completely complied with all of the terms of the credit, but Last National, knowing of the applicant's bankruptcy, wrongfully refuses to pay the credit as agreed. You are the attorney for Latek Steel, and the vice president in charge of marketing calls you with some questions. The market for steel is falling rapidly. Must Latek Steel resell the steel involved in this transaction immediately, or may it wait, hoping the bank will change its mind and pay what it owes? If it does resell, does that reduce the amount it can claim as damages from Last National? As to both these matters, see §5-111(a).

PROBLEM 101

At the request of its applicant, Octopus National Bank (ONB) issued an irrevocable letter of credit to Warren Crook, the beneficiary. The credit's terms required a bill of lading showing that the goods were loaded on board the *S.S. Titanic* by April 1, 2014. Crook cleverly drew up a phony bill of lading supposedly issued by the *Titanic* and presented it along with a draft on the bank to the issuer. ONB paid the draft. Can it collect from its applicant? See §5-108; also note §§5-110 (warranties on transfer and presentment), 5-111 (presenter's right to damages on wrongful dishonor of a draft), and 5-117 (subrogation rights of the parties). Could the applicant use the §5-110 warranties to sue the beneficiary?

PROBLEM 102

Luddite Technologies, Inc., wanted to build a new company headquarters. It hired Weekend Construction Company to do the job, requiring a standby letter of credit of $80,000 to be paid if Weekend failed to keep to the required schedule for completion of the building. At Weekend's request, Last

National Bank issued such a credit in favor of Luddite, payable, according to the terms of the credit, "on default by Weekend Construction Company in meeting the attached completion schedule and the beneficiary's presentation of an affidavit to that effect along with a draft drawn on us for $80,000." Weekend Construction dutifully performed its contractual duties, but the president of Luddite, needing money, sent the required draft and affidavit to Last National, wrongfully asserting that Weekend had missed timely completion of a part of the project. Last National paid the draft without investigating the truth of the assertions in the affidavit and now seeks reimbursement from the applicant, Weekend Construction. Can Weekend resist paying under the theory that Last National did not verify the default as the letter of credit required? See §5-108(g) and its Official Comment 9. White & Summers explain: "Where the documents commit the issuer to assess facts and events outside the documents presented, they disable the independence principle and topple the wall that separates presented documents from beneficiary-applicant disputes"; §21-6-g at 1112. If Weekend Construction has gone bankrupt since the bank honored the draft, can Last National pursue Luddite Technologies to get its money back? See §§5-108(i)(4), 5-110. How quickly must it act? See §5-115.

IV. FRAUD

Sztejn v. J. Henry Schroder Bank Corp.

New York Supreme Court, 1941
177 Misc. 719, 31 N.Y.S.2d 631

SHIENTAG, J.

This is a motion by the defendant, the Chartered Bank of India, Australia and China, (hereafter referred to as the Chartered Bank), made pursuant to Rule 106(5) of the Rules of Civil Practice to dismiss the supplemental complaint on the ground that it fails to state facts sufficient to constitute a cause of action against the moving defendant. The plaintiff brings this action to restrain the payment or presentment of payment of drafts under a letter of credit issued to secure the purchase price of certain merchandise, bought by the plaintiff and his coadventurer, one Schwarz, who is a party defendant in this action. The plaintiff also seeks a judgment declaring the letter of credit and drafts thereunder null and void. The complaint alleges that the documents accompanying the drafts are fraudulent in that they do not represent actual merchandise but instead cover boxes fraudulently filled with worthless material by the seller of the goods. The moving defendant urges that the complaint fails to state a cause of action against it because the Chartered Bank is only concerned with the documents and on their face these conform to the requirement of the letter of credit.

On January 7, 1941, the plaintiff and his coadventurer contracted to purchase a quantity of bristles from the defendant Transea Traders, Ltd. (hereafter referred to as Transea) a corporation having its place of business in Lucknow, India. In order to pay for the bristles, the plaintiff and Schwarz contracted with the defendant J. Henry Schroder Banking Corporation (hereafter referred to as Schroder), a domestic corporation, for the issuance of an irrevocable letter of credit to Transea which provided that drafts by the latter for a specified portion of the purchase price of the bristles would be paid by Schroder upon shipment of the described merchandise and presentation of an invoice and a bill of lading covering the shipment, made out to the order of Schroder.

The letter of credit was delivered to Transea by Schroder's correspondent bank in India, Transea placed fifty cases of material on board a steamship, procured a bill of lading from the steamship company and obtained the customary invoices. These documents describe the bristles called for by the letter of credit. However, the complaint alleges that in fact Transea filled the fifty crates with cowhair, other worthless material and rubbish with intent to simulate genuine merchandise and defraud the plaintiff and Schwarz. The complaint then alleges that Transea drew a draft under the letter of credit to the order of the Chartered Bank and delivered the draft and the fraudulent documents to the "Chartered Bank at Cawnpore, India, for collection for the account of said defendant Transea." The Chartered Bank has presented the draft along with the documents to Schroder for payment. The plaintiff prays for a judgment declaring the letter of credit and draft there under void and for injunctive relief to prevent the payment of the draft.

For the purpose of this motion, the allegations of the complaint must be deemed established and "every intendment and fair inference is in favor of the pleading." . . . Therefore, it must be assumed that Transea was engaged in a scheme to defraud the plaintiff and Schwarz, that the merchandise shipped by Transea is worthless rubbish and that the Chartered Bank is not an innocent holder of the draft for value but is merely attempting to procure payment of the draft for Transea's account.

It is well established that a letter of credit is independent of the primary contract of sale between the buyer and the seller. The issuing bank agrees to pay upon presentation of documents, not goods. This rule is necessary to preserve the efficiency of the letter of credit as an instrument for the financing of trade. One of the chief purposes of the letter of credit is to furnish the seller with a ready means of obtaining prompt payment for his merchandise. It would be a most unfortunate interference with business transactions if a bank before honoring drafts drawn upon it was obliged or even allowed to go behind the documents, at the request of the buyer and enter into controversies between the buyer and the seller regarding the quality of the merchandise shipped. If the buyer and the seller intended the bank to do this they could have so provided in the letter of credit itself, and in the absence of such a provision, the court will not demand or even permit the bank to delay paying drafts which are proper in form.... Of course, the application of this doctrine presupposes that the documents accompanying the draft are genuine and conform in terms to the requirements of the letter of credit....

However, I believe that a different situation is presented in the instant action. This is not a controversy between the buyer and seller concerning a mere breach of warranty regarding the quality of the merchandise; on the present motion, it must be assumed that the seller has intentionally failed to ship any goods ordered by the buyer. In such a situation, where the seller's fraud has been called to the bank's attention before the drafts and documents have been presented for payment, the principle of the independence of the bank's obligation under the letter of credit should not be extended to protect the unscrupulous seller. It is true that even though the documents are forged or fraudulent, if the issuing bank has already paid the draft before receiving notice of the seller's fraud, it will be protected if it exercised reasonable diligence before making such payment.... However, in the instant action Schroder has received notice of Transea's active fraud before it accepted or paid the draft. The Chartered Bank, which under the allegations of the complaint stands in no better position than Transea, should not be heard to complain because Schroder is not forced to pay the draft accompanied by documents covering a transaction which it has reason to believe is fraudulent.

Although our courts have used broad language to the effect that a letter of credit is independent of the primary contract between the buyer and seller, that language was used in cases concerning alleged breaches of warranty; no case has been brought to my attention on this point involving an intentional fraud on the part of the seller which was brought to the bank's notice with the request that it withhold payment of the draft on this account. This distinction between a breach of warranty and active fraud on the part of the seller is supported by authority and reason. As one court has stated: "Obviously, when the issuer of a letter of credit knows that a document, although correct in form, is, in point of fact, false or illegal, he cannot be called upon to recognize such a document as complying with the terms of a letter of credit." Old Colony Trust Co. v. Lawyers' Title & Trust Co., 2d Cir., 297 F. 152 at page 158, *certiorari denied*, 265 U.S. 585, 44 S. Ct. 459, 68 L. Ed. 1192....

No hardship will be caused by permitting the bank to refuse payment where fraud is claimed, where the merchandise is not merely inferior in quality but consists of worthless rubbish, where the draft and the accompanying documents are in the hands of one who stands in the same position as the fraudulent seller, where the bank has been given notice of the fraud before being presented with the drafts and documents for payment, and where the bank itself does not wish to pay pending an adjudication of the rights and obligations of the other parties. While the primary factor in the issuance of the letter of credit is the credit standing of the buyer, the security afforded by the merchandise is also taken into account. In fact, the letter of credit requires a bill of lading made out to the order of the bank and not the buyer. Although the bank is not interested in the exact detailed performance of the sales contract, it is vitally interested in assuring itself that there are some goods represented by the documents. Finkelstein, Legal Aspects of Commercial Letters of Credit, p. 238; O'Meara v. National Park Bank of New York, 239 N.Y. 386, 401, 146 N.E. 636, 39 A.L.R. 747, opinion of Cardozo, J., dissenting; Thayer, Irrevocable Credits in International Commerce, 37 C.L.R. 1326, 1335.

On this motion only the complaint is before me and I am bound by its allegation that the Chartered Bank is not a holder in due course but is a mere agent for collection for the account of the seller charged with fraud. Therefore, the Chartered Bank's motion to dismiss the complaint must be denied. If it had appeared from the face of the complaint that the bank presenting the draft for payment was a holder in due course, its claim against the bank issuing the letter of credit would not be defeated even though the primary transaction was tainted with fraud. . . .

Accordingly, the defendant's motion to dismiss the supplemental complaint is denied.

Is *Sztejn* still good law? Read §5-109 and its Official Comments carefully; see Mid-America Tire, Inc. v. PTZ Trading Ltd. Import and Export Agents, 2000 WL 1725415, 43 U.C.C. Rep. Serv. 2d 964 (Ohio App. 2000).

Note well that it has always been the law that if the draft is held by a holder in due course, the bank that issued the letter of credit is not allowed to allege the defense of fraud; see §5-109(a)(1) (expanding this idea to protect all innocent parties); Daiwa Products, Inc. v. NationsBank, N.A., 885 So. 2d 884 (Fla. App. 2004).

PROBLEM 103

Just as Octopus National Bank was about to honor a draft drawn on it by the beneficiary of its letter of credit, the bank's applicant called and demanded that the bank dishonor the draft because the beneficiary was guilty of "out-and-out fraud" on the underlying transaction between them.

The bank calls you, its attorney, for advice. The documents presented along with the draft exactly match the terms of the credit, and the bank officials are sure that there is no fraud in the documents. Look at §§5-108 and 5-109, and tell the bank what you think it should do. Cf. Emery-Waterhouse Co. v. Rhode Island Hosp. Trust Natl. Bank, 757 F.2d 399, 40 U.C.C. Rep. Serv. 737 (1st Cir. 1985) (punitive damages of $1,397,000 awarded against beneficiary who fraudulently drew against a letter of credit). If ONB dishonors the draft and this causes the beneficiary to lose millions of dollars on the underlying transaction, is ONB ever liable for *more* than the amount of the letter of credit? See §5-111.

In §5-109(a) the bank is given the option to honor or not as it wishes. As you can well imagine, banks tend to pay more attention to the applicant's request to dishonor if his name is Donald Trump than if her name is Jane Doe. If the bank decides to honor the draft, the applicant has two causes of action against the seller-beneficiary: the underlying obligation (normally the contract of sale, see Article 2) and the §5-110(a)(2) warranty.

Intrinsic Values Corp. v. Superintendencia de Administracion Tributaria

Florida Court of Appeals, 2002
806 So. 2d 616, 46 U.C.C. Rep. Serv. 2d 1092

SHEVIN, Judge.
Intrinsic Values Corporation appeals an order denying its motion to dissolve a temporary injunction. We affirm.

Superintendencia de Administracion Tributaria, the Guatemala tax administration agency, entered into a contract with Intrinsic, a Panamanian corporation, for the purchase of automobile license plates, decals and identification cards. At Superintendencia's request, Banco de Guatemala issued irrevocable letters of credit for Intrinsic's benefit; First Union National Bank and Barclays Bank, PLC, were the confirming banks.

Based on Intrinsic's failure to supply the goods, Superintendencia unilaterally canceled the contract, as provided therein. Superintendencia filed an action against Intrinsic in Guatemala, the forum selected in the parties' agreement. The Guatemala court issued an injunction barring Banco de Guatemala from paying on the letters of credit.

Subsequently, in Florida, Superintendencia brought an action pursuant to section 675.109(2), Florida Statutes (2001) to prevent First Union and Barclays from honoring the letter of credit. Superintendencia asserted that it had canceled the contract due to Intrinsic's failure to perform according to contract specifications, that the Guatemalan injunction was in force, and that honor of any presentment by Intrinsic would facilitate a material fraud. Intrinsic was not named in the complaint, nor served with notice. The court entered an agreed-upon injunction. Intrinsic learned of the injunction when it sought payment under the letter of credit. Intrinsic intervened in the action and sought an order dissolving the injunction. Following an evidentiary hearing, the court denied the motion.

The trial court properly denied Intrinsic's motion to dissolve the temporary injunction. In support of its request for a temporary injunction, Superintendencia presented two bases for the injunction: presentment would result in a material fraud; and comity militated in favor of the injunction. The temporary injunction was properly entered on those bases.

Section 675.109(2) provides:

> (2) If an applicant claims that a required document is forged or materially fraudulent or that honor of the presentation would facilitate a material fraud by the beneficiary on the issuer or applicant, a court of competent jurisdiction may temporarily or permanently enjoin the issuer from honoring a presentation or grant similar relief against the issuer or other persons only if the court finds that:
>
> (a) The relief is not prohibited under the law applicable to an accepted draft or deferred obligation incurred by the issuer;
>
> (b) A beneficiary, issuer, or nominated person who may be adversely affected is adequately protected against loss that it may suffer because the relief is granted;
>
> (c) All of the conditions to entitle a person to the relief under the laws of this state have been met; and
>
> (d) On the basis of the information submitted to the court, the applicant is more likely than not to succeed under its claim of forgery or material fraud and the person demanding honor does not qualify for protection under paragraph (1)(a).

As required under the statute, Superintendencia demonstrated that honoring a presentation would facilitate a material fraud by the beneficiary on the issuer or applicant. The record demonstrates as follows: Intrinsic did not perform in accordance with the contract; Superintendencia had canceled the contract; Superintendencia notified Intrinsic of cancellation, and had obtained an injunction against payment by the issuing bank; and Superintendencia had brought this action to prevent Intrinsic from committing a material fraud by presenting documents for payment of the letter of credit. Superintendencia also demonstrated, more likely than not, that it would succeed on the material fraud claim. Itek Corp. v. First Nat'l Bank of Boston, 730 F.2d 19 (1st Cir. 1984); Rockwell Int'l Sys. v. Citibank, N.A., 719 F.2d 583 (2d Cir. 1983); Touche Ross & Co. v. Manufacturers Hanover Trust Co., 107 Misc. 2d 438, 434 N.Y.S.2d 575 (Sup. Ct. 1980).

The Uniform Commercial Code Comment to section 675.109 addresses the propriety of awarding an injunction under the factual scenario in this case. "Material fraud by the beneficiary occurs only when the beneficiary has no colorable right to expect honor and where there is no basis in fact to support such a right to honor." U.C.C. §5-109 (1999) cmt. 1. Here, Intrinsic was aware that the contract had been canceled prior to presentment. Under these circumstances Intrinsic's demand for payment had "absolutely no basis in fact"; the Guatemala injunction forbid the issuer's payment on letters of credit based on this contract. Thus, the facts demonstrate the possibility of a "'fraud' so serious as to make it obviously pointless and unjust to permit the beneficiary to obtain the money." U.C.C. §5-109 (1999) cmt. 1 (quoting Ground Air Transfer, Inc. v. Westates Airlines, Inc., 899 F.2d 1269, 1272-73 (1st Cir. 1990)). Under this scenario, section 675.109 contemplates the issuance of an injunction. We, therefore, hold that the trial court properly denied the motion to dissolve the temporary injunction.

The temporary injunction is also properly granted based on principles of comity. A foreign decree "is entitled to comity, where the parties have been given notice and the opportunity to be heard, where the foreign court had original jurisdiction, and where the foreign decree does not offend the public policy of the State of Florida." Nahar v. Nahar, 656 So. 2d 225, 229 (Fla. 3d DCA), *review denied*, 664 So. 2d 249 (Fla. 1995). Here, the Guatemala court had jurisdiction, in accordance with the parties' contract, to resolve the controversy over Intrinsic's performance vel non, and Intrinsic had notice and opportunity to be heard in that forum. As Florida's jurisdiction and due process requirements had been met, the Guatemala injunction is entitled to comity. Absent the Florida injunction, the confirming banks would be required to honor payment requests under the letter of credit, but the Guatemala injunction would bar reimbursement from the issuing bank. As a result, the trial court properly enjoined payment on the letter of credit to render effective the Guatemala injunction and to preserve the status quo pending a final decree of the Guatemala court. See Cardenas v. Solis, 570 So. 2d 996 (Fla. 3d DCA 1990) (applying comity principles to enforce Guatemala court temporary injunction), *review denied*, 581 So. 2d 163 (Fla. 1991).

Based on the foregoing, the trial court's order denying the motion to dissolve the temporary injunction is hereby,

Affirmed.

NOTE

In deciding the liability of an issuer who refuses to honor a credit, the courts have placed great emphasis on the "real" reason the issuer wants out. If that reason is that the applicant is bankrupt, so that the issuer fears no reimbursement will be forthcoming, the courts will stretch to hold the issuer liable. After all, fear of applicant insolvency was the very reason the seller wanted a letter of credit in the beginning. On the other hand, where the issuer hesitates because it is afraid that honoring will violate §5-108, and the issuer will lose the right to seek reimbursement from its applicant, the issuer's conduct is more likely to receive favorable treatment from the court. For a fascinating example of these considerations at work, compare the district and appellate court opinions in Courtaulds N. Am., Inc. v. North Carolina Natl. Bank, 387 F. Supp. 92, 16 U.C.C. Rep. Serv. 1323 (M.D.N.C. 1975), *rev'd*, 528 F.2d 802, 18 U.C.C. Rep. Serv. 467 (4th Cir. 1975).

V. ASSIGNMENT

PROBLEM 104

Octopus National Bank issued a $50,000 letter of credit to Grey Goods of New York, payable to Grey Goods on presentation of a draft and certain documents demonstrating shipment of clothing to Ohio Wholesalers, the bank's applicant. Grey Goods needed money to finance its operations, so it borrowed $30,000 from Midwest State Bank (MSB), giving MSB a security interest in the proceeds of the letter of credit, and assigning the right to those proceeds to MSB, which promptly notified ONB of the assignment. Grey Goods had trouble filling the Ohio Wholesalers order, so those two parties agreed to lower the amount shipped and the price to $10,000 worth of clothing, and the letter of credit was amended to reflect this lower amount. When the clothing was shipped and the draft presented under the letter of credit, ONB was only willing to pay $10,000 to MSB. MSB calls you, its attorney. What are its rights here? See §§5-114 and 5-106, and Official Comment 2 to the latter.

VI. SUBROGATION

PROBLEM 105

Ebenezer Scrooge was the sole shareholder of Scrooge and Marley, Inc., a corporation that sold coal. In early 2016, the corporation signed a $2 million contract to buy mineral rights in a new coal tract in Pennsylvania from Frederick Bean, the owner of the land, agreeing that he would allow

Scrooge and Marley to mine the coal in the summer of 2009, sell it to others, and then pay the $2 million to Bean. In the meantime, Scrooge and Marley signed a promissory note for this amount payable to Bean, guaranteed personally by Ebenezer Scrooge, due June 1, 2016. Bean also required Scrooge and Marley to get a standby letter of credit in his favor for the amount of $2 million, payable if the corporation defaulted on its promissory note. The corporation had Dickens National Bank issue such a letter of credit, with Bean as the beneficiary. The transaction went as planned until the market for coal collapsed after Scrooge and Marley had mined the Bean tract and found itself unable to sell that coal at a profit. When the promissory note was not paid when it came due in 2016, Bean drew a draft on the bank under the letter of credit. Dickens National Bank has this draft in hand, and calls you, the bank's attorney. Scrooge and Marley has just filed for bankruptcy, and has no assets. Must it pay the letter of credit? If it does so, can it subrogate itself to Bean's rights against Ebenezer Scrooge? See §5-117;[4] JP Morgan Chase Bank v. Cook, 318 F. Supp. 2d 159, 52 U.C.C. Rep. Serv. 2d 999 (S.D.N.Y. 2004). Can it go after Scrooge *before* it pays Bean's draft? See §5-117(d).

---

4. In reading that section you should know that the Restatement (Third) of Suretyship and Guaranty calls sureties and similar parties "secondary obligors," and has complicated rules explaining under what circumstances they are entitled to subrogation. See the Official Comments to §5-117.